THE ELEMENTARY
STRUCTURES OF KINSHIP

CLAUDE LÉVI-STRAUSS

The Elementary Structures of Kinship

(Les Structures élémentaires de la Parenté)

Revised Edition
Translated from the French
by
JAMES HARLE BELL
JOHN RICHARD von STURMER
and
RODNEY NEEDHAM
Editor

BEACON PRESS

BOSTON

Published first in France under the title *Les Structures
élémentaires de la Parenté* in 1949. A revised edition under
the same title was published in France in 1967.

Translation copyright © 1969 by Beacon Press

Library of Congress catalog card number: 68–12840

First published by Beacon Press in 1969

First published as a Beacon Paperback in 1969

International Standard Book Number: 0–8070–4669–8

9   8   7

Beacon Press books are published under the auspices of the
Unitarian Universalist Association

TO THE MEMORY OF
LEWIS H. MORGAN

Contents

INTRODUCTION

I NATURE AND CULTURE   3

Nature and society. The problem of the transition from nature
to society. 'Wild children.' The superior forms of animal life.
The criterion of universality. The prohibition of incest as a
universal rule.

II THE PROBLEM OF INCEST   12

Rationalist theories: Maine, Morgan. Conclusions from
genetics. Psychological theories: Westermarck, Havelock
Ellis. Sociological theories I: McLennan, Spencer, Lubbock.
Sociological theories II: Durkheim. Antinomies of the
problem of incest.

PART ONE:
RESTRICTED EXCHANGE

1. THE BASES OF EXCHANGE

III THE UNIVERSE OF RULES   29

Consanguinity and alliance. Prohibition of incest, 'the rule as
rule'. The system of the scarce product: rules of alimentary
distribution. Transition to marriage rules: marriage and
celibacy.

IV ENDOGAMY AND EXOGAMY   42

Polygamy, a special form of reciprocity. True endogamy and
functional exogamy. Limits of the social group. The case of
the Apinayé. Exogamy and the prohibition of incest.

PART TWO:
GENERALIZED EXCHANGE

1. SIMPLE FORMULA OF GENERALIZED EXCHANGE

Figures

Editor's Note

An English edition of a major work such as *Les Structures élémentaires de la Parenté*, and one so difficult in argument and exposition, is of unusual importance, and some indication should therefore be given of how it was prepared and how authoritative it may be taken to be.

After a long and testing search Professor J. H. Bell and Mr. J. R. von Sturmer were decided upon as translators. They prepared their draft translation in Australia and sent it chapter by chapter, together with bibliographical and other queries, to the editor in Oxford. These drafts were rigorously collated with the French text, and certain of the original sources, and were recast. The annotated chapters were returned to the first translators for correction and any remaining verification of references. The amended and retyped drafts were then sent back to Oxford, where they were again revised against the text. The proofs were read in Oxford, and further improvements were made.

Bell and von Sturmer, with the aid of members of their university staff, not only traced the English sources and, reproduced the passages which Professor Lévi-Strauss had cited in French, but they also carried out nearly all of the wearisome bibliographical work which is more conventionally an editorial task. The editor, for his part, actually concentrated upon the scrupulous fidelity of the translation of the argument, and the ultimate responsibility for its accuracy, both grammatical and theoretical, is his.[1] Although he made numerous stylistic changes as well, increasingly as the work progressed, it is to be expected that the result may savour of committee English, and it must be recognized that the text can hardly possess the individual character or the literary polish which may be looked for when a work is interpreted by a single translator rather than by three.

But the great advantage of this procedure – and one which appears not to have been enjoyed by any other French work, from *La Cité antique* onwards, in a series of such translated contributions to 'Anglo-Saxon' social anthropology – is that *Les Structures élémentaires de la Parenté* has thus undergone two integral translations. The first translators checked each other in the preparation of their joint drafts, and then considered the cogency

---

[1] He would be greatly obliged for advice of any undetected defects and for the suggestion of possible improvements.

of the editorial emendations; the editor twice construed the entire work, in the course of collation and revision, and returned to particular passages for added confidence of accuracy. It is hoped that these circumstances will confer on the edition a special reliability which may far outweigh any minor awkwardnesses in the English.

Professor Lévi-Strauss, however, formally declined to examine the translation before it went to press, and he has likewise abstained from reading the proofs. He has had an opportunity to assess the degree of care and exactitude with which the edition has been prepared, but it can only be regretted that the work should have been deprived of the final stamp of authority which is claimed by its importance to scholarship.

The present version differs from the original French publication of 1949 in a considerable number of places, where the author has made corrections and has inserted additional arguments and other observations.[1] In the French second edition[2] these changes have been indicated by square brackets,[3] but at Professor Lévi-Strauss's instruction, countermanding the editor's intention, no such indications have been provided for readers of the English edition. A few rectifications of misprints and other minor points have been tacitly made by the editor, who has also compiled a general index.

The editor deeply thanks his collaborators in Australia for the professional spirit and the equanimity with which they readily acceded to the plethora of changes and suggestions which he made in their drafts. It is hard enough for working academics to devote themselves so intensively for more than a year, and to the detriment or exclusion of their own researches, to the propagation of the views of another man, however distinguished, without doing so under unremitting criticism; and the editor would wish the reader to take special account of the scholarly abnegation and sense of responsibility on their part which the production of this translation has demanded.

He also adds his own warm recognition of the services of Miss Janice McDonald, who, without the satisfaction of contributing intellectually to the wider recognition of an outstanding work of analysis, twice performed the exacting and indispensable labour of typing this lengthy book.

---

[1] A total, in fact, of approximately 180 corrigenda, deletions and interpolations, amounting to well over 9,000 words (not including Radcliffe-Brown's letter) and often materially affecting the original argument. These alterations are dated April, 1962. The author subsequently made a small number of other changes during the preparation of the English edition, which in these particulars thus varies slightly from the French revised edition.

Professor Lévi-Strauss's revisions, and the working draft of the translation, have been deposited in the Bodleian Library, University of Oxford (shelf-mark: MS. Eng. misc. c. 448).

[2] Paris and The Hague: Mouton, 1967.

[3] [This at least is what one would understand from the author's declaration in the French preface (p. xv). Actually, of all the corrigenda effected (not counting the correction of misprints and small grammatical points), nearly seventy per cent are not signalled in this way.]

Two of the editor's colleagues have at Oxford aided decisively in ensuring a dependable rendition of Professor Lévi-Strauss's work. Dr. P. G. Rivière has very generously and effectively carried out an additional reading of the proofs, and has at the same time subjected the translation to yet a further scrutiny at places throughout each chapter. Mrs. Francis Korn has made a special check of the tables, diagrams, and formulas, and has in other ways most kindly ministered to the editorial task.

RODNEY NEEDHAM

University of Oxford

Postscriptum. In the new preface, which he modified especially for this edition* and which was not supplied until after the translation and editing had been reported complete, Professor Lévi-Strauss indirectly charges the editor with a 'fundamental misunderstanding' of the very title and subject matter of the book, and imputes to him (admittedly in excellent company) a fallacious assimilation of elementary structures to prescriptive marriage which is alleged to have seriously misled later commentators on the theory.

Readers who may therefore be justifiably uneasy that the editor should have assumed particular responsibility for the theoretical accuracy of the rendering of the argument (p. xvii) will doubtless appreciate the assurance, for the present, that wherever the idea of prescription appears in this edition (see index s.v.) it is a literal translation from the French. For example, when in the opening lines of the work Professor Lévi-Strauss defines 'elementary structures' as 'those systems which prescribe marriage with a certain type of relative' (p. xxiii), this is a direct translation of his original and unamended words: '*les systèmes qui prescrivent le mariage avec un certain type de parents*' (1949, p. ix; 1967, p. ix).

It may be found informative, also, to refer to the only place at which Professor Lévi-Strauss has previously defended his argument, where he writes that if an alternative theory proposed by certain critics, in terms of psychological 'preference', were correct, matrilateral marriage would indeed be more frequent 'but it would not need to be *prescribed*'.†

R.N.

* The critical content, however, is in large part a repetition, made more specific in its application, of points already published in the author's Huxley Lecture, 'The Future of Kinship Studies' (*Proceedings of the Royal Anthropological Institute*, 1965, pp. 13–22). The preface has also appeared separately, under the title 'Vingt ans après', in *Les Temps modernes* (23ᵉ année, no. 256, September 1967, pp. 385–406).

† Claude Lévi-Strauss, *Anthropologie structurale* (Paris: Plon, 1958), pp. 344–5 n. 1; cf. English edition, translated by Claire Jacobson and Brooke Grundfest Schoepf, *Structural Anthropology* (New York: Basic Books, 1963), p. 322 n. 105. The italics are those of Professor Lévi-Strauss.

Few who will give their minds to master the general principles of savage religion will ever again think it ridiculous, or the knowledge of it superfluous to the rest of mankind. Far from its beliefs and practices being a rubbish-heap of miscellaneous folly, they are consistent and logical in so high a degree as to begin, as soon as even roughly classified, to display the principles of their formation and development; and these principles prove to be essentially rational, though working in a mental condition of intense and inveterate ignorance . . .

The tendency of modern inquiry is more and more towards the conclusion that if law is anywhere, it is everywhere.

E. B. Tylor, *Primitive Culture*
(London, 1871), pp. 20–2

ACKNOWLEDGEMENTS

We wish to acknowledge the help given by the following people in the preparation for this translation. Mrs. Barbara Bancroft of the Department of French in the University of New England willingly discussed many matters with us and offered suggestions which we feel have greatly improved the translation. Miss Gwenda Cane of the Department of Mathematics in the University of New England read chapter XIV. Miss Janice McDonald of the Faculty of Agricultural Economics in the University of New England typed the manuscript. Miss McDonald and Miss Mary Jackes of the Department of Sociology prepared many of the figures contained in the draft. To these people we make grateful acknowledgement.

J. H. B.

J. R. von S.

The University of New England,
Armidale, New South Wales
Australia

Preface to the First Edition

Elementary structures of kinship are those systems in which the nomenclature permits the immediate determination of the circle of kin and that of affines, that is, those systems which prescribe marriage with a certain type of relative, or, alternatively, those which, while defining all members of the society as relatives, divide them into two categories, viz., possible spouses and prohibited spouses. The term 'complex structures' is reserved for systems which limit themselves to defining the circle of relatives and leave the determination of the spouse to other mechanisms, economic or psychological. In this work, then, the term 'elementary structures' corresponds to what sociologists usually call preferential marriage. It has been impossible to retain this terminology, because the basic purpose of this book is to show that marriage rules, nomenclature, and the system of rights and prohibitions are indissociable aspects of one and the same reality, viz., the structure of the system under consideration.

The preceding definition would thus confine the term 'elementary structure' to those systems which, like cross-cousin marriage, lead to an almost automatic determination of the preferred spouse. On the other hand, systems, like several in Africa and our own contemporary society, which are based on a transfer of wealth or on free choice, would be classified as complex structures. This distinction will be largely retained, although several reservations must be made.

Firstly, there is no absolutely elementary structure, because only exceptionally can a system ultimately determine one sole individual as the prescribed spouse. Elementary structures allow for the definition of classes or the determination of relationships, but as a general rule a number of individuals, and the number is often large, are equally suited to make up the class and to satisfy the relationship. Consequently, even in elementary structures there is always some freedom of choice. On the other hand, no complex structure allows a completely free choice, the rule being not that one can marry anyone in the system, but only those not expressly forbidden. The limit of elementary structures lies in the biological possibilities which always provide many solutions to a given problem, in the form of brothers, sisters, or cousins, while the limit of complex structures is found in the incest prohibition, which excludes, by the social rule, certain solutions which are nevertheless biologically open. Even the strictest elementary structure retains a certain freedom of choice, while even in the vaguest of complex structures this choice is subject to certain limitations.

Elementary and complex structures thus cannot be wholly contrasted, and the line separating them is also difficult to define. Between those systems which determine the spouse and those which do not there are certain hybrid and ambiguous forms, where economic privileges allow a secondary choice within a prescribed category (marriage by purchase combined with marriage by exchange), or where there are several preferential solutions (marriage with mother's brother's daughter, and with wife's brother's daughter; marriage with mother's brother's daughter, and with mother's brother's wife, etc.). Certain of these will be examined, because they may clarify some of the simpler cases, while others indicating a change to complex forms will be ignored for the while.

Properly speaking, then, this work is an introduction to a general theory of kinship systems. Following this study of elementary structures there is need for another on complex structures, and perhaps even a third on those family attitudes expressing or overcoming, by conventional behaviour, conflicts or contradictions inherent in the logical structure such as are revealed in the system of nomenclature. However, it is essentially for two reasons that this book is published in its present form. Firstly, without being exhaustive, the study, in that it deals with principles, is complete. Even if some aspect of the problem treated in the work were developed no new idea would be introduced. For the elucidation of any special problem that the reader has in mind, the definitions and distinctions used here should be applied, and the same method followed.

Secondly, no claim is made that the work is free from errors of fact and interpretation. The social sciences have become so highly interrelated and complex, because of the vast mass of facts and documents on which they rest, that their development depends on collective effort. I have been obliged to deal with certain fields in which I am badly prepared, to risk hypotheses not immediately verifiable, and, lacking information, to ignore for the while problems whose solutions were essential to my purpose. Should but few ethnologists or sociologists, psychologists or linguists, archaeologists or historians, studying human phenomena either in the laboratory, study or in the field, read this work, and should their comments and criticisms correct some of the extensive and serious errors which we are the first to admit exist in it, the limitation of the inquiry, and the presentation of the preliminary results before attempting to seek subsequent implications, will have been justified.

II

A comparative sociological study faces two main difficulties, viz., the choice of sources, and the utilization of facts. The problem here arises principally from the wealth of material, and the hard necessity to limit it. On the first point, it will be appreciated that since it was written in the United States – where I was generously welcomed and given such exceptional working conditions – and in daily contact with American colleagues, this book made much use of Anglo-Saxon sources. Had I ignored this source of material, I should have failed my French colleagues who are especially interested in overseas developments in their science. While not neglecting old sources when they were absolutely necessary, an attempt has been made to renovate the traditional basis of the problems of kinship and marriage by avoiding another grinding-out of examples already exhausted by the past discussions of Frazer, Briffault, Crawley and Westermarck. For this reason, a large number of articles and books published in the last thirty years have been used. Thus, while possibly useless theoretically, the work may perhaps be excused because it provides easier access to some scattered and occasionally rare sources.

The second point poses a more ticklish problem. In using his material, the comparative sociologist constantly faces two criticisms. The first is that in amassing examples he strips them of substance and meaning by arbitrarily isolating them from their context, while the second is that in preserving their concrete nature and ties with other aspects of the culture, only a small number of facts may be considered, on which basis he cannot generalize. Westermarck is commonly accused of the first fault and Durkheim of the second. But by following the course so vigorously outlined by Marcel Mauss, it seems these two dangers might be avoided. In this book these two methods have been taken not as mutually exclusive, but as two different steps in the proof. The initial stages of this combined approach concern facts so general that the inquiry, at first, is directed towards setting up the hypothesis, guiding intuition, and illustrating principles, rather than with verifying the proof. So long as the phenomena considered are so simple, universal, and part of everyday life, it is no doubt justifiable, in that they are not required to fulfil any conclusive function, for examples to be amassed without undue concern for the context which gives each its particular meaning. For, at this stage, this meaning is almost identical for them all, and comparison with the subject's own experience as a member of a social group is almost always enough to restore the content. In this way, even isolated examples, borrowed from the most widely varying cultures, acquire an added value, attesting strongly to the similarity underlying the differences. Their particular rôle is to foster the impression and to define the atmosphere and colour permeating the truths, rather than the truths themselves, as these emerge in the beliefs, fears and desires of men.

But as this combined method progresses, and more complex relationships are arrived at, this first method ceases to be legitimate. The number of examples must be limited so that the particular significance of each may be thoroughly studied. At this point the proof relies upon a very small number of carefully chosen examples. The validity of any subsequent generalization will depend upon the typicality of these examples, that is, in so far as each example contains as many of the conditions of the problem as reasoning might determine. This is why the progress of the argument in this work is accompanied by a change of method. Beginning with a systematic exposition in which eclectic examples, chosen solely for their evocative value, are used, primarily to illustrate the reasoning and to encourage the reader to recall personal experiences of the same type, the horizon is gradually narrowed to allow for deeper analysis, so that the second part, the conclusion excepted, is almost in the form of three monographs, on the respective marriage organizations of Southern Asia, China and India. These preliminary explanations are necessary to justify this procedure.

This book would never have appeared without the help of the following people and institutions. The Rockefeller Foundation provided encouragement and material means for the undertaking; by lecturing at the New School for Social Research certain of my ideas were clarified and formulated, and through personal contact and correspondence with colleagues, facts were verified and hypotheses crystallized. The following are thanked for their encouragement: Robert H. Lowie, A. L. Kroeber, Ralph Linton, Paul Rivet, Georges Davy, Maurice Leenhardt, Gabriel Le Bras, Alexandre Koyré, Raymond de Saussure, Alfred Métraux, André Weil (who kindly added a mathematical appendix to Part I) and very especially, Roman Jakobson, who amicably insisted that the work be finished and to whom a great deal is owed for theoretical inspiration.

This work has been dedicated to the memory of Lewis H. Morgan for three reasons: to pay homage to the pioneer of the research method modestly adopted in this book; to honour the American school of anthropology that he founded and with whose work I was associated for four years; and perhaps also, in some small way, to try to discharge the debt owed to him, by recalling that this school was especially great at a time when scientific precision and exact observation did not seem to him to be incompatible with a frankly theoretical mode of thought and a bold philosophical taste. For the progress of sociology will be no different from its forerunners, and this must not be forgotten when we are beginning to glimpse, as through a glass darkly, the area where all these will eventually meet. Having quoted Eddington, 'Physics is becoming the "study of organization" ', Köhler wrote, almost twenty years ago: 'In this way . . . it will converge with biology and psychology.'[1] This work will have fulfilled its purpose if, after having finished it, the reader feels inclined to add, 'and sociology'.

New York, February 23rd 1947

---

[1] Köhler, 1930, p. 30.

Preface to the Second Edition

Seventeen years have passed since the publication of this book, and almost twenty since it was first written. During these twenty years, so much new material has appeared, and the theory of kinship has become so scientific and complicated, that the text would have to be wholly rewritten if it were to be brought up to date. On reading it today, the documentation seems tedious and the expression old-fashioned. If I had been more careful and less hesitant under the weight of my undertaking, I would doubtless have seen from the start that its very bulk would involve certain weaknesses, upon which, in fact, critics have dwelt with some malice. I would also have understood better the discreet warning contained in what was at first sight a flattering compliment paid me by Robert Lowie when he returned the manuscript, which he had been so kind as to peruse: he told me, in fact, that the work was 'in the grand style . . .'. Nevertheless I reject not one part of the theoretical inspiration or of the method, nor any of the principles of interpretation. This is why I have finally decided to keep corrections and additions to an absolute minimum. After all, the book wanted for reprinting by the publisher is the one brought out in 1949, not some other work.

In the first place I have corrected a considerable number of typographical errors which certain rather uncharitable scholars have been prepared to see as errors on my part. Such is the case with Lucien Malson, who, in his excellent little book, *Les Enfants sauvages*,[1] thus reproaches me for certain data for which I am not responsible, but which come from writers whom I quote and with whom he does not agree. Nevertheless, I do believe he is justified in considering the two or three short pages devoted to his own particular problem as of scant use, and the solution, right or wrong, that I adopt as adding very little to the question.

I admit to being an execrable proof-reader, who, when faced with the finished text, is inspired neither by the tender care of a writer for his work, nor by the aggressive inclination which makes for a good corrector. Once completed, the book becomes a foreign body, a dead being incapable of holding my attention, much less my interest. This world in which I have so passionately lived closes up against me and shuts me out. At times it is almost beyond my comprehension. If the typographic presentation of the first edition contains many more faults than now, it is because I had no help whatever.

[1] Union générale d'Éditions, collection 10/18, Paris, 1964.

Some factual errors were doubtless inevitable in a work which – as my card-index bears witness – required me to consult more than 7,000 books and articles. Some of the errors I have corrected as often as not had escaped my critics' notice. On the other hand, these self-same critics have been quick to seize upon passages which they have not fully understood through lack of familiarity with the French language. I have also been taken to task for ethnographic errors when the evidence itself comes from reputable observers whom I quoted without using inverted commas because the source reference was given a little later. I dare say these facts would have been received with greater consideration had they not been attributed to me.

Apart from correcting these details I have not substantially altered or expanded the original text except on three points.

In the first place I might have indicated the importance of a general study of so-called 'bilateral' or 'undifferentiated' systems of descent, even though I did not undertake such a study. These systems are far more numerous than was believed when I wrote my book, although, by a natural reaction, there has been perhaps too great a haste to include, in these new types, systems which are now being seen, more and more, as possibly reducible to unilateral forms.

With regard to the other two points, I have revised my whole discussion of the Murngin (chapter XII) and the Kachin (chapters XV–XVII) systems. Notwithstanding the criticisms which have been levelled against me and which I have had to refute, I consider the interpretations put forward in 1949, although not definitive, as having lost none of their validity.

If I have refrained from altering Sections II and III of Part II, which are devoted to China and India, it is for quite a different reason. I no longer have the necessary heart or incentive to tackle such large slabs of writing. Around 1945 there were relatively few works on the kinship systems of China and India. Without being too presumptuous it was possible to absorb them all, to synthesize them, and to isolate their meaning. Today this is no longer permissible, for sinologists and Indianists, in pursuing these studies, rely on a body of historical and philological knowledge which a cursory comparative approach cannot fully grasp. It is clear that the authoritative research of Louis Dumont and his school on kinship in India henceforth makes this a field on its own. I am thus resigned to letting the sections on China and India stand, begging the reader to take them for what they are, as stages outstripped by the progress of anthropology, but judged as being still of some interest by competent colleagues, viz., Louis Dumont himself and Alexander Rygaloff, who were kind enough to read them over again prior to republication.

As to the basic problems raised in the introduction, many new facts and the development of my own thought mean that nowadays I would no longer express myself in the same way. I still believe that the prohibition of incest is to be explained entirely in terms of sociological causes. Certainly, however, I have treated the genetic aspect in too casual a manner. A more accurate appraisal of the very high rate of mutations and the proportion which is harmful would call for some qualification of my statements, even if the deleterious consequences of consanguineal unions have played no part in the origin or the persistence of rules of exogamy. On the subject of biological causality I shall now do no more than repeat that social anthropology has no need of this hypothesis to explain marriage prohibitions.

As far as the contrast between nature and culture is concerned, the present state of knowledge and that of my own thought (the one, moreover, following upon the other) would seem in several respects to present a paradox. My proposal was to trace the line of demarcation between the two orders guided by the presence or absence of articulated speech. One might think that the progress of studies in cerebral anatomy and physiology would have given an absolute foundation to this criterion, since certain structures of the central nervous system peculiar only to man seem to control the capacity for giving objects names.

But on the other hand, the appearance of certain phenomena has made this line of demarcation, if not less real, then certainly more tenuous and tortuous than was imagined twenty years ago. Among insects, fish, birds and mammals, complex processes of communication, which now and then bring true symbols into play, have been discovered. We also know that certain birds and mammals, notably chimpanzees in the wild state, can fashion and use tools. In that period which science has pushed further and further back and which saw the beginning of what is still conveniently called the lower palaeolithic, different species and even different genera of hominoids, fashioners of stone and bone, seem to have lived together on the same sites.

The question then is just how far the contrast between nature and culture may be pushed. Its simplicity would be illusory if it had been largely the work of the genus *Homo* (antiphrastically called *sapiens*), savagely devoted to eliminating doubtful forms believed to border on the animal; inspired as it presumably was some hundreds of thousands of years or more ago by the same obtuse and destructive spirit which today impels it to destroy other living forms, having annihilated so many human societies which had been wrongly relegated to the side of nature simply because they themselves did not repudiate it (*Naturvölkern*); as if from the first it alone had claimed to personify culture as opposed to nature, and to remain now, except for those cases where it can totally bend it to its will, the sole embodiment of life as opposed to inanimate matter.

By this hypothesis, the contrast of nature and culture would be neither a primeval fact, nor a concrete aspect of universal order. Rather it should be seen as an artificial creation of culture, a protective rampart thrown up around it because it only felt able to assert its existence and uniqueness by destroying all the links that lead back to its original association with the other manifestations of life. Consequently, to understand culture in its essence, we would have to trace it back to its source and run counter to its forward trend, to retie all the broken threads by seeking out their loose ends in other animal and even vegetable families. Ultimately we shall perhaps discover that the interrelationship between nature and culture does not favour culture to the extent of being hierarchically superimposed on nature and irreducible to it. Rather it takes the form of a synthetic duplication of mechanisms already in existence but which the animal kingdom shows only in disjointed form and dispersed variously among its members – a duplication, moreover, permitted by the emergence of certain cerebral structures which themselves belong to nature.

II

Of the developments to which this book has given rise, doubtless the most unexpected from my point of view was that which resulted in the distinction, now almost standard in England, between the notions of 'prescriptive marriage' and 'preferential marriage'. To discuss this distinction somewhat embarrasses me, so great is my debt of recognition to the man who first formulated it, Rodney Needham, who has acted as my interpreter (and also, at times, my critic) to the English-speaking public in the energetic and perceptive prose of his *Structure and Sentiment*,[1] a book with which I would prefer not to express any disagreement, even if, as is the case, such disagreement as I feel bears on a limited problem. However, the solution proposed by Needham involves so complete a change from my own point of view that it seems absolutely necessary to return here to certain themes which, in deference to my British colleagues, I had made a point of first presenting in their language and on their soil, since, by conferring upon me the Huxley Memorial Lecture for 1965, they themselves had provided me with the opportunity for so doing.

It has long been known that societies which advocate marriage between certain types of kin adhere to the norm only in a small number of cases, as demonstrated by Kunstadter and his team through the use of computer simulations.[2] Fertility and reproduction rates, the demographic balance of the sexes and the age pyramid never show the perfect harmony necessary for every individual, when the time comes for him to marry, to be assured of finding a suitable spouse in the prescribed degree, even if the kinship nomenclature is broad enough to confuse degrees of the same type but unequally distant, often so much so that the notion of a common descent becomes purely theoretical: hence the idea of calling such systems 'preferential', a name which, as we have just seen, expresses the reality.

However, there are some systems which confuse several degrees in prescribed marriage categories, and in which it is not inconceivable to find

[1] Chicago: University of Chicago Press, 1962.
[2] Kunstadter, P., Buhler, R., Stephan, F. F. and Westoff, C. F., 'Demographic Variability and Preferential Marriage Patterns', *American Journal of Physical Anthropology*, n.s., vol. XXI, 1963, pp. 511–19.

even non-kin. This is the case in Australian aboriginal societies of the classical type and others, mostly in South-east Asia, in which marriage takes place between groups which are called and which call themselves 'takers' and 'givers' of women, the rule being that any group may receive women only from its 'givers', and may itself give women only to its 'takers'. As the number of these groups always seems quite large, there is a certain freedom of choice for each group, which is in no way obliged, from generation to generation, and even for marriages contracted by several men in the same generation, to have recourse always to the same 'giver'. In this way, the women married by two men belonging to consecutive generations (e.g., father and son) may, if they come from different groups of 'givers', have no kinship link between them. The rule is therefore very flexible, and societies which adopt it experience no real difficulty in observing it. Exceptional cases apart, they do what they say they must, hence the reason for calling their marriage system 'prescriptive'.

Following Needham, several writers today assert that my book is only concerned with prescriptive systems, or, to be more exact (since one need only glance through it to be assured of the contrary), that such had been my intention had I not confused the two forms. But if the champions of this distinction had been correct in believing that prescriptive systems are few and far between, a most curious consequence would have resulted: I would have written a very fat book which since 1952[1] has aroused all sorts of commentaries and discussions despite its being concerned with such rare facts and so limited a field that it is difficult to understand of what interest it could be with regard to a general theory of kinship.

Nevertheless, the very part which Needham has been so good as to take in the English edition of this book, and which gives him an added claim to my gratitude, shows that it has not lost all theoretical interest in his eyes. How could this be if the book discussed mere isolated instances? Were this the case I would have to admit that Leach is correct when he writes: 'Since the "elementary structures" which he discusses are decidedly unusual they seem to provide a rather flimsy base for a general theory', and in speaking of my book as 'a splendid failure'.[2] At the same time, however, it is puzzling to consider the motives which have prompted publishers, almost twenty years after it first appeared, to reissue both in French and in English a work which had failed, even splendidly.

If I have employed the notions of preference and obligation indifferently, even at times in the one sentence, for which I have been reproached, it is because, in my opinion, they do not connote different social realities, but rather, correspond to slightly differing ways in which man envisages the same

[1] The publication date of J. P. B. Josselin de Jong's work, *Lévi-Strauss's Theory on Kinship and Marriage*, Leiden, 1952.
[2] Leach, E., 'Claude Lévi-Strauss – Anthropologist and Philosopher', *New Left Review*, No. 34, 1965, p. 20.

reality. If we follow the example of their creators and define so-called prescriptive systems as we have just done, the only conclusion to be reached is that, on this count, they would not prescribe very much. Those who practise them know fully that the spirit of such systems cannot be reduced to the tautological proposition that each group obtains its women from 'givers' and gives its daughters to 'takers'. They are also aware that marriage with the matrilateral cross-cousin (mother's brother's daughter) provides the simplest illustration of the rule, the form most likely to guarantee its survival. On the other hand, marriage with the patrilateral cross-cousin (father's sister's daughter) would violate it irrevocably. It is on degrees of kinship that the system would turn, assuming the ideal situation in which the number of exchange groups, having fallen to the lowest possible figure, prevented the provisional opening or closing of secondary cycles.

That there is a divergence between the theoretical model and the empirical reality is nothing new. Gilhodes, one of the first observers of the Kachin, repeatedly emphasized this when describing how things happened, and even Granet's diagrams bring out the plurality of the cycles. My original edition was careful to take this into consideration. It is none the less true that the empirical reality of so-called prescriptive systems only takes on its full meaning when related to a theoretical model worked out by the natives themselves prior to ethnologists, and that this model cannot help but employ the notion of degree.

Moreover, is this not exactly what Needham is doing when he entitles an article 'The Formal Analysis of Prescriptive Patrilateral Cross-Cousin Marriage',[1] but at the cost of too close an approximation between model and empirical reality? To claim to show that no society, unless content with a low proportion of regular marriages, can permanently practise a rule of marriage with the patrilateral cousin, because of the intolerable restraints resulting from the change in the direction of the marriage exchanges in each generation, improves but slightly on the observations contained in chapter XXVII. On the other hand, those wishing to conclude that this type of marriage is contradictory would certainly be making a mistake. Indeed this is a cause which could only be pleaded (and then with certain reservations) if marriage exchanges were always between clans, a hypothesis by no means necessary and arbitrarily formulated. One should not start by introducing an impossible condition – as I proved when I showed[2] that marriage with the patrilateral cousin can never 'realise an overall structure', and that 'there is no law' for it – merely for the sake of rediscovering this impossibility. But apart from the fact that there is nothing *a priori* to prevent patrilateral systems from being maintained under precarious conditions, an adequate model of such systems exists at least in the minds of the many peoples who proscribe them. If they proscribe them they surely must have some idea of them.

[1] *Southwestern Journal of Anthropology*, vol. XIV, 1958, pp. 199–219.
[2] pp. 553–4 of the first edition.

Rather let us own that the notions of prescriptive and preferential marriage are relative: a preferential system is prescriptive when envisaged at the model level; a prescriptive system must be preferential when envisaged on the level of reality, unless it is able to relax its rule to such an extent that, if one persists in preserving its so-called prescriptiveness (instead of paying heed, rightly, to its preferential aspect, which is always apparent), it will finally mean nothing. One of two things can happen: either change the 'giver' group, and a former alliance will be renewed and consideration of the preferred degree will remain pertinent (e.g., the new wife will be a daughter of great-grandmother's brother's great-grandson, consequently of the same kind as a matrilateral cousin) or else there will be an entirely new alliance. Two cases can then arise: either this alliance foreshadows other alliances of the same type, and, by the same reasoning as above, becomes the cause of future preferences, expressible in terms of degree, or it remains short-lived, simply the result of a free and unmotivated choice. Accordingly if the system can be called prescriptive it is in so far as it is preferential first. If it is not also preferential its prescriptive aspect vanishes.

Conversely, a system which recommends marriage with the mother's brother's daughter may be called prescriptive even if the rule is seldom observed, since it says what must be done. The question of how far and in what proportion the members of a given society respect the norm is very interesting, but a different question to that of where this society should properly be placed in a typology. It is sufficient to acknowledge the likelihood that awareness of the rule inflects choices ever so little in the prescribed direction, and that the percentage of conventional marriages is higher than would be the case if marriages were made at random, to be able to recognize what might be called a matrilateral 'operator' at work in this society and acting as pilot: certain alliances at least follow the path which it charts out for them, and this suffices to imprint a specific curve in the genealogical space. No doubt there will be not just one curve but a great number of local curves, merely incipient for the most part, however, and forming closed cycles only in rare and exceptional cases. But the structural outlines which emerge here and there will be enough for the system to be used in making a probablistic version of more rigid systems the notion of which is completely theoretical and in which marriage would conform rigorously to any rule the social group pleases to state.

As Lounsbury has clearly shown in his review of *Structure and Sentiment*,[1] a fundamental misunderstanding is bound to arise if the opposition between 'elementary structure' and 'complex structures' becomes assimilated to that between 'prescriptive marriage' and 'preferential marriage', and if one is then substituted for the other.[2] I maintain, on the contrary, that an elementary structure can be equally preferential or prescriptive. Neither prescription nor

---

[1] *American Anthropologist*, vol. LXIV, 1962, pp. 1302–10.
[2] The same can be said for the likening of restricted exchange to mechanical solidarity

preference is the test of an elementary structure. Its one and only criterion rests in the fact that, preferred or prescribed, the spouse is the spouse solely because she belongs to an alliance category or stands in a certain kinship relationship to Ego. In other words, the imperative or desirable relationship is a function of the social structure. We enter the realm of complex structures when the reason for the preference or the prescription hinges on other considerations, e.g., the fact that the desired wife is blond, or slim, or intelligent, or belongs to a rich or powerful family. The latter certainly involves a social criterion, but its valuation remains relative, and the system does not define it structurally.

Consequently, in the case of both elementary and complex systems, the use of the term 'preferential' does not suggest a subjective inclination on the part of individuals to seek marriage with a certain type of relative. The 'preference' expresses an objective situation. If it were in my power to fix terminology I would use 'preferential' to describe any system in which, in the absence of a clearly formulated prescription, the proportion of marriages between a certain type of real or classificatory relative (taking 'classificatory' in a vaguer sense than defined by Morgan) is higher than were it the result of chance, whether the members of the group are aware of this or not. This objective proportion reflects certain structural properties of the system. If we were able to isolate these properties, they would turn out to be isomorphic with those which are directly knowable in societies which exhibit the same 'preference', disguised, however, as a prescription, and in practice obtaining exactly the same result. In the case of marriage with the matrilateral cross-cousin as well as with women from exclusively 'giver' groups, the result would be, on the one hand, alliance networks ideally tending to close themselves (although not necessarily doing so), and on the other hand, and more especially, relatively long networks, as compared with those to be observed or imagined in societies with preferential marriage with the father's sister's daughter, producing (even in the absence of any prescriptive rule) a correlative shortening of the cycles.[1]

---

[1] It is true that, following De Josselin de Jong, who made a similar remark many years before (loc. cit.), Dr. Maybury-Lewis ('Prescriptive Marriage Systems', *Southwestern Journal of Anthropology*, vol. XXI, 1965, pp. 207–30) believes he can assert that the theoretical model of a patrilateral system contains cycles which are just as long as those in the matrilateral model, the only difference being that, with the patrilateral model the cycles regularly reverse direction, while with the matrilateral model, they maintain the same direction. But those who read the diagram in this way are simply deluded by an optical illusion. That the mark of the patrilateral system is short cycles, reflecting the desire for the return, as promptly as possible, of a woman in exchange for the woman given in the previous genera-

---

and of generalized exchange to organic solidarity, adopted without discussion by Homans and Schneider. If a society with restricted exchange or generalized exchange is envisaged as a whole, each segment fulfils an identical function to each of the other segments. Consequently what we are dealing with is two different forms of mechanical solidarity. I dare say I myself have repeatedly used the terms 'mechanical' and 'organic' more loosely than Durkheim intended and than is generally accepted.

In other words, I do not dispute that there is an ideological distinction to be made between the prescriptive or preferential forms of a type of marriage. But the extreme terms always allow for a continuous series of intermediary applications. I postulate, therefore, that this series constitutes a group, and that the general theory of the system is only possible in terms of this group and not in terms of some particular application or other. The system should not be broken down, reduced by analysis to the various ways in which men may choose to represent it. Its nature arises objectively from the type of divergence engendered between the form taken by the alliance network of a society, and the form which would be observed in this same society if marriages were made at random. Fundamentally, the sole difference between prescriptive marriage and preferential marriage is at the level of the model. It corresponds to the difference which I have since proposed between what I call a 'mechanical model' and a 'statistical model';[1] i.e., in one case, a model the elements of which are on the same scale as the things whose relationships it defines: classes, lineages, degrees; while in the other case, the model must be abstracted from significant factors underlying distributions which are apparently regulated in terms of probabilities.

III

This search for a significant structure of marriage exchanges on which the society says nothing, either directly by means of rules, or indirectly by inferences to be drawn from the kinship nomenclature or by some other means, is still possible if the group concerned is small and relatively closed. In such a case the genealogies are decisive. But when the size and fluidity of the group increase, and its very limits become imprecise, the problem becomes singularly complicated. The group continues to stipulate what is not done, be this merely in the name of the prohibition of incest, but does it unsuspectingly do something more (or less) than would be the case if its members chose their spouses on the basis of their own personal histories, ambitions and tastes? It strikes me that the problem of the transition from elementary to complex structures, or if preferred, the problem of extending the anthropological theory of kinship to contemporary societies, is posed in these terms.

When I was writing my book, the method to be followed seemed simple. The first decision would be to reduce contemporary societies to those cases favourable to the inquiry, viz., the demographic isolates with a strong

---

[1] *Anthropologie structurale*, pp. 311–17; *Structural Anthropology* (New York, 1963), pp. 283–9.

---

tion (sister's daughter for father's sister) is amply attested to by the philosophy, not only of those who approve of it, but also of the much greater number who condemn it. It is better to accede to the universal judgment of those who are interested than to contradict not only oneself but the facts by simultaneously declaring that a patrilateral system forms long cycles as seen in the diagram, but, because of its very nature, fails to close even the shortest cycles. To reason in this way would lead to a confusion of empirical reality no longer only with the model but with the diagram.

coefficient of endogamy, and in which genealogical chains and networks of alliance intersecting at several points might be obtained. In so far as the proportion of marriages between relatives was determinable it would be possible to know whether these cycles were orientated at random, or whether a significant proportion belonged to one form rather than another. For example, are spouses who are kin (often without their knowledge) related in the paternal line or the maternal line, and if either is the case, are they born of cross-cousins or parallel cousins? Supposing that a trend did appear, it could be classed as a type with similar but better defined structures which anthropologists have already studied in small societies.

Nevertheless, the divergence between indeterminate types, which believe or wish themselves to be such, and the clearly determined systems which I have called elementary structures, is too great for the comparison to be decisive. Happily (or so I believed at that time), ethnography does provide an intermediary type, viz., systems which only set up preventions to marriage, but apply them so widely through constraints inherent in their kinship nomenclature that, because of the relatively small population, consisting of no more than a few thousand persons, it might be possible to obtain the converse, viz., a system of unconscious prescriptions which would reproduce exactly and in full the contours of the mould formed by the system of conscious prohibitions. If this operation were possible, the anthropologist would have at his disposal a method to be applied to cases in which the margin of freedom between what is prohibited and what is done widens, making it risky to deduce the positive from the negative when only the latter is given.

The systems just invoked are known in social anthropology as Crow-Omaha systems, because it is in these two North American tribes that their matrilineal and patrilineal variants respectively were first identified. It is through them that in 1957-8 I contemplated approaching the study of complex kinship structures in a second volume to which several allusions have been made but which doubtless I shall never write. I should therefore explain why I have abandoned this project. While still quite convinced that it will not be possible to generalize unless the Crow-Omaha systems are taken into consideration, I have come to see, more and more, that their analysis raises tremendous difficulties which are the province, not of the social anthropologist, but of the mathematician. Those with whom I have occasionally discussed this problem over the last decade are agreed. Some have declared that it can be solved, and others that it cannot, because of a reason of a logical nature which I shall indicate below. At all events, no one has felt the desire to take the time necessary to clear up the question.

Radcliffe-Brown and Eggan have taught us a great deal about these systems by showing that one of their essential characteristics was for membership of the lineage to have priority over membership of the generation. However, it strikes me that there is too much of a hurry to range Crow-Omaha systems with other systems which also give a single term to several members of a lineage, be they male or female, although they belong to consecutive generations, and which, like the Crow-Omaha systems, raise or lower by one or two generations certain members of two lineages which are arranged symmetrically on either side of a third containing Ego. Indeed, many writers class Crow-Omaha nomenclatures with that of societies with so-called asymmetrical marriage, i.e., prescriptive or preferential marriage with the matrilateral cross-cousin. As the theory of the latter systems poses no problem, it is assumed that it would be the same for the former.

Nevertheless, a curious anomaly must detain us. It is easy to construct the diagram of an asymmetrical system. It looks like a chain of successive connections, the orientation of which remains the same in each generation level, thus forming closed cycles one on top of the other, which can be traced on the wall of a cylinder and projected on a plane. On the other hand, no one has yet managed to give a satisfactory graphic representation of a Crow-Omaha system in a two- or even three-dimensional space. As one generation follows another new lineages are involved, and to represent these requires as many reserve planes as there are new lineages. Lacking complete genealogical information except for that explicitly provided by the system, the anthropologist is only entitled to make these planes intersect once in the space of three or four generations. As the rule holds for both sexes, and as a lineage includes at least one man and one woman in each generation (otherwise the model would not be in equilibrium), the result is that a diagram limited to even a few generations requires many more spatial dimensions than can be projected on a single sheet of paper. And to these is added a temporal dimension which does not figure in the model of an asymmetrical system. Radcliffe-Brown and Eggan have got round this difficulty but only by juxtaposing several diagrams which each illustrate a single aspect of, or instant in, the system. Even placed side by side they fail to tell the whole story.

Let us see how a discerning observer such as Deacon goes about describing a Crow system as found in Melanesia. Among the Seniang, he writes, 'the selection of a consort . . . is controlled by a number of prohibitions rather than injunctions', and he adds, 'theoretically . . . a man should not marry a woman belonging to a clan into which a man of his own group has married within living memory'.[1] One need only turn these two phrases round to obtain a perfectly satisfactory definition of asymmetrical marriage. Indeed, in this case, a single prescription is enough to determine the selection of a consort, viz., that which requires a man to marry a mother's brother's daughter or a woman from a 'giver' group. The 'giver' group, moreover, is recognized by the fact that there have already been similar alliances with it in living memory.

It would be impossible to conclude from this that all so-called Crow-Omaha systems necessarily refrain from issuing prescriptions or voicing

[1] Deacon, A. B., *Malekula: A Vanishing People in the New Hebrides*, ed. C. H. Wedgewood, London, 1934 (George Routledge and Sons), p. 132.

marriage preferences, just as it would be to conclude that there is complete freedom of choice within the approved clans. The matrilineal Cherokee prohibit only two clans, the mother's and the father's, and recommend marriage with a 'grandmother', i.e., with a girl from mother's father's clan or from father's father's clan. Among the Hopi, marriage was theoretically prohibited with any woman from any phratry to which belonged the mother's clan, the father's clan, or the mother's father's clan. If these societies comprised only four clans or phratries, i.e., one for each type of grandparent, their marriage system would be very similar to the Kariera or Aranda systems of Australia, in which, to find a suitable marriage partner, an individual rejects two or three lines and directs his attention to those one or two which remain. But Crow-Omaha systems always have more than four lines, there being seven clans among the Cherokee; ten among the Omaha; thirteen among the Crow, and probably more at one time; twelve phratries and about fifty clans among the Hopi; and thirty to forty clans among the Seniang. Since, as a general rule, marriage is allowed with all clans not subject to a formal prohibition, the Aranda-type structure, towards which every Crow-Omaha system would tend if the number of clans were approaching four, will remain submerged, as it were, beneath a flood of contingent incidents. It will never crystallize into a stable form. Here and there it will show through in a fluid and undifferentiated environment, but only as a faint and fleeting shadow.

Moreover, in general this phenomenon will not even occur if it is true that the most suitable manner of defining a Crow-Omaha system is to say that each time Ego chooses a line from which to obtain a wife, all its members are automatically excluded for several generations from among the spouses available to Ego's line. As every marriage means that the same thing happens, the system is in a continual state of turmoil which places it in contrast with the ideal model of an asymmetrical system in which the exchange mechanism is regularly ordered. On the whole an asymmetrical system resembles a clock with all its workings encased:[1] but a Crow-Omaha system is more like a lift-and-force pump fed from an external source, into the basin of which any surplus water which cannot be distributed is returned.

Nothing, therefore, could be further from the truth than to see Crow-Omaha systems and asymmetrical systems as identical, on the pretext that, in both systems, one type of cross-cousin is raised a generation and the other type lowered a generation, as this would be to overlook an essential difference. Asymmetrical systems make one cross-cousin a 'father-in-law' and the other a 'son-in-law', i.e., always a member of a line with which Ego can contract marriage or which is able to contract marriage with Ego's line. On the other hand, it will not unduly force matters to say that Crow-Omaha systems

---

[1] Or, to take into account the valuable analyses made by Needham, several clocks, each of which can engage any one at all of its wheels with the relevant part of any other, but all contained in the same case and functioning in such a way that there is always at least one dial working, even if whole portions of the cog-systems of each clock are temporarily still.

change these same persons into 'father' and 'son' respectively, thereby proclaiming that marriage between their and Ego's lineages has become impossible. Consequently, an asymmetrical system operates to change kin into affines, contrary to a Crow-Omaha system, which operates to change affines into kin. But in so doing, the two systems are seeking symmetrical and inverse effects: to make it possible or necessary either for the marriage alliance to be always between closely related persons or for alliance and kinship to become mutually exclusive, except (and as yet we do not know) for distant degrees.

It is in this sense that Crow-Omaha systems provide the connecting link between elementary and complex structures. They relate to elementary structures in so far as they formulate preventions to marriage in sociological terms, and to complex structures in so far as the nature of the network of alliances is aleatory, an indirect result of the fact that the only conditions laid down are negative. To return to a distinction which has already been mentioned, we can say that, like all elementary structures, they require a mechanical model on the normative level, but, as observed in complex structures, they require only a statistical model on the factual level.

No doubt some will object that the same is true of complex structures, since we are of the opinion that the prohibition of incest provides sufficient guarantee that a network of alliances, resulting in all other respects from free choices, will not compromise social cohesion. The incest prohibition persists in modern societies as a mechanical model. However, there is a difference: this model, which we continue to use, is much lighter than the model of Crow-Omaha systems in that, while ours covers a small number of very close degrees, the Crow-Omaha takes in whole lineages. On the other hand, the distribution of alliances in Crow-Omaha systems can be assumed to be less aleatory than in ours since these systems are concerned with small societies in which the mingling which is the consequence of massive prohibitions seemingly cannot avoid the appearance of a certain kinship between the spouses if the system has functioned regularly for several generations. Is this true, and if so, what form does it take and what is the mean distance of the degree? These are all questions of a major theoretical interest, but equally are all very difficult to answer for reasons which must now be given in detail.

IV

When we study systems with marriage classes (without giving this notion too technical a meaning), it is always possible and is generally easy to define *marriage types*, each type being represented by the marriage of a man from a determined class to a woman likewise from a determined class. If each class were given an index (a letter, number, or combination of both), there would thus be as many permissible types of marriage as there are pairs of indices, provided that all those which correspond to prohibited alliances are excluded in advance.

In the case of elementary structures, this operation is considerably simplified by the fact that there is a positive rule which lists the types or allows them to be deduced. But with the Crow-Omaha systems, things are doubly complicated. Firstly, the number of classes (if, for the sake of the argument, it is agreed to call exogamous units classes) increases appreciably and sometimes runs into the tens. More importantly, the system does not prescribe (or prescribes only partially and on rare occasions). It prohibits two or three types and allows all others, without telling us anything as to their form and their number.

Nevertheless, we can ask mathematicians to express Crow-Omaha systems in terms of elementary structures. If each individual were represented by a vector with as many indices as there are clan memberships made pertinent by the prohibitions of the system, all the vector couples which did not have the same index twice would then constitute the list of those types of marriage which are permissible, and these in turn would determine those permissible or not for the children born of these previous marriages, and for their own children. Bernard Jaulin, Head of the Mathematical Section of the Maison des Sciences de l'Homme, has kindly dealt with this problem and I thank him. Subject to possible errors which attach solely to the vague and clumsy way in which an anthropologist presents his data, it appears that a Crow-Omaha system which imposed only two prohibitions, viz., on the mother's and the father's clans respectively, would allow 23,436 different types of marriage if there were seven clans, 3,766,140 types if there were fifteen, and 297,423,855 if there were thirty. With three clan prohibitions the constraints would be stronger, but the number of types would remain in the same order of magnitude: 20,181; 3,516,345; and 287,521,515 respectively.[1]

These high figures give us food for thought. Firstly, it is clear that when we deal with Crow-Omaha systems we are dealing with vastly different mechanisms to those found in societies with marriage classes, in which the number of marriage types has nothing in common with the above figures. At first sight they seem to be more akin to the situation one might expect to find in modern societies in certain sectors, characterized by a strong coefficient of endogamy. If research in this direction confirmed the similarity, from the numerical point of view alone, Crow-Omaha systems would indeed form a bridge between elementary and complex structures, just as we supposed.

As far as their range is concerned, the combinative possibilities of Crow-Omaha systems also suggest such complicated games as cards, draughts and chess, in which the possible combinations, although theoretically finite, are so large in number that, for all useful purposes and on the human scale, they might as well be infinite. In principle, these games are unaffected by history, since the same synchronic configurations (in the distributions) and diachronic configurations (in the development of the moves) can reappear, even after thousands or millions of millenia, provided that imaginary

[1] The latter set of figures was also calculated by J. P. Schellhorn whom I also thank.

players keep at it for that length of time. Nevertheless, in practice such games remain in a continual state of flux, as is seen in the fact that whole works are written on the history of chess strategy. Although potentially present at all times, the entire range of possible combinations is too great for it to become an actuality except fragmentarily and over a long period of time. In the same way, Crow-Omaha systems reveal a compromise between the periodicity of elementary structures and their own determinism which relates to probability. The combinative possibilities are so vast that individual choices always preserve a certain latitude which is inherent to the system. The conscious or unconscious use to which this is put might even inflect the system if, as certain indications suggest, this margin of freedom proved to vary according to the composition of the vectors determining the place of each individual in the system. If such were the case, it would have to be said that, with Crow-Omaha systems, history finds its way into elementary structures, although, judging by what happens, their mission would seem to be to counteract its effects.

Unfortunately. the way to go about measuring this margin of freedom, and the limits between which it is liable to vary, remains largely unknown. Because of the very high number of combinations, computer simulations would have to be employed. However, in order to commence operations, an initial state would have to be determined. The danger then would be that of being trapped in a vicious circle, because in a Crow-Omaha system the state of possible or prohibited marriages is constantly determined by the marriages which have occurred in preceding generations. The only solution to the problem of determining an initial state which does not violate for certain one of the rules of the system would be a regression to infinity, unless one were prepared to wager that, despite its aleatory appearance, a Crow-Omaha system returns on itself periodically in such a way that, taking any initial state whatsoever, after a few generations a structure of a certain type must necessarily emerge.

But even assuming that the empirical data would allow us to prove *a posteriori* that this is how things actually happen, the problem would not be resolved. A difficulty of a demographic nature must be taken into account. Almost all societies with a Crow-Omaha system were small in population. The most studied of these, the American examples, had fewer than 5,000 persons. Consequently, the types of marriage which were actually practised in each generation could represent only an absurdly low proportion of the possible types. The result is that in a Crow-Omaha system the marriage types are not realized only at random, given the prohibited lineages. A factor of chance to the second power intervenes and chooses, from among all the potential marriage types, that small number which will become actual, and which will define, for the generations born of them, another range of possible choices, which, for the most part, are fated to remain merely potential in their turn. In the final analysis, a very strict nomenclature and negative rules which operate mechanically combine with two types of chance, one distributive, the other selective, to produce a network of alliances, the properties of which are unknown. This network of alliances probably differs little from the network produced by so-called Hawaiian-type nomenclatures which give generation levels priority over the lineages, and which define preventions to marriage in terms of individual degrees of kinship rather than by prohibiting whole classes. The difference with Crow-Omaha systems derives from the fact that the Hawaiian systems employ three heterogeneous techniques characterized by the use of a restricted nomenclature, the ambiguity of which is corrected by a very precise determination of the prohibited degrees, and by an aleatory distribution of alliances, a distribution guaranteed by prohibitions extending to the fourth collateral degree and on occasion beyond. On the other hand, Crow-Omaha systems, which employ the same techniques, give them a more systematic expression by integrating them into a body of solidary rules which ought more readily to permit the development of the theory of such games. Until the development of this theory with the help of mathematicians, without which nothing is possible, the study of kinship will mark time despite the ingenious attempts which have appeared during the last ten years, but which, turned as they are towards empirical analysis or towards formalism, equally fail to recognize that kinship nomenclature and marriage rules are complementary aspects of a system of exchanges whereby reciprocity is established and maintained between the constituent units of the group.

Paris, February 23rd, 1966

Introduction

A relative by marriage is an elephant's hip.

Rev. H. L. Bishop, 'A Selection of
ŠiRonga Proverbs', *The South African
Journal of Science*, vol. XIX (1922), p. 413

CHAPTER I

Nature and Culture

I

Of all the principles advanced by the forerunners of sociology, probably none has been so confidently repudiated as the distinction between nature and society. In fact, it is impossible to refer without contradiction to any phase in the evolution of mankind, where, without any social organization whatsoever, forms of activity were nevertheless developed which are an integral part of culture. But the distinction proposed can admit of more valid interpretations.

It was taken up by ethnologists of the Elliot Smith and Perry school to construct a theory, which, although questionable, clearly reveals, beyond the arbitrary detail of the historical outline, the profound contrast between two levels of human culture, and the revolutionary character of the neolithic transformation. With his probable knowledge of language, his lithic industries and funeral rites, Neanderthal man cannot be regarded as living in a state of nature. His cultural level, however, places him in as marked a contrast with his neolithic successors as, in another way, writers of the seventeenth century are to be distinguished from writers of the eighteenth. Above all, it is beginning to emerge that this distinction between nature and society,[1] while of no acceptable historical significance, does contain a logic, fully justifying its use by modern sociology as a methodological tool. Man is both a biological being and a social individual. Among his responses to external or internal stimuli, some are wholly dependent upon his nature, others upon his social environment. For example, there would be no difficulty in establishing the respective origins of the pupillary reflex, and the usual position of the horse-rider's hands on the reins. But the distinction is not always as easy. The physico-biological and the psycho-social stimuli often arouse similar reactions, and it may be asked, as did Locke, whether a child's fear of the dark is to be explained as revealing his animal nature, or as resulting from his nurse's stories.[2] Furthermore, in most cases, the causes themselves are not really

[1] 'Nature' and 'culture' seem preferable to us today.
[2] In fact, it seems that fear of the dark does not appear before the twenty-fifth month: cf. Valentine, 1930, pp. 394–420.

3

distinct, the subject's response representing an integration of the biological and social sources of his behaviour, as in the mother's attitude towards her child. Culture is not merely juxtaposed to life nor superimposed upon it, but in one way serves as a substitute for life, and in the other, uses and transforms it, to bring about the synthesis of a new order.

If this general distinction is relatively easy to establish, a twofold difficulty emerges when it has to be analysed. An attempt might be made to establish a biological or social cause for every attitude, and a search made for the mechanism whereby attitudes, which are cultural in origin, can be grafted upon and successfully integrated with forms of behaviour which are themselves biological in nature. To deny or to underestimate this opposition is to preclude all understanding of social phenomena, but by giving it its full methodological significance there is a danger that the problem of the transition from the biological to the social may become insoluble. Where does nature end and culture begin? Several ways can be suggested for answering this dual question, but so far all have proved singularly disappointing.

The simplest method would be to isolate a new-born child and to observe its reactions to various stimuli during the first hours or days after birth. Responses made under such conditions could then be supposed to be of a psycho-biological origin, and to be independent of ulterior cultural syntheses. However interesting the results which modern psychology has obtained by this method, their fragmentary and limited character cannot be overlooked. In the first place, only the early observations can be valid, for signs of conditioning are likely to appear within a few weeks or even days, and hence only such very elementary reactions as certain expressions of emotion can in actual fact be studied. Furthermore, negative proofs are always ambiguous, in that the question always remains open whether a certain reaction is absent because its origin is cultural, or because, with the earliness of the observation, the physiological mechanisms governing its appearance are not yet developed. Because a very young child does not walk, it cannot be concluded that training is necessary, since it is known that a child spontaneously begins to walk as soon as it is organically capable of doing so.[1] Analogies can be found in other fields. The only way to eliminate these uncertainties would be to extend observation over several months or even years. But insoluble difficulties would then be encountered, since the environment satisfying the strict isolation requirements of the experiment is no less artificial than the cultural environment it purports to replace, in that, for example, during the first years of life, maternal care is a natural condition in the individual's development. The experimenter is locked in a vicious circle.

It is true that sometimes chance has seemed to succeed where artificial means have failed. Eighteenth-century imaginations were greatly stirred by the instance of "wild children", lost in the countryside from their early years, and enabled, by exceptionally fortunate circumstances, to continue living

[1] McGraw, 1944.

and developing outside the influence of any social environment. But it seems clear enough from past accounts that most of these children were congenital defectives, and that their imbecility was the cause of their initial abandonment, and not, as might sometimes be insisted, the result.[1]

Recent observations support this view. The so-called 'wolf-children' found in India never reached a normal level. One of them never learned to speak, even as an adult. Of two children discovered together some twenty years ago, the younger remained unable to speak, while the elder lived till six years of age, but had the mental age of a $2\frac{1}{2}$-year-old, and a vocabulary of scarcely one hundred words.[2] A South African 'baboon-boy', discovered in 1903 when probably twelve to fourteen years old, was considered a congenital idiot in a 1939 account.[3] It must be added that as often as not the circumstances of discovery are unreliable.

Moreover, these examples must be dismissed for a general reason which brings us directly to the heart of the problems to be discussed in this Introduction. As early as 1811, Blumenbach noted in a study of one of these children, 'Wild Peter', that nothing should be expected of such phenomena, for he made the important observation that if man is a domesticated animal he is the only one who has domesticated himself.[4] While it can be anticipated that, if lost or isolated, a domesticated animal, such as a cat, dog, or farm animal, will return to the natural behaviour of the species prior to the outside interference of domestication, such cannot be expected of man, since the species has no natural behaviour to which an isolated individual might retrogress. A bee, Voltaire said, having roamed far from the hive, which it can no longer find, is lost, but for all that, has not become more wild. Whether the product of chance or experimentation, these 'wild children' may be cultural monstrosities, but under no circumstances can they provide reliable evidence of an earlier state.

Man himself, therefore, cannot be expected to exemplify types of precultural behaviour. Is a reverse approach then possible, of trying to find among the superior levels of animals, attitudes and manifestations recognizable as the preliminary indications and outline of culture? Superficially, the contrast between human and animal behaviour provides the most striking illustration of the difference between culture and nature. If the transition does exist, it is not at the level of the so-called animal societies, as encountered among certain insects, for the unmistakable attributes of nature, instinct, the anatomical features necessary to it, and the hereditary transmission of forms of behaviour essential to the survival of both the individual and the species, seem united nowhere better than here. In these collective structures there is not even a suspicion of what might be called the universal cultural model, i.e.,

[1] Itard, 1962; von Feuerbach, 1833.
[2] Ferris, 1902; Squires, 1927, p. 313; Kellogg, 1931, pp. 508–9; Kellogg, 1934, p. 149. See also on this polemic, Singh and Zingg, 1942; Gesell, 1940.
[3] Foley, 1940, pp. 128–33; Zingg, 1940, pp. 455–62.
[4] Blumenbach, 1865, p. 339.

language, tools, social institutions and systematized aesthetic, moral, or religious values. If any incipient stage to these human activities is to be discovered, attention must be directed to the other end of the animal scale, to the superior mammals, and more especially the anthropoid apes.

But research on the great apes during the last thirty years has been particularly discouraging in this respect. This is not to say that the basic components of the universal cultural model are entirely absent. With infinite trouble certain subjects can be made to articulate several monosyllables and disyllables but they never attach any meaning to them. To a certain extent the chimpanzee can use elementary tools and on occasions improvise with them.[1] Temporary solidary and subordinate relationships can appear or disappear within a given group, and certain remarkable attitudes might be recognized as suggesting unselfish forms of activity or contemplation. Recent experiments have established the existence, among chimpanzees, of certain rudimentary forms of symbolic thought. What is remarkable is that it is especially feelings, such as religious fear and the ambiguity of the sacred, normally associated with the noblest part of human nature, that are the most easily identified among the anthropoids.[2] But if these phenomena all plead by their presence, their paucity is even more eloquent and in quite a different way. The rudimentary outline they provide is less striking than the apparently utter impossibility, confirmed by all the specialists, of developing these hints beyond their most primitive expression. Consequently, the gap which a thousand ingenious observations were expected to close has in reality merely shifted, whereby it appears even more insuperable. When it has been shown that there is no anatomical obstacle to a monkey's articulating the sounds of speech, or even to his stringing syllables together, one can only be further impressed by the irremediable lack of language and the total incapacity to treat sounds uttered or heard as signs. The same must be acknowledged in other fields. This explains the pessimistic conclusion of an attentive observer, resigned after years of study and experimentation, to see the chimpanzee as 'a being hardened in the narrow circle of his own innate imperfections, "regressive" in comparison with man, neither desirous nor capable of tackling the path of progress'.[3]

But even the failures in the face of exact testing are not so convincing as the more general finding, which goes much more deeply into the problem, that general conclusions cannot be drawn from experiment. The social life of monkeys does not lend itself to the formulation of any norm. Whether faced by male or female, the living or the dead, the young or the old, a relative or a stranger, the monkey's behaviour is surprisingly changeable. Not only is the behaviour of a single subject inconsistent, but there is no regular pattern to

---

[1] Guillaume and Meyerson, 1930, pp. 92–7; 1931, pp. 481–555; 1934, pp. 497–554; 1938, pp. 425–48.
[2] Köhler, 1928, appendix.
[3] Kohts, 1937, p. 531; 1928, pp. 255–75; 1930, pp. 412–47.

be discerned in collective behaviour. Furthermore, in sexual life, as in other forms of activity, the external or internal stimulus, and rough adjustments, as influenced by successes and failures, seem to provide all the elements necessary to the solution of problems of interpretation. These uncertainties appear in the study of hierarchical relationships within the one group of vertebrates – a study, nevertheless, which can establish an order of subordination for the animals in their relations with one another. This order is remarkably stable, since the one animal retains the dominant position for anything up to a year. Yet frequent irregularities make systematization impossible. A fowl, subordinate to two others in the middle of the hierarchical table, nevertheless attacks the bird with the higher rank. Triangular relationships are observed in which A dominates B, B dominates C, and C dominates A, while all three dominate the rest of the group.[1]

It is the same with the relationships and individual tastes of anthropoid apes, among which such irregularities are even more pronounced: 'Primates are much more variable in their food preferences than rats, pigeons, and hens.'[2] In addition, the sex life of these anthropoids provides a 'picture that almost covers the entire field of sexual behaviour in man . . . all of the "normal" elements . . . also . . . the more conspicuous of the elements usually designated as "abnormal" in that they run up against social conventions.[3] The orang-utan, gorilla and chimpanzee especially resemble man in this individualization of behaviour.'[4]

Malinowski, then, is wrong when he writes that all the factors which define the sexual behaviour of male anthropoids 'are common to all individuals of the species. They work with such uniformity that for each animal species one set of data and only one has to be given . . . The variations . . . are so small and irrelevant that the zoologist ignores them and is fully justified in in doing so.'[5]

What then is the real state of affairs? Polyandry seems to prevail among the howler monkeys of Panama, since the proportion of females to males is 28 to 72. In fact, a female in heat has been observed to have promiscuous relations with several males, but without preferences, or an order of priority, or lasting bonds being definable.[6] The gibbons of the Siam forests live in relatively stable monogamous families, but sexual relations take place without discrimination between members of the same family group, or with an individual belonging to another group, thus proving, it could be said, the native belief that gibbons are the reincarnations of unhappy lovers.[7] Monogamy and polygamy exist side by side among the rhesus monkeys,[8] and while bands of wild chimpanzees observed in Africa vary from four to fourteen in number the question of their conjugal system remains unanswered.[9]

[1] Allee, 1942.　　　　[2] Maslow, 1933, p. 196.　　　　[3] Miller, 1931, p. 392.
[4] Yerkes, 1927, p. 181; Yerkes and Elder, 1936, p. 39.
[5] Malinowski, 1927, p. 194.　　　[6] Carpenter, 1934, p. 128.　　　[7] ibid. 1940, p. 195.
[8] ibid. 1942.　　　　　　　　[9] Nissen, 1931, p. 73.

It seems as if the great apes, having broken away from a specific pattern of behaviour, were unable to re-establish a norm on any new plane. The clear and precise instinctive behaviour of most mammals is lost to them, but the difference is purely negative and the field that nature has abandoned remains unoccupied.

This absence of rules seems to provide the surest criterion for distinguishing a natural from a cultural process. Nowhere is this suggested more than in the contrast between the attitude of the child, even when very young, whose every problem is ruled by clear distinctions, sometimes clearer and more imperative than for the adult, and the relationships among members of a simian group, which are left entirely to chance and accident and in which the behaviour of an individual subject today teaches nothing about his congener's behaviour, nor guarantees anything about his own behaviour, tomorrow. In fact, a vicious circle develops in seeking in nature for the origin of institutional rules which presuppose, or rather, are culture, and whose establishment within a group without the aid of language is difficult to imagine. Strictly speaking, there is consistency and regularity in nature as in culture, but these features appear in nature precisely where in culture they are weakest, and vice versa. In nature this is the field of biological heredity, and in culture, that of external tradition. An illusory continuity between the two orders cannot be asked to account for points of contrast.

No empirical analysis, then, can determine the point of transition between natural and cultural facts, nor how they are connected. The foregoing discussion has not merely brought us to this negative result, but has provided the most valid criterion of social attitudes, viz., the presence or absence of rules in patterns of behaviour removed from instinctive determination. Wherever there are rules we know for certain that the cultural stage has been reached. Likewise, it is easy to recognize universality as the criterion of nature, for what is constant in man falls necessarily beyond the scope of customs, techniques and institutions whereby his groups are differentiated and contrasted. Failing a real analysis, the double criterion of norm and universality provides the principle for an ideal analysis which, at least in certain cases and within certain limits, may allow the natural to be isolated from the cultural elements which are involved in more complex syntheses. Let us suppose then that everything universal in man relates to the natural order, and is characterized by spontaneity, and that everything subject to a norm is cultural and is both relative and particular. We are then confronted with a fact, or rather, a group of facts, which, in the light of previous definitions, are not far removed from a scandal: we refer to that complex group of beliefs, customs, conditions and institutions described succinctly as the prohibition of incest, which presents, without the slightest ambiguity, and inseparably combines, the two characteristics in which we recognize the conflicting features of two mutually exclusive orders.[1] It constitutes a rule, but a rule which, alone among all the social rules, possesses at the same time a universal character. That the prohibition of incest constitutes a rule need scarcely be shown. It is sufficient to recall that the prohibition of marriage between close relatives may vary in its field of application according to what each group defines as a close relative, but, sanctioned by no doubt variable penalties, ranging from immediate execution of the guilty parties to widespread reprobation, sometimes merely ridicule, this prohibition is nevertheless to be found in all social groups.

In fact, the famous exceptions and their small number which traditional sociology is often content to emphasize cannot be called upon here, for every society is an exception to the incest prohibition when seen by another society with a stricter rule. This being so, it is appalling to think how many exceptions a Paviotso Indian would record. When reference is made to the three classical exceptions, Egypt, Peru and Hawaii, and to several others which must be added (Azande, Madagascar, Burma, etc.), it must not be overlooked that these systems are exceptions only in comparison with our own, in that their prohibitions cover a more limited area. But the idea of exception is completely relative, with a very different meaning for an Australian aborigine, a Thongan or an Eskimo.

It is not so much, then, whether some groups allow marriages that others prohibit, but whether there are any groups in which no type of marriage whatever is prohibited. The answer must be completely in the negative, for two reasons: firstly, because marriage is never allowed between all near relatives, but only between certain categories (half-sister, to the exclusion of sister, sister to the exclusion of mother, etc.); secondly, because these consanguineous marriages are either temporary and ritualistic, or, where permanent and official, nevertheless remain the privilege of a very limited social category. Thus in Madagascar, the mother, the sister, and sometimes also the cousin, are prohibited spouses for the common people, while for the great chiefs and kings, only the mother, but the mother nevertheless, is *fady* or 'prohibited'. But there is so little 'exception' to the prohibition of incest that the native conscience is very sensitive about it. When a household is sterile, an incestuous relationship, although unknown, is taken for granted, and prescribed expiatory ceremonies are celebrated automatically.[1]

Ancient Egypt is more disturbing since recent discoveries[2] suggest that consanguineous marriage, particularly between brother and sister, was perhaps a custom which extended to the petty officials and artisans, and was not, as formerly believed,[3] limited to the reigning caste and to the later dynasties. But as regards incest, there is no absolute exception. One day my eminent colleague, Ralph Linton, told me that in the genealogy of a Samoan

[1] Dubois, 1938, pp. 876–9.   [2] Murray, 1934, p. 282.
[3] Amelineau, 1895, pp. 72–3; Flinders-Petrie, 1923, p. 110.

---

[1] 'If ten ethnologists were asked to indicate one universal human institution, probably nine would choose the prohibition of incest. Several have already formally designated it as the only universal institution' (cf. Kroeber, 1939, p. 448).

noble family studied by him, of eight consecutive marriages between brother and sister, only one involved a younger sister, and native opinion condemned it as immoral. Marriage between brother and older sister appears then as a concession to the law of primogeniture, and it does not exclude the prohibition of incest, since over and above the mother and daughter, the younger sister remains prohibited as a spouse, or at least not viewed with favour. Now one of the rare texts we possess in the social organization of Ancient Egypt suggests a similar interpretation. It is the Bulak Papyrus No. 5, which tells the story of a king's daughter who wished to marry her older brother, and her mother remarked, 'If I have no more children after those two, is it not the law for them to marry?'[1] Here also there seems to be a form of prohibition approving marriage with the older sister, but not with the younger. As will be seen later the scope of our interpretation is widened by ancient Japanese texts which describe incest as a union with the younger, to the exclusion of the older sister. The rule of universality, even in these perhaps extreme cases, is no less apparent than the normative character of the institution.

Here therefore is a phenomenon which has the distinctive characteristics both of nature and of its theoretical contradiction, culture. The prohibition of incest has the universality of bent and instinct, and the coercive character of law and institution. Where then does it come from, and what is its place and significance? Inevitably extending beyond the historical and geographical limits of culture, and co-extensive with the biological species, the prohibition of incest, however, through social prohibition, doubles the spontaneous action of the natural forces with which its own features contrast, although itself identical to these forms in field of application. As such, the prohibition of incest presents a formidable mystery to sociological thought. Few social prescriptions in our society have so kept that aura of respectful fear which clings to sacred objects. Significantly, as must be commented upon and explained later, incest proper, and its metaphorical form as the violation of a minor (by someone 'old enough to be her father', as the expression goes), even combines in some countries with its direct opposite, inter-racial sexual relations, an extreme form of exogamy, as the two most powerful inducements to horror and collective vengeance. But not only does this aura of magical fear define the climate in which this institution is evolving even yet in modern society, but on the theoretical plane as well, it envelops those debates with which sociology, since its inception, has, with an ambiguous tenacity, been concerned: 'The famous question of the prohibition of incest,' writes Lévy-Bruhl, 'this *vexata quaestio*, whose solution has been so sought after by ethnographers and sociologists, has none. There is no purpose in asking it. In the societies just discussed, it is useless wondering why incest is forbidden. The prohibition does not exist . . . There is no consideration given to prohibiting it. It is something that does not occur, or, if by some impossibility it does occur, it is unparalleled, a *monstrum*, a transgression

[1] Maspero, 1889, p. 171.

spreading horror and fear. Do primitive peoples recognize a prohibition on autophagy or fratricide? There is no more nor less reason for them to prohibit incest.'[1]

To find so ill at ease a writer who otherwise did not falter at the boldest hypotheses is not surprising if it is borne in mind that almost all sociologists exhibit the same repugnance and timidity in the face of this problem.

[1] Lévy-Bruhl, 1931, p. 247.

CHAPTER II

The Problem of Incest

I

The problem of the prohibition of incest displays all the ambiguity which, on a different plane, undoubtedly accounts for the sacredness of the prohibition itself. This rule is at once social, in that it is a rule, and pre-social, in its universality and the type of relationships upon which it imposes its norm. Man's sexual life is itself external to the group, firstly, in being the highest expression of his animal nature, and the most significant survival of instinct, and secondly, in that its ends are to satisfy individual desires, which, as is known, hold little respect for social conventions, and specific tendencies, which, although in another sense, also go beyond society's own ends. However, if the regulation of relationships between the sexes represents an overflow of culture into nature, in another way sexual life is one beginning of social life in nature, for the sexual is man's only instinct requiring the stimulation of another person. This point must be taken up later. That it should provide a transition, in itself natural, between nature and culture, would be inconceivable, but it does give one reason why the change can and must necessarily take place in the field of sexual life above any other. It is a rule which embraces that which in society is most foreign to it, but also a social rule which retains what in nature is most likely to go beyond it. The incest prohibition is at once on the threshold of culture, in culture, and in one sense, as we shall try to show, culture itself. Let it suffice for the moment to note the inherent duality to which it owes its ambiguous and equivocal character. Rather than accounting for this ambiguousness, sociologists have been almost exclusively concerned with reducing it. Their attempts fall into three principal types, which we shall distinguish and discuss here only in their essential features.

II

Following the popular belief of many societies, including our own, the first type of explanation attempts to maintain the dual character of the prohibition by dividing it into two distinct phases. For Lewis H. Morgan and Sir Henry Maine,[1] for example, the origin of the incest prohibition is really

[1] Maine, 1886, p. 228.

both natural and social, but in the sense that it results from a social reflection *upon* a natural phenomenon. The incest prohibition is taken to be a protective measure, shielding the species from the disastrous results of consanguineous marriages. This theory is remarkable in that it is required by its very statement to extend to all human societies, even to the most primitive, which in other matters give no indication of any such eugenic second-sight, the sensational privilege of knowing the alleged consequences of endogamous unions. This justification for the prohibition of incest is of recent origin, appearing nowhere in our society before the sixteenth century. Following the general pattern of his *Moralia* and impartially listing all possibilities without showing a preference for any one of them, Plutarch proposes three hypotheses, all sociological in nature, none referring to eventual defects in the descendants. Only Gregory the Great[1] can be quoted to the contrary, but his work does not seem to have had any influence on the thought of contemporaries or on later commentators.[2]

It is true that various monstrosities are threatened to the descendants of incestuous parents in the folklore of various primitive peoples, notably the Australian aborigines. But apart from the fact that this Australian aboriginal taboo is probably the least concerned with biological proximity (it permits unions, such as grand-uncle with grand-niece, the effects of which cannot be particularly favourable), it is sufficient to note that such punishments are, in primitive tradition, commonly expected for all those who break rules, and are in no way especially confined to reproduction. The extent to which hasty observations should be distrusted is well brought out in Jochelson's remarks:

> 'These Yakut told me that they had observed that children born from consanguineous marriages are generally unhealthy. Thus, my interpreter, Dolganoff, told me that it had been observed among the Yukaghir that in case of marriages between cousins – which are contracted regardless of the custom of *n'exi'yini* . . . – the children die, or the parents themselves are subject to disease which frequently result in death.'[3]

So much for natural sanctions. As for social sanctions, they are based so little upon physiological considerations that among the Kenyah and Kayan of Borneo, who condemn marriage with mother, sister, daughter, father's sister or mother's sister, and with brother's daughter or sister's daughter, 'in the case of those women who stand to him in any of these relations in virtue of adoption, the prohibitions and severe penalties are if possible even more strictly enforced'.[4]

Furthermore, it must be remembered that since the end of the paleolithic

---

[1] Muller, 1913, pp. 294–5.   [2] Cooper, 1932.

[3] Jochelson, 1910–26, p. 80. The Nuer call incest 'syphilis' because they see in one the punishment of the other (Evans-Pritchard, 1935, p. 11).

[4] Hose and McDougall, 1912, vol. I, p. 73. These authors remark that this observation demonstrates the *artificiality* of the rules concerning incest, ibid. vol. II, p. 197.

era man has increasingly perfected cultivated or domesticated species through the use of endogamous reproductive methods. If it is supposed that man was conscious of the results of such methods, and also that he had judged the matter rationally, what explanation could be given as to how, in the field of human relationships, he reached conclusions running counter to those which his everyday experience in the animal and vegetable kingdoms continually served to prove, and upon which his very well-being depended? Moreover, if primitive man had been conscious of such considerations, why, instead of setting prohibitions upon himself, did he not turn to prescriptions whose experimental results had, at least in certain cases, shown beneficial effects? Not only did he not do so, but we ourselves still recoil from any such undertaking, and it has been only in recent social theories, denounced moreover as irrational, that the planned reproduction of man has been recommended. The positive prescriptions most commonly encountered in primitive societies, in association with the prohibition of incest, are those which tend to increase the number of marriages between cross-cousins (the respective descendants of a brother and a sister), and which, in this way, place identical forms of marriage, from the point of view of proximity, at the two extreme poles of social regulation: the marriage of parallel cousins (descended from two brothers or two sisters) is likened to fraternal incest, and cross-cousin marriage, despite the very close degree of consanguinity between the spouses, is regarded as an ideal.

Nevertheless, it is striking to see how contemporary thought is loth to abandon the idea that the prohibition of relations between immediate consanguines or collaterals is justified for eugenic reasons, doubtless because, as we have experienced in the last ten years, it is in the field of biological concepts that we find the last traces of deductive reasoning still prevalent in modern thought. A particularly significant example comes from a writer whose scientific work has contributed most highly in dispelling the prejudices surrounding consanguineous unions. East, namely, has shown, in some admirable work on the reproduction of maize, that the creation of an endogamous line results first in a period of fluctuations during which the type is subject to extreme variations, undoubtedly because of the resurgence of recessive characteristics which are usually hidden. Then the variabilities gradually diminish, ending in a constant and invariable type. In a work destined for a wider audience, the author, having recapitulated these results, draws the conclusion that popular beliefs about marriages between near relatives are largely justified, laboratory work merely confirming the prejudices of folklore, for, as one old writer said, 'Superstition is often awake when reezon iz asleep.'[1] This is so because 'objectionable recessive traits are common in the human race as they are in maize'.[2] But, except for mutations, this troublesome reappearance of recessive characteristics is explicable only where work is being done on previously selected types, the characteristics which reappear

[1] East, 1938, p. 156.   [2] loc. cit.

being precisely those that the age-long effort of the stock-breeder has success-fully eliminated. With man, this situation is not to be found, since, as we have just seen, the exogamy practised in human societies is a blind exogamy. But more especially East's work has indirectly established that these supposed dangers would never have appeared if mankind had been endogamous from the beginning. If this were so, human races would probably be as constant and as definitively fixed as the endogamous lines of maize after the elimina-tions of variable factors. The temporary danger of endogamous unions, sup-posing such a danger to exist, obviously stems from an exogamous or pangenetic tradition, but it cannot be the cause of this tradition.

As a matter of fact, consanguineous marriages merely match up genes of the same type, while a system having the law of probability as its only deter-minant for the union of the sexes (Dahlberg's 'amphimixis') would mix them haphazardly. But the nature of genes and their individual characteristics remain the same in both cases. Consanguineous unions need only be inter-rupted for the general composition of the population to revert to what might be expected on a basis of 'amphimixis'. Consanguineous marriages con-tracted long before therefore have no influence; they affect only the generations immediately following. But this influence is itself a function of the absolute dimensions of the group. In any given population, a state of equilibrium can always be defined in which the frequency of consanguineous marriage is equal to the probability of such marriages in an 'amphimixis' system. If the population goes beyond this state of equilibrium, the frequency of con-sanguineous marriages remaining the same, then the number of carriers of recessive characteristics will increase: 'The enlargement of the isolate brings with it an increase of heterozygosity at the expense of homozygosity'.[1] If the population falls below the state of equilibrium, the frequency of consan-guineous marriages remaining 'normal' in comparison, the recessive charac-teristics are lowered at a progressive rate of 0·0572 per cent in a population of 500 with two children per family, and of 0·1697 per cent if the same population falls to 200. Dahlberg can thus conclude that 'as far as heredity is concerned these inhibitions do not seem to be justified'[2] from the standpoint of the theory of heredity.

It is true that mutations determining the appearance of a recessive defect are more dangerous in small than in large populations. In fact, the chances of a transition to homozygosity are greater in small populations. However, this same rapid and complete transition to homozygosity will sooner or later ensure the elimination of the dreaded characteristic. Consequently, in a small, stable, endogamous population, as exemplified by many primitive societies, the only risk in marriages between consanguines arises from the appearance of new mutations, a risk that can be calculated since the rate of appearance is known. But the chances of finding a recessive heterozygote within the group are slimmer than would attend marriage with a stranger.

[1] Dahlberg, 1937–8, p. 224.   [2] ibid. 1929, p. 454.

Even in connection with recessive characteristics arising from mutation within a given population, Dahlberg estimates that the rôle of consanguineous marriages in the production of homozygotes is very slight, because for every homozygote from a consanguineous marriage, there are an enormous number of heterozygotes which, if the population is sufficiently small, will necessarily reproduce among themselves. Hence, in a population of eighty, the prohibition of marriage between near relatives, including first cousins, would only reduce the carriers of rare recessive characteristics by 10 per cent to 15 per cent.[1] These considerations are important since they introduce the quantitative notion of population size. The economic systems of some primitive or archaic societies severely limit population size, and it is precisely for a population of such a size that the regulation of consanguineous marriages can have only negligible genetic consequences. Without fully attacking the problem to which modern theoreticians can only hazard provisional and highly varied solutions,[2] it can therefore be seen that primitive mankind was not in a demographic position which would even have permitted him to ascertain the facts of the matter.

III

The second type of explanation tends to do away with one of the terms of the antinomy between the natural and social characteristics of this institution. For a large group of sociologists and psychologists, represented principally by Westermarck and Havelock Ellis, the prohibition of incest is no more than the social projection or reflection of natural feelings or tendencies, which can be entirely expanded by human nature. Quite important variations may be noted among those supporting this position, some deriving the horror of incest, the postulated origin of the prohibition, from the physiological nature of man, and others rather from his psychic tendencies. As a matter of fact, the old preconception of the 'voice of blood' has merely been revived, and here expressed more negatively than positively. This alleged horror of incest can only be manifested when a kinship relationship is supposedly known, or later established, between the guilty parties, and this sufficiently substantiates that its source cannot be instinctive. There remains the interpretation that this horror is based upon actual attraction, or the lack of it. Thus Havelock Ellis explains the repugnance for incest by the negative effect of daily habits upon erotic excitability, while Westermarck adopts a similar but more strictly psychological interpretation.[3]

[1] Dahlberg, 1937–8, p. 220.

[2] Baur, Fischer and Lenz, 1927; Dahlberg, 1930–1, pp. 83–96; Hogben, 1931; Haldane, 1938; cf. also ch. VIII below.

[3] Havelock Ellis, 1906; Westermarck, 1891, vol. I, p. 20 et seq. and vol. II, p. 207 et seq. Westermarck's position provides curious variations. Moving away from the Havelock Ellis type of interpretation based on instinct, in the first edition of his *The History of Human Marriage*, he was to develop towards a more psychological conception, which is apparent in the second edition. However, towards the end of his life (Westermarck, 1934a, pp. 22–40), reacting against B. Z. Seligman and Malinowski, he returned not only to his 1891 position

The objection might be raised that these writers are confusing two forms of familiarization, the first of which develops between two individuals who are sexually united, generally bringing about a lessening of desire, and which a modern biologist declares, 'is one of the disturbing elements in every social system'.[1] The second prevails among near relatives and is thought to have the same result, although sexual activity, which plays the determining rôle in the first case, is obviously absent in the second. The proposed interpretation therefore begs the question, for without experimental verification there is no knowing whether the alleged observation on which it rests, viz., that sexual desire is less frequent among near relatives, is to be explained either by these relatives being physically or psychologically accustomed to one another, or as a consequence of the taboos which constitute the prohibition. Therefore, the observation is assumed at the very moment of its alleged explanation.

There is nothing more dubious than this alleged instinctive repugnance, for although prohibited by law and morals, incest does exist and is no doubt even more frequent by far than a collective conspiracy of silence would lead us to believe. To explain the theoretical universality of the rule by the universality of the sentiment or tendency is to open up a new problem, for in no conceivable way is this supposedly universal fact universal. Hence, if all the numerous exceptions were treated as perversions or anomalies, it would remain to be defined in what these anomalies consist, on the only level to which they might be referred without tautology, i.e., the physiological, which would undoubtedly be all the more difficult now that the attitude taken by an important modern school towards this problem runs completely counter to Havelock Ellis and Westermarck. Psychoanalysis, namely, finds a universal phenomenon not in the repugnance towards incestuous relationships, but on the contrary in the pursuit of such relationships.

Nor is it certain that familiarity is always regarded as being fatal to marriage. Many societies judge otherwise. 'The desire for a wife begins with the sister', an Azande proverb says. The Hehe justify their custom of cross-cousin marriage by the long intimacy between the future spouses, which is seen by them as the true cause of sentimental and sexual attraction.[2] And it is the very same type of relationship which Westermarck and Havelock Ellis regarded as the origin of the horror of incest that the Chukchee strive to make the model of exogamous marriage:

'Most of the marriages between relatives (that is, cousins) are concluded at a tender age, sometimes when the bridegroom and the bride are still infants. The marriage ritual is performed, and the children grow up,

---

[1] Miller, 1931, p. 398. This innate tendency of man to become tired of his sexual partner is common to him and to the higher apes, ibid. p. 386.   [2] Brown, 1934, p. 33.

but even to the belief that the ultimate origin for the prohibition was to be sought in a vague awareness of the harmful consequences of consanguineous unions (Westermarck, 1934*b*, p. 53 et seq.).

playing together. When a little older, they tend the herd together. Of course, the ties between them grow to be very strong, often stronger even than death: when one dies, the other also dies from grief, or commits suicide.

'Similar to these marriages are those between the members of families friendly to each other, though not connected by ties of blood. Sometimes such families agree to a marriage between their children even before the children are born.'[1]

Even among the Indians of the Thompson River in British Columbia, where marriage between second cousins is treated and derided as incestuous, this hostility to even distant consanguineous marriages does not prevent men from being betrothed to girls twenty years younger than themselves.[2] Facts such as these could be multiplied indefinitely.

But there is an infinitely more serious confusion underlying the attitude under discussion. Why, if it resulted from congenital physiological and psychological tendencies, should the horror of incest be expressed as a prohibition so solemn and so essential as to be found enveloped by the same aura of sacredness in every human society? There is no point in forbidding what would not happen if it were not forbidden. Two answers can be given to this argument. The first is that the prohibition is only meant for certain exceptional cases in which nature has failed. But what proportion is there between the exceptions, which *ex hypothesi* must be extremely rare, and the importance of the regulations directed against them? In particular, if these errings were not regarded as harmful and dangerous, why should they be prohibited, let alone punished, with such extreme severity in many societies? The origin of the prohibition of incest must be sought in the existence, or in the assumed existence, of this danger for the group, the individuals concerned, or their descendants. We are brought back inevitably to the previous explanation. It is true that a comparison could be made with suicide, against which multiple sanctions are levelled by morality and often the law itself, even though self-preservation is a natural tendency in all living beings. But the analogy between incest and suicide is only apparent, for if society prohibits them both this prohibition applies in the first case to a natural phenomenon found commonly among animals, and in the second, to a phenomenon which is completely foreign to animal life and which should be regarded as a function of social life. Society expressly forbids only that which society brings about. Next, and in particular, society condemns suicide because it considers it harmful to its interests, and not because it constitutes the denial of a congenital tendency. A better proof is that, while every society prohibits incest, there is none which does not make room for suicide and does not recognize it as legitimate in certain circumstances or for certain motives when the individual attitude happens to coincide with some social interest. Accord-

---

[1] Bogoras, 1904–9, p. 577.   [2] Teit, 1900, pp. 321, 325.

ingly, the reasons why incest is prejudicial to the social order still remain to be discovered.

IV

The third type of explanation and the one just discussed have this in common, that they both claim to do away with one of the terms of the antinomy. In this way, they both contrast with the first type of explanation, which keeps both terms while trying to dissociate them. However, while advocates of the second type of explanation choose to reduce the prohibition of incest to some instinctive psychological or physiological phenomenon, the third group adopts the similar but contrary position of seeing it as a rule whose origin is purely social, its expression in biological terms being accidental and of minor importance. Because this last point of view is subject to more variations among its authors it must be set out in a little more detail than the others.

Considered as a social institution, the prohibition of incest has two different aspects. Sometimes it is only a prohibition of sexual union between close consanguines or collaterals, while at others this form of the prohibition, based as it is upon a definite biological criterion, is only one aspect of a broader system which is apparently without any biological basis. In many societies the rule of exogamy prohibits marriage between social categories which include near relatives, but, along with them, a considerable number of individuals for whom it is impossible to establish all but the most distant consanguineous or collateral relationships. In this case, it is an apparent caprice of the nomenclature to assimilate individuals who fall under the prohibition to biological relatives.

Advocates of the third type of interpretation give their particular attention to the broad and social form of the incest prohibition. But let us discard, without further delay, Morgan and Frazer's suggestions that exogamous systems incorporate methods for preventing incestuous unions, which are actually only a small fraction of the unions that these systems do prohibit. In fact, as is proved by societies with neither clans nor moieties, the same result could be achieved without cumbersome rules of exogamy. If this first hypothesis provides a highly unsatisfactory explanation for exogamy, it provides no explanation at all for the prohibition of incest. Much more important from our point of view are theories giving a sociological interpretation of exogamy, or else leaving open the possibility that the incest prohibition may have derived from exogamy, or categorically affirming the existence of such a derivation.

In the first group are included the ideas of McLennan, Spencer and Lubbock,[1] and in the second those of Durkheim. McLennan and Spencer saw exogamous practices as the fixing by custom of the habits of warrior tribes among whom capture was the normal means of obtaining wives. Lubbock outlined an evolutionary transition from endogamous group marriage to

[1] McLennan, 1865; Spencer, 1882–96; Lubbock, 1870, p. 83 et seq.; Lubbock, 1911.

exogamous marriage by capture. As opposed to wives gained endogamously, wives acquired by capture would have the status of individual possessions, and only they, for this reason, would provide the prototype for modern individual marriage. All these ideas can be discarded very simply, since, if they do not establish any connection between exogamy and the prohibition of incest, they fall outside our study, and if, on the contrary, they do offer applicable solutions not only to the rules of exogamy but to that particular form of exogamy which is the prohibition of incest, they are still completely unacceptable, for they would then claim to derive a general law, the prohibition of incest, from some special and often sporadic phenomenon, no doubt associated with certain societies but having no possible universality. They have this and several other methodological defects in common with Durkheim's theory, which is the most conscientious and systematic interpretation from purely social causes.

The hypothesis advanced by Durkheim in the important work which inaugurated the *Année sociologique*[1] has three characteristics. Firstly, it is based upon the universalization of facts observed in a limited group of societies; secondly, it makes the prohibition of incest a distant consequence of rules of exogamy; and, thirdly, these rules of exogamy are interpreted by reference to phenomena of a different order. Durkheim believed that the observation of Australian societies, which were regarded as illustrating a primitive type of organization formerly common to every human society, would provide the solution to the problem of incest. As is well known the religious life of these societies is dominated by beliefs affirming an identity of substance between the clan and the eponymous totem. The belief in this substantial identity explains the special prohibitions imposed upon blood, which is considered as the sacred symbol and the origin of the magico-biological community uniting members of the one clan. This fear of clan blood is particularly intense as regards menstrual blood, and it explains why, in most primitive societies, women are subject, because of their menstrual periods, and then in a more general way, to magical beliefs and special prohibitions. Consequently, the prohibitions relating to women and their segregation, such as in the rule of exogamy, would only be the distant repercussions of religious beliefs which originally did not distinguish between the sexes, but which changed with the link which became established in men's minds between blood and the female sex. In the final analysis, if the rule of exogamy prevents a man contracting a marriage within his own clan, it is because otherwise he would risk coming in contact with that blood which is the visible sign and substantial expression of his kinship with his totem. Since the totem of others is unaffected by prohibitions and does not contain any magical force, there is no such danger for members of another clan, and accordingly there arose the double rule of interclan marriage and the prohibition of marriage within the clan. As conceived nowadays, the prohibition of incest is

[1] Durkheim, 1898.

only a vestige or relic of that complex collection of beliefs and prohibitions, with roots extending into a magico-religious system where ultimately the explanation lies. Consequently, by proceeding analytically, we see that for Durkheim the prohibition of incest is a remnant of exogamy, that this exogamy is explicable in terms of the special prohibitions relating to women, that these prohibitions originate in the fear of menstrual blood, that this fear is only a particular case of the general fear of blood, and finally, that this fear merely expresses certain feelings deriving from the belief in the consubstantiality of the individual clan member and his totem.

The strength of this interpretation proceeds from its capacity to systematize widely varying phenomena, which, when taken separately, are seemingly very difficult to comprehend. Its weakness lies in the fact that the connexions so established are fragile and arbitrary. Let us leave aside the prejudicial objection drawn from the non-universality of totemic beliefs. In fact, Durkheim postulates this universality, and it is highly probable he would maintain his position, in view of contemporary observations which in no way prove this theory, but which cannot give reasons to invalidate it either. But even accepting his hypothesis for the moment, we find no logical link between the various stages allowing them to be deduced from the initial postulate. The relationship linking each of the stages with its predecessor is arbitrary, and there is no *a priori* proof either for or against its existence. Take first the belief in totemic substantiality. We know that this belief poses no obstacle to the eating of the totem, but merely confers some ceremonial significance upon this eating. Marriage and, in very many societies, the sexual act itself have a ceremonial and ritualistic significance in no way incompatible with the claim that they represent a form of totemic communion. Secondly, the horror of blood, especially menstrual blood, is not universal.[1] Young Winnebago Indians visit their mistresses and take advantage of the privacy of the prescribed isolation of these women during their menstrual period.[2]

On the other hand, where the horror of menstrual blood seems to reach its culminating point, it is by no means obvious that the imourity should have predilections, or limits. The Chaga, a Bantu tribe living on the slopes of Mt. Kilimanjaro, have a patrilineal social organization. However, the instructions lavished upon girls during initiation put them on guard against the general dangers of menstrual blood, and not against the special dangers to which people of the same blood would be exposed. Moreover, it seems to be the mother, and not the father, who runs the gravest danger:

'Do not show it to your mother, for she would die! Do not show it to your age-mates, for there may be a wicked one among them, who will take away the cloth with which you have cleaned yourself, and you will be barren in your marriage. Do not show it to a bad woman, who will take

[1] Van Waters, 1913.   [2] Radin, 1920, p. 393.

the cloth to place it in the top of her hut . . . with the result that you cannot bear children. Do not throw the cloth on the path or in the bush. A wicked person might do evil things with it. Bury it in the ground. Protect the blood from the gaze of your father, brothers and sisters. It is a sin to let them see it.'[1]

The Aleutian does not copulate with his wife during her menstrual periods for fear of bad hunting, but if a father sees his daughter during her first menstrual period, she risks becoming blind and mute. The dangers are all for her, not for him.[2] As a rule, a woman is impure during her menses, not only for her clan relatives, but also for her exogamous husband, and for everyone in general. This point is vital since Durkheim claims to derive exogamy from a combination of customs and prohibitions relating to women, of which it is presumably in some way the consequence, and from difficulties to which it might provide a solution. However, these prohibitions are not lifted when the rule of exogamy is applied, and they are imposed indifferently upon endogamous as well as exogamous members of the group. Moreover, how did the rule of exogamy appear if prejudices relating to menstrual blood were its only source? The prohibition of sexual relations with the wife during her menses would be enough to avoid any risk of pollution. If the rules of exogamy have no other function, they are superfluous and incomprehensible, especially when one considers the innumerable complications which they introduce into group life. If these rules have arisen it is because they satisfy other demands and fulfil other functions.

The sociological interpretations of Durkheim, as well as of McLennan, Spencer and Lubbock, have one basic defect in common. They attempt to establish a universal phenomenon on an historical sequence, which is by no means inconceivable in some particular case but whose episodes are so contingent that the possibility of this sequence being repeated unchanged in every human society must be wholly excluded. In being the most complex, the Durkheimian sequence falls most heavily under this criticism. It is possible to imagine that, in a given society, the origin of some particular institution is to be explained by some highly arbitrary transformations. History provides examples. But history also shows that, according to the society considered, such processes may result in widely differing institutions, and that where analogous institutions have found independent origins in various parts of the world, the historical sequences leading up to their appearances are themselves highly dissimilar. This is what is termed convergence. But if the results of a succession of immutably repeated events were always identical (as in the physical sciences), the conclusion could be reached with assurance that these events are not the reason for the phenomenon's existence but point to a law which alone provides the explanation. Durkheim does not propose any law which might account for the necessary transition in the human mind

[1] Raum, 1939, p. 559.   [2] Jochelson, n.d., nos. 34–5.

from the belief in totemic substantiality to the horror of blood, from the horror of blood to the superstitious fear of women, and from this fear to the setting up of exogamous rules. The same criticism can be levelled at Lord Raglan's imaginary reconstructions. However, we have shown that there is nothing more arbitrary than this succession of transitions. Even if there were only these transitions at the origin of the incest prohibition, they would still have permitted other solutions, some of which at least should have eventuated, by the simple law of probabilities. For example, the prohibitions affecting women during their menstrual periods provided a very happy answer to the problem, and a number of societies could have been satisfied with it.

The ambiguity then is more serious than it seemed, bearing not solely or principally upon the validity of the facts involved, but also upon the way in which the prohibition itself must be conceived. McLennan, Lubbock, Spencer and Durkheim see the prohibition of incest, in comparison with current social conditions, as a survival from an altogether heterogeneous past. Consequently they are confronted with a dilemma, namely, if the whole institution is no more than a survival, how can the universality and vitality of the rule be understood, when only occasional formless traces of it might conceivably be brought to light, or does the prohibition of incest correspond in modern society to new and different functions? But this being the case, it must be acknowledged that the historical explanation does not exhaust the problem. Furthermore, might not the origin of the institution be found in those functions which are still current and are verifiable by observation rather than in a vague and hypothetical historical scheme? The problem of the incest prohibition is not so much to seek the different historical configurations for each group as to explain the particular form of the institution in each particular society. The problem is to discover what profound and omnipresent causes could account for the regulation of the relationships between the sexes in every society and age. Any different procedure would commit the same error as that of the linguist who believed that by studying the history of vocabulary he had exhausted the sum total of the phonetic or morphological laws governing the development of language.

v

This disappointing analysis at least explains why contemporary sociology has often preferred to confess itself powerless than to persist in what, because of so many failures, seems to be a closed issue. When it cannot tackle a problem of this importance, instead of admitting that its methods are inadequate and that its principles require revision and readjustment, it declares that the prohibition of incest is outside its field. It was in this manner that, in *Primitive Society*, where so many problems have been reopened, Robert Lowie came to the following conclusion regarding the question with which we are concerned: 'It is not the function of the ethnologist but of the biologist and psychologist to explain why man has so deep-rooted a horror of incest. . . The student of society merely has to reckon with the fact that the dread of incest limits the biologically possible number of unions'.[1] Another specialist writes on the same subject: 'It may be that it is impossible to explain or to trace the origin of any human custom that is universal; perhaps the most we can do is to correlate it with certain other conditions',[2] which amounts to the same thing as Lowie's renunciation. But the prohibition of incest would then clearly be the only case of the natural sciences being asked to account for the existence of a rule sanctioned by human authority.

It is true that, through its universality, the prohibition of incest touches upon nature, i.e., upon biology or psychology, or both. But it is just as certain that in being a rule it is a social phenomenon, and belongs to the world of rules, hence to culture, and to sociology, whose study is culture. In the Appendix to *Primitive Society*, Lowie, having perceived this very clearly, reconsiders the statement just quoted: 'Nevertheless, I do not believe, as formerly, that incest is *instinctively* repugnant to man . . . We . . . must consider his aversion towards incest as a former cultural adaptation.'[3] The almost general failure of theories gives no justification for the drawing of any other conclusion. Instead, analysis of the causes of this failure should lead to the readjustment of those principles and methods which provide the only possible basis for a viable ethnology. In fact, how could rules be analysed and interpreted if ethnology should confess its helplessness before the one pre-eminent and universal rule which assures culture's hold over nature?

We have shown that each of the early theoreticians who tackled the problem of the incest prohibition held one of the three following points of view. Some put forward the natural and cultural duality of the rule, but could only establish a rationally derived and extrinsic connection between the two aspects. Others have explained the prohibition of incest solely or predominantly if not in terms of natural causes, then as a cultural phenomenon. Each of these three outlooks has been found to lead to impossibilities or contradictions. Consequently, a transition from static analysis to dynamic synthesis is the only path remaining open. The prohibition of incest is in origin neither purely cultural nor purely natural, nor is it a composite mixture of elements from both nature and culture. It is the fundamental step because of which, by which, but above all in which, the transition from nature to culture is accomplished. In one sense, it belongs to nature, for it is a general condition of culture. Consequently, we should not be surprised that its formal characteristic, universality, has been taken from nature. However, in another sense, it is already culture, exercising and imposing its rule on phenomena which initially are not subject to it. We have been led to pose the problem of incest in connection with the relationship between man's biological existence and his social existence, and we have immediately established that the

[1] Lowie, 1961, p. 15.　　[2] Seligman, 1935, p. 75.　　[3] Lowie, 1935, pp. 446–7.

prohibition could not be ascribed accurately to either one or the other. In the present work we propose to find the solution to this anomaly by showing that the prohibition of incest is the link between them.

But this union is neither static nor arbitrary, and as soon as it comes into being, the whole situation is completely changed. Indeed, it is less a union than a transformation or transition. Before it, culture is still non-existent; with it, nature's sovereignty over man is ended. The prohibition of incest is where nature transcends itself. It sparks the formation of a new and more complex type of structure and is superimposed upon the simpler structures of physical life through integration, just as these themselves are superimposed upon the simpler structures of animal life. It brings about and is in itself the advent of a new order.

PART ONE
Restricted Exchange

Your own mother,
Your own sister,
Your own pigs,
Your own yams that you have piled up,
You may not eat.
Other people's mothers,
Other people's sisters,
Other people's pigs,
Other people's yams that they have piled up,
You may eat.

Arapesh aphorisms: M. Mead, *Sex and
Temperament in Three Primitive Societies*
(New York, 1935), p. 83.

CHAPTER III

The Universe of Rules

I

Even if the incest prohibition has its roots in nature it is only in the way it affects us as a social rule that it can be fully grasped. In form and in field of application it varies greatly from group to group. While highly limited in our society, in certain North American tribes it is extended to the most distant degrees of kinship. In this case there is no need to add that the prohibition is less concerned with true consanguinity, which is often impossible to establish, if at all, than with the purely social phenomenon by which two unrelated individuals are classed as 'brothers' or 'sisters', 'parents' or 'children'. The prohibition and the rule of exogamy, in this case, are therefore merged. Occasionally both institutions exist side by side. As has often been observed, exogamy by itself is not enough to prevent the marriage of a mother with her son in a patrilineal system, nor of a father with his daughter in a matrilineal system. But in many cases it is the rule of exogamy or the kinship system which is decisive, without taking real relationships, apart from those of the first degree, into account. It is the same law which in the marriage of cross-cousins likens one group of first cousins to brothers and sisters and makes the other half of these same cousins into potential spouses. The same system, and others also, highly recommends and sometimes prescribes marriage between the maternal uncle and his niece, and less commonly between the paternal aunt and her nephew, whereas similar behaviour by the paternal uncle or the maternal aunt would horrify just as much as would incest with the relatives to whom these collaterals are assimilated. It has often been noted that several contemporary legal systems omitted to register one or both of the grandparents among the prohibited degrees. This discrepancy can be explained by the high improbability of such marriages in modern societies, but among the Australian aborigines – otherwise so punctilious – and certain Oceanic peoples, such a union is not inconceivable, although other unions involving a more distant relationship are specifically forbidden. Hence, the prohibition is not always expressed in terms of degrees of real kinship but refers to individuals who use certain terms in addressing one another. This remains true even of those Oceanic systems which permit marriage with a classificatory 'sister', but distinguish immediately between

29

kave maori, or 'real sister', and *kave kesekese,* 'different sister', *kave fakata-fatafa,* 'sister set aside', *kave i take ŋaeŋa,* 'sister from another place'.[1] It is the social relationship more than the biological tie implied by the terms 'father', 'mother', 'son', 'daughter', 'brother', and 'sister', that acts as the determinant. For this reason especially, theories attempting to justify the prohibition of incest by the harmful consequences of consanguineous unions (including numerous primitive myths suggesting this interpretation) can only be regarded as rationalizations.

Considered from the most general viewpoint, the incest prohibition expresses the transition from the natural fact of consanguinity to the cultural fact of alliance. Nature by itself already moves to the double rhythm of receiving and giving, which finds expression in the opposition of marriage and descent. But, although present in both and in some way bestowing a common form upon them, this rhythm does not display the same aspect in both nature and culture. The characteristic of nature is that it can give only what has been received. Heredity expresses this permanence and continuity. However, in the sphere of culture, the individual always receives more than he gives, and gives more than he receives. This double disequilibrium is expressed by the processes of *education* and *invention,* one being the inverse of the other, and both contrasting with the process of heredity. It is certainly not our intention here to suggest that the vital phenomena should be considered as phenomena in equilibrium; the contrary is obviously true. But biological disequilibria only appear as such in their relationship with the physical world. In comparison with cultural phenomena, they show, on the contrary, stability, whereas dynamic synthesis is now applicable to the new phenomena. Seen thus, the problem of the transition from nature to culture is reduced to the problem of introducing the accumulatory processes within the repetitive process.

Based on natural facts, which hypothetically are all that are present, how is this introduction possible? As we have just emphasized, nature, like culture, moves to the double rhythm of receiving and giving. But the two moments of this rhythm, as produced by nature, are not viewed indifferently by culture. The first stage, that of receiving, as expressed through biological kinship, finds culture powerless, for a child's heredity is integrally inscribed in the genes transmitted by the parents; whatever they are, such will be the child. The transitory effect of the environment can leave its mark, but cannot make this permanent independently of changes in this environment. But for the moment let us consider marriage, which nature requires just as urgently as descent, if not in the same way or to the same extent. In the first instance, only the fact of marriage is required, but not, within specific limits, its determination. Nature assigns to each individual determinants transmitted by those who are in fact his parents, but it has nothing to do with deciding who these parents will be. Consequently, from the point of view of nature heredity is doubly necessary, firstly as a law – there is no spontaneous genera-

[1] Firth, 1936, p. 265.

tion – and secondly as a specification of the law, for nature not only says that one must have parents, but that one will be like them. As regards marriage, however, nature is satisfied with affirming the law, but is indifferent to its contents. If the relationship between parents and children is strictly determined by the nature of the parents, the relationship between male and female is left entirely to chance and probability. Thus, mutations aside, nature contains one solitary principle of indetermination, revealed in the arbitrariness of marriage. If, in keeping with the evidence, nature is acknowledged as being historically anterior to culture, it can be only through the possibilities left open by nature that culture has been able to place its stamp upon nature and introduce its own requirements without any discontinuity. Culture yields to the inevitability of biological heredity. Eugenics itself can barely claim to manipulate this irreducible fact while respecting its preconditions. But culture, although it is powerless before descent, becomes aware of its rights, and of itself, with the completely different phenomenon of marriage, in which nature for once has not already had the last word. There only, but there finally culture can and must, under pain of not existing, firmly declare 'Me first', and tell nature, 'You go no further'.

For much deeper reasons than already given, we are opposed to those concepts, such as held by Westermarck and Havelock Ellis, which credit nature with a principle of determination, even a negative one, for marriage. Whatever the uncertainties regarding the sexual habits of the great apes, and the monogamous or polygamous character of the gorilla and chimpanzee family, it is certain that these great anthropoids practise no sexual discrimination whatever against their near relatives. On the other hand, Hamilton's observations establish that sexual familiarity lessens desire even among the Macaques.[1] Either there is no link, therefore, between the two phenomena, or, in man, the transition from familiarity to aversion, regarded by Westermarck as the true origin of the prohibition, is accompanied by additional characteristics. How can this peculiarity be explained if, *ex hypothesi*, the intervention of any step of an intellectual, i.e., cultural, origin has been excluded? The supposed aversion would have to be seen as a specific phenomenon without any sign of corresponding physiological mechanisms. We consider that if this aversion were a natural phenomenon, its appearance would have been anterior or at least external to culture, and unaffected by it. It would be useless to wonder in what way or by what mechanisms the articulation of culture with nature, without which there could be no continuity between the two orders, was brought about. This problem becomes clear when nature's indifference to the modalities of relations between the sexes is acknowledged, an indifference witnessed to by the entire study of animal life, for it is precisely alliance that is the hinge, or more exactly the notch where the hinge might be fixed. Nature imposes alliance without determining it, and culture no sooner receives it than it defines its modalities.

[1] Miller, 1931, p. 392.

The apparent contradiction between the regulatory character of the prohibition and its universality is thus resolved. The universality merely expresses the fact that culture has at all times and at all places filled this empty form, as a bubbling spring first fills the depressions surrounding its source. For the moment, let it be enough to state that the content with which culture has filled it is the rule, the permanent and general substance of culture, without asking yet why this rule exhibits the general characteristic of prohibiting certain degrees of kinship, and why this general characteristic seems so curiously varied.

II

The *fact of being a rule*, completely independent of its modalities, is indeed the very essence of the incest prohibition. If nature leaves marriage to chance and the arbitrary, it is impossible for culture not to introduce some sort of order where there is none. The prime rôle of culture is to ensure the group's existence as a group, and consequently, in this domain as in all others, to replace chance by organization.[1] The prohibition of incest is a certain form, and even highly varied forms, of intervention. But it is intervention over and above anything else; even more exactly, it is *the* intervention.

This problem of intervention is not raised just in this particular case. It is raised, and resolved in the affirmative, every time the group is faced with the insufficiency or the risky distribution of a valuable of fundamental importance. Certain forms of rationing are new to our society and arouse surprise in minds cast in the traditions of economic liberalism. Thus we are prompted to see collective intervention, when it affects commodities vital to our way of life, as a bold and somewhat scandalous innovation. Because the control of distribution and consumption affects gasoline, we readily think that its formulation was only contemporaneous with the motor-car. But nothing is less true. 'The system of the scarce product' constitutes an extremely general model. In this and many other cases these periods of crisis, to which until recently our society was so unaccustomed, merely re-establish, in a crucial form, a state of affairs regarded as virtually normal in primitive society. Thus, 'the system of the scarce product', as expressed in collective measures of control, is much less an innovation, due to modern conditions of warfare and the worldwide nature of our economy, than the resurgence of a set of procedures which are familiar to primitive societies and necessary to the group if its coherence is not to be continually compromised.

It is impossible to approach the study of marriage prohibitions if it is not thoroughly understood from the beginning that such facts are in no way exceptional, but represent a particular application, within a given field, of principles and methods encountered whenever the physical or spiritual existence of the group is at stake. The group controls the distribution not only of women, but of a whole collection of valuables. Food, the most

---

[1] Porteus has clearly seen this point for Australia: Porteus, 1931, p. 269.

easily observed of these, is more than just the most vital commodity it really is, for between it and women there is a whole system of real and symbolic relationships, whose true nature is only gradually emerging, but which, when even superficially understood, are enough to establish this connexion. Thurnwald tells us that in Buin women feed the pigs, relatives lend them to one another, and the villages exchange them for women.[1] This continuity is possible only because it remains within the sphere of speculation. Primitive thought unanimously proclaims that 'food is . . . something that has to be shared'.[2] But this is because, from season to season, the native lives in accordance with the double rhythm of abundance and famine, passing 'through the whole range of sensations from inanition to repletion'.[3] From one set of conditions to another, from 'the hungry months' to 'the months of plenty', the change is brutal and complete.[4] These observations are not just true for Africa. Among the Svanetes of the Caucasus, 'if some family decides to kill a bullock or cow, or to sacrifice several dozen sheep, the neighbours come from all around . . . Having eaten, the Svanetes will fast for weeks, content to swallow down a little flour mixed with water. Then comes another feast . . . '[5] In view of this radical uncertainty, which might be illustrated by examples the world over, it is not unusual that primitive thought should be incapable of regarding food 'as something which could be procured, owned, and consumed by one individual alone. In childhood, or in subsequent dependent positions, it must be supplied by elders; throughout life it must be shared with contemporaries.'[6] This sharing follows rules which are interesting to consider because they reflect, and also specify, the structure of the familial and social group.

The Eskimo hunter of Hudson Bay 'who first strikes a walrus receives the tusks and one of the fore-quarters. The person who first comes to his assistance receives the other fore-quarter; the next man, the neck and head; the following, the belly; and each of the next two, one of the hind-quarters.'[7] But in times of scarcity, all rights of distribution are suspended, and the kill is regarded as the common possession of the community as a whole.

Another section of this work will describe the matrimonial organization of certain Burmese peoples. The reader need only refer to this section[8] to comprehend the extent to which the native mind sees matrimonial and economic exchanges as forming an integral part of a basic system of reciprocity. The methods for distributing meat in this part of the world are no less ingenious than for the distribution of women. These methods for distributing meat have been carefully described by Stevenson.[9] The recipient groups vary according to the importance of the feast, and those who receive meat during the *tsawnlam* feasts are not the same as those taking part in the hunting

[1] Thurnwald, 1934, pp. 119–41.
[2] Richards, 1939, p. 197.
[3] ibid. 1932, p. 165.
[4] ibid.; Evans-Pritchard, 1940, p. 83.
[5] Kowalewsky, 1890a, p. 53.
[6] Richards, 1939, pp. 199–200.
[7] Boas, 1901, p. 116.
[8] Pt. II, chs. XV and XVI.
[9] Stevenson, 1937, pp. 15–23.

or war dances. The system of obligations is again modified at the *Ruak hnah*, *Khan Tseh* and *Pual thawn* funeral feasts:

Recipients	*Khuang tsawi* feast	Animals killed in the hunt	Funerals
Father	+	+	
Brothers (class.)	+	+	+
Sisters	+ (6)	+ (1)	+ (3)
Mother's brother	+	+	+
Wife's brother	+	+	+
Ego (feast-giver, shooter of game, or heir of deceased)	+	+	+
Rual	+	+	+
Headman	+	+	+
Blacksmith	+	+	+
Gun-owner		+	
Beaters		+	
Previous givers of feasts	+		
Sangsuan		+	
Workers (at feasts)	+	+	+
Assistant (at feasts)	+		
Owner of *Khuang* bamboo	+		

Curiously similar rules have been described for Samoa.[1]

In the present example, three buffalo (*bos frontalis*) are sacrificed for the *Khuang tsawi* feast, and are cut up in the following manner (Fig. 1).

The distribution is made within the limits of the kinship group (Fig. 2).

Pa and *nau* receive three *alu* and three *amifi* (the heads to the closest relatives, and the joints to the more distant).

Farnu ngai get one *akawng* each.

Hlam hlaw farnu get one *ahnawi* each.

Nupu and *papu* share the *pusa*, or entrails.

Rual (ritual friends) get one *azang* each.

The assistants, the headman, the blacksmiths, and so on, get an equal portion from the distribution.

These rules and those determining the distribution of the bride-price are not formally of the same type, but are organically connected. There are at least two indications of this. A man is always paired with one of his sisters who is called his *ruang pawn farnu*, 'body-paired sister', whose bride-price he receives, and whose husband's *nupu* he becomes. On the other hand, the generosity expended in the feasts has the effect of raising the price which may be demanded for the marriage of the daughter.[2]

[1] Buck, 1930, pp. 119–27.
[2] Stevenson, 1937, pp. 22, 27. Other schemes for sharing may be found in Shirokogoroff, 1935, p. 220, and Lévi-Strauss, 1948a, fig. 17.

The organized distribution of alimentary products was apparently formerly applied by the Kaffirs to vegetable foodstuffs and milk as well as to meat. But even today 'the division of an ox upon the central place of the village, or

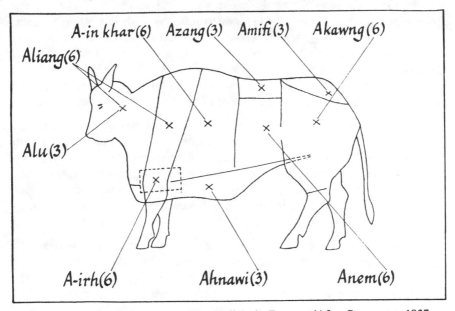

Fig. 1. Ceremonial carving-up of a buffalo in Burma. (After Stevenson, 1937, p. 19.)

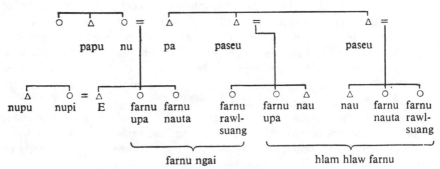

Fig. 2. Distribution of meat among relatives.

of the quarry slain in the hunt, must give young children a dramatic demonstration of the functions of kinship, and of the series of reciprocal obligations so entailed.'[1] The Thonga assign a hind-leg to the elder brother, a fore-leg to the younger brother, the other two limbs to the eldest sons, the heart and

[1] Richards, 1932, p. 79. Similarly, having recalled that any activity of an Australian tribe is founded on a network of personal relationships established on the basis of a genealogical system, Radcliffe-Brown, 1940, p. 7, adds: 'When an Australian blackfellow goes hunting he provides meat, not only for himself, but for his wife and children and also for other

kidneys to the wives, the tail and the rump to the relatives-in-law, and a piece of the loins to the maternal uncle. In certain regions of East Africa, the rules are infinitely more complicated since they vary for oxen, sheep or goats. In addition to the relatives, the headman and those who helped in getting the beast have the right to a portion. This distribution is made less ostensibly than the division in the village square whose end is 'that those who are eating, and those who are not, may be seen'.[1] Authority within the family is in fact based on 'the possession and control of food'.[2]

Finally, the same observer's description of the division of a great antelope among twenty-two adults and forty-seven children must be quoted:

'During the division of the animal the excitement was intense . . . Before the meal there was a buzz of expectation. Women ground extra flour with enthusiasm, "Because we have so much meat to eat with it" . . . Directly after the meal the women gathered near me talking in loud voices. They kept describing with ecstasy how full they felt . . . Another old lady cried light-heartedly, hitting her stomach, "I have been turned into a young girl again, my heart is so light . . . " '[3]

For some years we have doubtless become more aware of the dramatic import of such situations. In any case, the reader inclined to appraise them in the perspective of our traditional culture, which likes to contrast the pathos of unhappy love and the comedy of the full stomach, cannot be too carefully forewarned. In the great majority of human societies, the two problems are set on the same plane, since, with love as with food, nature presents man with the same risk. The lot of the satiated man is just as liable to excite emotion, and is just as much an excuse for lyrical expression, as the lot of the loved man. Moreover, primitive experience asserts the continuity between organic sensations and spiritual experiences. Food is completely riddled with signs and dangers. 'Warmth' can be the common denominator of states as different for us as anger, love, or repletion. Repletion, in its turn, hinders communications with the supernatural world.[4]

There is no need to call upon the matrimonial vocabulary of Great Russia, where the groom was called the 'merchant' and the bride, the 'merchandise'[5] for the likening of women to commodities, not only scarce but essential to the life of the group, to be acknowledged. The comparison seems less shocking if Richards's analyses of the systems of psycho-physiological equivalences in native thought are kept in mind: 'Food is the source of some of his most

[1] Richards, 1932, p. 80.   [2] ibid. p. 81.
[3] ibid. 1939, pp. 55–9.   [4] ibid. 1932, p. 162.
[5] Kowalewsky, 1890*b*, p. 480. The same symbolism is to be found among the Christians of Mosul where the marriage proposal is stylized: 'Have you any merchandise to sell us? . . . Upon my word, yours is excellent merchandise! We shall buy it.' Kyriakos, 1911, p. 775.

relatives to whom it is his duty to give meat when he has it.' Elkin, 1934, p. 9, uses much the same terms: 'Kinship rules also lie at the basis of the distribution of gifts; this explains why a native shares his earnings with others.'

intense emotions, provides the basis for some of his most abstract ideas, and the metaphors of his religious life . . . To the primitive man it may come to symbolize some of his highest spiritual experiences, and express his most significant social ties.'[1]

Let us first examine the feature of growing scarcity. There is a biological equilibrium between male and female births. Consequently, except in societies where this equilibrium is modified by customs, every male should have a very good chance of obtaining a wife. In such circumstances, is it possible to speak of women as a scarce commodity requiring collective intervention for its distribution? It is difficult to answer this question without posing the problem of polygamy, any discussion of which would go too far beyond the bounds of this work. We shall confine ourselves, therefore, to a few rapid considerations which will be less a demonstration than a brief indication of what seems to be the soundest position in this matter. For some years, the attention of anthropologists, especially those attracted by the diffusionist interpretation, has been drawn to the fact that monogamy seems to predominate in those societies which otherwise appear to be at the most primitive economic and technical level. From this and similar observations, these anthropologists have drawn more or less hazardous conclusions. According to Father Schmidt and his students, these facts must be seen as the sign of man's greater purity in the archaic stages of his social existence. According to Perry and Elliot Smith, they attest to the existence of a sort of Golden Age before the discovery of civilization. We believe that each author observed the facts correctly, but that there is a different conclusion to be drawn. At these archaic levels, it is the difficulties of daily existence, and the obstacle they present to the formation of economic privileges (which, in more highly evolved societies, are easily recognized as still providing the substructure of polygamy), which limit the cornering of women for the benefit of a few. Purity of soul, in the Vienna School sense, is never a factor in what might more readily be called a form of abortive polygamy rather than monogamy, for, in these societies as well as in those which favourably sanction polygamous unions, and in our own, the tendency is towards a multiplicity of wives. It was earlier indicated that the contradictory nature of the information about the sexual habits of the great apes does not allow any resolution, on the animal plane, of the problem of whether polygamous tendencies are innate or acquired. Social and biological observation combine to suggest that, in man, these tendencies are natural and universal, and that only limitations born of the environment and culture are responsible for their suppression.[2] Consequently, to our eyes, monogamy is not a positive institution, but merely incorporates the limit of polygamy in societies where, for highly varied reasons, economic and sexual competition reaches an acute form. The very small degree of social unity in the most primitive societies accounts very well for these particular characteristics.

[1] Richards, 1932, pp. 173–4.   [2] Miller, 1931, p. 392.

Even in these societies, moreover, monogamy is not a general rule. The Nambikwara, semi-nomads of western Brazil, who live for most of the year by collecting and gathering, sanction polygamy for their headmen and sorcerers. The securing of two, three or four wives by one or two important persons in a band of sometimes less than twenty people necessarily obliges their companions to be celibate. This privilege by itself is sufficient to upset the natural equilibrium of the sexes, since male adolescents occasionally can no longer find wives available from among the women of their own generation. Whatever the solution given to the problem – homosexuality among the Nambikwara, fraternal polyandry among their northern neighbours, the Tupí-Cawahib – the growing scarcity of wives does not appear less serious a problem in a society however predominately monogamous it might be.[1] But even in a strictly monogamous society, the considerations of the previous paragraph still retain their validity. This deep polygamous tendency, which exists among all men, always makes the number of available women seem insufficient. Let us add that, even if there were as many women as men, these women would not all be equally desirable – giving this term a broader meaning than its usual erotic connotation – and that, by definition (as Hume has judiciously remarked in a celebrated essay[2]), the most desirable women must form a minority. Hence, the demand for women is in actual fact, or to all intents and purposes, always in a state of disequilibrium and tension.

Considerations drawn exclusively from the study of relations between the sexes in our society could not reveal the truly tragic nature of this disequilibrium in primitive societies. Its sexual implications are secondary. Indeed, primitive society, even more than our own, provides many ways of overcoming this aspect of the problem. Homosexuality in some groups, polyandry and wife-lending in others, and finally, almost everywhere, the extreme freedom of premarital relations would prevent adolescents from experiencing any discomfort while waiting for a wife, if the wife's function were limited to sexual gratification. But, as often noted, in most primitive societies (and also, but to a lesser extent, in the rural classes of our own society) marriage is of an entirely different importance, not erotic, but economic. In our society, the difference between the economic status of the married man and the unmarried man amounts almost solely to the fact that the bachelor has to replace his wardrobe more frequently. The situation is altogether different in groups where the satisfaction of economic needs rests wholly on the conjugal society and the division of labour between the sexes. Not only do man and wife have different technical specializations, one depending on the other for the manufacture of objects necessary for their daily tasks, but they are each employed in producing different foodstuffs. Accordingly, a complete, and above all regular, food supply indeed depends on that 'pro-

[1] Lévi-Strauss, 1948*a*, and 1948*b*.
[2] Hume, 1886, p. 154. Likewise, 'If all were excellent here below, then there would be nothing excellent', Diderot, 1935, p. 199.

duction cooperative', the household. The Pygmies, who consider women and children as the most valuable of the active part of the family group, say that 'the more women available the more food'.[1] Likewise, Hottentot women, during the marriage ceremony, chorus the praise of the groom and of the men who, like him, are looking for a wife, 'since today they have enough to eat'.[2]

It would be almost impossible for an individual by himself to survive, especially at the most primitive levels, where hunting and gardening, as well as collecting and gathering, are made hazardous by the harshness of the geographical environment and the rudimentary nature of techniques. One of the deepest impressions which I retain from my first experiences in the field was the sight, in a central Brazilian native village, of a young man crouching for hours upon end in the corner of a hut, dismal, ill-cared for, fearfully thin, and seemingly in the most complete state of dejection. I observed him for several days. He rarely went out, except to go hunting by himself, and when the family meals began around the fires, he would as often as not have gone without if a female relative had not occasionally set a little food at his side, which he ate in silence. Intrigued by this strange fate, I finally asked who this person was, thinking that he suffered from some serious illness; my suppositions were laughed at and I was told, 'He is a bachelor.' This was indeed the sole reason for the apparent curse. This example could be multiplied many times. Denied food after bad hunting or fishing expeditions when the fruits of the women's collecting and gathering, and sometimes their gardening, provide the only meal there is, the wretched bachelor is a characteristic sight in native society. But the actual victim is not the only person involved in this scarcely tolerable situation. The relatives or friends on whom he depends in such cases for his subsistence are testy in suffering his mute anxiety, for, from the combined efforts of both husband and wife, a family often barely derives enough to avoid death by starvation. Hence, in such societies it is no exaggeration to say that marriage is of vital importance for every individual, being, as he is, doubly concerned, not only to find a wife for himself but also to prevent those two calamities of primitive society from occurring in his group, namely, the bachelor and the orphan.

We apologize for amassing a number of quotations and comments here, but it is essential to illustrate if not the generality of these attitudes, which doubtless no one would contest, then rather the vehemence and conviction of their expression in primitive thought everywhere. 'Among these Indians', write Colbacchini and Albisetti of the Bororo, where the observation contained in the previous paragraph was made, 'celibacy does not exist, and it is not even imagined, for its possibility would never be admitted.'[3] Likewise, Schebesta says, 'the Pygmy despises and jeers at bachelors as abnormal creatures.'[4] Radcliffe-Brown notes: 'One man was mentioned to me as being a

---

[1] Schebesta, 1933, p. 128 and 1936, pp. 138–9.
[2] Schapera, 1930, p. 247.
[3] Colbacchini and Albisetti, 1942, p. 51.
[4] Schebesta, 1936, p. 138.

bad man because he refused to take a wife after he had reached the age when it is considered proper for a man to marry.'[1] In New Guinea, 'The economic system, the traditional partition of labour between man and woman, make a community of life between the sexes a necessity. Indeed, all persons attain that state except cripples.'[2] 'With the Reindeer Chukchee, no man can live a tolerable life without a separate house of his own and a woman to take care of it . . . A man full-grown and unmarried is despised by the people, and in reality is looked upon as a good-for-nothing, a lounger, a tramp, idly wandering from camp to camp'.[3]

Gilhodes says of the Kachin of Burma:

'As to voluntary celibacy, they seem not to have even the idea of it. It is a glory for every Kachin to marry and to have children, and a shame to die without posterity. You find nevertheless some rare old boys or old spinsters; but nearly always they are half-witted people or of an impossible temper, and at their death they are given a ridiculous burial.'[4]

Again:

'Some rare cases, however, are found of old bachelors and old spinsters. In their lifetime they are ashamed of their condition and at their death they inspire fear chiefly to the young . . . Young men and young girls, for fear of not being able to settle themselves in the future, take no part . . . in the funeral meals; the ceremonies are chiefly done by the old men and women and in a somewhat ridiculous manner . . . The dances are done inside out.'[5]

Let us conclude this brief survey with a report from the Orient. ' "If a man has no wife, there will be no Paradise for him hereafter and no Paradise on earth" . . . If woman had not been created, there would have been no sun and no moon, no agriculture and no fire.'[6] Like the eastern Jews and the ancient Babylonians, the Mandaeans make celibacy a sin.[7] The unmarried of both sexes (and particularly monks and nuns) are given up defenceless to the dealings of demons 'and so [evil] spirits and goblins proceed from them which plague mankind'.[8] The Navaho Indians share the same theory. Even in the first three of the inferior Four Worlds, the distinction of the sexes and their relationships is maintained, so difficult do the natives find it to imagine a form of existence, be it the lowest and most miserable, which did not possess this benefit. But the sexes are separated in the fourth world, and monsters are the fruit of the masturbation to which each sex is reduced.[9]

There are no doubt several exceptions to this general attitude. Celibacy seems to be of some frequency in Polynesia,[10] perhaps because in this part of

[1] Radcliffe-Brown, 1933, pp. 50–1.   [2] Thurnwald, 1916, pp. 383–4.
[3] Bogoras, 1904–9, p. 569.   [4] Gilhodes, 1922, p. 225.
[5] ibid. p. 277.   [6] Drower, 1937, p. 59.   [7] ibid. p. 17.
[8] ibid. p. 65.   [9] Reichard, n.d., p. 662.   [10] Firth, 1936, *passim*.

the world the production of food is not a critical problem. Elsewhere, as among the Karen of Burma and the Tungus,[1] it is rather a consequence of the rigour with which these people apply their rules of exogamy. When the prescribed spouse is subject to a strict determination, marriage becomes impossible without there being a relative in exactly the required position. In this last case at least, the exception proves the rule.

What would happen, then, if the principle of collective intervention expressed purely formally by the rule prohibiting incest – without regard to particular circumstances – did not exist? It might be expected that privileges would arise in that natural aggregation called the family, by reason of the greater intimacy of its inter-individual contacts, and by the lack of any social rule tending to limit this family and to establish equilibrium in it. We are not suggesting that every family would automatically maintain a monopoly of its women. This would be to assert the institutional priority of the family over the group, a supposition far from our mind. We merely postulate, without posing the question of the historical precedence of the one over the other, that the specific viscosity of the family aggregation would act in this direction, and that the combined results would confirm this action. As has been shown, such an eventuality is incompatible with the vital demands not only of primitive society but of society in general.

[1] Bogoras, 1904–9, p. 570; Frazer, 1919, vol. II, p. 138.

CHAPTER IV

Endogamy and Exogamy

I

By establishing a general rule of obedience, whatever this rule may be, the group asserts its jural authority over what it legitimately considers an essential valuable. It refuses to sanction the natural inequality of the distribution of the sexes within the family, and on the only possible basis it institutes freedom of access for every individual to the women of the group. This basis is, in short, that neither fraternity nor paternity can be put forward as claims to a wife, but that the sole validity of these claims lies in the fact that all men are in equal competition for all women, their respective relationships being defined in terms of the group, and not the family.

This rule also has advantages for individuals, since, by obliging them to renounce a limited or very restricted share in the women immediately available, it gives everybody a claim to a number of women whose availability, it is true, is checked by the demands of custom, but a number which theoretically is as large as possible and is the same for everyone. If it is objected that such reasoning is too abstract and artificial to have occurred at a very primitive human level, it is sufficient to note that the result, which is all that counts, does not suppose any formal reasoning but simply the spontaneous resolution of those psycho-social pressures which are the immediate facts of collective life. In non-crystallized forms of social life, such as communities arising spontaneously out of accidental circumstances (bombardments, earthquakes, concentration camps, children's gangs, and so on), which still await psychological investigation – and are so rich in both elemental and universal processes – it is soon learnt that the perception of another's envy, the fear of violent dispossession, the distress resulting from collective hostility, and so on, can wholly inhibit the enjoyment of a privilege. The renunciation of a privilege need not be explained by the intervention of authority, nor as being calculated, but may be merely the resolution of an emotional conflict, the pattern of which has already been observed in the animal kingdom.[1]

Even when thus corrected, this method of posing the problem remains

[1] Zuckerman, 1932; Köhler, 1928, p. 88 et seq., 300–2; Yerkes, 1935, ch. 21; Nissen and Crawford, 1936, pp. 383–419.

approximate and provisional. We shall have an opportunity to specify and elaborate upon it later. However, even in this approximate form, it is sufficient to show that there is no need to assume an apprenticeship of thousands of years to understand that in the course of history savage peoples have clearly and constantly been faced with the simple and brutal choice, powerfully expressed by Tylor, 'between marrying-out and being killed out'.[1]

But for the demonstration to be effective, it must extend to every member of the group. It is this condition, in a most developed form, of which the prohibition of incest provides the ineluctable expression. Marriage is an eternal triangle, not just in vaudeville sketches, but at all times, and in all places, and by definition. Because women have an essential value in group life, the group necessarily intervenes in every marriage. It does this in two ways: firstly in the form of the 'rival', who, through the agency of the group, asserts that he had the same right of access as the husband, a right upon which the union is conditional and which must be shown to have been respected; and secondly through the group as a group, which asserts that the relationship which makes the marriage possible must be social, that is, defined in group terms and not in the natural terms having all the consequences incompatible with collective life which have already been indicated. Considered in its purely formal aspect, the prohibition of incest is thus only the group's assertion that where relationships between the sexes are concerned, *a person cannot do just what he pleases*. The positive aspect of the prohibition is to initiate organization.

Doubtless the objection will be made that in no way does the prohibition of incest fulfil any organizing function. Is it not true that in certain areas of Australia and Melanesia this prohibition is adapted to a virtual monopoly of the women by the old men, and, more generally, to polygamy, the results of which we ourselves have emphasized?

But these 'advantages', if one wishes to see them as such, are not unilateral, for, on the contrary, analysis shows that they always entail a positive counterpart. Let us return to the example cited above of the Nambikwara chief who jeopardizes the demographic equilibrium of his little band by monopolizing several women, who would normally have made as many monogamous wives for men of the following generation. It would be arbitrary to isolate the institution from its context. The chief of the band bears heavy responsibilities, since the group relies on him entirely to fix the itinerary for its nomadic life, to choose the camping places, to know every inch of the territory and the natural resources to be found there during each season, to determine the position and movement of hostile bands, to negotiate or fight with them, as the occasion arises, and finally, to organize sufficient reserves of arms and everyday objects so that everyone has what he needs. Without his polygamous wives, who are companions rather than wives, freed by their social status from the constraints of their sex, and always ready

[1] Tylor, 1889, p. 267.

to accompany and assist him in his reconnaissances, agricultural work or handicrafts, the chief could not face up to all his responsibilities. His plurality of wives, accordingly, is both the reward for and the instrument of power.

Let us push the analysis a little further. If the Nambikwara had combined their rule of bilateral cross-cousin marriage[1] with a strict monogamy there would be a perfectly simple system of reciprocity, both quantitatively, since the system would guarantee roughly a wife for every man, and qualitatively, since this general guarantee would result in a network of reciprocal obligations based on individual kinship relationships. But the polygamous privilege of the chief upsets this ideal formula. It results in an otherwise non-existent element of insecurity for every individual. Where, then, did this privilege originate, and what is its significance? By recognizing the privilege, the group has exchanged the *elements of individual security* which accompany the rule of monogamy for a *collective security* arising out of political organization. Each man receives the daughter or the sister of another man as his wife. The chief receives several wives from the group. In exchange, he gives a guarantee against want and danger, certainly not to the particular individuals whose sisters or daughters he has married, and not even to those perhaps condemned for ever to celibacy by the exercise of his polygamous right, but to the group as a group, for it is the latter which has suspended the common law in his favour.[2]

Polygamy, therefore, does not run counter to the demand for an equitable distribution of women. It merely superimposes one rule of distribution upon another. In fact, monogamy and polygamy correspond to two types of complementary relationship. On the one hand, there are the systems of prestations and counter-prestations which bind together the individual members of the group, and on the other hand, there are the systems of prestations and counter-prestations which bind together the group as a whole and its chief. This parallelism can become so transparent that in the Trobriand Islands, for example, the chief, who receives a wife from each of the subclans, is regarded as a sort of 'universal brother-in-law'. Political allegiance and the presentation of tribute are no more than just a particular case of that special relationship which in this part of the world places the wife's brother under obligation to his sister's husband.[3]

Besides, so far only the most summary aspect of the prohibition of incest has been considered, that is, from the viewpoint of a rule as a rule. Considered from this angle, the prohibition does not yet provide a solution to the problem. It is merely a preliminary measure, useless in itself, but necessary for future development. In short, the prohibition of incest asserts that natural distribution should not be the basis of social practice regarding women. What this basis should be still remains to be determined. To borrow an expression familiar to modern regulation (but eternal also in some ways) of

[1] For the definition of this marriage rule and its theoretical study, see below, ch. IX.
[2] Lévi-Strauss, 1944, pp. 16–32.   [3] Malinowski, 1929, pp. 131–32.

the 'scarce product', the first logical end of the incest prohibition is 'to freeze' women within the family, so that their distribution, or the competition for them, is within the group, and under group and not private control. So far this has been the only aspect of the prohibition examined. But it can also be seen to be the one primordial aspect coextensive with the whole prohibition. Passing from the study of the rule as a rule to the study of its most general characteristics, it now has to be shown how the transition from an originally negative rule to a collection of entirely different stipulations was accomplished.

II

Considered as a prohibition, the prohibition of incest merely affirms, in a field vital to the group's survival, the pre-eminence of the social over the natural, the collective over the individual, organization over the arbitrary. But even at this point in the analysis, the converse of this ostensibly negative rule has already appeared. When considered from this new point of view, the prohibition of incest appears so laden with positive modalities that this overdetermination is itself an immediate problem.

In point of fact, marriage rules do not always merely prohibit a kinship circle, but occasionally also fix one within which marriage must necessarily take place, under pain of the same scandal as would result if the prohibition itself were violated. There are two cases to be distinguished here: on the one hand endogamy, or the obligation to marry within an objectively defined group; and on the other, preferential union, or the obligation to choose as spouse an individual who is related to Ego in some particular way. It is difficult to make this distinction in classificatory kinship systems, for all individuals in a defined kinship relationship to each other, or to a given subject, fall into one class, and consequently it is possible to pass from preferential union to endogamy, properly so called, without any marked change. Any system of marriage between cross-cousins could thus be interpreted as endogamous if all the parallel cousins were designated by one term, and all the cross-cousins by another. This double appellation could hold good even after the disappearance of the marriage system considered, and consequently an exogamous system *par excellence* would make way for a new system, which, on the contrary, would offer all the appearances of endogamy. This artificial conversion of genuine exogamous systems into ostensibly endogamous systems may be seen in the field, and the difficulties it raises in the interpretation of certain Australian systems will be seen later.[1]

It is advisable then to distinguish between two different types of endogamy. One is merely the reverse of a rule of exogamy and is explicable only in terms of this rule; the other – or true endogamy – is not an aspect of exogamy but is always found along with the latter, although not in the same regard, but simply in connexion with it. From this point of view, any society is both

[1] cf. ch. XIII.

exogamous and endogamous. Thus among the Australian aborigines the clan is exogamous, but the tribe is endogamous, while modern American society combines a family exogamy, which is rigid for the first degree but flexible for the second or third degrees onwards, with a racial endogamy, which is rigid or flexible according to the particular State.[1] But contrary to the hypothesis examined above, endogamy and exogamy are not here complementary institutions and they could appear symmetrical only from a formal point of view. True endogamy is merely the refusal to recognize the possibility of marriage beyond the limits of the human community. The definitions of this community are many and varied, depending on the philosophy of the group considered. A very great number of primitive tribes simply refer to themselves by the term for 'men' in their language, showing that in their eyes an essential characteristic of man disappears outside the limits of the group. Thus the Eskimoes of Norton Sound describe themselves exclusively as the 'excellent people', or more exactly as the 'complete people', and reserve the epithet 'nit' to describe neighbouring peoples.[2] The generality of the attitude lends some colour of truth to Gobineau's hypothesis, according to which the proliferation of the fantastic beings of folklore – dwarfs, giants, monsters, and so on – is to be explained less by a rich imagination than by the inability of fellow-citizens to conceive of strangers in the same way as themselves. Certain Brazilian tribes identified the first black slaves imported to America as 'earth monkeys', in comparison with the arboreal species which was the only kind known to them. When certain Melanesian peoples were asked for the first time who they were, they replied: ' "Men," meaning that they were not demons or ghosts, but living men; and they did so because they did not believe their visitors to be men, but rather ghosts themselves, or demons, or spirits belonging to the sea.'[3] On their arrival in the New Hebrides, the Europeans were at first taken to be ghosts, and were so named. Their clothes were called 'ghost skins' and their cats 'the ghosts' rats'.[4] Lévy-Bruhl has collected other accounts of no less significance, such as horses taken for their riders' mothers, since they carried them on their backs, in contrast with missionaries who were called lions, because of their fair beards, and so on.[5]

In all these cases, it is merely a question of knowing how far to extend the logical connotation of the idea of community, which is itself dependent upon the effective solidarity of the group. In Dobu, the white man is considered as 'another kind', not really a human being in the native sense of the word, but as a being with different qualities. These differences, however, do not extend to yams, which are regarded as people. The order of affinities is therefore: the native group, *tomot*; yams, which reproduce in the same way as the group and allow the group to survive; and finally, white men, who are set completely outside the community. All this is because the group's continuity depends on the continuity of the vegetable lines. There are masculine

---

[1] Johnson, 1943.   [2] Rink, 1887, p. 333.   [3] Codrington, 1891, p. 21.
[4] Deacon, 1934, p. 637; Radcliffe-Brown, 1933, p. 138.   [5] Lévy-Bruhl, 1935, pp. 59–60.

and feminine gardens, each descended from ancestral seed, hereditarily transmitted from the mother's brother to the sister's son or daughter. If a 'race' of seeds is lost, the human line is in jeopardy, for the woman will not find a husband, nor will she raise children to succeed to her miserable inheritance and share the contempt attached to her destitution. A person deprived of his hereditary seeds cannot count upon charity, nor upon grain borrowed from outside: 'I knew of several women in this position. They were thieves, or fishers, sago workers and beggars.'[1] Thus yams are real persons, for to be without them is to be orphaned. When all is said and done, the economic and social structure of the group does justify the restrictive definition of itself as a community of tubers and cultivators. But let us not be deceived. The strict endogamy of the Mormons is based on formally analogous considerations, even although they are spiritual. If a girl cannot find a partner possessing the true faith, it is better for her to marry her father, for it is the possession of this faith which is the prime essential in their definition of a human being.[2]

Similar distinctions are found also in groups in which rank and fortune are rated highly. But in all these cases, endogamy is merely the expression of a conceptual limit and of a negative reality. It is only in the exceptional case of highly differentiated societies that this negative form can take on a positive aspect, viz., as a deliberate calculation to maintain certain social or economic privileges within the group. Yet this situation is still more the result of a concept of endogamy than its locus of origin. Generally, 'true' endogamy simply represents the exclusion of marriage outside the culture, which itself is conceived of in all sorts of ways, sometimes narrowly, sometimes broadly. The apparently positive formula of being obliged to marry within a group defined by certain concrete characteristics (such as name, language, race, religion, and so on) thus merely expresses a limit, socially conditioned, to the capacity for generalization. Beyond the precise forms just alluded to, the expression of the formula in our society is diffuse, since the proportion of marriages between cousins is known to be greater in general than would be the case if marriage were contracted at random.[3]

By contrast, the other form of endogamy previously distinguished might be called 'functional endogamy', since it is only a function of exogamy, or the counterpart of a negative rule. In cross-cousin marriage, for example, the class of possible spouses is never an exogamous category, in spite of the appearances emphasized earlier. Cross-cousins are not so much relatives who must intermarry, as they are the first persons among relatives between whom marriage is possible once parallel cousins are classified as brothers and sisters. This vital characteristic has often been misunderstood, for in certain cases cross-cousin marriage is not only sanctioned but obligatory. When

[1] Fortune, 1932, pp. 69–74, 102.
[2] 'Der sexuelle Anteil an der Theologie der Mormonen', 1914.
[3] Hogben, 1931, p. 152.

possible it is obligatory because it provides the simplest conceivable system of reciprocity. Indeed, we shall attempt to show later that cross-cousin marriage is essentially a system of exchange. But whereas, in this case, only two marriages are required to maintain the equilibrium, a more complex and consequently more brittle cycle becomes necessary, with less likelihood of the desired result, when the kinship relationship between the spouses becomes more distant. Marriage between outsiders is a social advance (because it integrates wider groups). It is also a venture. But the best proof that the class of marriageable cross-cousins is determined simply by eliminating the class that is forbidden (so that endogamy here is clearly a function of exogamy, and not the contrary), is that there is no trouble if a potential spouse of the required degree of cousinhood is missing, for a more distant relative can be substituted. The category of possible spouses in a system of preferential marriage is never closed, for what is not prohibited is permitted, though sometimes only in a certain order and to a certain extent. Moreover, this preference is explained by the mechanism of exchanges proper to the system considered, and not by the privileged nature of a group or class.

The difference between the two forms of endogamy is particularly easy to make when the marriage rules of strongly hierarchical societies are studied. 'True' endogamy is all the more marked when the social class practising it occupies a higher rank, as in ancient Peru, the Hawaiian Islands and certain African tribes. By contrast, it is 'functional endogamy' whenever the relationship is inversed, that is, when the apparent endogamy steadily diminishes as one rises in the hierarchy. The Kenyah and the Kayan of Borneo are divided into three unequally privileged classes, and while these are normally endogamous, the highest class is subject to village exogamy.[1] Thus, as in New Zealand and Burma, exogamy is specified at the top of the social hierarchy, and is a function of the obligation of feudal families to maintain and widen their alliances. The endogamy of the lower classes is one of indifference, and not of discrimination.

Finally the case must be considered where preferential union is not directly determined by a relation of kinship but by the membership of a clan or a marriage class. Here, there are constituted groups, and would it not appear that marriage obligations which pair these groups off one with another are equivalent to forming 'true' endogamous categories, each consisting of two clans or classes practising intermarriage? But in reality, things are less different than they seem. The classes and the sub-classes of the Australian aborigines are not so much groups defined in extension as positions which are alternately or successively occupied by the members of one line of descent or by the partners in an alliance. Among the Bororo Indians, whom I studied in 1936, the situation is less clear, for marriage preferences seem to make a direct pairing of the clans and not the classes. But then it is the very temporariness of these clans, their presence in one village, their absence in another,

[1] Hose and McDougall, 1912, vol. I, pp. 71, 74.

and their possible division or subdivision into sub-clans, which enables them to elude the fixity and strict delimitation of endogamous categories. One is tempted to see the clan preferences not as an outline of 'true' endogamy but simply as a technique of adjustment to ensure matrimonial equilibrium in the group, the clan itself continually changing to suit the demands of this equilibrium.[1]

The correlation between the concepts of endogamy and exogamy emerges elsewhere, and particularly clearly in the neighbouring example of the Apinayé Indians. These are divided into four exogamous groups, or *kiyé*, united by a system of preferential marriage, so that a man of A marries a woman of B, a man of B marries a woman of C, and man of C marries a woman of D, and a man of D marries a woman of A. This appears to be what is later described as a simple system of generalized exchange,[2] except that here the rule of descent makes the system static, with the first result that it excludes cousins from the number of possible spouses. With regard to the *kiyé*, boys succeed to their fathers' status, and girls to their mothers'. Hence, men of A and women of B are all descended from marriages between men of A and women of B; men of B and women of C are all descended from marriages between men of B and women of C; and so on. The apparent division into four exogamous groups thus conceals a division into four endogamous groups, viz., men of A and women of B, these being related to each other, men of B and women of C, these being related, men of C and women of D, these being related, and men of D and women of A, these also being related to each other. By contrast, there is no relation of kinship between the two groups, one of male kin, the other of female kin, which go into the formation of the *kiyé*.[3] Unlike Lowie,[4] we believe that this system is not exceptional, but is merely a particular application of a general formula, which will be studied in another work, and which is more typical than it would seem.[5] We confine ourselves here to this brief description, which is sufficient to show in a precise case that exogamous and endogamous categories have no objective existence as independent entities. Rather, they must be considered as viewpoints, or different but solidary perspectives, on a system of fundamental relationships in which each term is defined by its position within the system.

---

[1] Lévi-Strauss, 1936.   [2] cf. ch. XII.

[3] Nimuendajú, 1939, p. 29 et. seq. Our interpretation is in agreement with those of Henry, 1940 and Kroeber, 1942.   [4] Lowie, 1940, p. 468.

[5] Williams, 1932, pp. 15–81; and chs. XXVI and XXVIII of this work. Maybury-Lewis, 1960, p. 196, refers to the above sentence as a 'startlingly specific remark', because, he says, it does not take into consideration the difference between 'descent' and 'filiation'. Is there any need to emphasize that this book is concerned exclusively with models and not with empirical realities? It is only in connexion with the latter that this distinction, rightly criticized by Leach in his controversy with Fortes, can be said to have any meaning. With all due respect to Maybury-Lewis, Williams – almost thirty years before him – had fully isolated from the Melanesian data the theoretical principle of 'parallel descent' as it exists among the Apinayé, writing, in the article cited above: 'The essence of [sex affiliation] is that male children are classed with their father's group and female children with their mother's.' Williams, 1932, p. 51.

Furthermore, in certain cases the relative reciprocity of endogamous and exogamous relationships already appears in the vocabulary. For example, the Ifugao term for 'relative-in-law', *aidu*, corresponds to a root found in every area of Indonesia with the original meaning of 'the other group' or 'outsiders', and the derivative meanings of 'enemy' or 'relative by marriage'. Likewise, in other Malay languages, *tulang*, 'all kin of the same generation' as Ego, comes to mean, on the one hand, 'aborigines' (Formosa, Buginese), 'brother and sister', 'sister', 'woman', and on the other, 'relative-in-law', or 'spouse'.[1] Compare this with the Japanese *imo* which sometimes designates the sister and sometimes the wife.[2] May we assert, as do Barton and Chamberlain, that the ambivalence of certain ancient terms bears witness to the former existence of consanguineous marriages? The hypothesis does not seem improbable when it is noted, as above, that ancient Japanese texts, by limiting the definition of incest to marriage with the younger sister, would seem to legitimatize marriage with the older sister, as in Egypt and Samoa. The preference for marriage with the matrilateral cousin among the Batak and in other regions of Indonesia, and indications that the same system formerly existed in Japan,[3] would suggest another interpretation, while not, however, excluding the previous one. Although referred to by the same term, women of Ego's generation would be distinguished as to whether they were possible or prohibited spouses. In this regard it will be noted that in the vocabulary of the Batak, the term *tulang* is applied by a man to the mother's brother and to the latter's daughter, who is the preferred spouse, while a woman addresses outsiders as 'father's sister', or as 'mother's brother',[4] that is, the names given respectively to the clanswoman who marries elsewhere, or to the uncle whose sons a woman cannot marry.

If the most general meaning of *aidu* is 'stranger', and if its derived meanings are 'affine' and 'enemy', it is clearly obvious that these last two meanings are two distinct modalities of, or more exactly two ways of looking at, the same reality. Among the 'other groups' some are my affines, others are my enemies. They are both enemy and affine at the same time, but not for the same person. This relativist interpretation, which is clear in this particular case, can also be easily applied to the former without resorting to the hypothesis of a former marriage with the sister. It is sufficient to consider that, starting from the general meaning of *tulang* as 'girls of my generation', the latter are either 'sisters' or 'wives'. Just as a group of 'affines' is at the same time 'someone's enemy', a 'married woman' must necessarily have been, for me to have married her, 'someone's sister'.

Thus we have distinguished a 'true' endogamy, which is a class endogamy (in the logical sense, but in many of the societies practising it, in the social sense of the term class as well), and a functional endogamy, which might be called endogamy of relation, since it is merely the counterpart or positive

---

[1] Barton, 1941, pp. 540–9.   [2] Chamberlain, 1932.   [3] cf. ch. XXVII.
[4] Loeb, 1933, pp. 22, 25.

expression of exogamy and expresses the apparently negative nature of the latter.

But, as we have emphasized at the beginning of this chapter, complementary endogamy merely serves to recall to mind that the negative aspect is only the superficial aspect of the prohibition. A group within which marriage is prohibited immediately conjures up the idea of another group, with clearly defined features (the prohibition of incest joined with an exogamous system), or vague characteristics (simple prohibition without exogamy), with which marriage is merely possible, or inevitable, according to circumstances. The prohibition on the sexual use of a daughter or a sister compels them to be given in marriage to another man, and at the same time it establishes a right to the daughter or sister of this other man. In this way, every negative stipulation of the prohibition has its positive counterpart. The prohibition is tantamount to an obligation, and renunciation gives rise to a counter-claim. It can now be seen how impossible it is to consider exogamy and endogamy as institutions of the same type, as is often done. This is true only for what has been called functional endogamy, which is none other than exogamy itself seen in terms of its consequences. The comparison is only possible on condition that 'true' endogamy, a passive principle of limitation incapable of development, is excluded. By contrast, the analysis of the notion of exogamy sufficiently shows its far-reaching effects. The prohibition of incest is not merely a prohibition, as the previous chapter suggested, because in prohibiting it also orders. Like exogamy, which is its widened social application, the prohibition of incest is a rule of reciprocity. The woman whom one does not take, and whom one may not take, is, for that very reason, offered up. To whom is she offered? Sometimes to a group defined by institutions, and sometimes to an indeterminate and ever-open collectivity limited only by the exclusion of near relatives, such as in our own society. But at this stage in the research I believe it possible to ignore the differences between the prohibition of incest and exogamy: in the light of the previous considerations, their formal characteristics are in effect identical.

Furthermore, in the technical case of marriage 'by exchange' so-called, or in any other marriage system whatsoever, the result of the incest prohibition is fundamentally the same, viz., that as soon as I am forbidden a woman, she thereby becomes available to another man, and somewhere else a man renounces a woman who thereby becomes available to me. The content of the prohibition is not exhausted by the fact of the prohibition: the latter is instituted only in order to guarantee and establish, directly or indirectly, immediately or mediately, an exchange. It is now for us to show how and why.

CHAPTER V

The Principle of Reciprocity

I

The conclusions of the famous *Essai sur le Don* are well known. In this study, which today is regarded as a classic, Mauss sought to show that exchange in primitive societies consists not so much in economic transactions as in reciprocal gifts, that these reciprocal gifts have a far more important function in these societies than in our own, and that this primitive form of exchange is not merely nor essentially of an economic nature but is what he aptly calls 'a total social fact', that is, an event which has a significance that is at once social and religious, magic and economic, utilitarian and sentimental, jural and moral. It is well known that in many primitive societies, particularly those of the Pacific Islands and the North-west Pacific coast of Canada and Alaska, every ceremony celebrating an important event is accompanied by a distribution of wealth. Thus in New Zealand the ceremonial offering of clothes, jewellery, arms, food and various goods was a common feature of Maori social life. These gifts were made on the occasions of births, marriages, deaths, exhumations, peace treaties, crimes and misdemeanours 'and many other things too numerous to mention'.[1] Similarly, Firth includes among ceremonial exchanges in Polynesia 'birth, initiation, marriage, sickness, death and other social events, as well as much religious ritual'.[2] In a more limited section of the same region, another observer cites betrothal, marriage, pregnancy, birth and death, and describes the presents offered by the young man's father at the betrothal feast, viz., ten baskets of dried fish, ten thousand ripe and six thousand green coconuts, the young man himself receiving in exchange two cakes four feet square and six inches thick.[3]

These gifts are either exchanged immediately for equivalent gifts or are received by the beneficiaries on condition that at a later date they will give counter-gifts often exceeding the original goods in value, but which in their turn bring about a subsequent right to receive new gifts surpassing the original ones in sumptuousness. The most characteristic of these institutions is the *potlatch* of the Indians of Alaska and the Vancouver region. During

---

[1] Best, 1929, p. 36. [2] Firth, 1939, p. 321.
[3] Hogbin, 1931*a*, p. 28. See also the astonishing figures collected by Firth, 1929, p. 317 et seq.

the *potlatch* considerable valuables are transferred in this way, sometimes amounting to several tens of thousands of rugs handed over in kind, or in the symbolical form of copper plaques whose face value increases in terms of the importance of the transactions in which they have figured. These ceremonies have a triple purpose, viz., to return gifts previously received, together with an appropriate amount of interest, sometimes as much as 100 per cent; to establish publicly the claim of a family or social group to a title or prerogative, or to announce officially a change of status; finally, to surpass a rival in generosity, to crush him if possible with future obligations which it is hoped he cannot meet, so as to take from him his prerogatives, titles, rank, authority and prestige.[1] Doubtless the system of reciprocal gifts only reaches such vast proportions among the Indians of the North-west Pacific coast, virtuosi who display a genius and an exceptional aptitude for the treatment of the fundamental themes of primitive culture. But Mauss has been able to establish the existence of analogous institutions in Melanesia and Polynesia. For example, it is certain that the main purpose of the feasts of several New Guinea tribes is to obtain recognition of a new *pangua* by an assembly of witnesses,[2] that is, the same function which, according to Barnett, is the fundamental basis of the Alaskan *potlatch*. The same author sees the desire to go one better than anyone else as a characteristic peculiar to Kwakiutl ceremonies, and regards the interest-bearing loan as a preliminary transaction to the *potlatch*, rather than as one of its modalities.[3] Doubtless there are local variations, but the various aspects of the institution form a whole found in a more or less systematized way in North and South America, Asia and Africa. It is a question of a universal mode of culture, although not everywhere equally developed.

But it should also be stressed that this attitude of primitive thought towards the exchange of goods is not only expressed in clearly defined and localized institutions. It permeates every transaction, ritual or profane, in which objects or produce are given or received. Implicitly or explicitly, the double assumption is found everywhere that reciprocal gifts constitute a means – normal or privileged, depending on the group – of transferring goods, or certain goods, and that these gifts are not offered principally or essentially with the idea of receiving a profit or advantage of an economic nature. 'On birth ceremonies,' writes Turner of the refined Samoan culture, 'after receiving the *oloa* and the *tonga*, the "masculine" and "feminine" property, the husband and wife were left no richer than they were.'[4]

Hogbin remarks that neither partner acquires any real material benefit from such exchanges.

'Indeed, at times the gifts exchanged are of precisely the same kind. Thus a ball of sennit ceremonially presented may be returned by a similar

---

[1] Davy, 1922; Murdock, 1936, pp. 3–20; Barnett, 1938*b*, pp. 349–58.
[2] See later, ch. VI.   [3] Boas, 1897; Barnett, 1938*b*, p. 351 et seq.
[4] Mauss, 1925, p. 42.

ball of exactly the same size, presented with exactly the same ceremony. Or again, a parcel of food may be returned by another parcel of the same kind of food cooked according to the same recipe.'[1]

On the southern coast of New Guinea, the natives make long voyages to participate in a transaction which from an economic viewpoint seems totally meaningless. They exchange live animals.[2] It is the same with the exchanges that accompany a Yukaghir marriage: relatives who have received a reindeer give a reindeer.[3] In fact, the exchange does not bring a tangible result such as is the case in commercial transactions in our own society. The profit is neither direct nor inherent in the things exchanged as in the case of monetary profit or consumer gain. Or rather it is not so according to our own conventions. In primitive thought there is clearly something else in what we call a 'commodity' that makes it profitable to its owner or its trader. Goods are not only economic commodities, but vehicles and instruments for realities of another order, such as power, influence, sympathy, status and emotion; and the skilful game of exchange (in which there is very often no more real transfer than in a game of chess, in which the players do not give each other the pieces they alternately move forward on the chessboard but merely seek to provoke a counter-move), consists in a complex totality of conscious or unconscious manœuvres in order to gain security and to guard oneself against risks brought about by alliances and by rivalries.

Amundsen's misadventures show the cost of losing the meaning of reciprocity. From the generous gifts that Amundsen gave the Eskimo, in return for their presents, they quickly concluded that it was to their advantage to offer all their goods as presents. It soon became necessary to decline any present and to resort to proper commerce.[4] Likewise, Holm states that an exchange with one native opens a general claim on the part of all the others to the same gift: 'The natives explained that they always gave people everything they asked for.'[5] But the true meaning of this statement must be specified:

'When a person wishes to start one of these [i.e., a *pă-tukh-tûk*] he takes some article into the *kashim* [the men's house] and gives it to the man with whom he wishes to trade, saying, at the same time, "It is a *pă-tukh-tûk*." The other is bound to receive it, and give in return some article of about equal value; the first man then brings something else, and so they alternate, until sometimes two men will exchange nearly everything they originally possessed; the man who received the first present being bound to continue until the originator wishes to stop.'[6]

This passion for the gift, accompanied by the ritual obligation on the recipient to accept and to give, is found at the other end of the American continent, among the Yaghan.[7]

[1] Hogbin, 1932, p. 13.   [2] Williams, 1936, p. 137; Armstrong, 1920–1.
[3] Jochelson, 1910–26, p. 96.   [4] Boas, 1897, p. 374.   [5] Nelson, 1896–7, p. 309.
[6] ibid.   [7] Gusinde, 1937, p. 980 et seq.

Radcliffe-Brown's observation on gift exchange among one of the most primitive peoples known, the Andaman Islanders, answers the problem posed by Turner in the text quoted above, and which concerns a highly developed culture: 'The purpose that it did serve was a moral one. The object of the exchange was to produce a friendly feeling between the two persons concerned.'[1] The best proof of the supra-economic nature of these exchanges is that in the *potlatch* there is no hesitation in sometimes destroying considerable wealth by breaking a 'copper' or by throwing it into the sea, and that greater prestige results from the destruction of wealth than from its distribution, because however liberal it may be distribution always requires a similar return. Although it is always limited and qualified by the other aspects of the institution of exchange, the economic character still persists. 'It is not, however, the mere possession of wealth which gives prestige; it is rather its distribution. . . The amassing of wealth has as its sole aim the buying of high status.'[2] As a matter of fact, 'the idea of a free gift is alien to Malekula culture . . . A gift is at most a venture, a hopeful speculation.'[3] However, 'even when pigs are given for pigs and food for food, the exchanges are not wholly without economic significance, for they are definitely valuable as a stimulus to work and for the need to which they give rise for organized co-operative effort'.[4]

II

The idea that a mysterious advantage is attached to the acquisition of commodities, or at least certain commodities, by means of reciprocal gifts, rather than by individual production or acquisition, is not confined to primitive society. The Alaskan Indians distinguish objects of consumption or provisions which do not go beyond the circle of production and family consumption, and wealth – property *par excellence* – which the Kwakiutl call 'the rich food'. The latter includes painted rugs, horn spoons, bowls and other ceremonial containers, ceremonial clothes, and so on, any object whose symbolical value infinitely outweighs the value of the labour or raw material, and which alone can enter into ritual cycles of tribal and intertribal exchange. But a similar distinction still operates in modern society. There are certain types of object which are especially appropriate for presents, precisely because of their non-utilitarian nature. In some Latin countries these objects can only be found, in all their luxury and diversity, in stores set up especially for this purpose, such as 'casas de regalias' or 'casas de presentes', and which are similar to Anglo-Saxon 'gift shops'. It is hardly necessary to note that these gifts, like invitations (which, though not exclusively, are also free distributions of food and drink), are 'returned'. This is an example of reciprocity in our society. It is as if in our society certain non-essential goods, such as flowers, sweets and 'luxury articles', to which is attached a great psychological,

[1] Mauss, 1925, p. 62.   [2] Deacon, 1934, p. 199.   [3] loc. cit.
[4] ibid. p. 202.

aesthetic or sensual value, are thought to be more properly acquired in the form of reciprocal gifts rather than as individual purchases or for individual consumption.

In our society also certain festivals and ceremonies regulate the periodical return and traditional style of vast exchange transactions. In North American society, which often seems to seek the reintegration into modern society of the very general attitudes and procedures of primitive cultures, these occasions assume quite exceptional proportions. The exchange of gifts at Christmas, for a month each year, practised by all social classes with a sort of sacred ardour, is nothing other than a gigantic *potlatch*, implicating millions of individuals, and at the end of which many family budgets are faced with lasting disequilibrium. Richly decorated Christmas cards certainly do not attain the value of 'coppers', but the refinement shown in their selection, their originality, their price (which although individually modest, is none the less to be multiplied by the number), and the quantity sent or received, are the proof, ritually exhibited on the recipient's mantelpiece during the week of celebration, of the wealth of his social relationships or the degree of his prestige. The subtle techniques of gift wrapping must also be mentioned, all expressing in their way the personal bond between the giver and the gift, and the magical function of the gift, such as special wrapping paper, ribbons appropriate to the occasion, heraldic labels and so on. Through the uselessness of the gifts, and their frequent duplication because of the limited range of objects suitable as presents, these exchanges also take the form of a vast and collective destruction of wealth. Without calling upon the very significant theme in modern folklore of the millionaire lighting his cigar with bank notes, there are many little facts in this example to remind us that even in our own society the destruction of wealth is a way to gain prestige. The skilful merchant knows that a way to attract customers is to advertise that certain high-priced articles must be 'sacrificed'. The motive is economic, but the terminology retains an air of mystery.

Doubtless gambling provides, in modern society, the most striking picture of these transfers of wealth with the sole purpose of gaining prestige. Gambling really requires a special study by itself, but here we shall confine ourselves to a brief statement. During the last hundred years, gambling has shown exceptional development each time the means of payment were found considerably to exceed the local availability of commodities. The fabulous gambling stories of the Klondyke of Alaska, during the mining expansion, are echoed by those of the Amazon region during the great rubber period. Thus it seems as if money, which we have become accustomed to regard as a simple means of obtaining economic goods, found, when it could not be used up in this way, another archaic rôle, formerly attributed to precious things, viz., as a means of gaining prestige by the value of the gift or sacrifice, which has actually been made or simply mooted. This ritualization of the use of 'surpluses' corresponds with the regulation, already examined in chapter

III, of the use of 'scarce products'. Between these two extremes there is a kind of zone of indifference and freedom. Martius's remarks on the Arawak are well known: 'Although they may have the idea of individual property, what each possesses is so common and easy to obtain, that everyone lends and borrows without too much concern for restitution.'[1] The Yakut refused to believe that somewhere in the world people could die of hunger, when it was so easy to go and share a neighbour's meal.[2] Thus the refinements of sharing or distribution appear with the urgency or the absence of the need.

But there is still a general model here. In the significant field of the offering of food, of which banquets, teas and evening parties are modern examples, the language itself, as in 'to give a reception', shows that among ourselves, as in Alaska or Oceania, 'to receive' is to give. The characteristic of reciprocity is not the only justification for comparing meals and their rituals with the primitive institutions that we have considered:

> 'In economic and social relationships the expression *fai te kai*, "prepared food" is very frequently heard, and signifies the preliminary act of initiating the relationship, since a basket of food is the common medium of prefacing a request, atoning for an injury, or fulfilling an obligation. In native descriptions of how to act in a variety of situations the words "go to your house, prepare food . . ." often begin the instruction.'[3]

One 'offers' dinner to a person whom one wishes to honour, and this type of invitation is the most frequent way of 'returning' a kindness. The more the social aspect takes precedence over the strictly alimentary, the more stylized also is the type and presentation of the food offered; the fine porcelain service, the silverware, and the embroidered table-cloths, which are usually carefully stored away in the family cupboards and buffets, are a striking counterpart of the ceremonial bowls and spoons of Alaska, brought out on similar occasions from painted and decorated chests. The attitudes towards food are especially revealing. Even among ourselves what may be called 'rich food' has a function other than the mere satisfaction of physiological needs. When one 'gives' a dinner-party, the ordinary daily menu is not served, and the literature has copiously conjured up all the banqueting folklore, such as *saumon-mayonnaise*, *turbot-sauce mousseline*, *aspics de foie gras*, and so on. Moreover, if the occasion requires certain traditional foods, their very appearance, by a significant recurrence, calls for shared consumption. A bottle of vintage wine, a rare liqueur, a foie gras, pricks the owner's conscience with the claim of someone else. These are some of the delicacies which one would not buy and consume alone without a vague feeling of guilt. Indeed, the group judges with singular harshness the person who does this. During Polynesian ceremonial exchanges it is required that goods be exchanged within the group of near paternal relatives, but must as far as possible go to other groups and into other villages. To fail in this duty is called

[1] Von Martius, 1867.   [2] Sumner, 1901, p. 69.   [3] Firth, 1939, p. 372.

sori taŋa, 'giving into one's own basket'. And at village dances convention demands that neither of the two local groups consume the food which it has brought, but that they exchange their provisions and that each shall eat the other's food.[1] The action of the person who, like the woman in the Maori proverb, *Kai kino ana Te Arahe*, would secretly eat the ceremonial food, without offering any of it,[2] would provoke from his or her near relatives irony, mockery, disgust and even anger, according to the circumstances and persons. But each of these sentiments in its way rouses a faint echo of similar emotions, which we have referred to in the preceding chapters. It seems that the group confusedly sees a sort of social incest in the individual accomplishment of an act which normally requires collective participation.[3]

But the ritual of exchange does not take place only at ceremonial meals. Politeness requires that the dish, salt, butter and bread be offered to one's neighbour before serving oneself. We have often observed the ceremonial aspect of the meal in the lower-priced restaurants in the south of France, especially in those regions where wine is the principal industry and is surrounded by a sort of mystical respect which makes it 'rich food' *par excellence*. In the small restaurants where wine is included in the price of the meal, each customer finds in front of his plate a modest bottle of wine, more often than not very bad. This bottle is similar to his neighbour's bottle, as are the portions of meat and vegetables which a waitress passes around. Nevertheless, a remarkable difference in attitude towards the wine and the food is immediately manifested. Food serves the body's needs and wine its taste for luxury, the first serving to nourish, the second, to honour. Each person at the table eats, so to speak, for himself, and the noting of a trifling slight in the way he has been served arouses bitterness towards the more favoured, and a jealous complaint to the proprietor. But it is entirely different with the wine. If a bottle should be insufficiently filled, its owner will good-humouredly appeal to his neighbour's judgment. And the proprietor will face, not the demand of an individual victim, but a group complaint. In other words, wine is a social commodity, while the *plat du jour* is a personal commodity. The little bottle may contain exactly one glassful, yet the contents will be poured out, not into the owner's glass, but into his neighbour's. And his neighbour will immediately make a corresponding gesture of reciprocity.

---

[1] Firth, 1939, pp. 311, 321.   [2] Best, 1924, vol. I, p. 425.

[3] cf. the Greek and Cambodian versions of *Ass's Skin*, in which the king symbolically reveals his incestuous desires towards his daughter: 'A man has a lamb that he himself has raised or nourished. Is it better that he eat it himself or that another man eat it?' And in the Khmer version: 'Summoning his mandarins one day, he asked them if a man should eat or sell the fruit from a tree that he has planted.' Cosquin, 1922, p. 9. Inversely, among the Baiga of central India, incest is expiated by offering great feasts (Elwin, 1938, pp. 237-54). And the natives of the Trobriand Islands justify their indignant condemnation of father-daughter incest, which in a matrilineal system is not an infraction of the exogamous law and which is not punished by ritual illnesses, by saying that it is 'very bad because already he married her mother. Already he caught hold of the first marriage present.' Malinowski, 1929, pp. 530–1.

What has happened? The two bottles are identical in volume, and their contents similar in quality. Each person in this revealing scene has, in the final analysis, received no more than if he had consumed his own wine. From an economic viewpoint, no one has gained and no one has lost. But the point is that there is much more in the exchange itself than in the things exchanged.

The situation of two strangers less than a yard apart, face to face on both sides of a table in a cheap restaurant (an individual table is a privilege to be paid for, and is not granted below a certain tariff), is commonplace and sporadic. Nevertheless, it is highly revealing, for it offers an example, rare in our society (but many instances are found in primitive society), of the formation of a group, for which, doubtless because of its temporary nature, no ready-made formula of integration exists. The French custom is to ignore people whose names, occupations and rank are unknown. But in the little restaurant, such people find themselves in a quite close relationship for one to one-and-a-half hours, and temporarily united by a similar preoccupation. A conflict exists, not very keen to be sure, but real enough and sufficient to create a state of tension between the norm of privacy and the fact of community. They feel both alone and together, compelled to the usual reserve between strangers, while their respective spatial positions, and their relationships to the objects and utensils of the meal, suggest, and to a certain extent call for, intimacy. For a short time these two strangers are forced to live together, although not for as long or as closely as if sharing a cabin of a transatlantic liner, or a sleeping-car, but for this reason also no clear cultural procedure has been established. An almost imperceptible anxiety is likely to arise in the minds of these table-companions with the prospect of trifling disagreements that the meeting might produce. When social distance is maintained, even if it is not accompanied by any sign of disdain, insolence or aggression, it is in itself a matter of sufferance in that any social contact entails an appeal, an appeal which is a hope for response. This is the fleeting but difficult situation resolved by the exchanging of wine. It is an assertion of good grace which does away with the mutual uncertainty. It substitutes a social relationship for spatial juxtaposition. But it is also more than that. The partner who was entitled to maintain his reserve is persuaded to give it up. Wine offered calls for wine returned, cordiality requires cordiality. The relationship of indifference can never be restored once it has been ended by one of the table-companions. From now on the relationship can only be cordial or hostile. There is no way of refusing the neighbour's offer of his glass of wine without being insulting. Further, the acceptance of this offer sanctions another offer, for conversation. In this way a whole range of trivial social ties are established by a series of alternating oscillations, in which offering gives one a right, and receiving makes one obligated, and always beyond what has been given or accepted.

And there is still more. The person beginning the cycle seizes the initiative, and the greater social ease which he has displayed puts him at an advantage. For the opening always involves a risk, in that the table-companion may respond to the drink offered with a less generous glass, or the contrary risk that he will take the liberty to bid higher, obliging the one who made the first offer (and we must not forget that the bottle is small) either to lose his last trump as his last drop, or to sacrifice another bottle for the sake of his prestige. We are faced then with a 'total social fact' – on a microscopic scale, it is true – the implications of which are at once social, psychological and economic. This apparently futile drama, which perhaps the reader will think has been given a disproportionate importance, seems on the contrary to offer material for inexhaustible sociological reflection. We have already indicated our interest in the non-crystallized forms of social life,[1] viz., the spontaneous aggregations resulting from crises, or (as in the example just discussed) simply by-products of collective life, providing fresh traces of very primitive psycho-social experiences, and whose equivalent scale might vainly be sought in the irremediably inferior animal life, or in the much superior life of archaic or savage institutions. In this sense, the respective attitudes of the strangers in the restaurant appear to be an infinitely distant projection, scarcely perceptible but nevertheless recognizable, of a fundamental situation, that of individuals of primitive bands coming into contact for the first time or under exceptional circumstances meeting strangers. The characteristics of this very tense experience in primitive society have been shown elsewhere.[2] Primitive peoples know only two ways of classifying strangers. They are either 'good' or 'bad.' But one should not be misled by a naïve translation of native terms. A 'good' group is one accorded hospitality without question, and given the most precious goods. A 'bad' group is one from which one expects and to which is promised, at the first opportunity, suffering or death. With one there is exchange, with the other, fighting. It is in this light that the Chukchee legend of 'the invisible ones', in which mysteriously conveyed goods exchange themselves, must be understood. Nothing clarifies this better than a description of their former markets. Everyone came armed, and the products were offered on spear points. Sometimes a bundle of skins was held in one hand and a bared knife in the other, so that one was ready for battle at the slightest provocation. The market was also formerly designated by the one word, *Elpu'rIrkIn*, 'to exchange', which was also applied to the vendetta. A new verb, *vili'urkIn*, 'to trade', corresponding to the Koryak *vili'vikIn*, 'to make peace with', has been introduced into the modern language. The author to whom we owe these observations adds: 'The difference in meaning between the old and the new term is very striking.'[3]

III

Exchange, as a total phenomenon, is from the first a total exchange, compris-

---

[1] p. 42. above.   [2] Lévi-Strauss, 1948*a*.   [3] Bogoras, 1904–9, pp. 53–5.

ing food, manufactured objects, and that most precious category of goods, women. Doubtless we are a long way from the strangers in the restaurant, and perhaps it will seem startling to suggest that the reluctance of the southern French peasant to drink his own flask of wine provides the model by which the prohibition of incest might be explained. Clearly, the prohibition does not result from this reluctance. Nevertheless, we believe that both are phenomena of the same type, that they are elements of the same cultural complex, or more exactly of the basic complex of culture. Moreover, this basic identity is apparent in Polynesia, where Firth distinguishes three spheres of exchange in terms of the relative mobility of the articles involved. The first sphere comprises especially food of various types, the second includes plaited cord and bark-cloth, and the third, shell fishhooks, rope, turmeric cylinders and canoes. He adds:

'Apart from the three spheres of exchange mentioned a fourth may be recognized where goods of unique quality are handed over. Such for instance was the transfer of women by the man who could not otherwise pay for his canoe. Transfers of land might be put into the same category. Women and land are given in satisfaction of unique obligations.'[1]

Perhaps we shall be criticized on the ground of having brought together two dissimilar phenomena, and we will answer this criticism before proceeding. Admittedly, the gift is a primitive form of exchange, but it has in fact disappeared in favour of exchange for profit, except for a few survivals such as invitations, celebrations and gifts which are given an exaggerated importance. In our society, the proportion of goods transferred according to these archaic modalities is very small in comparison with those involved in commerce and merchandising. Recriprocal gifts are diverting survivals which engage the curiosity of the antiquarian; but it is not possible to derive an institution such as the prohibition of incest, which is as general and important in our society as in any other, from a type of phenomenon which today is abnormal and exceptional and of purely anecdotal interest. In other words, we shall be accused, as we ourselves have accused McLennan, Spencer, Lubbock and Durkheim, of deriving the rule from the exception, the general from the particular, and the function from the survival. Perhaps it will be added that there is only one common characteristic between the prohibition of incest and the reciprocal gift, viz., the individual repulsion and social reprobation directed against the unilateral consumption of certain goods, but that the essential characteristic of reciprocal gifts, i.e., the positive aspect of reciprocity, is entirely missing in the first case, so that strictly speaking our interpretation could be valid only for exogamous systems (and particularly dual organizations) which present this reciprocal characteristic, but not for the prohibition of incest as practised in our society.

We shall begin with the second objection, already alluded to in the previous

[1] Firth, 1939, p. 344.

chapter. We have maintained that the prohibition of incest and exogamy constitute substantially identical rules, and that they differ from each other only in a secondary characteristic, viz., that reciprocity, present in both cases, is only inorganic in the first, while it is organized in the second. Like exogamy, the prohibition of incest is a rule of reciprocity, for I will give up my daughter or my sister only on condition that my neighbour does the same. The violent reaction of the community towards incest is the reaction of a community outraged. Unlike exogamy, exchange may be neither explicit nor immediate; but the fact that I can obtain a wife is, in the final analysis, the consequence of the fact that a brother or father has given her up. But the rule does not say in whose favour the person shall be given up. On the contrary, the beneficiary, or in any case the beneficiary class, is delimited in the case of exogamy. The only difference then is that in exogamy the belief is expressed that the classes must be defined so that a relationship may be established between them, while in the prohibition of incest the relationship alone is sufficient to define continually in social life a complex multiplicity, ceaselessly renewed by terms which are directly or indirectly solidary. This transformation in itself poses a problem. This problem will have to be resolved, and we shall do so by showing that exogamy and the prohibition of incest must both be interpreted in terms of the simplest pattern, that provided by marriage between cross-cousins. But whatever solution will have to be proposed, it can be seen that the prohibition of incest does not differ from exogamy and from exchanges of prestations of another order.

The other objection touches an equally important point, for it is a question of choosing between two possible interpretations of the term 'archaic'. The survival of a custom or a belief can in fact be explained in two ways. Either the custom or belief is a survival without any other significance than that of an historical residue spared by chance or as a result of extrinsic causes, or else it has survived because through the centuries it has continued to play a rôle and because this rôle is the same as might account for its initial appearance. An institution can be archaic because it has lost its reason for existing, or, on the contrary, because this reason for existing is so fundamental that any transformation of its ways of acting has been neither possible nor necessary.

Such is the case with exchange. Its rôle in primitive society is essential because it embraces material objects, social values and women. But while in the case of merchandise this rôle has progressively diminished in importance in favour of other means of acquisition, as far as women are concerned, reciprocity has on the contrary maintained its fundamental function, on the one hand because women are the most precious possession (in chap. III we have justified the exceptional position they occupy in the primitive system of values), but above all because women are not primarily a sign of social value, but a natural stimulant; and the stimulant of the only instinct the satisfaction of which can be deferred, and consequently the only one for which, in the act of exchange, and through the awareness of reciprocity, the transformation from the stimulant to the sign can take place, and, defining by this fundamental process the transformation from nature to culture, assume the character of an institution.

IV

The inclusion of women in the number of reciprocal prestations from group to group and from tribe to tribe is such a general custom that a whole volume would not be sufficient to enumerate the instances of it. Let us note first of all that marriage is regarded everywhere as a particularly favourable occasion for the initiation or development of a cycle of exchanges. The 'wedding presents' of our society are obviously to be included in the group of phenomena studied above.

In Alaska and British Columbia, the marriage of a girl is necessarily accompanied by a *potlatch*, to such an extent that the Comox aristocrats organize pseudo-marriage ceremonies with no bride, for the sole purpose of acquiring rights in the course of the exchange rites.[1] But the relationship which exists between marriage and gifts is not arbitrary. The marriage itself is an inherent part of the prestations which accompany it. It forms merely the central motive (Fig. 3). Not so long ago it was the custom in our society 'to ask for' a young girl in marriage, and the bride's father 'gave' his daughter in marriage. 'To give away the bride' is an expression still used in English. And of the woman who takes a lover, it is also said that she 'gives herself'. The term 'gift', in the Germanic languages, still has the two meanings of 'present' and 'betrothal'. Likewise, in Arabic, *sadaqa* means alms, bride-price, justice and tax. Doubtless, in this last case the comparison can be explained by the custom of wife-buying. But marriage by purchase is a special institution only in its form. In reality, it is only a modality of that basic system analysed by Mauss, according to which, in primitive society and still partially in our own, rights, goods and persons circulate within the group according to a continual mechanism of prestations and counter-prestations. Malinowski has shown that in the Trobriand Islands, even after marriage, the payment of *mapula* represents on the man's part a counter-prestation intended to compensate for services provided by the wife in terms of sexual gratification. This still seems to be the function of the engagement ring in our society, since the custom is for it to be left to the wife in case of divorce, and not to be included in the property settlement.

Although less important than those associated with funerals, the astonishing complexity of the matrimonial exchanges illustrated in Fig. 3 deserves to engage our attention. This complexity is expressed both in the number of prestations and in the number of social ties that they involve. In fact, marriage involves five different types of family and social relationships. To the right

[1] Barnett, 1938*b*, p. 133.

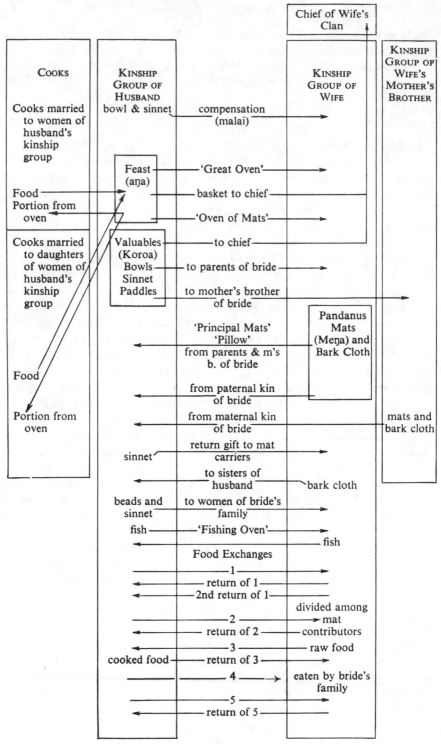

Fig. 3. Marriage exchanges in Polynesia (after Firth, 1939, p. 323).

of the husband's lineage there can be seen, firstly, the wife's lineage, and secondly, the wife's maternal uncle's lineage. The fact that the latter may be distinct from the former indicates that descent is patrilineal, as is actually the case in Tikopia from where this example has been taken.[1] To the left of the husband's lineage, the group of 'cooks' (or rather those called upon to play this rôle in this particular circumstance) is also subdivided, firstly into relatives by marriage with the women of the husband's lineage, and secondly into relatives by marriage with the women related to these affines themselves. When one of its members marries, the husband's lineage is then, as it were, supported by two groups of sons-in-law, the direct and the indirect sons-in-law, and its prestations are made to, and returned to it by, two groups of parents-in-law, viz., parents-in-law proper, and the parents-in-law of these parents-in-law.

In chapter XVIII we shall find this type of structure binding each lineage, in a system of directional exchanges, to its 'near sons-in-law' and to its 'distant sons-in-law' on the one hand, and, on the other, to its 'near parents-in-law' and to its 'distant parents-in-law'. The point of the comparison is to show that a society the study of which certainly pertains to complex kinship structures (for preferred degrees are unknown in Tikopia, and marriage between cousins is prohibited there) nevertheless conforms with our methods of analysis and can be defined, at least in a functional way, as a society with a long cycle, in the sense given to this term in chapter XXVII. From a more general point of view, it will be sufficient to note here that a new marriage renews all marriages concluded at other times, and at different points in the social structure, so that each connexion rests upon all the others and gives them, on its establishment, a recrudescence of activity.

Finally, it must be noted that the 'compensation' (*te malai*), which initiates the matrimonial exchanges, represents an indemnity for the bride's abduction. Even marriage by capture does not contradict the rule of reciprocity. Rather it is one of the possible legal ways of putting it into practice. The bride's abduction dramatically expresses the obligation upon any group holding girls to give them up. It shows clearly that they are *available*.

It would then be false to say that one exchanges or gives gifts at the same time that one exchanges or gives women. For the woman herself is nothing other than one of these gifts, the supreme gift among those that can only be obtained in the form of reciprocal gifts. The first stage of our analysis has been intended to bring to light this basic characteristic of the gift, represented by women in primitive society, and to explain the reasons for this. It should not be surprising then to find women included among reciprocal prestations; this they are in the highest degree, but at the same time as other goods, material and spiritual. This syncretic character of the conjugal bond and, over and above the conjugal bond and doubtless before it, of the alliance itself, emerges clearly from the protocol of the marriage proposal

[1] Firth, 1936, ch. XV.

among the Bushmen of South Africa. Approached by an intermediary, the parents of the young girl replied: 'We are poor, we cannot afford to give our daughter away.' The suitor then visits his future mother-in-law and says: 'I have come myself to speak to you. If you die, I will bury you, if your husband dies I will bury him.' And gifts immediately follow.[1] This expresses perfectly the total character, sexual, economic, legal and social, of this collection of reciprocal prestations which make up marriage. In Ontong Java, an island of the Solomon Archipelago, the ceremonial exchanges take place in the following way (Fig. 4).

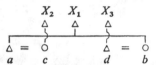

Fig. 4. Ceremonial exchanges in the Solomon Islands.

Suppose X_1 is the headman of the group of a and b; a is married to c, whose headman is X_2, and b is married to d, the headman of whose group is X_3. At one exchange, a and his brothers give fish to X_1, and c and her husband's brothers' wives give puddings to him. In return, a gets puddings, and c fish. At the same time, d gives fish to X_3, and b gives him puddings, and they receive the opposite in return. At the other exchange, a gives fish to X_2, and c gives him puddings, and each gets the opposite in return. At the same time, d gives fish to X_1, and b gives him puddings.[2] Thus, 'in one exchange the headman received fish from his male blood relatives, and taro puddings from his female relatives by marriage. In the other he received fish from his male relatives by marriage, and puddings from his female blood relatives. On both occasions he kept some of the gifts for himself and then gave to each person the opposite to what he or she had presented.'[3] Thus economic exchanges offer an ideal commentary on marriage transactions.

Analysing a special kinship relationship (to which we shall have to return) in force among certain groups in New Guinea, Seligman remarks:

'For example the folk of Beipaa (Veifa) feed pigs and bring up dogs but these pigs and dogs are not for them, they are for the village of Amoamo, their *ufuapie*, and in return the pigs and dogs from Amoamo come to Beipaa . . . The same condition holds in the matter of marriage; the girls of a village, according to the accepted rule, should not marry any others than the men of the *ufuapie*.'[4]

These examples, which might easily have been multiplied almost to infinity, show not only that the system of prestations *includes* marriage, but also

[1] Schapera, 1930, p. 106.
[3] ibid. p. 55.
[2] Hogbin, 1931*b*, p. 47.
[4] Seligman, 1910, pp. 363–4.

that it *keeps it going*. In Alaska the rivalry of the *potlatch* takes place essentially between the father-in-law and the son-in-law, and in the Andaman Islands the son-in-law is bound specially to honour his parents-in-law with gifts well after marriage. In New Caledonia, the sister's name perpetuates the memory of these exchanges at the same time that her status as exogamous wife guarantees their continuity. She is called *puneara*, 'the provider of food', and the expression indicates that any brother is welcome at a meal in the territory where his sister has married.[1]

In short, the system of prestations *results in* marriage.

On reaching puberty, the Konyak Naga boys begin to look for girls from the complementary clan to their own, and they exchange little gifts the value and nature of which are strictly fixed by custom. These gifts are of such importance that a boy's first question to the young girl whose favours he seeks is as follows: 'Will you take my gifts or not?' The answer being, perhaps: 'I will take them', or 'I have taken the gifts of another man. I don't want to exchange with you.' Even the wording of these overtures is fixed by tradition. This exchange of gifts initiates a whole series of reciprocal prestations which lead to marriage, or, rather, constitute the initial transactions of marriage, viz., work in the fields, meals, cakes, and so on.[2]

The small nomadic bands of the Nambikwara Indians of western Brazil are in constant fear of each other and avoid each other. But at the same time they desire contact, because it is the only way in which they are able to exchange, and thus to obtain products or articles that they lack. There is a link, a continuity, between hostile relations and the provision of reciprocal prestations. Exchanges are peacefully resolved wars, and wars are the result of unsuccessful transactions. This feature is clearly witnessed to by the fact that the transition from war to peace, or at least from hostility to cordiality, is accomplished by the intermediary of ritual gestures, a veritable 'reconciliation inspection'. The adversaries inspect each other and, with gestures which still hint of combat, examine the necklaces, earrings, bracelets and feathered ornaments of one another with admiring murmurs.

And from being arrayed against each other they pass immediately to gifts; gifts are received, gifts are given, but silently, without bargaining, without any expression of satisfaction or complaint, and without any apparent connexion between what is offered and what is obtained. Thus it is a question of reciprocal gifts, and not of commercial transactions. But a supplementary stage may be reached. Two bands which have thus come to establish lasting cordial relations can decide in a deliberate manner to join by instituting between the male members of the two respective bands the artificial kinship relationship of brothers-in-law. Given the marriage system of the Nambikwara, the immediate consequence of this innovation is that all the children of one group become the potential spouses of the children of the other group and vice versa. Thus a continuous transition exists from war to exchange,

[1] Leenhardt, 1930, p. 65.   [2] von Fürer-Haimendorf, 1938, p. 363.

and from exchange to intermarriage, and the exchange of brides is merely the conclusion to an uninterrupted process of reciprocal gifts, which effects the transition from hostility to alliance, from anxiety to confidence, and from fear to friendship.[1]

[1] Lévi-Strauss, 1943a; 1943b, pp. 398–409.

CHAPTER VI

Dual Organization

I

The fundamental characteristic of marriage as a form of exchange is seen particularly clearly in the case of dual organizations. This term defines a system in which the members of the community, whether it be a tribe or a village, are divided into two parts which maintain complex relationships varying from open hostility to very close intimacy, and with which various forms of rivalry and co-operation are usually associated. These moieties are often exogamous, that is, the men of one moiety can choose their wives only from the other, and vice versa. When the division into moieties does not regulate marriages, this rôle is frequently assumed by other forms of grouping. There may be a second bipartition of the group, parallel or perpendicular to this earlier division, the moieties may embrace exogamous clans, sub-clans or lineages, or, lastly, the modalities of marriage may depend upon specialized forms called marriage classes.

Dual organizations have numerous features in common apart from this direct or indirect exogamy. Descent is most often matrilineal; two culture heroes, sometimes older and younger brothers, sometimes twins, play an important part in the mythology; the bipartition of the social group is often continued into a bipartition of the universe into animate and inanimate objects, and the moieties are connected with such characteristic opposites as Red and White, Red and Black, Clear and Dark, Day and Night, Summer and Winter, North and South or East and West, Sky and Earth, Terra Firma and Sea or Water, Left and Right, Upstream and Downstream, Superior and Inferior, Good and Evil, Strong and Weak, Elder and Younger. Along with dual organizations there is sometimes a dichotomy of power between a secular chief and a sacred chief, or a secular chief and a military chief. Finally, the moieties are linked not only by the exchange of women, but by the furnishing of reciprocal prestations and counter-prestations of an economic, social and ceremonial nature. These links are frequently expressed in ritual games, which clearly show that double attitude of rivalry and solidarity which is the most striking feature of relationships between moieties. Sports races in North-east and Central Brazil, and ball games, with exactly the same function, in Australia and North, South and Central America provide examples of these. These similarities in detail have often suggested the hypothesis that dual organizations have spread from a single point of origin. We believe rather that these similarities rest on a common basis, reciprocity, which has a functional character and which must have an independent existence in countless human communities. As we shall try to show, the dual system does not give rise to reciprocity, but merely gives it form. This could at times have been a local discovery, subsequently imposed by conquest or borrowed for its convenience. It could never have spread if the basic conditions making its adoption desirable or facilitating its imposition had not been present everywhere.

The distribution of dual organizations has features which make this type of organization particularly remarkable. These features are not apparent among all peoples but are encountered in all parts of the world, and generally at the most primitive levels of culture. This distribution therefore suggests a functional character peculiar to archaic cultures rather than a single unique origin. Naturally, there are exceptions, but in support of this view it may be pointed out that in more numerous cases still it is possible to discern vague outlines or survivals of dual organization among neighbours evolved from groups which exhibit this organization more definitively. Thus in Indonesia, traces of dual organizations may be found among the Sakai of Sumatra, in the Macassar region, and in central and southern Celebes, on Sumba, Flores, Timor, and in the Moluccas. There is evidence and some suggestion that they existed, and still exist, in the Carolines and Palau of Micronesia. They are found in New Guinea, in the Torres Straits and the Murray Islands. In Melanesia, Codrington, Rivers, Fox and Deacon express their agreement in almost the same words, that dual organizations are the most archaic social structure. Finally, traces or embryonic forms have been observed in the Banks Islands, the New Hebrides, Fiji (by Hocart), Samoa, Tahiti, and perhaps even on Easter Island: 'The ten tribes or *mata* were split into two groups that were probably nothing more nor less than two hostile confederations', writes Métraux of the former social organization of this island.[1] Meanwhile, in another work, the same author points to the belief in a mythical dichotomy which accounts for the very origin of these tribes,[2] and he describes the forms of ritual co-operation between *Tuu* and *Hotu-iti*.[3] It is unnecessary to dwell on Australia, for the division into exogamous moieties is known to be a frequent feature of Australian aboriginal cultures and has nowhere else been subject to such refinements.

Writers of the sixteenth century had already pointed out forms of dualism in Central America and Mexico, and during the same period similar indications were forthcoming for Peru. In North America, moieties extend widely throughout the whole eastern zone, notably among the Creek, Chickasaw, Natchez, Yuchi, Iroquois and Algonquins. They are found in the cultures of the Plains, distinctly or as survivals, among the Sauk-Fox,

[1] Métraux, 1941, p. 70.   [2] ibid. 1942.   [3] ibid. 1940, pp. 124–5.

Menomini, Omaha, Kansas, Osage and Winnebago, and as less and less clear vestiges among the western groups. They are lacking in particular among the Arapaho and the Cheyenne, but reappear in the primitive cultures of central California. Finally, it has been only in the last ten years or so, but with a richness which has all the force of a proof, that dual organization has been observed in the most primitive cultures of South America. If dual organization, which is present at least in principle among the Nuer, the tribes of the Lobi branch, and the Bemba of Northern Rhodesia,[1] nevertheless seems less common in Africa than elsewhere, it could be shown that even where there is no dual organization certain mechanisms of reciprocity persist which are functionally equivalent to this type or organization. Among the Nuer of the White Nile, whose clans are still split even today into exogamous pairs, their origin is explained in the following myth:

'A certain Gau, who descended from heaven, married Kwong (according to one account an even earlier arrival from heaven), by whom he had two sons, Gaa and Kwook, and a number of daughters. As there was no one with whom these could marry, Gau assigned several daughters to each of his sons, and to avert the calamities that follow incest he performed the ceremony of splitting a bullock longitudinally, decreeing that the two groups might intermarry but that neither might marry within itself.'[2]

This myth obviously accounts for the theoretical origin of exogamous pairs. The same author tells us that among the Bari, where this dichotomy is unknown, the same 'splitting ceremony' is observed when there is some uncertainty as to the kinship relationships of the two who are engaged to be married. Here then, the theoretical risk of incest is avoided by an ideal reconstitution of a correlative and antagonistic couple. Moreover, the sacrifice of the bullock or goat to ward off an abnormal relationship between the spouses is widely spread throughout Africa, and elsewhere it has significant equivalents.

It is true that we might be guilty here of begging the question, since we seem to assume, instead of proving, as is our object, the basic identity of dual organization and customs which on the surface vary greatly. Nothing is more dangerous to a sound method of research than to adopt such a vague and elastic definition of the institution under examination that afterwards it is difficult not to read everything into it. The study of dual organization has especially suffered from this type of excess.

Wherever dual organization appears, it has a certain number of consequences. The most important of these is that individuals are defined in relationship to each other essentially by whether they belong or do not belong to the same moiety. This feature does not change, whatever the mode

---

[1] Evans-Pritchard, 1940; Labouret, 1931; Richards, 1937, pp. 188–93; Haekel, 1938, p. 654.

[2] Seligman and Seligman, 1932, p. 207.

of transmitting the moiety's name may be. Whether it be through the male or the female line, the mother's collaterals will always be grouped in one category, and the father's in another. Consequently, a single term will usually serve to designate the mother and her sisters, and likewise another for the father and his brothers. This system, which is usually far more complex, has been called 'the classificatory kinship system', and it can be seen that its specific nature is very readily accounted for by dual organization. For this reason, Tylor and Frazer have suggested that dual organization can always be postulated at the origin of the classificatory system. As the classificatory system exists, or can be found in almost all human societies, the seriousness of this hypothesis can be seen, since it implies nothing less than the universality of dual organization. We believe it impossible to hold this hypothesis in such a strict form, for we have already indicated that the essential thing, as we see it, is not dual organization but the principle of reciprocity of which it constitutes, in some way, the codification. But we agree that the classificatory system can be seen as proof of the generality, if not of dual organization itself, then at least of mechanisms, potentially more flexible and capable of functioning independently of any systematic apparatus, which none the less attest to the fundamental rôle of this principle of reciprocity.

II

Where does dual organization begin and where does it end? Moieties have this in common with clans, that descent is always unilineal. But we know of societies divided into clans and being without dual organization, societies with clans grouped into moieties, and lastly, societies with moieties not subdivided into clans. The principal difference between moieties and clans seems then to be one of size.

Let us take the simplest hypothesis – and the most favourable one – viz., that in which both clans and moieties are exogamous. An immediate distinction has to be made. For a clan to be exogamous does not inform us as to the marriage rules in the society considered. We would only know that an individual cannot seek his spouse in his own clan. To which clan should he turn? What degrees of closeness are permitted? Do preferential unions exist? This we do not know. The Crow Indians are divided into thirteen exogamous clans. All we learn from this is that a man can regard twelve out of every thirteen women as a possible spouse. Apart from the scale, the marriage rule is as indeterminate as in our own society.

The situation is wholly different in a society similarly divided into several unilineal groups, each of which, however, maintains defined marriage relationships with one or several others. For example, suppose that group *A* and group *B* always intermarry, and that it is the same for group *C* and group *D*, group *E* and group *F*, and so on; or else, that group *A* gives women to group *B*, which gives its women to group *C*, which in turn gives its women to group *D*, and so on . . . or any other analogous combination. In every instance here, the groups together represent a system, which was already true in the case of the previous hypothesis. But the system now has a stable structure, and a marriage law may be isolated for every combination, informing us completely as to the nature of the exchanges in whatever group is being considered. The term *clan* will be reserved for unilineal groupings which, in that they are exogamous, permit a purely negative definition, and the term *class*, or more exactly, *marriage class*, to those groupings which permit a positive determination of the modalities of exchange.

The distinction between the two forms is not always easy to make. There are clans which have none of the characteristics peculiar to classes. The Tupí-Cawahib of the Upper Madeira have such clans, each comprising one or more villages occupying an hereditary territory. There are twenty clans, and the only marriage rule is a recommendation to take a wife from outside. Thus each clan finds itself in the position of maintaining marriage relationships with several others, there being no limit to the number, no permanency in the alliances, and no marked preference for any particular combination. Obviously, in cases of this type, it cannot be said that the clan is not a functional unit. Its exogamous nature alone makes it such. But this functional rôle is reduced to a minimum and the factors determining the number of clans, their appearance and disappearance, their geographical location and their numerical importance, are more historical than anything else.[1]

With the Bororo, who have already been referred to,[2] the situation is more complex. The clans are unequal in number and importance. Their distribution and even their internal structure vary from village to village. Nevertheless, the clans are always distributed among two exogamous moieties and two other ceremonial moieties. Furthermore, the clans are linked in twos, or in more complex combinations, through marriage preferences which yet are not strict. Consequently, we are dealing with social categories possessing the characteristics of both clans and classes, without these characteristics completely overlapping. By contrast, among the Kachin of Burma marriage is regulated by two large groupings which are simultaneously both clans and classes.[3] Finally, in Australia there are marriage classes which are not clans, since the successive members of the same line of descent can be assigned to different classes.[4]

The distinction, however, is of great theoretical importance. If we try to interpret dual organization as a particular case of clan organization, and, more precisely, to compare moieties with a system with n clans in which $n = 2$, we meet with insoluble difficulties. As long as $n > 2$, the notion of

[1] Lévi-Strauss, 1948*b*.
[2] cf. pp. 48-9. The Mundurucu likewise have exogamous moieties, one (White Moiety) composed of nineteen clans, the other (Red Moiety) of fifteen clans. According to legend, these clans, formerly rival tribes, became 'brothers'. There are also clans which maintain closer relationships and are called *i-barip*, 'related', Kruse, 1934, pp. 50–7.
[3] cf. ch. XV.   [4] cf. ch. XI.

clan is not bound up with any positive determination, or only with very vague determinations. But when the number of groups falls to two, everything changes, negative determinations become positive, and instead of it being impossible for a man to marry into one group, he learns that he must marry into the other. Generally speaking, for every act of social life governed by dual organization, a *partner* is immediately identifiable. Hence Lowie's embarrassment in trying to treat moieties as clans: 'It is a puzzling question how this reciprocity is to be interpreted',[1] and his subsequent abandonment of this position.[2]

But moieties belong in fact, not to the 'clan' series, but to the 'class' series, and it is not enough that the number of clans be reduced to two, through demographic extinction or for any other reason, for a dual organization to emerge. Lowie rightly quotes the case of the Crow who today have only two military societies, the 'Foxes' and the 'Lumpwoods'. There were seven when Maximilian visited them.[3] The pseudo-dualism on this occasion has no significance from the dual organization standpoint. It would be the same if, as exemplified in South America, two clans surviving from a more complex organization together sought alliance with other villages or tribes. Thus the much discussed problem of whether clan organization resulted from a sub-division of moieties, or whether moieties were formed by an aggregation of clans has no significance whatsoever. Both are possible, as examples given below will show. Moreover, they are not the only possible methods. Dual organization may result from the establishment of organic ties between two villages, and even between two tribes. I myself have seen this happen between two tribes which did not speak the same language, and develop to such a point that only the names of the moieties were missing for there to be a characteristic and definite dual organization.[4]

These considerations perhaps provide an answer to a recent polemic on the unique or multiple origin of dual organization. Against Olson, who supports the former interpretation,[5] Lowie points out that institutions which are to all appearances heterogeneous are confused under the title of dual organization.[6] In North America alone the Iroquois have exogamous moieties consisting of several clans; the Hidatsa, non-exogamous moieties but also consisting of several clans; the Fox and the Yuchi, non-exogamous moieties, organized without any reference to clans; the Crow and the Kansas, indeterminate phratries; the Creek, ceremonial and non-exogamous moieties; the Keres and the Tewa, ceremonial moieties, tending to endogamy with the transfer of the wife to the husband's moiety if she does not belong there in the first place; and so on. In short, the one common characteristic of moieties is that there are two of them, and the duality is called upon to play

---

[1] Lowie, 1961, p. 133.   [2] ibid. 1934, p. 325.   [3] ibid. 1924, p. 87.
[4] Lévi-Strauss, 1943b; legend, as has been seen, attributes the same origin to the Mundurucu clans (cf. note 2, previous page).
[5] Olson, 1933, pp. 351–422.   [6] Lowie, 1961.

highly varying rôles as the circumstances require. Sometimes it governs marriages, economic exchanges and ritual, sometimes just some of these, and sometimes only sporting contests. There would thus appear to be as many different institutions as there are distinguishable modalities. Lowie even goes so far as to treat systems with patrilineal moieties and systems with matrilineal moieties, systems with exogamous moieties and systems with non-exogamous moieties, as virtually independent 'species'.[1]

The American sociologist is no doubt right in attacking certain abuses. Yet this attack must extend to the very nature of these abuses. Olson and his predecessors, principally Perry,[2] were doubly wrong. They defined dual organization in the most complex and most developed form that it is capable of attaining, and whenever they observed a hint or embryo of dualism they interpreted it as a vestige of this complex form and as a sign of its former existence. In that case, as Lowie once jokingly observed, the duality of political parties in the United States might be the survival of a former dual organization in which Democrats and Republicans acted as moieties.

But if dual organization rarely reaches the institutional stage, it nevertheless has to do with the same psychological and logical roots as all those sketchy or partial forms, sometimes simply outlines, which are formulations of the principle of reciprocity for the same reason (though not always as systematically) as dual organization is just such a formulation. Accordingly, dual organization is not in the first place an institution. If we wished to interpret it in this way, our search for its beginning and its end would be doomed as hopeless, and we would risk being thrown back on Lowie's atomism and nominalism. It is, above all, a principle of organization, capable of widely varying and, in particular, of more or less elaborated, applications. In some cases, the principle applies only to sporting competition. In others, it extends to political life (and the question of whether the two-party system is not an indication of dualism can be put without fear of absurdity), in others again, to religious and ceremonial life. Finally, it may extend to the marriage system. In all these forms, there is a difference of degree, not of kind; of generality, and not of type. To understand their common basis, inquiry must be directed to certain fundamental structures of the human mind, rather than to some privileged region of the world or to a certain period in the history of civilization.

It has been pointed out that we are ignorant of the origin and evolution of dual organizations, as well as their forms of decomposition. However, must the edict setting them up in some particular case be known for their functional validity to be affirmed? Inversely, must certain definite cases of dual organizations having undergone changes due entirely to contingent events such as wars, migrations, internal struggles, and so on, necessarily lead to the affirmation of their historical origin? American ethnologists were pleased to show how interpretations which are too theoretical can come to grief, when

---

[1] ibid. 1940, p. 427.   [2] Perry, 1923.

it was established that the number and distribution of exogamous units in certain systems had varied in a relatively short space of time. They concluded that such unstable structures elude all systematic analysis.[1] But this is to confuse the principle of reciprocity, which is always at work and always oriented in the same direction, with the often brittle and almost always incomplete institutional structures continually used by it to realize the same ends. The contrast, the apparent contradiction, we might almost say, between the functional permanence of systems of reciprocity, and the contingency of the institutional matter placed at their disposal by history, and moreover ceaselessly reshaped by it, is supplementary proof of the instrumentality of these systems. Whatever the changes, the same force is always at work, and it is always to the same effect that it organizes the elements offered or abandoned to it.

In this respect, discussion is no substitute for the three examples analysed in the following pages. They are drawn from three different regions, and reveal, firstly, how dual organization can arise, secondly, the crises to which it is exposed, and thirdly, the specific modifications which it causes in a social system which may be observed independently of its action.

III

The Motu and the Koita of New Guinea were originally two different tribes. Nevertheless, they tended to bring their villages together. The new village was either formed simply from two groups of houses, or the two villages remained distinct although contiguous. In certain cases, the Motu penetrated into Koita territory, and in others the opposite happened. However, marriage exchanges have in general been so frequent that it is difficult to find 'in the eastern moiety any considerable number of people of Koita blood who have remained pure for three generations'.[2] In particular, the social structure is so organized that one may no longer dare to distinguish the legacy of history from the conscious or unconscious ends of the system. Thus the centre of Poreporena today consists of four villages grouped into two sub-divisions, each comprising a Koita village and a Motu village.

Hohodai (K.)	}	Hanuabada			
Hanuabada (M.)					
			}	Poreporena	
Tanobada (M.)	}	Tanobada			
Guriu (K.)					

The reasons for each particular migration are to be found in demographic, political, economic or seasonal circumstances. Nevertheless, the general result gives proof of integrating forces which are independent of such

[1] Lowie, 1940; Kroeber, 1938, pp. 305–7.   [2] Seligman, 1910, p. 45 et seq.

conditions, and under the influence of which history has tended towards system.

The Mekeo, also studied by Seligman, provide an even more striking example. The plan of their social organization is a subtle and complex symmetry, and the historical vicissitudes to which its component elements have been exposed have never succeeded in abating its strictness. Legend connects the origin of the Mekeo with successive migrations caused in the first place by a quarrel as to the *ongoye* bird's laugh, which some said was oral and others supposed to be anal. In addition to the fights between factions and migrations, apparently alluded to in this legend, Seligman cites war, revenge, and transfers of territory. The history of the Inawi and Inawae villages is crammed full of such factors.[1]

And yet the villages coincide with social units whose nature, number and distribution cannot be the mere results of chance. The Mekeo are divided into two groups, *Ofa* and *Vee*. Each group is in turn subdivided into two *ngopu*, meaning 'group of common descent', and named Inawi and Inawae for the *Ofa*, and Ngangai and Kuapengi for the *Vee*. Each *ngopu* consists of one, two or several *pangua*, clans or local groups within the village, while the clan is divided into sections, each characterized by a men's house or *ufu*.

To a certain extent it is known how a *pangua* subdivides and gives rise to new units. A *pangua* normally consists of several *ikupu* or enlarged families. An *ikupu* can acquire a jural personality by proclaiming itself the 'younger section' (*ekëi*) of a *pangua*, and the other *ikupu* of the *pangua* are then known as the 'older section' (*fäangiau*). It can also break completely with its clan and found a new *pangua*. There is a third process of subdivision whereby the *pangua* gives rise to two groups, on the one hand *fäa aui* or *lopia aui*, which is always a segment of the older section and includes the political chief, and, on the other, *io aui*, which can be a segment of the younger section but always includes the war chief. Demographic pressure, internal quarrels, economic inequalities, political ambition or the desire for prestige, seem to be the principal motives in these processes of fission, and Seligman gives detailed examples of them.[2]

And yet, each *pangua*, or *ikupu* group within the *pangua*, maintains a particular type of relationship with certain *pangua*, or *ikupu* groups in the same or different *pangua*. Pangua or *ikupu* interjoined by this special tie are called *ufuapie*, or 'men's house from the other side of the village'. The *ufuapie* exchange prestations which are economic, legal, matrimonial, religious, or ceremonial as the case may be, and it is no exaggeration to say that the *ufuapie* relationship is the regulating principle for the whole social life of the Mekeo. In one sense, then, the *ufuapie* structure is the final cause of the complex system of *ngopu*, *pangua*, *ikupu* and *ufu*. There is so much truth in this that, in referring to the native theory which reduces the disorder and apparent confusion of present-day groups to two sections (*Biofa* and

[1] ibid. pp. 315–19.   [2] ibid. pp. 328–46.

Vee), each consisting in two *ngopu* which are *ufuapie* in relationship to one another, Seligman, at the end of a detailed analysis, acknowledges that 'the conditions actually existing . . . are almost exactly those required by the hypothesis founded upon native history'.[1]

Thus the social structure of the Mekeo has been modified by two factors, firstly, by migratory movements which have introduced allogeneous elements, and secondly, by an internal tendency: 'There is, and apparently always has been, a centrifugal tendency which, with the absence of a central dominating authority, has permitted the formation of a large number of *pangua* by fission from the parent stock.'[2] The ancient organization of the *Biofa* and the *Vee*, each divided into two exogamous moieties with reciprocal prestations, has been complicated and diversified. However, it is still revealed in the *ufuapie* relationship, which can be explained less as a historical survival than as a regulating principle which, though no doubt imperfectly, has nevertheless continued to exist.

IV

This respective independence of the principle of reciprocity and the temporary institutions in which it is expressed, whatever the society and whatever the moment in its history, stand out equally clearly among the Naga of Assam. Their northern and eastern representatives, the Konyak, are divided into two linguistic groups, Thendu and Thenkoh, and are also distinguished by peculiarities of clothing. Both groups are endogamous, whether they live in the same village[3] or in different villages.[4] But each village has a men's house or *morung*, some having two, others more. Each *morung* corresponds to a *khel* or subdivision of the village, and groups together several hierarchized clans among which marriage is forbidden. In certain cases at least, then, the *morung* functions as an exogamous unit. Nevertheless, the existence of clan exogamy does not prejudice the exogamy of the *morung*, and in certain villages, Wakching for example, the *morung* are coupled to form two exogamous pairs, viz., Oukheang and Thepong, on the one hand, and Balang and Bala on the other. Marriage is concluded by an exchange of gifts between the bridegroom and his parents-in-law 'which is repeated at intervals until his death and in some cases for even longer'.[5] This system of prestations between *morung* regulates the whole economic and ceremonial life of villages practising it. Thus, 'the *morung* of the Konyak Nagas are the centres of village life and the pillars of their social and political organization. The *morung* system regulates the relations of every man and woman with the other members of the community, and forms a framework for the numerous mutual obligations between individuals and groups. It strengthens the sense of social unity . . . and at the same time encourages competition . . . thus stimulating the activities of the whole village.'[6]

---

[1] Seligman, 1910, p. 352.   [2] ibid. p. 367.   [3] Hutton, 1921*b*, p. 114 et seq.
[4] von Fürer-Haimendorf, 1938.   [5] ibid. p. 362.   [6] ibid. p. 376.

This basic system of reciprocal rights and duties is at the constant mercy of conflicts and quarrels which necessitate a complete reorganization of the structure. According to custom, the Thepong boys once rebuilt the *yo* (the girls' dormitory) for the Bala girls. They thus acquired the privilege of courting these Bala girls in the *yo*. The Thepong boys became aware that the girls also received visits from some Ang-ban boys who had no such right. Their reproaches being ineffectual, the Thepong invaded the *yo* and cut down the bamboo bed platforms. The girls, outraged, then demanded a fine, which the boys refused to pay unless the girls also paid a fine for having illegally received the Ang-ban. Tempers were lost on both sides, and relations were completely broken off between the Thepong boys and the Bala girls. The two groups no longer sing or dance together, they go separately to the fields, and they no longer exchange gifts. In these circumstances, the Ang-ban clan has maintained good relations with both the Thepong and the Bala, and by interposing itself between the two has prevented interruption of the circuit of prestations. For their part, the Bala and Thepong have opened a new cycle of relationships with other *morung*.[1]

Another incident, which its narrators traced back to the beginning of the century, is equally typical. The men of the Bala *morung* had made themselves unpopular because of their arrogance and quarrelsome nature. One day one of them fell into a game pit dug by a man from Chingtang, and died from his wounds. Although this was only an accident, the Bala swore to take revenge. The other *morung* intervened with the Bala, asking that they be content with a heavy fine. The Chingtang said they were quite willing to pay, but the Bala refused, lay in ambush, and inadvertently killed a Wakching woman instead of the Chingtang they were expecting.

The other *morung* then lost their patience and demanded that the Bala should deliver the two culprits to Wakching, in order to avoid a war between the two villages. However, the culprits escaped, and the Bala satisfied Wakching by buying a slave whose head served to avenge the murder.

The incident might then seem to have been settled. However, relations between Bala and Thepong continued to worsen, and a quarrel about the rights in a certain song ended in an open fight. Both *morung* fought desperately, not only with clubs, which are generally used in fights of this type, but also by throwing stones. The Bala even attacked their adversaries with spears and wounded several of them. Furious at such a violation of the rules, the Thepong killed a Bala.

From then on all hope of peace was lost. The four *morung*, Oukheang, Thepong, Balang and Ang-ban, decided to finish once and for all with the trouble-makers. But since it is forbidden to destroy a *khel* of one's own village, they asked the Ang of Chi to do the job for them. The Ang of Chi agreed on condition that the people of Wakching place one of Chi's younger

[1] ibid. p. 364.

brothers at the head of their own Ang. It was in these circumstances that the Bala *khel* was burnt down and its members driven out.

However, the Bala did not entirely disappear. Some found refuge among the Balang, although the latter had participated in the conspiracy. But the Balang had attacked the Bala as a different *morung* to their own, not as their fellow-clansmen in that *morung*. As such, the Bala had a right to be protected by the Balang, and knowing this took refuge only with those *morung* with which they could not intermarry, and not with their relatives-in-law. The Bala *morung* had disappeared, but a good half of its numbers were accepted among the Balang and treated as such. Only fifteen years later was the Bala *morung* rebuilt and reopened.[1]

There is no doubt that in most cases such events do account for the present-day form of a social structure, but it would be singularly shortsighted not to see beyond this. Despite incident, conflict and destruction, the structures just considered still remain structures of reciprocity. Their true nature derives from those factors which cause them to survive as such, and not from the spasmodic history which continually forces them to readapt.

V

The Yokut and the Western Mono of California provide just as striking an example, since here is a group in which only certain elements are affected by dual organization, and then not to the same extent. In particular, where this dual organization does exist, it is superimposed upon a more general form of organization which it specifies and amplifies without being inconsistent with or replacing it. This general form of organization consists firstly in a system of patrilineages which it is agreed today is basic to the social life of Californian tribes, and secondly, in a continual demand for reciprocal prestations between persons, families, lineages, villages, or tribes: 'On all occasions of . . . jubilance or sorrow there was always a reciprocal group who supplied services or gifts which were balanced with gifts of equivalent value in the form of bead money, baskets, feather ornaments, furs, or foodstuffs.'[2] Roughly speaking there are, on the one hand, groups (or more exactly partners, since relationships of reciprocity exist between two groups, two persons, or even a person and a group, as in the case of propitiatory rites to the totem of an animal which has been hunted and killed), and on the other, a network of bilateral relationships between these partners. At the same time, marriage is prohibited between all the *ta.a'ti* or kin, including all cousins up to the second and sometimes even the third degree.

What happens in the Mono or Yokut tribes which superimpose a division into moieties upon this general organization? Nothing changes and nothing is omitted, but the moieties do add something: firstly, a further type of correlative opposition with a function analogous to the previous types;

[1] von Fürer-Haimendorf, 1938, pp. 366–7.   [2] Gayton, 1945, p. 416.

secondly, a principle of systematization allowing the grouping and simplification of the previous network of relationships; and, finally, a common method for handling relationships (such as marriage) which prior to this had not been consciously assimilated to reciprocity.

The moieties, like the lineages, are patrilineal, and the grouping of the lineages into moieties does not prevent them from keeping their respective totems. Nevertheless, the totems acquire an order or arrangement which they previously lacked, for they too are divided between the two moieties. 'For example, the Tachi assigned Eagle, Crow, Falcon, etc., to the *Tokelyuwiš* moiety, Bear, Raven, Coyote, etc., to the *Nutuwiš* moiety.'[1] A man whose patrilineage has the crow as its symbol is then both Crow (with respect to lineage) and *Tokelyuwiš* (with respect to moiety). He shows the customary respect for his own symbol, and at least perfunctory respect for all other symbols of his moiety. Likewise, on ceremonial occasions, the bipartite tribes classify the products from collecting and hunting into *Tokelyuwiš* (seeds and mushrooms) and *Nutuwiš* (berries, birds, game). The moiety 'owning' the food would collect the first fruits and offer them to the other moiety. This second moiety must take its share in order to lift the alimentary prohibition that would otherwise be imposed upon the first group. In the tribes without moieties redemption ceremonies for an animal killed during hunting are observed by the eponymous lineage. In tribes with moieties, these ceremonies become the business of one of the two principal divisions, the interested family having no more than an officiating rôle.[2]

There are other changes also. The official titles ('chief' and 'messengers') are the prerogative of the Eagle and Dove lineages in the tribes without moieties. In tribes with moieties, the Eagle lineage (*Tokelyuwiš* moiety) keeps the first place in the hierarchy. But a second chief, from the Coyote lineage, appears in the *Nutuwiš* moiety, and the Eagle–Coyote duality becomes characteristic of the whole organization. In this way, authority acquires a dual structure that it otherwise lacks. But the marriage system merits special attention. There is no complete rupture with the rules previously described. Cross-cousin marriage remains prohibited, and marriage within the moiety is possible when there is no known relation of kinship. However, a person tends to apply the term *ta.a'ti* to all members of his moiety. Moiety exogamy, without being compulsory, corresponds to a general tendency, 70 to 75 per cent of marriages among the Yokut being exogamous. The Yokut and Western Mono observe the annual mourning ceremony in conjunction with a neighbouring tribe which acts as partner for the exchange of prestations and counter-prestations. The guest tribe does not have to be the same one every year, but in tribes with moieties the reciprocal pairing must always be a *Tokelyuwiš* moiety of the host tribe and a *Nutuwiš* moiety of the guest tribe, or vice versa. However, reciprocity is not all embracing. It is not one moiety accepting another, but rather a

---

[1] ibid. p. 420.   [2] ibid. pp. 420–2.

general principle applying to all the constituents (families and persons) of both the respective groups. The family of the host chief receives the family of the guest chief, and, depending upon their particular relationship, the families are thus grouped into host and guest pairings. Thus the principle remains whereby the lineage continues to be the fundamental social unit, cutting across hamlet, village, homogeneous tribe, or tribe divided into moieties.[1]

As the author of these observations rightly says, the Californian moieties are not crystallized institutions corresponding to rigorously defined concepts. Rather, they reveal a principle of reciprocal grouping, according to associated or opposed poles, of the very same constituents found among peoples without moieties in the same region, viz., the person, the family, the lineage, or the tribe. There is a general preponderance of the patrilineage, and where there are moieties these serve only to intensify and extend the mechanisms of reciprocity which are equally characteristic of the whole region, without prejudice to the forms of organization which everywhere correspond to them.[2]

VI

These facts tally with others which might have been added in revealing dual organization less as an institution with certain precise and identifiable features than as a method for solving multiple problems. It is from this multiplicity of content that dual organizations draw their apparent heterogeneity. However, it would be wrong to confuse this basic diversity with the simple and constant form imposed upon it. On the contrary, the extreme generality of this form can be recognized without falling into those two traps of purely historical ideas, viz., general history and the monographic study.

Even in societies where the clan (as defined above) is the predominant form or organization, rough outlines of classes can be seen appearing when the normal system does not provide any ready-made solution to unexpected problems. Few people seem so far removed from dual organization as the Ifugao of the Philippines, who prohibit marriage between first cousins, and, apart from exceptions, between second and third cousins. Furthermore, in the case of such exceptions, a special ritual beginning with a sham fight must be observed. The bridegroom's family would proceed in arms to the bride's village, where her family, likewise armed, were waiting for them. The two groups would then start an argument more or less as Barton has reconstructed it:[3]

BOY'S KINDRED: We have come for the debt you owe us.
GIRL'S KINDRED: Debt? We owe you nothing. We borrow only within our own family!
BOY'S KINDRED: Is it lost? Have you forgotten?

[1] Gayton, 1945, pp. 420–4.   [2] ibid. p. 425.   [3] Barton, 1946, pp. 164–5.

GIRL'S KINDRED: Yes, of course it's lost because we never borrowed. Take your impudence to your own village and get out!
BOY'S KINDRED: What? Are you quarrelsome? Well, let's fight it out.

A sham fight would then ensue, but with real weapons, and although the weapons were not aimed at anyone in particular, the natives recount that it was best for a man 'to keep his eyes open because there might be bad shots'. A short time later someone would cry out: 'Enough, enough! Let's arrange it by an intermarriage, else a pity for our bodies.' Rites of pacification would then be celebrated, followed by invocations to the gods and ancestors: 'Ye ancestors are involved because we who were enemies are making peace . . . Let not the children who introduce an intermarriage (to terminate their enmity) become rusty or fat-sided.'[1] Consequently, for marriage to be possible within the exogamous group, there has to be a real, or at least, a simulated rupture of this group. This brings to mind those peoples of New Britain where the moieties are referred to as 'the boundaries of marriage',[2] or the people of Guadalcanal, who are divided into exogamous moieties, and who refer to marriage between members of the same division as having broken the moiety.[3] In Africa, as we have seen, the same mechanisms have a very general field of application.

This functional aspect of dual organization is not always as obvious as in the following example from a region where marriage is usually concluded between villages, and where the whole village helps pay the price for the marriage of each of its members. However,

> 'in one village where marriage within the village had occurred a row of logs across the centre of the village divided it into halves. These halves acted to each other with all the forms used between separate villages connected by marriage . . . In validating the marriage of another of their village members who had married normally outside the village both halves sank their division and worked together, the one for the other's business and reciprocally co-operating and pooling their wealth, instead of halving it and exchanging their half's respective pools, as they did when validating the marriage within the village.'[4]

Thus we can see emerge, on a purely empirical level, the notions of opposition and correlation basic to the definition of the dualistic principle, which is itself only one modality of the principle of reciprocity.

[1] loc. cit.
[2] Trevitt, 1939, p. 355.
[3] Hogbin, 1937, p. 78.
[4] Fortune, 1932, pp. 60–1.

CHAPTER VII

The Archaic Illusion

I

Up till now we have sought, though no doubt provisionally and schematically, to define certain very general frameworks of social life with which that universal institution, the prohibition of incest, and the various systems for regulating marriage, which are its modalities, might be connected. We are still at the stage of outlining and putting these frameworks into perspective, and it is not yet time to offer a complete proof of them. This proof is to be found in the book as a whole and is to be judged by the degree of coherency with which the facts have been interpreted. Nevertheless, we should pause and reflect for a moment on our premises. To assert, as we did in the last chapter, that a historical or geographical study could not exhaust the problem of the origin of dual organizations, and that for a better understanding of these organizations we must take into consideration certain fundamental structures of the human mind, would be a meaningless proposition if we were unable to perceive exactly how these structures were made up and what the method was by which we might apprehend and analyse them. Without wishing to undertake a task for which the sociologist is as yet imperfectly prepared, we believe a cursory look in this direction is essential, and it will be more than enough if the first results indicate that this undertaking is not completely without purpose.

What are the mental structures to which we have referred and the universality of which we believe can be established? It seems there are three: the exigency of the rule as a rule; the notion of reciprocity regarded as the most immediate form of integrating the opposition between the self and others; and finally, the synthetic nature of the gift, i.e., that the agreed transfer of a valuable from one individual to another makes these individuals into partners, and adds a new quality to the valuable transferred. The question of the origin of these structures will be taken up later. Whether or not they can account for the phenomena can only be answered from the whole work. Our sole intention at this point is to find out if they do exist, and to grasp them in their concrete and universal reality. Moreover, it is to this end that in the setting up of our hypothesis we have so far purposely avoided exceptional examples, or examples which, because their realization in some native society or other has been pushed to a very high degree of perfection, appear exceptional. By referring to our own society and to what appear to be trifling daily incidents, in an attempt to isolate certain basic structures, we have already outlined a demonstration of their generality.

But there is one field of experience which is even more universal than that resulting from the comparison of manners and customs. This is the field of infant thought, which provides a common basis of mental structures and schemes of sociability for all cultures, each of which draws on certain elements for its own particular model. Observations made on infant psychology reveal, in a concrete and striking form, mechanisms which, corresponding as they do to needs and very basic forms of activity and which for this reason are buried in the deepest recesses of the mind, are somewhat difficult to arrive at through theoretical analysis. These are apparent in the child not because his mind represents an alleged 'stage' of intellectual development, but because his experience has been less influenced than an adult's by the particular culture to which he belongs. Susan Isaacs's observations are particularly valuable from this point of view.

She begins by emphasizing 'the strength and urgency of the common wish of little children to have exclusive possession or at least the biggest share or main use of whatever properties are the centre of interest at the moment. The satisfaction of having things all one's own is deep, the chagrin at others having more than oneself very bitter.'[1] This attitude is felt not only for material objects, but also for immaterial rights, such as the hearing or singing of a song. Furthermore, 'taking turns' is one of the hardest lessons for children under five years to learn. All that the child 'knows is that the others "have got it", and he hasn't. A few minutes is an eternity when one is eagerly waiting'.[2]

Few ethnographic analyses are as engrossing as those of this author in her disentangling of the psychological mechanisms by which the notion of arbitration or intervention comes to be imposed on the infant mind. Susan Isaacs notes, with regard to a quarrel between two children about the exclusive use of a tricycle, 'that neither child was willing to accept arbitration until she had proved conclusively her inability to gain her will . . . by her own efforts'.[3] And she adds: 'Here the two children *could* teach each other that lesson, because they were so equally matched in power and persistence.'[4] This is the interpretation:

'If my enjoyment has to suffer limitations for someone else's pleasure, then I must have at the least as much as he. If *I* cannot be supreme, we must all be equal. *My* wish for exclusive possession is tamed by my fear of *his* encroachments and the hope that if I admit to equal rights he will take no more.'[5]

[1] Isaacs, 1933, p. 221.   [2] ibid. p. 223.   [3] loc. cit.
[4] loc. cit.   [5] loc. cit.

In other words: 'Equality is the least common multiple to these conflicting wishes and fears.'[1]

If this psychological development is possible, it is because, as Susan Isaacs has very clearly perceived, the desire to possess is not an instinct, and is never based (or very rarely) on an objective relationship between the subject and the object. What gives the object its value is the 'relation to the other *person*'.[2] Only food has any intrinsic value for someone who is starving. But few objects afford a constant interest at all times and in all circumstances. 'What is so desperately desired may be wanted only because someone else has it.'[3] An important object assumes 'great value . . . if another person begins to take an interest in it'.[4]

The desire to possess 'is essentially a *social* response'.[5] And this response should be 'understood in terms of power–or, rather, of *powerlessness*. I want to own it because if I do not it may not be there when I need it. . . . If another has it, he may keep it for ever.'[6] Hence, there is no contradiction between property and community, between monopoly and sharing, between the *arbitrary* and *arbitration*. All these terms designate the various modalities of one tendency, or of one primitive need, the need for security.

It can thus be said that the capacity for sharing or 'taking turns' is a function of the growing feeling of reciprocity, itself the result of a living experience of the collective fact, and of the deeper mechanism of identification with another.[7]

'One of the commonest and naïvest grounds for feeling friendly to other children is gratitude for gifts received.' But children 'do not so much love *for* the gift, as feel that the gift *is* love. They love for the giving, even more than for the gift. Both giving and gift are to them love itself.'[8]

Hence, 'the making and receiving of gifts remains the clearest, most unequivocal *sign* of love. . . . In a thousand ways, every patient shows that the deepest layer of meaning of "being loved" is still receiving a gift; and the primal meaning of being hated is being deprived, being robbed, since to the infant this means being destroyed.'[9] Beyond the intrinsic value of the thing given, there is the gift itself as a sign of love, and beyond that, the gift as a sign of the fact of being worthy of love:

'He who is denied feels that he has been denied *because* he is bad, because he is or has been hostile to the giver. This it is which brings poignancy to the child's gratitude for gifts, and bitterness to his sense of loss when he is left out of the giving. The gift is not only a sign that the giver loves and does not hate; it is also a sign that the recipient is believed to be loving, not hating and hateful.'[10]

This explains the child's desire to make enormous and magnificent gifts, 'a polar bear . . . a real one', 'a *big large* engine'. It is essentially a wish to be

---

[1] Isaacs, 1933, pp. 223–4.   [2] loc. cit.   [3] loc. cit.   [4] loc. cit.   [5] ibid. p. 225.
[6] loc. cit.   [7] ibid. p. 276.   [8] ibid. p. 272.   [9] ibid. pp. 272–3.   [10] ibid. p. 273.

potent in giving: 'If one has "big large engines" to give away, one is indeed both safe and good. One is no longer the helpless puling infant, dependent upon the gifts of others, and driven by helpless anxieties to rage and jealousy. . . . It is more blessed to give than to receive, because to be able to give is *not to need*.'[1]

These feelings apply to services, too: 'How warmly the children appreciated services done them . . . Tommy . . . calls out to the children who are jointly carrying a large plant pot "Don't go too quickly, so that I can help".' Such is the intensity of the 'great pleasure from being able (i.e., powerful enough) to be unselfish'.[2]

But this apparent generosity is merely the transposition of an initial situation which should not be overlooked. One loves, one hates; or more exactly, one loves because one hates: 'All children . . . feel other children to be actual or potential rivals.'[3] Children waver continually between desperate love and fierce hatred: 'There is no balanced feeling, no stable attitude.'[4] The steady friendship relationship begins only with the establishment of a steady hatred for someone else, and this may be spoken of as 'the reciprocal relation between loving one's friends and hating one's enemies'.[5] But hostility is still the primitive and fundamental attitude. 'It is hostility which provides the drama in the lives of little children, as in that of adults.'[6]

There is no need for us either to compare this infantile attitude towards gifts with the attitude of the Eskimo shamans that 'presents give strength',[7] or to recall the Hindu marriage hymn, 'It is love which has given her, it is to love that she has been given, etc.', to which we shall return later,[8] to show that we are not completely digressing here. Ethnographic inquiry could provide an almost unlimited commentary on all the preceding observations: an appeal to the rule to escape the intolerable suspense of the arbitrary; the desperate need for security which entails that one should never promise too much to another, and that one be ready to give everything to gain the assurance of not losing everything, and of receiving in one's turn; the personalization of the gift; the correlative opposition between the notions of antagonism and reciprocity; the division of beings into friends, to whom nothing is refused, and enemies: 'I shall take the first opportunity of killing him for fear he will kill me.'[9] All these attitudes reveal such a close analogy – except when pushed to its ultimate conclusions – between infant society and so-called primitive society that we cannot exempt ourselves from seeking reasons for them without running the risk of the most tragic mistakes.

II

The problem of the relationship between primitive and infant thought is

[1] ibid. p. 274. [2] loc. cit. [3] ibid. p. 231. [4] ibid. p. 251. [5] ibid. p. 252.
[6] ibid. p. 266. [7] Birket-Smith, 1936, p. 172. [8] cf. ch. XXIX.
[9] Radcliffe-Brown, 1913, p. 151. Compare with the observations of Searl (1932, vol. II, pp. 276–95), who describes among children the same pressing dichotomy being applied to beings and things.

not new, and has been posed in almost hard-and-fast terms by authors as divergent in other respects as the psychoanalysts and certain psychologists such as Blondel and Piaget. It is indeed tempting to see primitive society as approximating more or less metaphorically to man's infant state. The principal stages of this state, for both man in general and man the individual, would then also reappear in the intellectual development of the child. Freud was repeatedly attracted to this schema,[1] and some of his students accepted it categorically: 'Freud has shown that the sexual theories of children are a phylogenetic heritage.'[2] Roheim's handling of this interpretation is well-known. Blondel's work compares primitive, infant, and morbid consciousness, and constantly treats them as interchangeable realities.[3]

In this regard, Piaget's attitude is more subtle, but often lacks clarity. He unearths magic, animism and myths in infant thought, and he remarks that as regards sacrifice, analogies between the thought of the child and the primitive can be expected at every step.[4] Nevertheless, he believes that the child's idea of 'participation' differs from that of the primitive.[5] However, he admits to 'a certain parallelism between ontogeny and phylogeny', but 'we have never dreamt of seeing child thought as an hereditary product of the primitive mentality', for 'ontogeny explains phylogeny, as much as the inverse'. Nevertheless, Piaget maintains that 'child thought has a different structure from the adult's',[6] and at times the attraction of phylogeny seems to carry him away:

> 'Our belief that the day will come when child thought will be placed on the same level in relation to adult, normal, and civilized thought, as "primitive mentality", defined by Lévy-Bruhl, as autistic and symbolical thought as described by Freud and his disciples, and as "morbid consciousness" in the event of this last concept, which we owe to Blondel, being eventually identified with the former.'[7]

It is true he immediately adds: 'But we must beware of the danger of drawing parallels in which functional divergences are forgotten.'[8] This is wise and prudent advice that one would like to see followed more systematically.

Indeed, any foolhardy attempt at assimilation would run up against the very simple fact that not only are there children, primitives and lunatics, but also primitive children and primitive lunatics, and both primitive and civilized psychopathic children. This objection is valid, firstly against recent studies devoted to 'primitive' children, so-called not because they belong to different societies from ours, but because they reveal an inability to carry out certain logical processes. Moreover, these studies reveal a difference and not a

[1] cf. for example, *Totem and Taboo*, chs. II and IV.

[2] Klein, 1932, pp. 188, 196. Similarly, 'schizophrenic logic is identical with primitive, magical thinking, that is, with a form of thinking that also is found in the unconscious of neurotics, in small children, in normal persons under conditions of fatigue, as "antecedents" of thought, and in primitive man'. Fenichel, 1945, p. 421; cf. also p. 46 et seq.

[3] Blondel, 1914.   [4] Piaget, 1929, pp. 88 and 138–40.   [5] ibid. p. 132.

[6] ibid. 1928*a*, pp. 38–40.   [7] ibid. 1928*b*, p. 256.   [8] loc. cit.

resemblance between the anomalies of infant thought and normal primitive thought: 'Contrary to the magical thinking of a primitive man when the connexion between ideas is mistaken for the connexion between things, in this case the child takes the connexion between things for the connexion between ideas.'[1]

It is unnecessary to emphasize that primitive societies are composed, as ours is, of children and adults, and that the problem facing them of relationships between the two age groups is no different from ours. Primitive children differ from primitive adults, just as these differences exist among civilized peoples, and contemporary ethnology and psychology are devoting an increasing number of studies to them.[2] Some particularly striking examples of this can be found in a fine native autobiography which allows the laborious adaptation of a Hopi child to the demands of his particular culture to be followed step by step.[3]

The extent to which normal child thought differs irreducibly from normal adult thought in any given society remains moreover open to controversy. It has been noted that a child, of whatever age, may be incapable of perceiving the relative nature of a certain idea, while being perfectly able to grasp the same characteristic in some other idea. Young children often demonstrate indirectly that they have acquired the idea of relationship as such well before the eleven or twelve age-limit indicated by Piaget.[4] The relation of opposition seems to be acquired spontaneously from the eighth or ninth year, and one out of every two children can formulate it when he is five.[5] Inversely, Piaget's experiments were repeated on nineteen-year-old subjects, and the results obtained were identical with those provided by subjects six or seven years of age.[6] Even Bühler, who said he was prepared to use infantile language to reconstruct the history of human language, restricts the philosophical import of such an undertaking to its just proportions when he says:

'[The influence of ancient logic] has been exaggerated and given an unjustifiable place in the development of the individual and mankind in general. I am of the opinion that the ethnology of today, applied to some psychological data of the child and some quite sound general considerations . . . would be in a position to demonstrate that the theory commencing with this sentence: "In the beginning flourished ancient logic pure and whole", commits the fault of *hysteron proteron*.'[7]

The conclusions reached by Wallon[8] are almost identical to those of Guillaume:

[1] Vygotski, 1929, p. 425.
[2] Dennis, 1940a, pp. 202–18; 1940b, pp. 305–17; 1941; Griaule, 1938; Kluckhohn, 1939; 1945; Leighton and Kluckhohn, 1948.
[3] Simmons, 1942.
[4] Deshaies, 1937, pp. 113, 131.
[5] Kreezer and Dallenbach, 1929, pp. 432–41.
[6] Abel, 1932, pp. 123–32.
[7] Bühler, 1933, pp. 118–19.
[8] Wallon, 1934.

'There is no need to believe in some mysterious internal necessity whereby the development of the individual must pass through all the tortuous paths of history . . . Ontogenic "repetition" is a spurious history only: it is rather a selection of models offered by the language in its actual state.'[1]

Doubtless Piaget has always sought to protect himself from possible reproaches of this type, but his general scheme of interpretation is not proof against criticism. A recent quotation, which I believe should not be abridged, clearly summarizes its uncertainty. Affirming the existence of convergences 'more numerous than it would seem' between 'the clearly conceptual thought of the child and the thought of primitive or ancient societies', Piaget writes:

'We can, however, refer to the striking resemblances between the be-ginnings of rational thought in the child of from seven to ten and in the Greeks. We find, for example, explanation by identification of substances (stars which are produced by air or clouds, air and earth coming from water, etc.), by atomism resulting from this identification and the use of the ideas of condensation and rarefaction, and even the exact explanation of certain movements by reaction of the air ($\dot{\alpha}\nu\tau\iota\pi\epsilon\rho\dot{\iota}\sigma\tau\alpha\sigma\iota\varsigma$) used by Aristotle. Are we then to conclude that the archetypes which inspired the beginnings of Greek physics are inherited by the child? In our opinion it is infinitely simpler merely to assume that the same genetic mechanisms which account for the development of the thought of the child today were in action also in the minds of those who, like the pre-Socratics, were just emerging from mythological and pre-logical thought. As for the schema of "reaction of the air", it seems to have been borrowed by Aristotle from current representations, which may have been as widespread in a civilization prior to mechanization as they are among the children of today.

To sum up, where there is convergence between the thought of the child and historical representations, it is much easier to explain the latter by the general laws of infantile mentality than by reference to a mysterious heredity. However far back we go in history or pre-history, the child has always preceded the adult, and it can be assumed that the more primitive a society, the more lasting the influence of the child's thought on the individual's development, since such a society is not yet capable of trans-mitting or forming a scientific culture.'[2]

This whole passage is a criticism of Jung's hypothesis of the collective unconscious, but its interest for us is something else entirely. The author asserts that primitive societies are nearer to the infantile mentality than is our own. The facts we quoted at the beginning of the chapter seem to confirm this viewpoint. However, we believe that they must be given a different interpretation.

[1] Guillaume, 1927, p. 229.   [2] Piaget, 1951, pp. 197–8.

III

Far from the logical thought of the child being irreducible to the thought of the adult, Isaacs establishes that the 'cognitive behaviour of little children even in these early years, is after all very much like our own'.[1] The notion of maturation which Piaget so constantly appeals to is 'strictly confined to those aspects of growth which cannot be shown to be a function of experience'.[2] Basov reaches the same conclusion:

'In other terms, lower structures from the very beginning serve for the formation of higher ones. . . . Yet [this] . . . does not preclude the possibility of such lower structures' being formed as such and remaining in this mould without any alteration. If environment did not place the child under conditions which require higher structures, perhaps the lower structures might be the only ones it would be able to produce.'[3]

It is interesting to see psychologists make independent but similar criticisms of the 'primitive mentality' thesis, and fundamentally Piaget's formulation is no more than a formal equivalent of this thesis. Undoubtedly, there are some differences between primitive and civilized thought, but these are due solely to the fact that thought is always 'situational'. The differences disappear as soon as the stimuli (social, economic, technical, ideological, etc.) change.[4]

Isaacs criticizes Piaget for using the concept of maturation – as an irreducible 'structure' of child thought – without sufficient precautions, and thus coming 'to attribute to maturation certain phenomena which can be shown to be to a real extent a function of experience'.[5] Symptoms of phases of development associated by Piaget with more advanced age groups are actually found in very young children under suitable conditions. In particular Piaget fails to answer the question, vital to the sociologist, of the origin of social development. He distinguishes broadly between four main phases in the development of the child, firstly, the period of autism, secondly that of egocentrism, and thirdly, social life proper which begins about the age of seven, during which the child learns to adapt himself to others and acquires knowledge of his own mental processes. The key to this development is held to be the appearance of 'social instincts' at seven to eight years. But as Isaacs notes, this appearance is a real *mystery*, and Piaget offers no psychological interpretation at all for their genesis.[6] Freud has shown himself more clear-sighted in this regard, for these 'social instincts' undoubtedly have an individual history and a strictly psychological genesis, the roots of which plunge, not only into experience of the social world, but also into the pressure exercised by the physical world, which arouses an ardent and very positive interest in children who are less than five years old.[7]

[1] Isaacs, 1930, p. 57. [2] ibid. p. 57. [3] Basov, 1929, p. 288. [4] Luria, 1934.
[5] Isaacs, 1930, p. 58. [6] ibid. pp. 77-8. [7] ibid. pp. 79-80.

If the mind of the child is egocentric and precausal, it is so 'in large part because of its ignorance and lack of organized experience . . . The child has not yet the organized body of knowledge to be able to resist being pushed back into the realm of fantasy and egocentricity, below relational thought.'[1] Two conclusions can be drawn from these remarks, firstly, that the child's thinking is substantially no different from the adult's; and, secondly, that all the elements of social life are present from the beginning of infant life: 'The threads of social development can be traced backwards and forwards, and whilst the total picture at the age of, say, six or seven years is in many respects very different from that presented at, say, two years, it is nowhere essentially new.'[2]

Consequently, it is not because children differ from adults both in their individual psychologies and in their social lives that they are of exceptional interest to the psychologist and sociologists, but because, and to the degree that, they resemble them. The child is not an adult, not in our society nor in any other. In all societies the level of child thought is equally remote from the adult level of thinking, such that the distinction between the two might be said to cut along the same line in all cultures and all forms of organization. No coincidence can ever be established between the two levels, even if examples are chosen as distant in time and place as one could wish. The most primitive culture is still an adult culture, and as such is incompatible with infantile manifestations in even the most highly developed civilization. Likewise, psychopathological phenomena in the adult remain an adult fact with nothing in common with the normal thinking of the child. In our opinion, the examples of 'regression' to which psychoanalysis has given so much attention must be considered in a new light.

These examples – those which we ourselves have quoted at the beginning of this chapter, and those upon which Jung has based his theory of the collective unconscious – are impossible to interpret and can lead only to incredible or contradictory hypotheses if recognition is not given to the fact that adult and infantile thought differ in extension rather than in structure. Let us allow, once and for all, that a child is not an adult. But let us remain loyal to this assertion and not proceed to contradict it, as so many psychologists and psychiatrists seem to have done, by insinuating that the thinking of a civilized child resembles the thought of a primitive adult, or that the thinking of a normal child resembles that of an adult lunatic. Every field-worker who has had concrete experience of primitive children will undoubtedly agree that the opposite is more likely to be true and that in many regards the primitive child appears far more mature and positive than a child in our own society, and is to be compared more with a civilized adult. But this is not the question.

Once the distinction between the child and adult has been propounded – and, as we have seen, it must not be overestimated – what is the basic

[1] Isaacs, 1930, p. 94.   [2] ibid. 1933, p. 388.

relationship to be established between their respective mental manifestations? Adult thinking is built around a certain number of structures which it specifies, organizes, and develops from the single fact of this specialization, and which are only a fraction of the initial summary and undifferentiated structures in the child's thought. In other words, the mental schemata of the adult diverge in accordance with the culture and period to which he belongs. However, they are all derived from a universal resource which is infinitely more rich than that of each particular culture. Every newborn child provides in embryonic form the sum total of possibilities, but each culture and period of history will retain and develop only a chosen few of them. Every newborn child comes equipped, in the form of adumbrated mental structures, with all the means ever available to mankind to define its relations to the world in general and its relations to others. But these structures are exclusive. Each of them can integrate only certain elements out of all those that are offered. Consequently, each type of social organization represents a choice, which the group imposes and perpetuates. In comparison with adult thought, which has chosen and rejected as the group has required, child thought is a sort of universal substratum the crystallizations of which have not yet occurred, and in which communication is still possible between incompletely solidified forms.

Can this hypothesis be proved? We shall merely indicate the direction in which we believe it could be verified. The first stage would have a still negative validity, viz., that the thinking of the child appears from the earliest years with characteristics which are completely and integrally human, and this serves to separate them entirely from animal activity. The difficulties are well known which Brainard encountered when he wanted to repeat on his little daughter the experiments that Köhler conducted with monkeys, for example, to put a candy outside a window and see whether the child would discover a way of reaching it. But the experiments are impracticable, because the child reacts socially. Instead of trying, the child protests: 'Hi! Daddy, get it!' The father's attitude is thought perverse, and the theoretical problem can only be resolved later. As Brainard puts it: 'The chief difference between these experiments and those of Köhler lies in the fact that the child has already a high social development, particularly in the use of language and in getting others to do things for her.'[1] In fact, all the *experiments* are turned into *discussions* such as 'I can't', 'Yes you can', 'It's too hard', etc.; and when the child succeeds, she says to her father: 'I'm fooling on you'.[2]

If we have recalled these facts it is because learning a language presents the same problems as the infant's first steps into social life, and because these problems have received the same solution. The variety of sounds that the speech organs can articulate is almost unlimited. However, each language retains only a very small number of all the possible sounds. During the prattling period, before the introduction to articulated language, the

[1] Brainard, 1930, p. 268.   [2] ibid. pp. 271–2, 276.

child produces the total range of sound realizable in human language while his own particular language will retain only some of them. In the first few months of its life every child has been able to emit sounds which later he will find very difficult to reproduce, and which he will fail to imitate satisfactorily when he learns languages very different from his own.[1] Every language makes a selection and from one viewpoint this selection is regressive. Once this selection is made, the unlimited possibilities available on the phonetic plane are irremediably lost. On the other hand, prattling is meaningless, while language allows people to communicate with one another, and so utterance is inversely proportional to significance.

Likewise, the multifarious structures outlined in the thought and attitudes of the child in the realm of inter-individual relations still have social value, since they constitute the raw material for the formation of heterogeneous systems. However, each of these systems can only retain a small number of them to have any functional value. It is through the child's incorporation into his particular culture that this selection takes place.

If this interpretation is correct, it must be allowed that infantile thought represents a sort of common denominator for all thoughts and all cultures. This is what Piaget has frequently expressed in speaking of the 'syncretism' of child thought, which, however, seems dangerous to us since it admits of two different interpretations. If by syncretism is meant a state of confusion and undifferentiation in which the child's distinction between himself and another, between people and objects, and between the objects themselves, is poor, there is a risk of being content with a highly superficial view of things and overlooking the main point. This seeming 'primitive undifferentiation' is not so much an absence of differentiation as a different system of differentiation from ours, and furthermore the result of several systems being in co-existence, and the constant transition from one to another. But there are systems. The further we penetrate towards the deeper levels of mental life, the more we are presented with structures diminishing in number but increasing in strictness and simplicity. For this reason we should speak more readily of the 'polymorphism' of child thought, using this term as does the psychoanalyst when he describes a child as a 'polymorphous pervert'. But what is really meant by this? It means that the child presents in a rudimentary form, and co-existently, all the types of eroticism among which the adult will seek his specialization on the normal or pathological plane. Considering the relationship between the social attitudes of the child and the different types of organization in human societies the anthropologist should be similarly inclined to say that the child is a 'polymorphous socialite'.

When we compare primitive and child thought, and see so many resemblances between them, we are victims of a subjective illusion, which doubtless recurs whenever adults of one culture compare their children with adults of another culture. Indeed, being less specialized than the adult's thinking,

---

[1] Jakobson, 1941.

the thought of the child always provides the adult not only with a picture of his own synthesis, but also of all the syntheses possible elsewhere and under different circumstances. It is not surprising that in this 'panmorphism' the differences strike us more than the similarities, so that a society's own children always provide the most convenient point of comparison with foreign customs and attitudes. In the normal course of things, customs varying greatly from our own always seem puerile. The reason for this prejudice has been shown, but it must be added that it deserves to be called such only in so far as we refuse to acknowledge that there are just as valid reasons why our own customs must appear in exactly the same light to outside observers.

The analogies between primitive and child thought are not based on any so-called archaism of primitive thought, but merely on a difference of extension which makes child thought a sort of meeting place, or point of dispersion, for all possible cultural syntheses. The basic structures of primitive societies are better understood when compared with the social attitudes of our own children. But primitives do not abstain from the use of the same procedure, and from comparing us with their own children. Indeed, infantile attitudes provide them also with the best introduction to strange institutions, the roots of which are intermingled, at this level alone, with their own. Consider, for example, the following observation where the native applies to the white man the same method of infantile assimilation as we so often use as regards him:

'In the Navaho family, the art of weaving or jewellery-making is learnt from example. To the young native, to look is to learn . . . Whence the complete absence of a way of life so common among us, even among adults. . . . I mean the habit of asking questions such as "And that, why do that?" or "After that, what are you going to do?" It is this habit more than any other which has given natives their strange opinion of white men, for the Indian is convinced that the white man is fool.'[1]

For the primitive, the attitudes of the civilized man correspond to what we should call infantile attitudes, for exactly the same reason that we find hints or outlines, in our children, of attitudes whose full and developed picture is provided in primitive society. Consequently, the importance of child psychology studies for the anthropologist can be seen. In their freshest form they give him access to that common capital of mental structures and of institutional schemata which are the initial resources at man's disposal in the launching of social enterprises. For proof that he must take his stand at this very elementary level to penetrate the nature of institutions which appear strange on the surface, but the underlying principles of which at least are in fact very simple and universal, we need only the remarkable observation, communicated to me at the end of one of my courses of lectures by

[1] Reichard, n.d., p. 674.

a woman listener who was hearing of dual organization for the first time:

'Johnny A., aged four, of Alexandria (Egypt), lives in two imaginary countries, *Tana-Gaz* and *Tana-Pé*, where everything is magnificent. *Tana-Gaz* is above and is better than *Tana-Pé*. His mother lives in *Tana-Gaz*, but his father lives in *Tana-Pé*. When the sea is calm, and Johnny can go swimming, it is in *Tana-Gaz*. When it is rough, and bathing is prohibited, it is in *Tana-Pé*. People also move from one country to the other. Originally both countries were good. Subsequently, *Tana-Gaz* has remained good, while *Tana-Pé* has become inferior to *Tana-Gaz*, sometimes neutral, sometimes openly evil.

'When Johnny was seven years old, he was asked whether he remembered *Tana-Gaz* and *Tana-Pé*. He then became embarrassed and said he had forgotten.'

The interesting nature of this observation does not lie merely in the reconstruction of a dual system by a four-year-old child, with the division of things and beings into two categories, the inequality of moieties, the stylistic creation of place-names, so evocative of a Melanesian onomastic system, and even the curious suggestion of exogamy. If Johnny had been a little Australian aborigine he could have elaborated the same fantasy, but he would not have been ashamed of it later. It would have progressively found basis in the official dualism of his society. The logical requirements and social attitudes expressed in dual organization would have been satisfied normally in an institutional activity conforming approximately to the infantile model. But Johnny grows up in a group which does not use bipolar structures to express antagonisms and reciprocities, except superficially and ephemerally. In it, the model proposed by the infantile mind cannot acquire any instrumental value. Furthermore, in many ways it is contradictory to the selected model, and because of this it must be abandoned and repressed.

In these circumstances, it is easy to understand why ethnologists, psychologists and psychiatrists have each been tempted to set up parallelisms between primitive, infantile and pathological thought. In so far as psycho-neurosis can be defined as the highest form of mental synthesis on a purely individual level,[1] the sick person's thought resembles the thought of the child. These forms of thought no longer conform, or do not yet conform, to the selective structure of the particular group to which they belong. Consequently, the child and the sick person are both relatively free to elaborate their own particular synthesis. This synthesis is probably doomed to remain unstable and precarious, because its realization is on an individual plane and is not within the framework of any social environment. All the same, it is a synthesis, or if one prefers, a turning kaleidoscope of sketchy or deformed syntheses, never an absence of synthesis (except perhaps in the special case

[1] Delay, 1942, p. 123. The reservation formulated below for hebephrenia lost much of its value after the publication of the work of Séchehaye (1960).

of hebephrenia). Accordingly, the apparent 'regression' is not a return to an archaic 'stage' in the intellectual development of the individual or species. It is the reconstitution of a situation analogous to that presiding over the beginnings of individual thought. Pathological and primitive thought contrast with child thought in being adult, but, in their turn, pathological and child thought have something in common which distinguishes them from primitive thought. Primitive thought is as completely and systematically socialized as our own, while the others have a relative and individual independence which, of course, has a different explanation in each case.

CHAPTER VIII

Alliance and Descent

I

Let us return to our investigation of the concomitants of dual organization when it appears in its most explicit form. Whether descent is matrilineal or patrilineal, the children of the father's brother and of the mother's sister are found in the same moiety as Ego, while those of the father's sister and of the mother's brother always belong to the other moiety. Consequently, in an exogamous system, the latter are the first collaterals with whom marriage is possible. This remarkable feature is expressed in several ways. Firstly, the cousins descended from the father's brother or from the mother's sister cannot marry, for the same reason as brothers and sisters (in that they belong to the same moiety), and are designated by the same term as for brothers and sisters. Secondly, the cousins descended from the mother's brother or the father's sister belong to the opposite moiety and are called by a special term, or by the term for 'husband' or 'wife', since the spouse must be chosen from their division. Finally, the father's brother and the mother's sister, whose children are called 'brothers' and 'sisters', are themselves called 'father' and 'mother', while the mother's brother and the father's sister, whose children are potential spouses, are called by special terms, or by a term for 'father-in-law' or 'mother-in-law'. This terminology, of which we have given only the broad outlines, satisfies all the requirements of a dual organization with exogamous moieties. In fact, it might be an expression, in terms of kinship, of the social organization based on moieties. However, this same relationship may be expressed differently. Indeed, the dichotomous terminology we have just described coincides also with another very prevalent institution in primitive society, viz., preferential marriage between cross-cousins. It has just been seen how this terminology classes together as 'parents' the father's brother and the mother's sister (parallel uncle and aunt), and distinguishes them from the father's sister and the mother's brother (cross-uncle and aunt) who are designated by special terms. Members of the same generation are also divided into two groups: on the one hand, cousins (whatever their degree) who are kinsmen descended from two collaterals of the same sex, and who call each other 'brothers' and 'sisters' (parallel cousins), and, on the other hand, cousins descended from collaterals of different sex (whatever their degree), who are called by special terms and between whom marriage is possible (cross-cousins). As the dual organization, the kinship system we have just discussed, and the rules of marriage between cross-cousins are in perfect harmony, it might just as easily be said, reversing the previous proposition, that dual organization is the expression, on an institutional plane, of a system of kinship which itself derives from certain rules of alliance. Sociologists have generally favoured the first interpretation. These include Tylor, Rivers and Perry, who writes concerning cross-cousin marriage: 'This form of marriage probably is derived from the dual organization of society as defined in its sociological aspect.'[1] Why is this? Perry continues: 'It seems to be found only in cases where the dual organization exists or has existed in the past.'[2] To be true, he immediately makes this prudent reservation: 'But on this point there cannot be entire certainty.'[3] Indeed, for we do not believe that the relationship between the two institutions can reasonably be interpreted simply as a derivation. If most writers have thought differently it seems to have been for two reasons.

Firstly, in the light of our own ideas on prohibited degrees, the system of marriage between cross-cousins appears profoundly irrational. Why set up a barrier between cousins descended from collaterals of the same sex, and cousins from collaterals of different sex, when in respect to proximity both cases are the same? Nevertheless, to pass from one to the other makes all the difference between clearly marked incest (parallel cousins being likened to brothers and sisters) and unions which are not only possible but even those which are enjoined upon everybody (since cross-cousins are designated by the term for potential spouses). The distinction is incompatible with our biological criterion for incest. There has been no intrinsic reason isolated for the peculiar cross-cousin relationship, and from this it has been concluded that the whole institution must have been the indirect consequence of a different order of phenomena.

In the second place, the striking thing was that as often as not the native mythology described the institution of moieties as a deliberate reform (although this would certainly not give sufficient reason for believing that this was actually the case) and moreover that, in certain cases at least, this seemed to be affirmed by more authoritative evidence (e.g., Howitt for Australia, and ancient documents for the Huron of North America[4]). From this it has been inferred that dual organization was conceived of as a partially if not completely effective means of preventing incest. Indeed, the moiety system always prevents incest between brothers and sisters, and also between father and daughter in a patrilineal system, and mother and son in a matrilineal system. The irrationality of the division of cousins into two groups is then regarded as a fault in the system.

These very imperfections gave the defenders of this theory a feeling of

[1] Perry, 1923, p. 281.　　[2] loc. cit.　[3] loc. cit.　　[4] Barbeau, 1917, pp. 392–405.

security because it would have been difficult for them to imagine barbaric peoples finding a perfect solution to their problems. If, on the contrary, the distinction between cousins had been taken as the starting-point in tracing the origins of dual organization, firstly, it would have been impossible, or at least very difficult, to deduce the prohibitions in the reverse order. Secondly, and more particularly, in its systematic nature and the coherency with which its full consequences have developed in almost all groups, cross-cousin marriage reveals a logical power and a theoretical capacity which we are particularly unwilling to concede to the primitive in the present instance because we seem incapable of discerning the reason for the system. The diffusionist school of Elliot Smith and Perry affirms the priority of dual organization over cross-cousin marriage for reasons which are quite different, but there is no point in our discussing them here, for we are not so much concerned with dual organization in its codified form as with certain basic mechanisms which we believe to be universally subjacent.

The reader is no doubt aware that the hypothesis of the secondary character of cross-cousin marriage, which we have endeavoured to expound, involves certain postulates which played a considerable rôle in the human sciences during the latter half of the nineteenth and early twentieth centuries. These postulates may be summarized as follows. A human institution has only two possible origins, either historical and irrational, or as in the case of the legislator, by design; in other words, either incidental or intentional. Consequently, if no rational motive can be found for cross-cousin marriage it is because it is the result of a series of historical accidents which in themselves are insignificant. Psychology once argued along these lines. It argued that mathematical concepts were either innate properties, testifying to the superiority and irreducible nature of man's mind, or that they must have derived from experience by an automatic process of association. This antinomy was resolved once it was realized that even the lowly fowl can apprehend relationships. Once this was acknowledged, both associationism and idealism found themselves non-suited.[1] There was no longer any need for highly complex historical reconstructions to account for really primitive concepts. But at the same time it was realized that such concepts were in no way the crowning point of the structure, but merely its basis and the humble raw material of its foundations. It had been believed that the only choice was between accepting the origin of the concept as transcendent or reconstructing it from bits and pieces, which was impossible. This antithesis vanished before the experimental discovery of the immanence of relation.

The same change in attitudes is beginning to appear in the study of human institutions, which are also structures whose whole – in other words the regulating principle – can be given before the parts, that is, that complex union which makes up the institution, its terminology, consequences and

[1] Köhler, 1930, p. 7.

implications, the customs through which it is expressed and the beliefs to which it gives rise. This regulating principle can have a rational value without being rationally conceived. It can be expressed in arbitrary formulas without being itself devoid of meaning. It is in the light of such considerations that the relationships between dual organizations and cross-cousin marriage should be defined. We do not simply propose to inverse the hypothesis of the priority of dual organizations over this form of marriage. We believe that they both have their origin in the apprehension, by primitive thought, of those completely basic structures on which the very existence of culture rests. In this sense, it can be said, but can only be said, that cross-cousin marriage and dual organization correspond to different stages in the growing awareness of these structures, and that the practice of marriage between cross-cousins, which appears more as an attempt than as a codified system, constitutes, from this psychological viewpoint only, a process which does not require so complete and definitive an awareness as the institution of dual organizations. However, we have absolutely no intention of posing problems of anteriority which lose much of their importance when the common reality underlying both institutions is pursued rather than the institutions themselves.

II

In common with the dual system, cross-cousin marriage, without being universal, nevertheless does extend to almost every part of the world. But cross-cousin marriage is far more frequent than exogamous moieties. Indeed, as we have shown, a system of exogamous moieties necessarily authorizes cross-cousin marriage, which exists, moreover, in many groups which are not divided into moieties. Rivers has even shown that in Melanesia it is precisely the tribes without dual organization that practise this form of marriage. We shall return to this later. The wider distribution of cross-cousin marriage can be explained in two ways. Cross-cousin marriage is either the more basic system with dual organization appearing in certain parts only of its distribution area as a secondary development, or else it was cross-cousin marriage which was the derivative phenomenon, with the explanation for the more restricted distribution of dual organization to be found in its archaic nature. Both interpretations are obviously riddled with evolutionism, and their essential preoccupation is with which of the two phenomena preceded the other. We, on the contrary, believe that it is not the hypothetical succession of the two institutions which should be considered, but rather their structure. From this point of view, cross-cousin marriage has a less organized structure, for it merely represents a tendency, whereas the organization into exogamous moieties is more coherent and rigid. This assertion needs to be elaborated upon since the objection might be raised that the contrary is true, that dual organization sanctions marriage within a very broad category, including not only 'real' cross-cousins, but also more distant kinsmen. By contrast, the obligation for cross-cousins, defined in the strictest sense, to marry, is sometimes a striking feature of the other marriage system.

Dual organization, therefore, defines a very general class within which it is permissible to choose a spouse, while, in certain cases at least, the system of cross-cousin marriage determines very precisely the individual whom one is obliged to marry. But the difference is not exactly this, for dual organization defines a class with very strictly fixed boundaries, while the cross-cousin system attaches importance to a relationship between individuals, which is capable of being reinterpreted again and again. Even among the Toda and the Vedda, who attach a great importance to kinship, an individual who has no cross-cousins can contract another marriage, it being understood that the possible marriages are arranged in a preferential order, according to how far they conform with the ideal model. That only 30 per cent of the Fijian marriages analysed by Thomson complied with the strict definition of cross-cousins establishes the same thing.[1] It is exactly the same in Australia.[2] Thus, if the system of cross-cousins defines the relationship between the individuals more strictly, the individuals themselves are not so strictly defined. The opposite happens with dual organization, which leaves the relationship very vague, but strictly defines the class, and the individuals included within this class. What is the result of this analysis? Dual organization is a global system, binding the group in its totality. Marriage between cross-cousins, on the contrary, seems a very much more special process; it is a tendency rather than a system. Among the Hottentots, Hoernlé tells us,[3] marriage between cross-cousins does not seem to have been the object of any positive obligation; it was only that marriage between parallel cousins was strictly prohibited. And yet, it is rare to find a kinship system so faultlessly built up about the dichotomy of cousins and the intermarriage of two classes as the Hottentot system. In South America, where we find kinship systems which are equally precise, such as the Nambikwara, the same fact holds true.

Accordingly, it can now be seen what in our opinion is the theoretical relationship between dual organization and the marriage of cross-cousins. Both are systems of reciprocity, and both result in a dichotomous terminology which is broadly similar in both cases. But while dual organization with exogamous moieties defines the actual spouse vaguely, it determines the number and identity of possible spouses most closely. In other words it is the highly specialized formula for a system which has its beginnings, still poorly differentiated, in cross-cousin marriage. Cross-cousin marriage defines a relationship, and establishes a perfect or approximate model of the relationship in each case. Dual organization delimits two classes by applying a uniform rule guaranteeing that individuals born or distributed into these two classes will always stand in this relationship in its widest sense. What is lost in precision is gained in automation and simplicity.

The two institutions are in contrast, one being crystallized, the other

[1] Thomson, 1908, p. 187.   [2] Radcliffe-Brown, 1913, p. 158.   [3] Hoernlé, 1925*a*, pp. 1–24.

flexible. The question of chronology is completely foreign to this distinction. There is no reason why some groups should not have acquired the whole formula right away, while others adopted it as the result of a growing awareness of the structural law of cross-cousin marriage, which alone they had practised previously. There is no reason, either, why a group should not have made the transition from dual organization to the marriage of cross-cousins, which has the same fundamental functional value but acts deeper down in the social structure, and so is more sheltered from historical transformations.

The relationship just suggested between dual organization and cross-cousin marriage gives a satisfactory explanation to Rivers's remark on Melanesian institutions, that cross-cousin marriage appears (or reappears) precisely where dual organization is missing. As their functional value (viz., to establish a system of reciprocity) is identical, it can indeed be understood how the absence of dual organization can be compensated for by the presence of cross-cousin marriage.

III

The foregoing considerations will help us guard against an inflexible interpretation which has grown up in the last ten years, and which threatens to compromise not only the progress of studies in primitive sociology, but in sociology generally. It has become explicit more recently in connexion with the interpretation of cross-cousin marriage and the relationships of this form of marriage to dual organization. Accordingly, let us dwell on a question which is prejudicial only in appearance, for the answer given to it will imply a basic standpoint with regard to all the problems to be examined in this book.

For a long time sociologists have considered that there is a difference in nature between the family, as found in modern society, and the kinship groups of primitive societies, viz., clans, phratries and moieties. The family recognizes descent through both the maternal and paternal lines, while the clan or moiety reckons kinship in one line only, either the father's or the mother's. Descent is then said to be patrilineal or matrilineal. These definitions have been understood in the strictest sense, as indeed the observation of the obscured facts often suggested. A system with matrilineal descent does not recognize any social kinship link between a child and its father, and in his wife's clan, to which his children belong, the father is himself a 'visitor', a 'man from outside', or a 'stranger'. The reverse situation prevails in a system with patrilineal descent.

This regulation seems so schematic and arbitrary that certain writers, who have consciously or unconsciously accepted it as the true picture, have concluded that such unnatural customs could not have arisen spontaneously in different regions and at different times, and that they must rather be connected with some great cultural upheaval which occurred at some precise moment, and at some single point in the world, from which they spread by diffusion. Nevertheless, as early as 1905, Swanton observed that the other line was never completely ignored even in what seemed to be the most unilineal of tribes. On the one hand, the conjugal family is always recognized, sometimes in a limited sort of way, but always effectively, even when it is not expressed in the institutions. On the other hand, the subordinate line regularly plays its own peculiar rôle reflected indirectly by custom.[1]

The flood of monographic studies in the last thirty years has largely confirmed Swanton's remarks. Today we know that societies as matrilineal as the Hopi take account of the father and his line, and that this is so in most cases. Furthermore, there are societies whose unilineal character is more apparent than real, since the transmission of functions and rights operates partly through one line and partly through the other. Some writers, therefore, have been induced to discard the conclusions of traditional sociology and to consider that strictly unilineal societies, supposing them to exist, can only be considered as exceptions, whereas bilinealism, by contrast, through its highly varied modalities, offers an extremely general formula.[2]

The truth seems more complex to us, since the one term, bilinealism, is being used for quite different phenomena. If what is meant is that all human societies recognize that a link, if not juridical then at least psychological and sentimental, does exist between the child and each of its parents, we agree. It may readily be conceded also that the recognition of this double link is expressed at all times and places in spontaneous practices, and even in the non-crystallized forms of social life. Finally, there are certainly some societies for which these flexible structures might provide a sufficient basis for institutional structures which are destined to remain very simple, as among the Andamanese, Fuegians, Bushmen, Semang and Nambikwara. Far more uncommon are those groups which base a complex and systematic juridical apparatus on the recognition of the two lines. In 1935, Radcliffe-Brown had only one case of this, that of Germanic law, which he considered an exception.[3] However, other examples were quick to appear, such as the Abelam of the Sepik River, where if there is no son, the daughter inherits the landed property, and if there is no daughter, the sister's son inherits.[4] In the first edition of this book, we added: 'In any case, the list would not be very long.'[5] Today we have to acknowledge that this assessment was incorrect. Following Murdock, many writers have proved that cognatic systems, those in which both lines are equally recognized, do exist, especially in Polynesia (the field of Firth's early work), and also in Melanesia and Africa. Davenport calls them 'non-unilineal systems'[6] and they are certainly far more common than was suspected around 1940. They probably form at

---

[1] Swanton, 1905a, pp. 663–73; 1906.   [2] Murdock, 1942, pp. 555–61.
[3] Radcliffe-Brown, 1935a, pp. 286–303.
[4] Kaberry, 1941, pp. 233–58, 345–67; 1942, pp. 209–25, 331–63.
[5] First edition, p. 135.   [6] Davenport,1959, pp. 557–72.

least a third of the descent systems now known. Nevertheless, the principles of our interpretation do not seem to need any substantial modification. In 1947, we suggested leaving such systems aside, because, like Radcliffe-Brown we thought that they were exceptional. Although this no longer seems so, our reservations still remain justified. Even though they are common, these systems should not be considered here, because they have nothing to do with elementary structures. As Goodenough has already pointed out,[1] and as opposed to what Murdock seems still to believe,[2] such systems do not belong to the same typology as those which we call 'elementary structures of kinship'. Indeed, they introduce an additional dimension, for they no longer define, perpetuate and transform the method of social cohesion with regard to a stable rule of descent, but to a system of land rights. The difference between societies where these are found and societies where there is only unilineal descent is somewhat the same as between arthropods and vertebrates. In one, the skeleton of the society is internal. It consists in a synchronic and diachronic interlocking of personal statuses in which each particular status is strictly a function of every other status. In the other, the skeleton is external. It consists in an interlocking of territorial statuses, i.e., in a landed society. These real statuses are external to the individuals who can, from this fact, and within the bounds imposed by these constraints, define their own status with a certain margin of freedom. In justification of the preceding comparison, note that it is precisely such extra-skeletal organisms which can undergo several morphological changes in the one lifetime. It follows that cognatic systems differ from unilineal systems in a second way, viz., in them the diachronic and the synchronic are, to a certain extent, dissociated by the freedom of choice that they give each individual. They enable societies possessing them to achieve historical existence in so far as the statistical fluctuations cumulatively effected by the individual choices happen to be oriented in a certain direction.

But the principal thing is that these diffuse or precise forms of bilinealism should be clearly distinguished from one other with which they tend to be confused. In the examples quoted in the previous paragraph, the recognition of the two lines indicates that they are both fitted to play the same rôle, the transmission of the same rights and the same obligations. Name, social status, property and prerogatives can be received from both the father and the mother, or from either one or the other. It is not that each lineage is assigned a special rôle, such that, if certain rights are transmitted exclusively in one line, then other rights will always be transmitted exclusively in the other. This second system has been observed in many regions of the world, notably in West and South Africa, India, Australia, Melanesia and Polynesia. But this formula can immediately be seen to be very different from the preceding one, and it seems essential that they should be distinguished terminologically. We shall call systems in which the two lines of descent can

---

[1] Goodenough, 1955, pp. 71–83.   [2] Murdock, 1960.

be substituted one for the other, and in which these may be merged in a joint exercise of their functions, systems with *undifferentiated descent*. *Bilineal descent* is reserved for very precisely defined systems, examples of which will be found below, their characteristic being the juxtaposition of two unilineal rules of descent, each governing exclusively the transmission of certain rights.

There are certainly no watertight bulkheads between unilineal, bilineal and undifferentiated descent. Any system has the coefficient of diffuse non-differentiation resulting from the universality of the conjugal family. To a certain extent, moreover, a unilineal system always recognizes the existence of the other line. Conversely, it is rare to come across an example of strictly undifferentiated descent. Our society, which has gone far in this direction (inheritance comes equally from the father and the mother, and social status is received, and prestige derived from both lines, etc.), keeps a patrilineal inflection in the mode of transmitting the family name. Be that as it may, the importance of undifferentiated systems for anthropological theory is today unquestionable. They prove that the dividing line between societies which are traditionally called primitive and so-called civilized societies is not the same as between 'elementary structures' and 'complex structures'. We are deeply aware that so-called primitive societies include heterogeneous types, and that the theory of some of these types still remains to be worked out. Let us acknowledge then that a good number of so-called primitive societies, in fact, have complex kinship structures. However, as this book is limited to the theory of elementary structures, we consider we are right in leaving on one side examples of undifferentiated descent.

Furthermore, it is not so much these undifferentiated systems as the bilineal systems that have recently been used in a revival of the classical interpretation of cross-cousin marriage in terms of dualism. But here the dualism has been redoubled. To explain the origin of cross-cousin marriage by the supposition that the group is, or was at one time, divided into exogamous moieties is to run up against a serious difficulty. Dual organization accounts for the dichotomy of cousins into cross-cousins and parallel cousins, and explains why cross-cousins are possible spouses, and why parallel cousins are prohibited. But it does not make it clear why, as is often the case, the cross-cousins are preferred to all other individuals who, like them, belong to the opposite moiety to Ego. A man finds women in the opposite moiety to his own not only with the status of cross 'cousins', but also – among others – of cross 'aunts' and cross 'nieces'. All these women have the same quality of being exogamous. Why then are cross-cousins privileged spouses?

Suppose now that a second unilateral dichotomy of the dual organization is added to the first unilateral dichotomy, but follows the other line; e.g., let there be a system of matrilineal moieties, A and B, and a second division, this time patrilineal, between two groups, X and Y. Each individual will hold a status A or B from his mother, and a status X or Y from his father. Hence, each will be defined by two indices: AX, AY, BY, or BX. If the marriage rule is that the possible spouses shall differ as to both the maternal index and the paternal index, it can easily be established that only cross-cousins satisfy this requirement, while uncles or aunts, and cross-nephews or nieces, differ in one index only. For a detailed proof, the reader may be referred to chapter XI. Here we shall confine ourselves to a few examples.

The dual organization of the Ashanti, perhaps also of the Gã, the Fanti, and even the negroes of Surinam,[1] rests on the crossing of a patrilineal factor, the *ntoro* or 'mind', with a matrilineal factor sometimes called *mogya* or 'blood', or sometimes *abusua*, 'clan'. In fact, the natives say, *abusua bako mogya bako* meaning 'one clan, one blood'. It is the *ntoro* of the man mixed with the *mogya* of the woman which produces the child.[2] The terminology emphasizes the correlation between this system and the marriage of cross-cousins in the equations:

ase	mother's brother's wife	= mother-in-law
oyere	mother's brother's daughter	= wife
akonta	mother's brother's son	= brother-in-law.[3]

The Toda of India are divided into exogamous patrilineal groups called *mod*, and into exogamous matrilineal groups called *poljo:ḷ*. Because of this dichotomy, the two great endogamous classes which form the principal social units of this tribe are themselves subdivided, as follows: the *to:rδas* into five exogamous groups (*poljo:ḷ*), the *töûviḷj* into six. Accordingly, cross-cousin marriage seems to result from the prohibition of marriage between individuals whose kinship relationship is established exclusively in the maternal or in the paternal line.[4] A similar type of organization is found among the Yakö of Nigeria, who are divided into exogamous patrilineal groups, the *yepun*, and into less strictly exogamous matrilineal groups, the *yajima*. Rights and duties are divided between the two groups, without any possible conflict in ascription: 'a man eats in his *kepun* and inherits in his *lejima*', asserts the native maxim.[5] As the prohibited degrees are defined by the exogamy of the *kepun* and the *lejima*, they are practically confined to parallel cousins in the maternal line. But if the exogamy of the *lejima* were as strict as the other, obviously all the parallel cousins would be excluded.[6] Finally, the Herero have a positive predilection for cross-cousin marriage, which might result from the intersection of about twenty patrilineal, patrilocal and exogamous clans called *otuzo* by six to eight non-localized matrilineal clans called *eanda* (pl. *omaanda*).[7]

From these and many other examples it might easily be concluded that, at all times and in all places, cross-cousin marriage is to be explained by a double dichotomy of the social group, consciously expressed in the institutions, or acting as the unconscious spring of customary rules.

[1] Herskovits, 1928. [2] ibid. 1937, pp. 287–96.
[3] Mead, 1937, pp. 300–1. [4] Emeneau, 1937, p. 104.
[5] Forde, 1939*a*, p. 529; 1939*b*, pp. 129–61. [6] loc. cit. [7] Luttig, 1934, pp. 85–6.

IV

We do not wish to contest that this may sometimes be the case. But we do not believe it possible to give an account of a system as general as cross-cousin marriage by extrapolation from precise and limited instances, or by using a dichotomy which is seldom attested to in institutions and the native consciousness. What then is the connexion between the two phenomena?

Let us anticipate our examination of the Australian aborigines to which the final chapters of this first part are devoted. We do not hesitate to interpret the Kariera or Aranda systems in terms of a double and sometimes more complex dichotomy. But the whole point is whether Australia provides a special case by which the final nature of the rules of kinship and marriage, as they exist universally, may be unveiled, or whether we are not faced with some local theory (isolated examples of which are known elsewhere) which has been developed by the native as a formulation of his own problems, and is a sort of rationalization of existing phenomena. Here we are confronted by the fundamental problem of explanation in the social sciences. If it is true, as Boas has heavily emphasized, that all types of social phenomena (language, beliefs, techniques and customs) have this in common, that their elaboration in the mind is at the level of unconscious thought,[1] the same question must always be raised as to their interpretation. Does the way in which man has apprehended them truly reflect how they originated, or must it be seen merely as an analytical procedure which provides a handy account of the phenomenon's appearance and results, yet does not necessarily correspond to what has really happened? Let us clarify our thoughts on this point.

There is another field where individual statuses are interpreted in terms of a simple or complex dichotomy, and where the combined physical characteristics of a given subject are regarded as resulting from the combination of certain elementary characteristics inherited from the parents. This is the field of genetics. For example, if the characteristics carried by the sexual genes are considered, the analogy with the phenomena described above is striking. The female bears two identical sexual genes, and the male, one gene similar to these genes, and another, which is the differential characteristic of masculinity, namely, a double matrilineal index, XX, and a double patrilineal index, XY. Each individual necessarily receives a maternal and a paternal index. As the sons must have the differential masculine characteristic, their paternal index would be Y, and their X would always come from the mother, while the daughters would have the paternal X and one of the two maternal X.[2] All the characteristics carried by the sexual genes will thus be distributed among the descendants in accordance with the dialectic of this double dichotomy.[3]

[1] Boas, 1911, p. 67 et seq.   [2] Jennings, 1935.
[3] In *Critique de la raison dialectique* (p. 744), Sartre has called attention to this formula, in which he sees a confusion between dialectical and analytic reasoning. But we do not

But in genetics there is a strict correspondence between the process of analysis and its object. The analysis is conducted on the premise that chromosomes and genes exist, and the microscopic examination of reproductive cells shows that this is really the case. The Mendelian idea that the hereditary characteristics of individuals result in a perpetually renewed combination of elementary particles, does not merely provide a convenient method for statistical prediction. It provides a picture of reality. Likewise, the 'distinctive features', used by the phonological linguist to explain the characteristics of a phenomenon, have an objective existence from the psychological, physiological and even physical points of view.[1]

By contrast, consider a mathematician attacking a problem by the algebraic method. According to the rule of the *Discourse*, he also would divide the difficulty 'into as many parts as may be required for its adequate solution', and the value of the method would be gauged by the extent to which the result conformed with the facts. But the analysis of the difficulty into 'unknowns' does not imply that each of them has a corresponding objective reality. In other words, this analysis is purely ideological, and its legitimacy is to be weighed in terms of the result, rather than by how faithfully the real process, resulting in the situation studied, is reproduced in the mathematician's mind. It will be seen below that Weil uses sixteen elementary units representing the types of marriage in his determination of the characteristics of an Australian aboriginal system with eight marriage classes.[2] It is certain that he is justified in doing so, since it allows him to isolate some of the system's consequences which had not been seen by fieldworkers. However, one can be sure that in elaborating this system, the aboriginal mind never had recourse to these sixteen categories. Furthermore, we shall show that the eight classes themselves were a secondary development, and that the beginnings of the system can be very satisfactorily explained by an unconscious division into four categories.[3] Whenever a system of this type is encountered, i.e., where the position of the individual in the social structure seems to result from the combination of several elementary characteristics, the question must always be asked whether the sociologist – and on occasion also, the native – has acted like the geneticist, or like the mathematician. In other words, are these objective characteristics of the social structure, or do they merely provide a convenient method for ascertaining certain of its characteristics? There are always three possible answers to this question.

[1] Jakobson, 1938, pp. 34–41; Lévi-Strauss, 1945*a*, pp. 33–53.
[2] ch. XIV.
[3] ch. XII. It can be seen that in contrast to the criticism levelled at us on occasion by writers who obviously have not read what we have written (Berndt, Goody), we exclude in advance all interpretations akin to that of Lawrence.

conceive of dialectical reasoning in the same way as Sartre. As we see it, the dichotomous approach is in no way incompatible with dialectical thought, but clearly the contrary. See on this subject, Lévi-Strauss, 1966, ch. IX.

In certain cases, the elementary units do exist. There are matrilineal clans and patrilineal sections, both denoted by the terminology, by the rules by which rights and obligations are transmitted, and by certain other aspects of custom and institutions. When a detailed and critical examination of the facts leads to a positive conclusion, there is no reason to doubt the rôle of corresponding mechanisms. In most cases, however, nothing of the sort is to be found. It is the sociologist who, in order to account for a complicated law of division into possible and prohibited spouses, invents a hypothetical division of the group into unilateral classes. These classes embody all that is needed to interpret the marriage system as resulting from their interaction. This method of analysis may be suitable as one stage in the demonstration; but this appears dubious when one refers to works of this type leading to schemata which are made suspect by their very complication.[1] More particularly, these works contravene a well-known principle of logic, viz., a class which can be defined in extension can never be postulated. The existence of a class may be established, but it can never be deduced.

But there are more embarrassing predicaments. It may sometimes be the native himself, and not the sociologist, who is guilty of methodological contrivance. Indeed, certain cultures have indulged in a real labour of categorization in their own social institutions. Established in this way, the system cannot claim, on pretext of its native origin, to be a faithful representation of a reality which is just as likely to be revealed, in its unconscious and collective aspect, to the subject's as to the observer's analysis. Australia provides striking examples of this situation. The sociologist to whom it might give doubts should remember that he is not the first to have encountered it. The Logic of the Schoolmen was the work of people who thought, and believed, that they had discovered the laws which their own thinking obeyed. Despite the fact that in certain cases thought develops consistently with the models of classical logic, and that any intellectual processes may be interpreted in keeping with its requirements, it is known today, through closer observation, that in most cases, the laws governing the processes of thought are governed by very different laws. The grammarians of Port Royal believed they had discovered the true laws of speech, but we have since learnt that syntax and morphology rest on a substructure which has few points in common with the frameworks of traditional grammar.

The fact that classes exist elsewhere than in the mind of the sociologist has the same value as the fact that syllogisms exist for others than the logician, but no more than this. The existence of both forms must be acknowledged when attested to by experiment and observation. It does not follow from this that they are always the *raison d'être* for phenomena analogous to those produced when they are thus attested to. We shall propose a demonstration which seems to the point when we tackle the problem of alternate generations.

[1] e.g., the two articles by B. Z. Seligman: 1927, pp. 349–75; 1928, pp. 533–58.

This phenomenon, which corresponds so perfectly with a double patrilineal and matrilineal dichotomy that there has not generally been any doubt that the latter dichotomy was the cause of the former, will be seen under altogether different circumstances which are brought about by very short cycles of reciprocity.[1]

When the thesis that cross-cousin marriage results in a double dichotomy of the group is examined closely, it is realized that except in a few precise and determined cases the facts do not stand up to analysis. The Wa-Nyanja of Portuguese Africa are divided into exogamous matrilineal groups called *kamu*, cut across by similarly exogamous patrilineal groups called *chilawa*. As is to be expected, this system excludes parallel cousins as possible spouses, but it does not make cross-cousins preferred spouses.[2] Forde has been led to make a similar reservation about the Yakö whose social organization is described above.[3]

A rough analysis of the Ashanti facts shows the extent to which the bilateral thesis should be mistrusted, even when it seems firmly established. As Seligman[4] has rightly pointed out, the dialectic of the *ntoro* and of the *abusua* would entail the marriage of bilateral cross-cousins only if each category comprised two and only two exogamous groups. This is certainly not the case among the Ashanti, who have an indefinite number of clans and *ntoro*, and consequently, the structure of their system does not entail that the grandsons shall automatically reproduce the patrilineal and matrilineal affiliations of their grandfather. This point is essential, because Rattray believed he could explain cross-cousin marriage and its particular relationship to the social organization of the Ashanti, by metaphysical beliefs.[5] Cross-cousin marriage is necessary because in a bilineal system the grandson reproduces the grandfather and re-embodies his social status. In this way, every soul can be reintegrated with its clan and *ntoro* after skipping a generation. This dialectic of alternate generations will be analysed below, and we shall not linger here on its theoretical implications. It should merely be noted that when there is an indefinite number of exogamous, patrilineal and matrilineal groups, the rule of double exogamy is not sufficient to make all marriages conform to the ideal model of marriage between bilateral cross-cousins. Marriage with the mother's brother's daughter (matrilateral cross-cousin) is an absolute barrier to the reproduction of alternate generations (indeed, the descendants preserve the patrilineal or matrilineal group of their male or female ascendant, according to sex, and indefinitely acquire a new alternate group). Finally, if, as Rattray says, the purpose of the system lies in the metaphysical necessity of reincarnation through alternate generations, Seligman has rightly noted[6] that, given the concomitant social organi-

---

[1] chs. XIII and XXVII.   [2] Barnes, 1922, pp. 147–9.   [3] Forde, 1941, p. 15.
[4] B. Z. Seligman, 1925, pp. 114–21.
[5] cf. Clark, 1930, pp. 431–70.
[6] B. Z. Seligman, 1925, pp. 114–21.

zation, this necessity can only be met if marriage is with the father's sister's daughter (patrilateral cross-cousin).

The theoretical reasons for this phenomenon will be given below.[1] But, to confine ourselves to the present case, two observations are indispensable. The negroes of Surinam, descendants of escaped slaves, have developed an autonomous civilization in the Guianas, with borrowings from European and Indian cultures which, however, do not conceal the African basis. Their social organization is still reminiscent of the social organization of the Ashanti. The clan is matrilineal, but from their father children inherit the *tcina*, the whole of the hereditary alimentary prohibitions which if violated can lead to leprosy. However, marriage prohibitions affect only the maternal line. One can marry freely into the father's brother's lineage, or the father's sister's lineage.[2] Must the conclusion now be drawn that girls and boys inherit the *tcina* from the father, as Herskovits's text would have us suppose?[3] This is perhaps the case among the negroes of Surinam, but by contrast, we have a formal account concerning the Ashanti. Bosman wrote in 1795 that the son never eats what is forbidden to his father, and in these matters the daughter follows her mother's example.[4] It would seem then that there are not two but three different methods of hereditary transmission: where sons and daughters follow their father's *ntoro;* likewise, where sons and daughters follow their mother's clan; and, by contrast, where sons follow the *tcina* of their father, and daughters the *tcina* of their mother.

The objection might be raised that this third form of descent has no influence on the rules of marriage, and consequently that there is no need to take it into account. The objection would be justified if the dichotomy of the sexes were not such a common characteristic of unilateral systems of marriage, precisely because in such systems brothers and sisters do not marry in the same way. In a system of marriage with the patrilateral cross-cousin, the son reproduces his mother's marriage, and the daughter that of her father. Hence it is understandable that each receives from the other parent that fraction of status, in other words, personal duties, which are unrelated to the marriage. In this way we should discover the existence of marriage with the father's sister's daughter which had already been suggested by the metaphysical beliefs. The reader to whom this analysis seems too schematic should refer to Chapter XXVI, where a Hindu example of the same ambiguity is discussed more extensively.

Certainly we do not claim that Ashanti marriage does in fact conform to the suggested model. Our only aim is to show that if there is no categorical evidence of forms of grouping that lead automatically to a double dichotomy, the explanation of cross-cousin marriage by 'double descent' is an idle one.

[1] ch. XXVII.   [2] Herskovits, 1928.
[3] '. . . the children inherit their personal food taboos . . .', and further on, the whole passage devoted to the personal attachment that the son or the daughter can have for their father (ibid. 1928, pp. 719–20).
[4] ibid. p. 719, n. 14.

V

Should this be surprising? It is striking to see that even with the most precise and explicit examples of organizations with marriage classes (e.g., the moieties of the Australian aborigines) these classes are much less conceived of in extension, as groups of objectively designated individuals, than as a system of positions whose structure alone remains constant, and in which individuals may change position, and even exchange their respective positions, provided that the relationships between them are maintained.

Among the aborigines of South Australia, the function of the custom of *kopara* seems to be to maintain the balance of exchange between the groups with regard to material goods, women, human lives, injuries, or initiation rites. The *kopara* is a debt, which must be regulated according to an established formula, and which varies according to the nature of the injury: e.g., a gift not returned, a woman not provided in exchange for a girl of the clan, an unavenged death, or a non-compensated initiation. This custom is of particular interest to us in that a murder or an initiation 'debt' is normally settled by the gift of a woman. Moreover, there is temporary exchange of wives to celebrate the settlement of each *kopara*, and, except for near kinsfolk, men and women of the same exogamous group can on this occasion have sexual relations: 'Thus . . . Tiniwa husbands send their Kulpuru wives to Kulpuru men, and vice versa.'[1] Likewise, the members of a revenge party normally belong to the deceased person's moiety, but they can oblige the men of the other moiety to help them, by lending their wives, which again means to say that under these circumstances sexual relations are permissible between members of the same moiety. This is the analogous but inverse situation to that in Guadalcanal, where the greatest insult is to tell a man 'to eat the excreta of his sister'. It can be wiped out only by the blood of the offender. But if the offender belongs to the opposite moiety, it is the sister herself who must be killed, and the original offender must also kill his sister if he wishes to re-establish his reputation.[2] This native evidence is perhaps based upon myths but it corresponds to very similar observations made by Warner among the Murngin.[3]

These facts are important for several reasons. Firstly, they emphasize that matrimonial exchange is only a particular case of those forms of multiple exchange embracing material goods, rights and persons. These exchanges themselves seem interchangeable, viz., a woman replaces a payment for a debt which was in the first place completely different, say, a murder or ritual privilege; not giving a woman takes the place of vengeance, etc. Furthermore, no other custom can more strikingly illustrate the point, which seems crucial to us, concerning the problem of marriage prohibitions: the prohibition is defined in a fashion which is logically prior to its object. If there is a prohibition it is not because there is some feature of the object

---

[1] Elkin, 1931*a*, p. 194.   [2] Hogbin, 1937, p. 68.   [3] Warner, 1931, pp. 172–98.

which excludes it from the number of possibilities. It acquires these features only in so far as it is incorporated in a certain system of antithetical relationships, the rôle of which is to establish inclusions by means of exclusions, and vice versa, because this is precisely the one means of establishing reciprocity, which is the reason for the whole undertaking. Similarly, the custom called *ausaŋ* in New Britain prescribes ritual combats with the distribution of food between potentially hostile villages, 'to provide an opportunity for the settlement of grievances and quarrels.'[1]

Among the aborigines studied by Elkin, the conflict of moieties is not based upon any intrinsic characteristic in either one of them, but solely, and as is always the case, on the fact that there are two of them: 'The aborigines of this region have no desire to kill off all the members of any one clan, for this weakens the tribe as a whole; and further – as they say – where are their wives and children to come from if they do?'[2] Inversely, among the Orokaiva, it is asked: 'If a girl married a man of her own clan, where . . . would the pay or bride-price come from?'[3] Speaking objectively, a woman, like the moiety from which she derives her civil status, has no specific or individual characteristics – totemic ancestor, or the origin of the blood in her veins – which makes her unfit for commerce with men bearing the same name. The sole reason is that she is *same* whereas she must (and therefore can) become *other*. Once she becomes *other* (by her allocation to men of the opposite moiety), she therefore becomes liable to play the same rôle, *vis-à-vis* the men of her own moiety, as she originally played to the men of the opposite moiety. In feasts, the same presents can be exchanged; in the custom of *kopara*, the same women that were originally offered can be exchanged in return. All that is necessary on either side is the *sign of otherness*, which is the outcome of a certain position in a structure and not of any innate characteristic: 'The exchange of gifts [taking place on the occasion of the periodic settlement of grievances between the groups] . . . is not a business transaction – not a mere bartering – but a means of expressing and cementing friendship.'[4] The gesture defines its mode of conveyance.

VI

But although there is this apparently formal characteristic of reciprocity expressed in the primacy of relationships over the terms which they unite, it should never be overlooked that these terms are human beings, that these human beings are individuals of different sexes, and that the relationship between the sexes is never symmetrical. To my mind the essential defect in the interpretation criticized in the previous paragraphs lies in treating problems which cannot be dissociated from their context in a purely abstract way. There is no justification for fabricating unilineal classes at will, because

[1] Todd, 1936, p. 406.   [2] Elkin, 1931*a*, p. 197.   [3] Williams, 1930, pp. 131–2.
[4] Elkin, 1931*a*, pp. 197–8.

the question is really whether these classes actually exist or not; the classes should not gratuitously be attributed any matrilineal or patrilineal character, on the pretext that it amounts to exactly the same thing in the ultimate solution of the present problem, without research into what is really the case. Above all, in formulating a solution, matrilineal groups cannot be substituted for patrilineal groups, or vice versa, for apart from their common characteristic as unilineal classes, the two forms are not equivalent, except from a purely formal point of view. They have neither the same place nor rank in human society. To be unmindful of this would be to overlook the basic fact that it is men who exchange women, and not vice versa.[1]

This apparently obvious point has a greater theoretical importance than might be thought. In his penetrating analysis of the *buwa*, the Trobriand custom whereby a man must give small presents to his mistress, Malinowski notes that 'this custom implies that sexual intercourse . . . is a service rendered by the female to the male'.[2] It is then a cause of wonder to him that this is the reason for a practice which seems 'by no means logical or self-evident'.[3] He would expect rather to see sexual relations treated 'as an exchange of services in itself reciprocal'.[4] And this functionalist, whose whole work declares that everything in social institutions has an end, concludes with a singular superficiality: 'But custom, arbitrary and inconsequent here as elsewhere, decrees that it is a service from women to men, and men have to pay.'[5] Must the principles of functionalism then be defended against their founder? Custom is not inconsistent in this case any more than it is in any other. But no understanding of it will come through considering merely its visible content and empirical expression. Custom is only a superficial aspect of the system of relations, which is what must be isolated.

Sexual relations between man and woman are an aspect of the total prestations of which marriage provides both an example and the occasion. We have seen that these total presentations have to do with material goods, social values such as privileges, rights and obligations, and women. The total relationship of exchange which constitutes marriage is not established between a man and a woman, where each owes and receives something, but between two groups of men, and the woman figures only as one of the objects in the exchange, not as one of the partners between whom the exchange takes place. This remains true even when the girl's feelings are taken into consideration, as, moreover, is usually the case. In acquiescing to the proposed union, she precipitates or allows the exchange to take place; she cannot alter its nature. This view must be kept in all strictness, even with regard to our own society, where marriage appears to be a contract between persons. Set going by the marriage of a man and a woman, with its aspects set out in the

[1] Certain tribes of South-east Asia, which almost provide a picture of the inverse situation, can undoubtedly be used as an example. This would not be to say that in such societies it is the women who exchange the men, but rather that men exchange other men *by means of* women.

[2] Malinowski, 1929, p. 319.   [3] loc. cit.   [4] loc. cit.   [5] loc. cit.

marriage service, this cycle of reciprocity is only a secondary mode of a wider cycle of reciprocity, which pledges the union of a man and a woman who is either someone's daughter or sister, by the union of the daughter or sister of that man or another man with the first man in question. If this fact is kept in mind, the apparent anomaly indicated by Malinowski is very simply explained. In the total prestations of which a woman is only a part, there is one category whose fulfilment depends primarily on her goodwill, viz., personal services, whether they be sexual or domestic. The lack of reciprocity which seems to characterize these services in the Trobriand Islands, as in most human societies, is the mere counterpart of a universal fact, that the relationship of reciprocity which is the basis of marriage is not established between men and women, but between men by means of women, who are merely the occasion of this relationship.

The first consequence of this interpretation should be to prevent an error which is likely to occur if too strict a parallelism is established between systems of mother-right and systems of father-right. At first sight, the 'matrilineal complex', as Lowie calls it, leads to an extraordinary situation. No doubt there are systems with matrilineal descent and permanent and definitive matrilocal residence, e.g., the Menangkabau of Sumatra, where a husband is called *orang samando*, 'borrowed man'.[1] Over and above the fact that in such systems – and there is scarcely need to recall it – it is the brother or eldest son of the mother's family who holds and wields authority, examples of them are extremely rare. Lowie gives only two (Pueblo and Khasi), but even then with reservations about the second.[2] In all other cases, matrilineal descent is accompanied by patrilocal residence, after a more or less short delay. The husband is a stranger, 'a man from outside', sometimes an enemy, and yet the woman goes away to live with him in his village to bear children who will never be his. The conjugal family is broken and rebroked incessantly. How can the mind conceive of such a situation? How can it have been devised and established? It cannot be understood without being seen as the result of the permanent conflict between the group giving the woman and the group acquiring her. Each group gains the victory in turn, or according to whether matrilineal descent or patrilineal descent is practised. The woman is never anything more than the symbol of her lineage. Matrilineal descent is the authority of the woman's father or brother extended to the brother-in-law's village.

The correlation established by Murdock between patrilineal institutions and the highest levels of culture[3] changes nothing in the absolute priority of these institutions over matrilineal institutions. It is true that in societies where political power takes precedence over other forms of organization, the duality which would result from the masculinity of political authority and the matrilineal character of descent could not subsist. Consequently, societies attaining this level of political organization tend to generalize the paternal

---

[1] Cole, 1936, p. 20.   [2] Lowie, 1919, p. 35.   [3] Murdock, 1937, pp. 445–70.

right. But it is because political authority, or simply social authority, always belongs to men, and because this masculine priority appears constant, that it adapts itself to a bilineal or matrilineal form of descent in most primitive societies, or imposes its model on all aspects of social life, as is the case in more developed groups.

To treat patrilineal and matrilineal descent and patrilocal and matrilocal residence as abstract elements combined in chance pairings is a complete misappreciation of the initial situation, which includes women among the objects in the men's transactions. There are as many matrilineal systems as patrilineal systems, if not more. But the number of matrilineal systems which are also matrilocal is extremely small. Behind the variations in the type of descent, the permanence of patrilocal residence attests to the basic asymmetrical relationship between the sexes which is characteristic of human society.

If further proof were necessary, one would need only to consider the expedients that a matrilineal and matrilocal society, in the strictest sense, must employ so as to establish an order roughly equivalent to that of a patrilineal and patrilocal society. The *taravad* of the Nayar of Malabar is a matrilineal and matrilocal lineage, the owner of the land, and the repository of rights over things and people. But to put this formula into effect a marriage must after three days be followed by a divorce. Henceforth a woman has only lovers.[1] It is not sufficient to say, as Radcliffe-Brown puts it, that 'in all societies there is a general difference between the status of a man and that of a woman'.[2] The extreme maternal unilateralism of the Nayar is not symmetrical with the extreme paternal unilateralism of the Kaffirs, as Radcliffe-Brown also suggests.[3] Strictly maternal systems are not only more rare than strictly paternal systems, but they are never a pure and simple inversion of the second. The 'fundamental difference' is a one-way difference.

We shall risk then advancing a suggestion based on the preceding considerations, and perhaps containing an explanation for a peculiar phenomenon, viz., why dual organizations are more frequently matrilineal than patrilineal. If these systems were strictly symmetrical, the problem would be resolved only with great difficulty unless use were made of diffusionist theories. But we have just seen that the number of societies with matrilineal descent and matrilocal residence is very limited. Consequently, the only alternatives are, on the one hand patrilineal and patrilocal systems, and on the other, matrilineal and patrilocal systems. The exceptional cases of matrilineal and matrilocal systems, which are in conflict with the asymmetrical relationship between the sexes, may be assimilated to the latter. If the functioning of the first raises few practical problems, this is not so of the second. This is clearly recognized by ethnographers, for whom the study of a matrilineal society represents the promise of a complicated social organization, rich in strange institutions, imbued with an atmosphere of the dramatic,

[1] Radcliffe-Brown, 1935*a*, p. 291.   [2] loc. cit.   [3] ibid. p. 295.

and very different in this regard from what is to be expected of a society with father-right. These special characteristics, from the specialist's viewpoint, are explained only in part by the greater differences which separate these societies from our own. To a large extent, the characteristics depend on their specific structure, and it is no coincidence that almost all monographs which have had wide repercussions have been about matrilineal societies.

For a matrilineal society, even though patrilocal, and without marriage classes, has peculiar problems to resolve. Its exogamy can only be of the local clan, or the village. In other words, the woman will go to live in her husband's village, sometimes far from her own people, while she and her children will always be strangers within the group with which they are nevertheless associated. If a society is both matrilineal and matrilocal, either permanently or temporarily, as often happens, the husband belongs to the despised class of 'those-resulting-from marriage' or 'strangers', as opposed to 'the owners of the village'. Consequently, he is always aware of the precariousness of his residential title as compared with his wife and children.[1] It can easily be imagined that groups under pressure of the psychological and social conflicts attached to such systems may determine, more easily than groups which are not, to wipe out the opposition between rule of descent and rule of residence by the local juxtaposition of exchange units, whether pre-existing clans or villages. We have referred to an evolution of this type, precisely in a society which seems condemned by its structure to otherwise insoluble conflicts.[2] Dual organization provides a very simple solution to the problems which afflict such societies as Dobu or, in a different sense, Kiriwina. The geographical proximity of social units eliminates the difficulties inherent in residence. The latter can remain patrilocal, or even matrilocal, without the conjugal society being perpetually broken down. And the men's house, by reuniting husbands and brothers-in-law in a ritual and political collaboration, resolves the conflict between 'owners' and strangers. The 'reign of women' is remembered only in mythology, an age, perhaps more simply, when men had not yet resolved the antinomy which is always likely to appear between their rôles as takers of wives and givers of sisters, and making them both the authors and victims of their exchanges.

[1] Fortune, 1932, pp. 5–7.   [2] ibid. p. 106 et seq.

CHAPTER IX

The Marriage of Cousins

I

The very nature of the principle of reciprocity allows it to act in two different and complementary ways, either by setting up classes which automatically delimit the group of possible spouses, or by the determination of a relationship, or a group of relationships, so that in each instance it can be said whether a prospective spouse is to be desired or excluded. Both criteria are given simultaneously, but their relative importance varies. The class is of the greater importance in dual organizations or in societies with marriage classes, whereas on the other hand the relationship is used first of all, in a negative form, with the simple prohibition on incest.

But there is one special case in which both aspects of the principle of reciprocity co-exist, or rather have the same relative importance, and where they overlap exactly and cumulate their effects. This is marriage between cross-cousins. In this, more than any other, the class and the group of individuals determined by the relationship are co-extensive. This is why Morgan, Tylor and Frazer were led to observe that dual organization had the same kinship terminology as systems of cross-cousin marriage, and that the cross-cousins were distributed as if they belonged to different moieties. In fact, cross-cousin marriage is to be distinguished from the prohibition of incest in that the latter employs a system of negative relationships, and the marriage of cross-cousins a system of positive relationships. The incest prohibition says who cannot be married, while the other establishes which spouses are preferred. At the same time, cross-cousin marriage is to be distinguished from dual organization in that the latter has an automatic procedure (unilineal descent) for sorting out individuals into the two categories, while the other has a discriminatory procedure which it applies separately to each individual. Finally, cross-cousin marriage is the only type of preferential union which can function normally and exclusively and still give every man and woman the chance to marry a cross-cousin, wherever the kinship terminology divides all the members of the one generation, and of the other sex, into two approximately equal categories, viz., cross-cousins (real or classificatory) and brothers or sisters (including real brothers and sisters and parallel cousins). To our way of thinking, whenever sociologists

119

have grouped cross-cousin marriage with other systems, such as the levirate, the sororate, or avuncular marriage, under the general title of preferential union, they have failed to show the real importance and place of this form of marriage. The levirate, the sororate, and avuncular marriage are not *preferential unions,* because for obvious reasons they cannot constitute the exclusive or even preponderant rule of marriage in any group. We would prefer to call them *privileged unions,* since they presuppose other modes of marriage on to which they themselves are grafted.

For example, take the Miwok of California, Gifford supported the thesis that the marriage of cross-cousins in this group is a recent innovation, and that the former system of marriage was with the wife's brother's daughter. The first point will not be discussed here. In our opinion, the fact that the marriage system is or is not reflected in the kinship terminology (and Gifford establishes that it is not) cannot legitimately be used to support the anteriority or the posteriority of a system.[1] However, it is certain that marriage with the wife's brother's daughter has never been the normal form, for the simple reason that for someone to marry his wife's brother's daughter he must already have a wife. The wife, similarly, cannot be thus defined without there being a vicious circle. Consequently, this form of marriage can never have been more than a privileged form, and doubly so, firstly, because it is a privilege for a married man, whose wife has a brother, and whose brother has a daughter, to be able to claim this daughter as a second wife, and secondly, because this system has the quality, which struck Gifford so forcefully, of being reflected in twelve different forms of designation.

But for it to be possible to invoke this last fact in favour of the anteriority and generality of the system, it must needs be, as in our society, that individuals should never be united by just one kinship relationship. There are rare cases of this in societies with classificatory systems, but never in groups with a relatively low population density and in which marriages take place within a restricted circle. In such societies individuals must choose from among the multiple kinship ties which join each of them to all the others.[2] For example, there is nothing to prevent the father's sister from being at one and the same time the mother's brother's wife, if she marries her cross-cousin; a grandmother (if the father's mother's brother has a marriage claim to the sister's daughter); a mother-in-law (if someone marries the father's sister's daughter); and a wife (if someone has a marriage claim to the maternal uncle's widow). In this way the system allows five different terms to be applied to the one individual. In these circumstances, what determines the term chosen? It may be the fact that a form of marriage is old or general. Perhaps, however, it may also be the fact that it is exceptional. The holders of a privilege may wish to enshrine the principle of the matter by bringing

---

[1] cf. pt. II, ch. XXII.

[2] R. Firth has made similar observations concerning Polynesian societies, cf. Firth 1930, pp. 235–68; 1936, p. 266 et seq.

the corresponding term into common usage, or it may please the whole group to emphasize any marked oddity arising from the conflict between an exceptional form of marriage and a normal form.

For example, most of the kinship systems of South American tribes practising cross-cousin marriage identify grandparents with parents-in-law. This custom is easily explained by the practice of avuncular marriage. When a girl marries her maternal uncle, her parents-in-law and her grandparents are identical. However, this purely feminine perspective ought, from the male point of view, to result symmetrically in identifying the parents-in-law with the sister and the brother-in-law. Yet this does not happen. For a reason open to many different interpretations the feminine perspective is the one imposed upon the group. On the other hand, cross-cousin marriage establishes a third system of identification which is generally adopted, namely, that which groups the cross-uncle and the cross-aunt under the one term with the spouse's father and mother.

The Nambikwara have only one term for grandfather, mother's brother and father-in-law, and only one term for grandmother, father's sister and mother-in-law. The conclusion to be drawn is certainly not that in South America avuncular marriage is older than cross-cousin marriage, or vice versa, but that, in accordance with the circumstances and the groups, it is one possible solution to conflicts of terminology, and one which has prevailed over other equally acceptable solutions. Perhaps the adoption of the feminine perspective, identifying grandparents with parents-in-law, should even be interpreted as a reaction of·the cross-cousin terminology to that of avuncular marriage. The status of cross and parallel cousins would remain as it was if the terminological confusions resulting from avuncular marriage were transferred to the previous generation. It would not be so if this asymmetrical terminology prevailed in the generation in which the potential spouses, the brothers-in-law and the sisters-in-law, are bound together in reciprocal relationships. If this interpretation is correct it follows, not only that the system of nomenclature peculiar to avuncular marriage proves nothing in support of the priority of this form of marriage in South America, but that the peculiar modalities of this system reveal a concomitant and opposed form.

However, the exceptional importance of cross-cousin marriage, as we see it, does not derive merely from its unique position at the very hub of matrimonial institutions. Its importance is no longer limited to its rôle as the 'pivot' between the incest prohibition and dual organization. The interest of cross-cousin marriage lies especially in the fact that the division that it establishes between prescribed and prohibited spouses cuts across a category of relatives who, from the viewpoint of biological proximity, are strictly interchangeable. This point has often been used to prove that marriage prohibitions have no biological basis, but it seems to us that its full significance has never been clearly perceived.

It is precisely because cross-cousin marriage disregards the biological factor that it should be able to establish that the origin of the incest prohibition is purely social, and furthermore to reveal what its real nature is. It is not enough to repeat that the prohibition of incest is not based on biological grounds. What then is its basis? This is the real question, and while it remains unanswered the problem cannot be said to have been resolved. For the most part, an answer to this is very difficult to give because the prohibited degrees of kinship, taken as a whole, are biologically closer than the permitted degrees. Consequently, there is always a doubt as to whether it is the biological degree, or the social degree, which is the basis of the institution. The difficulty is completely eliminated only in the case of cross-cousin marriage, for if we can understand why degrees of kinship which are equivalent from a biological point of view are nevertheless considered completely dissimilar from the social point of view, we can claim to have discovered the principle, not only of cross-cousin marriage, but of the incest prohibition itself.

This method seems so obvious to us that it may be wondered why it was not used in the first place, and why cross-cousin marriage was regarded as a marriage system like any other, instead of as a phenomenon of another order, as we have proposed. The answer is simple. Sociologists have trapped themselves in their own argumentation. Because cross-cousin marriage is an arbitrary regulation from the biological viewpoint, they have proceeded to assert that it is arbitrary in the absolute, whatever viewpoint is adopted. Alternatively, but to the same effect, they have tried to reduce it to a secondary consequence of heterogeneous institutions, just as some people explain the Jewish and Moslem prohibition of the eating of pork by the risk of it being bad in old unhygienic civilizations. It is denied that the *raison d'être* of an institution might be found within the institution itself; instead, it is reduced to a series of contingent connexions, derived as often as not from dual organization and the practice of exogamy.

This intellectual position is particularly apparent in one of the extreme writers, who, in a highly tendentious frame of mind, it is true, has made a close analysis of cross-cousin marriage:

'The first form of exogamy, that of the dual organization, bears every trace of artificiality; certain groups of relatives are possible mates, while others are forbidden; the children of brother and sister, cross-cousins may marry, while those of two brothers or of two sisters may not marry. Such a rule is not founded on any prohibition devised for some other purpose.'[1]

We realize clearly that Perry, in making this statement, is merely attempting to find a basis for a preconceived system, and that this is even more riddled with historicism than are those of his predecessors. It is not a bad thing, however, to borrow a quotation from a writer whose work is generally

[1] Perry, 1923, p. 381.

denounced as an extravagant abuse of the historical method, for, from our present viewpoint, such illustrious predecessors as Tylor and Morgan are guilty of just as great an error in method, since it has led them to an analogous conclusion. Perry identifies cross-cousin marriage with dual organization, and he claims to explain them both historically. But Morgan and Tylor are no different, for when they analysed cross-cousin marriage they saw it simply as a residue of exogamous customs and dual organization. What should have been done, on the contrary, was to treat cross-cousin marriage, rules of exogamy, and dual organization as so many examples of one basic structure. This structure should have been interpreted in terms of its total characteristics, instead of being broken up into bits and pieces and set alongside one another in a juxtaposition which might justify an historical interpretation but would have no intrinsic significance. It was especially necessary to see that, of the three types of institution, cross-cousin marriage is the most significant, making the analysis of this form of marriage the veritable *experimentum crucis* in the study of marriage prohibitions.

II

If cross-cousin marriage is not a consequence of dual organization, what is its real origin? Swanton[1] has suggested that the origin is to be found in a desire to keep the most valuable possessions within the family. However, even if such an explanation were conceivable for the tribes of British Columbia or India, how could it be extended to the semi-nomadic bands of the Nambikwara of western Brazil, whose members are equally poor in material goods and in social prestige to hand on to their descendants? It is true that some people do not see any reason to treat the marriage practices of widely differing societies as the one and the same phenomenon. For example, Lowie concluded his analysis with these words: 'Cross-cousin marriage is in all probability not a phenomenon that has evolved from a single cause but one that has independently arisen in several centres from diverse motives.'[2]

A multiplicity of origins would in no way be excluded if the institution of cross-cousins were nothing but a highly specialized form of preferential marriage. For example, cross-cousin marriage is frequently encountered in the form of preferential marriage with the maternal uncle's daughter, and it is by no means certain *a priori* that, wherever this type of marriage is met with, its explanation should rest on a single unique cause. Rivers has given a plausible if not indubitable account of it, in the Banks Islands, as a form of matrimonial privilege over the girls of the group, handed on to the sister's son by the mother's brother. Also plausible but no more certain is Gifford's explanation for it among the Miwok, as a privilege over the wife's brother's daughter handed on to his sons by their father. But the question is not

[1] Swanton, 1905*b*, p. 50 et seq. In the same sense, Wedgwood, 1936*a*, pp. 612–13; Richards, 1914, pp. 194–8.   [2] Lowie, 1961, p. 31.

altogether posed in this way. Side by side with marriage with the mother's brother's daughter, there is, less frequently it is true, marriage with the father's sister's daughter. Moreover, in the great majority of cases, there is marriage with the father's sister's daughter who is *at the same time* the mother's brother's daughter (when the father's sister has married the mother's brother); there are innumerable cases, nevertheless, even where cross-cousin marriage does not exist, of the mother's brother's children and the father's sister's children falling into a common category, to be distinguished from the father's brother's children and the mother's sister's children who are called brothers and sisters. There are even more frequent cases of special terms, or a common term, being used to isolate the mother's brother on the one hand, and the father's sister on the other, from parallel uncles and aunts who are generally identified with the father and the mother. There are symmetrical cases – but not always – in which nephews and nieces descended from a brother or a sister of the same sex as the speaker are called sons and daughters, or are simply distinguished from nephews and nieces descended from a kinsman of the opposite sex and are called by different terms. There are the matrimonial privileges of the maternal uncle over the sister's daughter, and more rarely, of the brother's son over the father's sister. Finally, even when there are no matrimonial preferences and privileges, and sometimes when they are both expressly denied, there is a whole range of special relationships between cross-cousins, between cross-aunts and cross-uncles and cross-nephews and cross-nieces, characterized by respect or familiarity, authority or licence.

No doubt each of these features has its own particular history, and doubtless also its history can vary from group to group. At the same time, however, no feature is to be seen as an independent entity isolated from all others. On the contrary, each appears as a variation on a basic theme, as a special modality outlined against a common backdrop, and it is only the individual qualities in each which are to be explained by reference to causes peculiar to the group or the cultural area under consideration. What, therefore, is this common basis? The only one possible is a general kinship structure, more or less completely reflected in every system, but which all systems with any of the features enumerated in the preceding paragraph partially exemplify, though in differing degrees. As systems without any of these features are far less common than systems with at least one of them and probably more, and as the latter systems are scattered all over the world, no region being completely devoid of them, it is this general structure, of all the rules of kinship, which, second only to the incest prohibition, most nearly approaches universality.

III

The idea that kinship must be interpreted as a structural phenomena, and not simply as the result of a juxtaposition of terms and customs, is not new.

Goldenweiser asserted it when he remarked that there must be a way to approach the study of kinship systems which avoids their apparent and impossible complexity, and when he outlined how a particular example could be subjected to this structural analysis.[1] Spier has not only shown that this ought to be the sociologist's point of view, but that it might also be that of the natives. He says that it is with very good reason that the word 'system' is used for the collection of terms which serve to describe kinship relationships. It seemed clear to him that the Maricopa themselves conceived of kinship terms as a clearly defined system. He adds that the female informant needed to know only the sex and relative age of the brothers and sisters composing the lineages to give, without any hesitation whatsoever, the terms employed between any two kinsmen belonging to subsequent generations, however distant the degree.[2]

'In fact, it is partly as a theoretical formula that subsections are carried intertribally', says Stanner[3] of the Murinbata of Australia, and he adds: 'Those who doubt the aborigines' power of such abstract reasoning can never have heard them expounding to their tribe's fellows how ŋinipun (subsections) should work, by inference from the theory to the case under attention. In this way an abstraction becomes a flesh-and-blood reality.'[4] The same writer has given a fascinating description of how a complex system with marriage classes can be borrowed and learned in a theoretical form:

'One or two exceptionally intelligent natives are regarded by their tribes as experts in the new fashions. Each of them is a traveller, having roamed beyond the tribal homelands, often over very great distances. They have been schooled in alien camps until they know perfectly these verbal accounts of how the subsections work. One described to me how he had sat down for days at a time near the mosquito-ridden Victoria River and had been patiently instructed by his Djamindjung friends . . . His instructors had drawn marks in the dust, or broken twigs, each mark or twig a subsection or a man. This man was pointed out to him as his *kaka*, this one as his *ŋatan* (brother), that woman whose name was not even to be whispered was his *pipi ŋinar*. Each one was this or that "skin" who in turn "made" another "skin". In this way he learned. The formulae are in a real sense a book of rules.'[5]

Deacon gives evidence which helps to throw light on the theoretical nature of the native's conception of his own marriage system. Deacon's description is all the more significant because it refers to one of the most complex systems known, the six-class system of Ambrym.[6] On two different occasions the natives gave Deacon demonstrations, using diagrams. Once an informant placed three white stones equidistant on the ground, each

[1] Goldenweiser, 1913, pp. 281–94.   [2] Spier, 1933, p. 209.
[3] Stanner, 1936, p. 202.   [4] loc. cit·   [5] ibid. p. 208.
[6] The Ambrym system will be studied and discussed in another work.

representing a line joined to the other two by a unilateral marriage relationship. Another informant drew three long lines on the ground (D, E, F), each representing a man from one of the three lines (Fig. 5). The marriage of each man and his children were represented by lines of different lengths placed to the left of the principal line for the spouse and to the right for the children. Boys and girls were distinguished by the length of the linear symbols given them. The two marriage cycles were indicated by two circles closing in opposite directions. This diagram revealed the whole functioning of the system and agreed perfectly with hypotheses to be made from the theoretical system:

Fig. 5.

Diagram traced by the Ambrym natives to explain their kinship system. (The long lines stand for men, and the short for women; the arrows separate the 'lines' within the same bilateral group (*bwelem*).

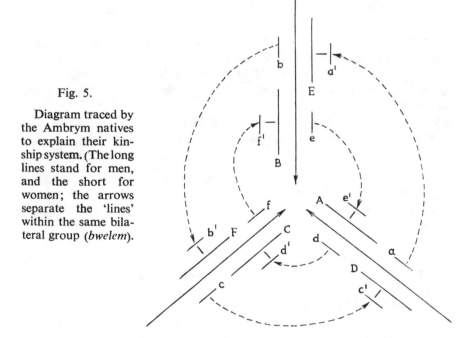

'It is perfectly clear that the natives (the intelligent ones) do conceive of the system as a connected mechanism which they can represent by diagrams . . . The way they could reason about relationships from their diagrams was absolutely on a par with a good scientific exposition in a lecture-room.'[1]

The same author describes similar experiences in Malekula, in the New Hebrides, and he adds:

'The old men explained the system [of marriage] to me perfectly lucidly; I could not explain it to anyone better myself . . . It is extraordinary that a

[1] Deacon, 1927, pp. 329–32 and n., p. 329.

native should be able to represent completely by a diagram a complex system of matrimonial classes . . . I have collected in Malekula, too, some cases of a remarkable mathematical ability. I hope . . . to be able to prove that the native is capable of pretty advanced abstract thought.'[1]

Bateson seems to be of the same opinion with regard to the New Guinea natives: 'Thus the culture is to a great extent in the custody of men trained in erudition and dialectic',[2] which are put to use in such quarrels as between the Sun and the Mother moieties. It is a question of which of these two great social units can claim ownership of the Night. One moiety claimed that Night was a positive reality in itself and could thus be appropriated freely, while the other moiety defined it as the negation of day, the consequence of the absence of the Sun totem, whence any claim by the Sun moiety must be a contradiction in terms.[3]

This logical versatility is ultimately reflected in the terminology. The study of kinship vocabularies shows that the native conceives of kinship phenomena as a system of relations rather than as a collection of statuses. Later we shall see how Radcliffe-Brown was induced to interpret Australian aboriginal kinship systems using an analysis, the basic elements of which are relationships (e.g., 'pairs', 'cycles' and 'couples'[4]), and not terms. But native theory preceded him in this discovery. The Kanakas have special terms for the combinations formed respectively by:

> husband and wife (pair): *duawe*
> father and son (couple): *duanoro*
> mother and daughter (cycle): *duaduwe*

and even for relationships which are still obscure for the theoretician:

> grandfather and grandson (alternate generations): *duaeri*
> maternal uncle and nephew (avuncular relationship): *duarha*.[5]

Likewise the Fijian system has nine dual terms each expressing a specific relationship between two persons, or two groups of persons, rather than the persons themselves; father and child; mother and child; brothers; sisters; brother and sister; grandfather and grandchild; grandmother and grandchild; uncle and nephew; cousins of the same sex; cousins of different sexes; husband and wife.[6] To this list may be added the term *veiqaravi*, 'those who stand opposite one another',[7] which expresses the relationship of partners which is implied in any ritual: between god and worshipper, victim and sacrificer, priest and acolyte, king and priest, etc.[8]

Primitive thought, therefore, is not incapable of conceiving of complex structures and apprehending relationships. Lowie called explicitly on these

---

[1] ibid. 1934, pp. xxii-xxiii. [2] Bateson, 1936, p. 227. [3] ibid. p. 230.
[4] cf. ch. XI. [5] Leenhardt, 1930, p. 59.
[6] Hocart, 1929, p. 34. [7] ibid. 1933. [8] loc. cit.

capacities when, in a now classic article,[1] he set out to question Rivers's interpretation of cross-cousin marriage in the Banks Islands, replacing Rivers's local and historical explanation with the permanent function of exogamy. In this particular case we believe such an appeal is most unreliable, but this is no place to start a debate on the problem. At all events, the general direction which Lowie gave to the study of kinship problems was right, just as he was right in showing that exogamy as a regulating principle, stripped of its historical or local modalities, is always likely to follow two different courses in its action, firstly confusing direct and collateral lines, and secondly confusing generations. It is in the same spirit that attention must be drawn to a third structural orientation, not limited to exogamy, although a necessary concomitant of it, and found also in a great number of systems without clans and dual organization. We mean the distinction between collaterals of the same degree, according as kinship is established through a relative of the same or of different sex. In other words, it is the idea that the *brother-sister* relationship is identical with the *sister-brother* relationship,[2] but that these both differ from the *brother-brother* and the *sister-sister* relationships, which are identical with one another. Even more succinctly, it is the principle whereby there are considerable differences of status attached to whether the structure of collateral relationships (from the point of view of the arrangement of the sexes) is symmetrical or asymmetrical.

In this way we arrive at the most general formula for the phenomena studied in the previous chapters. An uncle does not have the same status for his nephews if he is the brother of a father who is his own brother, or the brother of a mother who is for him a sister, and it is the same with the aunt. Nephews and nieces are distinguished according as they are the children of my sister (if I am a man), or of my brother (if I am a woman), or according as they are the children of my brother whose brother I am, or of my sister, whose sister I am. Finally, a female cousin or a male cousin, the child of a brother's brother, or a sister's sister, is to me, as it were, a brother or a sister, while if we are kinsfolk in an asymmetrical structure, sister's brother or brother's sister, he, or she, becomes something else entirely, perhaps even the person farthest removed from a kinsman, i.e., a spouse. *In a very great number of societies there are consequences, ranging from a mere difference in terminology to a transformation in the whole system of rights and duties, following from the fact that there is or is not a change of sex in passing from the direct line to the collateral line.* Let us repeat: undoubtedly, this principle and all the consequences arising from it coincide perfectly with dual organization; nevertheless, they cannot be explained as resulting from this type of social organization. Firstly, such an interpretation, as we have seen, would lead to cross-cousin marriage itself being made a consequence of dual

[1] Lowie, 1915, pp. 223–39.
[2] Except in the most endogamous systems in which marriage with the (older) sister is permitted only because the two relationships are not reciprocal; cf. ch. I, p. 9–10.

organization, but neither the facts nor the analysis of the respective theoretical characteristics of the two institutions would justify such a conclusion. Secondly, this distinction of the relationships between the direct line and the collateral line, according as they reproduce symmetrical structures or asymmetrical structures, is met with in societies which do not practise cross-cousin marriage and which have no division into moieties.[1]

It would be just as useless to invoke the levirate and the sororate, which are very widespread, because these institutions, for the same reason as the features listed earlier, are elements of an original complex to which they owe their existence but of which they embody but few of the characteristics. Therefore, supposing it were alleged that some of the characteristics of the complex could be explained by one institution, and some by another, and so on until they had all been exhausted, it would still have to be shown how this complex can have the structural nature on which we have insisted, and how this structure can be both simpler but richer in possibilities than the isolated elements which are claimed to be primary. Before the institutions, and as a condition of their existence, there is in fact the apprehension of a relationship, or more exactly the apprehension of the opposition between two relationships. These relationships concern both the direct line and the collateral line, and the difference emerges from the fact that these two lines can be linked through relatives of the one sex, or relatives of different sexes. Why is this difference seen as an opposition?

The characteristic feature of cross-cousin marriage cannot merely be reduced to the existence of a social barrier between biologically identical degrees. Neither is it a purely negative limit merely excluding parallel cousins from marrying, but a complete reversal in direction. The antipathy shown to parallel cousins does not simply disappear in the presence of cross-cousins; it is transformed into its opposite, that is to say, into affinity. Consequently, it is not enough to give a separate explanation for the prohibition of parallel cousins, nor would it serve any useful purpose to give an interpretation ignoring the fact that cross-cousins are included among the possible spouses. Positive and negative phenomena mean nothing by themselves, but form parts of a whole. If our general concept is correct, cross-cousins are recommended *for the same reason* that parallel cousins are excluded.

These difficulties are clarified if cross-cousin marriage is seen as the elementary formula for marriage by exchange, and if exchange is seen as the *raison d'être* of the system of oppositions the structural qualities of which were emphasized in the previous paragraphs. In our opinion, the source of all the uncertainties surrounding the problem of incest and the study of marriage prohibitions is none other than our tendency to think of marriage in terms

---

[1] By comparing the relationships of reciprocity between cross-cousins among the Azande, and father and son among the Pawnee, Hocart has clearly seen that both forms derive from a basic relationship between a male individual and a female individual. (Hocart, 1935, pp. 149–51.)

of our own institutions, as a unilateral act of transfer and as an asymmetrical institution, when in fact (and even among ourselves) it is a bilateral act and a symmetrical institution. The only difference is that preponderantly in primitive societies the symmetrical structure of the institution involves two groups, while in modern societies the symmetrical elements are on the one hand a class tending to be reduced solely to the individual, and on the other a class which extends so far as to be confused with the social group as a whole. We have already come across an analogous formula in accounting for polygamous marriage and the relationship of reciprocity between the chief and his band.[1] In this regard, the juridical basis of modern marriage appears as the generalization or democratization of a model with a more limited application. However, let us begin by determining the true nature of cross-cousin marriage.

Suppose there are two patrilineal and patrilocal family groups, *A* and *B*, united by the marriage of a *b* girl and an *a* man. From the viewpoint of group *A*, the *b* woman represents an acquisition, while for group *B*, she represents a loss. Thus, for group *A*, which benefits, the marriage is expressed by a change to a debit position, and for group *B*, which is decreased by the loss of one female member to the profit of group *A*, by the acquiring of a credit. Similarly, the marriage of each of the men of group *B* and of group *A* represents a gain for his respective group, and thus places the group in general, and the family involved in particular, in the position of debtor. By contrast, the marriage of each of the *a* or *b* women represents a loss, and thus opens up a right to compensation. Related women are women lost; women brought in by marriage are women gained. Each family descended from these marriages thus bears a sign, which is determined, for the initial group, by whether the children's mother is a daughter or a daughter-in-law. Families descended from a daughter and a son-in-law result from an impoverishment of the group, and, from the initial group's viewpoint, have a credit to their account. Families which derive from the marriage of a son and daughter-in-law are families of acquisition, and since they have gained, they must give. The sign changes in passing from the brother to the sister, since the brother gains a wife, while the sister is lost to her own family. But the sign also changes in passing from one generation to the next. It depends upon whether, from the initial group's point of view, the father has received a wife, or the mother has been transferred outside, whether the sons have the right to a woman or owe a sister. Certainly, in real life, this difference does not mean that half the male cousins are destined to remain bachelors. However, at all events, it does express the law that a man cannot receive a wife except from the group from which a woman can be claimed, because in the previous generation a sister or a daughter was lost, while a brother owes a sister (or a father, a daughter) to the outside world if a woman was gained in the previous generation.

[1] cf. ch. IV, p. 44.

A diagram will illustrate this analysis (Fig. 6). Each couple bears a (+) or (−) sign, according to whether it results from a woman being lost to or

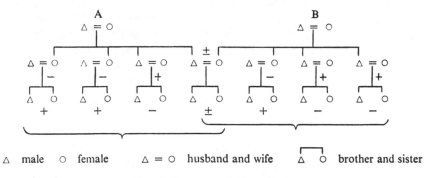

Fig. 6. Cross-cousin marriage.

The cousins who are in the (+ −) relationship are cross; those who are in the (+ +) or (− −) relationship are parallel.

acquired by line *A* or *B*. The sign changes in the following generation, the members of which are all cousins to one another. The pivot-couple, formed by an *A* man married to a *B* woman, obviously has two signs, according to whether it is envisaged from the viewpoint of *A*, or that of *B*, and the same is true for the children. It is now only necessary to look at the cousins' generation to establish that all those in the relationship (+ +) or (− −) are parallel to one another, while all those in the relationship (+ −) or (− +) are cross. Thus, the notion of reciprocity allows the dichotomy of cousins to be immediately deduced. In other words, two male cousins who are both in the credit position towards their father's group (and in the debit position with regard to their mother's group) cannot exchange their sisters any more than could two male cousins in a credit position with regard to their mother's group (and debit position with regard to the father's group). This intimate arrangement would leave somewhere outside not only groups which did not make restitution, but also groups which did not receive anything, and marriage in both would be a unilateral transfer. In the final analysis, therefore, cross-cousin marriage simply expresses the fact that marriage must always be a giving and a receiving, but that one can receive only from him who is obliged to give, and that the giving must be to him who has a right to receive, for the mutual gift between debtors leads to privilege, whereas the mutual gift between creditors leads inevitably to extinction.

There is nothing to prevent us from supposing in our theoretical diagram that exchange has already taken place in the parental generation. In this case, all the marriages will conform to the pivot-couple's marriage, that is, between *A* men and *B* women, or between *B* men and *A* women. Furthermore, the children will be cross or parallel in both the paternal and the maternal lines, instead of in only one, the general structure remaining the same. It might also be supposed that the initial exchange had taken place between the grandparents, the *A* grandmother being the sister of the *B* grandfather, and vice versa. In this case, the following generation (that of the parents) will already be composed of cross-cousins, and the children's generation will have the same structure as in the preceding case, for the exchange of sisters or daughters, wherever it takes place, makes cross-cousins. The children of cross-cousins are cross-cousins in relation to one another; children descended from an exchange of sisters between men without any kinship relationship are cross-cousins; and even children descended from an exchange between parallel cousins are cross-cousins.

It may have been noted that we have assumed what might be called, so as not to prejudge institutions, a paternal perspective. That is, we have regarded the woman married by a member of the group as acquired, and the sister provided in exchange as lost. The situation might be altogether different in a system with matrilineal descent and matrilocal residence, i.e., in which the children belong to the mother's group, or where the mother's group profits from the husband's services. But, whatever the system, the same phenomenon is always to be found, although it may be expressed in more or less complex ways. In fact, the advantages or losses resulting from marriage are rarely shared out as simply as we have supposed for the clarity of the diagram. Each group loses and gains at the same time, according to the way in which the rights are distributed. Descent may be gained while residence is lost, or vice versa, and material goods and social titles are not necessarily transmitted homogeneously. The essential thing is that every right acquired entails a concomitant obligation, and that every renunciation calls for a compensation. In marriage by exchange, these renunciations and acquisitions always affect both unions symmetrically, but inversely. Even supposing a very hypothetical marriage system in which the man and not the woman were exchanged, it would only be necessary to reverse all the signs in the diagram and the total structure would remain unchanged.

But there is no need, in this theoretical case, to postulate any precise type of institution. If there is any real case corresponding to this theoretical one it is clearly that of primitive bands composed of biological families set closely side by side, or, on the contrary, without regular contacts, and still at a very elementary stage of organization. As a matter of fact, our interpretative diagram does not imply the existence of stable institutions, or the establishment of a particular rule of descent or residence. It merely implies that women are regarded as valuables – a psychological attitude sufficiently attested to in the great majority of primitive societies, and by the relationships between the sexes at the animal level – and the apprehension by the individual of reciprocal relationships of the type: *A* is to *B* as *B* is to *A*; or again, if *A* is to *D* as *B* is to *C*, *C* must be to *D* as *B* is to *A*; that is, the two formulas for the exchange of sisters and for cross-cousin marriage. The acquisition of a capacity to apprehend these structures poses a problem, but a psychological, not a sociological one. We shall return to this point later. We know for a fact that structures of this type are conceived of by primitive thought.

CHAPTER X

Matrimonial Exchange

I

Frazer must be given credit for being the first to call attention to the structural similarity between marriage by exchange and cross-cousin marriage, and for establishing the real connexion between the two. His starting-point is the observation that in certain kinship systems requiring preferential marriage with only one of the cross-cousins (usually the mother's brother's daughter) there is nevertheless the double identification of the mother's brother with the father-in-law and the father's sister with the mother-in-law. However, it is impossible to understand this second identification unless there is marriage with the father's sister's daughter. Frazer remarks that this difficulty is cleared up if we suppose that the two female cross-cousins are identical, that is, if the mother's brother's daughter is also the father's sister's daughter,[1] a situation which arises automatically when the cross-cousins are descended from men who have exchanged their sisters. This connexion between cross-cousin marriage and marriage by exchange is very clearly understood in some cases: 'Thus in Mandla and Bastar a man thinks he has a right to his sister's daughter for his son on the ground that his family has given a girl to her husband's family, and therefore they should give one back. This match is known as *Dūdh lautāna* or bringing back the milk.'[2] In actual fact, among the same Gonds, 'milk money', or compensation for the cross-cousin, is owed if she marries a man other than the prescribed cousin.[3] The Marātha Brahmans have a proverb: 'At a sister's house her brother's daughter is a daughter-in-law.'[4] Among the Kachin of Burma, who prohibit marriage between all close relatives – except the mother's brother's daughter and the father's sister's son, who are obligatory spouses under pain of fine – marriage by exchange functions as a substitute for cross-cousin marriage, when the prescribed relatives are lacking.

However, it is in Australia particularly that the remarkable coincidence between marriage by exchange and cross-cousin marriage can be established:

'It may be safely laid down as a broad and general proposition that among these savages a wife was obtained by the exchange of a female relative . . .

---

[1] Frazer, 1919, vol. II, p. 104.   [2] ibid. pp. 120–1.   [3] ibid. p. 121.   [4] ibid. p. 124.

The most common practice is the exchange of girls by their respective fathers as wives for each other's sons, or in some tribes the exchange of sisters, or of some female relatives by the young men themselves.'[1]

Similar evidence is provided by Curr and Lumholtz. Among the Narrinyeri, says another writer also quoted by Frazer, it is considered a humiliation for a woman not to be '*given away* in exchange',[2] and a wife acquired in any other way has a status little different from that of a prostitute in our society. Moreover, it is a general fact in Australia that a man cannot hope to obtain a wife if he has no sister, daughter or god-daughter to give in exchange. Brough Smyth draws a moving picture of the condition almost of despair to which the bachelor who fails to obtain a wife is reduced in spite of himself in Australian aboriginal society: 'A man who has no female relations that can be exchanged for a young woman of another tribe leads an unhappy life. Not only must he attend to his own wants, and share the discomforts of the bachelors' quarters, but he is an object of suspicion to the older men, who have perhaps two or three young wives to watch . . . There is the discontent and unrest of such a life, which makes him a dull companion, a quarrelsome friend, and a bitter enemy.'[3] In actual fact, as Frazer puts it,[4] the 'poor and desperate' bachelor who cannot obtain a wife in the normal manner by exchange is forced to lead the life of an outlaw, for his only chance lies in carrying off one of the women of his group, or in capturing a woman from another group. In both cases, however, the group will turn against him, either out of solidarity with the injured member, or through fear of trouble with other groups. Furthermore, the question anxiously discussed in the council of elders will be the same in both cases: where is a woman to be obtained to give in exchange for the one carried off or captured, in order to appease the original possessor? All these observations immediately call to mind others from other societies.[5]

The remarkable coincidence between the exchange of wives and the marriage of cross-cousins is shown not only in the theoretical analysis with which we have been concerned, but also in the data assembled by Frazer. In these circumstances, how is it that the hypothesis first formulated by Frazer did not immediately gain a wide acceptance? How is it that his far-reaching theory explaining cross-cousin marriage in terms of marriage by exchange was not immediately and definitively accepted? Moreover, why today does it seem to be abandoned in favour of other explanations?[6] In our opinion, Frazer clearly saw the correct course to take, but he never followed it right to the end. He gathered facts with a lucidity which leaves nothing to be

---

[1] ibid. p. 195.   [2] ibid. p. 196.   [3] ibid. pp. 197–8.   [4] ibid. p. 199.   [5] cf. ch. III.
[6] cf. for example Wedgwood, 1936*a* and 1936*b*. Wedgwood's argument that Frazer is contradicted by the Torres Straits Islanders and the New Guinea natives who exchange wives but prohibit cross-cousin marriage is fallacious. From the fact that cross-cousin marriage is a marriage by exchange, it does not follow that every marriage by exchange is effected between cross-cousins.

desired, but the interpretation he gave them is strangely narrow and disappointing considering all the possibilities available to him.

Seeing the connexion between cross-cousin marriage and marriage by exchange should have led to the discovery of the universal, permanent, and basic structure of marriage. By contrast, Frazer saw cross-cousin marriage as an historical form of marriage, marriage by exchange as another such form, and he concentrated on placing these, together with other forms such as dual organization and the classificatory system, in a temporal sequence, and on setting up causal connexions between them. What we regard as the means of escaping from cultural history he attempted to interpret as cultural history. The very thing we see as a necessary condition of society, he sought to analyse into stages of social evolution. It seems moreover that Frazer has some inkling of the possibilities laid open by his theory, but he mentions them only to recoil immediately in horror. With regard to Australian marriage classes, which are always even in number, he writes:

'This suggests, what all the evidence tends to confirm, that these various groups have been produced by the deliberate and repeated bisection of a community, first into two, then into four, and finally into eight exogamous and intermarrying groups or classes; for no one, so far as I know, has yet ventured to maintain that society is subject to a physical law, in virtue of which communities, like crystals, tend automatically and unconsciously to integrate or disintegrate, along rigid mathematical lines, into exactly symmetrical units.'[1]

We certainly would never think of comparing societies with crystals. But if, as we try to show here, it is true that the transition from nature to culture is determined by man's ability to think of biological relationships as systems of oppositions: opposition between the men who own and the women who are owned; opposition among the latter between wives who are acquired and sisters and daughters who are given away; opposition between two types of bond, i.e., bonds of alliance and bonds of kinship; opposition in the lineages, between the consecutive series (composed of individuals of the same sex) and the alternate series (where the sex changes in passing from one individual to another); and if it is true, finally, that exchange is the immediate result of these pairs of oppositions and that the dichotomy of cousins reflects the exchange, then no doubt it could be said that: 'Human societies tend automatically and unconsciously to disintegrate, along rigid mathematical lines, into exactly symmetrical units.' But perhaps it must be acknowledged that duality, alternation, opposition and symmetry, whether presented in definite forms or in imprecise forms, are not so much matters to be explained, as basic and immediate data of mental and social reality which should be the starting-point of any attempt at explanation.

The first fault in Frazer's interpretation rests in the dissociation which

[1] Frazer, 1919, vol. II, p. 231.

he makes, within cross-cousin marriage, between two problems which according to him have only a contingent connexion. For him, the question why cross-cousins can marry has absolutely nothing to do with the question why parallel cousins cannot. He sees these questions as so distinct that he studies them in two different chapters, and has two different explanations, one to account for the preference, and one for prohibition. Frazer does not hesitate to generalize from facts found in Australian aboriginal society: 'It seems reasonable to suppose that in all Australian tribes which permitted or favoured the marriage of cross-cousins, such marriages were the direct consequence of the interchange of sisters in marriage and of nothing else. And that interchange of sisters flowed directly from the economic necessity of paying for a wife in kind, in other words of giving a woman in return for the woman whom a man received in marriage.'[1] As marriage by exchange is found in connexion with cross-cousin marriage in numerous other societies, for example, the Madiga and the Idiga of Mysore, several tribes from Barwani, and the district of Almora, in the United Provinces of India, and also several tribes from Assam and Baluchistan, and as, on the other hand, marriage by exchange is itself a widespread institution found among the western Torres Straits islanders, the Mowat, the Banaro of New Guinea, in Buin, among the Pededarimu of Kiwai, the Santal of Bengal, the Senoufo and Mossi of the Sudan, in Sumatra, and finally in modern Palestine, the conclusion can be reached that, as among the Kariera of Australia, where the connexion is particularly clear, 'the marriage of cross-cousins flows directly and simply in the ordinary course of events, from the interchange of sisters in marriage'.[2]

But why did Frazer, having thus set out the basic explanatory principle, abandon it immediately as being inadequate? As a matter of fact, he writes: 'But if we have found an answer to the question, Why is the marriage of cross-cousins so commonly favoured? we have still to find an answer to the question, Why is the marriage of ortho-cousins so commonly forbidden?'[3] As we shall see, not only does his answer to this second question have nothing to do with the first, but it seems that even in propounding it Frazer was caught up in a host of contradictions, and lost all the ground that he had previously gained. But first let us ask ourselves why exchange, which seemed to us to allow the dichotomy of cousins to be directly deduced, seems to Frazer to be connected exclusively with cross-cousins, and not at all with parallel cousins.

There are two basic differences between Frazer's concept of exchange and the concept which we ourselves have proposed. Both these differences arise from the fact that whereas we see exchange as a mere aspect of a total structure of reciprocity which (in circumstances still to be specified) was immediately and intuitively apprehended by social man, Frazer sees it as just one of many institutions in an evolutionary series. Let us elaborate this point.

[1] ibid. p. 209.   [2] loc. cit.   [3] ibid. p. 221.

For Frazer, marriage by exchange is not a primitive institution, but was preceded by other forms of marriage such as promiscuity, consanguineous marriage, and group marriage. It appeared only when the 'society progressed from group marriage, or from still laxer forms of commerce between the sexes, to individual marriage'.[1] In the second place, Frazer conceives of the exchange of wives as a convenient solution to the economic problem of how to obtain a wife. He repeatedly asserts that the exchange of sisters and daughters 'was everywhere at first a simple case of barter.'[2] He depicts the poor Australian aborigine wondering how he is going to obtain a wife since he has no material goods with which to purchase her, and discovering exchange as the solution to this apparently insoluble problem: 'Men exchanged their sisters in marriage because that was the cheapest way of getting a wife.'[3] This economic concept of exchange appears again in Frazer's conclusion, since, when all is said and done, his recognition of a necessary connexion between exchange and cross-cousin marriage is based on the universality of economic laws: 'For under the surface alike of savagery and of civilization the economic forces are as constant and uniform in their operation as the forces of nature, of which, indeed, they are merely a peculiarly complex manifestation.'[4]

In this work, we have constantly sought to show that, far from exchange being a form of purchase, purchase must be seen as a form of exchange. Because Frazer was happy to give his primitive man the mentality of the *Homo Œconomicus* as conceived of by nineteenth-century philosophers he completely failed to see the solidarity between the preference for cross-cousins and the prohibition of parallel cousins: 'Regarded from the purely economic point of view there seems to be no difference between the women',[5] he writes of the two kinds of cousins. But it is precisely from the economic viewpoint that exchange should not be envisaged. Frazer first postulates the existence of economic goods, including women, and he asserts that from the economic viewpoint it makes no difference whether sisters are exchanged between cross-cousins or between parallel cousins. There is no doubt but that it leads to an impasse. By contrast, our first postulate is the awareness of an opposition between two types of woman, or rather between two types of relationship in which a man may stand with a woman. She may, on the one hand, be a sister or a daughter, i.e., a woman given, or on the other, a wife, i.e., a woman received. To put it in other words, she is either a kinswoman or a relative by marriage. We have shown how this primitive opposition is used to build up a structure of reciprocity, according to which the group which has received must give, and the group which has given can demand. In this way we have established that, whatever the group, parallel cousins come from families in the same formal position, which is a position of static equilibrium, while cross-cousins come from families in conflicting

---

[1] Frazer, 1919, vol. II, p. 203.   [2] ibid. p. 220.   [3] ibid. p. 254.
[4] ibid. p. 220.   [5] ibid. p. 221.

formal positions, i.e., in relationship to one another they are in a dynamic disequilibrium, which is the inheritance of kinship, and which alliance alone has the power to resolve. The exchange relationship comes before the things exchanged, and is independent of them. If the goods considered in isolation are identical, they cease to be so when assigned their proper place in the structure of reciprocity.

Thus Frazer is faced with an insoluble difficulty when he comes across a marriage system such as among the Buin of the Solomon Islands, where the exchange of women, instead of being substituted for purchase, is, on the contrary, superimposed upon it. It is true that he suggests that when goods of identical value are transferred, the two purchases cancel one another out as if they did not exist: 'If two men pay each other half-a-crown, the net result is precisely the same as if they had neither paid nor received anything.'[1] But in Erromanga and several regions of central and eastern Asia, where exchanges of women are between districts and not families, it is not merely a question of goods of the same value being doubly transacted, but the same objects accompany the transfer of wives, both coming and going. It is therefore an operation which is not only null from the economic point of view, but absurd. By contrast, the whole thing becomes very clear when it is acknowledged that it is the exchange which counts and not the things exchanged. As Frazer puts it on another occasion, 'the strictly mercantile, not to say mercenary, character of these connubial transactions lies on the surface'.[2] But one can go further still, for Frazer's hypothesis is contradictory. He purports to prove the great antiquity of cross-cousin marriage by assuming the origin of the exchange of women to be in groups so primitive that women were the only objects of value available: 'In the general poverty characteristic of low savagery a man had practically no other lawful mode of obtaining a wife.'[3] From this he concludes that cross-cousin marriage began under a system of 'extreme ignorance and extreme poverty, if not in absolute destitution'.[4] We more than agree on the extreme primitiveness of marriage by exchange. In such circumstances, however, with Frazer supposing a form of humanity so rudimentary as to have no means of payment, how was exchange substituted for purchase? Where did the notion of purchase itself arise? In point of fact, Frazer pictures an abstract individual with an economic awareness, and he then takes him back through the ages to a distant time when there were neither riches nor means of payment. In this paradoxical situation he has him discover, in a prophetic vision, an anticipatory substitute for the woman's worth in the woman herself. But actually there is nothing in the exchange of women faintly resembling a reasoned solution to an economic problem (although it can acquire this function in societies which have already learnt in some other way what purchase and sale are). It is a primitive and indivisible act of awareness which sees the daughter or

[1] ibid. p. 220, n. 1.   [2] ibid. p. 218.
[3] ibid. p. 245.   [4] ibid. p. 220, n. 2.

sister as a valuable which is offered, and vice versa the daughter and sister of someone else as a valuable which may be demanded.

This false interpretation of the origin of exchange comes, as we have said, from the fact that Frazer sees exchange itself as a derivative phenomenon, arising from calculation and reflection. It is this same narrowly historical outlook which must have prompted him to seek the origin of the prohibition of marriage between parallel cousins outside exchange. According to him, its origin is to be found in dual organization, which is 'practically universal' in Australia, and 'sufficiently prevalent' in Melanesia to be recognized as a factor in this region also; and it will be remembered that in a system with exogamous moieties parallel cousins belong necessarily to the same moiety, and cross-cousins to different moieties. Frazer does not hesitate to infer that dual organization formerly existed in Asia, Africa and America, this being vouched for, according to him, by the wide diffusion in these regions of totemic exogamy and the classificatory kinship system.[1] Let us grant his suggestion that dual organization formerly extended through 'a half or more than a half of the habitable globe'.[2] What is its origin? Frazer replies that it is to prevent consanguineous marriages, firstly, between brothers and sisters (first division of the group into two classes), then between parents and children (second division of the group into two classes), and finally between cross-cousins (the Aranda system of Australia with the division of the group into eight marriage classes). There is no doubt that the dual system does lead to the placing of brothers and sisters in the category of prohibited spouses, nor that the organization with four marriage classes achieves the same result for that one of the two parents (the father in a matrilineal system, and the mother in a patrilineal system) who is not affected by the prohibition in a two-class system, nor finally, that the organization with eight classes extends the prohibition on parallel cousins to cross-cousins. This whole series of assertions is based on the following principle: 'At least these were certainly amongst the effects produced by the successive divisions, and from the effects it is legitimate to argue back to the intentions.'[3]

The least that can be said of this principle is that it constitutes a remarkably radical conversion to a sociological doctrine of final causes. But to us this conversion seems to go as far beyond what is admissible as the narrowly historical attitude of the preceding argument seemed to fall short. For intentions to be legitimately inferred from results, there must at least be a certain equivalence between the observed results and the supposed intentions. Thus it is possible that the division of the group into four marriage classes has its origin in a growing awareness, be it clear or confused, of a new system of oppositions replacing terms previously thought of as identical.

But how can the same reasoning be applied to the prohibition on marriage between brothers and sisters, and to the first (and also most widespread)

[1] Frazer, 1919, vol. II, pp. 222–3.   [2] ibid. p. 223.   [3] ibid. pp. 232–3.

division of the group into two exogamous moieties? In this case, the supposed intention corresponds to only a very small part of the result, and if the result is to be expressed in terms of intention this intention must be supposed to have been very different.

Dual organization finds expression in a division of collateral relatives into two categories, those with whom it is possible to contract marriage, and those with whom it is impossible. This latter category includes brothers and sisters together with parallel cousins. Accordingly, it is arbitrary to decide that the purpose of the institution is to prohibit marriage between brothers and sisters, and that the prohibition of parallel cousins appears in the picture only as an accident. The opposite could just as well be true. If the intention was only to prohibit brother and sister incest, all that would have been needed was to prohibit it quite straightforwardly, without setting up a prodigiously cumbersome institution which eliminates one, two, or three undesirable spouses only by prohibiting at the same time roughly half the available men or women. If dual organization, which forbids me to marry half the women of my group, had really been instituted only to prevent me from marrying my sister, it must be recognized that there is a remarkable incoherency in the minds of those who thought it up interspersed with the foresight so freely attributed to them. Actually, dual organization is either useless – which is a defensible thesis – or else it is useful precisely because of its result, and it is entirely useful in this regard. To claim, on the one hand, that dual organization was consciously intended and conceived of, and on the other, that it was intended and conceived of for only a small fraction of its attendant results (even though this fraction might so easily have been ensured by other means, as indeed it has been in many societies), is an unacceptable position both from the point of view of the historical succession of institutions and from the point of view of a legislative will. But if, as we believe, the function of dual organization is solely to produce those consequences which it actually does produce, then it must obviously be acknowledged that this function is not to eliminate a degree of kinship as being too close. Brothers and sisters are closer than the parallel cousins with whom they are identified, while parallel cousins are as close as the cross-cousins from whom, however, they are differentiated. If there is any *raison d'être* of dual organization, it is to be found only in a common quality, shared by brothers and sisters and by parallel cousins, whereby both these groups are opposed *in exactly the same way* to the group of cross-cousins. This common quality cannot be biological proximity. We have found this common quality in the fact that brothers and sisters, like parallel cousins, are similarly oriented, and bear the same sign within a structure of reciprocity, in some way thus cancelling one another out, while cross-cousins bear opposite and complementary signs. Keeping to this metaphor, it could thus be said that they attract each other.

We shall let Frazer himself expose the greatest weakness in his system:

'The general cause which I have assumed for the successive changes in marriage customs which we have now passed under review is a growing aversion to the marriage of persons nearly related to each other by blood. Into the origin of that aversion I shall not here inquire; the problem is one of the darkest and most difficult in the whole history of society.'[1]

In short, then, he saw cross-cousin marriage and marriage by exchange as originating in the prohibition of incest. The exchange of sisters, and the consequent preference for cross-cousins, are seen as an increasingly general practice, resulting from widespread condemnation of marriage between brothers and sisters. The prohibition of parallel cousins results immediately from the setting up of dual organization, which itself is enacted to sanction the growing public feeling. Consequently, the immediate origins of the preference and of the prohibition are different, one deriving from morals, the other from law. But their primary origin is held to be the same, in both cases being an answer to 'the growing aversion' in the group against consanguineous marriage. We shall not even insist upon the fact that the hypothesis of consanguineous marriage as a social institution is purely hypothetical, as too is the hypothesis of group marriage which Frazer invokes to account for the classificatory kinship system. Actually, this whole reconstruction is circular: the appearance of marriage by exchange put an end to group marriage; the establishment of cross-cousin marriage was a consequence of marriage by exchange; the appearance of dual organization sanctioned the practice of cross-cousin marriage; finally, 'the classificatory system of relationship flows directly from the organization of society in two exogamous classes'.[2] Nevertheless, when he posed the question of the origin of the classificatory system, Frazer's answer was extremely precise: 'It appears to have originated in, and to reflect as in a mirror, a system of group marriage.'[3]

Above all, the interpretation proposed by Frazer hangs upon the thread of an enigma, for if cross-cousin marriage was introduced as a preliminary attempt at eliminating incestuous unions, there is nothing to explain why these incestuous unions themselves were regarded as an evil which had to be suppressed. Frazer merely made repeated reference to the 'growing sentiment' against this type of marriage. It is this unexplainable and unexplained 'growing sentiment' which ultimately is the cornerstone of the system. By contrast, we have maintained that a rigorous analysis of cross-cousin marriage should reveal the ultimate nature of the incest prohibition.

II

However, we have been careful to eliminate all historical speculation, all research into origins, and all attempts to reconstruct a hypothetical order in which institutions succeeded one another. By according cross-cousin marriage

[1] Frazer, 1919, vol. II, pp. 245–6.   [2] ibid. p. 245.   [3] ibid. p. 230.

the prime position in our demonstration we have postulated neither its former universality nor its relative anteriority with respect to other forms of marriage. Furthermore, we do not believe that our assertion that there is a connexion between cross-cousin marriage and the exchange of wives leaves us open to the criticisms levelled at Frazer's conception, which is at least superficially analogous. The fact that marriage by exchange often coincides with a prohibition against marriage between all types of cousins has been invoked against this conception. To our way of thinking, Frazer was right in being on his guard against cases where cross-cousin marriage seemed to be excluded. Recent sociological inquiries in South America clearly prove that, as Frazer foresaw, cross-cousin marriage is even more widespread than formerly suspected. These are often groups about which little has been known and about which negative and sometimes contradictory evidence has been given. Thus it is wise, as Frazer recommends, when faced with sources relating to a given group, some stating that marriage between cross-cousins is prohibited and others expressly stating that it is allowed, to keep in mind that some early observers would have paid attention solely to the prohibition of marriage between parallel cousins, while others would have seen only the concomitant practice of cross-cousin marriage. In a theory such as ours, in which the apprehension of a certain logical structure is made the fundamental basis of marriage customs, it is important to note that this structure is often visible even in systems in which it has not materialized in a concrete form.

Cases which Frazer himself noted of marriage by exchange in which, however, cousins are indiscriminately grouped among the prohibited degrees could prove more troublesome. In certain Torres Straits islands and in New Guinea the exchange of wives is also associated with the prohibition of cousins. But once again, these facts can be advanced against Frazer who makes marriage by exchange a historical stage in the evolution of marriage, the marriage of cross-cousins another such historical stage, and establishes a cause and effect relationship between the two. There may be good cause to wonder why it is, if cross-cousin marriage is a consequence of marriage by exchange, that one may be found without the other being necessarily associated with it. But we have asserted nothing of the sort. We have seen exchange, considered not in the technical form of the institution called 'marriage by exchange' but in its general aspect as a phenomenon of reciprocity, as the *universal form* of marriage. Further, we have not studied cross-cousin marriage as a primitive, archaic, relatively ancient, or recent expression of this form, but as a *special case* showing particularly clearly that reciprocity is present behind all marriages. We have given proof of this characteristic of cross-cousin marriage by adopting a double viewpoint: firstly by showing that the dichotomy of cousins into assigned and prohibited spouses may be directly deduced from the relationship between two or more families, once this relationship is conceived of as a structure of reciprocity; and secondly by emphasizing that through its logical qualities, the institution of cross-cousin marriage occupies an exceptional position, placed as it were at the bifurcation leading to two extreme types of reciprocity, viz., dual organization and the prohibition of incest.

But to insist that this special case was the first to appear, or that, at one time or another, it had universal existence, is wholly unsubstantiated. The physicist who formulates a law knows well that strictly it will never be proved, except in the laboratory, and that only approximate examples of it are to be found in nature. In this, the sociologist is more fortunate than the physicist – an opportunity so rare that it would be wrong not to try to extract the greatest possible advantage from it. Social experiment frequently gives rise to cross-cousin marriage in a very pure form, and its very frequency would in itself be enough to warrant surprise. If cross-cousin marriage had not been practised by any of the earth's people, it would no doubt have been much more difficult to determine the law of reciprocity at the origin of marriage rules. But supposing this law had been discovered, there would have been no difficulty in deducing *a priori* the formula for cross-cousin marriage, as providing the simplest conceivable expression of the law. The fact that this formula had not been discovered by any human society would easily have been explained by the gap separating theory from humble reality, and no one would have asked why crude and primitive populations failed to conceive of such a simple but precise method. The large number of societies which successfully elaborated this strict expression certainly may be admired, but it should not cause surprise that others were never successful.

The conception we propose has the advantage of accounting not only for the dichotomy of cousins, but also for all the other systems of identification or dissociation usually accompanying it. The principle of reciprocity explains the distinction of uncles and aunts, male and female cousins, and nephews and nieces, into cross and parallel, instead of the usual constraint to interpret the dissociation appearing in the generation preceding that of Ego, and in the succeeding generation, as a consequence of the dissociation operating in Ego's own. In point of fact, the principle of reciprocity acts simultaneously on three levels. Let us first consider the generation preceding Ego's. In the structure of reciprocity, the father's brother occupies the same position as the father (both have received wives and given sisters) and the mother's sister occupies the same position as the mother (both have been, or may be, received as wives and given as sisters). But the mother's brother occupies an inverse position to that of the mother, for whatever the system of descent may be, one is the giver or receiver, the other is the received or given, and the same relationship exists between the father and the father's sister (although not strictly, as we shall see elsewhere). Thus, returning to the formula in Fig. 6, it can be said that the sign remains the same whether it be $(+)$ or $(-)$, in passing from the father to the father's brother or from the mother to the mother's sister, whereas the sign changes in passing from the mother to her brother or from the father to his sister. The former are identifiable in a terminology based on a system of oppositions, while the latter must be distinguished. We have already shown how the oppositions of sign and the parallelisms are reversed in the following generation, the general structure remaining the same. This constant configuration, in passing from the preceding generation to Ego's generation, obviously continues, at the price of a new inversion of signs, in passing from Ego's generation to the nephews' generation, as seen in the example (Fig. 7), in which Ego has a right to his sister's daughter,

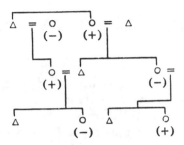

Fig. 7. The concept of crossing.

because he has given his sister to be his niece's mother, while he must give away his own daughter because he has received his daughter's mother as his wife. If we had taken Ego's maternal uncle as our subject and not Ego, the general structure would remain the same, all the signs, however, being reversed, as can easily be seen.

2 · *Australia*

CHAPTER XI

The Classical Systems

I

The term 'restricted exchange' includes any system which effectively or functionally divides the group into a certain number of pairs of exchange-units so that, for any one pair X-Y there is a reciprocal exchange relationship. In other words, where an X man marries a Y woman, a Y man must always be able to marry an X woman. The simplest form of restricted exchange is found in the division of the group into patrilineal or matrilineal exogamous moieties. If we suppose that a dichotomy based upon one of the two modes of descent is superimposed upon a dichotomy based upon the other the result will be a four-section system instead of a two-moiety system. If the same process were repeated, the group would comprise eight sections instead of four. This is a regular progression and embodies nothing faintly resembling a change in principle or a sudden upheaval. We have already considered the first stages in this process during our analysis of the connexions between unilineal and bilineal descent.[1]

At that stage we made an observation which should now be developed, viz., that the transition from a moiety system to a four-class system does not necessarily modify the rules of marriage. The preferred spouse tends to be defined in a more strict and limited way in one case, and in a vaguer and more tolerant way in the other, as one or other cross-cousin (the father's sister's daughter or the mother's brother's daughter), who may be (and most probably is) one and the same. Of course, a class system and the marriage rules do not always coincide. For example, the Dieri, with their dual organization, have the same marriage prohibitions as the Aranda with eight subsections. This is also the case in certain groups having the four-class system. For the time being the discussion of this problem, which led Radcliffe-Brown to deny that classes had anything to do with the regulation of marriage, will be left entirely to one side. The fact remains that in an eight-class system of the Aranda type, marriage between cross-cousins is automatically impossible, while there is nothing in a four-class system (except contingent marriage prohibitions and the kinship system) to prohibit it. From this negative standpoint, the two-class and the four-class systems are equivalent.

[1] ch. VIII.

In both, the class system considered as such prohibits the same types of collateral relatives (brothers and sisters and parallel cousins) and leaves the same types in the category of spouses sanctioned by the system (cross-cousins and those identified with them). Restricted exchange thus poses a quite disturbing theoretical problem: what is the relationship between the moiety system and the four-class system? How does it come about that in passing from one to the other there is no dichotomy of possible spouses? More especially, how is it that systems of restricted exchange do not take into account the duality between patrilateral and matrilateral cross-cousins?

Australia is ideal for studying these questions, for two reasons. Firstly, it provides particularly precise and explicit examples of the different systems of restricted exchange, viz., dual organization, the four-section system, and the eight-subsection system. Secondly, some Australian tribes distinguish between patrilateral and matrilateral cross-cousins, a distinction, however, which does not seem to follow from any of the preceding types. This occurs in several north Australian tribes, particularly those in Arnhem Land studied by Warner and Webb. These groups have an eight-class marriage organization sometimes disguised as a four-class organization, but only, it would seem, because the subsections are not always named.

Generally known as the Murngin system, these forms attract our attention for a special reason. This system has often been distinguished from other Australian systems as excluding the exchange of sisters. Our whole interpretation of kinship systems has the notion of exchange as its universal and fundamental basis. On a continent which otherwise seems most favourable to our thesis, the Murngin system poses an important problem which cannot be ignored.

The immense amount of work carried out in the last few years in Australia by Radcliffe-Brown and the famous *Oceania* team has given incomparably rich and detailed information on Australian kinship systems, to a large extent obviating the sociologist's reliance upon the often obscure pioneer studies of Howitt, Mathews, Spencer and Gillen, etc. But even among modern investigators there is no one who would claim that the typology of the systems is perfectly clear, or that their relationships have been definitively established. In this respect, the last fifteen years seem rather to have complicated the situation. In 1931, Radcliffe-Brown proposed the following general classification:

1. Systems with two matrilineal exogamous moieties
2. systems with two patrilineal exogamous moieties
3. four-section systems:
   (*a*) with named matrilineal moieties
   (*b*) with named patrilineal moieties
   (*c*) without named moieties
4. eight-subsection systems

   5. systems with four named patrilineal semi-moieties
   6. systems with two endogamous alternating divisions, and
   7. systems without named divisions.[1]

However, several years later Lawrence came to the conclusion that there were eleven systems divided into two principal groups: on the one hand, systems without marriage classes, comprising five types, and on the other, systems with marriage classes, comprising six types, the latter themselves divided into three categories:

I. Systems without classes:
   (*a*) unilateral marriage without the exchange of sisters
   (*b*) systems without classes or matrilineal dichotomy
   (*c*) systems with matrilineal clans
   (*d*) systems without matrilineal clans, and
   (*e*) systems with alternating generations.

II. Systems with classes:
   A. *Eight-class systems:*
   (*a*) eight named subsections
   (*b*) four named sections divided into eight unnamed subsections, and
   (*c*) four patrilineal semi-moieties divided into eight unnamed subsections.

   B. *Four-class systems:*
   (*a*) four sections, and
   (*b*) two patrilineal moieties divided into four unnamed sections.

   C. *Two-class systems:*
   (*a*) two matrilineal moieties.[2]

These differences derive from differences in the interpretation of two basic points, viz., the relationship between patrilineal and matrilineal descent on the one hand, and systems with classes and systems without classes on the other.

II

Radcliffe-Brown has shown very clearly that the basic unit of Australian aboriginal society is the local group, or 'horde'. The horde consists of a group of brothers, their sons and unmarried daughters, and their sons' daughters. Although living in the horde, their wives and their sons' wives actually come from a neighbouring horde, because of the law of exogamy, and they continue to belong to their fathers' and brothers' group. The horde can thus be defined as a patrilineal group, exploiting a certain territory over which it has exclusive rights. There is no political unit superimposed upon the horde. The tribe is defined purely linguistically: it includes all the hordes speaking roughly the same dialect, but it does not exist beyond this awareness

---

[1] Radcliffe-Brown, 1931, pp. 41–2.   [2] Lawrence, 1937, pp. 319–54.

of a linguistic community. It has neither political organization nor territorial rights. Strictly speaking, if there is such a thing as a tribal territory, it is only in so far as 'the territory of the tribe is the total of the territories of its component hordes'.[1]

Hence, the basis of Australian society is held to be territorial and patrilineal. Accordingly, Pink was able to speak of the Northern Aranda as 'landowners', among whom the 'ancestral clan estate' and the patrilineal line by which it is transmitted together with the ritual, play a leading rôle in both the collective and individual life: 'It not only binds families, using that word in its most limited sense . . . but also the whole clan.'[2] We must turn to her analysis of relationships of reciprocity between different totemic clans in order to reply to the objection formulated by Thomson who asserts that the clan came before the horde. The horde, he says, consists of all the male members of the clan. Their wives, who are members of the horde but not of the clan must be added, and their daughters and married sisters, who are members of the clan but have left the horde, must be subtracted: 'It is clear, therefore, that although the horde is the war-making group, the clan, and not the horde, is the landowning group; a clan is a stable, permanent, structural unit of society; but the horde is unstable; it is a sociological entity the membership of which is constantly changing.'[3] Thus, the solidarity of the clan based on descent, the totemic cult, and the territory is contrasted with the solidarity of the horde based on marriage, the family, the sexual division of labour, and war. In point of fact, however, the importance attached by the Northern Aranda to the *kutuŋula* relationship[4] between a man and his father's sister's son is enough to show that the two types of organization are not antagonistic.

The question is not so much whether it is the horde or the clan which should be considered the real landowning group, but which of these two patrilineal groups is at the basis of the social organization. All contemporary observers agree that a double matrilineal and patrilineal dichotomy exists and functions in Australian societies. Radcliffe-Brown and Lawrence are at one on this point, but they disagree on the question of priority. Lawrence proposed a hypothetical sequence: matrilineal totemic clans without moieties – moieties with matrilineal clans – sections with or without matrilineal clans – subsections.[5] This is in complete disagreement with the basic rôle which Radcliffe-Brown ascribes to the patrilineal horde. Nevertheless, there is no question that 'the vast majority, and perhaps all of the peoples of Australia were organized primarily on a basis of patrilocal-patrilineal land-holding hordes'.[6] Consequently, it is argued, the rule of descent (patrilineal or matrilineal) is secondary to the rule of residence.

As we see it, the disagreement is only a question of method. When

---

[1] Radcliffe-Brown, 1931, p. 36.   [2] Pink, 1936, p. 303.
[3] Thomson, 1935, pp. 462–3, n. 4.   [4] Pink, 1936, p. 291.
[5] Lawrence, 1937, p. 346.   [6] Kroeber, 1938, pp. 302–3.

Radcliffe-Brown starts with the concrete observation of groups and asserts the generality of the horde and its sociological and psychological reality, the validity of his observation can scarcely be doubted. Lawrence starts with a more formal point of view and adopts the notion of the exchange of sisters as the common basis of all Australian systems. Consequently, it is the matrilineal dichotomy, considered as the constant form of dichotomy (since the local sections may vary in number) which seems vital to him. Lawrence is justified in adopting the notion of exchange as the starting-point of his analysis. But he interprets it exclusively in terms of restricted exchange, thus making the Murngin system unintelligible, as is shown in the following passage dealing with regions practising 'unilateral' marriage (i.e., with the mother's brother's daughter exclusively):

'The latter are of recent discovery, and are as yet ill understood. In each case the report is inadequate, yielding no proper explanation of how marriages complete a cycle through the hordes nor any acceptable articulation of kinship terms either to patri-clans or to divisions resembling those of neighbours who practise marriage by sister exchange. This seems to indicate some measure of antiquity with local modification by borrowing. Further comment appears premature pending accurate description.'[1]

But it is Lawrence's conception of sister-exchange which is defective, not the descriptions of the Murngin system. We shall try to show that the latter system is also based upon exchange, and for this reason we shall have to widen considerably Lawrence's narrow definition of exchange, taken in the restricted sense. At the same time, it will appear that exchange, in its generalized form, can take place between patrilineal hordes as well as between matrilineal moieties, and that, in terms of formal analysis, the question of priority is secondary. Kroeber made an observation on this point but it is possible to subscribe to it only in part. He says of four-class or eight-class systems that

'the concepts patrilineal and matrilineal become wholly inapplicable, except where moiety names persist in addition to sectional or subsectional names, and in many cases they do not. In brief, where there are four sections or eight subsections the patrilineal or matrilineal moieties appear to be names or historical relics rather than socially functioning units.'[2]

From this he concludes that exogamy, dual organization, clans and totemism are epiphenomena, secondary to the basic structures, the most important of which he sees as the rule of residence.[3] His whole conclusion should be quoted:

'I submit that, in addition to unilateral descent reckoning, much of the formalized social organization of primitive peoples is in the nature of unconscious experiment and play of fashion rather than the core or

[1] Lawrence, 1937, p. 345.   [2] Kroeber, 1938, p. 305.   [3] ibid. p. 307.

substance of their culture. In certain cases, as in Australia, it may well represent the pinnacle of their achievement, just as experiment and play with abstractions, words, and plastic forms resulted in the pinnacles of Greek civilization, while science, technology, and the control or exploitation of nature are those of our own. But pinnacles are end products, not bases.'[1]

Kroeber has taken up the same idea in a recent study where he compares the complex forms of social organization in certain primitive societies with 'the play of earnest children.'[2]

In this text, which is one of the most important to be found for the illustration of certain intellectual attitudes of contemporary sociology, there is a strange mixture of perspicacity and caution. If patrilineal or matrilineal descent, dual organization, etc., are really in a sense (and contrary to traditional sociological thinking) secondary phenomena, this secondariness arises not from their being compared with obviously primary phenomena, but in respect of the relationships uniting them. These relationships, and these alone, can be said to be the true 'raw materials' of social life. We, too, have compared dual organization with children's games,[3] not to relegate it to any insignificant and secondary position, but just the opposite, to show that behind dual organization, regarded as an institution limited in its forms and in its distribution, there are a certain number of logical structures the recurrence of which in modern society, and at different ages in life, proves it to be both fundamental and universal.

For us, then, the question of the priority in Australia of the patrilineal or of the matrilineal dichotomy respectively is much less important than the fact that it is possible, according to the standpoint adopted, to make a choice of either view. Radcliffe-Brown's 'local group' interpretation has the great advantage at least of showing that territorial rights are not incompatible with primitive forms of life and organization.[4] But it does not follow from our previous remarks that the logical and historical approaches are interchangeable. To interpret the system using either approach has irrevocable consequences once the choice has been made.[5] In the following chapters we shall see that the transition from a restricted to a generalized conception of exchange does away with this apparent contradiction, and that logical analysis and historical analysis are both possible when the local group, considered as the basic element in Australian systems, is used as the starting-point.

The second question raised at the beginning of this chapter – viz., whether organizations without classes are more or less primitive than those with classes – must be treated in the same way. The study of geographical distri-

---

[1] ibid. p. 309.   [2] ibid. 1942, p. 215.
[3] cf. ch. VII.   [4] cf. on this point Davidson, 1928a, pp. 614–31.
[5] cf. ch. XIX which is a development of this point of view with regard to the evolution of the Chinese system.

bution would readily suggest the former possibility. The tribes with neither moieties nor sections occupy six coastal, i.e., peripheral, areas in the north, west and south of the Australian continent. From this it might readily be concluded that classless systems are the older form.[1] However, the areas without marriage classes are not homogeneous, and more often than not the marriage rules practised there are the same as those which would result from classes or sections. Radcliffe-Brown accordingly considers them to be later developments, as modified forms of a Kariera-type system.[2] Howitt also believed this but for a less legitimate reason: for him the absence of classes implied individual marriage, which he thought was derived from group marriage.[3]

We shall return to this problem in detail when we discuss the Mara system.[4] For the time being we shall limit ourselves to a general statement: to answer the problem too dogmatically would be to overlook certain striking features in the development of Australian systems. There is nothing to prove that this development extended over hundreds or thousands of years or that it is necessary to give to systems without classes and to systems with classes an absolute position in time. They have the same result but employ different methods, based sometimes on the notion of class and sometimes on that of relation. But it is perfectly conceivable that one and the same group, while maintaining a basically stable system of reciprocity, might frequently have oscillated, over a period of time, between one method and the other. The absence of class is not a negative characteristic but the result of a preference for another procedure of similar functional value. It is a superficial or, in Kroeber's sense, secondary characteristic. These views are not wholly theoretical. There are cases in which tribes with eight classes have reverted to a four-class system, tribes with four classes have reverted to a two-class system, and tribes with two classes have adopted a new regulation of marriage between clans of the same moiety.[5] Above all, recent observations have revealed the rapid diffusion of marriage systems from one group to another, and efforts at adaptation between different systems, all of which supposes a good deal of original invention.

III

In this regard the Murinbata along the northern coastline are a striking example of how Australian aboriginal systems (and no doubt many others) must have originated and spread. Today the Murinbata have a system characterized by a division into eight subsections, matrilineal totemic groups, and preferential marriage with the sister's son's daughter. Radcliffe-Brown considers this form of marriage to be peculiar to the north-western coast of

---

[1] Davidson, 1926, pp. 529–48; 1928b; Lawrence, 1937, pp. 345–6.
[2] Radcliffe-Brown, 1931, p. 368.   [3] Howitt, 1907, p. 284.   [4] cf. ch. XIII.
[5] Lawrence, 1937, p. 346.

Australia.[1] However, it is to be noted that it corresponds with the theoretical conditions of marriage in societies with eight subsections. If my sister has married according to this type of marriage (i.e., in the second ascending generation), my preferential wife will be both my sister's son's daughter and my father's mother's brother's son's daughter. Nevertheless, Stanner has shown that the whole Murinbata system has been borrowed, and his description of the psychological atmosphere in which systems which might appear to be pure abstractions evolve deserves to remain a classic.

Tribes living on the fringe of the subsection area feel inferior for not having subsections and for not understanding how they work. The belief that they marry *wadzi*, 'wrongly', is implanted in their minds, and the imposing apparatus of subsections, together with the corresponding marriage rules and forms of totemism, seems somehow superior to their traditional system.[2] The Murinbata and the Nangiomeri frankly admit that their new system still puzzles them:

> 'Informants are continually being checked and corrected by other informants. Less knowledgeable natives than the "heads" clumsily try to bequeath the matrilineal *ŋulu* totems patrilineally, much as they tend to think of the subsections as descending on indirect patrilineal instead of indirect matrilineal principles.'[3]

The Murinbata experience particular difficulty in understanding that the *ŋulu* totems can belong to members of the two patrilineal moieties, a theory borrowed from the Djamindjung during the last twenty years. One aborigine, returning to his group after ten years in prison, found himself in an almost pathetic predicament. He knew nothing of the new order, of the workings of the *ŋulu* (totems) and of the *ŋinipun* (subsections), and for this was ridiculed by the young reformers. And further, meanwhile, the belief is becoming established that there are physical likenesses between members of the same totemic clan.[4]

The original system[5] was of the Kariera type, except that cross-cousins of the first remove were prohibited as spouses and were called 'mother' and 'mother's brother'. Hence, classificatory cross-cousins were the only conventional spouses, and only two patrilineal lines were recognized, as in the Kariera system, viz., that of the mother's father (*thamun*) and that of the father's father (*kangul*). Consequently, the problem for the Murinbata is how to make a system with eight classes, and its concomitant marriage and totemic rules, function in a system which in part at least renders the subsection system superfluous. The question whether the subsections are basically totemic groups or marriage classes is meaningless, for 'the subsections are

[1] Radcliffe-Brown, 1931, p. 53.   [2] Stanner, 1936, p. 186.
[3] ibid. p. 196.   [4] ibid. pp. 199, 202.
[5] The reader unfamiliar with the theory of Australian systems would be well advised to leave the study of the Murinbata example until he has finished reading the chapter.

spreading specifically as marriage groupings ... [and] as a new marriage convention'.[1] This supports our theoretical position.

The first step in this adaptation is a gradual adjustment of the vocabulary of the system, but it has been only partially successful. The subsection system is as follows:

Fig. 8. Murinbata marriage rules.

Masculine subsections are in upper case, feminine subsections are in lower case. The arrows indicate indirect matrilineal descent and the = sign denotes preferential marriages.

In the new system, a *TJANAMA* must regard a *nauola* as his only possible wife (in doing so, he acquires his sister's son's daughter, who will usually be *nauola*). At the same time he continues to regard a classificatory cross-cousin (in this case *nangala*) as an appropriate spouse. Likewise, a *TJALYERI* will waver between a *namira* and a *nabidjin*. There seems then to be a movement towards a polygyny based upon the adding together of the previous alliances (classificatory cross-cousins) and the new alliances (sister's son's daughter, mother's brother's daughter's daughter's daughter). From this arise difficulties which obsess the aborigines, and, as Stanner notes of another phenomenon, appear to them 'as ... riddles of which only others know the answers'.[2] For example, in a normal eight-subsection system the grandson would reproduce his father's father's subsection by marriage with the mother's mother's brother's daughter's daughter. The wavering of the Murinbata between the traditional system and the new order ends in practice with the identification of the mother's brother's daughter and the mother's mother's brother's daughter's daughter as the possible marriage partner, i.e., for *TJANAMA*:

nangala = nauola

Hence, a *TJIMIJ* man marries a *namij* woman. The father maintains that his daughter is *nalyeri* (which is the 'conventional' subsection). However, a *namij* woman is by kinship *purima*, a 'marriageable' daughter of the sister's

[1] Stanner, 1936, p. 198.   [2] ibid. p. 205.

son, but according to the subsections she is a 'sister'. Consequently, her daughter is *nabidjin*, for according to the aboriginal rule, formulated in a matrilineal idiom: '*namij* makes *nabidjin*'. From this the conflict arises of whether the subsections are patrilineal or matrilineal.

The general attitude of the aborigines, says Stanner, is that the problems will find their own solution:

'The attempts to make the subsections descend patrilineally will almost certainly not succeed as a general practice, but there is strong reason to believe that the Murinbata will establish as formal conventions variations in the pattern of subsection descent which occur in other tribes only as the result of "alternative" marriages',[1]

i.e., a five-generation patrilineal cycle. This phenomenon will be studied in detail in the following chapter. The notion of cycle is already present in the native mind:

'Informants are fond of showing how one subsection "comes back" by tracing it through both patrilineal and matrilineal lines. The Warramunga do this by actual genealogical references, the Nangiomeri and Murinbata by reciting the verbal accounts they have learned from neighbouring tribes. They have not possessed the subsection system long enough to be able to give genealogical proof.'[2]

Until such time as a new system can integrate the needs of the traditional and borrowed systems, provisional methods are contrived in order to straighten out irregularities, For example, in one concrete case, the Murinbata decided that a *nangala* daughter of *TJANAMA* and *nangari* (which is incorrect) would marry a *TJAMIRA* or *DJABIDJIN* man, and that her children would be regarded as *TULAMA* and *nauola* instead of *TJALYERI* and *nalyeri*, as should have resulted from the mother's subsection. But the aborigines say that this *nangala* girl is 'all the same *nangari*', or to use an informant's pidgin, 'she no more come up nothing herself', for she is daughter of *TJANAMA*, and by refusing to take her mother's *nangari* into account she is classed in the *nangari* or *nalyeri* subsection, in which she would have been had her father been correctly married.[3] Thus a solution is sought by treating descent as patrilineal (in accordance with former ideas), even though the present system is matrilineal.

IV

This example, to which others might be added,[4] is enough to show that systems should not be treated in isolation with their individual peculiarities seen as indissociable attributes. Underlying concrete systems, geographically localized and evolving through time, there are simpler relationships allowing

[1] ibid. p. 207.   [2] ibid. p. 210.   [3] ibid. p. 214.   [4] Elkin, 1940*a*, p. 22.

every type of change and every type of adaptation. For the present, we intend to consider groups only as providing ideal examples for attacking, analysing, and defining those elementary relationships which they illustrate. This is what Radcliffe-Brown did when he distinguished between two basic types which he called I and II, resulting from the existence of complex organizations cutting across both the horde and the tribe. These organizations, which are two, four, or eight in number, are generally called 'marriage classes'. Radcliffe-Brown proposed the use of more specialized terms, viz., 'moieties' when there were only two divisions in the group; 'sections' when there were four; and finally 'subsections' when there were eight. The moieties may be matrilineal as in eastern or western Australia, or patrilineal as in central Victoria. In both cases they are governed by the rule of exogamy, i.e., the men of one moiety can take wives only from the other moiety and vice versa. We have repeatedly stressed that this moiety system always leads to the classification of brothers, sisters and parallel cousins in the same category as Ego, these persons all belonging to the same moiety, while cross-cousins necessarily belong to the other moiety. This fact does not in itself entail that cross-cousins shall become sanctioned or prescribed spouses, though this is most frequently the case. The Dieri of South Australia, however, have a moiety system and prohibit cross-cousin marriage, yet even in this case the notion of cross-cousins is used to determine the possible spouse, in that instead of cross-cousins it is the children of cross-cousins who marry. Whatever the rule of marriage, it can thus be said that the moiety system leads necessarily to the dichotomy of cousins and that the preferred spouse must necessarily stand in a kinship relationship to Ego which is equivalent to the relationship of cross-cousin, or which is established through this relationship.

A system distributing members of the tribal group into four sections is to be found in both western and eastern Australia. For example, the Kariera belong to one or other of the following sections:

> Banaka
> Karimera
> Burung
> Palyeri.

Banaka necessarily marries Burung, and Karimera, Palyeri. The rule of descent is that the children of a Banaka man and a Burung woman are Palyeri, while the children of a Burung man and a Banaka woman are Karimera. Likewise, the children of a Karimera man and a Palyeri woman are Burung, and reversing the sexes with the classes remaining the same they are Banaka. This system is summarized in Fig. 9 where the = sign joins sections which intermarry, and the squared arrows link the mother's section with her children's section. It can thus be seen that there are three types of relation between the sections, and Radcliffe-Brown has given them special names. The sections of the husband and the wife are a *pair*, the sections of the father and his children are a *couple*, and the sections of the mother and her children are a *cycle*. There are always four pairs, viz., *AB* and *CD*, *BA* and *DC*; four couples, viz., *AD*, *BC*, *CB*, and *DA*; and four cycles, viz., *AC*, *BD*, *CA*, *DB*. As each of these types is based upon the combination of only four terms, they might be simplified and reduced to two pairs, two couples and two cycles. It will be seen later why the expanded form is to be preferred.

Given this, the law of descent for a four-section system can be formulated as: if a man belongs to a given section, his children necessarily belong to the alternate section of his own couple.

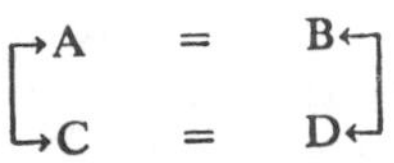

$$\begin{bmatrix} \rightarrow\!A & = & B\!\leftarrow \\ \rightarrow\!C & = & D\!\leftarrow \end{bmatrix}$$

Fig. 9. Kariera marriage rules.

One need only analyse this formula to see the connexion between a Kariera-type system and the simpler organization in matrilineal moieties. Men of sections *A* or *C* can only marry women from sections *B* or *D*. Moreover, a woman, her daughters, her daughters' daughters, etc., alternate indefinitely between sections *B* and *D*, if the mother is *B* or *D*, or between *A* and *C*, if the mother is *A* or *C*. In other words, the cycles *AC* and *BD* operate respectively as two matrilineal moieties. What does the Kariera system add to the division into two matrilineal moieties? A different division, perpendicular to the preceding division, into patrilineal moieties: a man, his sons, his sons' sons, etc., will oscillate indefinitely between sections *A* and *D*, if the father was *A* or *D*, and between sections *B* and *C*, if the father was *B* or *C*. The couples *AD* and *BC* respectively operate, therefore, as two patrilineal moieties, cutting across the two matrilineal moieties *AC* and *BD*. The discovery that a division into matrilineal moieties is always subjacent to a system of marriage classes, even if these matrilineal moieties are not explicitly named, is one of the most valuable achievements in Australian sociology in recent years.[1]

Let us now ask ourselves what marriage institutions correspond to this four-class system. Radcliffe-Brown has shown that the class does not automatically lead to the determination of the spouse:

'The classes of the Kariera tribe are groups of related persons. The rule that a man of one class may only marry a woman of one of the other classes is the result of the more fundamental rule that a man may only marry a woman bearing to him a certain relation of consanguinity, namely, the daughter of his mother's brother. Marriage is regulated by consanguinity and by consanguinity alone.'[2]

[1] Radcliffe-Brown, 1931, p. 39.   [2] ibid. 1913, p. 158.

He also insists that many tribes with a four-section system practise the same marriage prohibitions as groups which, with eight subsections, are obliged to prohibit twice as many of the possible spouses than would theoretically be necessary with four sections:

'Two tribes may both have a system of four sections, even with the same names, and yet have very different kinship systems and a very different regulation of marriage.'[1]

Thus, the same regulation of marriage (of the Aranda type) is found among the Dieri, who have a moiety organization, the Talaindji, with four sections, the Waramanga, with eight subsections, and the Mara, with four semi-moieties. On the other hand, two tribes with an identical four-section social organization have respectively a Kariera system (Ngaluma) and an Aranda system (Mardudhunara). Nevertheless, as we shall see in connexion with the Mara system, these assertions would seem not to be strictly correct: there are differences in the regulation of marriage, which correspond to differences in the social structure. On the other hand, it does not follow, from the fact that differing kinship nomenclatures and marriage regulations may coexist with the same type of social structure, that any system of nomenclature, or any regulation, may correspond with any type of structure. Of these three types of phenomena, structure is always the simplest. It consists of a symbolic whole which is capable of expressing different significations, though it is undeniable that there is always a functional correlation between that which signifies and that which is signified. There are cases in which this correlation is so rigid, and where 'the membership in subsections is correlated with the classificatory grouping of kin' so completely, that 'the subsection names may be used as terms of address between kin, and the natives naturally make use of the subsection terms in discussing marriage rules of the kinship system'.[2]

Warner made the same observation of the Murngin:

'Frequently the native confuses the kinship term with the subsection term in the mother's father's and mother's mother's brother's lines of descent. The fact that there are two names for each of these individual relatives (the kin and section name) indicates that the native does see them as separate and distinct systems, but also the confusion of such names shows further that they are looked upon somewhat as the same thing and serve the same general functions.'[3]

Elkin notes that: 'In the great number of tribes in which sections or subsections have been established for a considerable time, even though they may have been, or are, primarily totemic in function, the kinship terms are correlated with them.'[4]

In this work we have attempted to define two methods for determining

---

[1] Radcliffe-Brown, 1931, p. 58.   [2] Sharp, 1935, pp. 161–2.
[3] Warner, 1933, p. 81.   [4] Elkin, 1940a, pp. 21–2.

the spouse, viz., the method of classes and the method of relations.[1] We then showed that these two methods never correspond exactly and that even in the simplest system, such as exogamous moieties, inter-individual relationships must always be taken into consideration. None the less, the very fact that classes do exist proves, it seems to us, that they are not entirely without use and that there should be at least a certain degree of equivalence between the two systems. Not all the members of the class are possible spouses, and even between possible and preferred spouses there are differences which can only be explained in terms of consanguinity, whereas such differences are non-apparent in terms of class. Nevertheless, no possible spouse is to be found outside the class, and this alone indicates that from the point of view of marriage rules the class does have a function. This function is simple and wide when the number of classes is small, but gains in refinement and precision, without ever becoming perfect (since the number of kinsmen is theoretically unlimited, while a system with too many classes would be useless because of its complication), when this number increases. But the function is the same in all cases, viz., to act as a 'sorting-office' in the determination of the spouse. Seen in this way the Kariera system (including the division into four sections and the kinship system) might be said to be a particularly satisfactory logical model since the first relatives selected by the method of classes are also the preferred spouses according to the method of relations. This, incidentally, seems to be the reason why Radcliffe-Brown made the Kariera system the prototype of his kinship system and called it type I.

The Kariera enjoin marriage with the mother's brother's daughter (matrilateral cross-cousin), who need not be, but generally is, the father's sister's daughter (bilateral cross-cousin), since the Kariera practise sister-exchange. This leads to the following diagram, showing the partial coincidence at least of the class system and the kinship system (Fig. 10). A crucial problem now faces us, for if the general structure in Fig. 10 is considered, it can be seen that it does not differ as much as might be expected from that of a group divided into two moieties. In this case, too, marriage is principally between cross-cousins, who are normally bilateral cousins. The superimposition of a matrilineal dichotomy upon the patrilineal dichotomy changes nothing from the point of view of marriage rules between cousins. However, one would normally expect something entirely different. Since the first division of the group into two moieties results immediately in the division of the women into two groups, one including possible wives, the other prohibited wives, i.e., in dividing the number of spouses by two, it would be natural that a second division should repeat the process, or, putting it another way, that it should divide the number of spouses regarded as possible in the first dichotomy again into two.[2] Must it thus be acknowledged that the introduction of a

---

[1] cf. ch. VIII.

[2] There is no need to state that here we are only dealing with marriage rules between persons of the same generation, and that for the time being we shall disregard the case,

four-class system is foreign to the regulation of marriage? If not, what is its effect on this regulation?

A moment ago we said that a four-class system results from the super-imposition of a matrilineal dichotomy upon a patrilineal dichotomy. However, these two dichotomous rules do not operate in the same way in the deter-mination of descent. A four-class system recognizes both of them, but not in the same connexion; each applies to its own sphere. While the matrilineal rule is followed in connexion with descent, the patrilineal rule determines residence, or more exactly local origin. Indeed, the local group, or horde, it will be remembered, is constituted on a patrilineal basis. Moiety systems ignore this local group in determining descent; only the matrilineal moiety

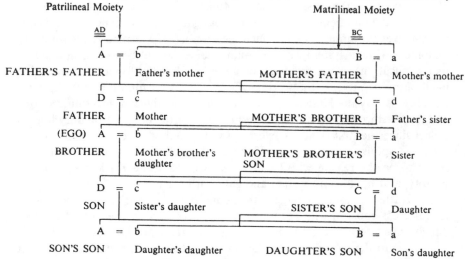

Fig. 10. Kariera system.

matters. By contrast, four-section systems employ both elements: they retain the mother's moiety but also take the father's group into consideration. It is the introduction of this new element which brings about the change from a two-class to a four-class system.

Let us illustrate this change with an example. Let us suppose that all the inhabitants of France are divided into two families, the Duponts and the Durands, and that, contrary to the custom of this country, the children always take their mother's name. In this way we would have a system roughly resembling a matrilineal moiety organization, which would also be exogamous if the law were that all Durands must marry Duponts, and all

which will be considered elsewhere, of dual organization allowing marriage with a classifi-catory 'mother' or 'daughter'. This is always theoretically possible, and is sometimes found in a moiety system, but it is strictly prohibited in a section system. However, we are of the opinion that so-called 'oblique' phenomena pose problems of a new order, which will be touched on in the second part of this book. It should be added that Kroeber has emphasized the uncommonness of plural marriage with mother and daughter (Kroeber. 1940, pp. 562–70).

Duponts, Durands. After a certain number of years, the result of such a system would be that every French city would comprise a certain number of Duponts and a certain number of Durands. There would be no rule to say that these Duponts and Durands must intermarry within the same city or that they should seek their spouses in other cities.

Let us now assume that the heads of two cities, for example, Paris and Bordeaux, have previously established co-operative ties between their cities. To cement these ties they extend the law that the Duponts marry solely with the Durands, and vice versa, by stipulating that the Duponts of one city must marry only the Durands of the other city, a rule naturally holding for the Durands also. It has already been stated that the family name is transmitted in the maternal line, but if the custom was formerly that women went to live with their husbands, the family name will be added to a place name transmitted through the paternal line, since it is the father's place of residence which determines the family's place of residence. Hence, there are four parties to the agreement, viz., the Duponts of Paris, the Duponts of Bordeaux, the Durands of Paris and the Durands of Bordeaux. Let us next examine the consequences of possible marriages by applying the twin rule that children take their family name from their mother and the name of their place of origin from their father. We would have the following combinations:

If a man:	*marries a woman:*	*the children are:*
Durand of Paris	Dupont of Bordeaux	Dupont of Paris
Durand of Bordeaux	Dupont of Paris	Dupont of Bordeaux
Dupont of Paris	Durand of Bordeaux	Durand of Paris
Dupont of Bordeaux	Durand of Paris	Durand of Bordeaux

By applying the symbols A, B, C, D, respectively to the Durands of Paris, the Duponts of Bordeaux, the Durands of Bordeaux and the Duponts of Paris, a Kariera-type formula is found (Fig. 11):

$$
\left[
\begin{array}{l}
\rightarrow \text{Durands of Paris} \quad (A) = (B) \quad \text{Duponts of Bordeaux} \leftarrow \\
\hookrightarrow \text{Durands of Bordeaux} \ (C) = (D) \quad \text{Duponts of Paris} \quad \ \leftharpoondown
\end{array}
\right]
$$

Fig. 11. An illustration of the Kariera system.

Thus the four classes are nothing more than the four possible combinations of two couples of opposite terms in each respective couple: a couple of nominal terms, and a couple of place names, it being given *ex hypothesi* that the nominal terms are transmitted in the maternal line and the place names in the paternal line. Each section is divided into two linked elements, i.e., a name term and a place name, as in the convenient formula used by

Lawrence[1] (Fig. 12) in which *A* and *B* are the names of moieties and *X* and *Y* the names of hordes of origin.

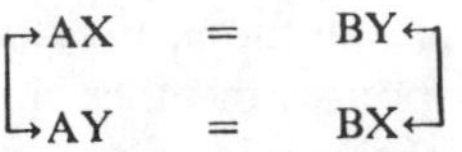

$$\left[\begin{array}{ccc} \rightarrow AX & = & BY \leftarrow \\ \rightarrow AY & = & BX \leftarrow \end{array}\right]$$

Fig. 12. Descent and residence in the Kariera system.

We can easily imagine in this way what the change is which brought about the transition from a moiety system to a four-section system. It is clear that there is nothing new as regards the kinship relationship of the possible spouses: in both cases they are cross-cousins. But while in the first case these cross-cousins, the Durands and the Duponts respectively, will risk marrying solely or primarily among themselves, either as Parisians or as Bordelais, in the second case a cross-cousin from Paris will necessarily marry a cross-cousin from Bordeaux, and vice versa. In other words, a new link will be superimposed upon the simple link established by the moiety division between the Duponts and the Durands, which will not only continue to unite them as in the past, but will also unite Paris and Bordeaux. A dialectic of residence, both reducing and reaffirming the social ties, will be added to the dialectic of descent. This is what is expressed by the fact that among the Kariera a local group always includes members of only two sections, some groups being Banaka-Palyeri and others Burung-Karimera. Consequently, a marriage necessarily establishes a relationship both between the members of two moieties and between the members of two groups. Instead of combining the benefit of three different types of social link – descent, alliance and locality – these are employed for different ends. Originally we had two groups (matrilineal moieties) united by three different types of link. We now have four groups (matrilineal moieties plus local groups with paternal descent), interrelated in such a way that one group is joined to another by at least two links, viz., descent plus marriage; marriage plus locality; or locality plus descent. The links are less numerous, but the number of things linked together is increased.

v

It is convenient to interpret the more complex eight-subsection systems in the same way. The essential difference is that, instead of interrelating two moieties and two groups, eight-class systems establish a connexion between two moieties and four groups. This is expressed by the fact that among the Aranda, for example, as described by Spencer and Gillen, the local group always contains members of only two subsections, together making up a patrilineal couple. Consequently, four groups are necessary for a complete cycle to be closed within the system. If the same symbols used earlier to

[1] Lawrence, 1937.

designate sections are retained, and if the two subsections resulting from the dichotomy of the original section are given respectively the signs 1 and 2, the following formula results:

If a man of subsection:	marries a woman of subsection:	the children belong to subsection:
A_1	B_1	D_2
A_2	B_2	D_1
B_1	A_1	C_1
B_2	A_2	C_2
C_1	D_1	B_1
C_2	D_2	B_2
D_1	C_1	A_2
D_2	C_2	A_1

This represents the application of the law that, if a man belongs to a given subsection, his children belong to the alternate subsection of the same couple (keeping to the technical meaning of the term 'couple' as defined above). All this may be expressed in the following diagram (Fig. 13). Suppose

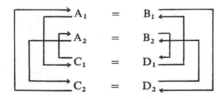

Fig. 13. Aranda rules of marriage.

there are eight pairs, A_1–B_1, A_2–B_2, C_1–D_1, C_2–D_2; B_1–A_1, B_2–A_2, D_1–C_1, D_2–C_2 which could be reduced to four if direction were not taken into consideration. Suppose there are also eight couples, likewise reducible to four on the same grounds: A_1–D_2, A_2–D_1, B_1–C_1, B_2–C_2; D_2–A_1, D_1–A_2, C_1–B_1, C_2–B_2; and finally two cycles, each comprising the four subsections of one matrilineal moiety, viz., A_1–C_1–A_2–C_2, then back to A_1, and B_1–D_2–B_2–D_1, then back to B_1. Note that in an eight-subsection system the parallelism with a four-section system extends to the pairs and the couples (with the one difference that there are twice as many of them), but that it stops at the cycles. There are two cycles in both systems, the difference being that in the eight-subsection system these cycles have twice the number of component elements. Accordingly the very structure of the cycle is changed, while the structure of the pairs and of the couples remains the same.

This structure can be illustrated in the same way as was done with the

Kariera system. Let us return to our two families, the Duponts and the Durands, who are obliged by the rule of exogamy to intermarry, and who transmit their names matrilineally. Let us further suppose, however, that there are four towns, Caen, Laon, Lille and Lyons, and that after marriage women go to live at their husband's place of residence. The double stipulation that the family name be transmitted in the maternal line, and the residential name in the paternal line, gives the following combinations:

If a man:	*marries a woman:*	*the children will be:*
Durand of Caen	Dupont of Laon	Dupont of Caen
Durand of Laon	Dupont of Lille	Dupont of Laon
Durand of Lille	Dupont of Lyons	Dupont of Lille
Durand of Lyons	Dupont of Caen	Dupont of Lyons
Dupont of Caen	Durand of Lyons	Durand of Caen
Dupont of Laon	Durand of Caen	Durand of Laon
Dupont of Lille	Durand of Laon	Durand of Lille
Dupont of Lyons	Durand of Lille	Durand of Lyons

This could readily be represented by the theoretical diagram of the Aranda system given above:

A_1 (Durand of Lille) $=$ (Dupont of Lyons) B_1

A_2 (Durand of Caen) $=$ (Dupont of Laon) B_2

C_1 (Durand of Lyons) $=$ (Dupont of Caen) D_1

C_2 (Durand of Laon) $=$ (Dupont of Lille) D_2

Fig. 14. Illustration of the Aranda system.

We have noted that the change from a moiety system to a four-section system does not, *in itself*, bring about any innovation with regard to the degree of kinship sanctioned or prohibited by marriage. But this is not so in passing from a four-section system to an eight-subsection system. The consequences are important and can be directly deduced from a consideration of the system. Again let us repeat that in this as in previous cases the class mechanism does not automatically determine the spouse (since the one class can contain both prescribed and prohibited spouses). Nevertheless, the system of classes can at least permit the automatic determination of a certain number of marriage prohibitions. Seen in this way, our assertion amounts to saying that the consideration of a four-section system cannot lead to the exclusion of more potential spouses than was the case – in the same generation – under a moiety system. To the contrary, the machinery of an eight-subsection system automatically excludes twice as many possible spouses as do moieties or sections. Let us construct the kinship system which corresponds to structures with eight subsections, and examine the position of various

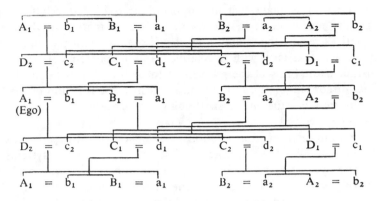

Fig. 15. Aranda system.

relatives in relation to this structure (Fig. 15). It is easy to see that in a system of this type the cross-cousins, whether unilateral or bilateral, can never fall into classes which are pairs (i.e., practising intermarriage), whereas the opposite is automatically brought about in the case of cousins descended from cross-cousins. This does not mean that cousins descended from cross-cousins become prescribed spouses because of this. But it does mean, at least, that the preferred spouse (in this case, the mother's mother's brother's daughter's daughter) belongs to the class of cousins descended from cross-cousins (Fig. 16).

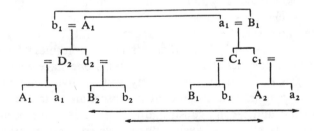

Fig. 16. Marriage of cousins descended from cross-cousins.

We are now in a position to review the question of the connexions between marriage classes and kinship systems. It does not follow from the mechanism of marriage classes that their end or even their result is the automatic determination of the prescribed spouse. Indeed, the opposite is true, since a class may contain both permitted and prohibited spouses, Thus, in the final analysis, it is the relationship of consanguinity which plays the principal rôle, while class membership, at least in practice, is secondary. Nevertheless, this is true only when the positive aspect of spouse selection is being considered, for the whole weight of evidence is agreed that, from the negative point of view, class plays just as important a rôle. The relationship of consanguinity means more than class in the determination of the spouse, but the natives regard the violation of class exogamy with the same horror as they regard marriage with a relative of a forbidden consanguineous relationship. If the basis of the problem is to be found in the consideration of degrees of consanguinity, rather than in classes, the function of the latter is not substantially different, even though the relation between them still remains to be specified.

The determination of this relationship, however, raises an extremely difficult problem. We have repeatedly observed that all class systems lead to the dichotomy of members of the group into permitted and prohibited spouses. In a system without classes, theoretically no spouse is prohibited except those falling under the incest prohibition. A system with exogamous moieties not only divides the group into two moieties but divides all the men and women into possible and prohibited spouses, a division which is expressed in the dichotomy of cross and parallel cousins. As we have just seen, an eight-subsection system further reduces by half the number of available spouses, since it establishes a new dichotomy between first cross-cousins and second cross-cousins. But none of this corresponds to the four-section system. In other words, if one considers only Ego's generation, it can be established that a moiety system divides the possible spouses by two, that an eight-subsection system again divides these by two, but that a four-section system leaves these untouched. We have interpreted this by pointing out that a four-section system has recourse to twice as many elements in defining the status of the individual within the family group. Accordingly, the effect of doubling the classes is annulled by doubling the factors.

For all that, however, the problem is not resolved. If we no longer consider the marriage class systems, but the successive dichotomies of spouses, we shall perceive that the dichotomous process skips one stage which nevertheless seems logically necessary. The moiety system divides all first cousins into cross and parallel cousins; the eight-subsection system divides cross-cousins into first and second cousins. But there must have been an intermediate phase, when cross-cousins were divided into matrilateral and patrilateral cousins, for just as there are two types of cousins, so there are two types of cross-cousin (sister's brother's children and brother's sister's children). The following process might thus have been expected: the first dichotomy distinguishes cross and parallel cousins and excludes the latter; the second dichotomy distinguishes matrilateral and patrilateral cross-cousins and excludes one or the other of these two groups; and finally, the third dichotomy distinguishes all cross-cousins as cross-cousins and as cousins descended from cross-cousins, and excludes the former. Only the first and third stages come into effect in a system with marriage classes, the first through moieties, the third by means of the subsections. The second stage is absent, because the sections to which theoretically it would have had to correspond do not themselves effect any dichotomy in Ego's generation. Consequently, we have to answer two questions: How is it that there is no dichotomy between cousins in a four-section system? What explanation is there for the fact that there is no stage answering to the distinction between the two types of cross-cousin in the dichotomous process corresponding to the series: two moieties – four sections – eight subsections?

CHAPTER XII

The Murngin System

I

These questions would probably have remained unanswered if tribes which practise precisely this dichotomy of cross-cousins had not been discovered in the north of Australia, in Arnhem Land to the west of the Gulf of Carpentaria. The Murngin, studied by Warner,[1] prescribe marriage with the mother's brother's daughter and prohibit it with the other cross-cousin, the father's sister's daughter. It is essential, therefore, to know how the Murngin organization stands in relation to the classical systems of moieties, sections and subsections. But here the difficulties begin.

In fact, the Murngin system of classes does not conform to any of the classical types. Sometimes it has been interpreted as a Kariera system (i.e., with four classes), but in this case no distinction between the two types of cross-cousin has been found, any more than it has been in the Kariera system itself. Sometimes it has been conceived of as an Aranda system (i.e., with eight subsections), but without taking into account the considerable differences which separate it from the latter. Thus, most authors are agreed in classing the Murngin system as an aberrant system ('off pattern', as Lawrence puts it[2]). One might then wonder how a marriage rule (the cross-cousin dichotomy), which seems a logically necessary term in a given series, may not be derived from systems constituting this series, while at the same time resulting from another system which is itself irreducible. Either the series is poorly constructed, or the Murngin system has been insufficiently analyzed.

The Murngin system resembles the Kariera system because it has four sections, and the Aranda system because these four sections are divided into eight subsections. But it differs from both in that these subsections always exist, although they are not always named. On the other hand, the subsections do not function as in an Aranda system; instead of resulting in the elimination of cross-cousins from the number of possible spouses, they retain them. In other words, the Murngin system differs from the Kariera system in that it has eight classes, and from the Aranda system in that these eight classes function as if there were only four.

[1] Warner, 1930, pp. 207–56; 1931, pp. 172–98. [2] See above, p. 150.

Let us leave to one side those groups in which the subsections, although real, are not named, and consider those, described by Webb, in which the subsections are explicitly designated. The tribes of eastern Arnhem Land are divided into two patrilineal moieties, Yiritcha and Dua, and each horde, of course, is exclusively in one or the other.[1] Each of these moieties is divided, in turn, into four subsections, thus making a total of eight subsections. For the sake of simplicity, we shall ignore the fact that there are two names for each subsection, one for males and one for females, because these have no influence on the system. Taking only the masculine name, we have the following list:

Yiritcha Moiety		*Dua Moiety*	
Subsections:	Ngarit	Subsections:	Buralang
	Bulain		Balang
	Kaijark		Karmarung
	Bangardi		Warmut

So far everything seems normal. But as soon as we consider the marriage rules, we find an anomaly characterizing every system in the region: instead of a man being required to seek his wife in only one subsection of the other moiety, he has a choice between the two subsections composing the one section. For example, a Ngarit man can marry either a Balang woman or a Buralang woman; a Bulain man may choose between a Buralang woman and a Balang woman; a Kaijark man marries either in the Warmut sub-section or in the Karmarung subsection, etc. Whatever the type of marriage practised, the children belong to the same section (the alternate section to the father's in the same moiety), but, within the section, to one or the other of the subsections. Thus a Ngarit man marrying a Balang woman will have Bangardi children, while if the woman is Buralang the children will be Kaijark. From a Buralang wife, a Bulain husband will have Kaijark children, and from a Balang woman, Bangardi children, etc. There is then a fixed relationship between the children's subsection and the type of marriage made by the father, and an equally fixed relationship between the children's subsection and the mother's subsection, but not between the father's sub-section and the children's subsection. Indeed, only the children's section maintains a fixed relationship with the father's section, the subsection depending on the type of marriage practised. This may be expressed by saying that there is a stable relationship between the pairs and the cycles, and a stable relationship between the pairs and the couples, but not between the cycles and the couples. Webb interprets this as proving that descent in the subsection is matrilineal, but Elkin has described this phenomenon more correctly as a case of indirect patrilineal descent. As a matter of fact, Elkin differentiates the two types of possible marriage as regular and alternate

[1] Webb, 1933, pp. 406–17.

types, and he then formulates the following law which satisfactorily accounts for this complex system: 'In the case of alternate marriage . . . the children belong to the subsection of the father's moiety to which they would have belonged had their *actual mother* been regularly married according to the strict subsection rule. Thus, the father is "thrown away" as far as the subsection is concerned.'[1] It is of relevance, moreover, that the alternate wife always comes from the same section as the regular wife (Fig. 17).

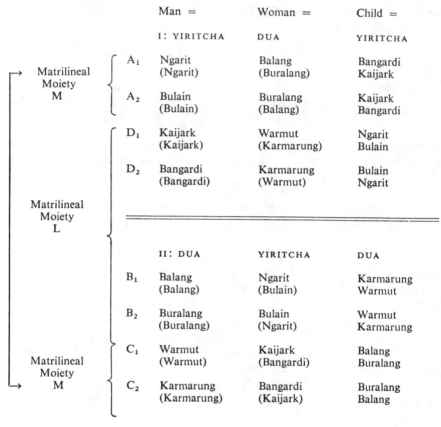

		Man =	Woman =	Child =
		I: YIRITCHA	DUA	YIRITCHA
Matrilineal Moiety M	A_1	Ngarit (Ngarit)	Balang (Buralang)	Bangardi Kaijark
	A_2	Bulain (Bulain)	Buralang (Balang)	Kaijark Bangardi
	D_1	Kaijark (Kaijark)	Warmut (Karmarung)	Ngarit Bulain
	D_2	Bangardi (Bangardi)	Karmarung (Warmut)	Bulain Ngarit
Matrilineal Moiety L				
		II: DUA	YIRITCHA	DUA
	B_1	Balang (Balang)	Ngarit (Bulain)	Karmarung Warmut
	B_2	Buralang (Buralang)	Bulain (Ngarit)	Warmut Karmarung
Matrilineal Moiety M	C_1	Warmut (Warmut)	Kaijark (Bangardi)	Balang Buralang
	C_2	Karmarung (Karmarung)	Bangardi (Kaijark)	Buralang Balang

Fig. 17. Structure of the Murngin system. (After Webb, 1933, pp. 406–17.)

For this reason, it has sometimes been considered that the subsections had nothing to do with the regulation of marriage, and that the Murngin system operated as though the sections and not the subsections were paired. Warner suggests this in his theoretical representation of the Murngin system (Fig. 18),[2] which, in our opinion, reveals its essence. The important fact is not that each system, the regular and the alternate, separately produce the same results,

[1] Elkin, 1933, p. 412.   [2] Warner, 1931, pp. 172–98.

but that they are two in number. To ignore this duality takes away all means of understanding its *raison d'être*.

Let us therefore construct two independent diagrams, one corresponding to the regular system, the other to the alternate system (Fig. 19). They need only be compared to show that the analogy between the Murngin system and the Aranda system, as represented in Fig. 13, is only apparent. The directions of the arrows, that is, are not the same. While the arrows on the

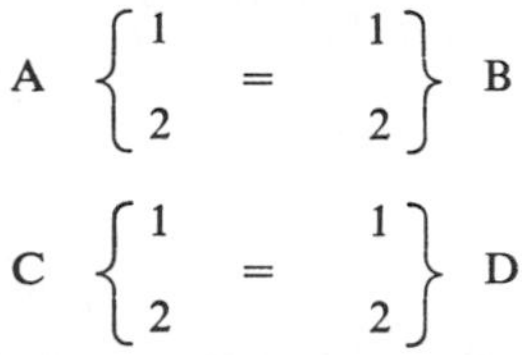

$$A \left\{ \begin{matrix} 1 \\ 2 \end{matrix} \right. = \left. \begin{matrix} 1 \\ 2 \end{matrix} \right\} B$$

$$C \left\{ \begin{matrix} 1 \\ 2 \end{matrix} \right. = \left. \begin{matrix} 1 \\ 2 \end{matrix} \right\} D$$

Fig. 18. Murngin marriage rules (after Warner, 1931, p. 183).

right of both Murngin diagrams are the same as on the right of the Aranda diagram, the arrows on the left point in the opposite directions. Elkin clearly saw this structural difference, which in the Murngin system has the effect that 'the cycle of a man of any one subsection is not completed until by marriage and descent all eight subsections have been gone through, and

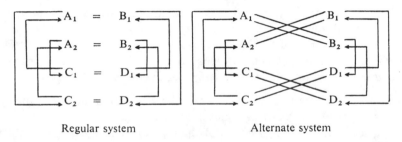

Regular system   Alternate system

Fig. 19. Murngin marriage rules.

until by descent alone all four subsections of his own moiety have been gone through'.[1] By contrast, in a classical eight-subsection system of the Aranda type, the cycle is formed in four subsections by descent and marriage, and by descent alone, in only two subsections, of the moiety of the man considered. This difference is seen in Fig. 20, which should be interpreted as follows: in the Aranda system a man always falls into the same class as his grandfather (his father's father) and he always finds his grandson (his son's son) in the same class as himself. In the Murngin system, on the contrary, a man falls into the same class only after five generations, i.e., a man, his father's father's father's father, and his son's son's son's son are in the same class.

[1] Elkin, 1933, p. 413.

Is there a relationship between this structural difference in the class system, and the marriage rule by which a man marries only his mother's brother's daughter, and not his father's sister's daughter? Elkin believes that the

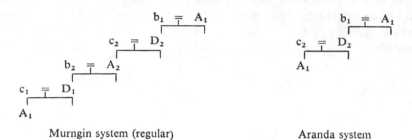

Murngin system (regular)   Aranda system

Fig. 20. The Murngin system and the Aranda system.

extension of the cycle of masculine descent, in the Murngin system, would directly explain the special regulation of marriage. Rightly insisting upon the importance, underestimated by Warner, of the subsection system, Elkin writes:

> 'Indeed, it is so important that it has been most carefully arranged to fit in with the rule of marriage with the mother's brother's daughter. Theoretically, this has been regarded as impossible, as, of course, it is, if the typical rule of the marriage and descent of the subsections be adhered to. The aborigines of this area were not so bound by theory, and faced with the practical problem, they seem to have solved it in a most ingenious manner by doubling the normal length of the cycle.'[1]

Let us ask, then, if a link really does exist between the doubling of the cycle and the regulation of marriage, and if so, what this link is.

First, let us take the hypothesis of the regular system, and seek in it the approved and the excluded spouses (Fig. 21).

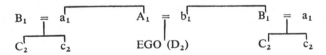

Fig. 21. Murngin marriage rule (regular system).

As, in the regular system, D_2 and C_2 form a pair, it may be seen that both cross-cousins fall into the class from which Ego may obtain a wife. That is, the class system does not take into account the distinction made by the Arnhem Land tribes between the matrilateral cross-cousin and the patrilateral cross-cousin.

[1] Elkin, 1933, p. 416.

Now what happens in the alternate system (Fig. 22)? As D_1 and C_2 form

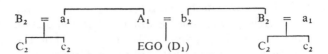

Fig. 22. Murngin marriage rule (alternate system).

a pair in the alternate system, it may be seen that the two cross-cousins are no more distinguished from each other than in the regular system. Both equally fall into the class of possible spouses.

II

Thus, there is no direct relationship between the specific character of the Murngin system (the doubling of the masculine cycle), and the regulation of marriage prohibiting the patrilateral cousin, and prescribing the matrilateral cousin. In actual fact, the doubling of the cycle has its own consequence, but this is quite different, viz., the restoration of both cross-cousins (or the bilateral cross-cousin) to the class of possible spouses. In other words, it annuls the specific effect of an eight-subsection system organized on the classical model. It is easy to see the reason for this. The doubling of the cycle is equivalent to dividing the number of classes by two. The cycle being twice as long, the system works as though there were four classes instead of eight. From the point of view of the regulation of marriage, the Murngin system, taken in isolation, revives purely and simply the conditions of the Kariera system. Whether it be the regular or the alternate type of marriage, as sanctioned by the Murngin system, the first relative fulfilling the class conditions required to be a possible spouse is the mother's brother's daughter, or the father's sister's daughter, or the cross-cousin who is both.

Faced with the Murngin system, must we then concede the complete absence of any connexion between the class system and the regulation of marriage? This regulation establishes, ostensibly by itself, a basic distinction which is reflected in the whole system: we shall see shortly that preferential marriage with the mother's brother's daughter gives the Murngin kinship system quite exceptional characteristics, unmatched in the majority of Australian tribes. However, because of this fundamental feature, the class system is of no effect. Both cross-cousins fall into the same class, that of possible spouses, but only one may be married. Is the preferred spouse wholly and solely determined, therefore, by the degree of relationship?

Before resigning ourselves to this negative conclusion, let us examine the problem further. The Murngin are distinguished from other groups with eight subsections, both by the functioning of the subsections and by the regulation of marriage. Even if it has to be agreed that the two orders are heterogeneous, this does not alter the fact that if there is a change in one there will be a change in the other. We have been unable to discover any relationship between the class mechanism and marriage preference. But the problem can be posed differently, viz., since a difference in the class mechanism is given simultaneously with a difference in marriage preferences, is it not possible to establish a connexion between the differences themselves? For it would be truly surprising if, quite independently, an anomaly were to develop in the class-system, and another anomaly in the regulation of marriage, without there being some degree of correlation between them. On the other hand, if this correlation does exist, it means that the regulation of marriage is not completely independent of the class system.

The difference in the regulation of marriage consists in the dichotomy of cross-cousins. The change in the system of classes consists in two things: firstly, there are two forms of marriage instead of one; and, secondly, each of these forms functions as though the system comprised four classes instead of eight. Unfortunately, we do not have any indication of the conditions in which the aborigines use these two forms. Both Webb and Warner say merely that a man of a given subsection marries within a particular subsection of the opposite moiety, and that he may also marry a woman from another subsection according to the alternate form of marriage. But let us take a hypothetical situation in which these two forms would be employed alternately in both the direct and the collateral lines. That is, if my father has married according to the alternate type, my son marries according to the regular type, my son's son according to the alternate type, and so on. It follows from this that if I marry in conformity with the regular type, my sister marries according to the alternate type, and vice versa. Hence, the result of this simple rule, the assumption of which is sufficiently suggested by the presence of the two forms, even in the absence of any positive information, is that the mother's brother's daughter automatically falls into the class of prescribed spouse, and the father's sister's daughter, also automatically, into the opposite class. There is thus a relationship between the anomaly of the class system (two forms to match the classes) and the anomaly of marriage (dichotomy of cross-cousins). At the same time, the peculiar functioning of the class mechanism becomes clear. We have said that the Murngin system, like the Aranda, has eight classes, but functions as if it had four as in the Kariera system. Nothing could be drawn from this peculiarity if there were only one form. But if there are two forms, and they function alternately, the system will develop characteristics of both types, or rather these will be compounded within the system. Elkin saw one aspect at least of this law when he noted that where an alternate marriage follows a regular marriage, there is a return to the classical cycle of class succession in the patrilineal line. But in fact there is no such return. Nothing would be gained by it, since there would only have been a change from a system indiscriminately sanctioning both cross-cousins, to one eliminating them both. The result in fact is intermediate between the four-class and the eight-class systems. The system, which originally functioned as a four-class system, begins to function as an eight-class system in one respect (i.e., by eliminating the patrilateral cross-cousin), and continues to function as a four-class system in the other (by keeping the matrilateral cross-cousin in the class of possible spouses). This emerges clearly from Fig. 23, which also shows that

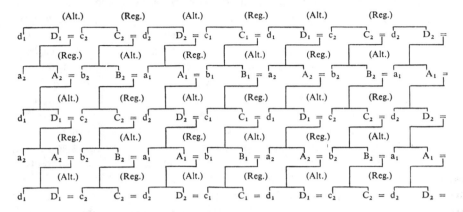

Fig. 23. The combined regular and alternate Murngin systems.

if the law of alternation between the regular and the alternate forms is followed in the direct line, it automatically extends to the collateral line and vice versa.

As may be seen, every marriage is with the mother's brother's daughter, while the father's sister's daughter is automatically eliminated by the alternative application of the two forms. There is scarcely need to emphasize that, whatever the modes of this alternative usage, the matrilateral cousin is always retained and the patrilateral cousin excluded. In other words, the system is entirely oriented in one direction, orientation in the opposite direction being impossible. The reason for this phenomenon will be given in chapter XXVII.

The connexion between the regulation of marriage and the class mechanism peculiar to the Murngin is thus clear. But still this connexion has been established only at the expense of extreme complication and with the elaboration of a burdensome and inconvenient system. To arrive at a dichotomy of cousins intermediate between that resulting from a moiety system and that peculiar to an eight-subsection system, the following procedure might be said to have been followed. Firstly, the eight-subsection system was adopted; then it was modified to function as a simpler system; and, finally, it was doubled to obtain a form of dichotomy intermediate between that of the simple system and that of the complex system. In other words, it seems that the more complicated form has been directly achieved and then even further complicated in order to make it function as a simpler form. This procedure strongly suggests that the Murngin system is not a direct codification of the marriage rule characteristic of this society, but rather that it is the result of a sort of compromise between a pre-existing marriage rule and a fully developed class system introduced from outside.

This hypothesis accords with Stanner's remarks on the marriage system of the Nangiomeri, living a few hundred miles from Arnhem Land. Until quite recently, the Nangiomeri had neither sections, moieties, nor any other form of marriage classes. Thus marriage took place with both cross-cousins, or with the bilateral cross-cousin. Within recent years these aborigines have acquired from tribes to the south and south-west a complex system of matrilineal totemic subsections, and a new form of marriage with the sister's son's daughter (provided that she is not the child of one's own daughter, who may marry the sister's son). The analogy with the functioning of the subsections in the Murngin system is brought to light by Stanner's observation that Ego's father's father is in the same subsection as Ego's son's son, while in a classical system Ego's father's father falls into the same subsection as Ego himself. In contrast, among the Nangiomeri, Ego falls into an intermediate subsection, and it is his son's son who completes the cycle. Thus, as among the Murngin, the cycle is doubled. And Stanner comments: 'These people quite frankly admit they do not yet understand [this new system] . . . [which] they were *taught* . . . by the Fitzmaurice and Victoria River tribes.'[1]

In another work on the same group this author says:

'What has happened is much the same as Warner has reported from Arnhem Land. The Nangiomeri are trying to apply, and have more ingeniously done so to a Kariera type of social organization, a subsectional system elaborated by a much more complex society probably related to the Aranda type. That is, a systematization of a kinship system of Aranda type has spread to them without the system upon which it is based itself having been adopted. The Nangiomeri do claim, however, to have adopted with the subsectional system marriage with the sister's son's daughter.'[2]

Stanner's last statement leaves untouched the question of the ultimate relationship between the class system of the Nangiomeri and their regulation of marriage. For even if, as is suggested, they borrowed both at the same time it would still need to be known in what conditions both types of phenomena came to coexist among their original owners. If the Murngin and the Nangiomeri systems could be traced back to their earliest beginnings, it seems almost certain that a group would be found, at the source, which had done its best to make an original marriage system coincide with an eight-subsection mechanism borrowed from elsewhere.

If this assumption is correct it produces an important consequence, viz., that although the two institutions may have been made to function together

[1] Stanner, 1933a, p. 417.   [2] ibid. 1933b, pp. 397–8.

satisfactorily, the Murngin class system does not constitute the Murngin marriage law, in the sense that the physicist uses the word law. If this word does not mean the rule as conceived of by the legislator (for, in this case, it is evident that the class system is a law) but a constant relationship between variables, then the question is posed whether the modes of Murngin marriage, which are relatively simpler than those of Aranda marriage, might not be expressed also in a formula simpler than that of the Aranda instead of in a more complicated form as seemingly they are. That the aborigines are not conscious of the postulated law should not be used as an argument against seeking it. For there is no need to be conscious of linguistic laws to be able to speak, nor of laws of logic to think. None the less, these laws exist, and the theoretician rightly strives to discover them. In this regard the sociologist's attitude should be no different. As Shirokogoroff notes of a people who offer but one particular illustration of a general phenomenon:

'From the description and analysis of the Tungus ideas and attitudes towards the phenomena of social organization and ethnical relations it may be seen that the Tungus treat them as other natural phenomena. They observe the facts, some of which are cognized while others escape their attention . . . Social phenomena may exist and function without being cognized.'[1]

On the other hand, the importance of the discovery of the law of preferential marriage with the mother's brother's daughter far exceeds the discussion of the solitary Murngin problem. The great majority of people practising cross-cousin marriage reveal a preference for the matrilateral cousin. Since we have made the analysis of cross-cousin marriage the crucial experiment for the problem of the incest prohibition, we cannot exempt ourselves from accounting for such a striking peculiarity. Finally, it has been shown that the classical Australian series of successive dichotomies between preferred and prohibited spouses contains a lacuna. This gap is revealed by the anomalies of the classical systems but they themselves are unable to define the missing term. We should seek whether the law of preferential marriage with the matrilateral cross-cousin does not provide it.

III

Let us consider the three classical Australian systems, viz., moieties, sections and subsections. These systems have a basic structure which is unaltered by any difference in the number of classes. This common characteristic may be formulated as follows: whether the class considered be a moiety, a section, or a subsection, marriage always conforms to the rule that if a man of A can marry a woman of B, a man of B can marry a woman of A. Thus there is reciprocity between the sexes within the classes; or, if preferred, the marriage

[1] Shirokogoroff, 1935, p. 104.

rules are indifferent to the sex of the spouses. What is true for marriage rules is obviously not so for the rules of descent, but there is no need to consider these for the moment.

Systems exhibiting this characteristic, whatever the number of classes, are called *systems of restricted exchange*, meaning that the systems can operate mechanisms of reciprocity only between two partners or between partners in multiples of two.

The immediate result is that a system with two exogamous moieties must always be a system of restricted exchange. Indeed, if we are limited to two groups *A* and *B*, and if marriage is impossible within each group, the only solution for *A* is to seek its spouses in *B*, and for *B* reciprocally to seek its spouses in *A*. But what is true for a two-class system is not true for a four-class system. In a system with four exogamous classes we have, in fact, the choice between two theoretical possibilities. The first is realized in the Kariera system, in which the classes are split into two pairs, each governed by a law of restricted exchange. The link between the two pairs is secured by descent, the children of parents who are of one of the pairs always belonging to a section of the other pair. That is, an *A* man marries a *B* woman (pair no. 1), the children are *D* (pair no. 2); a *B* man marries an *A* woman (pair no. 1), the children are *C* (pair no. 2).

But there is a second possibility satisfying at the same time the exigencies of class exogamy and those of the division, formulated or unformulated, into moieties. This possibility may be expressed by the formula: if an *A* man marries a *B* woman, a *B* man marries a *C* woman. Here the link between the classes is expressed simultaneously by marriage and by descent. We propose to call the systems using this formula, *systems of generalized exchange*, indicating thereby that they can establish reciprocal relationships between any number of partners. These relationships, moreover, are *directional relationships*. For example, if a *B* man depends for his marriage upon class *C*, placed after his own, a *B* woman depends upon class *A*, placed before.

Such a system may be illustrated by Fig. 24, where the arrows represent one-way pairs (going from the man to the woman), while the same system turns symmetrically but inversely if considered from the point of view of the other spouse (Fig. 25).

Fig. 24. Generalized exchange.   Fig. 25. Generalized exchange.

Let us examine this system from the point of view of the pairs, the couples and the cycles. Firstly, four types of possible marriage are implied, viz.,

A with *B*, *B* with *C*, *C* with *D*, and *D* with *A* (or, from the woman's point of view, *B* with *A*, *C* with *B*, *D* with *C*, and *A* with *D*, which amounts to the same thing). Thus, following Radcliffe-Brown's terminology, we have four pairs. But these pairs do not have the same character as in systems of restricted exchange in which the notion of pair implies a double marriage relationship, such that, for the pair *AB*, the relationship is of an *A* man with a *B* woman, and of a *B* man with an *A* woman. In a system of generalized exchange, by contrast, the pairs are univocal instead of reciprocal. That is, they unite only the men of one section with the women of the other. As we have seen, it is the reciprocal character of the pairs which allows their reduction to two in a Kariera system. In this regard, the difference is that in the type of system being described here there are four univocal or directional pairs.

Let us now consider the couples. Whatever the relationship uniting the father's section and that of his children, the couples remain the same. The same may be said of the cycles, i.e., the relationship between the mother's section and that of her children has no influence on the rule of marriage. In other words, the rules of marriage and of descent are not functionally related. The former – by which an *A* man marries a *B* woman, a *B* man a *C* woman, a *C* man a *D* woman, and a *D* man, an *A* woman – remains the same, whether it is decided that the children of a man *A* shall fall into section *A*, *B*, *C*, or *D*. The only condition is that the rule of descent, once chosen, shall be applied systematically.

Let us suppose, for example, that the children belong to the section immediately following that of the mother. This form is particularly convenient since it implies, in the preceding figures, that two consecutive arrows indicate, for the same conjugal family, firstly, the rule of marriage, and secondly, the rule of descent. Four types of relationship between the father's section and that of his children are found, viz., *AC*, *BD*, *CA*, and *DB*. Finally, there are four cycles, viz., *BC*, *CD*, *DA* and *AB*. It is easy to see that these cycles have the same structure as the pairs, that is, a rotating structure, while the couples have an oscillatory structure (Fig. 26).

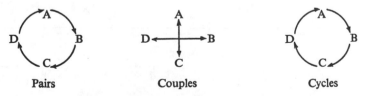

Pairs   Couples   Cycles

Fig. 26. Pairs, couples and cycles.

This means that in a four-class system of generalized exchange there are always two explicit or implicit patrilineal moieties, but no matrilineal moiety. Further, in such a system the rotary structure appears twice (in the

pairs and in the cycles) and the oscillatory structure only once (in the couples).
If the same analysis is applied to the Kariera system it may be established
that the rotary structure is entirely absent, the pairs, couples and cycles all
being based on the oscillatory type. On the other hand, in an Aranda system
the oscillatory structure appears twice (in both cycles) and the rotary structure
also twice (in the pairs and in the couples). From the point of view of formal
analysis, the four-class system of generalized exchange is thus in an intermediate position between the two systems of restricted exchange, one with
four classes, the other with eight classes. Is it the same in regard to the
regulation of marriage?

It is sufficient to construct a model to see the marriage form sanctioned by
a four-class system of generalized exchange (Fig. 27).

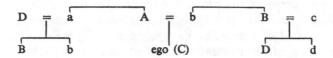

Fig. 27. Matrilateral marriage.

The rule of marriage being that a *C* man marries a *D* woman, it may be
seen that Ego can marry the mother's brother's daughter, who is always
in the class immediately following his own, but not the father's sister's
daughter, who is always in the class immediately preceding his own.
This characteristic structure is reversed when passing from the sister to
the brother, so that Ego cannot marry his patrilateral cross-cousin, but the
latter's brother (who is also *B*) can marry Ego's sister (who is *C*). Indeed, Ego's
sister is the matrilateral cross-cousin of her patrilateral cousin. In this type of
system, marriage relationships are always like a theoretically indefinite chain,
in that my patrilateral cross-cousin marries my sister, I marry my matrilateral
cross-cousin, her brother marries his matrilateral cross-cousin, and so on.
In fact, four families are sufficient to close the cycle, since there are four
classes or any multiple of four (Fig. 28).

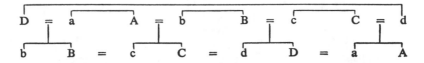

Fig. 28. Generalized exchange among four classes.

It may therefore be seen that a four-class system of generalized exchange
is the theoretical model of preferential marriage with the mother's brother's

daughter. It expresses most simply the law of the dichotomy of cross-cousins.[1] We have thus reached the theoretical form of Murngin marriage. At the same time we have found a term, missing in the classical series, which can be inserted between the moiety system and that of eight subsections, a place which the four-section system of the Kariera type falsely occupied, and which explains the transition from the prohibition of parallel cousins to the prohibition of all first cousins. This intermediate term is the four-section system, but with generalized exchange, the function of which is to eliminate half the cross-cousins.

Is it now possible to attribute to the system of generalized exchange a value other than that of a theoretical formula? There is no doubt the Murngin seem unconscious of the existence of this system. But it seems possible, firstly, to show that certain peculiarities of the Murngin kinship system are unintelligible if the effect of an implicit system corresponding to the definition of generalized exchange, underlying the explicit system, is not postulated; and, secondly, to explain why the system of generalized exchange has remained subjacent and why the explicit system is formulated in very different terms.

IV

The Murngin kinship system requires seven patrilineal lines united by the marriage of the father's sister's son with the mother's brother's daughter. It also recognizes five generations, viz., two ascending generations above that of Ego, and two descending generations below. The second ascending generation is called the 'head' of the kinship system, the second descending generation is the 'foot', and the lines are the 'paths'. It is seen that the extension of the system, in both senses, is enormous, and Warner, surprised by this, stated that it seemed 'unexplainable and almost fantastic'.[2] Actually,

---

[1] On the hypothesis of the prior existence of a division into patrilineal moieties, of course. Otherwise, three classes suffice.

The symbols used in Figs. 26, 27 and 28 have led J. P. B. de Josselin de Jong to credit me with the idea—which he considers odd, and with good reason—that the Murngin system derived from four classes, with the assignation of the son to the class of the mother's brother's wife (de Josselin de Jong, 1952, pp. 37, 39–40). In fact, I suppose nothing of the sort, for, firstly, I was not dealing at this point with the Murngin system, but with a hypothetical model of generalized exchange; secondly, it was only a matter of convention, and as a means of making it easier to read, that I supposed—as explained on page 179—that the rule was that children belong to the class following that of the mother. Consequently, Fig. 30 does not represent *a stage in the system* (as de Josselin de Jong seems to believe), but a rule of *conversion* from one stage to another. It is a simple operational procedure, not the picture of a society. De Josselin de Jong, it is true, questions the liberty I took in choosing a conversion rule solely by virtue of its simplicity, because it contravenes the notion—which I use in another connexion—of unilineal descent (ibid. p. 40). However, as I have repeatedly indicated, and as my eminent critic himself recognizes, I define unilineal descent in a purely formal way. Take any element of personal status, and unilineal descent involves no more, as far as this element is concerned, than a constant relationship between this element and the same element of the status of both of the parents or of one of them.   [2] Warner, 1931, p. 181.

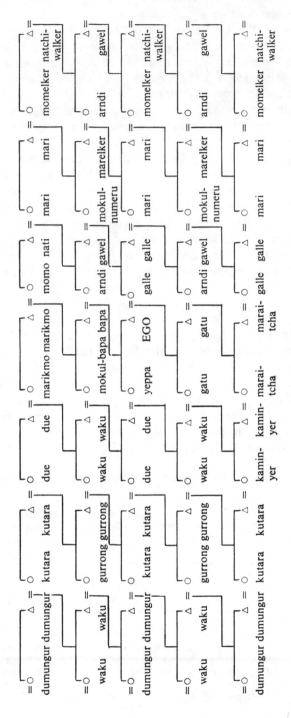

Fig. 29. Murngin kinship nomenclature.

marriage with the unilateral cross-cousin theoretically requires only three lines, viz., those of Ego, his mother, and his sister's husband.

From these three indispensable lines we might expect a symmetrical system as among the Kariera.[1] However, the system is extended to the right, beyond the maternal line, by two supplementary lines (the *mari-mokul-marelker* line, and the *momelker-natchiwalker-arndi-gawel* line), and to the left, by two supplementary lines, also beyond the brother-in-law's line (the *kutara-gurrong* line, and the *dumungur-waku* line). Besides, it should immediately be noted that in both directions the last line is a reflection or echo of the last but two. Warner very clearly shows that *dumungur* is a diminutive of *due* (while *waku* repeats *waku*), that *momelker* is a diminutive of *momo*, and *natchiwalker* of *nati* (while *arndi* repeats *arndi*, and *gawel*, *gawel*).

Warner attempts to explain the enormous extension of the Murngin kinship system in psychological terms. According to him, the two supplementary lines are added to both ends to resolve tensions which, without them, would arise in the group. Given marriage with the matrilateral cross-cousin, the sister's son (*waku*) depends, in fact, on the mother's brother (*gawel*) to obtain a wife. He is in a suppliant position with respect to him, a psychologically weak position. By contrast, the position of the mother's brother, father of the cross-cousin, is strong. If the kinship system were limited to the three central lines of descent, the theoretically essential ones, the social groups would be in a state of psychological disequilibrium. The structure would terminate at one end in a *gawel* person, i.e., an individual in the strong position, and at the other end in a *waku* person, an individual in the weak position. This is avoided by adding a supplementary line to both ends of the system. The *kutara* (sister's daughter's son) is to the *waku* (sister's son) as the *waku* is to Ego, and symmetrically Ego is not, as regards his *gawel* (mother's brother) in a weaker situation than the latter is to Ego's *mari* (mother's mother's brother). Thus 'through the *mari-kutara* tie there is strength between *gawel* and *waku*, so that a solid bond is established from *mari* in the second ascending generation and second lateral line to the right of Ego, and *kutara* in the second descending generation and second lateral line to the left of Ego'.[2] Indeed, *mari*, who plays the rôle of faithful friend to Ego, is *gawel* to Ego's own *gawel*: 'the *mari-kutara* reciprocal creates an equilibrium in the kinship structure by balancing the inequalities of the *gawel-waku* reciprocal'.[3] Using an argument of the same type Warner purports to account for the two succeeding lines, one added to the right of the *mari* line, the other to the left of the *kutara* line:

'*Momelker* and *natchiwalker* are important because the former is the mother of Ego's mother-in-law, and the latter because he is the brother of this woman. *Dumungur*, reciprocal of these terms, is emotionally important because, from the point of view of *momelker* and *natchiwalker*,

---

[1] Warner, 1931, p. 182.   [2] ibid. p 179.   [3] ibid. p. 182.

he is the person who has a feeling of taboo for them since the woman is his mother-in-law's mother.'[1]

This interpretation seems to us to entail an arbitrary and dangerous teleology, in that it amounts to explaining the unconscious bases of social life by conscious or semi-conscious superstructures, and primary phenomena by secondary and derivative phenomena. All the specialists on Australia have stressed the importance of the kinship system, by showing that kinship relationships define the respective status of individuals in the group, and their rights and duties to each other. This general observation would lose all meaning if, as Warner suggests, it is psychological needs that determine the existence or non-existence of certain degrees of kinship. For then we should be trapped in a circular argument, the kinship system giving rise to attitudes, and these attitudes modifying the kinship system. Even if the relationships of *kutara* and *mari*, and of *momelker* and *dumungur*, were not in the terminology, there would always be someone occupying the place which these terms designate. The function of equilibrium, fulfilled by *kutara* and *mari*, would thus be no less assured within a system whose structure and terminology would simply be different. Conversely, if supplementary columns were indefinitely added, a definite function would appear in the system for each new kinship relationship thus created.[2] To justify the addition of supplementary classes, Warner reasons, as we have seen, as if the Murngin system could function with only three lines, and as it is clear that, in this case, the system would terminate abruptly on both sides, he suggests a hypothesis which is neither necessary nor adequate. It is not necessary, since theoretically, and allowing for the existence of the moieties, the functioning of the system depends not on three lines but on four. On the other hand, the psychological hypothesis is not adequate, since although it is propounded in order to avoid leaving the system with its ends hanging in the air, it assures nothing of the kind. Whom does *natchiwalker* marry, and who marries *dumungur*? The information given by Warner on this point is obscure:

'This asymmetrical cross-cousin marriage causes a male relative in the third patrilineal line to the left of Ego and a female relative in the third patrilineal column to the right of Ego to go unmated (in the kinship system) or a never-ending addition to this system to bring about a sym-

[1] Warner, 1931, p. 152.

[2] Leach, 1961*a*, p. 77, protested as early as 1951 against this criticism of Warner, asserting that Warner's psycho-sociological interpretation was perfectly structural and that he himself accepted it. However, in order to perceive the artificial character of this kind of argument, one need only note that Warner, while constructing a model in equilibrium, wavers between five and seven lines, while Leach–who claims to adopt Warner's interpretation–uses only four (which, moreover, are not the same as those chosen by Warner). This confirms my thesis that 'functionalist' reconstructions of this type are tautological; too many of them can be put forward for any one of them to be any good.

metrical form, but as one line is added to each side of the system a new one is necessary, unless some device is created to throw this additional line back into the kinship. This has been done by the natives. *Natchiwalker* marries *mari* (not *mari* as mother's mother); *gawel* marries a distant *mokul* and to the left of Ego *dumungur* marries another *kutara*, and *waku* another *gurrong*.'[1]

This passage can be interpreted in different ways. Either we are faced simply with an extension of the nomenclature, the terms concerned having little meaning except in differentiating between 'affines' on the one hand and 'affines of affines' on the other, i.e., between lineages as they belong to one or other of the moieties; or the statement refers to the actual closing of the cycle of matrimonial exchanges. In this latter case, we would have to have demographic information – which we lack – on the empirical structure of the cycles of reciprocity among the Murngin in order to be able to make a correct interpretation of Warner's information, which has been confirmed both by Elkin[2] and by Berndt.[3] The theoretically circular model which is presupposed by the rule of marriage with the matrilateral cousin can in practice be either broken down into several cycles or lengthened indefinitely. We shall return to this later. Because we do not have more precise information on the empirical modalities of the marriage cycles, we shall be reduced to constructing hypotheses about the empirical structure of the system, and it is with this reservation that the following observations are presented.

It has been seen that the Murngin kinship system has seven lines, while the Aranda system has only four (the father's father's, which is Ego's line; the mother's father's; the father's mother's brother's; and the mother's mother's brother's) and the Kariera system has only two (the father's father's, which is Ego's line; and the mother's father's). These proportions are similarly reflected in the number of kinship terms used in each of the systems. While the Kariera system employs twenty-one different kinship terms, the Aranda employs forty-one, and the Murngin system seventy-one. How is it that the Murngin system, which brings about an intermediate dichotomy between that of the Kariera and the Aranda systems, requires almost double the number of kinship terms as that of the more complex system?

This difficulty is exactly analogous to that met with when comparing different class systems. We stated then that the Aranda system seemed to result from the doubling of the Kariera system, but that nevertheless a necessary stage in the progressive dichotomy of spouses was skipped in passing from one to the other. At this point, we see that there is also a relationship between the degree of dichotomy realized and the number of kinship terms used: the Aranda system, which divides the dichotomy of spouses as used by the Kariera into two, also has twice as many terms as the latter. Logically, then, the Murngin system, the dichotomy of which is intermediate

---

[1] Warner, 1931, pp. 210–11.　　　[2] Elkin, 1953.　　　[3] Berndt, 1955.

between the two, should also have an intermediate number of kinship terms. In fact, it has seventy-one of them, which is a much larger number than theoretical analysis would have predicted. This difficulty is insoluble, as long as the Murngin system is seen as a form of the Aranda system, unless we rely upon psychological arguments such as Warner's, which depend upon considerations which are foreign to the structure of the system. By contrast, the problem becomes clear once we discern behind the explicit system (double system of restricted exchange with eight classes) what has been referred to above as the implicit system (system of generalized exchange with four classes) which is the law of the Murngin system. Let us then reproduce the structure of the kinship system by replacing the kinship terms by the classes into which each kinsman would fall in a system of generalized exchange (Fig. 30).

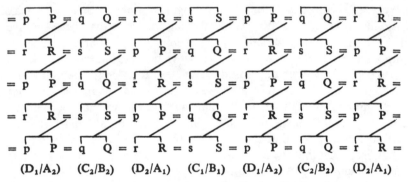

Fig. 30. Murngin system in terms of generalized exchange.

To facilitate comparison with Fig. 23, showing the distribution of classes by the alternate use of the regular and the alternate systems of eight sub-sections, Fig. 30 reproduces, at the bottom of each line, the patrilineal couple which characterizes it in the preceding figure. It may be seen that there is complete coincidence between both forms, as the following list of equivalences between the patrilineal couples in both shows:

Generalized exchange (Four classes)		*Restricted exchange* (Alternate usage of two systems with eight classes)
PR	corresponds to	D_1-A_2
QS	„ „	C_2-B_2
RP	„ „	D_2-A_1
SQ	.. „	C_1-B_1

This system of equivalences makes possible a decisive step in the argument.

It does not merely show that the system of generalized exchange coincides in all respects with the system of restricted exchange of which it provides the simplest and most intelligible expression, but it also provides the reason for, and the means by which, the change from one to the other is effected.

Fig. 31. Descent and residence in generalized exchange.

Two identical but inverse couples in the system of generalized exchange always correspond to two different couples in the system of restricted exchange. Thus, $PR = D_1-A_2$, and $RP = D_2-A_1$, and on the other hand, $QS = C_2-B_2$, but $SQ = C_1-B_1$. This may be expressed as follows: an inversion of the terms of a couple of sections, in a generalized system, corresponds to an alternation of the subsections of one and the same couple, without the inversion of the sections, in a restricted system. Indeed, if the subsections were ignored, we would have PR or $RP = DA$, and QS or $SQ = CB$.

If, instead of establishing the equivalence between couples, we try to establish it between terms comprising the couples, it will then be seen that to each term of the generalized system there always correspond two terms of the restricted system:

P corresponds to D_1, A_1
Q   „   „ C_2, B_1
R   „   „ A_2, D_2
S   „   „ B_2, C_1

since the change in position of a term in one system corresponds to a change of term, without a change in position, in the other. This means that the subsections of the restricted systems are simply the result of the doubling of the original sections of the generalized system. Why is there this doubling?

When a formal analysis of the four-class system of generalized exchange was made, it was noted that this system functioned as if the group were divided into two patrilineal moieties, without a matrilineal dichotomy.

Let us now suppose that this group proposes to add a division into matrilineal moieties (explicit or implicit) to the existing division (explicit or implicit) into patrilineal moieties. This change will, firstly, be necessarily expressed by the splitting of each section into two subsections relating to one or other of the matrilineal moieties, which we shall call x and y. Instead of four sections, P, Q, R, S, there will then be eight subsections, P_x, P_y, Q_x, Q_y, R_x, R_y, S_x, and S_y.

Let us now suppose that the correspondence between *one* section of the generalized system and *two* subsections of the restricted system is explained by this splitting of the sections under the influence of the new matrilineal dichotomy. We shall then have the following system of equivalences:

Patrilineal moiety I

$$P_x = A_1 \qquad P_y = D_1 \qquad R_x = A_2 \qquad R_y = D_2$$

Patrilineal moiety II

$$Q_x = C_2 \qquad Q_y = B_1 \qquad S_x = C_1 \qquad S_y = B_2$$

and the form of marriage and descent, in the system of generalized exchange, will be established, as in Fig. 31, the conventions being the same as in Figs. 24 and 25. This can be expressed equally well in the type of diagram used for the Murngin system, by placing each subsection x or y of the generalized system of exchange in the place of the corresponding subsection of the system of restricted exchange (Fig. 32).

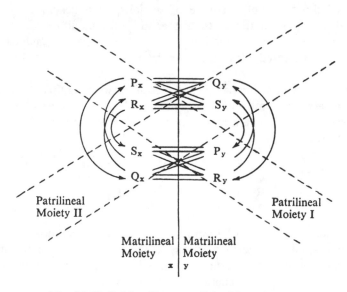

Fig. 32. Definitive diagram of the Murngin system.

By applying the double law of the exogamy of both the patrilineal and the matrilineal moieties, we thus have:

$$P_x \text{ man marries a } Q_y \text{ woman, the children are } R_y$$

R_x	,,	,,	,, S_y	,,	,,	,,	,, P_y
S_x	,,	,,	,, P_y	,,	,,	,,	,, Q_y
Q_x	,,	,,	,, R_y	,,	,,	,,	,, S_y

and

P_y man marries a Q_x woman, the children are R_x
Q_y „ „ „ R_x „ „ „ „ S_x
R_y „ „ „ S_x „ „ „ „ P_x
S_y „ „ „ P_x „ „ „ „ Q_x

a formula which establishes the ultimate identity of the system of generalized exchange, split by the introduction of the matrilineal dichotomy, and the eight-subsection Murngin system as it has been described above. This identity is now perfectly clear. At the same time we discover the reason for the juxtaposition of the two systems which have been called respectively regular and alternate, and also the verification of the law, which was proposed as a working hypothesis, that preferential marriage with the mother's brother's daughter entails the alternate use of these two systems. The principle of generalized exchange bequeaths an inheritance to the new system, in that the latter continues to be a directional system in which the directions are irreversible. The pairs are not formed in the same way, but vary according to the angle from which they are viewed, viz., when read from x to y the pairs conform to the regular system, when read from y to x they conform to the alternate system. That is to say, as we have postulated, that one out of every two marriages conforms to one of the systems, while the other marriage conforms to the other system. Instead of the real symmetry of the Kariera and Aranda systems, there is a pseudo-symmetry which may be reduced, in fact, to two superimposed asymmetrical structures.

V

It is in this structure, which is not simple but double, that the reason for the difficulty mentioned at the beginning of the chapter must be sought. We have remarked upon the enormous extension of the Murngin kinship system, coinciding with almost twice the number of kinship terms found in the most complex systems of the Aranda type. These peculiarities are explained if it is accepted that the Murngin system was originally an asymmetrical structure, and that it later reproduced, as it were, twin structures, in order to satisfy a law of symmetry. This point will perhaps be clearer if the following image is used, though it has, of course, no more than metaphorical value. A four-class system of generalized exchange may be considered as a three-dimensional geometrical structure. For the cycle is completed by moving from P to Q, Q to R, R to S, and finally back to P in the opposite direction from that in which it started. In short, exactly as one might travel from Paris to Moscow, from Moscow to Shanghai, from Shanghai to New York, and finally from New York back to Paris. In contrast, a system of restricted exchange may be represented geometrically in only two dimensions. Whatever the number of classes, there are never more than two points, directly linked by a fixed route which may be covered in both directions.

When the addition of matrilineal moieties changes the original generalized system to give it at least the appearance of a system of restricted exchange, a problem of representation, well known to geographers, is posed. How is the external aspect of a three-dimensional body to be represented on one plane? To cope with this, cartographers have at their disposal different methods of projection, none of which, however, provides a perfectly satisfactory solution. Thus, instead of showing only a half the earth's surface, two hemispheres are placed side by side in contact, one representing the eastern world, the other, the western. The most western part of one hemisphere, and the most eastern part of the other, which meet in reality, are shown as being farthest away from each other.

To meet this difficulty, an additional artifice is introduced. In order that the continuity between the extreme right and the extreme left of the map shall be perfectly clear, part of the territories represented on the left is repeated on the right, and vice versa. The countries in the middle of the map are thus represented only once, but those on the edges twice, once 'really', and once 'as a reminder'. We believe that an analogous artifice explains the peculiar development of the Murngin kinship system. Not that the aborigines effected this duplication consciously and voluntarily: the resulting complication is too great and too useless for this assumption to be accepted. Rather, the doubling is explained by the logical difficulty that was found, after the introduction of matrilineal moieties, in conceiving the system simultaneously as a kind of both restricted exchange and of generalized exchange. Everything suggests that the mind of the native had vainly sought to represent one and the same structure simultaneously in three dimensions and on one plane, and to see it under the dual aspect of continuity and alternation. What then is the end result?

Let us represent the sections of a system of generalized exchange on the equator of a sphere (Fig. 33).

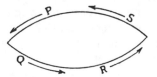

Fig. 33. A four-class cycle.

Starting from R, it is obviously possible to get to S by two different directions. But these directions are not equivalent for Ego. For by following the route *S–P–Q–R*, he proceeds, as it were, in the direction of rotation of the system. He always faces in the direction which he had to take in seeking a wife. By contrast, in following the route *Q–P–S–R*, Ego proceeds in the wrong direction; he must turn about, and face in the direction in which not he but his sister is directed to find a spouse. In attempting to represent this directional structure on one plane, aboriginal thought has thus naturally doubled, to the right and left of Ego, these two routes which have such different meanings. Starting from Ego's section, R, it swings the curve S–P–Q back to the right, the direction prescribed by the system, and the curve Q–P–S to the left in the prohibited direction. Ego's patrilineal cycle (C_1–B_1 for an Ego of section R), is therefore represented only once, while the three other cycles are each represented twice, once to the right and once to the left. There are then, on the right, the successive lines D_1–A_2, C_2–B_2, and D_2–A_1, and on the left, identical lines succeeding each other in inverse order, or, as it were, backwards, i.e., D_2–A_1, C_2–B_2, and D_1–A_2. The structure in space has been projected on to the plane, so that the point in space occupied by Ego's section corresponds to one and one point only on the plane, while each of the remaining three points of the structure in space, representing the three remaining sections, corresponds to two symmetrical and opposed points on the plane projection.

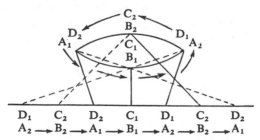

Fig. 34. Plane projection of a cyclical system.

The three central groups, D_2–A_1, C_1–B_1 and D_1–A_2, are not affected by the change, and form the common and immutable base of the generalized system, and of its transposition under a restricted form. The group C_2–B_2 which in the generalized system had the function of completing the cycle by furnishing wives for D_1–A_2, and husbands for D_2–A_1, is doubled in two groups C_2–B_2, flanking, on the right and on the left, the stable set composed by the three central groups. Finally, on the other side of C_2–B_2, each of the stable groups D_2–A_1 and D_1–A_2 is reflected, one to the extreme right, the other to the extreme left of the system. On the basis of their function in the system, the three central groups are thus the 'real' groups, and the same is true of one of the two groups C_2–B_2, either one being equally able to play this rôle according to the point from which the system is viewed. But the two extreme groups, which reproduce in a symmetrical but inverse position the two terminal groups of the central triad, are unable to be anything other than echoes or reflections. Therefore, all the kinship terms which are applied to them are the literal repetitions, or diminutives, of kinship terms belonging to the homologous line. Ego, looking left, sees in succession D_2–A_1 (real) and D_1-A_2 (reflection), but he does not see D_1-A_2 (real), which is to the right. Likewise, in looking right, he sees D_1-A_2 (real) and through it D_2-A_1 (reflection), but he does not see D_2-A_1 (real), which is to the left. Thus the terminology of D_1-A_2 (reflection) repeats that of D_2-A_1 (real), which is the same as regards the sections, if not the subsections. And the terminology of D_2-A_1 (reflection) repeats that of D_1-A_2 (real), which stands in the same relationship.

We have already said that the theory of the Murngin system will not be brought to a conclusion until there is precise information on the way in which the marriage cycles are closed. But we can see even now that the Murngin kinship system is to all appearances a system with four patrilineal couples in which, in order to resolve a problem of representation, three of the couples have had to be reproduced twice. Only Ego's couple remains undivided, and the reason for this is clear, viz., that Ego is unable to see himself, and his own line, simultaneously as subject and as object.

On the basis of the phrase, 'the way in which the marriage cycles are closed', Leach has accused me – and Berndt and Goody in his wake – firstly, of confusing, as did Lawrence and Murdock, 'local lines' and 'descent lines', and secondly, of mistakenly postulating the circularity of the Murngin system.

With regard to the first point, it is sufficient to consider Fig. 34 and the comments thereon to see that, far from having ignored the difference between 'local lines' and 'descent lines', I was not only the first to formulate it, although in different terms, but also the first to reduce the number of 'real' groups (in my terminology) to $3 + 1 = 4$, a result which Leach has done no more than borrow from me, while at the same time gratuitously imputing to me a conception of a different kind.

However, Leach has not been aware of the fact that the particular formulation which he adopts would have to be just the opposite to be correct: 'local lines' are fixed in number but the number is unquestionably high. It is the 'descent lines' and not the 'local lines' which number four, i.e., three which every individual applies unequivocally to concrete 'local lines', and one, which he can choose to apply to a fourth, which may be either to his extreme right or to his extreme left. All the other 'descent lines' are terminological reduplications of the preceding 'descent lines', and Ego projects them, as it were, on to 'local lines' which are even more indirectly allied to his, so as to be able to give them a name.

Consequently, it is false to follow Leach and to say that the Murngin system comprises seven 'descent lines' and four 'local lines'. In point of fact, Murngin society, observed at any one time, has a finite (but high) number of 'local lines', the actual number of which is unknown to us. To define his kinship relationships, Ego has at his disposal four 'descent lines', three of which are fixed and one not, enabling him to place himself in relation to four 'local lines': his own, the line of those who give him wives, and that of those who take wives from him; plus one, which is at his own discretion, either that of the wife-givers of his wife-givers, or that of the wife-receivers of his wife-receivers. As it seems that the cycles of exchange involve more than four local groups, Ego has been led to coin supplementary terms (though derived from pre-existing terms) to designate possible 'local lines', sometimes wife-giving lines or wife-givers of his own wife-givers, sometimes wife-taking lines or wife-takers of his own wife-takers. Finally, if the cycles extend even further he can always repeat the same process *ad lib.* or, if they are less extensive, he can always drop certain remote names in favour of closer ones; on the sole condition, however, that the cycle shall be effectively closed, i.e., that it comprise an even number of 'local lines' $\geqq 4$ (because of the existence of the patrilineal moieties).

Elkin and Radcliffe-Brown have argued about cycles $\geqq 10$ (i.e., never closed), while Lawrence and Murdock have elaborated a special terminological solution to a cycle = 8, but, paradoxically, by misinterpreting an observation by Webb in reporting (as Elkin suspected) a cycle = 6. All these arrangements are possible at the price of a statistical fluctuation in the relationship between regular marriages and alternate marriages, a fluctuation which would not jeopardize the equilibrium of the system provided that somewhere there were an equal and opposite statistical fluctuation.

This much said, the distinction between 'local lines' and 'descent lines' is still over-simplified. In point of fact, three things must be distinguished: the *obligatory* 'descent lines', which number $3+(1)$; the *optional* 'descent lines', which number $4-(1)$; and the 'local lines', the number of which is unknown to us, since it varies according to the time and place, but which could not be less than four, and (because of the range of the terminological system) must as a general rule be much higher.

The second criticism brought against me – that I mistakenly postulated the circularity of the system – derives from a misunderstanding between what is meant by model and what is meant by empirical reality. The model of a generalized system necessarily implies a certain circularity although this may be simple or complex, and may assume various forms. But the empirical reality is far more flexible. Of all the empirically observable cycles of alliances, a certain proportion will be found to be circular, either short term (three are absolutely necessary, at least four among the Murngin because of the division into moieties) or long term; and others, which never 'join up' because they are 'lost'. All that is needed for the model to remain valid, broadly speaking, is for the number 'lost' in one direction to be approximately equal to the number 'lost' in the other direction, so that negatively as well as positively the losses balance out. As Leach has acknowledged, I have fully explained, with regard to the Kachin, the flexible conception of empirical circularity which must be held. The latter must always be distinguished from the theoretically strict circularity of the model, be it the native's or the ethnologist's. When (following Warner, moreover) I raise the question of the circularity of the Murngin system, I do not think of it as an empirical circularity, but as an objective model of circularity by means of which the natives conceptualize their system. The anomaly in the Murngin system which, like Murdock and Lawrence, I bring to light from this viewpoint is that the model of circularity appears clearly in the class system, but not in the terminological system; an anomaly which, as I have demonstrated, disappears on the assumption that there is an alternation between regular marriage and alternate marriage.

Accordingly, I not only anticipated Leach by distinguishing the 'descent lines' from the 'local lines', and by showing that one of these categories should not exceed four terms; but I likewise anticipated the solution to the subsequent controversy, between Leach and Berndt, over the exact number of lines (four according to one, three according to the other), by showing that four lines can be analysed into three fixed and one not, only three having an objective existence, and the choice of the fourth being a function of Ego's particular outlook.

To claim, as Leach does, that a system of matrilateral marriage is not necessarily circular, at least in theory, is the same as asserting that a cyclist who kept the handle-bars of his bicycle turned in the same direction would not go round in a circle. Admittedly, he might never return exactly to his starting-point, but it can be taken as statistically probable that, if several cyclists complete a large enough number of revolutions in the one direction, they will inevitably cross over the starting-point of one of them, and a great number of times at that. For a matrilateral system to be totally devoid of circularity, the number of 'local lines' would have to be infinite. The fewer they are, the greater will be the chance of an approximate circularity being manifested. As a matter of fact, the circularity of asymmetrical systems does not result from a preordained ordering of the 'local groups', but from the fact that, in whatever way they establish relationships among themselves, the genealogical space in which they move is 'curved'.

Consequently, even if we agree on the distinction between the 'local lines' and the 'descent lines', it remains a fact that a definitive interpretation of the Murngin system still eludes us because our ignorance of, firstly, the number of 'local lines' at any one time, and, secondly, the extent of the networks of alliances uniting them (short or long? closed or not?). If all these possibilities were to be realized, how frequent and in what proportion would they be?

Only if these questions were answered could there be any glimpse of the solution to a problem which Murdock and Lawrence on the one hand, and Berndt and Leach on the other, have too casually believed they could tackle in opposite ways, viz., one party by affirming the equivalence of 'descent lines' and 'local lines', the other by entirely rejecting this idea.

The truth seems to be that, although the lines are theoretically distinct, one set being on the conceptual plane, the others on the demographic plane, they must in practice be capable, to a certain point, of being *adjusted* to each other. As I emphasized in the first edition of this book, we do not know exactly how the Murngin set about this. The structure of the system is such that there are 'local lines', and these 'local lines' can be organized into cycles of alliance. Therefore, empirically, we must encounter cycles of various lengths, but never odd in number (owing to the division into patrilineal moieties). If these cycles = $7+1$, $7+3$, $7+5$, etc., the nomenclature applicable to them is that which was observed by Warner and Elkin; and it is clear that Webb's claim to the contrary, which has been disputed but which is nevertheless perfectly plausible, deals with a particular case in which the cycle of 'local lines' = $7-1$.

In the final analysis, the Murngin paradox is reduced to the fact, of which pages 189–92 have already provided the explanation, that an odd-numbered conceptual system ('descent lines') is used to describe an even-numbered actual system ('local lines'); the adjustment can be carried out either by reduplicating (Elkin, Radcliffe-Brown), or by eliminating (Webb), certain conceptual series. But there is no theoretical reason why either procedure should be used exclusively, for it would be equally incorrect to assert, as the observers have implicitly done, but in a mutually contradictory manner, either that the 'local lines' are never cyclical, or that they are always cyclical with the same periodicity. Without ever having visited the Murngin, one can assert that the truth is to be found half-way between these two postulates, something which no observer seems to have suspected that he could easily verify empirically by means of what might be called 'lateral' genealogies, i.e., by establishing a certain number of concrete examples of networks of alliance between 'local groups'. In the preface to the second edition of *A Black Civilization*, Warner criticizes me – obviously without having read my work, since the rather casual argument he puts forward by-passes the problems on which I have centred my discussion – for not basing my analysis on the study of genealogies. I might reply: Very well, but whose fault is that? It is clear that his admirable book consists entirely of abstract models of the empirical reality, but that concrete data (genealogical and demographic) are most woefully lacking. I do not doubt that Warner might have used them to construct his models; but since by not publishing his data he has studiously refrained from giving us the opportunity to draw deductions other than his own, he is not in a very strong position to criticize me for not having used them.

My interpretation is directly confirmed by McConnel's observations among the tribes of Cape York Peninsula, which have matrilateral marriage, like the Murngin, but recognize, according to the groups, only five or six lines. Nevertheless, the terminology of the system extends to seven lines, as in the Murngin system, and the author indicates that the seventh line to the left is only the reflection of the first to the right.[1] Thus the real cycle is shorter than it appears from a superficial examination of the terminology. In fact, in the table of the Wikmunkan system, the third line to the right of Ego's,

[1] McConnel, 1940, p. 445.

and the third line to the left, doubles Ego's line, if certain terminological differences in Ego's generation and in the two immediately consecutive generations in ascending and descending order are excepted. These differences can be explained by the fact that, as we shall see in the following chapter, each line is subdivided into two branches, older and younger respectively, and that the third line to the left is represented by an elder branch, and the third to the right by a younger branch. The probability, therefore, is that the Wikmunkan system is in fact a system with three lines, as the Murngin system is a system with four.

The reason for the abnormal extension of the system and of the considerable number of kinship terms can be seen. The extension, which in itself is incomprehensible, of the system so as to include seven lines is explained when we conceive of it as a system with four lines prolonged by its own reflection. If we consider the kinship terms, we can understand that each line, extending over five generations and requiring one term for the masculine group and one for the feminine group in each generation, needs ten terms. If we then add a supplementary term to Ego's line, because Ego may be a man or a woman, we have forty-one kinship terms for the four basic lines, i.e., the same number as in an Aranda-type system. But as each line is produced twice, except Ego's line with its eleven terms, we easily arrive at the figure of seventy-one, which no longer appears mysterious.

CHAPTER XIII

Harmonic and Disharmonic Regimes

I

If our analysis is correct, the problem of peripheral systems which are without classes or have an aberrant number of classes needs to be seen in a new light. A typology based exclusively on the Kariera and Aranda systems would prove inadequate in the north and south of Australia, where there are systems with not two, four, or eight lines but an odd number, e.g., three in the south, and three, five, six (considered as a multiple of three), and seven in the north. Furthermore, these systems practise the dichotomy of cross-cousins into patrilateral and matrilateral, although this seemed impossible in the previous systems.

The Karadjeri of Lagrange Bay in north-western Australia recognize only three lines, those of the father's father, the mother's father (identified with the father's mother's brother) and the mother's mother's brother. As marriage is prohibited with the father's sister's daughter but sanctioned with the mother's brother's daughter, there .is a structure of the following type (Fig. 35).

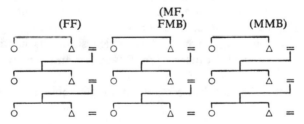

Fig. 35. The Karadjeri System.

The characteristic feature of the system as Elkin sees it lies in the prohibition of the exchange of sisters.[1] It is undoubtedly prohibited according to the formula in force among Kariera or Aranda type systems. It remains to be seen whether it is not the very notion of exchange, as it may be elaborated on the basis of these systems, which should be changed in order that new modalities may be integrated into it.

[1] Elkin, 1940b; 1931b, pp. 299–312.

Another tripartite system most likely of the same type is known among
the Tiwi of Bathurst and Melville Islands, to the north-east of Port Darwin.
The Tiwi are divided into twenty-two matrilineal totemic clans, which are
grouped into three unnamed exogamous phratries.[1] Their system is probably
not unrelated to that of the Larakia and Wulna, which is similar to but
simpler than the Murngin system. There are neither moieties nor sections
and the system recognizes only five lines (as among the Yir-yoront), joined
according to the formula of generalized exchange (marriage with the mother's
brother's daughter).[2]

The Mara system deserves particular attention, not only because of its
coastal and northern distribution, which makes the Mara and the Anula
neighbours or almost neighbours of the Murngin, but also because of its
peculiar characteristics. At the bottom of the Gulf of Carpentaria and at the
mouth of the Roper River there is a group of tribes with a kinship terminology
of the Aranda type, but with only four named divisions instead of eight
subsections. Furthermore, the son remains in his father's division, and this
gives the four divisions the appearance of patrilineal lines grouped by pairs
into two moieties.[3]

The marriage rules state that a man cannot marry into his own division,
or into the alternate division of his moiety, or into his mother's division.
Thus, the only marriage possible is with a woman of his mother's moiety,
and of the alternate division of this moiety. If we call the four divisions P,
Q (moiety I) and R, S (moiety II), a P man can marry only an R woman
if his mother is S, and an S woman if his mother is R. Consequently, the
wives of the men of one patrilineal line P will be R and S alternately.

Radcliffe-Brown and, following him, Warner have tried to bring the social
structure and the kinship terminology into harmony. They use the alternation
of classes in the mother's series as the ground for recognizing two unnamed
divisions in each named division, allegiance to one or the other leading to
different matrimonial destinies. In other words, the division P conceals an
unformulated subdivision into Pa and Pd which shows its hand, however,
in the fact that a man of Pa marries an R woman, and a man of Pd an S
woman.

There would thus be, not four sections, but eight subsections, viz.,

Murungun a ... $\}$ (P)	Purdal b ... $\}$ (R)
Murungun d ...	Purdal c ...
Mumbali a ... $\}$ (Q)	Kuial b ... $\}$ (S)
Mumbali d ...	Kuial c ...

[1] Hart, 1930a, pp. 167–80; 1930b, pp. 280–90.
[2] Warner, 1933, pp. 73–4 and table VII.
[3] Radcliffe-Brown, 1931, p. 41; Warner, 1933, pp. 78–9.

The marriage system would thus be identical with that of an Aranda system (Fig. 36). Radcliffe-Brown concludes: 'It can be shown that in this way each of the four semi-moieties consists of two groups which are exactly equivalent to the subsections of other tribes.'[1]

We were faced with a similar problem with the Murngin system but we had to resort to another solution. We felt that this system, with its eight named or unnamed subsections, should be interpreted as resulting from an

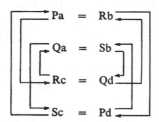

Fig. 36. The Mara System (after Warner, 1933, p. 79).

attempt to adapt a four-class system of a different type to the Aranda formulas. The presence of the Mara system in a neighbouring region makes this hypothesis seem very likely. Furthermore, the question must be asked whether the Mara system itself should not be interpreted in this way, i.e., as a system effectively with four classes and a borrowed Aranda-type terminology. An argument immediately presents itself in support of this interpretation. If the Mara system differed from an Aranda system only in that the subsections were unnamed, the rules of marriage would be strictly identical in both. But this is not so. Sharp has established that there is an alternative marriage formula in the Mara-type systems studied by him in north-western Queensland: 'The marriage rule is of the normal Aranda type by which a man and his sister marry the daughter and son of a mother's mother's brother's daughter. Exceptionally, however, they may marry the daughter and son of a mother's brother.'[2] This being so, one may well ask oneself if the two systems are not structurally different.

There is a system in another part of the world which is similar to the Mara system, but independent of any Aranda system. This is the Munda system of northern India.[3] This system distinguishes two patrilocal groups, each divided into two marriage classes. If we call the two divisions of one group P and R, and the two divisions of the other group, Q and S, the following rule of marriage is established: if one generation practises marriages of the type $P = Q$ or $R = S$, marriage in the following generation should be according to the formulas $P = S$ and $R = Q$. Yet we must add that while the marriage rule $P = Q$ is in force, R can take advantage of an alternative marriage with either Q or S, and vice versa. Sharp has noted a similar

---

[1] Radcliffe-Brown, 1931, p. 41.   [2] Sharp, 1935, p. 158.
[3] cf. ch. XXVI.

development among the Laierdila of the islands and coast of Queensland. Their system is of the Mara type but has two additional marriage possibilities, one with the mother's brother's son's daughter, and the other with the father's father's sister's daughter.[1]

'It is thus possible for an A_1 man to marry a woman of any of the sub-sections B_1, B_2, C_1 or C_2, or any woman of the moiety opposite to his own',[2] the subsections no longer determining where the children belong by reference to the mother's subsection. It seems that the situation is the same among the Munda, since the type of marriage prescribed for one generation determines the type prescribed for the following generation, however the father happens in fact to have married.

When we come to analyse the Munda system, we shall show that the only way to interpret it satisfactorily is to treat it as a four-class system prescribing marriage with the father's sister's daughter. Furthermore, we shall see what the basic relationship is between patrilateral and matrilateral marriage. Consequently, the question arises seriously whether the Mara system, like the Murngin system which we saw as a four-class system with matrilateral marriage, expressed by a complex set of formulas in terms of the Aranda system, should not similarly be considered as a four-class system with patrilateral marriage, also expressed in terms of an Aranda-type system. In fact, as we have seen, the alternative form of Mara marriage still preserves this type of marriage.

Moreover, in the Cape York Peninsula of Queensland both forms of marriage, matrilateral and patrilateral, exist side by side. It is particularly significant that the Wikmunkan, who are matrilateral, nevertheless sanction marriage with the father's sister's daughter as with the mother's brother's daughter, and strictly prohibit it only with the bilateral cross-cousin. Their eastern neighbours, the Kandyu, practise patrilateral marriage exclusively.[3]

Thus, the principal difference between the Mara system and the Murngin system seems to be that the latter has openly adopted eight classes in order to preserve its specific orientation, while the Mara system, because it has kept to its primitive structure, has had to allow its patrilateral orientation to be submerged in the apparently bilateral form of its alternate marriage, which is of the Kariera type: the father's sister's daughter is also the mother's brother's daughter, as is brought out clearly in chart II of Sharp's article.[4]

It is true that Sharp has shown that the Laierdila effectively distinguish their semi-moieties, if not in the regulation of marriage, then at least in their particular totemic system. Moreover, Elkin has made similar observations: 'We do know, however, that sections and subsections and moieties are frequently totemic in nature, and that in some regions at least, they have

---

[1] Sharp, 1935, p. 161.   [2] ibid. p. 162.
[3] McConnel, 1940, p. 437. On her interpretation of these differences, and our criticism, cf. ch. XXVII. Since this book was written it no longer seems so certain that patrilateral marriage exists among the Kandyu.
[4] Sharp, 1935, p. 171.

spread or are spreading as a system of totemism.'[1] But only the four groups, *P, Q, R, S,* are objectively named among the Laierdila. From the fact that the subsection couples are regarded as units, it in no way follows that this unity should be seen as the unity of a couple. At all events, there is nothing in Sharp's analysis to justify such a conclusion. Nevertheless, it is to be expected that the notion of subsection will be formulated in coincidence with the degree of success with which the system is converted to the Aranda formula. The important point lies elsewhere. Until more information is available, the Mara system should not be regarded as an Aranda system which has lost some of its superficial characteristics, but as an original and heterogeneous system upon which Aranda features are gradually being imposed.

II

Do the aberrant groups of southern Australia confirm, in the same respects as do those of the north, this view of the matter?

The Arabana recognize three lines, those of the father's father (classified with the mother's mother's brother), the father's mother's brother, and the mother's father. The fact that the father's father is classified with the mother's mother's brother, while the father's mother's brother is distinguished from the mother's mother's husband, would suggest an original system of marriage with the father's sister's daughter.[2] The natives energetically deny, contrary to what Spencer and Gillen have indicated,[3] that any form of marriage between cross-cousins has been practised. And yet children's spouses continue to be identified with the sister's children, a typical equation in a system based on cross-cousin marriage. To complicate the situation, Spencer and Gillen noted a terminological identification, viz., father's sister = father's mother, which Elkin was unable to rediscover, although a usage of the same type still exists among the Yaralde and Ungarinyin.[4] The identification of relatives belonging to two or more consecutive generations is, as we shall see, characteristic of systems based upon marriage with the mother's brother's daughter, and the Arabana terminology even today maintains certain asymmetries which are in accord with such a system; thus, although the father's father is identified with the mother's mother's brother as *kadnini*, their respective lines are called by different terms, and the same happens with the mother's mother and the father's father's sister. Although the terminology recognizes only three lines, the rules of marriage and descent distinguish four. The fact that the present system is in a 'broken-down condition' and

---

[1] Elkin, 1940*a*, p. 24; 1937. [2] ibid. 1940*b*, pp. 441–8.
[3] Spencer and Gillen, 1899, pp. 59–68.
[4] Needham (1960*a*, p. 285, n. 33) mistakenly disputes this assertion. I do not say 'the same usage' but 'a usage of the same type', namely the use of a consecutive terminology to designate women belonging to the same lineage and of two generation levels. In fact, it is not myself, but Elkin, who rightly compares the Arabana case cited with the terminology of the Yaralde and the Ungarinyin (Elkin, 1940*b*, p. 438).

'in a stage of transition'[1] prevents Spencer and Gillen's information from being completely refuted. The identification of the father's sister with the father's mother suggests that the three lines were originally matrilineal, as the totemic clans are even now in the north-western part of South Australia. A structure featuring marriage with the father's sister's daughter and matrilineal descent would be of the type shown in Fig. 37, in which the three

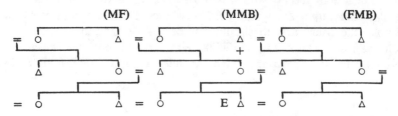

Fig. 37. The Aluridja system.

+ : Father's father, mother's mother's brother.

elementary lines are easily discoverable, and in which also the identification of the father's father with the mother's mother's brother can be understood. Consequently, Elkin's hypothesis that this original form of marriage was once allowed among the Arabana seems to be correct, even though this form of marriage is now prohibited.

In regulating marriage the Aluridja use two reciprocal terms, *tanamildjan* and *ŋanandaga*. The first is used between members of the same generation. It is also used between an individual and the members of his grandfather's generation on the one hand, and the members of his grandson's generation on the other. The second is used reciprocally between members of two consecutive generations in ascending or descending order (i.e., between a man and his father, or between a man and his son). The alternate generations are grouped together in 'lines', and the marriage rule requires that both spouses shall belong to the same 'line'.[2] A similar system exists among the Northern Aranda,[3] and another has been observed by Bateson in New Guinea.[4] They may all usefully be likened to the classification of alternate generations into *ŋanandaga* (grandfather; Ego; grandson) and *tanamildjan* (father; son) in western South Australia. Not only can a man marry only a *ŋanandaga* woman, but the alternation of generations forms the basis of ritual, and of reciprocal prestations.

The southern Aluridja practise, at least occasionally, marriage with the father's sister's daughter. That it could once have been a general practice is suggested by the fact that under no circumstances is the identification of the mother's brother with the wife's father acceptable. Patrilateral marriage is also known among the Wailpi.[5] Elkin considers these consequences as

[1] ibid. 1940*b*, pp. 446, 447.   [2] ibid. pp. 213–24; 1940*a*, p. 23, n. 5.
[3] ibid, 1940*b*, pp. 200–1.   [4] Bateson, 1931, pp. 245–91.   [5] Elkin, 1940*b*, pp. 380–1.

anomalies. And yet if we look at Fig. 37, which illustrates this form of marriage, we shall see that the Aluridja arrangement of 'lines' corresponds exactly to the structure of patrilateral marriage. In a system of marriage with the father's sister's daughter, that is, one generation in two marries in one direction, and one generation in two marries in the other. In other words, an individual can, without upsetting the system, take a wife from his own generation or from his grandfather's generation or from his grandson's generation, both of which relatives in these two latter generations make marriages of the same type as in his own. But he is absolutely forbidden to marry into the generations immediately before or after his own, which are destined to a different type of marriage. In other words, the Aluridja formula is structurally identical with the Mara formula, except that the structure of one is expressed in vertical terms (lines) and the structure of the other in horizontal terms (generations). Both can be and in actual fact are affected by other types of system; yet their specific character remains apparent. Furthermore, an important theoretical statement must be made. The system of alternate generations does not result exclusively, or necessarily, from bilateral descent. It is also an immediate function of patrilateral marriage, which is a simple structure of reciprocity.[1] This point will have to be remembered when we discuss the archaic Chinese system. As Elkin excellently remarks: 'It is, of course, theoretically possible that the section-system was evolved . . . as a means of preserving alternate generation-levels and preventing cross-cousin marriage, but these are both done quite efficiently where there are no such groupings.'[2] We shall have to emphasize repeatedly that all the effects of the different forms of marriage class systems may occur when there are no such systems, by the appropriate determination of the underlying relationships: 'Moieties and sections are not universal and inevitable developments from the kinship-system and associated marriage-rules.'[3]

The system in the neighbourhood of Southern Cross in Western Australia should probably be interpreted in the same way. The group is divided into two endogamous moieties. A man marries within his moiety, but the children belong to the alternate moiety. As Radcliffe-Brown says, each division 'is equivalent to one intermarrying pair of sections' (Fig. 38).[4]

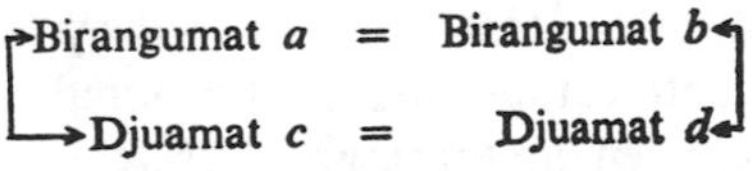

$$\begin{array}{rcl} \text{Birangumat } a & = & \text{Birangumat } b \\ \text{Djuamat } c & = & \text{Djuamat } d \end{array}$$

Fig. 38. The Southern Cross system.

But why does the system have this peculiar form? This question can only be answered if the system is considered as originally a four-class system with patrilateral marriage, later converted to bilateralism.

[1] cf. ch. VIII and ch. XXVII.
[3] loc. cit
[2] Elkin, 1940*a*, p. 23.
[4] Radcliffe-Brown, 1931, p. 41.

III

Of all the kinship systems known at the present time, that of the Dieri of South Australia is one of those which are the most difficult to interpret. Nevertheless, the differences between the information given by Howitt and that collected by Elkin thirty-two years later[1] are very slight. The system seems to be stationary, or at least to have completed its evolution. This makes it all the more difficult to reconstruct its evolutionary stages.

The Dieri have two matrilineal moieties, and totemic clans which are also matrilineal. They apparently do not have sections or subsections. Yet, from the point of view of marriage rules, their system functions as an Aranda system, with the prohibition of marriage between cross-cousins, and preferential marriage between the four types of second cousins descended from cross-cousins (mother's mother's brother's daughter's daughter; mother's father's sister's daughter's daughter; father's father's sister's son's daughter; father's father's brother's son's daughter). There are also reciprocal terms between members of the second ascending generation and the second descending generation (viz., father's father = son's son; mother's father = daughter's son; father's mother = son's daughter; mother's mother = daughter's daughter; respectively, *yenku, kami, nadad, kanini*). Finally, father's father's sister and mother's father's sister are classified with, and may actually be, father's mother's brother's wife and mother's mother's brother's wife respectively.[2]

However, there are some differences. In the Dieri system, as in the Arabana, cross-cousins are classified with father's mother and her brother (*kami*), which is not the case in the Aranda system. Furthermore, the Dieri differentiate between the mother's mother's brother and his son's son (respectively *kanini* and *niyi*), whereas the Aranda see them as identical. Finally, the Dieri system has only sixteen kinship terms and this has no correlation whatsoever with the Aranda terminology or with the Kariera terminology, or with the figure which might be calculated, on the basis of these two last, for a simple moiety system.

That the system cannot be regarded as an Aranda system, in contrast to Radcliffe-Brown's attempts,[3] emerges clearly from the table presented by Elkin (Fig. 39). The system is systematic only in appearance, and contingent lines are needed in order to close a malformed cycle. At the same time, a certain number of identifications are to be noted which are possible, in essence at least, in the given circumstances. Thus:

tidnara   =   *taru* (by marriage);
ngatamura =   *paiera* (by marriage);
ngatata   =   *yenku* (passing through *kaku, yenku's* sister and *kami's*
                          wife).

[1] Elkin, 1940b, pp. 52–3.   [2] ibid. p. 54.
[3] Radcliffe-Brown, 1931, p. 58. Radcliffe-Brown has also tried to interpret the Dieri system as a system with four unnamed sections. See Radcliffe-Brown, 1914.

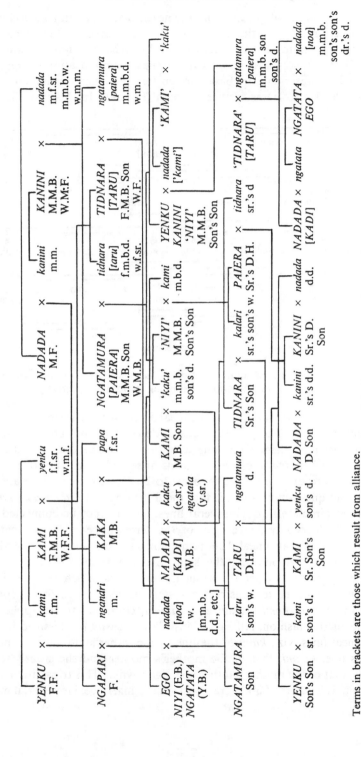

Fig. 39. The Dieri system (after Elkin, 1940*b*, p. 53).

Terms in brackets are those which result from alliance.

Inverted commas signify that the relationship is not 'own' or of the first degree, but tribal or distant.

If the terminologies of groups from the north-east of Australia are compared with the terminology of the Dieri,[1] it is found, moreover, that the Arabana have only one term *kadnini*, whereas the Dieri have *yenku* and *kanini*. On the basis of these equations, one can attempt a simplification of the system, which, while preserving the basic sixteen terminological distinctions, nevertheless provides a clearer picture of them (Fig. 40). In this way the system

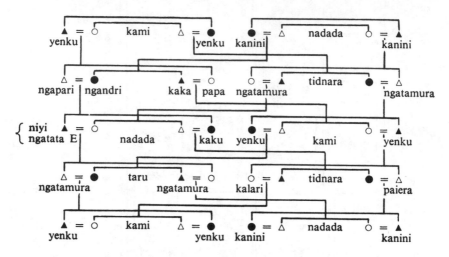

Fig. 40. Simplified representation of the Dieri system. The two moieties are distinguished by white and black symbols respectively.

appears to be based on four patrilineal lines, with a system of restricted exchange and marriage between cousins descended from cross-cousins.

Two questions then claim our attention. Whence does the dichotomy preventing the marriage of cross-cousins arise? The structure of the system is powerless to explain it, and it seems to be a sort of needless elaboration. The second question is how it is that the four terms *yenku, nadada, kami* and *ngatamura* circulate through several lines. This cannot be connected with a patrilineal dichotomy (since each of the terms appears in two patrilineal lines), or with a matrilineal dichotomy (since these terms designate alternate generations within one and the same matrilineal line). The first task in attempting to reconstruct the sequence of events which resulted in these anomalies would be to construct a system in which each of the four line-indicators *yenku, kami, kanini* and *nadada*, continues to be applied in its own distinctive fashion. All Ego's kinsfolk can easily be classified into three matrilineal lines, viz., *kami* of the line of the father's mother and the cross-cousins line, *kanini*, that of the mother's mother and the sister's son, and *nadada*, that of the mother's father and Ego's wife.[2] This tripartition suggests an original structure of unilateral cross-cousin marriage. However, if marriage

¹ Elkin, 1940*b*, p. 63.   ² ibid. p. 61.

were with the father's sister's daughter, the wife's clan would be identical with that of the father's mother, and if it were with the mother's brother's daughter, the mother's father's clan and the father's mother's clan would be the one and the same. On the other hand, the *yenku* line, i.e., Ego's patrilineal line, disappears completely from the picture.

For the time being, let us pass over these difficulties. In a system with patrilateral marriage, as we know, the wife's clan is not constant. The existence of a matrilineal clan, *kanini*, which permanently includes the wife and her brother, thus gives an assurance in favour of matrilateral marriage. Let us adopt this as a working hypothesis. We shall then have an archaic system of the type in Fig. 41, in which the matrilineal line *yenku* is added as a

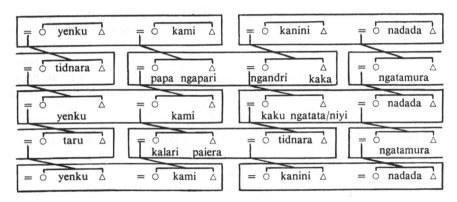

Fig. 41. Reconstruction of the hypothetical evolution of the Dieri system.

fourth (as a matter of fact, *yenku* marries *kami*, *kalari* marries *taru* (= *tidnara*)), and in which all the marriages conform, by and large, to the present system, except for the univocal nature of all the relationships.[1]

If such a system had passed directly to direct reciprocity (restricted exchange), it would automatically have been reduced to two dual systems in which *yenku* and *kami* on the one hand, and *kanini* and *nadada* on the other, would have constituted two independent exchanging pairs, with cross-cousin marriage in each pair. Yet, all the same, the repetition of terms in alternate generations would still be incomprehensible.

But if, on the contrary, the same system had had to adapt itself to a Mara-Aluridja formula, or had wished to do so, the whole thing would become clear. The four matrilineal and matrilocal lines, instead of exchanging by pairs and hence giving rise to the fission of the group into two sub-societies, would preserve the unity of the social group according to the Mara formula: an exchange between *P* and *R* in one generation would lead to an exchange

---

[1] Even at the present time, the prohibition of marriage between cross-cousins is not as strict as the system would seem to require. (Elkin, 1931*c*, p. 55; 1931*d*, p. 494.)

between P and S in the following generation, with a return to the formula $P = R$ in the generation after; likewise Q marries R and S alternately. In changing in this way, the system passes from generalized to restricted exchange. Marriage with the unilateral or bilateral cross-cousin becomes impossible, and makes way for the obligatory marriage of the children of cross-cousins. The alternation of terms corresponds to the alternation of forms of marriage: the exchange couple of the granddaughter reproduces the exchange couple of the grandmother. Finally, the characteristic terms of one matrilineal line can appear in two distinct patrilineal lines, since each line exchanges according to two different formulas.

Consequently, we propose the following sequence of events in explanation of the present-day characteristics of the Dieri system; firstly, an archaic system with four matrilineal and matrilocal lines based on generalized exchange (marriage with the mother's brother's daughter); secondly, the adaptation to a Mara-Anula system; and, finally, the present system. This is undoubtedly a purely hypothetical sequence but it is the only one allowing the anomalies of the system to be understood. In fact, it explains all of them. The Dieri system, is therefore, not a modality of the Aranda system; it is a specific system, and its similarities with the Aranda system are the result of convergence.

Chapter XXIII provides an incidental proof of our hypothesis when we give a similar interpretation (but admitting of direct proof) of the Manchu system. The Manchu and Dieri systems differ considerably in several ways, but they are both systems of generalized exchange which have turned into restricted exchange. The similarity in their respective developments has resulted in certain characteristics being curiously common to both. One cannot help but be struck by the fact that the Dieri, in order to determine a kinship relationship, employ several terms in the terminology as indicators of generation and of collaterality: 'The term for mother's mother's brother's son's son might be given as yenku kanini ngatata (that is, father's father, mother's mother's brother, younger brother).'[1] It will be seen that this procedure is basic to the Manchu terminology. When we study the Manchu system we shall find the same problem of lineal indicators, like the Dieri terms *yenku*, *kami*, *nadada* and *kanini*, reappearing in different patrilineal lines, so that we shall be forced to designate them, not as the names of lines, but as indicators of lineal series, i.e., terms allocated to segments of different lines. In both cases, this feature is to be interpreted in the same way, i.e., that lines integral with a system of generalized exchange have had to be fitted together as separate pieces into a structure of restricted exchange, so that each line of the new system is composed of segments of several former lines of the old system The extent to which this similarity goes is shown by the fact that in both system certain kinship relationships are expressed by the juxtaposition of two different lineal series indicators: e.g., among the

[1] Elkin, 1940*b*, p. 56.

Dieri, *yenku kanini* ('father's father *kanini*' = older brother) for mother's mother's brother's son's son, and, in Manchu, *nahundi eskundi* ('*nahundi* brother') for father's mother's brother's son's son.[1]

The Dieri system is not the only one to exhibit similarities with the Manchu, for others just as striking are encountered in certain systems in the Cape York Peninsula. These systems are still subject to the rule of unilateral marriage, but the change-over to restricted exchange is largely under way. Such is the case of the Wikmunkan, the Yir-yoront, and the Kandyu, which, as we have seen above, exemplify various modalities of cross-cousin marriage; either preferential marriage with the mother's brother's daughter (Wikmunkan and Yir-yoront), or marriage with one or the other unilateral cousin, the bilateral cousin being always excluded (the Kendall-Holroyd tribes), or, finally, preferential marriage with the father's sister's daughter (Kandyu). These tribes thus provide the living picture of a process of development which we could no more than reconstruct as far as the Dieri are concerned.

The Wikmunkan practise a characteristic form of marriage with the mother's younger brother's daughter; the mother's older brother's daughter is prohibited.[2] The structure of alliance and kinship thus does not simply possess the cyclical form of systems of generalized exchange, as we saw it among the Murngin, for the cycle takes on the additional appearance of a spiral, a man always marrying into a younger branch, and a woman into an older branch. The adjustment is made by closing the cycle with an absolute displacement of three generations in every six lines (Fig. 42). This is made possible by means of a system of alternating generations (as among the Aranda) in one direction only (unlike the Aranda). Among the Wikmunkan, for example, a man can marry a woman in his grandson's generation, but never in his grandfather's generation. Men marry into the generations below their own, and women into the generations above. At the same time, Ego cannot compete with his grandson, because of the rule: 'Men marry women of their own generation in a younger line, or of a younger generation in an older line, they cannot marry women of an older generation in a younger line.'[3] Consequently, when Ego marries his grandson's cousin, she necessarily belongs to the older branch of the grandson's generation, while the grandson can take a wife only in the younger branch of the same generation.

The subdivision of each generation into two age classes, 'older' and 'younger', is thus in direct correlation with the possibility of two men vying for the one woman. This competition is avoided by limiting their respective claims to two different age classes, the members of which are either real or classificatory parallel cousins. We shall have frequent cause to show that this dichotomy of generations always appears in such circumstances, and that it must be seen as a normal function of systems of alternate marriage. In fact, among the Cape York tribes, there is not one alternate marriage, but two. In association with matrilateral marriage there is, in a weakened form

---

[1] cf. p. 384.   [2] McConnel, 1940, p. 440.   [3] ibid. p. 448.

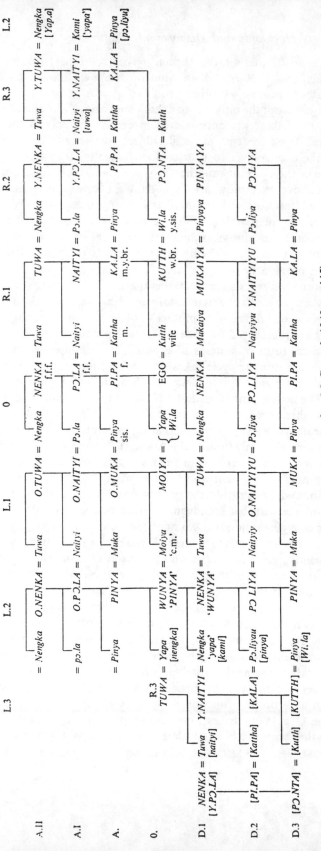

Fig. 42. Wikmunkan system (after McConnel, 1940, p. 445).

Descent line L.3 coincides with R.3 by marriage between women of L.2.0 with men of R.3. A.II coincides with R.2; L.4 coincides with R.1 and L.6 with EGO's line.

it is true (since in the second case the cousin can only be classificatory), a patrilateral type of marriage. This emerges clearly from statements by McConnel's informants:

> 'My mother's *younger* brother is my *KALA* . . . My *KALA'S* daughter, my *moiya*, I take for my wife . . . I may marry a woman from a distant ground given by a "*KALA*". We two "change hands". I give my sister (*yap.a* or *wi.la*) to my *KUTTH* (*KALA'S* son). I exchange with him. Now I call my *KUTTH*, *MOIYA* (sister's husband) and my *KUTTH*, he calls my father *KALA*.'[1]

Thus, in the Wikmunkan system, which originally had a structure of generalized exchange, patrilateral marriage has been joined with the prior matrilateral marriage, with two results. The first is a gradual transition from generalized to restricted exchange: 'A man usually gives a *younger* half-sister from his own family or clan to the man who gives him his sister for a wife.'[2] In the second place, the gradualness of this change is apparent in the fact that if a man marries his real unilateral cousin (mother's brother's daughter – see the aboriginal informant's statement below – or father's sister's daughter), and if the marriage is accompanied by an exchange, at least one of the two cousins must be classificatory. This is what McConnel expresses, but in a way which does not seem to be fully in keeping with her description, when she writes: 'Exchange of wives takes place between distantly related clans.'[3] It seems quite clear, in fact, that one of the two women might be a first cousin. In this case, a very important theoretical consequence must follow, viz., that a twofold exchange of this type may in fact be a threefold exchange, i.e., I marry my cross-cousin, and I borrow from a parallel line a woman whom I give in exchange to my brother-in-law. Accordingly, for each woman there are two marriage possibilities: either in a direct cycle of generalized exchange, or in an indirect cycle of restricted exchange.

In this respect, the similarities with the Manchu system are striking. Like the Wikmunkan, the Manchu divide each line into older and younger branches. One need only compare McConnel's and Shirokogoroff's tables to see their similarity (Fig. 43).

Moreover, the Manchu and Wikmunkan systems are based on the recognition of six lines. There is no doubt as to the correspondence between three of the Manchu lines and the three central or 'real' lines of the Wikmunkan system represented here in the same way as in Fig. 42:

Wikmunkan	*Manchu*	
0	*enendi*	Ego and his descendants
L.1	*inadi*	sisters' descendants
R.1	*nakundi*	mother's brother's descendants.

If we keep to our hypothesis on pp. 195-6, that the other three Wikmunkan

[1] McConnel, 1940, p. 439.   [2] ibid. p. 451.   [3] loc. cit.

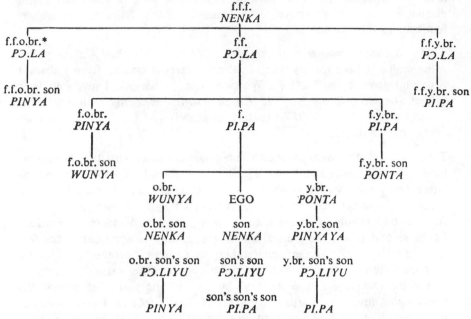

DIAGRAM I. AGE LINES
A. FATHER'S LINE

f.f.f.
NENKA

f.f.o.br.*
PƆ.LA

f.f.
PƆ.LA

f.f.y.br.
PƆ.LA

f.f.o.br. son
PINYA

f.f.y.br. son
PI.PA

f.o.br.
PINYA

f.
PI.PA

f.y.br.
PI.PA

f.o.br. son
WUNYA

f.y.br. son
PONTA

o.br.
WUNYA

EGO

y.br.
PONTA

o.br. son
NENKA

son
NENKA

y.br. son
PINYAYA

o.br. son's son
PƆ.LIYU

son's son
PƆ.LIYU

y.br. son's son
PƆ.LIYU

PINYA

son's son's son
PI.PA

PI.PA

* m.m.br. and w.m.f. rank as f.f.br. with analogous age lines.

DIAGRAM I. AGE LINES
B. MOTHER'S LINE

m.f.f.
TUWA

m.f.o.br.*
NAITYA

m.f.
NAITYA

m.f.y.br.
NAITYA

m.f.o.br. son
MUKA

m.o.br.
MUKA

m.

m.y.br.
KALA

m.f.y.br. son
KALA

MOIYA

m.o.br. son
MOIYA

m.y.br. son
KUTTH

KUTTH

TUWA

o.sis. son
TUWA

y.sis. son
MUKAIYA

MUKAIYA

NAITYIYU

o.sis. son's son
NAITYIYU

y.sis. son's son
NAITYIYU

NAITYIYU

MUKA

o.sis. son's son's son
KALA

y. sis. son's son's son
KALA

KALA

* w.f.f., sis.hus.f.f. and f.m.br. rank as m.f.br. with analogous age lines. Sister's son is from half *MUKA*, not full *MUKA*.

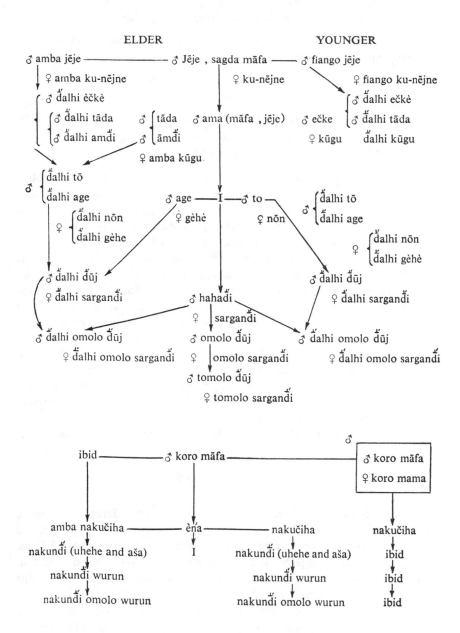

Fig. 43. The Manchu and the Wikmunkan systems.

On the left, the father's clan (at the top) and the mother's clan (at the bottom) in the Wikmunkan system. (After McConnel, 1940.) On the right, the father's clan (at the top) and the mother's clan (at the bottom) in the Manchu system. (After Shirokogoroff, 1924, Tables I and VIII, pp. 35 and 42 respectively.)

lines result from a division of those principal lines with which they coincide terminologically, we can complete the table of correspondences:

Wikmunkan	*Manchu*	
L.2	*eskundi*	father's collateral descendants
R.2	*dalhidi*	my collateral descendants
R.3	*tehemdi*	my mother's collateral descendants.[1]

The priority of generalized exchange over restricted exchange in both systems follows from the common preference for the matrilateral first cousin, and from a common repugnance for the daughter of the older class of the father's clan. When restricted exchange is practised by the Wikmunkan, says McConnel, it is only between distant clans.[2] Likewise, the Manchu are repelled by exchanges between clans which are already allied.[3] Finally, both systems have the same dialectic of age classes and generations. In the Manchu system, a man can marry a woman belonging to a generation senior to his own, or to the older branch of his own generation, while women from the younger class of his generation, or members of younger generations, are prohibited.[4] The 'age spiral' of the Wikmunkan has its symmetrical but inverse model among the Manchu. Our interpretation of the Manchu system as resulting from a change from generalized to restricted exchange will thus confirm similar interpretations given by us for so-called 'aberrant' Australian systems (which are aberrant only because of an incomplete classification). In the same way, this particular interpretation will be called upon in the second part of this work to elucidate certain theoretical problems of systems in the Far East.

IV

If our analysis is correct, there was originally a considerable difference between systems of the Dieri type and systems of the Kariera or Aranda types. In the latter, descent and residence are transmitted in separate lines. By contrast, we have suggested that the archaic Dieri system must have had a purely maternal determination for residence and for descent. This point must be carefully examined.

A system of exogamous moieties can function, whatever the rule of descent. It can also function whatever the rule of residence, and, finally, whatever the relationship between the rule of residence and the rule of descent. In other words, a moiety system does not take residence into account, or, because of its special structure, need not take it into consideration.

If, on the contrary, one seeks to define the social status of the individual

---

[1] cf. ch. XII, pp. 189-96.   [2] See above, p. 211.
[3] cf. ch. XXIII.   [4] Cch. XXIII, p. 386.

in terms of descent and residence, the consequences vary greatly according to whether the regime of the system under consideration is harmonic or disharmonic. A harmonic regime is one in which the rule of residence is similar to the rule of descent, and a disharmonic regime is one in which they are opposed. A system with matrilineal descent and matrilocal residence is harmonic, and so too is a system with patrilineal descent and patrilocal residence. By contrast, systems in which one of the factors follows the paternal line, while the other follows the maternal line, are disharmonic. Accordingly, there are two types of harmonic regimes, patrilineal and patrilocal, and matrilineal and matrilocal; and two types of disharmonic regimes, patrilineal and matrilocal, and matrilineal and patrilocal.

We have seen what happens under a disharmonic regime, or what comes to the same thing, since the Kariera system, with its matrilineal moieties and two patrilocal groups falls into this category. As we know, a matrilineal dichotomy leads to a division into four sections sanctioning marriage with the two unilateral cross-cousins, and with the bilateral cross-cousin. What happens under a harmonic regime?

Suppose there is a system with patrilocal residence comprising two patrilineal moieties, A and B, and two local groups, 1 and 2. The formula for marriage and descent will be:

If a man:	*marries a woman:*	*the children will be*
A_1	B_2	A_1
B_2	A_1	B_2
A_2	B_1	A_2
B_1	A_2	B_1

In other words, the system will function as two dual systems juxtaposed. Instead of one, there will simply be two, and the degree of integration in the total system will remain unaltered. If we have four local groups instead of two, the same situation will arise, i.e., each group will split in two, joining with one half of a neighbouring group to reconstitute a new system of two moieties. Thus we shall have started with four local groups, each divided into exogamous halves, and have ended up with four local groups, each composed of exogamous halves (i.e., moieties). What does this mean? It means that the factor of residence, in the case of harmonic regimes, is unproductive. Taking only descent and residence into account, harmonic regimes are incapable of going beyond the stage of moiety organization.

Is the harmonic regime then doomed to remain at that primitive stage of group integration which is represented by dual organization? It is true that under such a regime there is nothing to be gained by exchanging wives among people of different origins, instead of among people of the same origin. But another possibility remains open, namely that of changing, not the groups between which a certain form of exchange operates, but the relationship according to which exchange is effected between the groups, i.e., changing from a double system of direct exchange according to the formula, $P = Q$, $R = S$, to a simple system of indirect exchange, according to the formula $P = Q = R = S \ (= P)$; or, finally, to put it in another way, to pass from a system of restricted exchange to a system of generalized exchange. In this way we arrive at a general table (Fig. 44).

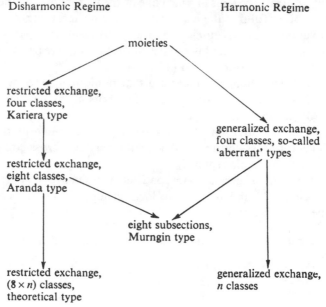

Fig. 44. Classification of the principal types of kinship systems, evolved from dual organization.

The relationship between the generalized system and the Aranda system becomes clear. The generalized system goes beyond the Kariera system, since it employs the same number of elements as the Aranda system, if not of the same nature: two moieties (patrilineal in one case, matrilineal in the other), and a four-component complex (of lines in one, and local groups in the other). The generalized system and the Aranda system are equally complex in terms of the number of elements they employ. On the other hand, however, the Aranda system represents the second dichotomy of the disharmonic regime, whereas the generalized system represents the first dichotomy of the harmonic regime. Furthermore, the arrangement of the elements in the Aranda system is twice as complex as in the generalized system: the same number of elements are combined in one to form eight subsections, and in the other to form four sections. The generalized system is like a Kariera system in the sense that they both employ, within their respective regimes, the dichotomy of the first degree, but it is like an Aranda system in that the dichotomy of the first degree in the harmonic regime requires the distinction of the same number of elements as does the dichotomy of the second degree in the disharmonic regime. In other words, the generalized system employs forty-one kinship terms like an Aranda system, and four sections like a Kariera system. What reason is there for this? Why can we not have a generalized system based solely on the distinction of only two moieties and two lines? The answer is obvious: in that case the lines would be merged with the moieties.

It can thus be said that harmonic regimes are unstable, while disharmonic regimes are stable. What do we mean by this? A disharmonic regime, in becoming more and more complex, can be expressed through forms of organization (moieties, sections, subsections) which represent a continuous progression within one and the same series. By contrast, harmonic regimes cannot reach a complex form of organization. This explains why class systems are so rare wherever marriage is determined by a law of generalized exchange. In point of fact, we shall see that in the vast majority of cases the preference for the matrilateral cross-cousin does not involve a structural system of such a kind.

Let us look at Fig. 44 in more detail. First we see that the relationship between the generalized system and the Murngin system is symmetrical, but inverse, to that between a moiety system and a Kariera system. The moiety system is based solely upon descent, and the harmonic or disharmonic features of the corresponding regime are confused. The transition to the Kariera system is brought about by the introduction of a local dichotomy, and as a consequence the disharmonic character appears. Conversely, the generalized system is based solely on line. There is thus a hiatus which expresses the fact that within each regime this regime is not unique. As we have seen, the disharmonic series lacks a stage in the dichotomous process (the distinction between both types of cross-cousin). Symmetrically, the harmonic series, which has the missing stage, reveals another hiatus, that of a four-factor system, represented in the disharmonic series by the Kariera system. We have established that the generalized system is unintelligible if an attempt is made to reduce it either to the Kariera system, which has a less complex structure, or to the Aranda system, which has a more complex function. Furthermore, we have established that it is impossible to see it as an intermediate form of the same type. In reality, the generalized system is similar in one respect to the Kariera system, and in another to the Aranda system. The system itself is not intermediate between the two, because it belongs to a series of a different order. Its function, however, is clearly intermediary.

These considerations may be extended to the entire gamut of Australian systems. The traditional error has been to admit only groups with disharmonic regimes, such as the Kariera and Aranda, as basis for classification. Accordingly, any hope of understanding harmonic regimes is lost, and one is forced either to treat them as monstrosities, or to try to reduce them to the previous forms, which is obviously an impossible undertaking.

But harmonic regimes do exist, and short of producing indefinitely an increasing number of reducible societies,[1] they have to be based on patrilateral or matrilateral marriage, but not on bilateral marriage, which is at the immediate disposal of disharmonic regimes alone. A harmonic *regime* can thus choose between two *systems* of marriage, patrilateral or matrilateral. Each of these two systems is itself compatible with two *modes* of descent, patrilineal or matrilineal. Thus we have:

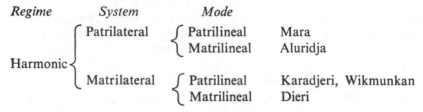

Regime	System	Mode	
	Patrilateral	Patrilineal	Mara
		Matrilineal	Aluridja
Harmonic			
	Matrilateral	Patrilineal	Karadjeri, Wikmunkan
		Matrilineal	Dieri

These systems can fall under the influence of disharmonic regimes, and evolve towards an apparent form of eight subsection *structure*. This seems to have happened among the Murinbata, who gave up their *system* for the sake of their *structure*, and perhaps also among the Murngin who never fully realized their *structure* because they remained faithful to the *system*. Or else the patrilateral and the matrilateral systems act concurrently, as in the present-day forms of the Arabana, Mara, Dieri and perhaps Murngin systems.

Thus, when they have completed their respective evolutions, harmonic and disharmonic regimes present convergent characteristics. Several harmonic regimes have made the transition from the *formula* of generalized exchange to the *formula* of restricted exchange. Moreover, patrilateral marriage *systems* and disharmonic regimes are both of the alternating *type* (the generations being reproduced, in all or part of their defining features, in every second generation), while matrilateral systems are always of the continuous *type* (consecutive generations being identical in all respects). This alternating type, which is common to both, makes the transition from patrilateral systems to the formula for restricted exchange easier than it is for matrilateral systems. This explains why the Mara and Dieri systems can have a terminology and marriage rules which are of the Aranda type, or close to it, without apparent subsections, while a Murngin system has to adopt the subsections, without succeeding, for all that, in changing its rules and its terminology. However, at the end of their development, the harmonic regimes have converged towards the disharmonic regimes, sometimes in structure (Murngin), sometimes in terminology (Mara), and sometimes in respect of the system and the marriage rules (Dieri). What is the reason for this evolution? Is it the result of geographical diffusion in neighbouring groups, or did it arise in the prestige attached to complex regulations among peoples whose

---

[1] See following chapter.

attention is traditionally drawn towards such problems? As we have seen, this seems to be the case among the Murinbata. On the other hand, the peripheral distribution of all the harmonic regimes which possess, or most probably used to possess, forms of generalized exchange,[1] strongly suggests that unilateral systems are more archaic than bilateral systems. Contrary to what Elkin believes,[2] it might thus be supposed that bilateral systems have themselves evolved from unilateral systems.

It belongs to the specialists in Australia to elucidate this problem. The first stage seems to be to fix the exact location of every system which is or used to be unilateral. So far there has been a tendency to interpret doubtful systems in bilateral terms, and this for several reasons: firstly, because the Australian typology is based on Radcliffe-Brown's types I and II, which are bilateral; and secondly, because any terminology with alternating generations has at once been considered as a proof of bilaterality. We hope we have established that the alternation of generations results from a system of patrilateral marriage just as much as from a double patrilineal and matrilineal dichotomy. In our opinion, there is no doubt that a careful reconsideration of instances of the alternation of generations would result, in a good number of cases, in the recognition of the immediate functions of patrilateral marriage. Since, moreover, matrilateral systems are distinguished by the employment of a consecutive terminology in opposition to patrilateral systems, which are distinguished by an alternating terminology, we foresee that this contrast may prove a valuable means of investigation in an attempt to arrive at a preliminary classification. In this connexion the existence of a consecutive terminology among the Yaralde and Ungarinyin[3] and traces of it among the Dieri, and of an alternating terminology among the Macumba and Aluridja may prove very instructive.

It is highly probable that a growing importance will be attached to harmonic regimes with unilateral systems in the typology of Australian societies. The autonomy of the Kariera system cannot be doubted, but it is a point to consider, on the basis of Radcliffe-Brown's frequent statement that this system shows a marked preference for matrilateral marriage, whether there has not been a certain overhastiness in including adjacent unilateral forms under the same heading: 'The discovery of the Kariera system by myself in 1911', writes Radcliffe-Brown, 'was the result of a definite search, on a

---

[1] The peripheral types with neither moieties nor sections are: the Narrinyeri, the Kurnai, the Yuin, the Melville Islanders, the Bard of Dampier Land and the Nanda of the western coast (Davidson, 1928*b*; 1937, pp. 171–4).

[2] Elkin, 1940*b*, pp. 379–83, and particularly n. 129, p. 382.

[3] Disputed by Needham (1960*a*, p. 285, n. 33); but I do no more than paraphrase Elkin, 1940*b*, p. 384: 'The kinship system has in terminology a vertical form such as is fully developed in the Ungarinyin tribe, north-west Australia.'

It may conveniently be reported here that in 1951 Radcliffe-Brown proposed a new classification of Australian systems which assigns a place to unilateral systems, which he designated by the name of Karadjeri. Radcliffe-Brown's article is usefully rounded off by a personal letter, which is published here for the first time. [See Appendix, p. 499]

surmise, made before visiting Australia, but after a careful study of Australian data in 1909, that some such system might very well exist and that Western Australia would be a reasonable place in which to look for it.'[1] That success should have crowned the bold hypothesis of the great English sociologist may justifiably encourage all those who believe that an internal logic directs the unconscious workings of the human mind, even in those of its creations which have long been considered the most arbitrary, and that the appropriate methods to be applied to it are those usually reserved for the study of the physical world. At the same time, however, a doubt intrudes itself, certainly not concerning the reality of the Kariera system, but about its exclusive existence in the enormous territory which has been assigned to it.[2]

In any case, the one fact remains. A formal study of the notion of exchange, such as sociologists have so far employed, has shown us that it did not succeed in embracing the facts in their integrity. Rather than deciding to lend a sterile discontinuity to phenomena which are, after all, of the same type, we have preferred to seek a wider and modified conception of exchange in an attempt to arrive at a systematic typology and an exhaustive explanation. It is the Australian facts, i.e., those taken from the classic region of restricted exchange, which have forced us to develop the notion of exchange and have, as it were, imposed upon us the notion of generalized exchange. What is the connexion between restricted and generalized exchange? Are they to be seen as two independent forms, yet capable of interacting one upon the other when the chances of culture contact bring them together, or do they represent two related stages in one process of evolution? In so far as the concern is with the solution of regional problems, this is a problem for the ethnographer and cultural historian. Our own intention is limited to making a structural study of the two types and their interrelations, and we must now attempt to isolate, in a simple and directly observable form, the formula of generalized exchange, the theoretical necessity for which has become apparent even before we have succeeded in discovering it in the facts.

[1] Radcliffe-Brown, 1931, p. 15, n. 5.
[2] cf. map in Radcliffe-Brown, ibid.; and in Lawrence, 1937.

CHAPTER XIV

Appendix to Part One

ON THE ALGEBRAIC STUDY OF CERTAIN TYPES OF MARRIAGE
LAWS (MURNGIN SYSTEM)

by André Weil

University of Chicago

In these few pages, written at Lévi-Strauss's request, I propose to show how a certain type of marriage laws can be interpreted algebraically, and how algebra and the theory of groups of substitutions can facilitate its study and classification.

In the societies in question, the individual men and women are divided into classes, each person's class being determined, according to certain rules, by those of his parents. According to the respective classes of a man and of a woman, the marriage rules indicate whether they can marry or not.

In such a society, the totality of possible marriages can thus be divided into a certain number of distinct types, which, if there is only one formula indicating to a man of a given class, the class in which he has the right to choose his wife (or in other words, the class in which he can marry a man's sister) is equal to the number of classes into which the population is divided. However, if there are several formulas, alternating in a predetermined manner, the number of possible marriage types may be double, triple, etc., the number of classes.

At all events, let the number of types of marriage be n. We arbitrarily designate them by n symbols, e.g., $M_1, M_2, \ldots, M_n$. We consider only the marriage laws satisfying the two following conditions:

(A) For any individual, man or woman, there is one and only one type of marriage which he (or she) has the right to contract.

(B) For any individual, the type of marriage which he (or she) may contract depends solely on sex and the type of marriage from which he (or she) is descended.

Consequently, the type of marriage which a son descended from a marriage of type M_i (*i* being one of the numbers *1, 2, . . . , n*) may contract is a *function* of M_i, which, following the normal mathematical notation in such cases, can be designated by $f(M_i)$. It would be the same for a daughter, the corresponding function, which we shall designate by $g(M_i)$, usually being distinct from the former. From the abstract point of view, knowledge of the two functions, f and g, completely determines the marriage rules in the society studied. These rules can thus be represented by a table with three lines, the first listing the marriage types $M_1, . . . , M_n$, the second and the third giving the corresponding values of the two functions f and g respectively.

Take a simple example. Let us suppose a four-class society, with generalized exchange, of the following type:

There are four types of marriage: (M_1) *A* man, *B* woman; (M_2) *B* man, *C* woman; (M_3) *C* man, *D* woman; (M_4) *D* man, *A* woman. Let us further assume that the children of a mother of class *A, B, C, D* are respectively of class *B, C, D, A*. Our table is then as follows:

(Parents' marriage type)	$M_1\ M_2\ M_3\ M_4$
(Son's marriage type)	$f(M_i) = M_3\ M_4\ M_1\ M_2$
(Daughter's marriage type)	$g(M_i) = M_2\ M_3\ M_4\ M_1$

Furthermore, as may be seen from the above example, f and g are substitutions, or, as is also said in such cases, *permutations* of $M_1, . . . , M_n$. This means that in our table the second line (which gives the values for f) and the third (which gives the values for g) are formed from symbols $M_1, . . . , M_n$, like the first line, but differ simply in being in a different order. Indeed, if this were not so, certain marriage types would disappear from the second generation onward. It is already clear that our study depends on the theory of the permutations of *n* elements, a theory which goes back to Lagrange, and Galois, and which has been further developed since.

We now introduce a new condition:

(C) Any man must be able to marry his mother's brother's daughter.

Let us express this condition algebraically. Let us consider a brother and a sister, descended from a marriage of the M_i type. The brother will have to contract an $f(M_i)$ marriage, so that his daughter will contract a $g[f(M_i)]$ marriage. The sister must contract a $g(M_i)$ marriage, so that her son will contract an $f[g(M_i)]$ marriage. Condition (C) will thus be expressed by the relationship:

$$f[g(M_i)] = g[f(M_i)]$$

This condition is known, in the theory of groups, as the *permutability* of the substitutions f and g. The pairs of permutable substitutions can be studied and classified according to known principles. In the language of the theory of groups (which it is unfortunately almost impossible to express in non-technical terms without going into very long explanations), the *group of permutations* generated by f and g is an Abelian group, which, having two generators, is necessarily cyclic or else is the direct product of two cyclic groups.

A new condition is introduced at this point and we shall express it by means of the following definition. We shall say that a society is *reducible* if it can be differentiated into two or more sub-populations, such that there is never any kinship tie between the individuals in one and the individuals in the other. In the opposite case, the society will be said to be *irreducible*. From the standpoint of the purely abstract study of types of marriage laws, we need only consider irreducible societies, since a reducible society operates as if each sub-population were a distinct society, in itself irreducible. For example, consider a system of restricted exchange:

with four types of marriage: (M_1) A man, B woman; (M_2) B man, A woman; (M_3) C man, D woman; (M_4) D man, C woman. Let us further suppose that all children are of the same class A, B, C, or D as their mothers. This society is obviously reducible, and consists of two sub-populations, one formed by the classes A and B, and the other by the classes C and D. The table of the functions f and g for this society is as follows:

$$
\begin{array}{cccc}
 & M_1 & M_2 & M_3 & M_4 \\
f(M_i) = & M_2 & M_1 & M_4 & M_3 \\
g(M_i) = & M_1 & M_2 & M_3 & M_4
\end{array}
$$

To suppose we are dealing with an irreducible society is to suppose, in the language of the theory of groups, that the group defined above (Abelian group of permutations generated by f and g) is *transitive*. Such a group, if cyclic, is of an extremely simple structure. If it is a direct product of two cyclical groups, the possibilities are more varied, and the principles of classification to be employed are more complicated; in any case, these questions can be treated using known methods. At this stage we shall merely state the results obtained in the case of a cyclic group. To this end it is necessary to indicate the well-known principle of the modulus n numeration.

Let *n* be any integer. The use of the modulus *n* means replacing a number at all times by the remainder when this number is divided by *n*. For example, 'the proof by 9', well known in elementary arithmetic, consists in using the modulus 9 in calculations. Similarly, in a calculation modulo 10, by adding 8 and 7 we get 5; multiplying 3 by 4 we get 2; adding 8 and 7 we get 5; multiplying 2 by 5 we get 0, etc. These are written: $8+7 \equiv 5$ (mod 10); $3 \times 4 \equiv 2$ (mod 10); $2 \times 5 \equiv 0$ (mod 10), etc. In all such calculations, it is usual to replace the sign = by the sign ≡ 'congruent to'. Calculating by modulus 10, we never have 10 or a number greater than 10, so that in this form of calculation, there are only 10 numbers, namely 0, 1, 2, . . . , 9.

Let us return to the case of an irreducible society with a cyclical group. In this society it is then possible to distinguish a certain number, *n*, of classes, numbered from 0 to $n-1$, such that a man of class *x* always marries a woman of class $x+a$ (mod *n*), and the children of a woman of class *x* are always of class $x+b$ (mod *n*), *a* and *b* being two fixed numbers, and all calculations being made modulo *n*. For example, in the system of generalized exchange described above, $n = 4$, $a = 1$, $b = 1$, as is seen by numbering the classes *A*, *B*, *C*, *D* as 0, 1, 2, 3 respectively.

We now go on to show how a more complex example can be formulated and discussed algebraically. We suppose a system with eight classes, with two marriage formulas to be applied alternatively:

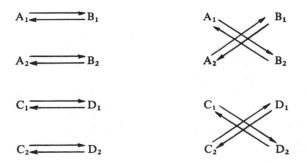

We further assume that the children's class is determined by the mother's, as follows:

(Mother's class)	A_1	A_2	B_1	B_2	C_1	C_2	D_1	D_2
(Children's class)	C_2	C_1	D_2	D_1	A_1	A_2	B_1	B_2

Finally, for our method to be applicable there must be a rule of alternation, between the formulas (I) and (II), satisfying condition (B) above. At this point, for mathematical convenience, we shall make a more precise hypothesis, which is perhaps unduly restrictive, but which will serve: i.e., the marriage formula, (I) or (II), to which any given individual must conform, depends solely on his sex and on the formula, (I) or (II), by which his parents married.

There are in this case sixteen types of marriage, according to the class of the spouses and the formula being applied. We shall not number them from 1 to 16, but in a way which is arithmetically more convenient. In all that follows, *the calculations must be seen in terms of the modulus 2*. In numeration modulus 2, there are only two numbers, 0 and 1. The multiplication table is as follows: $0 \times 0 \equiv 0$, $0 \times 1 \equiv 0$, $1 \times 0 \equiv 0$, $1 \times 1 \equiv 1$. The addition table is as follows: $0 + 0 \equiv 0$, $0 + 1 \equiv 1$, $1 + 0 \equiv 1$, $1 + 1 \equiv 0$.

Given this, we annotate each class by a triple index (a, b, c), each being one of the numbers of numeration modulo 2, i.e., 0 or 1. This follows these rules:

(1) a is 0 if the class is A or B, 1 if it is C or D

(2) b is 0 if the class is A or C, 1 if it is B or D

(3) c is 0 for the sub-class 1, and 1 for the sub-class 2.

For example, if a man or a woman is of class C_2, we would say, in our notation, that he or she is of class $(1, 0, 1)$.

Each marriage type is annotated by a quadruple index (a, b, c, d), whereby (a, b, c) represents the husband's class, and where d is 0 if the marriage follows formula (I), and 1 if it follows formula (II). Thus, in a marriage $(1, 0, 1, 1)$ the husband is of class $(1, 0, 1)$, that is C_2, and if the marriage follows formula (II) the woman is of class D_1, that is $(1, 1, 0)$. Furthermore, the children are of class B_1, that is $(0, 1, 0)$.

Generally speaking, in formula (I) marriages, if the husband is of class (a, b, c), the wife is of class $(a, b+1, c)$ and in formula (II) marriages, if the husband is of class (a, b, c) the wife is of class $(a, b+1, c+1)$, all this being verified by direct examination of individual cases. Thus, in a marriage (a, b, c, d), the husband is of class (a, b, c), and the wife is of class $(a, b+1, c+d)$.

On the other hand, if a woman is of class (x, y, z), her children are of class $(x+1, y, x+z+1)$, this again being confirmed by direct examination. It follows that, in a marriage (a, b, c, d), the children are of class $(a+1, b+1, a+c+d+1)$.

It is now necessary to specifiy our hypothesis on the alternation between the formulas (I) and (II). We shall assume one of the four following cases: (i) the children always follow the parents' formula; (ii) the children always follow the opposite formula to the parents', so that the formulas alternate from generation to generation; (iii) the sons follow the parents' formula, and the daughters the opposite formula: (iv) the daughters follow the parents' formula, and the sons the opposite formula. Each of these cases will be annotated with a double index, (p, q), as follows: p is 0 if the son follows the formula of the parents (case (i) and (iii)), and 1 in the opposite case (case (ii) and (iv)); q is 0 if the daughter follows the parents' formula (case (i) and (iv)), and 1 in the opposite case (case (ii) and (iii)).

This being so, we find, by direct verification on the basis of the results obtained above, that the functions f and g previously defined can be expressed at this point by the following formulas:

$$f(a, b, c, d) \equiv (a+1, b+1, a+c+d+1, d+p) \qquad \text{(mod 2)}$$
$$g(a, b, c, d) \equiv (a+1, b, a+c+q+1, d+q) \qquad \text{(mod 2)}$$

It remains to be stated that these substitutions are permutable, this expressing, as we know, that marriage with the mother's brother's daughter is always allowed. It is an easy calculation to make and gives:

$$(a, b+1, c+d+1) \equiv (a, b+1, c+d+q+1) \qquad \text{(mod 2)}$$

This shows that q cannot be 1. Condition (C) thus excludes cases (ii) and (iii), the only possible cases then being (i) and (iv). The first of these is that of a reducible society, composed of two sub-populations, one of which always marries following formula (I), and the other always following formula (II). If we leave this case to one side, there remains case (iv), in which $p = 1, q = 0$. The functions f and g are then as follows:

$$f(a, b, c, d) \equiv (a+1, b+1, a+c+d+1, d+1) \qquad \text{(mod 2)}$$
$$g(a, b, c, d) \equiv (a+1, b, a+c+1, d) \qquad \text{(mod 2)}$$

By means of these formulas, all the questions relating to this marriage law can easily be submitted to arithmetic examination. For example, let us ask ourselves if marriage with the father's sister's daughter is possible. In this general case, it is easy to see that a necessary and sufficient condition for it to be possible is that f and g shall satisfy the relationship:

$$f[f(M_i)] = g[g(M_i)]$$

For the law just examined, an immediate calculation shows that this relationship is not verified for any choice of indices a, b, c, d. Thus, no man in the society in question can marry his father's sister's daughter. A similar calculation shows that this type of marriage would always be allowed, by contrast, in a society which always applied either formula (I) or formula (II).

Finally, let us find out if the society above is irreducible. There are general methods for treating such a problem, but here it is easier to note that the combination $b–d$ is constant for the substitutions f and g, i.e., it has the same value respectively for the four-index symbol (a, b, c, d), and for symbols deduced from it by the substitutions f and g. This implies the existence of two distinct sub-populations, one composed of all the possible spouses for marriages of the type (a, b, c, d) where $b–d \equiv 0$, that is, $b = d$, and the other comprising the spouses for marriages (a, b, d, c) where $b–d \equiv 1$, that is, $b \neq d$. In other words, we are dealing here with a reducible society, which breaks down into the two following sub-populations:

$$1 \begin{cases} \text{Men of class A or C who marry according to formula (I)} \\ \text{Men of class B or D who marry according to formula (II)} \\ \text{Women of class A or C who marry according to formula (II)} \\ \text{Women of class B or D who marry according to formula (I)} \end{cases}$$

$$2 \begin{cases} \text{Men of class A or C who marry according to formula (II)} \\ \text{Men of class B or D who marry according to formula (I)} \\ \text{Women of class A or C who marry according to formula (I)} \\ \text{Women of class B or D who marry according to formula (II).} \end{cases}$$

Of course, as we have already noted above, these calculations are only valid if the alternation between formulas (I) and (II) follows the simple rules indicated earlier. If it were not so, the calculation would have to be modified. Further, if the rules of alternation did not satisfy condition (B), the problem could no longer be suitably treated by our method.

II

COMMENTARY

This mathematical examination of the Murngin system calls for a number of comments. Firstly, the discovery that a Murngin type system, if it functions under the strict conditions which alone allow it to be interpreted systematically, gives rise to the fission of the group into two irreducible societies, shows that a system of generalized exchange cannot evolve beyond its own formula. Doubtless, the system can be conceived of with any number of classes, but whether there be 3, n, or $n+1$, the structure remains unchanged. If an attempt is made to change the structure there are two possibilities open: either the change is made, and the formula for generalized exchange comes to an end (as with the Dieri system), or the formula is preserved, and then it is the change of structure which proves illusory. In acquiring eight subsections, the Murngin system succeeds only in functioning under the theoretical conditions for two juxtaposed systems of generalized exchange, each with four classes. We came to this conclusion in the previous chapter, using a purely structural analysis, and it is confirmed by the mathematical analysis. The extent to which Elkin was mistaken can be seen when, letting himself be misled by a Malinowski-inspired empiricism, he wrote: 'And generally speaking, the study of the merely formal element in Australian kinship is hardly worth doing . . . After all, it is of little satisfaction and affords no real understanding of the life of the tribe.'[1]

In connexion with Murngin society properly speaking, it is difficult to imagine that a society should function in the circumstances suggested by the theory and still maintain its individuality. On the other hand, if Murngin society was actually split into two sub-societies, this would not have passed

[1] Elkin, 1941, p. 91.

unnoticed by observers of the quality of Warner and of Webb. In point of fact, the Murngin must adhere to a formula which allows them to preserve the unity of the group. Thus we were justified in supposing that the system, as expressed in the complicated rules of subsections and optional marriage, should be considered as a theory elaborated by the natives while under contradictory influences, and as a rationalization of these difficulties, rather than as an expression of the reality. The reality of the system lies elsewhere, and we have attempted to disclose the nature of this reality.

It remains to be seen how the Murngin manage to avoid the danger of their theoretical system, which can only be done by applying it incorrectly. In these circumstances, the gaps in the observations, the ambiguous nature of the information on the various ways in which the cycles of exchanges can in fact be closed, perhaps do not arise solely from a lack of informants. It is possible that they are an indication of an intrinsic limit to the structure, which cannot be carried to its logical conclusion without compromising the unity of the group. Is the mark of this limit the fact that the real cycles are shorter or longer than those which would be implied by the existence of seven lines? This is possible, though it is difficult to see how this reduction would in itself constitute a solution. It is also possible that the cycle is closed with a displacement of one or more generations, as is the case among the Wikmunkan. However this may be, the apparently Aranda-type codification must always remain incomplete, or the social group must be segmented.

Consequently, it is perhaps not absolutely arbitrary that the systems in the neighbourhood of Southern Cross give the appearance – an illusory one, moreover – of two endogamous moieties, and that the Yir-yoront are at least partially endogamous. The Yir-yoront are divided into two patrilineal moieties and 'all the men of *Pam Lul* clans marry into the other moiety; but men of certain *Pam Bib* clans marry into *Pam Lul* clans, the others marrying into clans of their own *Pam Bib* division'.[1] These facts should be closely re-examined, in the light of this mathematical study and its theoretical conclusions.

In any case, there is one tribe in which we know that a system of generalized exchange in the course of evolving tends to bring about the subdivision of the group into sub-societies. This is the Apinayé of Central Brazil. It may be remembered that the tribe is divided into four *kiyé*, i.e., four 'sides' or 'parties'. The rule of marriage is typical of generalized exchange: an *A* man marries a *B* woman, a *B* man a *C* woman, a *C* man a *D* woman, and a *D* man an *A* woman. Furthermore, boys follow their father's *kiyé* and girls their mother's *kiyé*, i.e., *kiyé A* comprises, on the one hand, the sons of *A* men and of *B* women, and on the other, the daughters of *D* men and of *A* women. In these circumstances, as we have already noted, all *A* men, and all *B* women, originate from one type of marriage (between *A* men and *B* women) which they are obliged to perpetuate. Although cousins of the first

[1] Sharp, 1934, p. 19.

degree are prohibited spouses among the Apinayé (which may be considered as a partial defence against the consequences of the system), it is none the less true that the *kiyé*, which seem exogamous, really function as endogamous units.[1] It is probable that a careful examination of cases of the same type, which must be more numerous than a too exclusive attention to the 'exogamous' side of the phenomenon would allow us to suppose, would provide a useful method of approach for the study of systems of generalized exchange. We shall return to this problem of the relationships between endogamy and generalized exchange in Part II.[2]

[1] cf. ch. IV above. Maybury-Lewis has given a very different interpretation of the Apinayé system (1960), to which the reader is referred.
[2] cf. chs. XXVI to XXVIII.

PART TWO

Generalized Exchange

The earth, it is true, is in good condition, but roads are yet wanting; Ningkong is going to open them; he takes under his arm his sister, 'Ndin Lakong, a ball of twine, unwinds part of it on China, and re-enters his palace; henceforth there is a fine road to China. He then goes towards the Shan countries, again unwinds his sister, and it is the Shan road. In the same way he opens the Kachin, Burmese and Kala roads . . .

Kachin Myth of Creation: C. Gilhodes, *The Kachins: Religion and Customs* (Calcutta: 1922), p. 18

1 · Simple Formula of Generalized Exchange

CHAPTER XV

The Givers of Wives

I

We have isolated a wider formula of exchange than that to which this term has so far been confined. Alongside and beyond exchange in its restricted sense, i.e., involving only two partners, there may be imagined, and there exists, a cycle which is less immediately discernible, precisely because it involves a more complex structure. It is to this that we give the name 'generalized exchange'. The analysis of forms of marriage in Australia, and the contradictions which appear in the traditional typology based exclusively on the notion of restricted exchange, have made us perceive the more complex formula, and the impossibility of understanding the marriage rules without integrating the two forms of exchange in the overall system which implies them both. But, so far, the formula of generalized exchange has appeared to us rather as a theoretical necessity. It has still to be discovered in the facts, and this is what we propose to do, by adopting a double viewpoint.

We must first present concrete systems based clearly and simply upon a structure of generalized exchange, and this will be the aim of the first chapters of Part II. But, to justify the object of this work, which is to find the origin and regulatory function of kinship in exchange in all its forms, something more must be done, viz., to show that kinship systems and types of marriage which until now have been considered incompatible with what is currently called 'marriage by exchange' do in fact depend on exchange, for the same reason as do forms of marriage which are more literally known by this term; and also to show that all known and conceivable types of kinship and marriage can be integrated into one general classification, as methods of exchange, either restricted or generalized. It is the notion of generalized exchange which will allow us to make this reduction, or, if one prefers, to extend the structure of exchange to types and customs which might seem completely foreign to this notion. For the time being, however, we shall keep to the first of these tasks, namely, the examination of generalized exchange, as it appears in fact, in its simplest form.

It was Hodson, in 1922, who first formulated the hypothesis that groups allowing marriage with the matrilateral cross-cousin, to the exclusion of the patrilateral cross-cousin, are structurally different from those allowing marriage with both.[1] He took up this hypothesis more systematically in 1925, and great credit goes to his short article, published in that year, for being the first to propose the theoretical distinction between dual organizations with bilateral cross-cousin marriage, and what he called tripartite organizations (composed of three sections, or a multiple of three), characterized by asymmetrical marriage between sister's son and brother's daughter.[2] The term, 'tripartite organization', is too narrow, since the Kachin system, which Hodson sees as the most perfect example, requires, at least on the level of the model, five elementary sections. In fact, systems of generalized exchange can incorporate any number of sections, but only if a given group is subdivided into an odd number of marriage classes or functionally analogous units (or if this number, although even, is a multiple of three), can its presence be presumed *a priori*.

Nevertheless, we shall come across systems of generalized exchange with four sections. Moreover, this is generally the case when dealing with a moiety system with generalized exchange – a formula already encountered among the Murngin[3] – the possibility of which, however, eluded Hodson. Nevertheless, he was able to distinguish the two basic formulas; he understood the correlation between marriage rules and social structure (although he believed that tripartite organizations must always be patrilineal,[4] when, as we have seen, they need only be *harmonic*, as defined in chapter XIII); and he divined that the formula of generalized exchange was more widely distributed than the facts at his disposal indicated. Moreover, Hodson discovered the typical examples, and his conviction that the Kachin system was a particularly favourable illustration is still just as valid.

In fact, in the Far East we find not one but two characteristic forms of generalized exchange, which are distributed – and this contrast itself poses a problem – at opposite extremes of the Pacific coast: on the one hand, among the Kachin of Burma and several tribes of Assam, and on the other, among the Gilyak of eastern Siberia.

II

There are numerous sources on the Kachin, and also a commentary on their kinship system by Granet.[5] It is not always easy to reconcile the texts, which date from widely differing periods, often dealing with different groups, and all relating to a period during which we know the system had begun to disintegrate.

[1] Hodson, 1922.   [2] ibid. 1925.
[3] cf. ch. XII.   [4] Hodson, 1925, p. 174.
[5] Granet, 1939, pp. 211–12, 238–42.

The Kachin live grouped in domains of a roughly feudal character. They are patrilineal and patrilocal, and practise polygamy. Their kinship system has been compiled by Wehrli from numerous sources dating before 1900.[1] There is also an analysis of their kinship system by Gilhodes,[2] and there are various pieces of information in Hanson[3] and Hertz.[4]

These were the only available sources when I wrote the present work. Shortly after its publication, Leach began, firstly in the form of articles, later in a book, to publish the results of his fieldwork among the Kachin. It scarcely needs to be said that his fieldwork was conducted in a much more up-to-date and systematic manner than was that of his predecessors. Because of this, we have been faced with a problem in deciding whether or not it was advisable to retain in the present edition a chapter which was prepared from sources which were now out of date. Would it not be better to use Leach's work as the basis for an entirely new text? I ruled this out for several reasons which should be briefly declared. In the first place, it is this book and not any other which the publishers wish to have translated. In the second place, this chapter, in its original form, contained a detailed summary of the older writers which is not to be found in Leach's publications, except as incidental references. It seems to me that in spite of the period when they worked, and their lack of ethnographic training, these older writers deserve much more credit than such treatment would have us suppose. In the third place, and most importantly, what I published in 1949 on the Kachin has been vigorously attacked, and on now re-reading the original text, it seems to me that it has much more often been distorted than really contradicted. It is true that, since his highly polemical article of 1951, Leach has been anxious to emphasize that he has drawn considerably closer to my point of view, but as he has republished this article unchanged in his book of 1961, I believe it necessary, without wishing to seek a retrospective quarrel, to justify what I originally wrote.

There is one initial point on which I shall again hasten to pay tribute to Leach. His analysis of the Kachin kinship system is much more firm, complete and precise than his predecessors'. The latter left many points in doubt and I was obliged therefore, in the first edition of this book, to devote two pages[5] to discussing certain contradictions between the sources, and to attempt to fill in the gaps by hypothetical reconstructions. Although the system I arrived at in this way was very close to that reported by Leach, it is quite clear that his is infinitely preferable, and I shall content myself, therefore, with reproducing it here, with very slight modifications. This is to be found in the new Fig. 45.

This much said, I shall proceed to discuss the many criticisms made by Leach in his 1951 article, none of which, in fact, seems to me to have any serious basis.

[1] Wehrli, 1904. [2] Gilhodes, 1913, pp. 363–75; 1922. [3] Hanson, 1896; 1913.
[4] Hertz, 1915 [5] pp. 294–5.

The first and most grave of these is that in this chapter I am held to have continually confused two distinct peoples, on the one hand the Kachin, and on the other the Haka Chin:

> 'There can be no doubt at all that he [Lévi-Strauss] has assumed that Head's statements about the Haka Chins are applicable to the Kachins [cf. L.-S., pp. 297, 322 ff., 377, etc.]. There can be no excuse for this blunder. Not only are the Chins geographically remote from the Kachins, they do not so far as we know even practise Kachin type marriage.'[1]

I freely admit having been perhaps over-eager in combining the two types, without always distinguishing, as far as I should have done, the sources of the information I used in constructing the model of generalized exchange. But is this amalgamation really inexcusable, as Leach claims? In order to assert this, it would be necessary to be able to demonstrate that the Kachin on the one hand, and the Chin on the other, are ethnically, linguistically and culturally two homogeneous entities which can be clearly differentiated. This hardly seems demonstrable in the case of the Kachin, about whom Leach writes: 'This population speaks a number of different languages and dialects and there are wide differences of culture between one part of the area and another.'[2] In fact, and in Leach's very own words, the term Kachin designates a highly heterogeneous population consisting of about 300,000 people scattered over an area of 50,000 square miles, a rectangle roughly 250 miles long and 170 miles across. The distance to the nearest Chin, who inhabit the hills on the other side of the Irrawaddy valley, is little more than 175 miles as the crow flies. In other words, the southern Kachin are closer to the Chin than they are to the northern Kachin. This conglomeration of local groups, sometimes without any contact with one another and scattered as they are over an enormous area, are arbitrarily grouped together in the literature as the Kachin. What actually do they have in common? As Leach himself acknowledges, it is not language, or dress, or culture. Leach succeeds in isolating only one criterion in justification of the collective and distinctive name of Kachin, and that is the existence of a common social structure within all the groups so designated: 'I assume that within a somewhat arbitrarily defined area – namely the Kachin Hills Area – a social system exists. The valleys between the hills are included in this area so that Shan and Kachin are, at this level, part of a single social system.'[3] If Leach sees the existence of a common social system as justifying the amalgamation of peoples as different in language, culture and history as the Shan and the Kachin, he is surely unwarranted in criticizing me for having likewise used a common social structure in bringing together the Kachin and the Chin groups, which certainly differ much less from one another than the Kachin differ from the Shan.

It is true that in 1951 Leach disputed the existence of a social system

[1] Leach, 1961a, p. 78.   [2] ibid. 1954, p. 1.   [3] ibid. p. 60.

common to the Kachin and to the Haka Chin. He wrote: 'So far as we know [the Chins do not] even practise Kachin type marriage'.[1] He immediately added a note: 'The Haka Chins are neighbours to the Lakher on one side, who do practise Kachin type marriage, and to the Zahau Chins on the other, who do not. Concerning the Haka themselves there is no evidence.'[2] Nevertheless, Leach already seemed to have had a doubt in this article about the presumed heterogeneity of the social structures, since he wrote a few pages later: 'Although Lévi-Strauss confused Kachin practice with Chin, he might still I think argue that the scale of Kachin bride-price payments is paradoxically large.'[3] However, a remarkable change has taken place in Leach's thinking on the close affinity of the Kachin and Haka Chin systems which I postulated in 1949, and to which he took exception in 1951 on the plea that there was no evidence on Haka Chin rules of marriage. Some years later he wrote of:

'The Lakher, an Assam tribe who are neighbours to the Haka Chin of Burma, whom they closely resemble in general culture. These last live some hundreds of miles to the south-west of the Kachin groups and are not in direct contact with them. Kachin and Haka Chin cultures are, however, so similar in their general aspects that at least one distinguished anthropologist has confused the two groups (Lévi-Strauss, 1949).'[4]

Leach thus took six years to realize that there was some justification for the liberty that I had taken in constituting a type of social structure by borrowing elements from peoples who were undeniably geographically distinct (although not so much as he himself suggests). He simply forgets to give me credit for having demonstrated this identity between the social structure of the Kachin and that of the Haka Chin. The very fact that I was able to deduce the structure of the Haka Chin marriage system solely from their system of economic prestations shows that, contrary to Leach's assertions, I never isolated the former from the latter. Indeed, it is not because I confused them that I thought them similar; it is because I had established that they were similar that I asserted that – as far as the marriage system was concerned – it was justifiable to merge them. Therefore, I have done no differently than Leach, when he recognizes that the category 'Kachin' rests neither on language, nor on culture, nor on geographical proximity, but solely on a common social structure. This is a suitable juncture at which to recall that, as Leach rightly remarks without realizing the consequences for himself: 'The assiduous ethnographer can find just as many "tribes" as he cares to look for.'[5]

Another charge made against me by Leach is that of having considered that the Kachin system contained a paradox, and having concluded from this that the model of the system was necessarily in disequilibrium. There are two

[1] ibid. 1961a, p. 78.   [2] ibid. n. 2.   [3] ibid. p. 88, n. 3.
[4] ibid. p. 116.   [5] ibid. 1954, p. 291.

aspects to be distinguished in his argument. In the first place, Leach disputes that the Kachin system tends to heighten the inequality between wife-receivers and wife-givers. According to him, the marriage prestations consist essentially of cattle,

> 'and cattle, among the Kachin, are a consumable commodity. On balance the chief does tend to accumulate wealth in the form of cattle. But prestige does not come from the owning of cattle; it derives from the slaughter of animals in religious feasts (*manau*). If a chief becomes rich as a consequence of marriages or other legal transactions he merely holds *manau* at more frequent intervals and on a larger scale, and his followers, who partake of the feast, benefit accordingly. Here then is the element which is necessary to complete the cycle of exchange transactions, the absence of which struck Lévi-Strauss as paradoxical.'[1]

Leach himself indicates, however,[2] that prestations are far from consisting chiefly of cattle, since they also include free labour, and it is difficult to see in what form restitution is made for this. In particular, moreover, it is wrong to say that restitution for the cattle provided is somehow made in the form of feasts. That the chief, thanks to his cattle, is in a position to give feasts means a gain in his prestige, which is literally capitalized. There is thus a constant tendency for chiefs to increase their prestige by means of that which the givers are not in a position to acquire on their own account since they part with cattle in the course of making marriage payments. Here as elsewhere, Leach seems gradually to have seen the inadequacy of his early views, since he writes much more justly some years later, contradicting the passage just quoted: 'Social climbing . . . is the product of a dual process. Prestige is first acquired by an individual by lavishness in fulfilling ritual obligations. This prestige is then converted into recognized status by validating retrospectively the rank of the individual's lineage.'[3]

Actually, in the passage previously quoted and in others[4] Leach seems to attribute to me the absurd idea that, in Kachin society, women are exchanged for goods. I have never said any such thing. It is clear that, as in all other social systems, women are exchanged for women. The reason I claim the Kachin system to be basically unstable is completely different. It does not relate to the economic nature of an alleged counterpart to prestations of women, but to the distortion of matrimonial exchanges in a system of generalized exchange. In fact, the longer the cycle of exchanges tends to become, the more frequently it will happen, at all stages, that an exchange unit, not being immediately bound to furnish a counterpart to the group to which it is directly in debt, will seek to gain advantages either by accumulating women or by laying claims to women of an unduly high status. The first aspect of Leach's argument that the model of Kachin society is in equili-

[1] Leach, 1961*a*, p. 89.   [2] ibid. p. 83.
[3] ibid. 1954, p. 164.   [4] ibid. 1961*a*, pp. 90, 101, 103.

brium, owing to the fact that the cattle given by the receivers of women in return for wives are redistributed to these receivers in the form of feasts, does not hold good. Restitution can be made for the meat but not for the prestige gained in this distribution.

Most important, however, it seems that Leach, having asserted in his 1951 article, contrary to me, that the model of Kachin society is in equilibrium and is not subject to any instability ('the system . . . is neither contradictory nor self-destructive';[1] 'He [Lévi-Strauss] is led to attribute to the Kachin system an instability which it does not in fact possess'[2]) came to a different interpretation, in his 1954 book, which in point of fact coincides with the one I had put forward five years earlier.

It is clear, in fact, that in the 1951 article it is only one form of organization in Kachin society which is being considered. Indeed, Leach writes before beginning his analysis: 'What follows applies primarily to the Kachin *gumsa* type of political organization. In an alternative type of system known as *gumlao* the structure is somewhat different.'[3] Nowhere, however, is this second type discussed. By contrast, in his 1954 book Leach emphasized the duality of the two types. He shows that, depending on the region and some-times even the village, Kachin society may be organized either on an egali-tarian basis (*gumlao*) or a hierarchical and semi-feudal basis (*gumsa*). He also shows that the two types are structurally linked and that, theoretically at least, it could be conceived that Kachin society continually oscillates between the two types. With regard to the question which is our present concern, it is strange that Leach in analysing each form emphasizes, on the one hand 'a basic inconsistency in *gumsa* ideology'[4] and adds, on the other: 'yet the *gumlao* system is equally full of inconsistencies'.[5] He continues:

'Both systems are in a sense structurally defective. A *gumsa* political state tends to develop features which lead to rebellion, resulting, for a time, in a *gumlao* order. But a *gumlao* community . . . usually lacks the means to hold its component lineages together in a status of equality. It will then either disintegrate altogether through fission, or else status differences between lineage groups will bring the system back into the *gumsa* pattern.'[6]

Having therefore asserted, in 1951, that Kachin society was in equilibrium, Leach acknowledged, in 1954, that it alternates, that it constantly oscillates, between two contradictory forms, each in itself involving a contradiction ('self contradictions of *gumsa* and *gumlao*'[7]). Leach so clearly realizes that he is thus merely adopting my own interpretation that he adds, not without embarrassment:

'The hypothesis that there might be such a relationship [between the Kachin *mayu-dama* marriage system and the class structure of Kachin

[1] ibid. p. 88.   [2] ibid. p. 90.   [3] ibid. p. 82, n. 2; cf. also p. 185, n. 1.
[4] Leach, 1954, p. 203.   [5] loc. cit.   [6] ibid. p. 204.   [7] ibid. p. 231.

society] originates with Lévi-Strauss . . . [who] made the further suggestion that the existence of a *mayu-dama* type marriage system, while leading to a class stratified society, would for that very reason result in the breakdown of Kachin society. The material I have assembled here partly supports Lévi-Strauss' argument though the instability in Kachin *gumsa* organization is not, I think, of quite the type that Lévi-Strauss supposed'.[1]

Leach might well have added that this empirical confirmation of my interpretation completely invalidates what he himself advanced in 1951. To be sure, I could not possibly have known of the existence of the two types, *gumsa* and *gumlao*, which had not been described by the older writers, and for which Leach deserves great credit in observing them in the field and in putting them in their correct perspective. But the pages which follow need only be read to show that, while unaware of this distinction, I nevertheless deduced it from a theoretical analysis of the formal conditions of Kachin marriage. However, from the fact that the *gumlao* distinguish the *mayu* and *dama* categories although 'there is nothing in their political system which calls for such separation',[2] I do not conclude, as does Leach, that there is a paradox, but that this dichotomy is not the result of a political system. Rather it is the cause: 'Empirically, *gumlao* groups . . . seem to revert rather rapidly to class differentiation on a lineage basis.'[3]

Even in 1954, in fact, Leach adhered to an interpretation which was insufficiently structural. The connexion between the feudal structure of *gumsa* type and matrilateral marriage seemed a contingent one to him, when I had shown them to be structurally related.

I shall pass more quickly over another of Leach's criticisms,[4] that in my discussion of the Kachin system I did not distinguish clearly between hypergamy and hypogamy. The reason for this is that, from a formal point of view, there was no need to distinguish between the two. To make this point clear, in the pages that follow I shall use the term anisogamy, from botany, which simply means marriage between spouses of different status without any implication as to which of them, to the man or the woman, is higher or lower. Here again, Leach, who in 1951 considered that hypergamy was a structural aspect of the Kachin systems, seems in 1954 to be drawing appreciably closer to my point of view:

'Matrilateral cross-cousin marriage is . . . a correlate of a system of patrilineal lineages rigged into a class hierarchy. It does not necessarily follow that the bride-givers (*mayu*) should rank higher than the bride-receivers (*dama*); but it does follow that if class difference is expressed by marriage, then *mayu* and *dama* must be exclusive and one of the two must rank above the other.'[5]

[1] Leach, 1954, pp. 287–8.   [2] ibid. p. 203.
[3] loc. cit.   [4] ibid. 1961*a*, p. 80, n. 1.
[5] Ibid. 1954, p. 256.

Indeed, it seems to me that in the same way that matrilateral and patrilateral marriage are both consistent with the two modes of descent, although patrilateral marriage is more likely in a regime with matrilineal descent (because of its structural instability which makes it prefer short cycles), and matrilateral marriage more likely in a patrilineal regime (which more easily allows the cycles to be lengthened), so hypogamy (representing the maternal aspect of anisogamy), in a regime with patrilineal descent, is the sign of a relatively unstable structure, and hypergamy of a stable structure. Hypogamy is therefore a sign of instability in a patrilineal society inclined towards feudalism, because its practice characterizes lineages which seek, in alliance (i.e., in a recognition of cognates), a means of affirming their position as agnates. It thus makes cognation a means to agnation, whereas hypergamy more logically assumes that, in an agnatic system, cognatic relatives are not pertinent. Consequently, to make the Kachin hypogamic configuration a historical and local result of the assimilation 'of Shan ideas about class difference'[1] is to fail to recognize that hypogamy represents an immense structural phenomenon, universally attested to in the taboos on parents-in-law, and that it corresponds to a state of *tension* between paternal and maternal lineages, the latter not yet in disequilibrium to the sole benefit of the first as with true hypergamy. In his 1951 article in which, concerning another problem, he proposes an interpretation, which this time is purely structural, of the relationship between 'affinal tie' and 'sibling tie', Leach seems finally to have found the principle for a typology which could usefully be extended to the classification of *gumsa* and *gumlao*, in which exchanges of women are still inseparably part of the general system of prestations.

I shall end with the last criticism made against me by Leach in 1951, namely, that of attempting to establish a conjectural history of all Asiatic societies.[2] Here again, it is Leach himself who, hostile to all historical reconstructions in 1951, states, as soon after as 1954, that it is very difficult when faced with systems of this type (referring to a periodic model, thus one which is interpretable only in diachronic terms) not to attempt to check the synchronic interpretation by historical considerations: 'I move on now from semi-history to pure speculation. We do not know how Kachin society grew to be what it is, but I am going to guess. My guess must fit with the historical facts which I have outlined above, it must also be consistent with known facts of Asiatic ethnography.'[3] Once again, time has done its work, but, contrary to Leach's assertion[4] that I regard the Kachin system as a borrowing from an archaic Chinese system, I have never said any such thing, but merely that the Kachin system, even today, attests to the existence of a type of social structure which must formerly have spread over an enormous part of Asia, including China.

After this long discussion, we can now take up the examination of the

---

[1] ibid.
[2] ibid. 1961*a*, pp. 77 and 103.
[3] ibid. 1954, p. 247.
[4] ibid. p. 249.

Kachin system from the beginning, i.e., by commencing with the kinship system (Fig. 45).

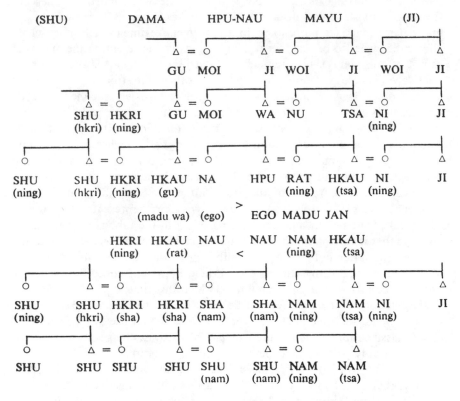

Fig. 45. The Kachin system (after Leach, 1961a, p. 41).

The terms in parentheses are those used exclusively by a female Ego.

This system is even more firmly structured than Leach seems to believe. Indeed, Leach is troubled by the collective designations of *dama* as 'grand-children' and *mayu* as 'grandparents', which he tries to justify by saying: 'Those who do not do so [i.e., which are neither *hpu-nau* ("brothers") nor *mayu* nor *dama*] by strict cognate or affinal relationship are treated much as if they were remote relatives of Ego's own clan.'[1] But they are strictly cognates, at least at the level of the model. When Ego was a child, the only cognates that the last line to the right (*mayu* of *mayu*) could contain were 'grandparents': father's mother's mother, mother's mother's father; and, when Ego gets older, he will find in the last line to the left (*dama* of *dama*) cognates who will be 'grandchildren': his daughter's daughter's children. The terms for the extreme lines are thus structurally a function of the rule of

[1] Leach, 1961a, p. 82.

marriage. They mean: 'line in which I have (great) grandparents', 'line in which I have (great) grandchildren'.

The terminology thus reflects completely the rules of alliance, which must now be examined.

'In all that concerns marriage, Kachins are divided into two groups: mayu ni and dama ni. Mayu ni are the tribe or the tribes which furnish women; dama ni, those where husbands are found.'[1] Strictly, the names *mayu ni* and *dama ni* designate families of which two members at least are united by marriage, but they also have a more general connotation. They are applied to all families or tribes which can intermarry, or which are in a proper relationship with one another for intermarriage.

'A tribe or family which is dama with regard to the mayu ni, tribe which gives it women, is its dama tribe. So, in the village of Matau, there are three principal families or branches: Chyamma ni, Latsin ni and Kawlu ni. The first takes a wife from the second, the second from the third and the third from the first.

'Chyamma ni are dama ni of Latsin ni, who are dama ni of Kawlu ni, who are dama ni of Chyamma ni.

'As also Latsin ni are mayu ni of Chyamma ni, who are mayu ni of Kawlu ni, who are mayu ni of Latsin ni.

'According to this arrangement, women remain only one generation in the same family; they turn so to speak from one tribe to another, whilst husbands remain stationary. So in the foregoing example, Latsin damsels become Chyamma ladies, whose daughters become Kawlu ladies, whose daughters become Latsin ladies, etc.'

It obviously 'follows that the nearest relative a young man can marry is only a cousin, daughter of a maternal uncle . . . In his mayu tribe, he can meet only cousins issued of maternal uncles, and according to custom, it is good, but not obligatory, that his choice fall on one of them.'[2] The same information is found in Hanson and in Carrapiett: 'The Kachins have clearly defined families who are said to be Dama or "husband-giving", and others who are said to be Mayu or "wife-giving" families.'[3]

The passages cited are important for several reasons, firstly, because they establish the marriage rule with the mother's brother's daughter, and the general formula of which it is the application, and secondly, because they show that the exchange cycle can be closed after a minimum of three stages, which directly eliminates any possibility of dual organization (which would require at least four stages). Here then is an absolutely simple formula of generalized exchange, not derived (as it was with the Murngin) from a previous organization into exogamous moieties.

The normal Kachin marriage then is with the mother's brother's daughter,

---

[1] Gilhodes, 1922, p. 207. [2] ibid. pp. 207–8.
[3] Carrapiett, 1929, p. 32; Hanson, 1913, pp. 181–2.

who, however, is denoted by the same term as the wife's brother's daughter. There is also marriage with a classificatory 'wife' of the father,[1] as well as the levirate and the sororate. Among the Haka Chin, the first is called *Nu Klai*, to marry a relative by marriage.[2] Gilhodes also describes successive sororal polygyny. Thus it seems that the preferred marriage results, not so much from a prescribed and precise degree of relationship, as from a general relationship between all the men of a lineage, creditors in wives, *dama ni*, and a debtor lineage, *mayu ni*, in respect of all its daughters and sisters. This is just the state of affairs represented to us by the observers. Carrapiett says: 'There is a word in Kachin – *kha* – which has been defined as a "debt". Every breach of the honour of a Kachin, every injury caused to him directly or indirectly, results in a "debt" which must be satisfied some day or other.'[3] Debts and claims are handed on for generation after generation. 'Nine out of ten cases can be traced, either directly or indirectly, but generally directly, to a woman.'[4] A note by Barnard in the same work adds this valuable comment: 'A Kachin woman, though actually married to an individual, is taken for a clan, and on becoming a widow passes to another male of the clan who exercises marital rights over her. Hence, according to true Kachin custom, there is no such thing as divorce . . . The best way to settle such cases is to provide another wife.'[5] Conversely, if a suitor asks for the younger sister before the elder sister he must pay a higher price, e.g., an extra buffalo.[6] The same author adds that, in the case of trouble in the household: 'Sometimes, to end the trouble, the parents exchange the first wife who is impossible against one of her younger sisters whom they hope will be more easily satisfied; the elder sister must then make over to her younger sister all her jewels, and the younger one takes her place.'[7] It is also stated that brothers commonly marry their brothers' widows, and that a father-in-law marries his daughter-in-law if she is widowed. This clearly shows that practice coincides with the terminology. 'If a woman refuses to live with her husband and all efforts by her people to induce her to return to him have failed, her family are required to give him another woman.'[8] Carrapiett cites a case judged before the district court, which clearly shows the collective and reciprocal aspect of the conjugal claim: 'Plaintiff is widow of respondent's cousin who died a year ago. She sues to be divorced from respondent's family as none of the male members remaining have taken her to wife.'[9] Conversely, if the mother's brother has no daughter to give in marriage, he must look for a wife for his nephew from among his other kin. If, on the other hand, a nephew refuses to marry his cousin, he must pay a fine to the offended

---

[1] Carrapiett, 1929, p. 96; Gilhodes, 1922, p. 209.

[2] Head, 1917, pp. 8–9.   [3] Carrapiett, 1929, p. 4.   [4] ibid. p. 5.   [5] ibid. pp. 35–6.

[6] Gilhodes, 1922, p. 212, a *mithan* or *bos frontalis*, cf. also Carrapiett, 1929, p. 73: 'It is considered an insult if a younger sister marries before her elder sister; and every endeavour is made (though not always successfully) to avoid this happening.'

[7] ibid. pp. 222–3.

[8] ibid. 1929, p. 37.   [9] ibid. p. 117.

uncle. If the wife dies after marriage, her husband has the right to demand another woman from his parents-in-law (uncle and aunt), who give him a daughter or a kinswoman as wife. Moreover, in the case of adultery the seducer's clan is jointly responsible for the fine payable to the offended husband.[1]

That one never marries an individual is brought out clearly in the customary form of the marriage proposal.

'The first step is to send Sălangs (elders) to the chosen family . . . If the parents are agreeable, the Sălangs surreptitiously take some personal ornaments or garments of all the eligible daughters – e.g., a flower, betel, tobacco, head-dress – which is brought to the man's village.

'Here a Ningwawt divines . . . which of the daughters is the most suitable.'[2]

Gilhodes gives other information: 'Woman, by marriage, enters into the family of her husband of whom she becomes so to say the property. So, at her husband's death, she is not free to return to her parents' house, or to re-marry with one of her choice; she remains at the disposal of the dama ni.'[3] The alternatives are marriage to a brother-in-law, or to a cousin of her husband, or to a married brother-in-law, as a second wife, or to a son from one of her husband's previous marriages. It is only if none of the *dama ni* wants her that she may return to her own family, who must give back part of the price paid for her.

III

What then are these groups between which marriage prestations are made in a way which is in principle unchangeable and directional? The older writers agree in reporting that the Kachin are subdivided into five principal groups: Marip, Maran, Nkhum, Lahpai and Lathong. Myth has it that they derive from a common ancestor. However, it is highly doubtful whether these are actually clans. These groups have certain ethnic differences, of dialect, dress and custom. The bond between them is established through a common tradition, and a real or theoretical kinship uniting the noble families of each group. However, George, quoted by Wehrli, adduces precise examples to show that the affiliations no longer have anything to do with real or mystical kinship relationship. For example, a Szi-Lepai who settles in the neighbourhood of a Maran chief becomes a Maran, together with all his descendants. Although nowadays the groups are more or less intermingled, it seems still possible to find a geographical centre for each of them which is perhaps the trace of a more rigid spatial division: the Lathong are to the

[1] Wehrli, 1904, p. 28. [2] Carrapiett, 1929, pp. 32–3.
[3] Gilhodes, 1922, p. 227. Reservations must be held concerning this interpretation, which does not seem to correspond to reality, cf. below, pp. 260-61.

far north, the Lahpai in the mountains on both sides of the Irrawaddy, the Maran are gathered together to the east of these, along the Chinese border; the Nkhum are found especially to the far north-west, and the Marip are situated to the south of the Nkhum.[1] Most observers call these groups 'tribes', which is hardly satisfactory considering the complete lack of political organization. Political organization appears only at the level of the domain or the free villages. The domains unite a small number of villages under a common authority, and their territories are clearly delimited from those of neighbouring groups. These domains are no more clans than are the principal groups, and Wehrli is undoubtedly right in distinguishing them from the Naga *khel*.[2] They are small political units subdivided into families or 'houses'.[3]

Within the domain, the chiefs (*du ni*) must be distinguished from the common people (*tarat ni*). The chiefs belong directly or indirectly to the chiefly family, and they enjoy a corresponding prestige: when two Chingpaw (i.e., Kachin) meet, the first question asked is: 'Are you a chief or a commoner?'[1] Moreover, the chiefly families have, as will be seen, a mythical origin, and their power is based upon this myth.

The chiefly families seem to have only the names of the five principal groups to which they belong, with the addition of a specific place-name. The commoners, by contrast, have a family or clan name. It should not be forgotten that the principal families all trace their genealogies back to the mythical founders of the principal groups whose name they can boast. The ordinary people are divided into a great number of clans which are not territorial units. The members of the one clan may belong to different principal groups and even domains, and to their clan name they add that of the principal group, and possibly that of the chief on whom they depend.[2] The clan name, properly speaking, is always kept: 'When a Szi-Chumlut, that is a member of the Szi tribe (a group showing marked affinities with the Kachin proper) and of the Chumlut clan, sets himself up in the territory of a Maran chief, be becomes a Maran-Chumlut.' Wehrli and George reach the same conclusion that the clan organization was historically prior to the division into five groups predominating today.[3]

The facts taken together suggest an evolution of the same type as that which seems to have taken place in pre-Columbian Peru, where an organization based originally on clans had a system of lineages, increasingly feudal in character, gradually superimposed upon it. In point of fact, analysis of Kachin society reveals three principal social forms: firstly, the clan, which no longer exists except among the common people and even then only as a

---

[1] cf. the map in Wehrli, 1904.   [2] cf. ch. XVII.
[3] Generally the household includes three generations living under the same roof, which can provide shelter for twenty to forty people. It is the household which is the economic unit of the chiefdom (Wehrli, 1904, p. 29).   [4] ibid. p. 25.
[5] For example, 'a branch of the Lathong tribe governed by a chief of the Sana family will be called Sana-Lathong, or named after the geographical peculiarities of its territory'. (ibid. p. 24.)   [6] ibid. p. 26.

name transmitted in the paternal line; secondly, the five great divisions, based upon a mythical genealogy; finally, the domains, which, within each of these divisions, are connected by additional links with this same genealogy. It is hardly to be doubted that these domains represent lineages, which increase in number through the departure of the eldest sons of the principal houses, who leave at regular periods to set up their own houses in new areas. For in fact it is the youngest son who inherits the chiefdom:

'The youngest son is the chief heir. He succeeds to the high position of the chief and takes possession of the family house and the right to the land. The older son of a Duwa, who does not inherit, joins friends who are in a similar position, emigrates, and founds a new settlement. The systematic extension of the Chingpaw group is probably a consequence of the law of inheritance, and it is this which perhaps also explains the dispersion of each branch into several chiefdoms.'[1]

There is a similar situation among the Lushai:

'Each son of a chief, as he attained a marriageable age, was provided with a wife at his father's expense, and given a certain number of households from his father's village and sent forth to a village of his own. Henceforth he ruled as an independent chief . . . The youngest son remained in his father's village and succeeded not only to the village, but also to all the property.'[2]

This continuous parthenogenesis of lineages, joined with the possibility, for each lineage, of adopting dependants of foreign origin who take its name, must gradually reduce the oldest lineages to non-homogeneous conglomerations, united only by the inheritance of peculiarities of custom, and a vague ancestral tradition.[3] This is clearly the appearance made by the principal groups. The absence of any additional clan name suggests that they themselves were formerly clans which have become political and territorial units, firstly by the impetus of enterprising chiefs, and then under the hegemony of a leading family. This is very much the same as the evolution of the

---

[1] ibid. p. 33.　　　　　　　　　　　　　[2] Shakespear, 1912, p. 43.

[3] These clients, who at times remind us of the Incan institution of 'Yanakona', are probably of the same type as those described by Shakespear under the name of *boi*. Among the Lushai, only a chief may have *boi*, who are divided into several categories: those who have come to seek refuge with the chief, driven by hunger and need; hunted criminals, who exchange their own and their children's freedom for the chief's protection; finally, deserters from enemy factions. It depends on the category to which he belongs whether the *boi* can or cannot buy back his freedom, and whether the status of his children is free or conforms to his own. It is not uncommon, says Shakespear, for an intelligent youth to be raised from *boi* to the status of private counsellor to the chief; a favourite *boi* may be adopted. (Shakespear, 1912, pp. 46–9.) One is reminded of the dependent feudal families which Granet believed helped form the *sing* of ancient China (Granet, 1939, p. 122), and of the basic social unit of the Sema Naga, the 'manor', founded on the relationship between the 'chief' (= father) and his 'orphans' whom he feeds and marries off (Hutton, 1921*a*, p. 144. et seq.)

Incas of Peru. On this interpretation, there was thus an archaic clan organization, which today has almost entirely disappeared except among the peasants; certain clans of this original organization evolved, and continued to evolve, into lineages, leaving behind them the schema of an original structure, viz., the five principal groups; and, finally, these lineages continually brought about new developments: domains, houses and families.

The vital point, in our opinion, is that the marriage system functions at all stages of this complex reality: the 'five tribes are in their turn, subdivided into branches and sub-branches . . . All these families are intercalated one between the other yet without being mixed; they live separately in groups dispersed in different villages, each a different territory.'[1] These statements probably go too far. Nevertheless, they do throw light upon the connexion of all the elements of the social group in a cycle, or a series of cycles, of marriages. The basic cycle is formed around the five principal groups: the Marip take their wives from the Maran, the Maran from the Nkhum, the Nkhum from the Lahpai, the Lahpai from the Lathong, and the Lathong from the Marip.[2] According to the bards (the *jaiwa ni*), this distribution goes back to the sons of Washet wa makam, the first chiefs of the five 'tribes'. We are undoubtedly dealing with a model here. Its coincidence with the empirical reality can never be other than partial and precarious. However, all the quotations collected here from the older writers show that these were well aware of this feature. Leach is only repeating what they said when he writes: 'The Kachin themselves undoubtedly tend to think of their total society as being composed of some seven or eight major groupings of this [clan] type.'[3] 'The first five of these are generally regarded as being of superior status, and are recognized throughout the Kachin hill area.'[4]

Gilhodes and Hanson agree that the system operating among noble families is more complex, each family of one group receiving wives from two families belonging to two other groups. 'This arrangement was somewhat modified later on; in the beginning Du ni had as mayu ni only one tribe, now they have generally two . . . The Tarat ni are always allowed to take a wife according to the ancient classification; for them, nowadays, the same tribe is subdivided into several families ranking as mayu ni and dama ni.'[5] For the time being let us leave to one side the commoners, and consider only the feudal families. Gilhodes gives as *mayu ni*: Maran and Lahpai for Marip; Lathong and Maran for Lahpai; Nkhum and Lathong for Maran; Nkhum and Marip for Lathong; finally, Marip and Lahpai for Nkhum. Hanson gives the same information, except that he reports a reciprocal relationship between Lahpai and Lathong, which obliges him to leave Nkhum out of the secondary cycles. Both facts seem highly improbable. No writer refers

---

[1] Gilhodes, 1922, p. 141.
[2] Carrapiett, 1929, p. 32; Gilhodes, 1922, p. 207; Hertz, quoted by Hodson, 1925, p. 93; Hodson, 1925, p. 166.
[3] Leach, 1954, p. 128.   [4] ibid. p. 128, n. 34.   [5] Gilhodes, 1922, p. 208.

to any special situation as far as the Nkhum are concerned, and reciprocity between the first two groups would imply a marriage between bilateral cross-cousins, in flagrant contradiction to the information given by all the observers, Hanson included. It is probable that Hanson constructed his schema from contradictory information, arising from the modern disintegration of the system. Examples of this will be found later. Rather than attempting to resolve these contradictions hypothetically by reference to a theoretical and primitive system, it will be preferable to confine ourselves to the data given by Carrapiett and Gilhodes, which tally and give a perfectly balanced picture (Fig. 46). However, Granet has raised a considerable problem on this subject.

Fig. 46. Feudal cycle of Kachin marriage.

The arrows unite groups which are givers of men to the groups which are givers of women.

IV

Granet, always on the look-out for possible verification of his hypothesis of an ancient eight-class Chinese system,[1] has attempted a reconstruction of the Kachin system based on certain of Hanson's remarks. Hanson indicates that the marriage rules and the relative order of exchange groups in the general cycle are justified by a mythical formula 'hierarchizing the families by indicating the *order of birth* of their founders, brothers descended from the same hero'.[2] There are five chiefly families, but there were eight brothers. The three youngest each founded a family which was annexed by a family descended from three of the five oldest. Thus, Nkhum, Lathong and Maran are each composed of a major and a minor section. Only the Marip, the descendants of the first-born, and the Lahpai, who today are the most powerful, have only one section. Granet relates the number of eight brothers to the fact that two families do not have any minor section and concludes that the original structure must have been more symmetrical, and more in harmony with the mythology, the only rôle of which is to justify customs

[1] ch. XIX.   [2] Granet, 1939, p. 239.

Everything would be clear if the eight brothers had originally founded four major sections and four minor sections; it would hence be understood why each group in the exchange cycle is linked with two groups and not one: 'Each group being the supplier of another group, each section must give to two linked sections, and receive from two linked sections.'[1] Granet does not hesitate to amend Hanson and Gilhodes's formulas in order to re-establish an ideal system with the double cycle: Marip—Lathong A—Nkhum A—Maran A—Lahpai—Lathong B—Nkhum B—Maran B—(Marip); and: Marip—Lathong B—Nkhum A—Maran B—Lahpai–Lathong A—Nkhum B—Maran A—(Marip).

There is little doubt that the system, as observed in the second half of the nineteenth century and the first half of the twentieth century, represents a much changed formula. Carrapiett reproduces the rules validated by Hertz 'over a generation ago',[2] and adds: 'As a general rule this order still remains true.'[3] But if reference is made to a note by Wilson in Carrapiett's book a different conclusion is reached.

'The Măyu-Dama custom of giving and taking wives, has been considerably relaxed within the last three or four generations. Sub-tribes or clans of Mărips intermarry with other Mărip sub-tribes, e.g., the Hkansi family who are Hkansi Mărips have taken wives from N'Ding Mărips. Lăhpais also intermarry. Shādan-Lăhpais sometimes take wives from Wawang-Lăhpais. A case in point is Shādang Kawng (father of N'Lung La, the present Alan Duwa) who married Ja Tawng, the daughter of a former Wawang Lăhpai Duwa.

In villages with mixed inhabitants, i.e., Chinghpaws, Atzis, Lăshis, and Mărus, intermarriage is becoming common. Atzi-Lăhpais sometimes take wives from Krawn Lăhpais. The Wawchun Duwa is an Atzi-Lăhpai and his wife is a Krawng Lăhpai.'[4]

There have been other contributing factors in the evolution of the system, and beside the greater freedom taken by the feudal families,[5] the fear of sterility, likewise strong among the commoners, must also be taken into account.

'Custom requires that the dama ni, whether du ni (nobles) or tarat ni (commoners), choose for themselves a companion among their respective mayu ni; not to conform oneself to this custom were, they say, to cover oneself with shame and to expose oneself to remain without posterity. However, when it happens that the first wife has no children, or dies young, or becomes mad, they sometimes take a new wife in a family with which they had up to that time no connexion and which they add in that way to the number of their mayu ni.'[6]

---

[1] Granet, 1939, pp. 239–41.   [2] Carrapiett, 1929, p. 32.   [3] loc. cit.
[4] ibid. p. 36.   [5] cf. above p. 248.   [6] Gilhodes, 1922, pp. 208–9.

It can thus be taken for granted that the original system must have differed considerably from that functioning more recently. There is still the question of how far Granet's rather facile conjectures on the form of this primitive system may be retained with some likelihood of truth. His whole hypothesis rests on the eight brothers ascribed to the mythology by Hanson. The version given by Hanson tallies with Wehrli,[1] but not with Carrapiett or Gilhodes, who speak of nine brothers and not eight. Carrapiett mentions seven tribes descended from nine brothers (the first tribe having three ancestors)[2] while Gilhodes gives a detailed account of the mythological antecedents of the kinship system.

V

The Kachin see the creation of the world as a series of procreations: 'Karai Kasang . . . creates through the agency of fathers and mothers, whoever exists on earth.' Consequently, the myths are of exceptional interest, since we can anticipate finding, at close hand, the ideas of marriage and kinship, as conceived by the native mind. The very beginning of things goes back to the meeting of a male element, Wawm Wawm Samwi, a mist or vapour, and a female element, perhaps a bird, Ningpang Majan, who gave birth to a great many mythical beings, viz., great cutlass, knife, spearhead, chisel, great needle, and many other supernatural entities, such as columns serving to separate heaven and earth, cords and vital nerves of the earth, and extremities of the earth. The next generation includes the *embryos* of all things, and the following generation, the *fathers and mothers* of the animal and vegetable species. The fourth generation is composed of the sky and the earth in their physical form (as opposed to their previous form) the tools and instruments and the great Nats or Spirits.[3] There are also four brothers (born to the third generation) who forge the world with the tools: with the great cutlass, Ningkong Wa cuts 'Kumli Sin, his brother without head, without neck, and who is shaped like a pumpkin',[4] into two, and out of one half, with the great chisel he carves out man and out of the other half he carves out woman. This is the origin of the *tarat ni* or common people.[5]

The princes and kings descend from incest between Ningkong Wa's brother, Daru Kumsan and sister, Shingra Kumjan, hidden by their mother until the earth became habitable.[6] A barely disguised second incest follows the destruction of the world by Ningkong Wa, and man is born from the fragments of the body of the incestuous child.[7] From this point the figure nine appears insistently. There are nine brothers, nine tribal ancestors and nine sons of the sun. The mythical heroes Khra Kam and Khra Naung conquer the crocodile with nine heads by means of nine bars and nine ropes of iron. The ogre-serpent has nine serpents as servants, the ogre-vulture, nine vultures.

---

[1] Wehrli, 1904, p. 13 et seq.   [2] Carrapiett, 1929, p. 2 et seq.
[3] Gilhodes, 1922, pp. 3–10.   [4] ibid. p. 19.   [5] loc. cit.   [6] loc. cit.   [7] ibid. pp. 22–4.

The Kachin chiefs descend directly from Ningkong Wa, who becomes Ka-ang Du-wa, and has a son, Ja Rua, and a daughter, Ja Pientingsa, who gives birth to Shingra Prawja. The latter marries Madai Jan Prawna, who begets Kumjaun Maja and Jan Praw Shen, who, following the example of their incestuous ancestors, have a son called Washet Wa Makam. He takes three wives. Magaun Kapan, Kumdi Shakoi and Anang Kashy, who bear him nine children, the first humans in this long genealogy. The nine sons are the first chiefs of the great Kachin tribes, according to the following division:

> La'n Kam commands the Marip
> La'n Naung commands one branch of the Lathong
> La'n La commands the Lahpai
> La'n Tu commands one branch of the 'n Khum
> La'n Tang commands one branch of the Maran
> La'n Yawng commands one branch of the 'n Khum
> La'n Kha commands one branch of the Lathong
> La'n Roi commands one branch of the Maran
> La'n Khyn commands one branch of the Maran.[1]

There are thus one Marip group, two Lathong groups, one Lahpai group, two 'n Khum groups, and three Maran groups. Unfortunately, Gilhodes shows little concern for the transition from the mythical structure to the contemporary reality which involves only five principal groups, since he merely notes: 'It is by mistake that I have in the introduction to the Mythology, divided the Kachins into some ten tribes; the Kachins properly so called, comprise only five principal families.'[2]

Wehrli, relying on the same traditions as those which most probably inspired Hanson, lists eight brothers, the sons of Wakyetwa, the son of Sana-Tengsan, who is himself one of the eight sons of the god Shippawn-Ayawng. The eight brothers have the same names and ascriptions as those listed by Gilhodes, except that La'n Roi, chief of the third Maran branch, is missing.[3] The five oldest brothers were the original chiefs of the five principal groups, and the direct ancestors of their respective lords. By contrast, the descendants of the three youngest brothers have combined with the popular classes. It is going a bit too far to accept Granet's conclusion that the Nkhum, Maran and Lathong were divided into two sections, one from an older brother, the other from a younger brother, more especially since Hanson – and Granet uses Hanson's evidence – represents the Nkhum in one exchange cycle only. Need we add that although the noble groups practise a double exchange, no one suggests that this requires two effectively distinct sections? On the contrary, everything indicates that it is the one group taken in its entirety which has the benefit of the option. Finally, when the previous ascriptions are compared with the list and ascriptions of the nine brothers as proposed by Carrapiett, similarities, but also signifi-

[1] Gilhodes, 1922, pp. 83–4.   [2] ibid. p. 144.   [3] Wehrli, 1904, p. 13.

cant differences, are to be noted. There is agreement on the three oldest. However, in Carrapiett's list, La'n Tang and La'n Roi are grouped with the first born, as common ancestors of the Marip, and this reduces the Maran to a single group, commanded by the youngest brother who is, indeed, Maran in the other lists. Only the Lathong remain subdivided into two groups, that of the Lathong proper, commanded by the second brother, and that of the Lathong Lase commanded by the seventh. Furthermore, the Nkhum are reduced to a single group, because the fourth brother is assigned to a new group, the Sasen, easily recognizable as the Sassan whom George[1] considered descendants of one of the five principal groups, probably the Lathong or the Nkhum. But, Wehrli adds, it is certain that the Sassan are well and truly mixed with the Marip. As for the Lathong Lase, they probably form one of the numerous branches described for this group.[2]

These agreements and disagreements suggest that the primitive mythological theme has often been manipulated by various groups and in various regions to bring it into accord with the general appearance of the distribution of families in the area in which any particular version was collected. Nothing seems more dangerous than to use any one of these versions to reconstruct a system which is both general and original. Accepting Granet's viewpoint, i.e., the search for possible prototypes of an archaic system, the nine-brothers version would be by far the most attractive, since it is difficult not to compare the triple marriage from which they are descended, in Gilhodes's version, with the triple marriage of the Chinese feudal lord, involving nine women in all. This comparison gains added force when it is remembered that the Kachin live largely on the Yunnan frontier, in precisely that region where non-Chinese tribes still practised this type of marriage in the seventeenth century.[3] Finally, the repeated occurrence of nine to which we have already called attention in Gilhodes's version reinforces the opinion that the account containing the nine brothers is the oldest.

However, it is especially important to realize that the formula for marriages between the principal groups is only a particular case of a more general formula which seems to function at all levels of the social reality. We have already cited evidence establishing that the division into *mayu ni* and *dama ni* is the rule, not only for the five 'tribes' as most writers call them, but for the smaller units, the subgroups and families, into which they are divided. So it is that Gilhodes gives the example of a ternary cycle between Chyamma, Kawlu and Latsin,[4] which are, according to him, families of the village of Matau, but the more general allegiance of which he does not indicate. However, it is most likely that these names are the equivalent of Chinese *sing*, i.e., clan names. Besides, we do have more precise information on this

[1] 1892, cited by Wehrli, 1904, p. 15.
[2] ibid. pp. 15–16. Leach has synthesized all the versions of the myth of origin which need be referred to (Leach, 1954, pp. 268, 278).   [3] See below, ch. XXI.
[4] Gilhodes 1922, p. 207.

point. Following such reliable informants as George and Parker, Wehrli says that, among commoners with only a clan name, people with the same clan name cannot marry. He adds:

'In some tribes, the clans are united by special rules of alliance (*connubium*). Among the Szi-Lepai, George lists the following clans: Malang, Laban, Thaw Shi, Hpau Hpau-Yan, Mislu and Sin Hang, which can marry women of Chumlut clan. The latter receives its wives from several other clans: Num Taw, Tum Maw, Jang Maw, Lumwa, Hupanvu, and Hpu Kawu. The custom of other Chingpaw corresponds to other forms of the same rule of alliance in which a women from the mother's brother's family is the prescribed spouse.'[1]

This is not, therefore, a system with a limited extension, and fixed form. Clans – if they really are clans – and, at all events, lineages, families and houses, are united by a complex system of matrimonial alliances, of which the general formula – viz., generalized exchange – is the one fundamental and unchanging characteristic.[2]

The Kachin system poses problems, but in an entirely different direction. In two aspects it reveals contradictory features, or more exactly strange antinomies which are undoubtedly something more than mere curiosities. We now intend to examine them, and to attempt to find out their significance.

[1] Wehrli, 1904, pp. 26–7.
[2] This paragraph, unchanged from the first edition, makes short shrift of Leach's charges that I confused the five 'clans' model with the empirical situation (Leach, 1961*a*, pp. 80, 81, 88). Actually, the distinction has always been made, and like myself Leach has merely re-endorsed the analyses of the earlier writers. I am not, therefore, in complete agreement with Salisbury (1956, pp. 639–41), who attributes the divergence between Leach and myself to the use respectively of a statistical model and of a mechanical model. In a society like that of the Kachin, the marriage model is clearly always mechanical; it is only when the number of exchange units and the permanency of the ties which unite them are considered that a statistical model, as used by us and by our predecessors, is necessary.

CHAPTER XVI

Exchange and Purchase

I

The first thing one is struck by in the Kachin marriage rule is its simplicity. It seems that the declaration of preferential union with the mother's brother's daughter is enough for the formation of a subtle and harmonious cycle, within which the great as well as the smallest social units automatically find their place, and, without compromising their general agreement, may also improvise more limited developments, such as the ternary cycles of feudal families, which fit so easily within the quinary cycle which embraces all the groups. Thus the simple formula of the division into *mayu ni* and *dama ni* seems rich in possibilities, and it suffices to bring a balanced order into a complex reality. To all intents and purposes this formula dominates the whole social life, and what Sternberg said of the identical formula governing Gilyak institutions might equally be said of it, viz., that the origin of these institutions must lie in some unique and simple principle, some categorical imperative acceptable to the native mind, and the seed from which the complex organization of native institutions has grown.[1]

Indeed, the law of generalized exchange seems to extend even beyond marriage:

'It were very shameful and very serious if a young man had intercourse with a girl of his own family or of his dama tribe, even were she only a distant relative of his. According to the old people, those cases are very rare and always severely punished because such a union . . . can never become legitimate. But a dama boy may without dishonour, if not without danger, have intercourse with a mayu girl . . .'[2]

In neighbouring tribes, the same law inspires the rules of distribution. Among the Rangte, the bride's paternal uncle has the right to receive a buffalo called *mankang:* 'If there be three brothers, A, B and C, B will take the *mankang* of A's daughters, C that of B's, and A that of C's.'[3] Even the form of the vendetta among the Haka Chin and the Kachin reminds one of generalized exchange. An offended group *A* can only take its revenge

---

[1] Sternberg, n.d., p. 117.　　[2] Gilhodes, 1922, p. 209.　　[3] Shakespear, 1912, p. 146.

on the offender *B* through a third group *C*, *B*'s enemy. This is the institution of the *sharé*, or the hired murderer,[1] a striking equivalent of which is found in Africa.[2] But unlike the marriage cycle, the vendetta cycle is reversible. 'If the proposed victim discovers the *Sharé's* intentions, he may hire him in turn – on the same terms as the first instigator and the *Sharé* must comply; otherwise he will incur a "debt" against himself.'[3] However, there is a sort of 'cycle of vengeance' comparable to the cycle of exogamy. Among the Haka Chin, failure to transfer a vendetta would leave an evil spell over a family for two or three generations.[4]

In the previous chapter we deliberately stressed the features which reveal the total nature of the institution, and the simple relationship it established or perpetuated between groups rather than individuals. 'If [part of a woman's skirt is] sent by Mayus to Damas . . . it would mean that a woman was available for marriage and could be claimed.'[5] Conversely: 'If the divorce is not the result of a mutual agreement, the husband may demand that in lieu of the return of his presents some other member of the family be given him as wife, either a sister, a cousin, or an aunt. If the parents or family consider the divorced husband eligible, this is done.'[6] The bond thus forms a reciprocal obligation, and if one of the groups means to evade it, so as to forge a new alliance also conforming to the prescribed type, a special procedure must be observed, which attests, over and above the general obligation arising from the solidarity of all the groups in the same cycle of exchange, to the particular obligations binding groups which are traditionally allied:

> 'No Dama family may take a wife from a family other than Mayu without the consent of the latter; and vice versa, no Mayu family may give one of its daughters in marriage to any other than a Dama family. When it is proposed to deviate from the customary law the family proposing to do so sends a packet of Yu ma yawn, nga ma yawn, to the family to be ignored and asks for its consent. Such permission is given by means of such presents as an elephant's tusk and a gong. Having received permission in this manner, the family which has received it then approaches the family from which a wife is desired. To safeguard itself against a "debt", the other family requires proof of consent and the presents which have been received are produced.'[7]

The opening present consists of rat meat[8] and buffalo meat, which are normally included in the suitor's present, and are cooked by the bride's mother and offered to the elders if the family is favourably disposed to the proposal.

---

[1] Head, 1917, p. 29; Carrapiett, 1929, pp. 29–31.　　　[2] Doke, 1923, p. 36.
[3] Carrapiett, 1929, p. 31.　　　[4] Head, 1917, p. 29.
[5] Carrapiett, 1929, p. 72.　　　[6] ibid. p. 35.
[7] ibid. p. 70.　　　[8] On the symbolism of the rat, cf. Leach, 1954, pp. 180–1.

Such a strict and well regulated plan of action, containing rules of procedure even for possible liberties, could not, it seems, leave any room for uncertainty. The type of potential spouse is prescribed, but at the same time is defined sufficiently broadly, in terms of the family and not the individual, for an equally orthodox replacement to be possible if necessary. Consequently, Kachin marriage must appear an almost automatic process, devoid of fuss and bother, and leaving no room for doubt or breaches. As it happens, this is not at all the case. Superimposed upon the clear regulation of prescribed degrees, there is a casuistry of purchase which is almost unbelievably complicated. For not only must the bride be chosen, she must also be paid for. The wonderful simplicity of the rules governing the choice contrasts most astonishingly with the multiplicity of the rules now to be considered.

II

Gilhodes was the first to show us that the marriage is not as simple as the rules of the preferential union might lead one to conclude: 'It is the parents, more often the fathers alone, who busy themselves with the future of their children. Every marriage takes more or less the form of a sale in which the price of the wife varies according to her rank.'[1] The importance given to this aspect of the problem in native thought is expressed in the songs of rejoicing at the birth of a child: 'Let him grow up! Let him become father of many children', the father exclaims if it is a boy; and if it is a girl: 'Let her grow up! May she be able to be given in marriage, and bring to her family buffaloes, gongs, brandy, clothes, etc.!'[2] Gilhodes makes the following comment on this: 'Kachins earnestly desire to have children: boys to continue and propagate the family, girls to draw profit from them especially at their marriage . . .'[3]

Various articles figure in the marriage prestations: food, especially meat and drink; domestic animals such as buffaloes and pigs; everyday objects, e.g., mats and blankets. Finally there are the *sumri*. These are special objects, so called because the evil 'spirits believe they are the vital nerves, sumri, which Karai Kasang holds in his hands, and seeing they are so solid, they dare not bite them and run away'.[4] The *sumri* are not negotiable. They consist especially of old weapons, halberds called *ningpha*, and ceremonial swords called *shatun re*, ordinarily hung above the fireplace of the parents' room. They are used to frighten the spirits in cases of serious sickness and at the birth of a child, etc., and the only way they can be transferred is by being given by the wife's parents, *mayu ni*, to the husband's parents, *dama ni*, on the day of the marriage, as part of the ritual exchange of presents.[5] They have their equivalent among the Gilyak, as we shall see.[6]

We have seen that the bride-price depends on the bride's rank, but not only on rank, it seems, for the *mayu ni*, by making arbitrary demands, get

---

[1] Gilhodes, 1922, p. 211.   [2] ibid. pp. 177–8.   [3] ibid. p. 185.
[4] ibid. p. 175.   [5] loc. cit.   [6] ch. XVIII.

back at least part of the freedom of which they had apparently been deprived by the fixing of preferred degrees. Among the Haka Chin a suitor who asks for a daughter in marriage is not refused, but is asked an exorbitant price.[1] The bride-price proper varies between two buffaloes, two gongs, two pieces of silk, several pieces of linen, a silken vest, and four or five 'jugs of grog', if it is the daughter of a commoner, and three or four times greater, if the girl is well-born, including an elephant tusk, a slave, a gun, two pounds of silver, etc.[2] Wehrli quotes Anderson who also emphasizes the considerable price paid for the daughters of chiefs: a slave, six buffaloes, a cooking pot and two sets of clothing.[3] Of course, these prestations are made between groups, not individuals: on the man's side, because the father is aided by his family in finding the price of the son's marriage; on the woman's side, on the one hand, because there are a number of beneficiaries or persons liable (for the return-gifts), and on the other, because, however considerable it may be, the bride-price is only one of the innumerable payments to be made when there is a marriage, or a death, or any other important occasion involving a relationship between two or more groups.

That unappreciated mine of contemporary ethnography, W. R. Head's *Handbook of the Haka Chin Customs*, must be read for the almost fantastic complexity of matrimonial exchanges in systems of this type to be understood. For them to be analysed in detail, Head's treatise would have to be reproduced in full, and so we shall merely give some specimen samples. If marriage is contracted between inhabitants of the same village, the prestations include the following payments: *ta man*, the brother's or the cousin's price; *pu man*, the uncle's price; *ni man*, the aunt's price; *nu man*, the mother's price; *shalpa man*, the slave's price. If the bride and the groom live in different villages, the following should be added: *ké toi*, price for walking (to the brother, uncle and aunt) and *don man*, price for the meeting (to the brother, uncle and aunt). Finally, in villages of the south, *in kai man*, price for marrying into a family. All this is merely preliminary to the *man pi*, the great payment (to the father or his heir), and to the *pun taw*, the daughter's price (to the father or his heir, transferable, in case of the husband's death before payment, to the wife's brother who will later collect the *pun taw* of the older daughter).[4]

All this seems already complicated enough. But let us consider just one of these payments, the *ni man*, or the aunt's price: this in itself includes three prestations, viz., the sacrifice of a pig; the *mante* or little payment; and the *man pi* or big payment. For want of space, we shall analyse only the little payment. It is split up as follows: (1) the aunt escorts her niece to the husband's house, and demands a knife, because it is thought that she must have used her own to cut her way through the forest; (2) the aunt asks for a bead for going inside the enclosure of the bridegroom's house; (3) she receives a gift for climbing the outside ladder; (4) she receives some

[1] Head, 1917, p. 1.   [2] Gilhodes, 1922, pp. 211–12.
[3] Wehrli, 1904, p. 28.   [4] Head, 1917, pp. 2–7.

iron, for 'licking the iron', a ritual of friendship; (5) she is given a mat for sitting down in the house; and (6) a cup, for offering drink to those who have discussed the price with her; (7) she must now be presented with other propitiatory gifts, to dissuade her from returning home with her niece, and be given in addition: (8) coral beads; (9) a copper belt; (10) a rug to replace the one she wore out in carrying her niece, when she was a baby; (11) a pig; (12) a special payment for having drunk outside the village with the husband and his family.[1]

Considering that we have given only one example and that the *pu man*, or the uncle's price which comes next, splits up into as many payments as there are uncles, and that the *hring man*, the birth price, is often added to the *pu man*;[2] that, on the bride's side, there are also multiple prestations, such as pig sacrifices, and dowry (paid by the wife's brother); and finally, that these obligatory presents, which do not stop even with death (since there is a *shé*, death price, which legend sets apart for the indemnification of the parents-in-law by the husband for the symbolic right to sleep with his wife's corpse), do not prevent the existence of veritable 'potlatches', which are optional but recommended, viz., the *vwawk a*, 'to kill pigs', and the *puan pa*, 'to spread out cloths', and modify the whole future equilibrium of the debts and obligations, it will then be acknowledged that this is an unusual development, with extraordinary characteristics which demand an explanation.

Prior to the marriage of daughters, there are feasts held in honour of the future bride with the effect of raising her price.[3] Similar ceremonies, which take place, however, at the marriage itself, change the juridical form of the contract. A custom which is not obligatory, says Head, but rather is made in sort of homage by the father or the brother to a daughter or a sister, its observance contributing to the glory of the person liable, is a feast, during which any number of pigs may be killed, and an equal number of cloths spread out for the husband and wife to trample underfoot. The same number of baskets of grain are also offered. After this ceremony is over, the bride-price can only be returned if the wife should divorce her husband.[4] The principal offerings are accompanied by a considerable number of accessory prestations, and they call for counter-prestations from the husband.

In the Kachin marriage ceremony also bad grace and obstinate refusal contrast with the ineluctability of the preferred degrees. The *mayu ni* are the givers of women and the *dama ni* the petitioners for women, both preordained to each other by an ancestral and in a sense, divinely ordered system. And yet, the day before the marriage, an intermediary, *lakya wa*,

---

[1] ibid. pp. 10–11.

[2] To complicate things further, the right to the *pu man* depends on an initial prestation by the uncle, who must kill and sacrifice a pig. If he did not do this, neither he nor his heirs could claim the *pu man*. The husband replies with a second pig sacrifice (Head, 1917, pp. 11–12). These opening and closing presents, upon which the practice of a more vital rite is conditional, have their equivalent in the *kula* ritual in Melanesia.

[3] Stevenson, 1937, p. 24.   [4] Head, 1917, pp. 15–16, 31 et seq.

is sent to the bride's house and asks for her in these terms: 'Great friendship has always united us and till now you have given brides to our sons . . .' The parents reply: 'We cannot give her.' The intermediary pretends to go away, returns, is again refused, leaves again, returns and pretends to give up. It is only at the fourth request that the *mayu ni* give their consent,[1] but then they make huge claims as to the price. The agreement is reached only after all this ritualistic bargaining.[2] The innumerable payments, such striking examples of which are provided by the Haka Chin and the Lakher, seem to be stipulated in order to instil the idea that the thread, which has been ordered since the beginning of the world to lead the bride to the bridegroom's home, the *mayu ni* to the *dama ni*, may break at any moment (and, in the creation myth, the sister is herself a ball of twine which unwinds, forming the road leading to far-off countries). The bride and her retinue pause at every obstacle, at every step of the way. They are ready to give up and return. In this way, the retinue demands presents on arriving at the altar of the bridegroom's village, then at the house of a *kasa* (marriage-broker), then at the conjugal home. The bride's kin try to prevent the sacrificer from performing his duty, by snatching his swords one after the other, etc.[3] The journey is an interrupted succession of crises which can only be overcome by repeated payments. But are these payments ever effective? Gilhodes tells us that even for two or three years after the marriage, the young wife stays with her parents and only visits her husband. It is only by means of incessant pressure that the *dama ni* finally constrain her to live with them.[4] Henceforward, on the slightest pretext the wife runs away to her parents, who naturally take her part, and keep her with them until the *dama ni* are better disposed towards her.[5] Among the Haka Chin, if a girl marries outside her village, the husband must find a house for his bride's father and brother in his own village. The owner of the house will eat a pig offered by the bridegroom, and by this gesture he will be adopted as a male relative, or even a brother, of the bride, and she will seek refuge in his house if she quarrels with her husband, and he will look after her in case of illness.[6]

The wife then always remains under the protection of her family, who can at any moment call her back home. If the husband wants her back, he must pay an indemnity, and so long as it remains unpaid he has only a right of sexual access to his wife, under a regime of matrilocal residence.[7] This fact, together with others (e.g., the retention of the child by the wife's family in case of non-payment of the bride-price), shows that the bride-price has less to do with sexual rights (which are exclusively in terms of preferential degrees among the Kachin, with their very great pre-marital freedom) than with the permanent loss of the wife and her offspring. Proof of this lies in the system of marriages by capture (*fan*). If the couple have children before the matter

---

[1] Gilhodes, 1922, p. 214.   [2] loc. cit.   [3] Carrapiett, 1929, pp. 33–4.
[4] Gilhodes, 1922, p. 221.   [5] ibid. p. 326.   [6] Head, 1917, p. 4.
[7] ibid. p. 18.

is regularized by the payment of the bride-price, the children belong to the wife's brother or to the closest male relative.[1] In general, it is striking that the brother seems to exercise as great a right over his sister as the father, if not greater. The wife goes by preference to her brother's house to seek refuge.

Mayu ni and *dama ni* may then be preordained affines, but the alliance between them is coupled with a latent hostility. No other system better illustrates Brown's delightful definition: 'Marriage is . . . a socially regulated act of hostility.'[2] We have seen that the *dama ni* is all-powerful in exacting a wife, and any other spouse who may be substituted if the first one named is not suitable. On the other hand, however, the *mayu ni* jealously watch over their son-in-law. During the first year at least (even if the many payments have been made regularly), the young husband must help his parents-in-law 'to prepare the rice-fields, and at another time, to rebuild their house'.[3] In case of divorce, when the husband is to blame, he must give his wife a *dah* (sword) and a buffalo which is sacrificed by his parents-in-law to celebrate their daughter's return, and if the divorce is the wife's fault her family must return all the presents and give a buffalo which is sacrificed by the husband as evidence of the return of the presents. However, says Gilhodes, in the case of adultery it is always the man who is responsible and he it is who pays the fines, *sumrai kha*.[4] He adds: 'The punishments that follow adultery are enormous considering the poverty of the Kachins, and reduce to rapid destitution, the family of the guilty man.'[5] One can see the extent to which these attitudes of hostility, and the modalities of the system of purchase and 'debts', sometimes arbitrary, sometimes exorbitant, contrast with the harmonious chain of matrimonial preordinations expressed in the terminology.

Before passing to the second antimony of the Kachin system, let us again remark on the rules of purchase. It has been seen that matrimonial prestations are distributed between several members of the bride's family, and that the uncle and the aunt are among the principal receivers. It is the same among the Haka Chin for the death price. When the father dies, it is the maternal uncle who claims the *shé*, i.e., he is the beneficiary of the mother's *pun taw*. The mother's *shé* is claimed by her brother, who has received the *pun taw*.[6] The word uncle here certainly means mother's brother, as is obvious from Head. The aunt can only be his wife, since the mother's sister is called by the same term as the mother, and the father's sister is the bridegroom's mother and is thus a member of the house which offers the presents. However,

---

[1] For the Kachin, Gilhodes, 1922, pp. 219–20; and for the Haka Chin, Head, 1917, p. 18.

[2] Brown, 1934, pp. 30–1. Moreover, all the facts that we have just described have known African parallels. Cf. for example the description of the bride's journey, with its many breaks and successive payments in order to keep her going, in Kavita Evambi (1938, p. 345).

[3] Gilhodes, 1922, p. 221.   [4] ibid. p. 223.   [5] ibid. p. 224; Carrapiett, 1929, passim.

[6] Head, 1917, p. 30; cf. also pp. 12–13.

the mother's brother's lineage and his wife's lineage are different, not only from each other but also from the bride's, and these two lineages have no right to the girl who is to be surrendered. Why then should their members be indemnified? It would be understandable in a system compatible with bilateral cross-cousin marriage, or patrilateral cross-cousin marriage, or finally avuncular marriage. But these are expressly excluded in systems of the type considered here. There is thus an enigma, which, having brought it to the reader's attention, we shall for the time being leave to one side. As a matter of fact, the reader will see that, far from being an anomaly peculiar to the Kachin system, this apparent contradiction seems to be a common characteristic of all systems based on generalized exchange. Accordingly, it is only after the basic features of these systems have been isolated that it will be possible to propose an interpretation.

III

The second antimony referred to above can now be expressed as follows. Kachin kinship terminology is of a remarkable simplicity: 'All the members of a group of families of the same name or blood, consider themselves brothers and sisters, and consider as brothers-in-law and sisters-in-law all the persons of the families with which, according to custom, they may unite themselves by marriage.'[1] With the help of a few qualifiers a very limited number of elementary terms suffice to express the principal categories of family relationships which, in a system allowing triadic exchange, could never be numerous. There is not even any kinship taboo or privilege. How then is it that whereas the terms of reference are of a marked asceticism there is a veritable riot of terms of address? We have seen that there is only one term of reference for 'child', but we find no fewer than eighteen terms of address (*mying madung*: fundamental names) for the first nine sons, and the first nine daughters. Following Gilhodes's list, which is identical with Wehrli's but more complete, they are:

Order of Birth	Son	Daughter
1	Kam	Kaw
2	Naw, Naung	Lu
3	La	Roi
4	Tu	Thu
5	Tang	Kai
6	Yau, Yaung	Kha
7	Kha	Pri
8	Roi	Yun
9	Khying	Khying

[1] Gilhodes, 1922, p. 199.

which are prefixed by *Sau, Nang* (prince, princess) in the aristocracy, and by *ma* or *'n* for both sexes among the commoners.[1] The *mying madung* are 'used only by the parents, the grandparents and the paternal uncles; another person using them, would sometimes cause pain to the child, who then would answer: "But I am not your child, nor am I your slave!" '[2] We similarly find a set of thirty terms of address, distinguishing maternal and paternal uncles and aunts, and brothers and sisters, according to order of birth, with five differential terms for each group.

The *mying makhaun*, praise names, must be added to this list. A child cannot have the same name as its father or mother without risking misfortune and perhaps death, although it can be called after one of its grandparents. It is interesting to note in passing this striking illusion of a system of alternate generations in a group in which any hypothesis as to a former dual organization can be resolutely denied. The fact has a particular importance, in the light of discussions, based on similar information, on the possible existence of an ancient system of alternate generations in China.[3] Be that as it may, if the first children die, the conclusion is reached that the names being used by the family are unfavourable, and they are replaced by the names of foreigners: *Mi-wa*, Chinese; *Mien*, Burmese; *Sham*, Shan; *Kala*, stranger; *Mayam*, slave; etc.[4] Finally, there are nick-names, *mying khaut*, which are not in constant use,[5] and religious names which are attached to the ordinary names, e.g., the oldest daughter, *Nang Kaw*, is given the combination *Jatsen Nang Koi*.[6]

We are thus confronted with two oppositions, one between the simplicity of the rules of the preferential union and the complexity of the system of prestations, and the other between the paucity of terms of reference and the wealth of terms of address.[7] We can immediately perceive a relationship between the two first parts of each antithesis. There are few terms of reference because the rule of marriage assimilates affines to a certain type of kin, which results in an initial terminological economy, and because family relationships are thought of in terms of groups (*mayu ni* and *dama ni*), so that individuals need be denoted only summarily, and with respect to their position in the structure. Is there also a relationship between the two second elements of each antithesis? In other words, does the multiplicity of the terms of address bear any relation to the system of prestations? The answer must undoubtedly

[1] ibid. pp. 93–4. [2] ibid. p. 194. [3] cf. ch. XX.
[4] Gilhodes, 1922, p. 195. [5] ibid. p. 196. [6] ibid. pp. 197–8.
[7] 'An error of the literature', asserts Leach on this subject (1961*a*, p. 78, n. 3). But, even putting the number of terms of reference as high as eighteen, the system is still very impoverished. As to the objection that the 'terms of address' are in fact proper names. I can only refer the reader to my book, *The Savage Mind* (1966), in which several chapters are devoted to discussing the theoretical implications of the notion of 'proper name' and, I hope, to dissolving it. In any case, it is clear that a society which had only nine proper names for each sex (Leach, 1961*a*) would have a notion of proper name which was quite incompatible with that of the grammarians, and clear also that such 'proper names' would be, even more obviously than our own, assimilable to classificatory terms.

be yes. Each child must be clearly ranked in order of birth, because of the complexity of the right of inheritance, which is a consequence of marriage by purchase. We have seen that the various prestations made at a marriage involve a considerable mass of wealth, to which must be added a mass of debts, which arise occasionally from incidents in married life. In a family with several sons, an important part of the patrimony will already have been transferred to the *mayu ni*, when the older sons married, before the younger ones reach marrying age. That the preferential right of the youngest son to the inheritance is, in this way, a consequence of the economic aspects of this type of marriage, emerges clearly from several passages in Head: among the Haka Chin, it was the youngest son who formerly inherited the *hmunpi*, or family house, and if he died without descendants, the oldest succeeded him. However, in the case where there are five brothers, the oldest being married and living in his own house and the other three, still unmarried, living in the *hmunpi* with their younger brother, if the latter dies, it is the fourth who inherits the *hmunpi*. The oldest brother, being married and having left the *hmunpi*, loses all his rights. In the case of five unmarried brothers, the order of succession is: first, the youngest; in his absence the oldest; otherwise, one of the other three, from the youngest to the second oldest, in order of birth. But if four of the brothers are married, the order changes: first, the youngest (the only bachelor), next, the oldest, and if not, in descending order to the second youngest. When the inheritance is large, the oldest brother recalls all the marriage prestations still due, pays the price of his own marriage and of all his younger brothers' marriages, and if anything is left he takes two-thirds and gives one-third to his youngest brother. The order of births is equally important for the sharing of the price paid for the sisters. If there are four brothers and three sisters, the oldest and the youngest have the right to the first two prices of the brother (*ta man*), and the intermediate brother to the third. If there are three brothers and five sisters, the oldest and the youngest each take two *ta man*, and the intermediate brother only one. It can be seen that the privileged position of the youngest is clearly a function of the system of matrimonial prestations, and that the regulation of the right of inheritance described by Head, involving a detailed differentiation of the beneficiaries, is intimately connected with marriage.[1]

The two oppositions are thus reduced to only one, but one which appears under a double aspect, according to whether one considers social conduct or vocabulary. But how is the fundamental opposition to be explained, namely, the antinomy inherent in the system, which is expressed in two modalities of marriage (prescribed degree and disputed purchase) and sometimes in two aspects of the nomenclature (simplified terms of reference,

---

[1] Head, 1917, pp. 20–3. Among the Lhota Naga, the youngest son also has priority over the inheritance (three rice granaries to the youngest brother against one half to the oldest and one to the intermediate), because, says Mills, he still has his marriage price to pay (Mills, 1922, p. 98).

expanded terms of address)? In order to understand it, we must consider from a more general point of view the principle of generalized exchange.

IV

Generalized exchange establishes a system of operations conducted 'on credit'. *A* surrenders a daughter or a sister to *B*, who surrenders one to *C*, who, in turn, will surrender one to *A*. This is its simplest formula. Consequently, generalized exchange always contains an element of trust (more especially when the cycle requires more intermediaries, and when secondary cycles are added to the principal cycle). There must be the confidence that the cycle will close again, and that after a period of time a woman will eventually be received in compensation for the woman initially surrendered. The belief is the basis of trust, and confidence opens up credit. In the final analysis, the whole system exists only because the group adopting it is prepared, in the broadest meaning of the term, *to speculate*. But the broad sense also implies the narrow sense:[1] the speculation brings in a profit, in the sense that with generalized exchange the group can live as richly and as complexly as its size, structure and density allow, whereas with restricted exchange, as we have seen, it can never function as a whole both in time and in space. The latter, by contrast, is obliged, sometimes from the spatial point of view (local groups), sometimes from the temporal (generations and age classes), and sometimes from both at once, to function as if it were divided into more restricted units, even though these themselves are interconnected by the rules of descent. These rules, however, only succeed in restoring unity by, as it were, spreading it out in time, in other words at the price of a *loss*, i.e., the loss of time.

By contrast, generalized exchange gains 'at every turn', provided, of course, it takes the initial risk. But the element of chance is to be seen in it in more ways than one. Born as it is out of collective speculation, generalized exchange, by the multiplicity of the combinations which it sanctions, and the desire for safeguards which it arouses, invites the particular and private speculations of the partners. Generalized exchange not only results from chance but invites it, for one can guard oneself doubly against the risk: qualitatively, by multiplying the cycles of exchange in which one participates, and quantitatively, by accumulating securities, i.e., by seeking to corner as many women as possible from the wife-giving lineage. The widening of the circle of affines and polygamy are thus corollaries of generalized exchange

---

[1] See for example, among the Kachin, the sophisticated rules for lending with interest. A lent pig must be repaid when it is due by an animal which is a prescribed number of 'fingers' and 'fists' bigger which varies with the length of the loan. After one year, the pig returned must be a 'fist' bigger than the pig lent. After two years, three 'fingers' must be added. After three years, two more, and so on. If two *rel* of grain are borrowed, four are owed at the end of one year, and sixteen at the end of three. The debt may thus increase up to three hundred *rel*, which is equivalent to a large buffalo, but this is the limit.

(although not exclusive to it). Polygamy is all the more tempting in that the claim applies, as we have seen, to all the women of a lineage rather than to a predetermined degree of kinship. In other words, generalized exchange seems to be in particular harmony with a society with feudal tendencies, even if of a very undeveloped kind. At all events, it must, from the very fact of its existence, develop these tendencies and push the culture concerned in the corresponding direction. This is what we have formulated more abstractly, and at the same time perhaps adducing the theoretical reason for it, by showing that generalized exchange can only originate in a harmonic regime. Indeed, a social system with feudal tendencies, with a disharmonic regime, would appear to be something of a contradiction.

But here we touch on the very nature of the opposition within the Kachin system, viz., that generalized exchange presupposes equality, and is a source of inequality. It presupposes equality, since the theoretical condition for the application of the elementary formula is that the operation, *c marries A*, which closes the cycle, is equivalent to the operation, *A marries b*, which opened it in the first place. For the system to function harmoniously, an *a* woman must be equivalent to a *b* woman, a *b* woman to a *c* woman, and a *c* woman to an *a* woman; i.e., that the lineages *A*, *B*, *C* shall be of equal status and prestige. By contrast, the speculative character of the system, the widening of the cycle, the establishment of secondary cycles between certain enterprising lineages for their own advantage, and, finally, the inevitable preference for certain alliances, resulting in[1] the accumulation of women at some stage of the cycle, are all factors of inequality, which may at any moment force a rupture. Thus one comes to the conclusion that generalized exchange leads almost unavoidably to anisogamy, i.e., to marriage between spouses of different status; that this must appear all the more clearly when the cycles of exchange are multiplied or widened; but that at the same time it is at variance with the system, and must therefore lead to its downfall.

This analysis is doubtless theoretical, but the Kachin provide a striking verification of it. Even in this rather primitive society, we continually run up against anisogamy. Kachin society is divided into four principal classes: the *du* or chiefs (Gilhodes's *du ni*); the *darat* (Gilhodes's *tarat ni*) or commoners; the *surawng*, the descendants of a free-man and a slave; and the *mayam* or slaves.[2] 'There is a lack of information' says Wehrli, 'on how the choice of a wife is made . . . There are marriages with slaves and others between members of *duwa* families and commoners.'[3] This is among the southern Chingpaw. Elsewhere, members of *duwa* families can marry only

---

[1] The words 'resulting in' should have prevented Leach's gratuitous reproach for my 'erroneous view' 'that [for Lévi-Strauss] polygyny is highly esteemed for its own sake' (Leach, 1961a, p. 84). As he acknowledges in the next sentence, Kachin polygyny is the consequence of political manœuvres. I have said nothing different.

[2] Carrapiett, 1929, p. 99.   [3] Wehrli, 1904, p. 27.

persons of their same class.[1] More can be added to this unambiguous information. The children of a free-man and a slave woman are free, but those of a slave man and a free-woman are slaves, as is to be expected, since descent is patrilineal.[2] There is even a sort of moral and aesthetic transposition of anisogamy: 'According to my old *jaiwa* [bard], two married people of the same character are not long happy: one of them is carried off by a premature death; but Karai Kasang, the supreme being, often manages for a good-natured man to marry a woman of a difficult character, or vice-versa, and so the marriage is prosperous'.[3] If a youngest son among the Haka Chin marries below his rank without the consent of his parents, his inheritance is reduced to that of an intermediate son.[4] The rule of polygamy is also characteristic. The proverb says: it is not good to take two wives at once.[5] Nevertheless, it is also said *du num shi, tarat num mali,* a noble may have ten wives, a commoner four.[6] Among the Haka Chin, polygamous marriages rarely exceed two or three wives, whom the husband may occasionally place in different villages, and who may have different statuses, e.g., *nupi tak,* principal wife, *nupi shun,* subordinate wife, a mere concubine without official status, and *nupi klai,* subsidiary wife, married after the death of the principal wife. Head adds that if a man divorces his *nupi tak,* or if she dies, he can raise his *nupi shun* to the rank of *nupi klai* by performing an appropriate ceremony, but once this is done, when he performs the propitiatory rite to the *nats* (spirits) his relatives will be able to take part, while he will be prevented from attending their ritual, having married beneath his rank and lost his status.[7] During other ceremonies, the sacrificer must use arrows to kill a buffalo held on a cord by relatives, or by persons of a higher status than his own, or else he will lose rank and quarrels will ensue.[8]

In the light of these observations, we can better understand the contrast between the rules of preferential union and the modalities of purchase, between the terminology of reference and that of address. The fantastic development of prestations and exchanges, of 'debts', claims and obligations is, in a way, a kind of pathological symptom. But the disorder it reveals and for which it acts as a kind of compensation is inherent in the system; viz., the conflict between the egalitarian conditions of generalized exchange, and its aristocratic consequences. The simple rule of prescribed degrees has maintained the former, while the subtleties of purchase give the latter their chance and the possibility to express themselves. If it is true that the Kachin marriage rule obliges all the clans to follow the general route, each, however, travelling over only a section of it, and thus subjects them to a relay system, each clan has, on the contrary, its own particular track to the spirit

---

[1] loc. cit.   [2] Carrapiett, 1929, p. 94.   [3] Gilhodes, 1922, p. 212.
[4] Head, 1917, p. 24.   [5] Gilhodes, 1922, p. 92.
[6] Leach (1961a, p. 80, n. 1), takes me to task for this gloss. But it is Gilhodes's not mine, and on Gilhodes's and Leach's respective linguistic competence I carefully refrain from expressing an opinion.
[7] Head, 1917, pp. 24–5.   [8] ibid. p. 32.

world.[1] Generalized exchange can provide a formula of organization of an exceptional clarity and richness, a formula which can be widened indefinitely and can express the needs of as complex a social group as may be imagined; its theoretical law can function uninterruptedly and without fail.[2] The dangers which threaten it come from outside, from concrete characteristics, and not from the formal structure of the group. Marriage by purchase, by substituting itself, then provides a new formula which, while safeguarding the principle of the formal structure, furnishes the means of integrating those irrational factors which arise from chance and from history, factors which the evolution of human society shows to follow – rather than precede – the logical structures which are elaborated by unconscious thought, access to which is often more easily gained through very primitive forms of organization.

[1] Carrapiett, 1929, pp. 44–5.
[2] 'An interesting feature about the single cousin marriage system is that it is capable of almost indefinite expansion according to this formula: $(A+b)$ $(B+c)$ $(C+d)$ . . . $[(R-2n) + (r-n)]$ $[(R-n) + r]$ $(R+a)$' (Hodson, 1925, p. 173).

CHAPTER XVII

External Limits of Generalized Exchange

I

Generalized exchange, in a more or less pure form, extends over a vast area of Southern Asia. It is found among the so-called 'Old Kuki' groups of Manipur,[1] where, although it has been less well studied, it appears in a form which seems to be very close to that of the Kachin. Shakespear does not report the marriage formula uniting the five exogamous lineages of the Aimol, but is more explicit about the Chiru. In this group, which also comprises five lineages, there are the following combinations: a Danla man can marry a Dingthoi or Shangpa woman; a Dingthoi man, a Chongdur or Danla woman; a Rezar man, a Danla woman; a Shangpa man, a Dingthoi or Danla woman; a Chongdur man, a Danla woman. The system has obviously changed, since we do not know which lineage receives its women from the Rezar. Besides, Danla and Dingthoi on the one hand, and Danla and Shangpa on the other, are engaged in a cycle of restricted exchange. However, the primitive system of generalized exchange can be discerned (Fig. 47), and it emerges even more clearly from the work of Bose.[2]

According to Bose, the Chiru are divided into five exogamous and patri-lineal groups, viz.: Danla, Rezar, Chongdur, Shampar and Dingthoi. The Danla are regarded as superior, and provide the village with its headman. The Rezar come next, and provide the deputy headman. The other three groups are on an equal footing. All are split into a number of families. The enjoined type of marriage is with the mother's brother's daughter. The patrilateral cross-cousin is strictly prohibited. Consequently, generalized exchange is beyond doubt, and the question whether marriage classes exist (as Bose is reluctant to admit, given the contradictions which appear among the villages) is not essential, since in every system of generalized exchange the notion of marriage class is identical with that of lineage.[3] Bose describes a single village, Nungsha, which comprises ten Khurung families, six Danla,

---

[1] Shakespear, 1912, pp. 153 et seq.　　　　[2] Bose, 1937, pp. 160–2.

[3] I have often been criticized for this formula. In fact, it is acceptable only on the level of the most abstract model: e.g., when the Kachin conceive of the lineage 'as a localized group identified with one particular place and having a special ranking status in respect to that place' (Leach, 1954, p. 167). Needham's criticism (1961) is therefore misdirected,

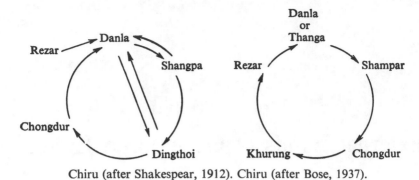

Chiru (after Shakespear, 1912). Chiru (after Bose, 1937).

Chawte (after Shakespear, 1912). Tarau (after Shakespear, 1912).

Fig. 47. Marriage cycles of the Chiru, the Chawte and the Tarau.

five Shampar, four Chongdur and five Rezar. The formula is as follows: a Rezar man marries a Thanga or Danla woman; a Thanga or Danla man marries a Shampar woman; a Shampar man, a Chongdur woman; a Chongdur man, a Khurung woman; and a Khurung man, a Rezar woman. Thanga is identical with Danla, and so there is a perfect quinary cycle (Fig. 47). The much altered formula which Shakespear gives for the Chawte

because it postulates that the notion of marriage class implies that of exogamous moieties. This would be true only for Australian 'classical' systems. But, from start to finish in this book, I adopt a much broader definition of marriage class; i.e., class is defined unequivocally, such that the members of the class have certain marriage constraints which are different from those imposed on the members of another class. Consequently, in an asymmetrical system with matrilateral marriage, two classes *a* and *b* are distinct, once the class containing the matrilateral cousins (real or classificatory) of the men of *a* class is itself distinct from the class containing the matrilateral cousins (real or classificatory) of the men of *b* class. Of course, we are dealing with a conceptual tool intended to simplify the study of the ethnographic reality, and to isolate a model from it, though not necessarily from an objective part of this reality. This distinction corresponds in part to Needham's distinction (1958) between '*structural group*' (= class, in my terminology) and '*descent group*'. Needham's argument that today it is no longer the clans but the lineages that are the 'structural groups' supports my 1949 formula.

obviously conceals something similar, viz., Marem marries Makhan; Makhan marries Irung; Kiang marries Makhan or Marem; Irung marries Marem, Thao or Kiang; Thao marries Makhan;[1] i.e., a quaternary cycle within which there are two ternary cycles.

The Aimol-Kuki of the Burmese frontier have moieties which were formerly exogamous, and clans which have remained strictly exogamous. The moieties (and consequently the clans which form them) are separated by considerable differences in status. The 'superior' moiety enjoys a political and religious pre-eminence, and the 'potlatch'-type feasts which allow prestige to be gained are solely the prerogative of its members.[2] Descent is patrilineal, and although the correct marriage is with the mother's brother's daughter, marriage with the father's sister's daughter being strictly prohibited, the multiplication of terms of reference for the degrees involved is a sign of the deterioration following on the partial endogamy of the moiety.

For the interpretation of the system, the reader is referred to Needham[3] whose analysis is subtler than the one which I merely outlined in the first edition of this book. My only reply to Needham's criticism is that, by his own admission, he has not been able to give a coherent interpretation of the Aimol kinship system either. From this point of view, the method I followed, viz., pointing out the anomalies found, and the one he has employed, viz., clearing away anomalies so as to leave only the coherent aspects of the terminology, can both be dismissed as non-suited. It seems to me today that such analyses have only a limited interest, because the indispensable ethnographic documentation is lacking. What emerges from an analysis of Aimol kinship nomenclature comes down to several very general and provisional hypotheses: (1) Certain terms (*'aou'*, *nai*, *tu*) are used especially to indicate generation levels; (2) certain terms are peculiar to the asymmetrical formula of marriage between 'clans'; (3) other terms are peculiar to the symmetrical formula of exchange between moieties; (4) other terms still seem to relate to the partial endogamy of the moieties, reported by Bose; and (5) finally, an essential feature of the system and one not seen in its full importance by Needham, lies in the differential terminology for older and younger in the parents' and Ego's generations. If this distinction corresponded, as I have often hypothesized, to a formula of alternative marriage (in fact, if not necessarily legally), it would provide the means for the integral interpretation of the model of a society with exogamous moieties, each made up of several clans or lineages, united by a formula of asymmetrical marriage, but of different types according as the lineages are classed as 'older' or 'younger'. In the case of the Aimol, however, speculation of this sort would be unfounded, because of the insufficiency of the evidence.

There is a tradition that the Tarau of Manipur were originally from Burma. They are divided into four lineages united by a simple relationship of general-

---

[1] Shakespear, 1912. p. 154.   [2] Bose, 1934*b*, pp. 1–9.
[3] Needham, 1960*b*.

ized exchange: a Panchana man marries a Tlangsha woman; a Tlangsha man marries a Thimasha woman; a Thimasha man marries a Khulpu woman; a Khulpu man marries a Pachana woman.[1] It is regrettable that little is known of the marriage system of a so-called 'New Kuki' group, the Thado. Certain information suggests that the marriage of cousins is prohibited. Nevertheless, there is a structural asymmetry which must necessarily correspond to a more complex system of generalized exchange, viz., the families are divided into 'families which sacrifice a sow' and 'families which sacrifice a mithan'. The sacrificers of mithans freely marry the daughters of the sacrificers of sows, but the opposite does not occur, at least as a general rule.[2] The custom is undoubtedly connected to the custom of the *longman*, the price which must be paid by a man to his wife's closest male relative when she dies, or when one of her sons dies. Shakespear gives an example in which three cycles of prestations and counter-prestations are spread over four consecutive generations. Each transaction consists of a pig-sacrifice offered by the wife's family to the husband's family, and in return the latter respond with a mithan-sacrifice. Thus, the pigs circulate from the wife's brother to the husband and the mithans from the sister's husband to the brother. It appears as if the sacrificers of pigs and the sacrificers of mithans were two types of affines, united (and at the same time differentiated) in an asymmetrical and unilateral relationship.

The Mikir, a Tibeto-Burman group in Assam, are divided into three geographically localized sections, viz., the Chingtòng in the Mikir hills, the Rònghàng in the Cachar and the Nowgong districts, and the Āmrī in the Khasi and Jaintia hills.[3] The last section once had an inferior status to the two others. However, the real exogamous units are the *kur*, which are four or five in number, viz., Ingti, Teràng, Lèkthē, Timung, which are themselves subdivided into smaller groups; these *kur* are represented in the three principal sections. These clans or lineages are patrilineal and patrilocal, and the preferred marriage, 'formerly the most usual match', is with the mother's brother's daughter. In the past the custom was so strict that, if the young man sought another wife, the maternal uncle could thrash him soundly.[4] It is clear that the matrilateral cross-cousin is merely the most satisfactory representative of the women of a lineage. In fact, when the suitor comes to propose, his maternal uncle questions him on the reason for his visit and the presents that he brings, and the young man's father replies: 'Your sister is becoming old and cannot work, so we have brought our son to marry your daughter.'[5] The same term, *ong*, is used to designate the maternal uncle, the maternal uncle's son, and the wife's brother (in the last two cases, with a diminutive suffix: *ong-so*). But the nomenclature distinguishes the wife's

---

[1] Shakespear, 1912, pp. 173–4.   [2] ibid. pp. 198–9.   [3] Stack and Lyall, 1908, p. 15.
[4] ibid. p. 18. This privilege, which has now fallen into disuse, is still remembered in the folklore, e.g., in the story of the orphan and his uncles (ibid. pp. 48–55).
[5] ibid. p. 20.

brother and the sister's husband (who is called brother, as among the Lakher).

Bose states categorically that the Garo, a matrilineal tribe of Assam, have a tripartite organization, like the 'Old Kuki' tribes, Chote, Chiru, Purum and Tarao.[1] As a matter of fact, Playfair notes three exogamous divisions or *katchi*, viz., Momin, Marak and Sangma, the first confined to one geographical area, the others represented in all regions.[2] This no doubt explains why Hodson[3] attributed a dual organization to the Garo. Nevertheless, the essential form of exogamy is not that of the *katchi*, but that of the *machong*, or matrilineal lineage, which exists in considerable numbers. It is the girl who makes the marriage proposal, except when she marries her father's sister's son, when it is an automatic procedure. When there is no patrilateral cross-cousin, she must marry a man in a similar position in the paternal lineage. There is no bride-price. That the preferential union, as among the Mikir and the Kachin, results from a relationship between lineages rather than from a prescribed degree between certain individuals, appears clearly among the Garo in that the son-in-law marries his widowed mother-in-law, 'thus assuming the anomalous position of husband to both mother and daughter.'[4] However, in the type of systems being considered here, there is nothing abnormal in the situation; quite the contrary. Whether the privilege is over the wife's mother (Garo), or the wife's brother's daughter (Miwok), we are only faced with matrilineal or patrilineal facets of the same institution, which itself is only one element in a total structure to which the type of descent is unimportant.[5]

With the Garo, we have in fact passed from patrilineal and patrilocal groups to a matrilineal and matrilocal group. Their Khasi neighbours also belong to this latter category. We are told that the Khasi can marry the maternal uncle's daughter after the maternal uncle's death but, however, that although there is no religious prohibition on marriage with the father's sister's daughter after the father's death, 'such unions are looked upon with disfavour by the Khasis. In the Wár country, however, such marriages are totally prohibited.'[6] It can be clearly seen therefore that the structure of generalized exchange does not depend at all on descent, but solely on the harmonic character of the regime considered.

It is true that Hodson contrasts the Khasi and Wár marriage customs. This interpretation seems contrary to Gurdon's text in that the latter notes only a difference of degree in the condemnation of marriage with the patrilateral cousin. The important point is that, even among the Khasi, the mother's brother's daughter is a permitted spouse, the father's sister's daughter a disapproved spouse. But Hodson found himself in a difficult position with regard to the Khasi system, because he believed that generalized exchange was tied to patrilineal institutions. It was therefore very important, from his point of view, that Gurdon drew attention to the existence, in the

---

[1] Bose, 1934*a*.   [2] Playfair, 1909, p. 64.   [3] Hodson, 1922.
[4] Playfair, 1909, p. 68.   [5] cf. ch. XXII.   [6] Gurdon, 1914, p. 78.

Wár country of undivided families, the *seng*, and that one region was known as the *ri lai seng* 'land of the three clans', these three clans, as legend has it, descending from three men, U Kynta, U Nabein and U Tangrai, thus suggesting a patrilineal descent for the *seng*.[1] But Gurdon, just as Hodson himself recognized, established that the *seng* existed among the Khasi, among whom the manager of the collective lands is the maternal uncle of the youngest daughter of the undivided family. Because of this, the uncle's house is called *ka üng seng*, and it is there that the remains of the deceased members of the lineage are carefully wrapped and preserved.[2] The only conclusion to be drawn from this information is that the *seng* can be either patrilineal or matrilineal, and that here as with the marriage system the structure is completely independent of descent.

The Lakher of eastern Assam, near the Burmese border, present one exceptional point of interest. They reveal (in an extraordinarily pronouced fashion) all the characteristics of generalized exchange which we found associated with it among the Kachin. The Lakher are made up of six sections subdivided into clans which are themselves hierarchized into three classes. The clan is not necessarily exogamous.[3] The kinship nomenclature seems extraordinarily impoverished, as among the Kachin, and it is especially noteworthy for its clear system of equations:

maternal uncle = wife's father;
maternal uncle's wife = wife's mother;
father's sister = husband's mother;
mother's brother's son = mother's brother = wife's brother;
mother's brother's wife = mother's brother's son's wife.[4]

As is indicated by the nomenclature, which reproduces the now familiar structure of a system of lineages with generalized exchange, the prescribed marriage is with the mother's brother's daughter, while marriage with the father's sister's daughter is condemned.[5] Marriage with the maternal uncle's

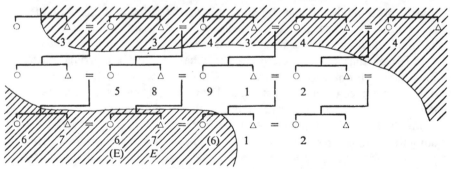

Fig. 48. Lakher system (reduced model).

[1] Gurdon, 1914, pp. 88–90; Hodson, 1925, pp. 163–4.
[2] Gurdon, 1914, pp. 88 and 141–2.   [3] Parry, 1932, p. 232.   [4] ibid. p. 241.
[5] ibid. p. 293.

wife is prohibited (since descent is patrilineal, and she thus does not belong to the consecutive lineage), but there is at least one of its two matrilineal equivalents, viz., the inheritance of the father's wife, which, Parry adds, is typical of the whole region.[1]

As among the Haka Chin, marriage is accompanied by multiple prestations which are perhaps even more complicated than those of the former. The principal 'prices' are: the *angkia*, paid to the father (thirty-six different prestations); the *puma*, paid to the maternal uncle (twenty-one prestations); the *nongcheu*, paid to the mother's oldest sister (eighteen prestations); the *nonghrihra*, paid to the mother's youngest sister (sixteen prestations); the *nangcheu*, paid to the father's sister (sixteen prestations); finally, the *tini*, the aunt's price (twenty prestations).[2] There is evidence of a marked form of anisogamy:

> 'The advanced age, as regards males, at which marriage takes place is due to the recognized obligation on the part of every male to marry the daughter of a house of higher standing than his own, with the consequently disproportionate advance in the amount of the marriage price. Too frequently a male on coming into his inheritance is occupied during his years of vigour in paying off the debt of his mother's marriage price, and can only afford to take a wife of a higher station than his own when he is no longer capable of becoming a father.'[3]

In point of fact, there are six royal clans, seventeen aristocratic clans and sixty-four plebeian clans. Unfortunately, Parry does not indicate what is the situation of the clans at the top of the scale, but we shall meet this problem again when we look at the theoretical implications of anisogamy.[4] All we are told is that chiefs and rich people tend to seek their wives in other villages, in order to establish their influence there, and thus to increase indirectly the influence they already have in their own villages.[5] It is highly probable that statuses are no more crystallized in a fixed hierarchy than they are among the Garo:

> 'It is the custom for a successful party in litigation to celebrate a victory by giving a feast, to which the opposite party replies with another in defiance. The first party then endeavours to eclipse its opponents in a feast of yet greater magnificence, and this goes on until the entertainments assume great proportions and prove a ruinous tax on the means of the litigants.'[6]

[1] ibid. p. 294.
[2] ibid. p. 321; see also pp. 231–338, and the detail of the bride-price in Shakespear, 1912, pp. 218–20.   [3] Whalley, quoted by Shakespear, 1912, pp. 216–17.
[4] cf. ch. XXVIII.   [5] Parry, 1932, p. 232.
[6] Playfair, 1909, p. 74. The feudal nature of matrilateral marriage also emerges among the Lushei, where the marriage prestations are very complex. The Lushei do not have prescribed or (except the mother and the sister) prohibited degrees, although marriage between patrilateral cross-cousins is viewed with disfavour. Nevertheless, among the chiefs 'the desire to marry another chief's daughter limits the young man's choice, and marriage amongst first cousins is more frequent than among commoners.' (Shakespear, 1912, p. 50.)

Harmonic lineages, generalized exchange, struggles for prestige, anisogamy, the simplicity of the prescribed degree (mother's brother's daughter), and the complexity of the purchase system have all been observed among the Kachin, and clearly appear through the study of other groups to be organically linked with one another.[1]

II

It remains for us to examine a collection of northerly groups which lie to the west of the Kachin and practise generalized exchange, which, while still conforming to its simple formula, no longer appears pure, but mixed with a formula of restricted exchange. We speak of the Naga, who live to the west of the Chindwin River and to the south of the Brahmaputra. They are split into several regional groups, the principal of which are the Sema, the Angami, the Rengma, the Lhota and the Ao.

The Naga systems are peculiar because all groups have two types of organization: some are split into three or six sections, others split into two sections, these from time to time themselves consisting of pairs of smaller units. Hutton points this out clearly in his introduction to Mills's book on the Lhota Naga:

> 'Even more than their customs the social constitution of several Naga tribes suggests a diversity of origin. In more than one tribe we find traces of a dual division crossed by a triple one, and indicating a division into three elements, either as three separate groups or as two primary groups, one of which is again split making three.'[2]

Thus, the Ao are divided into two linguistic groups, Chongli and Mongsen, who live in the same villages even though their vocabularies often differ-especially with regard to kinship terms. Across this division, there is another into three theoretically exogamous clans, Pongen, Langhkam and Chami, which are encountered in both linguistic groups. These clans are hierarchized through differences of status.

The same situation is found among the southern Konyak. Here the two linguistic groups are called Thendu and Thenkoh and are further distinguished by tattoos, while a tripartite division is to be found in both. The Rengma villages comprise members of both linguistic groups, Intensi-Kotsenu and Tseminyu, the latter subdivided into two sub-groups which use different terms for the mother, *avyo* and *apfsü*. The Angami are also divided into two groups which use different terms for the mother, with one group made up

---

[1] Another clue for recognizing these affinities is the comparison between the custom of *nokrom*, notably among the Garo (adopted son-in-law, in the absence of the marriage corresponding to the preferred degree), and that of the daughter-heir. We shall take up this discussion again with regard to Indo-European systems. On the *nokrom*, see Playfair (1909, pp. 68–73), the discussion between Bose (1936) and Mookerji (1939), and the Chinese equivalents (Granet, 1939, pp. 142–4).

[2] Mills, 1922, p. xxx.

of a pair of sub-groups.[1] Among the Memi Angami there is a third division (Cherhechima) of inferior status. Among the Memi Angami proper the first two groups do not marry with this inferior group whose members, however, have no difficulty in marrying into other Angami groups. Finally, the Lhota have two divisions using the term *oyo* for the mother, while a third employs the term *opfu*. These three divisions are named respectively Tompyaktserre, or 'Forehead-clearing men', Izumontserre, 'Scattered men' and Mipong-sandre, 'Fire-smoke-conquering men'. Hutton considers that they have different geographical origins.

Before going any further, we should discover if the duality between these two types of social structure affects the marriage system, i.e., if it is reflected in the kinship terminology. Among the Rengma, Mills found no trace of tripartite organization, but only of a former dualism.[2] Nevertheless, the clans are divided into six exogamous groups, and the kinship terminology reveals characteristics which are in direct contrast with each other. For example, some equations suggest marriage between bilateral cross-cousins, while, by contrast, other terms differentiate between the mother's brother's lineage and the father's sister's husband's lineage. There is firstly the identification of the father's sister (*anü*) with all the women married to a man of the mother's clan, and more particularly with the mother's brother's wife,[3] and the identification of the father's sister's husband with the men of the mother's clan, more particularly the mother's brother. If the equations, wife's father = mother's brother, and wife's mother = father's sister, are added, there is extremely strong presumptive evidence of marriage between bilateral cross-cousins.

But at the same time, the nomenclature contains equations which are typical of a system of lineages oriented in a one-way cycle. They are: mother's brother's son (older than Ego) = mother's brother; mother's brother's daughter (older than Ego) = mother. Apart from that, the terminology for brothers-in-law and sisters-in-law is very limited, and there are no special terms for the matrilateral cross-cousin, which always suggests alliance. By contrast, there are special terms for the patrilateral cross-cousins: *achagü* designates the father's sister's children; the sister's children (man speaking); and grandchildren. These indications culminate in a certainty with the following equation: wife's brother = mother's brother's son,[4] as opposed to the eastern Rengma where wife's brother = sister's husband,[5] indicating bilateral marriage. According to the terms considered, there are thus two types of nomenclature, corresponding predominantly, perhaps, with the eastern Rengma and the western Rengma, one suggesting a system

---

[1] ibid. pp. xxxi–xxxii.
[2] Mills, 1937, pp. 11–14. [3] ibid. p. 129.
[4] The term for mother's brother, wife's brother and mother's brother's son, is *ami*. 'The word *ami* conveys to the speaker's mind a man of a different clan, potentially hostile in a clan quarrel, debarred for ever from co-heirship; and the father of a girl with whom sexual relations are permissible.' (Mills, 1937, p. 138.) [5] ibid. p. 136.

of restricted exchange, the other a system of generalized exchange (Fig. 49).

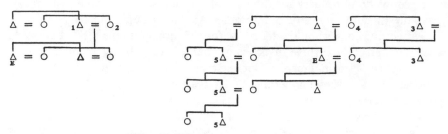

Fig. 49. The Rengma Naga system.

This contrast is clearer still among the Lhota, whose marriage rules are better known, although it is also a case of 'an exogamous system which is in the process of breaking down.'[1] The Lhota Naga are divided into three exogamous phratries, subdivided into twenty-seven clans or *chibo*, each comprising several lineages (*mhitso* = tail). Myth has it that the three principal phratries are descended from three brothers, but, on the other hand, gives various geographical and legendary origins to the clans, with some at least descending from forest savages. Phratry exogamy implies constant knowledge of the clan to which the possible spouse belongs, and there is a system of correspondence between the clans with different names in the various Naga tribes.[2]

Mills reports that marriage with the mother's sister's daughter, the sister's daughter, and the father's sister's daughter is always prohibited even though the latter do not belong to the same phratry as Ego. On the other hand, marriage is possible with the mother's brother's daughter, and she or a woman from the mother's clan is the recommended spouse. This type of marriage is not obligatory, but to act otherwise incurs the risk of offending the maternal clan. If a man whose first wife belonged to the mother's clan remarries into another clan, he is obliged to pay a fine called *lolang 'ntyakma*, 'price for not taking from the mother's clan'.[3] On the other hand, remarriage with the father's widow, viewed with disfavour by the Lhota, is approved by the Sema.[4]

This preference for asymmetrical marriage with the maternal clan is doubly expressed, in the rules of marriage and in the kinship terminology. Marriage requires prestations of service from the bridegroom to his father-in-law. However, the bridegroom is also entitled to the help of the men who have married women of his clan.[5] These men, therefore, cannot also be the beneficiaries of the marriage prestations, as would be the case in a system of restricted exchange. Further, there are the equations:

[5] Mills, 1922, p. 87.   [2] ibid. pp. 88–93.   [3] ibid. p. 95.
[4] loc. cit.   [5] ibid. p. 149.

wife's father = mother's brother = wife's brother;
wife's mother = mother's brother's wife;
wife's brother = wife's brother's son = son's wife's parents;
wife's sister = wife's brother's daughter (Fig. 50).

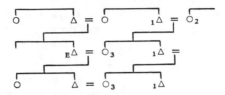

Fig. 50. The Lhota Naga system (reduced model).

But at the same time the nomenclature reveals a most uncommon duality which is worth close examination. This duality is not so much a distinction between younger and older in Ego's and his parents' generations, but rather is to be seen in the existence of two terms for younger and for older, i.e., for each level in the one generation. In this way we have:

omoramo: father's older sister's husband (if he is of the mother's clan)
onung: father's older sister's husband (if he is of another clan)
omonunghove: father's younger sister's husband (if he is of the mother's clan)
onung: father's younger sister's husband (if he is of another clan)
ongi: mother's brother's wife (if she is from a clan other than Ego's; if not,
the consanguineous term is retained.

If the father's sister's husband belongs to the mother's clan, and if the mother's brother's wife belongs to Ego's clan, the system will no longer be one of generalized exchange with unilateral marriage, but a restricted system with bilateral marriage. This new possibility is confirmed by the terminology applied to the children's generation:

sister's son and daughter = wife's brother's son and daughter (man speaking)
brother's son and daughter = husband's sister's son and daughter (woman speaking) (Fig. 51).

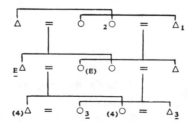

Fig. 51. Another aspect of the Lhota Naga system.

In this work we have continually interpreted the distinction between older and younger in the one generation as an indication, or a vestige, of an alternate system of marriage (i.e., in which two classes of men can compete for the same class of women), the solution to which was sought in the complementary allocation of the elder and of the younger. Accordingly, the force of this differentiation among the Lhota is an added indication that two types of marriage clearly correspond to the heterogeneity and complexity of the social structure. Two spouses are always possible, one corresponding to a formula of restricted exchange, the other to a formula of generalized exchange.

The Sema Naga system presents great similarities with the system just described. Nevertheless, the local groups, in this case villages or village wards, seem to play a more important rôle in the social organization than do the twenty-two exogamous patrilineal clans into which the Sema are distributed. The most important of these clans tend to become endogamous, and the rule of exogamy then applies to the subdivisions of the principal clan.[1] This rule of exogamy operates very strictly, extending to cousins of the third degree in the paternal line. Although marriage is permitted with the father's sister's daughter and the mother's brother's daughter, the former type is regarded as unfruitful, and the latter is always preferred: 'The reason given is that such marriages conduce to domestic concord owing to the relationship between the parents of the couple, who see that their children behave well to one another.'[2] This rationalization, which has its equivalent in China,[3] is not very satisfactory, since both types of cross-cousin are equally descended from a brother and from a sister.

The kinship system is simple:

1. *apuza*   all grandparents other than *asü*
2. *asü*   father's father (= tree, stock)
3. *apu*   father, father's brother
4. *aza*   mother; mother's sister; mother's brother's daughter
5. *amu*   elder brother; father's brother's son
6. *afu*   elder sister; father's brother's daughter older than speaker; wife's sister
7. *atükuzu*   younger brother; father's brother's son, younger than Ego (man speaking)
8. *apëu*   younger brother; father's brother's son, younger than Ego (woman speaking)
9. *achepfu*   younger sister; father's brother's younger daughter, younger than Ego (woman speaking)
10. *atsünupfu*   younger sister; father's brother's younger daughter, younger than Ego (woman speaking)
11. *atikeshiu*   sister's children; father's sister's children (man speaking)

[1] Hutton, 1921*a*, pp. 122–9.   [2] ibid. p. 132.   [3] Hsu, 1945, pp. 83–103.

12. *anu*   son, daughter; grandson, granddaughter; younger brother's children (man speaking)
13. *akimi*   husband
14. *anipfu*   wife
15. *ani*   father's sister; wife's mother; husband's mother; husband's elder sister; elder brother's wife (woman speaking); husband's elder brother's wife
16. *angu*   mother's brother, mother's brother's son, wife's father; wife's brother (in the west), husband's brother
17. *achi*   father's sister's husband; wife's brother (in the east); elder sister's husband; elder brother's wife (man speaking); sister's husband (woman speaking)
18. *ama*   younger sister's husband (man speaking)
19. *amukeshiu* younger brother's wife; son's wife (sometimes also called *anipa*)
20. *anipa*   wife's sister's husband, husband's younger brother's wife, son's wife
21. *atilimi*   (= seed, fruit) grandchildren
22. *angulimi*   male relatives by marriage (mother's family, also wife's and husband's family)
23. *atazümi*   brethren (man speaking)
24. *apelimi*   brethren (woman speaking)

According to relative age, the father's brother's wife is called *aza* or *achi;* the mother's brother's wife, *aza* or *afu;* the mother's sister's husband, *apu* or *amu*. A man uses the term *atikeshiu* with the general meaning of a person related through his mother, a member of our family (= comes from our seed). There are no special terms for the following relatives: daughter's husband; sons' wife's parents; daughter's husband's parents; wife's brother's

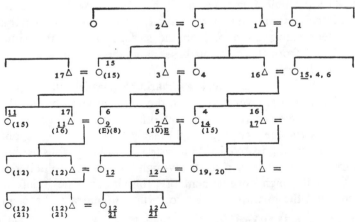

Fig. 52. The Sema Naga system (reduced model).

children; husband's brother's children; wife's sister's children; husband's sister's children; mother's sister's children; sister's daughter's husband. Only 'friend' or the above terms of respect are used.[1]

If the hypothesis of preferred marriage with the mother's brother's daughter is adopted, the result is a restricted and unsatisfactory model (Fig. 52), in which the recurrence in different lineages of terms 4, 6, 11, 15 and 16 can be taken as an assurance that, as Hutton points out, patrilateral marriage is also practised. This is another example, then, of the combination of the formulas of restricted exchange and generalized exchange.

III

The situation is even more complex among the Ao Naga.

It is probable that their perhaps legendary predecessors, whom Mills, however, is inclined to see as the Konyak, had a tripartite division into Isangyongr, Nokrangr and Molungr.[2] At present, the Ao comprise three groups of clans. Th e Chongli are divided into three exogamous phratries, the 'oldest' two of which are Pongen (ten clans) and Lungkam (eleven clans), and the youngest, Chami (sixteen clans). The status of this last phratry is clearly inferior to that of the first two, and Mills sees it as the remains of peoples conquered by the other Chongli.[3] The second group, Mongsen, also comprises three strictly exogamous phratries, but they are unnamed. Their respective strengths are eleven, seven and eight clans. Mongsen and Chongli admit to an equivalence between their respective phratries, and the members of corresponding sections cannot intermarry. The last group, Changki, does not have any obvious division, and Mills regards it as the first to occupy the region. Among the Chanki, only eight clans can be recognized, four of these acting as one section, and the other four as four exogamous units,[4] All familiarity is prohibited between members of the same clan and of the same phratry. The prohibited spouses are: the father's widow; the mother's sister; the father's sister's daughter. Mills adds: 'Nor may a woman marry her father's sister's son.'[5] Therefore, on the surface at least, this situation is clearly different from the previous cases, and the kinship system must be examined much more attentively.

The difficulties it presents provide a remarkable parallel with the complexity of the social structure. Over and above the differentiation between younger and older in the one generation, we sometimes find two, three, or even four different terms for the one degree of kinship, the terms corresponding to various matrimonial possibilities. In a system as full of pitfalls as this one, it is not surprising to discover a relatively high number of prohibited degrees, and an unusually high development of prohibitions. One is left with the impression that the mixture of the two formulas (generalized exchange and

[1] Hutton, 1921*a*, p. 139 et seq.   [2] Mills, 1926. p. 11.   [3] ibid. p. 13.
          [4] ibid. pp. 21–6.   [5] ibid. p. 163.

restricted exchange) has reached saturation point. The Ao system is of exceptional interest because it shows us how heterogeneous a kinship system can become without breaking down. Let us see how far this is the case.

As in all the Naga systems, it seems that there is one term for the paternal grandparents, 1, and one for the maternal grandparents, 2. The father's brother's wife is designated by one term if she belongs to the mother's phratry (*uchatanuzü* = sister, 3), and another term if she belongs to Ego's phratry in the female line (*amu*, 4).

The father's sister's husband is designated by one term (*anok*, 5) if he is descended, through his mother, from a man of Ego's phratry. He is identified with the maternal uncle (*okhu*, 6) if he is descended from a man of Ego's mother's phratry.

The mother's brother's wife is identified with the father's sister (*onü*, 7) if she belongs to Ego's phratry; with the maternal grandparents *otsü*, 2, if she belongs to Ego's maternal grandmother's phratry; she is called *amu*, 4, if she belongs, through her mother, to Ego's phratry.

The mother's sister's husband, as a member of Ego's phratry is *obatambu* or *obatanubu* (father's elder or younger brother, 8); as a member of another phratry, he is *okhu* (maternal uncle) if older than Ego, *anok* (father's sister's husband) if younger.

The wife's father is called *okhu*, when he belongs to Ego's mother's phratry; *anok*, when his mother belongs to Ego's phratry.

The wife's mother can be: *onü* (Ego's phratry); *uchatanuzü* (Ego's mother's phratry); identified with the father's mother, 1, if she comes from the same phratry; called *amu* in all other cases.

The father's sister's son is called *anok*, her daughter, *amu*. The mother's father's son is identified with her father (*okhu*); the daughter, with a younger sister of the mother (*uchatanuzü*). The wife's brother can belong through his mother to Ego's phratry, and he is then called *anok*. In all other cases, he receives the name of *okhu* (mother's brother), 'the necessary relationship through the speaker's mother being assumed'.[1] This information is vital, in the general uncertainty regarding the marriage formula, since it suggests that marriage must always be matrilateral, i.e., of the generalized exchange type, at least. If the wife's sister belongs through her mother to Ego's section, she is *amu*; if not, *uchatanuzü*.

The husband's brother is called *okhu*, and, in certain villages, *anok*, if his mother belongs to the wife's phratry. The husband's older brother's wife can belong: to Ego's section, and she is then called elder sister, *oya*, 9; to Ego's mother's section, and called *uchatanuzü*; to another section, and called *amu*. It is the same for the husband's younger brother's wife, with the respective names of younger sister (*tünü*, 10), *uchatanuzü*, and *amu*.

For the wife's brother's wife, we have: Ego's phratry, *oya*; Ego's mother's phratry, *uchatanuzü*; any other phratry, *amu*. The husband's sister's husband

[1] ibid. p. 167.

has the term for elder or younger brother (*uti*, 11, *topu*, 12), depending on his age, if he belongs to Ego's phratry; if not, *okhu*.

The sister's husband (man speaking) is *okhu* if he belongs to Ego's mother's phratry, and in other cases, *kabang*, 13, or *anok*, depending whether his wife is older or younger than Ego. When it is a woman speaking, she calls her sister's husband *okhu*, when he belongs to her mother's phratry; if not, *küthang*. The brother's wife is *uchatanuzü* (mother's phratry) or *amu* for both sexes.

The wife's brother's son is called *opu*, 1, if he belongs to the grandfather's phratry; otherwise he is called *anok*. The wife's brother's daughter can be *otsü* (when Ego's wife belongs to the grandmother's phratry); otherwise she is *amu*.

The husband's sister's son is called elder brother (when he belongs to Ego's phratry); if not, he is identified with the younger brother.

If the husband's sister's daughter is a member of Ego's phratry and older than him, she is called elder sister; if not, younger sister. The daughter's husband is called *anok* (a member, through his mother, of Ego's phratry); if not, *abang*, 15. The son's wife can be *uchatanuzü* (mother's phratry) or *amu*.

All the grandchildren are called *samchir*, 16; parallel cousins are identified with brothers and sisters; parallel nephews and nieces, with sons and daughters.[1]

The terminology, in itself, is simple: 'Broad categories typical of the group system of relationship are the rule. A man puts all men of his clan of his father's generation into the father-category, those of his own generation into the brother-category, all women of his mother's clan and generation into the mother-category, and so on.'[2] Furthermore, appellations relating to direct kinship are always preferred to those relating to alliance. Thus the three terms, *okhu*, *anok* and *amu* connote respectively: all the men of the mother's phratry; all the wife's sons of Ego's phratry; all the wife's daughters of Ego's phratry:

'These general terms cover all relationships outside the phratry for which there are no special terms. If no relationship can be traced through the father, some can be traced through the mother if you go back far enough. The Ao simply does not contemplate relationships solely by marriage, with no blood-relationship whatever on either side.'[3]

This means that even if, as Mills states, marriage with the patrilateral or matrilateral cross-cousin is prohibited, marriage with a cousin of a more distant degree is obligatory. To be convinced of this, one need only note that the wide collective designations, *anok* and *okhu*, correspond exactly to the *dama ni* and the *mayu ni* of the Kachin. If the *dama ni* are here distinguished into *amu* and *anok*, it is because of the mixture of restricted exchange which

---

[1] Mills, 1926, pp. 164–74.   [2] ibid. p. 174.   [3] ibid. p. 175.

evidently occurs among the Ao, and which brings the sisters of sons-in-law into the cycle.

In certain respects, the terminology coincides admirably with a system of generalized exchange (Fig. 53), with the recurrence of the terms *amu*, for the wife's brother's wife, and *okhu* for the husband's sister's husband even providing a suggestion of a cycle of three stages. Nevertheless the equations:

father's sister's husband = mother's brother;
father's sister = mother's brother's wife;
wife's father = father's sister's husband;
wife's mother = father's sister;
wife's brother = father's sister's son;
wife's sister = father's sister's daughter;
husband's brother = mother's brother's son;
sister's husband = mother's brother's son

all indicate a patrilateral marriage, or, taking into consideration the previous information and the fact that patrilateral marriage is excluded,[1] a bilateral marriage.

Finally, the existence, for certain degrees, of three or four terms referring to different lines of descent, proves that marriage can take on other forms still. This is in no way surprising for the Ao are caught between two conflicting demands, viz., the first, to marry only relatives, their system being a mixture of the simple forms of restricted exchange and of generalized exchange; the second, to extend the prohibited degrees incessantly, in an attempt to escape the confusion resulting from the combined use of the two formulas, and one of the more serious consequences of which is the spreading

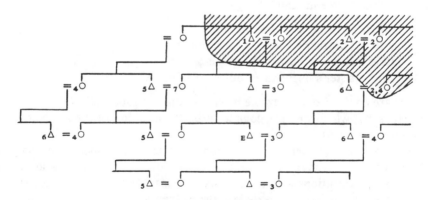

Fig. 53. The Ao Naga system (reduced model).

of familial prohibitions. We shall give only one example. Among most Naga the maternal uncle is the object of an important taboo. Among the Ao, the

[1] ibid. p. 163.

taboo is diffused surprisingly quickly: 'A man is expected to show respect and obedience to his parents-in-law and brothers-in-law. A quarrel with an elder blood relation such as father, mother, uncle, aunt, elder brother, elder sister and so on is a serious thing, and is believed to entail illness, poor crops and other evil fortune,'[1] i.e., the precise consequences which other Nagas attach to quarrels with the maternal uncle.

All the Naga systems thus present the same hybrid character. The feature is sometimes expressed in the fact that a double (sometimes triple, and even quadruple) terminology corresponds to the possible choice between two types of marriage, matrilateral or bilateral, and sometimes, in the extension of the same terms to two categories of relatives, according to the type of marriage actually chosen. In both cases, we note the contrast between two groups of terms, or two ways of using them, one corresponding to a simple formula of restricted exchange, the other to a simple formula of generalized exchange. More often than not the former group is illustrated by equations identifying the maternal uncle and the father's sister's husband, the husband's father, and the mother's brother; the latter, by terms differentiating between two categories of affines, paternal relatives *who are not identified* with maternal relatives.[2] In systems of generalized exchange, this contrast is usually expressed by a pair of antinomous terms, with a very wide extension, e.g., the *dama ni* and the *mayu ni* of the Kachin, with their corresponding pairs of correlative oppositions in all Naga nomenclatures: *achagü* and *ami* (Rengma Naga); *onung* and *omo* (Lhota Naga); *anok* and *okhu* (Ao Naga); and *achi* and *angu* on the one hand, *atikeshiu* and *angulini* on the other, among the Sema Naga. We will find the same pairing among the Gilyak, in the following chapter, with the *imgi – axmalk* opposition. Furthermore, there are the following equations:

> mother's brother = wife's father;
> mother's brother's wife = wife's mother;
> father's sister = husband's mother;
> father's sister's husband = husband's father,

which are confirmed, in the systems under consideration in the table prepared by Hodson,[3] which we have completed by the addition of the Ao Naga and Aimol Kuki terms.

The hybrid character of the kinship systems corresponds to a complex social structure, resting on the one hand on dual organizations, and on the other on organizations with three or six sections.[4] What do both correspond to, and what connexions are there between them?

[1] Mills, 1926, p. 175.
[2] 'How many herds and herds of brothers-in-law he had!' says the proverb which distinguishes between 'wife's brothers' and 'sister's husbands' (Gurdon, 1896, p. 38).
[3] Hodson, 1922, p. 94.
[4] A general tabulation of the tribes of Assam and Burma with dual or tripartite organizations, or both, has been outlined by Bose (1934a).

IV

In his excellent description of the Angami Naga who live to the north of the
Barak river, Hutton makes the clan the fundamental unit: 'The real unit of
the social side is the clan. So distinct is the clan from the village that it forms
almost a village in itself, often fortified within the village inside in its own
boundaries and not infrequently at variance almost amounting to war with
other clans in the same village.'[1] The clans are arranged in two divisions,
except among the Memi Angami who have three exogamous divisions, the
first two exchanging wives, and the third marrying only with the Angami

	Tarau	Chawte	Kachin	Sema	Ao	Aimol Kuki
Mother's brother	Pu*te*	Pu	Tsa	Ngu	Khu	Pu
Father's sister	Ni	Ni	Moigyi	Ni	Nü	Ni
Mother's brother's wife	Pi*te*	Pi	Ni	Za or Fu	Tsü	Pi
Father's sister's husband	Marang	Rang	Ku	Chi	Nok	Rang
Husband's mother	Ni	Ni	Moi	Ni	Nü	Tarpi
Wife's father	Pu	Pu	Tsa	Ngu	Khu	Pu
Husband's father	Marang	Arang	Ku	Ngu	Nok	Tarpυ
Wife's mother	Pi	Pi	Ni	Ni	Tsü	Pi

who are not of the Memi group, and are of a different ethnic origin, or so
says Hutton. The Angami moieties are called *kelhu*, which usually means
'generation.' Until recently they were exogamous. The term *khel*, current in
Assam, is easily recognized. It designates the exogamous divisions of the
Ahom, corresponding to the clans (*thino*) of the Angami. Finally, an increasing place must be made within the clan for the *putsa* (<*apo*, 'father',

[1] Hutton, 1921*b*, p. 109.

and *tsa*, 'side') which is, as its name indicates, a patrilineal and exogamous lineage.[1] Thus, among the Angami, there are three types of grouping, in addition to the village, viz., *kelhu*, *thino* and *putsa*; and the four are, in varying degrees, exogamous units.

The Lhota have three exogamous phratries, and villages subdivided into two or more *khel*: 'In some villages these "khels" mark the division of clans ... But this is not common. Usually a "khel" appears to be nothing more than a convenient division of a village in which men of various clans live.'[2] One lives in the *khel* of one's ancestors, but change is possible. In fact, the clan proper is called *chibo*, and is subdivided into lineages, *mhitso*.[3] Accordingly, in spite of the terminological difference in the use of the word *khel*, there is a parallel between the social organization of the Angami and that of the Lhota. With the latter, there are also four types of grouping: village, phratry, clan and lineage.

Among the Sema, for whom the village seems to play the fundamental rôle in the social structure, the exogamous clan bears the name *ayeh*, and the village group is called *asah* (= *khel*). Moreover, there are traces of dual organization, and although the clans at present number twenty-two, legend has them descending originally from six clans descended from six brothers.[1]

As for the relationship uniting these various types of grouping, they admit of two possible interpretations, one historico-geographical and the other genetic. With respect to the Ao, who, it will be recalled, are arranged in three groups of clans, the first two of which alone are divided into three exogamous phratries, Mills provides a commentary, which is a good example of the tendency to interpret in the historico-geographical fashion:

'Thus, assuming, as I think we may, that the Changki, Mongsen and Chongli groups represent three waves of invasion of which the Changki group was the first and the Chongli group the last, we get the common Naga threefold division into phratries non-existent in the first wave, somewhat vague in the second and clear cut in the last.'[2]

Indeed, the arrangement of Mongsen clans into three phratries apparently gives rise to certain misgivings. At the beginning of his book on the Rengma, Mills likewise notes that he was unable to discover any trace of a tripartite organization, but that there were some traces of a moiety system.[3] The implicit conclusion is that the dual structures represent an archaic type, and the tripartite structures more recent formations, resulting essentially from the warlike or peaceful incorporation of new groups. 'Even more than their customs the social constitution of several Naga tribes suggests a diversity of origin,'[4] says Hutton also in his introduction to *The Lhota Nagas*.

---

[1] Hutton, 1921*b*, pp. 110–16. [2] Mills, 1922, p. 24. [3] ibid. p. 87.
[4] Hutton, 1921*a*, pp, 121–6. [5] Mills, 1926, p. 26. [6] ibid. pp. 11–14.
[7] ibid. 1922, p. xxx.

In fact the arguments to be drawn from the diversity of customs would scarcely be convincing. Like the five fundamental groups of the Kachin system, the divisions of the tripartite groups of the Naga are differentiated by dialect and by particulars of dress. This should not cause any surprise, since all systems of generalized exchange derive from harmonic systems, i.e., the sections are distinguished from one another by both descent and residence. Generalized exchange can thus provide a specially favourable formula for the integration, within one and the same social structure, of ethnically and geographically remote groups, since it is in such a system that they have to renounce the least of their peculiarities. But the system also favours differentiation, even when it does not exist originally, because it reduces exchanges between the groups to a minimum, and, by reason of its competitive nature, invites the partners to assert themselves. Diversity can therefore be a determining factor, as well as a result, of generalized exchange.

Much more important, in our opinion, are the considerations derived from the respective vitality of dual and of tripartite organizations. The latter are sometimes absent, or exist only in vestigial form; they never come into being before our eyes. It is quite the contrary with moieties and the subdivisions of moieties. Among the Naga they present, as it were, an experimental character, which makes these tribes a privileged field for the study of dual organizations.[1] The prolificity of these organizations seems almost inexhaustible: the Rengma are divided into two groups, one of which is again subdivided; the Angami have two moieties, Thevoma and Thekronoma, also called Pezoma and Pepfüma, from the terms that they use to designate the mother, and the Pezoma are further divided into Sachema and Thevoma.[2] In this respect, the moieties are not distinguishable from clans. Hutton says of the clan, 'it ought not to be regarded in the light of a rigid institution incapable of fluctuation or development. On the contrary, it is always tending to split up into component clans.'[3] The Sema Naga provide a good example of the same phenomenon:

'The Chishilimi have long been divided into the descendants of Chuoka and those of Kutathu, which superseded the Chishilmi as exogamous groups and are themselves ceasing to be exogamous. The Chophimi, again, have ceased to be exogamous (if they ever were so), being at present composed of two subdivisions at least, Molimi and Woremi; and most if not all of the other larger clans have lost their exogamous nature, the exogamous rule having been replaced by a working system under which marriages between persons of the same clan are not forbidden, provided that the parties to the marriage have no common ancestor in the direct paternal line for five generations. Sometimes four generations is given as the limit. It is true that this rule is usually regarded as applying to parties from different villages only.'[4]

[1] See ch. VI.   [2] Mills, 1922, pp. xxxi–xxxii.   [3] Hutton, 1921b, p. 109.
[4] ibid., 1921a, p. 130.

If one considers that moieties also can lose their exogamous character, as among the Angami[1] and the Aimol Kuki,[2] it is very tempting to regard moieties, clans and lineages as stages, or moments, in a single social process. Hutton has stated this very clearly in connexion with the Angami: 'We thus have a series of groups each split in its turn into more groups . . . losing, as it splits up, its formerly exogamous character. The *kelhu* breaks up into the *thino*, which again splits up into new *thino*, which in their turn lose their exogamous status to the *putsa* into which they are divided.'[3] At the present time, he adds, exogamy is at an intermediate stage between the *thino* and the *putsa*, i.e., between the clan and the lineage. The closely related *putsa* do not marry among themselves. In a like manner, the Chalitsuma are divided into five *putsa*: Vokanoma, Morrnoma and Ratsotsuma, descended from three brothers and not marrying among themselves, and Rilhonoma and Seyetsuma who can marry between themselves and with any of the other three. Among the Mao of Manipur, Shakespear has also noted the division of the *khel* into exogamous groups.[4]

Moreover, the phenomenon can be directly observed. The Awomi were divided into two groups:

'in the last generation by Kiyelho of Seromi, father of Kivilho, the present Awomi chief of that village. He said that his ancestors, though incorporated with the Awomi clan, came from Yetsimi and were not of the same stock as the original Sema nucleus, and that in future he and they would intermarry with the rest of the Awomi at will and form a separate clan. Immediately after, however, he lost his head to a hostile village, and this was regarded as a judgment on his impiety, and no more was heard of his proposed split.'[5]

Nevertheless, there are other formerly exogamous clans which, having split, have become endogamous. Similarly among the Lhota: 'Some clans are still undivided. Others have split up into two kindreds which intermarry and call themselves "big" and "little", e.g., Ezongterowe and Ezongstsopowe. Others, again, are divided into many kindreds.'[6]

This does not mean that, contrary to what we maintained with regard to the Kachin, clans, or here moieties, must be seen as more recent formations than tripartite organizations. It is possible, and in certain cases probable, that they are historically older, but we believe that their intervention in the marriage system is recent. In other words, historical antiquity and functional primacy must be distinguished. From this viewpoint, the phenomena of restricted exchange, in the Naga systems, appear to be secondary to those of generalized exchange. But here again, it is less a question of historical than of logical precedence. It is perfectly conceivable that, on the basis of an old clan organization certain clans should have changed into feudal lineages

[1] Hutton, 1921*b*, p. 113. [2] cf. p. 271. [3] Hutton, 1921*b*, p. 116.
[4] ibid. p. 117, n. [5] ibid. 1921*a*, p. 130. [6] Mills, 1922, p. 91.

united by a structure of generalized exchange, while the others continued to function, in the background and in remote areas, according to a reciprocal formula. Restricted exchange is free to reoccupy first place when the feudal system reaches its period of crisis, which is sufficiently attested to by certain Naga customs: the assimilation of prowess in love to head-hunting among the Angami;[1] child marriages among the eastern Angami nobles;[2] the extreme development of rules of purchase among the Lhota, who in this respect resemble the Kachin and the Lakher;[3] and, finally, the considerable rôle of sacred 'valuables' or wealth among the Ao Naga.[4]

At all events, the village seems to be the most recent exogamous unit. '*Khels*, living side by side in the same village, would stand so far apart in hostile feelings that no effort would be made by one to check the massacre, within the village walls of another.'[5] Again: 'The *khels* composing [the village] exist in a state of bitter feud . . . The inter-khel feuds were and are far more bitter than inter-village feuds.'[6] Describing the conflicts, half-symbolic, half-real, which occur at a marriage between members of different villages, Mills notes that the bridegroom leads his expedition accompanied by 'the men of his own clan and of his mother's clan, and men who have married women of his clan';[7] i.e., the group of men constituting, as it were, 'the marriage unit' (my own clan, its *dama ni*, and its *mayu ni*, to use the Kachin terminology) in a system of generalized exchange, the pre-eminent position of which is thus clearly affirmed. The members of villages which have quarrelled cannot share the same meal, however remote the original incident; but this prohibition in no way prevents intermarriages.[8] More striking still is the case of the Rengma:

> 'When two villages were at war each hated the other heartily, [but] this hatred was not extended to women from the enemies' village who were married to men in the haters' village. Such marriages were quite common, and a woman would be allowed to go and visit her parents even though her husband was at war with them. She took two or three men of her husband's village with her, and all carried bunches of leaves. While in hostile territory they were sacrosanct.'[9]

In such systems one can see that marriage alliances are the essential basis of the social structure. As the proverb puts it: 'Marriage is the strongest of all knots.'[10]

---

[1] ibid. 1926, p. 58; Hutton, 1921*b*, p. 52.   [2] Mills, 1937, p. 213.   [3] ibid. 1922, p. 155.
[4] ibid. 1926, pp. 66–70.   [5] Godden, 1896, p. 167.   [6] ibid. 1897, p. 23.
[7] Mills, 1937, p. 210.   [8] ibid. 1922, p. 101 and n. 1.   [9] ibid. 1937, pp. 161–2.
                    [10] Gurdon, 1896, p. 71.

CHAPTER XVIII

Internal Limits of Generalized Exchange

I

The social organization of the Gilyak has been the subject of a study by Sternberg, published in Russian, but of which there is an English version in the American Museum of Natural History[1] which kindly allowed me to use it. It is a work of exceptional value and insight, although the precision of the observation is sometimes impaired by rash historical interpretations.[2] Nevertheless, Sternberg was fully conscious of the uniqueness of the Gilyak system, and of the problems it poses.

Because of its extreme importance, and the difficulty of gaining access to the text, a detailed analysis of the kinship nomenclature will be given here.

The Gilyak are divided into patrilineal, patrilocal and exogamous clans. They practise marriage by purchase, the bride-price being paid to the bride's father, or to her brothers.

Sternberg distinguishes fourteen principal terms, added to which are a certain number of terms which he considers secondary, either because they are used regionally, or because they are intended to make a secondary distinction between relatives identified by the principal term.

1. *tuvn*   own brothers and sisters; parallel cousins; half-brothers and sisters:

   (a) *akand*: elder *tuvn* (male)
   (b) *asxand*: younger *tuvn* (male); husband's younger *tuvn's* wife; brother's child (woman speaking) (?)
   (c) *nanaxand*: elder *tuvn* (female); father's sister, and father's *tuvn* (female); husband's mother, and husband's mother's *tuvn* (female); mother's sister (exceptionally)
   (d) *ranī*: sister (in relation to brothers) ⎱   terms of
   (e) *kiun*: brother (in relation to sisters) ⎰   reference only

2. *imk*   mother; father's 'wives'; father's *tuvn's* wives; mother's 'sisters' (mother's female *tuvn*); wife's father's 'sisters' (*tuvn*); brother's father-in-law's 'sisters' (*tuvn*)

[1] Sternberg, n.d.   [2] ibid. 1912.

3. *itk*   father; mother's 'husbands'; father's 'brothers' (western Gilyak); father's 'younger brothers' (eastern Gilyak); mother's 'sisters' ' husbands, and these husbands' *tuvn* (male); wife's father's sister's husbands; brother's wife's father's sister's husbands:

    (a) *pilan*: father's younger *tuvn* (eastern Gilyak), in the general meaning of 'older' (borrowed from the Tungus)

4. *atk*   father's father, and his *tuvn* (male); father's father's father, and his *tuvn* (male), etc., in the ascending line; father's elder *tuvn* (eastern Gilyak); alternative to *axmalk* (cf. 10)

5. *ack*   wives and sisters of grandfathers and great-grandfathers; mother's brother's wife, and his other 'wives'; wife's 'mothers', and wives of the men of wife's clan; wives of an *axmalk*; husband's grandmothers and great-grandmothers; husband's paternal aunts and great-aunts

6. *oglan*   son and daughter; brother's children (man speaking); sister's children (woman speaking); wife's sister's children; brother's wife's sister's children (man speaking); maternal uncle's daughter's children (man speaking); children of a male *oglan*. It is used, further, as a term of affection for sister's son (man speaking), brother's daughter (woman speaking), and by an old man addressing a boy

7. *angey*   wife; wife's sisters; elder *tuvn*'s wives; all *tuvn*'s wives' sisters; mother's brother's daughter, and mother's brother's *tuvn*'s daughter (man speaking):

    (a) *ivi*: in the western dialect and under Tungus influence, wives of all *tuvn*; wife's sisters; father's younger brother's wife (Ego's potential wife among the Tungus)

8 *yox*   son's wife; younger *tuvn*'s wife (man speaking); bride (man speaking)

9. *pu*   husband; sister's husbands; husband's brothers (Gilyak of the Amur River and of north-east Sakhalin); husband's younger brothers (other regions); father's sisters' sons (woman speaking)

10. *axmalk* my mother's clansmen; my wife's clansmen; my clansmen's wives' clansmen:

    (a) *atk*: (western dialect, a term of Tungus origin?) – *for a man*: mother's brother, her *tuvn* (male) and all her male clan ascendants (my maternal uncles, grandfathers, great-grandfathers and grand-uncles); father-in-law and all his male clan ascendants; all my *axmalk* of the older generation; wife's elder brothers (when the occasion arises); – *for a woman*: husband's father, his male *tuvn*, and his male clan ascendants; husband's older *tuvn* (eastern Gilyak); *axmalk* of the older generation

(b) *navx*: all the *axmalk* of my generation and their male clan descendants (man speaking); alternative to *atk* (woman speaking)

11. *imgi* term used by a man, his *tuvn,* and their wives, to designate: daughter's husband and his *tuvn;* sister's son and his *tuvn;* sister's husband and his *tuvn;* father's sister's husband and his *tuvn:*

     (a) *navx*: *imgi* of Ego's generation and their clan descendants

     (b) *okon*: among the Gilyak of the Amur River, older sister's husbands, and father's sisters' husbands (man speaking)

     (c) *ora*: among the Gilyak of the Amur River, daughter's husband, and younger sister's husband (man speaking)

     (d) *ola*: daughter's husband (woman speaking)

12. *oragu* plural of *ora,* all the *axmalk* and *imgi* taken together (Gilyak of the Amur River)

13. *navx* reciprocal term between women; between wife and husband's sisters; between wife and father's sister's daughters; between brothers' wives (Gilyak of the Amur River)

14. *nern* sisters' husbands' sisters (*tuvn*), or daughter's husband's sisters; sister's daughter (*tuvn*); father's sister's daughter; sister of an *imgi* of Ego's generation or younger; wife's younger sister (should the occasion arise) – man speaking: husband's sister's daughter; husband's father's sister's daughter – woman speaking.

The western Gilyak terms: *okon* (husband), *ivi* (brother's wife, man speaking), *ora* (son-in-law, brother-in-law) are borrowed from the Tungus (Olchi).

The implications of such a system are perfectly clear, and Sternberg confirms them as follows: 'Let *A* be my clan and *B* my mother's brother's clan: the latter, taken as a whole, is "father-in-law" (*axmalk*) of clan *A,* which is itself "son-in-law" (*imgi*) of clan *B.* Most importantly, this relationship between the two clans is established once and for all: at all events, clan *B* could not become "son-in-law" of clan *A.*'[1]

All mother's sisters are father's 'wives', and are thus regarded as 'mothers'. Similarly, my maternal uncle's sons' daughters are my sons' wives, and my brothers' sons' wives, 'and so on: in each generation all the men of my clan and all the women of my mother's brother's clan, are husbands and wives respectively'.[2] Thus, the men of clan *A* take their 'wives' from clan *B,* while the men of clan *B* find their 'sisters' (*tuvn*), 'daughters' (*ogla*), 'aunts' (*ack*) and 'nieces' (*nern*) in clan *A* – because of patrilocal residence – but

---

[1] Sternberg, n.d., p. 27.   [2] ibid. p. 25.

never their 'wives' (*angey*). A man calls father's sister 'older sister' or 'aunt', and she calls him 'younger brother': 'and at the same time, she and her husband's clan adopt the same relationship to me and my clan as we have with my mother's brother's clan',[1] i.e., my clan and I are the *axmalk* of the members of my father's sister's clan, who are themselves our 'sons-in-law' (*imgi*). Thus it is clear that we are faced with a system based on generalized exchange, and the following passage from Sternberg shows this even more clearly:

'We have seen that the relationship between *axmalk* (*B*) and *imgi* (*A*) clans is permanent, but the members of clan *B* must in turn have another clan (*C*) which is *axmalk* to them, while the members of clan *A* must have their *imgi* clan (*D*). These four clans thus become affines. Each clan has two *axmalk* clans and two *imgi* clans, which are distinguished in the nomenclature by the qualificatives *hanke* [? – illegible in the manuscript] or *mal* (= near), and *tuyma* (= distant). Thus clan *B* is *hanke axmalk* to clan *A*, and *tuyma axmalk* to clan *D*, and so on, but the kinship nomenclature does not extend beyond these general terms for members of distant *axmalk* or *imgi* clans.'[2]

Furthermore, the relationship of 'son-in-law' or 'father-in-law' does not exist exclusively between two given clans. Each clan is engaged with several others in various cycles of generalized exchange, each conforming to the above model. Finally, to avoid inevitable confusions as much as possible, the terms *axmalk* and *imgi* are restricted to families rather than clans, and the relationships connoted by these terms are restricted to individuals of the first two generations. We shall come back to this vital point. At present it should be noted that the system, expressed from the viewpoint of prohibited degrees and preferential forms of marriage, amounts to this: that the sister's son has a preferential right over the brother's daughter, but that a brother's son should not marry a sister's daughter.[3] In other words, marriage is always contracted with the matrilateral cross-cousin, and never with the patrilateral cross-cousin. This feature is also noted by Czaplicka.[4] But the relationship under consideration is still an inclusive relationship between the clans, and not a kinship relationship between possible spouses: 'Particular attention must be given to the remarkable fact that the sexual norms regulating relationships between the children of a (real or classificatory) brother and a (real or classificatory) sister do not apply only to these children, who are cousins, but to the two clans considered in their totality. The laws and prohibitions applied to the children of a "sister" and of a "brother" extend to all generations of the two clans – the brother's clan and the sister's husband's clan. Thus, only one woman has to marry into a given clan for all the women of this clan to be forbidden to the men of her own clan.'[5] But the system has

---

[1] ibid. p. 27. [2] ibid. pp. 29–30. [3] ibid. p. 63.
[4] Czaplicka, 1914, p. 99. [5] Sternberg, n.d., pp. 63–4.

not just a negative result: 'The number of clans forbidden to clan *A* increases with the number of clans whose members take wives from *A*. But each new clan, in which the members of clan *A*, in turn, go and seek their wives, means an additional batch of potential wives (*angey* = wives) for the clans which are already the *axmalk* of clan *A*.'[1] It is this multiplication which is likely at any moment 'to gum up', as it were, the complex mechanism of deferred exchanges, all the particular cycles of which are interdependent. Also, as just pointed out, a convention places a two-generation limit on the asymmetrical rule of exogamy which, given two intermarrying clans, prohibits one from taking its wives (because it must give its daughters) and the other from giving daughters (because it already gives husbands). After two generations, the rule disappears, and the cycle may therefore be reversed or discontinued. Besides, within the clan, or rather the lineage, there is an hierarchical classification by generations. Men of the father's generation are classified as *nerkun cvax*; those of the second ascending generation, as *mesvax*; of the third, *cesvax*; of the fourth, *nisvax*; of the fifth, *tosvax*; the men of my generation are my *tuvn*, and those of my sons' generation are *nexlunkum cvax*.[2]

Among the Gilyak there is thus a rule of exogamy limited to two generations, and this limit is only meaningful and intelligible in terms of a system of generalized exchange with marriage with the mother's brother's daughter. In a very vast area, actually the whole of the Far East, there is a rule of the same type, although the prescribed duration varies, viz., three generations in Indonesia,[3] four or five in Assam,[4] five in the China of the Shang,[5] and five, seven and nine in various parts of Siberia.[6] There is strong presumptive evidence at least that wherever this rule exists it is a function of a system of generalized exchange, as in fact it is in Indonesia. But even where the system has disappeared, or is not explicitly described, the limiting of the rule of exogamy to a certain number of generations seems a valuable indication of the underlying structure.

II

The Gilyak system, as described by Sternberg, can be represented in the model depicted in Fig. 54, which reveals hiatuses. In fact, contrary to what Sternberg says, certain particular terms apply to the clans of distant 'sons-in-law' and 'fathers-in-law'. However, there are only a small number of these terms. The numerous connotations of the term *ack*, 5, which is applied to ascendants belonging to five different clans are to be noted. This assimilation seems contradictory to the system, but it is found in most systems of generalized exchange. The nomenclature is clear enough when seen from Ego's (male) viewpoint: 1 applies to the members of my clan and generation, 6 to the members of my clan of later generations than mine, 3 and 4 to my clans-

[1] Sternberg, n.d., p. 65.   [2] ibid. pp. 18–19.   [3] cf. p. 462.
[4] cf. ch. XVII.   [5] cf. ch. XIX.   [6] cf. ch. XXIII.

men of earlier generations than mine. This whole male line of the clan from which I take my wife is grouped under 10, and the male line of the clan into which my sister marries is grouped under 11. 7 and 8 are possible spouses, 5 and 14 the women of distant clans, or distant relatives of near clans. A considerable complication appears with a female Ego, because women use the men's nomenclature in a similar way, but – the system being asymmetrical

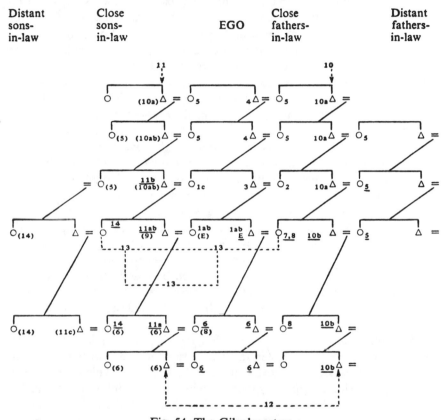

Fig. 54. The Gilyak system.

Ordinary numbers: terms used indifferently by E̱ and (E)
Underlined numbers: terms used by E̱ only
Bracketed numbers: terms used by (E̱) only
.... : reciprocal terms
------------------ →: terms applied to one or two masculine lineages

– apply it to different individuals. Thus, a man applies 10 to his wife's male line, i.e., to her brother, father, grandfather, etc., and to her brother's son, grandson, etc. Ego's sister does the same, but from her own viewpoint, i.e., she classifies her husband's ascendants under 10. Consequently, the term *axmalk*, 10, has a double meaning, expressing on the one hand the univocal relationship uniting one clan with another, and, on the other, simply meaning 'parents-in-law'. The wife actually uses the term for her parents-in-law without taking into account the fact that they are also the 'sons-in-law' of her clan. The same ambivalence is found in terms 14, 11, 6 and 5, which shift from one clan to another in the cycle according to as they are used by a man or a woman. This division of the nomenclature into two is obviously only possible because of the rigid and inclusive relationship between 'sons-in-law' clans and 'fathers-in-law' clans. Within this fixed framework in which the clans are objectively located, individuals use the same terms, not to express the invariable order of the cycle, but their relative position (variable as to sex) in this order. Be that as it may, the division appears particularly significantly in the use of two corresponding reciprocal terms, one for each sex, viz., *oragu*, 12, or *pandf* is used between my clan and its *imgi*, on the one hand, and my clan and its *axmalk* on the other; it is used for all three together; and in designating the relationship between *axmalk* and *imgi* of the one clan,[1] i.e., it is used for the cycle of affines. *Navx*, 13, is used between wife, sister, and sister's husband's sister on the one hand, and between women of the *imgi* clan and women of the *axmalk* clan on the other; i.e., it applies to the identical but inversely oriented cycle of affines.[2]

The projection of identical terms upon members of different clans could nevertheless be interpreted more simply if the Gilyak possessed, or had in the past possessed, exogamous patrilineal moieties as well as clans. If this were the case, *axmalk* and *imgi* would then always belong to the alternate moiety to my own. Their grouping under the generic name of *pandf*, and the double incidence of series 10, could then be readily understood.[3] This question poses an extremely ticklish problem, given the attitude taken by Sternberg on the subject of moieties. His argument deserves close examination.

'We have seen', Sternberg writes, 'that the clan is not self-sufficient. The existence of a clan must be seen in organic relationship with that of at least two others which are connected to it, viz., the clan from which it receives its wives, and the clan to which it should give its daughters in marriage. Furthermore, these two clans cannot be confused, since reciprocal exchange is prohibited.'[4] Consequently there are always three interrelated clans, viz., those of Ego, the 'fathers-in-law', *axmalk kxal*, and the 'sons-in-law', *imgi kxal*, all three grouped under the name of 'men of the same descent', *pandf*. According to Sternberg, this three-clan grouping forms a phratry in which

---

[1] Sternberg, n.d., p. 18.

[2] 'The term *navx*, which is used between *imgi* and *axmalk* of the one generation, in the long run becomes the term which a Gilyak uses to greet a stranger' (ibid. p. 335); cf. ch. XV for the same extended meaning of the term *hkau* among the Haka Chin.

[3] In his *Specimens of Gilyak Folklore* (in Russian, 1904), Sternberg makes *pandf* the participial form of a verb *pand* meaning 'to shoot up', 'to grow up', the equivalent, in the passive, of the active *vand*, 'to raise', 'to cause to grow up'. The approximate meaning of *pandf* could then be 'those who have grown up together'.

[4] ibid. p. 129.

all husbands and wives are like cousins in the maternal line, i.e., 'a veritable phratry of cognates'.[1]

The situation would thus be simple, if there were not a further rule of marriage, viz., the asymmetry of the prohibited degrees is valid not only for close *axmalk* and *imgi* but also for distant *axmalk* and *imgi*. If the men of clan *A* marry women of clan *B*, and if the men of clan *B* marry women of clan *C*, clan *C* becomes *tuyma axmalk* (distant father-in-law) of clan *A*. Thus, just as it is not possible for men of *C* to take wives from *B* (their *imgi*), no more is it possible for them to take wives from *A* (their distant *imgi*). To put it differently, a woman cannot take a husband from the clan which provides women to the clan in which her own brother finds his wife. In the

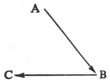

Fig. 55. Generalized exchange with three clans.

case under examination, clan *C* is condemned to remain without women, and clan *A* without men. Accordingly, the only solution is to bring in a fourth clan which might ask *A* for wives and provide *C* with spouses, without breaking the rule of 'parents-in-law'. In the clans which are *tuyma axmalk* to each other (*A* and *D*, and *B* and *C* respectively), the husbands clearly remain cross-cousins, and the wives cross-cousins, but in the second degree: 'as in Australia the remoteness of the degree of kinship beyond a certain range appears to be an obstacle to marriage'.[2]

The fundamental problem is therefore the prohibition of the *tuyma axmalk*. Sternberg says that he began by believing that the explanation of this problem lay in the necessity to maintain a reserve of women in the third clan which could be called upon if the second clan died out. However, he abandoned this functional interpretation for a hypothesis based on the supposed evolution of the Gilyak system.[3] Like Kohler and Crawley, he sees cross-cousin marriage as a consequence of dual organization. The latter is supposed to have derived from an earlier stage of promiscuity with marriage between brother and sister, continuing even after the prohibition of sexual relations between parents and children: 'The marriage formula then becomes the union between brother's and sister's children, who are themselves husband and wife, and parents of the young couple.'[4] Dual organization is then simply a survival of marriage between brother and sister descended from

---

[1] loc. cit. cf. the Chukchee *vǎ' rat*, 'the collection of those who are together', describing the group of families united by marriage, which Bogoras notes as being 'an embryo of a clan' (Bogoras, 1904–9, p. 541), and Jochelson's remark that the marriage alliance provides 'a veritable outline of the social group' (Jochelson, 1908, p. 761).

[2] Sternberg, n.d., p. 138.   [3] loc. cit.   [4] ibid. p. 158.

brother and sister. But the transition from marriage between bilateral cross-cousins to the unilateral marriage of the Gilyak is still to be accomplished. Sternberg sees it as an original solution to a problem likewise facing the Australian aborigines. To restrict the prohibited degrees, the latter determined upon preserving the principle of exchange; consequently, they were forced to abandon the first degree. The Gilyak wanted to preserve the first degree, but they were forced to forgo exchange;[1] hence the abandonment of dual organization.

In short, Sternberg regards the Gilyak system, like the Aranda system, as being derived from dual organization. The appeal to four clans, when theoretically three could have sufficed for a system of marriage with the matrilateral cousin, must be explained by the existence initially of dual organization.[2]

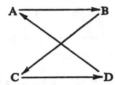

Fig. 56. Generalized exchange with four clans.

There is quite an evolutionist influence in this construction. But in Sternberg's case the observer is worth more than the theoretician, and nowhere is it to be gathered from observation that the marriage cycle is confined to four clans. If this were so, the problem of the *tuyma axmalk* would be resolved, but there would still be one difficulty, viz., with regard to a given clan *A*, a single clan *C* would be both *tuyma axmalk* and *tuyma imgi*. If we refer to Fig. 54, we shall see that both clans are at least partially distinguished by the terminology. Further, none of Sternberg's information gives any reason for us to think that the two *tuyma* are not objectively different: 'Each clan is linked with at least four others by very close kinship relationships.'[3] This obviously makes an elementary cycle of five and not four clans. In these circumstances, any hypothesis of dual organization vanishes.

And what remains of it in the face of a passage as precise and eloquent as the following?

'Any clan which carries on marriage relationships, even with a single member of another clan outside the four initial clans, becomes *axmalk* or *imgi* to the whole clan. Then again we know that every *axmalk*, or *imgi*, is not only in alliance with the clans with which he carries on direct marriage relationships, but also with the *axmalk* and the *imgi* of these clans. Thus, each clan has in addition to its *axmalk* and *imgi* of the first degree, those of the second, the third degree and so on. All these clans are called *pandf*, i.e., persons of the same origin . . .

[1] Sternberg, n.d., p. 164.   [2] ibid. pp. 165–75.   [3] ibid. p. 299.

Thus, the fundamental principle of the family and the clan, according to which a man prefers to marry his mother's brother's daughter is as simple and clear as it may be and establishes its ties and sympathies, not only within its own clan, but also in the form of wider unions between groups, finally extending to the whole tribe.'[1]

It is evident from this passage that the cycle of alliance requires a minimum of five clans, but can include many others. Consequently, the hypothesis of a division into moieties is not only useless, but contradicts the facts as recounted by Sternberg.

III

The complete similarity of this system with those described in the previous chapters, particularly the Kachin system, need not be stressed. Properly speaking the Gilyak clan seems to be much less a clan than a lineage, as its name, *kxal*, suggests, for the latter means 'cover', or 'sheath', with the gloss, 'we have the same father-in-law, the same son-in-law'.[2] Far from being an 'astonishing form',[3] marriage with the mother's brother's daughter, the veritable 'seed from which the whole complex structure of Gilyak institutions has sprung forth',[4] reproduces a simple type of generalized exchange which is repeated in the far north and in the far south of eastern Asia. The similarities are not confined to the forms of marriage and the characteristic traits of the kinship system, but are also found in the particulars of marriage by purchase.

Among the Gilyak, even marriage by purchase is a function of marriage with the matrilateral cross-cousin. It appears only when the relationship of the future spouses does not conform to the preferred type, the only one which is 'absolutely pure and sacred'. Sternberg makes the following comment: 'As soon as a son is born to her, the mother's first care is to do all in her power to bring about his betrothal with the daughter of one of her brothers.'[5] If she succeeds, there will be no *kalim*, or bride-price. On the contrary, the future wife's father will give gifts to the bridegroom, given the extraordinary privileges a man has over his mother's brother.[6] As it happens, the bride-price is very high, and poor people cannot hope to obtain a wife outside the institution of preferential marriage. Moreover, sexual relations are sanctioned between a man and his unmarried *angey*, and although the husband's rights must be respected with regard to a married *angey*, fraternal polyandry is practised by common assent. On the other hand, if there is a prohibition on sexual relations with a stranger, yet 'from one end of the region to the other, wheresoever a man may find his *angey*, he finds, at the same time, a conjugal home. All he needs is to know the kinship relationships.'[7] Legends strongly suggest that there was no marriage ceremony, this being easily understood

[1] ibid. p. 327.   [2] ibid. p. 271.   [3] ibid. p. 337.   [4] ibid. p. 117.
[5] ibid. p. 79.   [6] ibid. pp. 81–2.   [7] ibid. pp. 86, n. 1, 87.

since the prescribed degree is the necessary and sufficient condition for marriage.

We must dwell a moment on the terminology of marriage by purchase. The usual Gilyak word for 'to pay' is *yuśkind*, which comes from *uskind*, synonymous with *fuxmund*, meaning 'to fight', 'to resist', 'to avenge'.[1] By contrast, bride-price is designated by another word, *kalim*, which means 'to offer'. This peaceable connotation is backed up by the affectionate relationship between *navx*, young men belonging to clans united by marriage: 'when walking, they go one behind the other, like lovers'.[2] The truth is that, among the Gilyak, 'marriage accompanied by bride-price is not regarded as a buying or selling transaction'.[3] Besides, the bride's family is kept to counter-prestations which spread out over several years, for 'it is discreditable to return the equivalent of the *kalim* to the bridegroom as gifts'.[4] In the case of unorthodox marriage, the deferred exchange of prestations is more a symbol of friendship, a guarantee against evil magical influences. Its principal if not exclusive aim is the artificial creation of ties which are lacking.[5]

The Gilyak have a special class of valuables, *šagund*, a term which Sternberg translates as 'the precious goods'. At this juncture it is impossible not to call to mind the 'rich foods' of the Kwakiutl.[6] Once these specific goods have been acquired – usually from Chinese or Japanese pedlars – they can be neither negotiated nor traded.[7] They are employed solely for the bride-price, and as minor prestations when the dowry is handed over, when ransom payments are made, and when there is a funeral. They are divided into iron *šagund*, i.e., cooking pots, spears, Japanese swords, coats of mail, etc., fur *šagund*, i.e., furred cloaks and goods, and silk *šagund*, which are usually Chinese goods.[8] The wife receives a dowry, which should be equivalent to the *kalim* and remains her property, transferable on her death to her daughters or to her brother.

Neither purchase nor anisogamy seems to play the same rôle among the Gilyak as among the Kachin. Nevertheless, there is a striking similarity between 'the precious goods', *šagund* in one, and *sumri* in the other. The inequality of lineages is obvious in both groups. The only difference is that, among the Kachin, this inequality is always expressed in the rules of purchase (since there is both purchase and prescribed degree), while among the Gilyak it is expressed in the fact that purchase, which dispenses with the need to observe the prescribed degree, gives the privileged lineages a wider choice. The poor would be unable to marry if there were not a prescribed degree, so high is the bride-price.[9]

Moreover, although the inequalities of status inherent in the system clearly exist among the Gilyak, as the text quoted above overwhelmingly proves, the Gilyak seem to have tried to deal with them more democratically than is the

---

[1] cf. ch. V, p. 601.   [2] Sternberg, n.d., p. 331.   [3] ibid. p. 251.   [4] loc. cit.
[5] ibid. p. 252.   [6] cf. ch. V.   [7] Sternberg, n.d., p. 253.
[8] ibid. p. 286, n. 1.   [9] ibid. p. 82.

case with the Kachin chiefdoms. There is a statutory relationship between *imgi* and *axmalk*, which, apart from all economic and social considerations, places each *axmalk* in a subordinate position to his *imgi*. A maternal uncle, i.e., father-in-law, is more affectionate towards his nephews/sons-in-law than towards his own children. He must give them part of his bag at the hunt, and is obliged to invite them to the ceremonial feasts for the bear-sacrifice, whereas the converse is not true.[1] But, of course, the *imgi* is bound down to this same one-sided obligation as regards his own *imgi*, to whom he himself is *axmalk*: 'In this way there is a continuous chain linking the whole series of clans in their social and religious feasts.'[2] This alternating structure, from father-in-law to son-in-law, in a continuous series of positive and negative attitudes, the exact equivalent of which has been described by Warner among the Murngin,[3] has parallels among the tribes of Assam.[4] It is obviously the structure best fitted for equalizing, among the groups, inequalities which must inevitably result from a system of generalized exchange, and it is not surprising to find it so highly developed and so rigorously formulated in more or less democratic societies practising marriage with the mother's brother's daughter. In societies which employ the same type of marriage, but have given free rein to the feudal consequences of the system, these inequalities can at least act as a brake or governor.

But Gilyak marriage by purchase is always unorthodox, i.e., it involves the renunciation of an old alliance. Because of this, part of the *kalim* is returned by right to the *axmalk* clan, i.e., to the clan from which wives had usually been taken. The *kalim* is received by the bride's mother's brother, less commonly by her father: 'and sometimes the payment is made more strikingly. A younger sister is given to the mother's brother, or one's own daughter is given to the wife's brother, so that these persons also receive a *kalim* . . . Furthermore, if the mother has several brothers and if a nephew has several sisters, a sister is given to each uncle.'[5] These are remarkable anomalies in the system, since descent is patrilineal, and since there is no such thing as patrilateral marriage. Sternberg interprets them as a survival of a matrilineal regime, or of a former marriage between bilateral cross-cousins.

These peculiarities are not restricted to the Gilyak, and their equivalent at least is found among the neighbours of the Gilyak, the Gold tribe of the Amur River.[6] There a woman cannot marry her mother's brother's son, for this 'would carry back to her mother's clan some of her mother's blood',[7] but a man can perfectly well marry his mother's brother's daughter. In this way, the maternal clan, which has already given him its blood, continues to provide new blood, from the same source, for his children. It is impossible to express the principle of generalized exchange more forcefully and neatly.[8]

---

[1] ibid. pp. 81–2 and 268.   [2] ibid. p. 333.   [3] cf. ch. XII.   [4] cf. ch. XVI.
[5] Sternberg, n.d., p. 256.   [6] Lattimore, 1933.   [7] ibid. p. 49.
[8] The Gold legends speak of men of 'Three Clans' (ibid. p. 12), thus suggesting tripartite organizations. Cf. the 'land of the three clans' among the Wár (cf. p. 274).

The Gold, therefore, like the Gilyak, have a system of asymmetrical marriage. It is impossible to marry the father's sister's daughter, the mother's blood being unable to return to the clan, while a woman by marrying her father's sister's son is only following in her aunt's footsteps. Moreover, the Gold have special terms for matrilateral cousins only, while patrilateral cousins seem to be identified with brothers and sisters.[1] Must we adopt Lattimore's viewpoint and see these rules as Chinese in origin? An opinion on this can be formed while reading the following chapters. At all events, the Gold claim these rules as their own, and, says Lattimore, so do the Manchu. This assertion poses a singular problem, as will be seen in Chapter XXIII. But, however precise the Gold marriage rules may be, there are indications among the natives of the same problem as regards bilateral marriage as found among the Gilyak. Lattimore has collected them from the Chinese in the form of legends. They say that the Gold first offer a girl to her mother's brother and only if he refuses her can another marriage be considered. This commemorates a myth in which a woman is carried off by a bear, by whom she has a daughter. This woman's brother finds her, kills the bear, and frees her and her child, whom he marries. We shall come across the same theme in Manchuria.[2] Another time a Chinese told Lattimore: 'You know, the Tartars always offer a girl first to her mother's brother in marriage, because only on the mother's side are they of human ancestry; their ancestor was a bear.'[3] However, the Gold deny this interpretation, and Lattimore is inclined to apply it to the Gilyak.[4] The customs to which it alludes certainly have their counterparts among the latter.[5]

It would be tempting to interpret the maternal uncle's participation in the bride-price strictly in terms of the Gilyak system. The bride's maternal uncle is the close *axmalk* of the bride's lineage, and therefore the distant *axmalk*, *tuyma axmalk*, of the bridegroom's lineage. In this way the rules of purchase seem to indicate that marriage not only involves close *imgi* and *axmalk*, but also distant *axmalk* and *imgi*, since such is the relationship uniting the bridegroom's lineage and the bride's maternal uncle's lineage. Consequently, everything happens in the marriage prestations as if the partners were *axmalk* and *imgi*, taking both terms in their widest meaning.

Such an interpretation, however, runs up against the rule of the *tuyma axmalk*, by which the latter cannot receive wives from the *imgi*. Thus there is clearly a sort of inherent contradiction in the system, and consideration must be given to whether this contradiction is apparent or real, or, at all events, to whatever significance the facts in which it is expressed may have had.

---

[1] Lattimore, 1933, pp. 49 and 72.   [2] cf. ch. XXIII.   [3] Lattimore, 1933, p. 50.   [4] loc. cit.

[5] Among the Gilyak, lovers belonging to prohibited categories have no course open other than suicide. It is interesting that a song which Sternberg quotes in support concerns a woman who becomes her uncle's mistress. Her sister calls her 'a bitch' and calls her lover 'a devil', and her sister, father and mother never stop shouting to her: 'Kill yourself, kill yourself!' (Sternberg, n.d., p. 107.)

The twin rôle of the maternal uncle in the Gilyak system, as protector of his niece against the exogamous 'bear' and as recipient in the marriage contract, has an exact equivalent in the south Asian systems with generalized exchange which have been studied in the previous chapters. Parry states that the Lakher, when addressing a chief, use the term *papu*, which means 'maternal uncle', the greatest honorific in the language.[1] Indeed, the maternal uncle enjoys a respect equal to, if not greater than, that shown by an individual towards his parents. The maternal uncle has a particular interest, not only in his nephews, but also in his nieces. It is he who receives the *puma* when his niece marries, and this payment is often greater than that received by the father, which he must share with his sons. A remarkable thing is that the tie between the uncle and his nieces seems closer than that between him and his nephews. He owes his nieces a portion of all the animals he kills while hunting, and it is only when there is no niece that he is occasionally expected to give a gift to his nephews. The maternal uncle is forbidden (*ana*) to curse or insult his nephew. If this prohibition were ever broken, it would require a sacrifice in expiation of the crime, which otherwise would heap the worst misfortunes imaginable upon the family. Under no pretext may a nephew marry his maternal uncle's widow, for either the marriage would be childless, or the children would be cretins, lame, blind or mad.[2]

Shakespear defines the term *pu* among the Lushai as meaning 'grandfather, maternal uncle, and every other relation on the mother's or wife's side. It is also used for a person specially chosen as a protector or guardian.'[3] The maternal uncle receives a portion of the bride-price, the *pushum*, which can be worth as much as a buffalo.[4] The Kolhen go even further, since the bride-price is paid exclusively to the mother, the brothers and the maternal uncle, the father being left out entirely. Shakespear asks himself the same question about this custom as Sternberg asked in connexion with the Gilyak: 'Can it be a survival of mother-right?'[5]

Mills likewise interprets the special relationships with the mother's brother among the Rengma Naga as a matrilineal survival. To quarrel with a maternal uncle is the greatest sin, for the natives say: 'A mother's brother is like a god'. He can exploit his nephews and nieces, deprive them of their movable goods, and make them ill by his curse.[6] One portion of the bride-price goes to the bride's maternal uncle. It is paid after the consummation of the marriage and requires a counter-prestation of a gift of meat from the beneficiary. If the marriage is childless, an extra gift is offered to the uncle, who is believed to have it in his power to prevent his niece from conceiving.[7]

[1] Parry, 1932, pp. 239–44.   [2] ibid. p. 243. See also Shakespear, 1912, pp. 217–19.
[3] Shakespear, 1912, p. xxii.   [4] ibid. p. 51.   [5] ibid. p. 155.
[6] Mills, 1937, pp. 137–8. From this undoubtedly comes the proverb: 'If the uncle dies first, I shall look for the devil second' (Gurdon, 1896, pp. 70–1).
[7] Mills, 1937, pp. 207–8.

The Sema Naga have the same prohibition between the maternal uncle and his nephews and nieces. When the niece marries, there is an exchange of gifts. The uncle makes his niece a gift, and receives one from her husband in return.[1]

From these few facts it can be seen that the rôle of protector, or of dominator, played by the maternal uncle, and his often preferential right to the bride-price, are found, with identical characteristics, in all the simple systems of generalized exchange that we have examined. Consequently we are not dealing with a mere peculiarity of some particular group, explicable in terms of the history of this group, but with an important structural phenomenon, which can only be accounted for in general terms, viz., that *although, in a system of generalized exchange, A is debtor solely to B from whom he receives his wives and, for the same reason, B is debtor solely to C, C to n, and n to A, when there is a marriage it is as if B had also a direct claim over n, C over A, n over B, and A over C.*[2] The fact that, among the Gilyak at least, this second debt is paid in women, suggests that it is of the same type as the first.

In most systems of generalized exchange in Southern Asia, this phenomenon is accompanied by another and symmetrical phenomenon, viz., the rôle played by the father's sister, and her husband's and her children's lineage, in the marriage of her nephew. It is the bridegroom's father's sister in particular who makes the ritual requests to the bride to call at the bridegroom's parents' house.[3] She also plays a leading rôle in the marriage ceremony, whereas the father is excluded from the wedding procession,[4] and acts as intermediary when negotiations are opened.[5] Further, we must not forget that, among the Lhota Naga, the husbands of women of the bridegroom's clan help the bridegroom fulfil his obligations towards his future parents-in-law.[6] Finally, among the Haka Chin and the Kachin, one well remembers that the bridegroom's sisters (in any case the eldest sister) help him pay the bride-price, and also that the bride's parents completely refrain from participating in the ceremony.[7] On the other hand the young woman is assisted by the maternal lineage, the uncle and aunt moreover receiving a considerable portion of the price in the form of the *pu man* and the *ni man.*[8]

There is certainly no necessity, or even excuse, for treating these peculiarities as matrilineal survivals. But do they not express a sort of female reaction to, or viewpoint on, the system taken as a whole? These patrilineal and patrilocal regimes, which condemn women to the hard fate of exile, theoretically for ever, in foreign households, often different in language and customs, do not exclude, however, a certain solidarity in the female line; perhaps they are even the cause of it. We have already described the latent antagonism

---

[1] Hutton, 1921*a*, p. 137.

[2] Whatever may be justified in Lane's confused hypothesis (1961) has already been expressly formulated in this passage which, if she had read it, would have spared her some discomfiture (cf. Leach, 1961*b*).   [3] Mills, 1937, p. 211.   [4] Hutton, 1921*a*, p. 241.
[5] Mills, 1937, p. 209.   [6] Mills, 1922, p. 149.
[7] Head, 1917, p. 2; Carrapiett, 1929, p. 34; Gilhodes, 1922, p. 217.   [8] ch. XVI.

between *mayu ni* and *dama ni* among the Kachin, and the multifarious methods of the *mayu ni* to ensure their right of control and power of protection over their daughters, even after marriage.[1] More than this, although the successive female generations in the one household have as many different origins as there are partner groups in the cycle of matrimonial exchanges, it seems that the female lines give a glimpse of something more or less like a desire to assert themselves as homogeneous formations. Among the Haka Chin, the daughter answers for the *pun taw* (the principal price) of her mother.[2] On the other hand, it is the maternal uncle who claims the *shé* (the death price) of the mother[3] but with the following reservation, viz., when a second relative dies, the tomb of the previous deceased is opened up, and the objects of value which were buried with him are withdrawn and go to the deceased's sisters, or in their absence, to his daughters. If the male relatives claim the valuables, the women retaliate by depriving them of their *shé* or their *pun taw*.[4] In certain circumstances, the daughters can, when their mother dies, inherit a part of what is still owing of their mother's *hlawn*. The *hlawn* is the dowry given to the young wife by her brother, and if he defaults she seizes the *pu man*, which was paid for her, on behalf of her daughters.[5]

These customs undoubtedly indicate a latent antagonism between feminine and masculine lineages, whether the latter consist of fathers and brothers, or uncles and brothers-in-law. Above all, they are particularly revealing of an attitude towards the system. A woman cannot place her mother's lineage, for which she no doubt feels a certain nostalgia passed on by her mother, on a par with the lineage in which she will go and live the remote and lonely life which is the fate of daughters born into patrilineal and harmonic regimes. The whole of Gilyak mythology – human maternal ancestors, animal paternal ancestors, the uncle who saves his sister and his niece from the claws of the bear – is deeply imbued with a poetry which might well be called feminine. This seems in fact to represent the marriage system as seen by the women, or at the very least by the brothers of these women, who always tend to exaggerate the loss they sustain in relinquishing their sisters, in comparison with the profit they make in procuring wives. Let us state this more clearly. The mythology is that of a linear system as opposed to a family and agnatic system, in which the rights of the brother over his sister (as repeatedly shown) are equal to or greater than those which the father exercises over his daughter. We shall have to remind ourselves of this when we come to consider the Shang of ancient China, among whom brother succeeded brother before son.[6]

'The significant thing . . .', writes Granet in connexion with a more recent period, 'is that the most powerful feeling aroused by the practice of exogamy was the feeling of banishment among the women. The ancient songs express it in verse: "Every daughter who marries – leaves far behind brothers and

---

[1] cf. ch. XVI.   [2] Head, 1917, p. 7.   [3] ibid. p. 30.
[4] ibid. pp. 30–1.   [5] ibid. p. 13.   [6] cf. ch. XX.

parents" . . . When love songs exalt the happiness of husband and wife they do so by saying that they have a *brotherly* understanding . . . But, conversely, one of the characteristic features of conjugal life in its initial stages, as much among the Chinese as among their Barbarian neighbours, is the great difficulty in reconciling the married couple [joined by an exogamous union]. No less than three years are needed for the marriage to be finalized, among these Barbarians as well as among the ancient Chinese. Among the latter, it took three years for a husband to receive his first smile from his wife. Among the Barbarians, the newly wed woman (who enjoys complete sexual freedom) leads the life of a young girl for three years. We are told that her brothers at the time show themselves to be extremely jealous. In China, in songs about the *unhappily married woman*, the wife who cannot pride herself on getting on as well with her husband as with a brother, makes the curious exclamation: "My brothers shall not find out: they would laugh and mock me." [1]

Such, briefly, is the attitude which finds its highest development among the Yakut in the custom – embellished by an efflorescence in folklore around the theme of the 'sister-mistress' – called *chotunnur:* the brothers deflower their sister before relinquishing her in exogamous marriage. [2] An echo of this is found as far afield as the Caucasus, among the Pschav, where an only daughter 'adopts' a temporary brother who plays the brother's usual rôle as her chaste bedfellow. [3] If the Gilyak system admitted of similar implications, there would be little difficulty in interpreting the curious distinction between various forms of incest among animals: 'Actually, the Gilyak are so deeply convinced that their marriage rules are based on nature that they even apply them to their domestic animal, the dog. They believe that among dogs as well, brothers and sisters cannot copulate. The rare exceptions which occur are attributed to the influence of an evil spirit, *milk*, and consequently, if a Gilyak chances to witness an incestuous act between dogs, he must kill the animal, for fear of committing the same offence himself. The execution of the dog is a religious ceremony. It is strangled and its blood is cast to the four corners of the earth. For the dog, however, this ceremony is only in punishment of the incest. It is curious to note that the Gilyak tolerate incest between dogs of consecutive generations, between mother and son, etc.' [4]

Finally, these considerations are essential for a good interpretation of ancient east European systems, which are full of this fraternal solidarity, and in which it is also the maternal uncle to whom the bride turns in tears on the eve of her departure. [5] As we shall show, these similarities attest to the typological unity of a vast system which from this point of view might be called Euro-Asiatic.

Over and above all that has been said of these customs, there is yet some-

---

[1] Granet, 1939, pp. 148–52. We have found all these customs still operating in Southeast Asia (cf. ch. XVI).

[2] Czaplicka, 1914, p. 113.

[3] Kowalewsky, 1893, pp. 259–78.

[4] Sternberg, n.d., p. 62.

[5] Volkov, 1891, pp. 160–84, 537–87.

thing else. On the one hand, the bride's maternal uncle plays an even more important rôle than her brother, and on the other hand, in certain systems at least, this rôle seems to be one of the terms in an opposition, the other position being occupied by the father's sister of the groom. The mother's brother (sometimes his wife) protects the bride and through his demands hinders her departure for her new home (we may recall the behaviour of the aunt in Haka Chin marriage). On the other hand, the father's sister of the bridegroom makes the advances, and tries to force the bride to join the household of her parents-in-law. Thus the two functions are at once correlated and opposed. What does this mean? All the systems with which we are concerned impose or enjoin marriage with the mother's brother's daughter, and all of them disapprove or prohibit marriage with the father's sister's daughter. The two protagonists are, as it happens, the bride's maternal uncle and the bridegroom's paternal aunt, i.e., those who, if there were no such asymmetric regulation, would have a direct, not indirect, interest in the marriage; the former, because his son could marry the bridegroom's sister, and the latter, because her nephew could marry her own daughter. Consequently, in their twin negative and positive aspects their rôles express the abandonment or affirmation of a claim, all this resulting from the fact that, of two corresponding types of marriage, one is prescribed and the other prohibited. But, although prohibited, the latter type (patrilateral marriage) appears in marriages in spectral form; it gnaws at the social conscience with a kind of nostalgia and remorse which, in the final analysis, can be seen as the underlying cause of the apparently abnormal rôle played by the bride's mother's brother, contrary to all indications given by the system. These considerations may seem vague, and even metaphorical, but we hope to be able to demonstrate their rational basis when we formulate our theoretical conclusions on the nature of generalized exchange. Before we reach that stage we must try, if possible, to connect the two geographically isolated but formally similar occurrences of simple forms of generalized exchange which we have observed and described for both extremities of the Asian continent.

2 · The Chinese System

CHAPTER XIX

Granet's Theory

I

Contemporary sociology offers some strange paradoxes. *The Elementary Forms of the Religious Life* was written by a man soundly prepared in the study of the philosophy and history of religions, but as ignorant in direct experience of Australia as of any other region of the world inhabited by primitive peoples. What today is the reputation of his general theory of the origin of religious life, based on the analysis of the Australian material? As a theory of religion, *The Elementary Forms of the Religious Life* is unacceptable, but on the other hand Radcliffe-Brown and Elkin, the most distinguished specialists of Australian sociology, are agreed in finding it a constant source of inspiration.[1] Thus Durkheim failed where he was best prepared, while the more adventurous part of his undertaking – the reconstruction, from literary evidence, of the social and spiritual life of a primitive group – has, after thirty years, lost nothing of its value. Granet's *Catégories matrimoniales et relations de proximité dans la Chine ancienne*[2] provides us with a similar but inverse situation.

In this work, a sinologist provides a decisive contribution to the general theory of kinship systems, but he presents his discoveries in the guise of Chinese material, and as interpretations of this material. However, when considered from this particular angle, these interpretations seem confused and contradictory, and sinologists have received them suspiciously, even when their own analyses were not contrary to them. Here, then, is a specialist who perhaps exceeds his proper rôle, but he succeeds in arriving at theoretical truths of a greater and more general significance.

What are these truths? Granet, more than anyone else, helps to dispel the error in traditional sociology that unilateral descent is a fundamental principle of primitive kinship: 'The Chinese facts . . . in no way lead us to imagine that kinship organization was first regulated by a principle of *unilateral descent*.'[3] Then, reconsidering the over-simplified hypothesis, propounded in his *Chinese Civilization*,[4] of the priority of matrilineal descent,

---

[1] Radcliffe-Brown, 1935*b*, p. 394; Elkin, 1937*b*, pp. 119–20.   [2] 1939.
[3] Granet, 1939, p. 2.   [4] 1930.

Granet, using, it must be owned, highly suspect Chinese facts, arrives at the system of alternate generations resulting from a regime of bilateral descent, and found today in many parts of the world.[1] He writes: 'In what circumstances could a system governed by the necessities of parallelism and exogamy have functioned if the family name depended on the men, and the personal names on the women?'[2] These circumstances are subsequently defined with a theoretical exactness which observation of groups using this system confirms in all respects. In the third place, Granet, while apparently unaware of similar suggestions by Williams and by Fortune,[3] formulates a positive and structural theory of the incest prohibition and of exogamy:

> 'The Chinese facts . . . do not lead us . . . to suppose that customs pertaining to matrimonial matters were initially governed by the desire to *prohibit* certain marriages in terms of certain rules of descent. These customs reflect a tendency to regulate the *circulation* of those especially effective prestations, women, so as to obtain regular returns, a favourable factor in maintaining a certain equilibrium between traditionally associated groups.'[4]

No doubt this view comes straight from *The Gift*, but Granet has developed and illustrated it with extraordinary force and conviction.

Taking as his basis this idea that marriage rules are always destined to establish a system of exchange, Granet has attempted to reconstruct the evolution of the Chinese system. Leaving aside for one moment the question of the value of his reconstruction with regard to the Chinese material, he should be given full credit for having formulated a classification ('chassé-croisé' and 'deferred exchange') which we are concerned to demonstrate, in this book, as showing the only possible positive basis for the study of kinship systems ('restricted exchange' and 'generalized exchange'). Granet's work here seems to have been independent, for there is nothing to indicate that he was familiar with Hodson or with Held, the only people at the time with any inkling of the problem and its solution. This only makes his discovery all the more remarkable. However, the theoretical implications of his work have passed unnoticed, because nowhere were they presented as such. Granet believed he was merely discovering unusually interesting features of Chinese sociology, found nowhere else in the world, and so of even more value, in his opinion as a sinologist. As it happens, he re-invented, allegedly as a transitional Chinese system which, however, probably never existed in China (hence the suspicion of his colleagues) the Murngin system of which he was very likely ignorant – but which does exist in Australia. For this he deserves the admiration of sociologists.[5]

---

[1] cf. ch. XIII.   [2] Granet, 1939, p. 105.
[3] Williams, 1936, pp. 167–70; Fortune, 1935, pp. 620–2.   [4] Granet, 1939, p. 2.
[5] There seems to me today to be no doubt that Granet, although he did not cite him, was influenced by Van Wouden (1935). But Granet has so many other claims on the admiration of sociologists that the above need not be changed.

What explanation is there for this paradoxical situation? The reasons in detail will emerge during our analysis. But already we can underline some general features which have a methodological interest. Granet had an admirable knowledge of Chinese sociological literature. The same flair for finding traces of cross-cousin marriage in the *Érh ya* put him on the track of other peculiarities, which are uncommonly difficult to interpret (as will be seen in the following chapter). Be that as it may, an adequate familiarity with kinship problems, not only in China but in the rest of the world, would have served as a lead. It is precisely this familiarity that Granet lacks. In fact, apart from the Kachin material, which is essential and which he found, the only facts he seems to have known with exactness are the Australian. More serious still, he believed this knowledge was sufficient, being still completely steeped in the Durkheimian idea that the Australian organization is the most primitive known and imaginable. A double error follows from this. Granet continually insists on the idea that a four-class marriage system (i.e., one based simultaneously on descent and on the distinction of consecutive generations) is the simplest possible system: 'When analysis is made of the system of nomenclature followed by the Chinese in the matter of close relationships, it seems that the Chinese have started with the stablest (and simplest) cohesive regime known.'[1] Later he says:

'The whole nomenclature *appears* to be explained by the division of endogamous communities into two exogamous sections, each section subdivided into two *in such a way as to distinguish the consecutive generations* and marriages being *obligatory* between *exogamous* SECTIONS and *parallel* GENERATIONS.

'This mode of division and this system of matrimonial alliance are well-known as well as being the *simplest* that are known.[2]

Nothing could be further from the truth than this statement, which with a single stroke does away with dual organization with exogamous moieties. There is no lack of examples from all parts of the world of societies in which the reciprocity of matrimonial exchanges neglects generations and is based solely on a distinction into two phratries. We shall take only a single example, the Bororo. There is no doubt that these natives have a form of preferential marriage with one or more determined clans belonging to the phratry prescribed by the rule of exogamy. But there is no distinction between generations, two frequent forms of marriage being avuncular marriage (with the father's sister) not excluding an earlier marriage in Ego's generation, and marriage simultaneously or consecutively with a woman and her daughter. In such a case, reciprocity is treated in a total fashion as an exchange *en bloc* between the phratries. No allowance is made for the necessity (which

[1] Granet, 1939, p. 159.
[2] ibid. p. 166. In this quotation and those following we shall keep to Granet's Mallarmé-style typographical system.

appears to be a logical refinement) of compensating for the prestations of wives between adults in the present generation by making counter-prestations in the following generation. Accordingly, Granet's starting-point for this reconstruction is a system (the Kariera system) which is already highly complex. It should be no surprise that later he is obliged to construct even more complex systems, so complex, indeed, that they are no longer verified by the facts.

The second aspect of Granet's error results from his interpretation of the Australian systems (and particularly the Kariera system) as systems of great antiquity. When he thinks that he has discovered traces of the same type of systems in China, he immediately puts them in the most archaic period, because there is no doubt in his mind that the 'australoid' aspect of Chinese sociology is also the most primitive. Such views were quite common at the end of the nineteenth century, but today we know that the archaic nature of the material culture of the Australian aborigines has no correspondence in the field of social institutions. By contrast, their social institutions are the result of a long series of deliberate elaborations and systematic reforms. In short, the Australian sociology of the family is, as it were, a 'planned sociology'.[1] Had Granet been aware of this aspect of the question, he would undoubtedly have drawn a parallel which would have greatly modified his schema. The history of mankind perhaps contains no set of circumstances more reminiscent of the palavers and councils of the old men during the elaboration of the Australian aboriginal systems than China during the period of Confucian reform. China of this period and Australia are both striking examples of societies attempting to formulate a rational code of kinship and marriage. What this immediately suggests, together with the fact that the modalities of family organization are not unlimited in number, is that it was in this period that the Chinese and Australian systems, proceeding from a like rationalist preoccupation, must have presented convergent aspects. The appearance in the *Êrh ya* of a terminology suggesting bilateral marriage with the cross-cousin and the exchange of sisters is quite straightforward when this view is adopted. By contrast, Granet sees himself as obliged to place the corresponding system in a completely unsupported archaic past, while neglecting even the approximate date of the work cited.

There is a third methodological error to be added to the others, and it too is due to what might be called 'the Australian deformation'. When Granet writes that 'there is no reason to suppose that the so-called four-class system was preceded by any other',[2] he not only asserts the priority of this system over all other class systems, but excludes the existence of any system of matrimonial exchange not involving classes implicitly or explicitly. Thus, bilateral marriage between cross-cousins would be impossible without a division of the group into four classes, and, adopting his particular assumption, so would unilateral marriage with the mother's brother's daughter without a system of eight classes. These two things are obviously not linked.

[1] cf. ch. XI.   [2] Granet, 1939, p. 169.

A system of classes is only one possible means of establishing a certain form of reciprocity. Another such method is preferential marriage, and its results are identical. It may well be said that in a society practising marriage with the bilateral cross-cousin it seems as if a four-class system were in force; but it in no way follows that possible spouses are actually distributed into four named or unnamed classes. The existence of a class system can never be postulated from its effects, because similar effects can always be obtained in another way. Specialists in Australian sociology are familiar with this problem.

Granet himself had too shrewd and penetrating a sociological intuition not to have at least an inkling of this. Though his criticism of the traditional terminology of cross-cousin marriage is full of the ambiguity to which we have just drawn attention, he seems at times to have clearly seen the problem: 'The categories are defined in terms referring to . . . relationships', and also: 'These terms note *categories of relationships* rather than *classes of individuals.*' Consequently, he proposes to speak of categories, and not classes. But what remains of the distinction when the *categories* are defined as *closed groups*? 'We shall say then that in the olden days Chinese communities seem to have been *closed* groups divided into four [matrimonial] *categories.*'[1] The whole work shows well enough the extent to which Granet is dominated by the theory of classes. His criticism of the notion of 'cross-cousin'[2] misses the point precisely because it interprets in terms of the logic of classes a notion which pertains to a logic of relations. Classes or categories, it matters little. The important thing is that primitive society governs marriage exchanges either by establishing classes *or* categories, or by defining the kinship relationships to be preferred. The two methods can have equivalent results. When there is no external evidence, it is impossible to work back from the result, whether it be given or inferred, to the method actually employed. Let us give an example to clarify our reasoning. There may be genuine reasons for supposing that a people now extinct had a religious cult, but there would be no justification for concluding from this that this people built temples, unless an archaeologist had uncovered traces of buildings. A temple is one means of practising a cult, but not the only one. Similarly among the Chinese, Granet discovered traces suggesting marriage of a certain type, This is entirely insufficient for the existence of precise institutions bringing about this type of marriage to be deduced, since this marriage can be realized otherwise than by these institutions.

This misunderstanding has seriously impaired the influence which Granet's sociological ideas ought rightly to have exercised. His critics have often been exasperated by his tendency to speak of certain hypothetical Chinese institutions (four-class system, eight-class system) as objective realities, when the available documents contain nothing to attest to their existence. The conclusion has sometimes been reached that Granet's work was pure fantasy.[3]

[1] ibid. pp. 169–71. [2] ibid. pp. 166–8.
[3] cf. the following chapter.

This is to neglect those observations which, although the basis of Granet's arbitrary reconstruction, still provide the sociologist with profitable food for thought.

Having cleared the ground with these preliminary remarks, we can move on to the study of the facts assembled by Granet. We propose to show that these facts have perhaps no connexion with the marriage system, as has been suggested by certain of his adversaries, or that if they do they should be interpreted differently. Either they are related to heterogeneous cultures and rules of marriage coexisting in China at the same time, or they are arranged in the opposite historical sequence to that proposed by Granet. Which of these hypotheses corresponds the better to the known facts is for sinologists to judge. From the particular viewpoint adopted in this work, both have the same result, viz., that at a certain period of Chinese history, or at least in certain regions of China, marriage rules based on generalized exchange must have provided the bridge between the identical systems of the Kachin in the far south and the Gilyak in the far north.

II

Granet's argument can be summed up as follows: a considerable number of facts, taken principally from the organization of the ancestor cult and from the regulation of degrees of mourning, suggest that the ancient Chinese conceived of kinship not as a series of *degrees*, but as a hierarchy of *categories*.[1] On the other hand, the fundamental distinction between *internal close relatives* (all the members of the same agnatic clan, and women married into the clan), and *external close relatives* (all other close relatives who are members of different clans) implies that a system of equivalences should be established between the two categories. This system of equivalences has to meet a double condition, viz., that marriage shall take place between bearers of *different* family names and members of *identical* generations. Only then can the system function. This is the reason, in Chinese family law, for an even stronger horror of marriages between members of two consecutive generations than of incest proper.[2] 'To avoid all obliquity and imbalance, it would be enough for marriages *always* to take place between non-agnatic cousins.'[3] Even in the modern Chinese Civil Code, Article 983, '*entirely implicitly*, by an artificial arrangement of the text',[4] gives a legal stamp to the sororate and the levirate, the usual concomitants of cross-cousin marriage, and to marriage between cousins (affinal or consanguineous) other than agnatic, i.e., including cross-cousins.

Such a system, based on cross-cousin marriage and the opposition of consecutive generations, can easily be interpreted in terms of the principle of alternate generations. In groups practising bilineal descent (i.e., in which

[1] Granet, 1939, p. 22.   [2] ibid. pp. 34–49.
[3] ibid. p. 37.   [4] ibid. p. 14.

the local name is transmitted in the maternal line and the family name in the paternal line, or vice versa), the civil status of each individual is expressed by a binomial, comprising but one term of the paternal binomial and one term of the maternal binomial. The parents' binomial is recomposed only in the generation of their children's children. Consequently one can say that children are *opposed* to their parents, but that grandchildren *reproduce* their grandparents.

The whole theory of Australian aboriginal systems has been clarified by the introduction of the notion of alternate generations[1] and similar facts have been gathered from several other regions of the world.[2] Since Granet paid little attention to references, it is a question whether he knew of these facts or whether he independently reinvented the theory in connexion with the Chinese evidence. Be that as it may, he relies on two arguments in postulating the archaic existence, in China, of a system of alternate generations. Firstly, there is the *chao mu* order, involving the appearance in the ancestral temples of father and son always in different categories, and grandfather and grandson in identical categories.[3] We shall return to this order later. Secondly, there is the ancient tradition by which the personal name is given by the mother, and the family name by the father.[4] This tradition is confirmed by the more recent practice of *pei fen tzu*, which specifies the individual members of the one family according to generation and relative age.

Thus from this there emerges the hypothesis that the archaic Chinese system *could have been* based on the reciprocal alliance of two exogamous groups, exchanging their daughters according to the principle of the equivalence of generations, specifically a four-class marriage system, with intermarriage between the two classes of the older generation (i.e., parents), and between the two classes of the younger generation (i.e., children), each joined in pairs. Such a system would obviously be based on marriage with the bilateral cross-cousin; or, more exactly, all cross-cousins descended from this system would be bilateral. Granet then turns to the nomenclature to seek proof that such a system really existed. The term *ku* means both 'mother-in-law' and 'father's sister', and the term *chiu* both 'father-in-law' and 'mother's brother'.[5] However, 'men and women classify their Father's Brothers (*fu*) with their Father, and their Mother's Sisters (*mu*) with their Mother'.[6] The same dichotomy is repeated in the younger generation, so that only four terms are required to designate the members of the generation above Ego's, or the members of the generation below: 'The result of this *seems* to be that, *since "Fathers" and "Mothers" are husbands and wives*, "Uncles' and "Aunts" are *also* husbands and wives . . . This nomenclature appears to be conceived for *an endogamous and bipartite community* with two *exogamous sections*.'[7] The term *sheng* has a double meaning corresponding to the twin meanings of the terms *ku* and *chih*: 'A man calls both "his Sister's Son" and "his

---

[1] cf. ch. XI. [2] cf. ch. VIII. [3] Granet, 1939, pp. 3–6. [4] ibid. pp. 83–102.
[5] ibid. p. 43. [6] ibid. p. 165. [7] loc. cit.

Daughter's Husband", "*sheng*". Only the term "*chih*" has the one meaning of "Niece". This exception seems to be explained by the development of the institution of polygyny.[1] Granet is alluding here to the custom of simultaneously marrying sisters and their niece. We shall return to this point later.

These terminological inferences have a considerable value. But Granet was convinced, on the one hand, that the system of alternate generations, with marriage between bilateral cross-cousins, was the simplest conceivable system, and, on the other hand, that a system with Australian aboriginal features could only belong to an extremely primitive period of Chinese society. He is thus led to declare that it is earlier than any other form to be discerned in the language and institutions. Because of this, he is forced to regard all facts which do not fit in with the original formula as indicating a later development. But why an historical development, and not simply the co-existence in the same period of heterogeneous forms in various regions or social strata? This is a problem which would take us too far outside the field of this study. Granet was always highly attentive to the historical co-existence of the Chinese proper and the Barbarians. On the other hand, the plan of his whole work was aimed, at least in part, at revealing the contrast between peasant mores[2] and feudal institutions,[3] or, as he puts it in the *Catégories*, between *customs* and *rites*. In the introduction to *Festivals and Songs*, he is undecided on the meaning of this contrast, viz., whether it is a contrast between two cultures, or between stages in the one development. Moreover, if he recognizes the two hypotheses as equally 'ideological',[4] it is immediately clear which direction he is going to take:

'I think . . . I have shown that it is possible (in spite of defective evidence and with the help of justified extrapolations) to write an *evolutionary history* of Chinese institutions . . . Having practised, with the organization based on clans, a system of total alternative prestations, securing the general mechanism of social life – having passed through the regime of the potlatch and having created chiefdoms – China finally built up a feudal system based on the principle of conventionally regulated exchanges . . . while, proceeding apace, the family, paternal authority, and individual kinship appeared.'[5]

The *Catégories* indisputably represents the crowning point of this evolutionist ardour – the credit for which is ascribed to (and is doubtless, alas, merited by) the sociological school.

III

'In China, the *rites* and the *laws* limit marriage choices only by prohibiting all endogamous or oblique unions . . . Between this relatively free regime

---

[1] Granet, 1939, p. 166.　　[2] ibid. 1932.　　[3] ibid. 1926.　　[4] ibid. p. 23.
[5] ibid. pp. 58–9.

and the regime of strict predestinations imposed by the division into four categories a transitional regime seems to have made a certain *freedom* of movement possible.'[1] Granet's starting-point is thus rather the recognition of a logical necessity than the setting-up of a certain historical evolution. There must have been at least one transitional form between the strictly determined regime, which he postulates as representing the archaic state, and the modern lack of restraint, and it is this transitional form which he proposes to reconstruct. Let us consider this point for a moment. The so-called four-class regime is found nowhere in China (although ancient documents and present-day observations suggest that at one time, or in certain regions of China, it is highly probable that it was *as if* there was – even recently – such a system in force). However, the reality of the system is an assumption only, and when one acknowledges, as does Granet, that the internal logic of the assumption requires a second assumption which has an infinitely weaker objective basis than the first, one is setting up an edifice which, although tempting to a certain logical aesthetic, is unacceptable to historical criticism. When all is said and done, it is the weaker assumption which will take the burden of the construction. To borrow again one of Granet's terms, the method he follows is essentially 'ideological'. One feels continually obliged to fight against the uneasiness which his approach provokes, in order not to begrudge the facts – or the embryo facts – which here and there emerge, their full credit. What are these facts? We shall try to follow Granet's often obscure exposition as closely as possible.

The hypothetical splitting of the four-class system (itself hypothetical) into a system with eight classes is at first suggested by the form of the *chao mu* order among the nobles. Not only are the consecutive generations opposed, but there is a sub-distinction between the grandfather and the grandson, pushing ancestor worship back to the great-great-grandfather.

'When the "Grandsons" must be *distinguished* from the "Grandfathers", when the Great-great-grandfather cannot be identified with the Grandfather, and when *four generations of Living People* are set over against *four generations of Ancestors, comprising the whole of* ANY *religious grouping*, would not the reason for it be that some bipartition had resulted in the number of categories being multiplied by two?'[2]

For the hypothesis to be acceptable, it must obviously not affect the attested terminology. We recall the double meanings of the terms *chiu, sheng*, and *ku*, and the meaning of the term *chih*. But the analysis of these terms must be completed with an additional note. When *chiu* and *sheng* are used as terms of address, they can only be used (since they are reciprocals) between men, and likewise *ku* and *chih* can only be used between women. Thus the terminology coincides with an exclusive system of marriage between bilateral cross-cousins, on condition that the women continue to marry their father's

[1] ibid. 1939, p. 187. [2] ibid. p. 184.

sister's son, and the men their mother's brother's daughter. In other words, there is a dichotomy between matrilateral and patrilateral cross-cousins. Thus Granet can formulate his hypothesis: '*Is it sufficient to admit that –* ceasing to marry their [paternal] "Aunts" ' Daughters . . . *the men remain the predestined husbands of their [maternal] "Uncles" ' Daughters . . . to be able to give a full – and apparently the only possible – explanation of* the rules of the ancestral temple and of those of "the *chao mu* order"?'[1]

Pages 187 to 200 of the work are given over to one of the rare theoretical analyses of the elementary forms (restricted exchange and generalized exchange) of marriage exchange at present to be found in the literature, and there are only two reservations to be made on its general excellence. The first is the excessive complexity of the symbols used, which obscures the argument. The second and the more important is the evolutionist distortion, which prevents Granet from seeing that restricted exchange and generalized exchange are two elementary modalities, and not two stages in the one process. He sees generalized exchange as a transformation of restricted exchange towards greater complexity. As he begins by adopting a far too complex formula of restricted exchange (the four-class system), he is unable to construct the formula of generalized exchange other than as an eight-class system, which is a more complex form still. Here is a fundamental error, for in passing from restricted exchange to generalized exchange it is not at all the nature of the quantity of the things exchanged which is altered, but solely the mode of exchange. In other words, there is no need to conceive of an eight-class system in order to account for generalized exchange. Even in a community organized into exogamous moieties, four classes arranged in rotation are sufficient. The theoretical aspect of this problem has been studied in its entirety in chapter XIII, to which the reader is referred. Nevertheless, Granet has let himself be drawn towards an eight-class system by the need for four generations of ancestors in the temples of the nobility, as borne out by the Chinese custom whereby a new lineage can be initiated at the fifth generation. To make a long story short, he concludes with the hypothesis of a transitional system, characterized by marriage with the mother's brother's daughter, and the division of each community into four matrilineal groups and two patrilineal moieties, all exogamous (Fig. 57).

It can be seen that in such a system the descendant reproduces the ascendant in the male line only every five generations, since the patrilineal line conforms necessarily to the model: $D_2-A_2-B_2-C_2-D_2$. In this way an explanation is thought to be given for the extension of the *chao mu* order to the great-grandfather (the father continuing to be opposed to the son) in the temples of the nobility, i.e., the class which tends more and more to give a patrilineal cast to a system which was originally matrilineal (or, at all events, bilateral). At the same time, other traces of Chinese nomenclature can be understood. In the system just described, each lineage had two types of affines, those from

[1] Granet, 1939, p. 186.

which it receives wives, and those to which it gives wives. 'The Chinese quite rightly use a *double* expression to designate affines, viz., *hun yin*, the first term (*hun*) designating those from whom wives have been received, and the second (*yin*) those who have been provided with wives.'[1] Thus, in the preceding schema, line *D* is *yin* and line *B* is *hun* to line *A*. Generally speaking, a given line has *yin* on the left and *hun* on the right. It is true – and Granet notices it immediately – that the expression *hun yin* 'implies *neither* that alliances (as a rule) are perpetual nor that there are only two affines, a donee, and a donor''. However, apart from the distinction between 'elder' and 'younger', the only other distinction between men is between *chiu* (maternal uncle; father-in-law) and *sheng* (sister's son; son-in-law). Even further, a man uses *chiu* not only for his maternal uncle but also for his wife's brother, who will give a wife, either to himself (according to noble practices) or to his son: 'These "Wives"' Brothers are regarded in advance as "Fathers of Daughters-in-law"'.

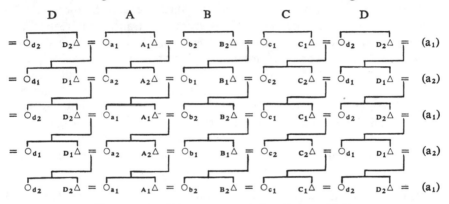

Fig. 57. The Chinese system (after Granet, 1939).

Similarly, the appellation *sheng* applies to nephews/sons-in-law and to sisters' husbands, retrospectively treated as fathers' sons-in-law. Thus the terminology seems to attest to the existence of two dynasties of *hun* and *yin*: 'In the four-category system, *chiu* and *sheng* designate *two* GENERATIONS *of affines;* when there are eight categories and one-way alliances, *chiu* and *sheng* designate *two* SORTS *of affines.*' Similarly, for women there is an identification between father's sisters and husband's sisters under the same term *ku*.[2]

Granet's argumentation is such that we are obliged to end with perhaps an over-long quotation in order to appreciate its validity:

'A system of *two-way* alliances was succeeded by a system of *one-way* alliances. Still governed by the double rule of exogamy and parallelism, it corresponds to the division of the members of the community into eight categories, the four categories of each of the two sections being distributed

[1] ibid. p. 210.   [2] ibid. p. 211.

into *two couples. There is reason to believe that membership of a particular category was determined by Mothers*: but (whatever the custom was that governed this detail) the existence of *four couples of categories* is connected with a division into *four groupings* (simple or complex) which can be arranged so as to constitute (four female dynasties, or, just as well) *four male dynasties. On the other hand, a rule of the game as regards marriage prestations enforced the exportation of girls.* Thus, *territorially speaking*, the distribution into eight categories meant a division of the community into FOUR GROUPS (divided by two into two exogamous sections) the male members of which *formed a dynasty of Fathers and Sons*, while their wives – Daughters-in-law and Mothers-in-law to one another – formed *a dynasty of "Aunts"* (Fathers' Sisters) and of "Nieces" (Brothers' Daughters). An *agnatic formula* can be used, on the "women's" side as the "men's", to define the closeness of persons who are to live *in the same territory* because of marriages required by a rule which seems to be formulated in terms of *uterine relationships.*[1] It is from this transitional regime that agnatic institutions have been able to develop. These institutions deserved this name only when the masculine dynasties of the family Fathers succeeded (by attacking the principle of invariability of alliances) in breaking the unity of the feminine dynasties originally of "Matrons", interconnected – just as the "Fathers" were interconnected – by ties which could be formulated in agnatic terms. But *in itself* the organization expressed by a division into eight categories does not attribute (any more than does the organization expressed by a division into four categories) any primacy to (either) agnatic (or uterine) *descent.*'[2]

This passage is surprising in several regards. Firstly one finds that scarcely is an eight-category system constituted than it seems to dissolve into a four-category system in which, as we have suggested above,[3] a difference in cohesion replaces the difference in complexity arbitrarily attributed to the regime of deferred exchanges, instead of being superimposed upon it, as Granet still maintains.[4] Secondly, the notion of unilateral descent, intensely criticized by Granet as not representing a primitive phenomenon, is denied, as it were, any kind of reality, being reduced to the rôle of a retrospectively applied, if not invented, convention. Let us begin by examining this latter point.

---

[1] Granet is not the first to have raised this difficulty. 'The scheme ignores all ties through female kin. The daughter of the maternal uncle belongs to her father's exogamous division and is therefore eligible as a spouse to a man of the exogamous division to which her father's sister went—to her father's sister's son. It may be that the explanation lies in the complete merger of the woman with her husband's exogamous division. Kinship may be traced *per capita* or *per stirpes* only by both computations' (Hodson, 1925, p. 174). But nothing is further from the truth than the idea that juridical, social and psychological ties between a woman and her line are abolished in a system of generalized exchange (cf. ch. XVIII.

[2] Granet, 1939, pp. 214–15.   [3] ch. XIII.   [4] Granet, 1939, p. 215.

One of Granet's main contributions to the general theory of kinship is to have shown that marriage rules are not dependent on the idea of unilateral descent, but are logically, and doubtless also historically, prior to it. The fundamental principle is a regular circulation of marriage prestations between groups. That is all very well. But when the question arises of the definition of the groups, and of the relationships uniting them, in order to ensure the permanence and the substantial identity of these groups throughout fluctuations in their individual compositions, their members are necessarily defined in terms of their membership, i.e., it is necessary to determine a mode of descent, which can be undifferentiated, unilateral (here, either patrilineal or matrilineal), or bilateral (i.e., in which each individual will be given both a patrilineal reference and a matrilineal reference). The idea of descent is a derivative idea, well enough, but from the moment it is elaborated it exists.[1] It is impossible that it should not be elaborated (for in this case the balance of matrimonial exchanges could no longer be maintained); and for any given group, its elaboration conforms to a certain type which from this point has just as real an existence as the notion itself.

Let us admit, therefore, with Granet, that the origin of the four-class system lies not in a unilateral conception of descent, but in the structural requirements of a system of prestations and counter-prestations between the groups. It is none the less true that in elaborating a four-class system there must come into effect a double patrilineal and matrilineal dichotomy, one dealing with residence and the other with name. This point was developed in chapter XI with regard to the Kariera system. In the particular case of China, Granet has himself repeatedly insisted on the probability of residence being transmitted in the maternal line (husbands/sons-in-law, cult of the land, etc.) this implying, also in agreement with Granet, a patrilineal transmission of the *sing*, i.e., of clan names.

In other words, the four-class system which Granet proposes to reconstruct for ancient China is formally of the Kariera type (disharmonic regime with four classes), but is actually the reverse (matrilocal groups, patrilineal moieties). Once assumed, it remains once and for all, and should survive objectively through all subsequent transformations. It may be a convention, but it is one which is basic to the structure of the social group once it is established, and cannot thus be regarded as a 'detail'.[2]

In these circumstances, it would be a system composed of *two matrilocal groups* and of *two patrilineal moieties* that would be found at the origin of the alleged eight-class system. How does this transformation come about? Four matrilocal groups[3] (Granet's 'categories') have to be assumed, and two patrilineal moieties (Granet's 'couples'). Things have either actually happened like this, or not at all. But to attempt, as does Granet, to change the four matrilocal groups into four patrilocal groups, on the ground of a supposed change in convention, is to confuse an ideological manipulation with an

[1] cf. ch. VIII.　　　　[2] loc. cit.　　　　[3] cf. ch. XI.

historical development, the stages of which are strictly conditioned by an objectively given initial state. Such a change is conceivable, of course, but it is only so as the last stage in a revolution substituting an harmonic regime (patrilineal local groups and moieties) for an earlier disharmonic regime. Such a change is theoretically possible, but only by the transition from a system of restricted exchange with four classes to a system of generalized exchange also with four classes, which brings about with one fell stroke the collapse of the whole hypothesis of the eight classes. Indeed, the hypothesis of the eight classes is bound up with the hypothesis of a development through composition, not by substitution.

Let us try to translate the eight-class system represented in Fig. 57 in terms of agnatic dynasties (Fig. 58). This new diagram either means nothing (since the lines are no longer objectively distinct, except as to the moieties), or it amounts to saying that, given four classes, *A, B, C, D*, an *A* class man marries a *B* class woman, a *B* class man marries a *C* class woman, and so on. Scarcely are they conceived than the eight classes disappear, and with them the possibility of a logical transition from one system to the other.

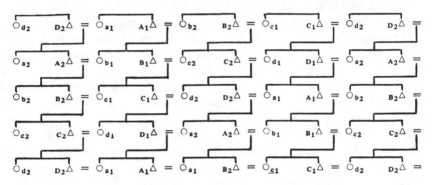

Fig. 58. Another aspect of Granet's hypothesis.

Thus Granet's whole argument amounts to using the nomenclature to infer the existence in ancient China of two types of marriage, one with the bilateral cross-cousin, the other with the matrilateral cross-cousin, and to asserting the historical anteriority of the first over the second. At no time is this transition clearly demonstrated except in an ideological construction with no objective basis. What we are to think of the hypothesis, thus reduced in breadth and significance, must now form the subject of our examination.

CHAPTER XX

The Chao Mu Order

I

In this analysis of the Chinese kinship system, we shall follow in the main the work of Han-Yi Fêng[1] and we shall keep to his transcription of the terms.

If certain terms, or certain usages of terms connected with their use in conversation (Fêng's 'referential modifiers' and 'vocatives'), are left aside, the Chinese system can be said to employ two types of terms: elementary terms ('nuclear terms') and determinant terms ('basic modifiers').

The previous chapter showed Granet trying to reduce the elementary terms to eight, grouped into four pairs, viz., father and mother as opposed to son and daughter; and mother's brother and father's sister as opposed to sister's son and brother's daughter. To this list he adds the equally elementary terms which divide Ego's generation into senior and junior, but which are not immediately required for his argument. Kroeber,[2] commenting upon the study of Chen and Shryock on the same subject,[3] retains twenty-two or twenty-five terms which he considers elementary. Fêng gives twenty-three:

tsu	father's father, ascendant
sun	son's son, descendant
fu	father, man of the generation above Ego's
tzŭ	son, man of the generation below Ego's
mu	mother, woman of the generation above Ego's
nü	daughter, woman of the generation below Ego's
hsiung	older brother, older man of Ego's generation
ti	younger brother, younger man of Ego's generation
tzü	older sister, older woman of Ego's generation ($\neq$ *tzŭ* = son)
mei	younger sister, younger woman of Ego's generation
po	father's older brother; husband's older brother
shu	father's younger brother; husband's younger brother
chih	brother's son, descendant from male collateral
shêng	sister's son, descendant from female collateral

---

[1] 1937, pp. 141–275.   [2] Kroeber, 1933, pp. 151–7.
[3] Chen and Shryock, 1932, pp. 623–69.

ku	father's sister and female relatives comparable with father's sister; husband's sister
chiu	mother's brother and male relatives comparable with mother's brother; wife's brother
i	mother's sister and female relatives comparable with mother's sister; wife's sister and female relatives comparable with wife's sister
yo	wife's parents and relatives comparable with wife's parents (term not included in Kroeber's list; Kroeber treats it as determinant)
hsü	daughter's husband; husband
fu	Ego's husband; husband
ch'i	Ego's wife; wife
sao	older brother's wife and female relatives comparable with older brother's wife
fu	son's wife; wife.

There is general agreement among all the authors that these elementary terms are the remains of an archaic system of the type frequently encountered among primitive peoples all over the world, and characterized by several distinctions, viz., between elder and younger in the one generation (preserved only in Ego's generation); between the direct line and the collateral line, and, within the latter, between maternal and paternal relatives; finally, the sex of the relative through whom the bond expressed by the term is established is taken into account.[1] The extreme likelihood of a former marriage between cross-cousins is also suggested by this nomenclature, as indicated in the previous chapter.

The originality of the Chinese system stems from the fact that this primitive nomenclature, instead of being abandoned or transformed, has been preserved and integrated in a more precise and complex system formed by the introduction of determinants. The seventeen determinants given by Kroeber are reduced to ten by Fêng:

kao	high, revered (modifying indicator of the fourth ascending generation)
tsêng	added, increased (third ascending and descending generation)
hsüan	distant (fourth descending generation)
t'ang	hall (collaterals in the paternal line)
ts'ung	to follow (same meaning as *t'ang*, but more general and more archaic)
tsai-ts'ung	to follow a second time (third collateral line)
tsu	clan, tribe (fourth collateral line and beyond)
piao	outside, external (descendants of father's sister, mother's brother and mother's sister)
nei	inside, inner; wife (descendants of wife's brother and wife's brother's paternal cousins)

[1] Kroeber, 1933, pp. 151–2, 155; Fêng, 1937, pp. 168–70.

wai   outside (reciprocal modifier between mother's parents and daughters' children).

Given the elementary terms and the determinants, they need only be combined for any degree of kinship to be defined with all desirable exactness and precision. The elementary terms provide a fundamental structure, except for the terms referring to parents and children, and to husband and wife, which are used to indicate sex (*fu* 父, *mu, tzu, nü;* and *fu* 夫, *fu* 婦, *hsi, hsü*).[1] The determinants of collaterality and descent are prefixed to the elementary term, while the determinants of sex are suffixed. The choice of the elementary term depends firstly on generation, and secondly on descent.

Fêng gives as an example the formation of the term for 'father's father's sister's son's daughter's son', a difficult case, since it involves a change of descent from the female line to the male line, with a subsequent return to the female line. With regard to generation, the individual designated belongs to the son's generation. Therefore, the elementary term can only be *chih* or *wai shêng*. But, as the closest relationship with Ego is established through the intermediary of a female of the same generation, *chih* must be eliminated, and *wai shêng* remains the only possible term. Moreover, the relationship expressed is consanguineal although not clan-based, and descent is traced from the father's father's sister, who is assimilable to the father's sister. Consequently, the determinants *ku* and *piao* have to be added. Lastly, the determinant *t'ang* indicates that the third collateral external line is involved, giving finally the complete term: *t'ang ku piao wai shêng*. If an individual of the female sex is involved, *nü* is added; for a woman related by marriage, *fu* is added instead of *nü;* for a man related by marriage, *hsü* is added instead of *fu*.[2] The reader may refer to Fêng[3] and Kroeber for detailed illustrations of the same principle.

It is difficult to define the Chinese system by reference to the traditional typology. Morgan wavered between what he called the 'Malayan' and 'Turanian' forms.[4] Kroeber is of the opinion that the Chinese system results from a combination of a 'classificatory' system and a 'descriptive' system which he regards as a later superimposition. Finally, Fêng proclaims the originality of the system: 'It must first be understood in the light of its own morphological principles and historical development'.[5] Although it is difficult to deny Kroeber's argument that the system reduced to elementary terms was originally 'classificatory', we must nevertheless ask, as did Fêng, wherein lies the originality of the evolution which led to the present-day system. As he so well puts it:

'The architectonic structure of the Chinese system is based on two principles: lineal and collateral differentiation, and generation stratification. The former is a vertical, and the latter a horizontal, segmentation. Through

---

[1] Fêng, 1937, p. 151, n. 23; Kroeber, 1933, p. 153.   [2] Fêng, 1937, pp. 151–3.
[3] ibid. pp. 153–4.   [4] Morgan, 1871, p. 431.   [5] Fêng, 1937, p. 269.

the interlocking of these two principles, every relative is rigidly fixed in the structure of the whole system.'[1]

Granet uses almost exactly the same terms: 'Every near relative is designated by (a word or) an expression indicating his place in the table, i.e., as often as not, by a *binomial* evoking the two *co-ordinates* which determine this place, viz., the *generation* (level, horizontal) and the *line* (column, vertical)'.[2] It is a remarkable thing, as will be discussed later, that this description – which agrees so exactly with Fêng's formula – is applied in Granet's writings not to the kinship system proper, but to the list of degrees of mourning.

Kroeber has dwelt at great length on the richness and exactitude of the system. He is not far short of regarding it as the most perfect system conceivable to mankind. Recalling that Chen and Shryock report 270 terms, and that their list could be considerably enlarged by making new combinations of the same elements, he adds:

'To be sure, not all of the 270 terms are in customary use; but apparently they would all be readily understood. It would be going too far to say that the Chinese apparatus suffices for the unambiguous designation of every conceivable variation of relationship within the seventh or eighth degree. But it certainly does specify a very much larger portion of the total possibilities than do any European systems.'[3]

Morgan had similarly noted that the Chinese system 'has accomplished the difficult task of maintaining a principle of classification which confounds the natural distinctions in the relationships of consanguinity, and, at the same time, of separating these relationships from each other in a precise and definite manner'.[4]

In point of fact, the Chinese system, which allows any kinship situation to be expressed with an almost mathematical exactness, appears to be an *overdetermined system*; and Kroeber has clearly seen that in this regard, it should be contrasted with European systems, with their marked tendency towards *indetermination*: 'We are like a people whose number system is so deficient that when they want to add or multiply above ten they have to fall back on manipulating counters.'[5] By contrast, the Chinese system is 'at once inclusive and exact'.[6] The Chinese 'have built up a rich system where ours is deliberately impoverished'.[7] This *overdetermination* of the Chinese system deserves close examination for its nature and origin to be understood.

The rationality of the system is attested to by a curious fact. When Davis and Warner set out to develop a system of universal formulas allowing all kinship systems to be expressed in a common language, they recreated purely and simply the Chinese system, or its equivalent, notably the two axes of

[1] Fêng, 1937, p. 160.   [2] Granet, 1939, p. 32.   [3] Kroeber, 1933, p. 156.
[4] Morgan, 1871, p. 414.   [5] Kroeber, 1933, p. 156.   [6] loc. cit.   [7] ibid. p. 157.

co-ordinates, and the definition of a relationship by a (theoretically unlimited) compounding of elementary terms or determinants.[1]

We have elsewhere criticized this ingenious undertaking which, as philosophers say, confuses 'reasoning reason' and 'reasoned reason'. Warner and Davis's conceptual system cannot help us grasp the structures of kinship any more than traditional grammar can perfectly express the operations of language, or Aristotelian logic permit the real functioning of thought to be understood.[2] However, the fact remains that, like Aristotle or the grammarians, a people (or, more likely, a scholarly élite) have undertaken the same task, in a new field, of putting a certain type of data into analytical form. The very perfection and artificiality of the Chinese system are sufficient indication that it is not, and cannot be, the result of a spontaneous and unconscious evolution. Everything about it suggests that it is a promulgated system. It has been fabricated, and fabricated with a certain end in view.

II

Both Granet and Fêng have brought out the fact that the ritual works, the *Li*, contain the best information on the kinship system:

> 'These ritual works are important sources for the functional study of the Chinese kinship system, because they deal with kinship in action. Such are the *I Li* and the *Li Chi*, works of the second half of the first millennium B.C., that treat kinship *in extenso*, especially in connexion with mourning rites, ancestor "worship", and other aspects of ritual. In all later works on ritualism . . . kinship is the basic subject of discussion.'[3]

Thus there is a relationship between the mourning system and the kinship system. Granet, who begins his study with an analysis of the Chinese theory of mourning, seems to proceed from the mourning system to the kinship system.[4] The former of these systems, he says, 'is very old'. It is from the analysis of the degrees of mourning that he draws the fundamental characteristics of the archaic kinship system, viz., the distinction of internal near kin and external near kin, the notion of category taking precedence over the notion of degree, and the importance of generation, which is as great as, if not greater than, that of descent.[5] Thus everything happens as if Granet, from the characteristics of the most ancient system attested to in the literature (the mourning system), inferred the very same characteristics for a more ancient system still, since it is not attested to (the kinship system). This is a quite different conception of the relationship between the two systems than the facts and Fêng's excellent commentary seem to suggest.

The mourning system, he remarks, is based on the clan distinction (internal close relatives and external close relatives), and on the differentiation of

---

[1] Davis and Warner, 1935, pp. 291–313.
[2] Lévi-Strauss, 1945*a*, pp. 33–53.
[3] Fêng, 1937, p. 145.
[4] Granet, 1939, p. 22 et seq.
[5] ibid. p. 37.

kinship degrees. The obligation to mourn for (internal) clan relatives is removed after the fourth collateral line, and after the fourth ascending or descending generation counting from Ego: 'There is, consequently, in the kinship system, a sharp differentiation of the first four collateral lines, and an indefinite grouping of all further collaterals in the *tsu* relationship.'[1] Corresponding to these five distinctions, there are five grades of mourning, viz., three years, one year, nine months, five months and three months. More exactly, there is a *unit of mourning* which is of a year, the longest periods being an 'increasing mourning', the shortest a 'decreased mourning'. Mourning begins with the closest relatives, who receive three *ch'i*, or units. The basic mourning for the father, is a year; for the grandfather, nine months; for the great-grandfather, five months; and for the great-great-grandfather, three months. In the descending order, it is one year for the son, nine months for the grandson, five months for the great-grandson, and three months for the great-great-grandson. Mourning for the brother lasts one year; for the father's brother's son, nine months; for the father's father's brother's son's son, five months; for the father's father's father's brother's son's son's son, three months. The terms *shang shai* (ascending decrease), *hsia shai* (descending decrease) and *p'ang shai* (horizontal decrease) correspond to these three decreasing hierarchies. All non-clan relatives, however closely related, receive three months, with a possible increase (five months for the mother's sister, and three months only for the mother's brother).

This system has two remarkable features. It transforms qualitative differences of forms of kinship into quantitative differences of length of mourning. In order to do this, it reduces degrees of removal which are expressed sometimes in the order of the generations and sometimes in the order of the collateral lines to a common denominator. The close correspondence in this connexion between the system of mourning and the system of kinship is made clear by comparing the two diagrams borrowed from Fêng[2] (Figs. 59–60). Of the two diagrams, it is obviously the former which provides the more rational and satisfactory picture. Thus we must look to the system of mourning to find the reason for the logical appearance of the kinship system. Fêng clearly understands this:

'Mourning grades of a simpler kind must have existed long before the Chou period, but their elaboration began only when they fell into the hands of the Confucianists. Using the family and the sib as the bases for their ideological structure, the literati elaborated the mourning system with a view to the maintenance of sib solidarity. In the course of this elaboration of the mourning system they also standardized its basis, the kinship system, for a carefully graded system of mourning rites requires a highly differential kinship nomenclature, lest an awkward incommensurability ensue.'[3]

[1] Fêng, 1937, p. 178.   [2] ibid. diagrams III and IV (pp. 166 and 182).   [3] ibid. p. 181.

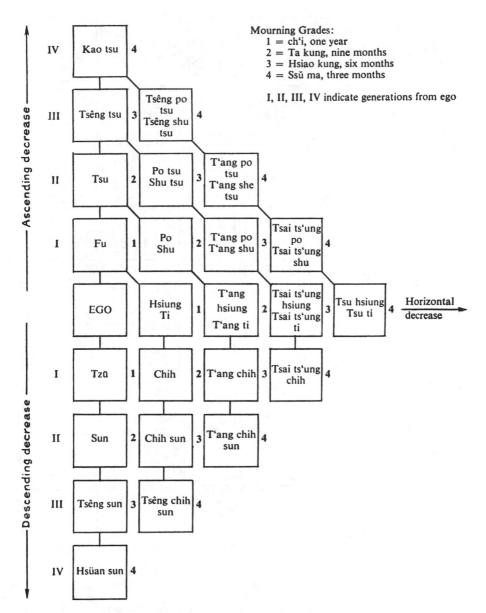

Fig. 59. Simplified table of mourning grades (Fêng, 1937, p. 182).
Only male relatives are given.

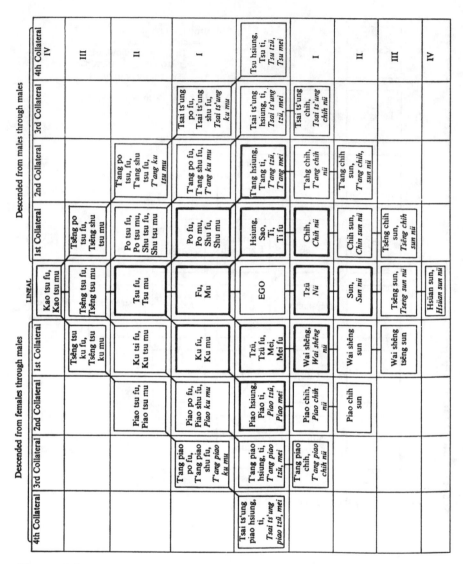

Fig. 60. Diagrammatic representation of the Chinese kinship system (Fêng, 1937, p. 166).

The heavy squares represent the nuclear group of relatives. Those in italics indicate their descendants have not been carried over into the next generation, e.g., the children of *nü* are *wai sun* and *wai sun nü* but are not given in the succeeding square. The Roman numerals represent ascending and descending generations.

Fêng finds proof that things really did happen in this way by comparing the ancient nomenclature of the *Érh ya* and that of the more recent *I Li*. The correspondence is more difficult to establish between the nomenclature of the *Érh ya* and the mourning system, for this nomenclature is 'inconsistent and less differential'.[1] It is because the *I Li* represents 'a later but rationalized system worked over to conform with the mourning system'.[2] In the light of these preceding remarks, the artificiality of the Chinese kinship system becomes apparent. The *analytical* kinship system is, in fact, a function of a *quantitative* system of mourning. Whatever the archaic system of kinship may have been, the one now before us, from the *Érh ya* and the *I Li*, is a methodical elaboration, and the result of a rationalizing effort.

This discussion helps to clear up one of Granet's confusions. It is the theory of mourning which accounts for the rigorous stratification into generations which is characteristic of the kinship system. Granet considers that an archaic system of kinship can be perceived through the system of mourning, while to us the kinship system, as found in the *Érh ya* and the *I Li*, appears to be the result and not the cause of the system of mourning. By adopting the opposite view, Granet has transposed into the hypothetical kinship system of the archaic period a feature – the stratification into generations – which actually belongs to the system of mourning, and which is comprehensible only in terms of it: one year for the father, nine months for the grandfather, five months for the great-grandfather, etc. In fact, we must wait for the T'ang Code (about A.D. 600) in order to find articles categorically prohibiting marriage between relatives of different generations.[3] This is why the prohibition was not so rigorously applied. But it was imposed with an increasing force, as the funeral rites developed and became popularized, until their zenith under the T'ang.[4] By projecting the principle of parallelism into the archaic period, Granet has been victim of a historical illusion. The stratification into generations should be placed not before the Confucian period, but after.

We have already stressed the fact that a Kariera-type system, as conceived by Granet to account for the origins of the Chinese family, is by no means, as he believes it to be, the simplest which can be conceived of or which can exist. In point of fact, anything in the *Érh ya* which seems to be a survival of cross-cousin marriage can be explained by the hypothesis, often formulated by Granet, that the primitive Chinese communities were divided into two exogamous moieties. Contrary to what Granet believed, this *by no means* constitutes a Kariera system. However, we do not go so far as to agree with Hsu,[5] who, in an excess of intellectual pharisaism, treats Radcliffe-Brown's evidence as purely hypothetical. The English sociologist considers highly probable the ancient existence of marriage between bilateral cross-cousins

[1] Fêng, 1937, p. 181.   [2] loc. cit.
[3] ibid. p. 165. However, M. J. Escarra tells me that legislative texts dating from the Han period already noted this prohibition.   [4] ibid. p. 181.   [5] Hsu, 1940–1, p. 357, n. 22.

'linking together two clans of a single village or two villages each of one clan',[1] as in Shan-si and Ho-nan still today. It is clear enough how, at a certain time, a rationalist reformation of such a system or similar system could have given it the appearance of a pseudo-Kariera system, which, in Australia, itself represents a similar transformation, but not for the same reasons. In Australia it involved the superimposition of a matrilineal dichotomy on a patrilineal dichotomy.[2] In China, short of admitting a similar but reverse transformation, which would appear to be a pure postulate, the stratification of the generations reveals itself as the cause, and not the result, of the transition to a more complex type.

That the Confucian reformation ran up against marriage between bilateral cross-cousins, and was ultimately obliged to make a place for it, is clearly indicated by some of Fêng's statements:

'Theoretically and ritually, it [this type of marriage] has been disapproved since the beginning of the first century A.D. Legal prohibition, however, came rather late, the first definite clause being found in the Ming Code. Since the enforcement of this law proved rather difficult, in the Ch'in Code this interdiction was invalidated by another clause, immediately following it, which allowed such marriages.'[3]

The exact texts are: 'A man cannot marry the children of his aunt on the father's side, or of his uncle or aunt on the mother's side, because though of the same generation they are within the fifth degree of mourning . . . In the interest of the people it is permitted to marry with the children of a paternal aunt or of a maternal uncle or aunt.'[4] While denying the current practice of cross-cousin marriage in modern China, and its survival in the modern nomenclature,[5] Fêng nevertheless considers that the *Êrh ya* and the *I Li* offer unequivocal proof of its practice in ancient times. For Fêng, Granet and Kroeber, the ambivalence of the terms *chiu*, *ku* and *shêng* indubitably establishes 'cross-cousin marriage of the bilateral type, coupled with sister exchange'.[6]

An essential feature of the system of mourning suggests, however, a connexion with very archaic forms of family organization. This is the rule which stops mourning at the fourth ascending or descending generation, or at the fourth collateral line. Granet notes that the ancient documents tell of a period when clan exogamy stopped at the fifth generation. Indeed, according to the *T'ai p'ing yü lan*, this limit – the principle of which will be found again in the peripheral systems[7] – was introduced in the Hsia and Shang periods (*c.* 1700–1100 B.C.):

'The institution of strict sib exogamy was traditionally attributed to Chou

---

[1] Radcliffe-Brown in a letter of Hsu, ibid.　　　　　　　　　[2] ch. XI.
[3] Fêng, 1937, pp. 183–4.　　　　　　　　　　　　　　　　[4] ibid. p. 184, n. 41.
[5] ibid. p. 184, n. 43. (This is contrary to Chen and Shryock, 1932.)　　[6] ibid. p. 185.
[7] cf. ch. XXIII.

Kung (*c.* 1100 B.C.), who instituted it for the maintenance of sib solidarity. Nevertheless, there is abundant evidence to show that even during the Chou period, this interdiction was neither universal nor strictly enforced. It was only after the overthrow of the feudal system and the transformation of the sib organization that absolute sib exogamy gradually prevailed. From the middle of the first millennium A.D. to the present this rule has been vigorously enforced by law.'[1]

By contrast, Hsu quotes Creel[2] as suggesting that, if we know nothing of the organization of the family prior to the Shang, it seems clear, on the other hand, that the Shang and the Chou represent entirely different cultures.[3] The agnatic family (*chung fa*) did not exist among the Shang. Brother succeeded brother, members of the father's generation were all 'fathers', and members of the grandfather's generation were all 'grandfathers' (*chu*). Consequently, the agnatic family must have suddenly appeared with the Chou. It is necessary perhaps to relate this information to Creel's statement[4] that the grouping by five, so frequent in the late Chou period, is completely lacking in the more ancient literature.

This raises a host of problems. As we have seen, the Chinese system, according to Granet, has developed from a strict clan regulation which has given way to a freedom gradually established by the transition to the agnatic family. The historical facts not only clearly suggest a change (not gradual, but abrupt) to the agnatic family, but also the replacing of a relative freedom by rigorous regulation. It is never clear in Granet over what period of time the following sequence applies: *four-class system – eight-class system – modern period*. If it is of long continuance it does not correspond to the facts. On the other hand, the rule of the five generations should appear in connexion with the eight-class system. Consequently, the latter must be contemporaneous with the Hsia and Shang periods, or even earlier. This would relegate the four-class system to a mythical past to which the Hsia themselves also belong.[5] Consequently, we would have to admit to the following sequence: *four classes – eight classes – relative freedom* (with the limit of five generations) – *a return to a strict clan exogamy* (under the influence of the Confucian reformation) – and *direct development towards the modern stage of freedom*, this being an infinitely more complex picture than that postulated by Granet. Secondly, we must accept the hypothesis that the system of the *Êrh ya* and of the *I Li* attest to an evolution effected several millennia before these works were written, and that the various stages of this evolution – themselves separated by very considerable spaces of time – have persisted in these works as vestiges, and are there presented on the one level. Fêng, it is true,

---

[1] Fêng, 1937, p. 175.   [2] 1941, p. 360.   [3] cf. Creel, 1937*a*.
[4] ibid. p. 97, n. 2. The Shang king offers sacrifice to his 'several fathers', which suggests an identification of all the men of the father's lineage and generation (Creel, 1937*b*, p. 128).
[5] loc. cit.

considers that it 'is still very doubtful whether the Hsia and the Yin peoples had any exogamy at all'.[1] However, this reservation only adds to the obscurity of the picture.

III

To cap this discouraging situation, we must introduce the question of the *chao mu* order, which, according to Granet, preserved a trace of the eight-class system and of the five generations up till modern times, a truly remarkable survival, and in itself an enigma. In the ancestral temples of the nobles of feudal China, the tablets representing the agnatic ancestors must be arranged in two vertical columns, *chao* and *mu*; in no circumstances can close relatives belonging to two consecutive generations be placed in the same column. If the father is *chao*, the son must be *mu*. Some noble families can only retain the tablets of ancestors of the two most recent generations, one *chao*, the other *mu*, but in seignorial families the *chao* and *mu* columns are each subdivided into two levels. This development nevertheless represents a restriction, viz., the tablets of ancestors older than the great-great-grandfather must be placed together and mixed up in a stone chest, beside the founder of the noble house.

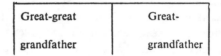

Fig. 61. The *Chao Mu* order.

As a rule, all the tablets of agnatic ascendants must be accompanied by those of their wives. If, on the other hand, the tablet of a close relative cannot be represented in the level reserved for his generation, it must be placed, not in the parent's generation, but in that of the grandparents.[2]

Granet interprets these rules as follows: the *chao mu* order expresses, firstly, a fundamental opposition between members of two consecutive generations, one necessarily *chao* the other necessarily *mu*. On the other hand, it seems to imply a secondary opposition between grandfather and grandson, who figure in the same *column*, but at different levels. A simple matrilineal dichotomy (or vice versa), would account for the fundamental opposition. But in order to explain the secondary opposition, a new dichotomy must be invoked, one cutting across the four-class system resulting from the previous formula, and transforming it into an eight-class system. Indeed, in such a system as seen on page 324, a patrilineal line is distributed among the four matrilineal sub-sections of the one patrilineal moiety, and

[1] Fêng, 1937, p. 175, n. 14.   [2] Granet, 1939, pp. 3–5.

it is only the son's son's son's son's son who reproduces, as to moiety and to subsection, the father's father's father's father's father. Thus, it is argued, the two characteristics of the *chao mu* order, and the restriction placed after the great-great-grandfather, can be explained. Indeed, the linear cycle terminates with the great-great-grandfather. The ancestor following is renewed in the head of the cult; the latter marries into the same subsection and moiety as the ancestor whom he reproduces. Thus, like the ancient literature, we can say that there was a regime in which the rule of exogamy disappeared after the fifth generation.

Rules of mourning, ancestor worship and kinship system thus converge in the hypothesis of the eight-class system, which accounts for all their peculiarities. Seligman is drawn towards the same conclusion when she writes:

'It is significant that the early terms for the affinal relatives, which in modern terminology are descriptive are typical of a classificatory system with cross-cousin marriage. When it is also recalled that in the old system after the fifth generation (inclusive) marriage was allowed within the sib, and that now mourning for ascending and descending generations ceases in the fifth generation, and the mourning cycle begins again, there appears to be more than presumptive evidence for a former class system with alternation of generations, as in Australia.'[1]

This is the beginning of Granet's whole theory.

Granet bases himself on other arguments, taken from the kinship nomenclature. We have already encountered them. They refer to the distinction of affines into *hun* and *yin*, and the respective male and female specialization of the reciprocal couples *chiu* and *shêng*, *ku* and *chih*. Further, *chiu* applies, not only to mother's brother/wife's father, but to brother-in-law, *hun* (wife's brother). Similarly, *shêng* designates brother-in-law, *yin* (sister's husband) as well as sister's son/daughter's husband. Both Granet and Fêng[2] interpret this extension in meaning as a case of teknonymy, a problem discussed in the next chapter. However, Granet also sees it as a survival of marriage with the mother's brother's daughter, and a few remarks are required on this subject. Taking first *chiu*, the extension of this term to the wife's brother appears for the first time in the *Hsin T'ang Shu*, a work of the eleventh century A.D.,[3] a period when the existence of the so-called eight-class system is completely out of the question. (This perhaps does not apply to marriage with the mother's brother's daughter, which is still practised in Yunnan, as Hsu was forced to admit later.) *Shêng* clearly appears in the *Êrh ya*, with the triple meaning of daughter's husband, sister's son and sister's husband, but according to Fêng the term also designates, in this period, the wife's brother,

---

[1] Seligman, 1939, p. 498.
[2] Granet, 1939, p. 210; Fêng, 1937, p. 194 et seq.; Fêng, 1936, pp. 59–66.
[3] Fêng, 1937, pp. 195–6; Hsu, 1940–1, p. 263.

the father's sister's son and the mother's brother's son. This can only be
explained as a survival of marriage between bilateral cross-cousins.[1] The
symmetry postulated by Granet therefore does not seem a strict one. The
terms have a wider connotation than he invokes, and furthermore the symmetry only appears after a gap of ten or twelve centuries. Finally, the only
other case in the *Êrh ya* where the one term is applied to members of two
consecutive generations, viz., *shu* for father's younger brother and husband's
younger brother, would have to be explainable in the same way.[2] Contrary
to Fêng, we believe that this practice can, if necessary, be explained without
recourse to teknonymy, by the hypothesis of marriage with the mother's
brother's daughter *and* a rule of matrilineal descent. But once again we run
up against the marked bilaterality in the *Êrh ya*.

The problem of the *chao mu* order has been taken up in its entirety by
Hsu in his minute but often narrow study of Granet's theory.[3] His sources
are the *Li Chi* and the *I Li*. According to the *Li Chi*, the emperor had seven
temples, nobles had five, and high officials had three (two for inferior
officials and one for minor officials). It is clear, says Hsu, that the first
temple is that of the founder of the dynasty, but what the next two (*A* and *B*)
represent is not clear. Some say that they represent the second and third
emperors, and in this case the occupants would be irremovable and outside
the *chao mu* cycle. Others, including the great commentator of the Sung
period, Chu Tzŭ, point to the sixth and seventh generations. This would be
inconsistent with Granet's hypothesis of a quinary cycle.

A greater obscurity still hangs over the subject of the feudal lord. The
Li Chi declares that the great-great-grandfather receives sacrifices with each
change of season, and the other ancestors every month (Fig. 62). Among
the high officials, finally, the *chao mu* order is violated, since temple number
four, which should be in the middle, is not that of the founder, but that of
the great-grandfather, who is thus 'neither *chao* nor *mu*'. Finally, a text of
the *Yi Li Yi Su* assigns the sacrifice to the great-great-great-grandson, i.e.,
a generation beyond what Granet's system admits of. Hsu even denies
Granet's statement that the tablets of ancestors above the fifth generation were
mixed together. The *Li Chi* requires the invocation of ancestors up to the
seventh generation:

'When prayer was made by the feudal lord . . . he invoked the ancestor
"6" on a specially built platform (*T'an*) and "7" on a specially marked-out
piece of ground (*Ch'an*). In the case of the high officials, ancestor "5",
was invoked on such a specially built platform, and the founder of the
family line (*T'ai Chu*) was offered sacrifices on another platform. In the
case of the officials of lower ranks, who had only two temples, ancester
"4" was invoked on such a platform. Thus not only was there no question
of a constant number of 2 or 4 generations upwards or downwards, but

[1] Fêng, 1937, p. 190.   [2] ibid. n. 72.   [3] Hsu, 1940–1; cf. also Hsu, 1940*a*.

different social classes offer sacrifices to their ancestors according to their own social ranks.'[1]

With regard to the permanent opposition between father and son, inferred by Granet, Hsu justifiably refuses to follow Radcliffe-Brown, who asserts that this opposition (and the correlative bond between grandson and grandfather) are 'nearly universal'.[2] We must add that a logical opposition, as seems to result from the *chao mu* order, is another thing entirely to the affective correlation which the English sociologist has in mind. Hsu likewise remarks that there are two methods of arranging the tablets when a new generation is added (Fig. 63). That is to say, when the head of the cult dies,

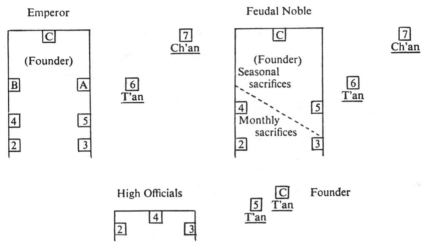

Fig. 62. The ancestral temple (after Hsu, 1940–1, pp. 256–7).

Note. Left and right must be determined with respect to the founder.

theoretically he can replace 3 or 2. Taking the first alternative, 3 then replaces 5, 5 is placed in the stone chest with the older tablets, and the other column remains unchanged: 'In this possibility a man's order *Chao* or *Mu* does not change.'[3] Taking the second alternative, 1 replaces 2, 2 replaces 3, 3 replaces 4 and 4 replaces 5: 'Thus upon the entry of each new generation into the ancestral temple there would be a complete change of the order *Chao* or *Mu* for every individual.'[4] *Chao* means 'a bigger light' and *mu* 'a smaller light', and the *Li Chi* and the *I Li* both associate the first term with the left side (place of honour) and the second with the right side, according to the saying, 'Tso Chao Yu Mu'. Hsu then asks can a son be supposed to be *chao* and his father *mu?* The father must always be *chao* to his son and that is enough to rule out the first hypothesis. But the second solution implies

[1] ibid. 1940–1, pp. 256–7.   [2] ibid. p. 357, n. 20.   [3] ibid. p. 257.   [4] loc. cit.

that *chao* and *mu* do not have an intrinsic meaning for individuals considered as such. They are relative positions, corresponding to temporary modalities by which the status of ancestors is expressed: 'In other words . . . the order of *Chao Mu* only referred to the relationship between fathers and sons.'[1]

In fact, two consecutive generations are always found in two different vertical columns, and in the same horizontal row. Further, there is no barrier between the columns, as Granet suggests. The diagram can be drawn in two

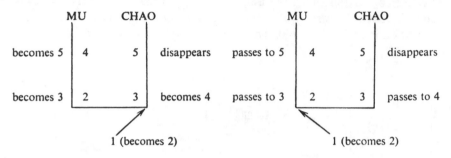

Fig. 63. The permutation of ancestors in the *Chao Mu* order.

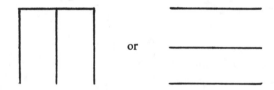

Fig. 64. Rows and columns.

ways (Fig. 64). Hsu prefers the second form, it being understood that the left side of the row corresponds to the 'bigger light', the place of honour, age, the exalted position (*Chun*), and the right side to the 'smaller light', the second place, youth, and the inferior position (*Pei*): 'But to stand expressly in the relation of *Chun* and *Pei* the two individuals must be closely related. Between a bigger light and a smaller light there is no difference of quality but only of quantity. Each horizontal column is a unit by itself, and *Chao Mu* does not refer to grandfather and grandson.'[2] Finally, in the house of the high official the great-grandfather is at the centre. Is he then *chao*, or *mu*, or both? Posed in this way the question is insoluble. But 'if we take every two consecutive generations as a complex unit with *Chao* and *Mu* merely indicating the relative position between a father and a son . . . then the placing of one ancestor in the middle and on top of the others is simply a result of the hierarchical conception of the kinship organizations.'[3] In fact, the unit of mourning is the category *father/son*.

[1] Hsu, 1940–1, p. 259.　　　　　[2] ibid. p. 354.　　　　　[3] loc. cit.

Hsu's observations are extremely interesting, but they are not altogether convincing. We have claimed that the Chinese system evolved from the quantitative to the qualitative, from the notion of kind to that of degree. If, as we admitted above with Fêng, the active force was the regulation of mourning, there is nothing surprising in the latter superimposing its arithmetical exigencies on those of a more ancient qualitative logic. Doubtless survivals can be found wherever one wishes. Nevertheless, Hsu's interpretation is neglectful in the extreme of the systematic nature of the classification of temples into three types (emperor with seven, noble with five, high official with three) corresponding so significantly with the triple circle of mourning in the *I Li*, expressing purely and simply the progressive weakening of the bond of kinship because of social remoteness.

Having looked at Hsu's analysis we must doubtless admit that the question of the *chao mu* order is more obscure than it appears to be in Granet's work. For all that, however, the ancient cycle of mourning does recommence after the fifth generation, and even when ancestors are invoked after the fifth generation it is a supplementary invocation, according to other modalities, and outside the temple, these additional ancestors forming, as it were, an annexe. The texts are particularly striking in this regard:

> 'The head of the empire established seven rooms, an altar and an area for his ancestors. He had a room for his father, one for his grandfather, one for his great-grandfather, one for his great-great-grandfather, and one for the most ancient of his ancestors; every month he made offerings in each one of them. In addition, he has two communal rooms for his remote ancestors. He only made them general offerings once each season. (When he wished to make particular offerings to his great-great-great-grandfather or his great-great-great-great-grandfather) he removed their tablets from the communal rooms and prepared an altar for the first, and an area for the second.'[1]

Hsu's ingenious argument that *chao* and *mu* are not individual attributes but relative positions, supports rather than weakens Granet's thesis.

Moreover, a note by Couvreur in his translation of the *Li Chi* was already clear on this point:

> 'On the death of an emperor, his tablet replaced his father's. The latter replaced . . . the grandfather's, the grandfather's replaced the great-grandfather's, which replaced the great-great-grandfather's. The great-great-grandfather's was placed in the room of Wenn Wang or of Ou Wang, with the tablets of the more remote ancestors who no longer had a special room of their own.'[2]

This relativity of *chao* and *mu* positions fits in very much better with Granet's hypothesis than a fixed order for every individual. If *chao* and *mu* are the

[1] *Li Chi*, trans. S. Couvreur, XX, vol. 2, p. 262. [2] ibid. vol. 1, p. 288, n. 1.

survivals of a former exogamous dichotomy, they can only attest to the existence of a former relationship, and certainly without reflecting the terms in which it was expressed. In this latter case, an individual would sometimes be *chao* and sometimes *mu*, and the fixed order would become totally unintelligible. However, there are more serious difficulties.

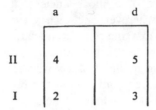

Fig. 65. The system of positions in the *Chao Mu* order.

No matter how the *chao mu* order is represented, whether by vertical columns, as does Granet, or by horizontal rows, as preferred by Hsu, it nevertheless remains true that the position of each tablet or group of tablets is determined by two factors, viz., the *chao* or *mu* position, and the higher or lower level. If the columns were called *a* and *d*, and the levels, I and II, the distribution would then be as in Fig. 65, i.e., a given patrilineal line would have the sequence, $d_2-a_2-d_1-a_1$, in which the couple *A/D* would obviously represent a patrilineal moiety, and the cycle *1/2* two matrilineal subsections. The eight-class system reconstructed by Granet using the *chao mu* order as his basis by no means gives such a sequence. If we refer to Fig. 57 we see that the patrilineal sequence is $a_1-b_1-c_1-d_1$, or $a_2-b_2-c_2-d_2$, and that only these two sequences are compatible with the system. Expressed in terms of the *chao mu* order, it amounts to saying that four consecutive members of the one patrilineal line must either occupy four levels of one single column, or four positions on the same row, and that the intervention of two columns and two rows at the one time is inexplicable. If the *chao mu* order had any relationship whatsoever to the kinship system (which is doubtful), it would mean that the father and the son would be identical as to row and opposed as to column, with grandfather and grandson identical as to column and opposed as to row. In Granet's kinship system, we see, on the contrary, that great-great-grandfather, great-grandfather, grandfather and father are *all* identical from one viewpoint (the patrilineal moiety), and *all* different from another (the matrilineal section). Thus, not only is the hypothesis a risky one, but it does not account for the facts which it is meant to explain.

Is there another kinship system the characteristics of which might better be expressed in the *chao mu* order? It is curious to note that there is one, viz., the Murngin system, functioning according to either the regular formula or the alternate formula. In both cases we find the sequence $d_2-a_2-d_1-a_1$. Let us therefore compare Granet's system and the Murngin system (Fig. 66).

In the diagram on the left (Murngin), the sign = joins the husband's sub-section with his wife's subsection, the sign → the mother's subsection with her children's subsection. In the diagram on the right (Granet) the internal sign → joins the husband's subsection with the wife's subsection and the external sign → the father's subsection with the children's subsection. We have seen that the Murngin system results from the superimposition of a matrilineal dichotomy on a patrilineal dichotomy, while Granet's system can only be explained by assuming the reverse, the original dichotomy being matrilineal and the secondary dichotomy patrilineal.

Murngin (Regular)   Granet

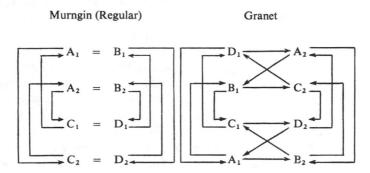

Fig. 66. Murngin marriage rules compared with Chinese marriage rules (according to Granet, 1939).

Let us now consider the patrilineal sequence corresponding to the *chao mu* order, i.e., $d_2-a_2-d_1-a_1$. This sequence is clearly found in the Murngin system, but only when it functions according to one of the two formulas, regular or alternate, which it has at its disposal. It will be remembered that in this case marriage is still possible with the bilateral cross-cousin,[1] since the eight classes function as if there were only four. It is only on the hypo-thesis that the system functions alternately according to the two formulas that marriage with the matrilateral cross-cousin takes place, but in this case the patrilineal sequence becomes $d_2-a_1-d_2-a_1$, i.e., father and son are com-pletely different, grandfather and grandson are completely identical; and this does not correspond to the *chao mu* order either. In other words, if an attempt is made to construct a system corresponding to the *chao mu* order, we find an eight-class system with marriage with the bilateral cross-cousin, which makes the eight classes unintelligible. If the eight classes are distributed so as to be given a functional value (marriage with the matrilateral cross-cousin), the system ceases to account for the characteristics of the *chao mu* order. Not only are we launched on a hazardous course but it leads nowhere.

Must we come to Hsu's conclusion that the *chao mu* order has nothing to do with a former kinship structure? We have much hesitation in admitting it. In the last few years, the principle of alternate generations has taken on

[1] cf. ch. XII.

such an importance in the interpretation of obscure phenomena that there must be a bias in favour of its intervention whenever there is a hint or trace of opposition between consecutive generations and of identification of remote generations. However, we have seen that the phenomenon is open to a different interpretation. Be that as it may, all that could be admitted is that the general characteristics of the *chao mu* order suggest a structure based on a certain alternation of generations. What type of alternation is this? It is impossible to say. The *chao mu* order, as we know it from the *Li Chi* and the *I Li* and the commentators, represents an institution which has already come under the influence of the hierarchial organization and the religious ritual. To hope to verify, in all its aspects, a clearly defined law of a certain kinship system would be a fruitless undertaking.

Through the observation of modern customs ethnography may perhaps be able to shed light on this problem. Here again, it is to be deplored that Hsu, without examination, should have rejected Radcliffe-Brown's suggestion that the *chao mu* order should be studied in the light of the practices of Fu Kien, where even today marriage with the patrilateral cousin is strictly prohibited[1] and where ancestors are still placed alternately to the right and left of the founder.[2] One is hard put to it to claim *a priori* that there is no connexion between these customs and the *chou* ritual as described by Maspero:

'The first ancestor was at the very head, facing east, his son to his left, facing south, and his grandson to his right, facing north, with all the descendants arrayed thus in two lines, the *chao* to the left, the *mu* to the right below the son and grandson respectively, each generation further from the ancestor than the previous . . . All the *mu* descendants of the Wen king in a line to his left, all the *chao* descendants of the Wu king in a line to his right, and all the *mu* and *chao* before these two kings . . . in two rows to the left and right of the original ancestor Heou-tsi.'[3]

If we add that, in a society as highly suggestive of ancient dynastic China as the Inca empire, with its funeral rituals which must constantly be compared with the corresponding archaic Chinese ceremonies, we come across what seems to be an alternate arrangement: 'On both sides of the Image of the Sun were the bodies of their deceased kings, all placed in order of their antiquity . . .'[4] one feels inclined to admit the existence of a general structural phenomenon, the theory of which escapes us at our present level of knowledge of these two civilizations. We certainly know that the inhabitants of Cuzco, and perhaps other regions, were divided into two groups, the High moiety, and the Low moiety (Hanan and Hurin). In this regard, De la Vega's text should be placed alongside other evidence:

'All the people of Cuzco came out [for the harvest rites], according to their tribes and lineages . . . They sat down on their benches, each man

---

[1] Lin, 1945–7, p. 94.　　　　　　　　　[2] Hsu, 1940–1, p. 258, n. 7.
[3] Maspero, 1927, pp. 251–2.　　　　　　[4] De la Vega, 1787, vol. I, p. 167.

according to the rank he held, the Hanan-Cuzcos being on one side, and the Hurin-Cuzcos on the other . . . The priests came in procession and the families of Hurin and Hanan Cuzco, each with the embalmed bodies of their ancestors.'[1]

Again: 'They brought all the huacas into the square, as well as the bodies of the dead Yncas, to drink with them: placing those who had belonged to the Hanan Cuzco on the side where that lineage was stationed, and the same with those of Hurin Cuzco. Then they brought food and drink to the dead bodies.'[2] Cuzco's geographical structure at least suggests a double dichotomy, the axis separating the Hanan from the Hurin being cut perpendicularly, from north to south, by the imperial road. Here also the hypothesis of alternate generations, with its two mutually exclusive implications of bilateral descent and patrilateral marriage should be closely examined.

[1] De Molina, 1873, pp. 26–7.   [2] ibid. pp. 47–8.

CHAPTER XXI

Matrilateral Marriage

I

There is a great deal of information suggesting the existence in ancient China of a system of bilateral cross-cousin marriage involving the exchange of sisters. Let us quickly refresh our memory as to this information. In the first place, there is the terminology preserved in the *Êrh-ya*, with its system of identifications, and the division of kin and affines into four lines. Secondly, there are the facts relating to archaic peasant life, as brought out by Granet in his *Festivals and Songs of Ancient China*: 'The essential feature of the ancient festivals is the sexual orgy which makes possible matrimonial exchanges . . . The matrimonial bonds will maintain the solidarity of the federated groups.'[1] It is a system of this type which Radcliffe-Brown believes survives in Shansi and Honan. This is also the system put forward by Chen and Shryock when, reviving the whole question of cross-cousin marriage in ancient China, they quote a poem by Po-chu-yi (A.D. 772–846) concerning a village of the Kiang-sou, the name of which consists of the names of two united clans:

> In Ku-feng-hsien, in the district of Ch'u chou
> Is a village called Chu Ch'en
> There are only two clans there
> Which have intermarried for many generations.[2]

Therefore, despite Hsu's qualms, one feels prepared to agree with Granet, Chen and Shryock, and especially with Fêng, from whom we borrow this chronology, and to admit that marriage between bilateral cross-cousins was practised in China (or certain regions of China) at least till the end of the first millennium B.C. This implies an implicit or explicit division of communities into two exogamous groups, or a grouping of local communities into twos for matrimonial purposes, but not, as Granet believed, a four-class system, which is vaguely suggested by certain facts (possible bilateral descent, and certain features of the *chao mu* order) but is not a necessary hypothesis, for it is not a logical necessity, or an inevitable historical stage, or a general feature of the geographical area under consideration.

[1] Granet, 1932, p. 221.　　[2] Chen and Shryock, 1932, p. 629; Granet, 1939, p. 179.

There are other facts besides these, with which, moreover, they are hardly compatible. There are firstly what Granet groups as phenonema of obliquity, viz., the seignorial practice of marriage with women belonging to two different generations, and certain equations in the nomenclature identifying kin of affines of two consecutive generations. Above all, there are the double classification of affines into *yin* and *hun*, and the specialization of certain terms of appellation used reciprocally between men or between women, suggesting that the group has an asymmetrical structure.

These indications of obliquity or asymmetry in the nomenclature have been specially analysed by Fêng.[1] There are five terms which apply to members of two consecutive generations:

chiu　mother's brother, wife's brother
yi　　mother's sister, wife's sister
po　　father's elder brother, husband's elder brother
shu　father's younger brother, husband's younger brother
ku　　father's sister, husband's sister.

All these relationships were originally distinct and their assimilation can generally be dated. For example, the extension of *chiu* to the wife's brother dates from the tenth century A.D., and nowadays determinants are being introduced to distinguish the two usages, viz., *chiu fu*, mother's brother, and *chiu hsiung* or *chiu ti*, wife's brother. In other words, a distinction is made between the *chiu* of the father's generation, and the *chiu* of the brother's generation.[2] The assimilation might strictly be interpreted as a result of marriage with the wife's brother's daughter, but Fêng argues, apparently conclusively, that *chiu* had lost the meaning of 'wife's father' at least a millennium before it was applied to the wife's brother. The extension of *po* and *shu* appears inexplicable to Fêng in terms of all known practices. We can disagree with him on this point, which, it must be added, has only a purely theoretical interest. A system of matrilineal lineages, with marriage with the mother's brother's daughter, can allow the grouping of the father's brothers and the husband's brothers, as the men who take wives from my lineage, Ego being female.[3] *Ku* would then normally designate the sisters

---

[1] Fêng, 1936, pp. 59–66.　　　　　　　　　[2] ibid. p. 61, n. 2.

[3] In an excellent study devoted wholly to the systems being discussed, Fei describes the system of his own native region, Wukiang, in which he notes the paucity of terms for the group of men who have married the clan's women. In practice there are only descriptive terms. Fei interprets this lack of terms as a possible indication of the former existence of a dual organization (p. 133). Here one is rather put in mind of a former system of lineages that Fei himself analysed from the system of Shanghai, with the differentiation of kin and affines into: men and women of my clan; women who have married into my clan; men who have married women of my clan; the mother's clan, the wife's clan (no special terms, the wife's nomenclature being used); husband's clan (the same situation, the husband's nomenclature being used). The clans actually appear to play the rôle of lineages. A most remarkable feature of the systems described by Fei is the complete absence of kinship terms for the generations younger than Ego's; only personal names are used. (Fei, 1936–7, pp. 125–48.)

of *po* and of *shu*. But a similar interpretation could only be extended to *chiu*, *shêng* and *yi* if Ego (male) adopted a matrilineal viewpoint, which would entail the greatest difficulties. In fact, the extension of *po* to the husband's elder brother is a late practice dating from the tenth century A.D., and is therefore incompatible with such a form of marriage (unless the practice could be localized, as no author in fact does, in Yunnan). Likewise, *ku* was not applied to the husband's sisters until about the fourth century A.D. As to *yi*, this term is confined to the wife's sister in the *Êrh ya*, and its extension to the mother's sister is attested to only after 550 B.C. The possible explanation in terms of marriage with the father's widow is nowhere verified.[1]

No doubt these dates cannot be accepted without some reservations. When practices appear in the literature, it is only because they have been in use for a long time. There can also be the question of local usages, which spread into a new region or are incorporated into the general usage, following a war of conquest, or the colonization of peoples possessing their own customs. Be that as it may, it is impossible to reduce the five extensions listed above to a single form of marriage, or to a precise system of kinship. Like Chen and Shryock, Fei has suggested that they should be interpreted in terms of teknonymy, i.e., in calling the brother-in-law *chiu*, or *po* or *shu*, men and women merely pay them the respect of the terminology which is used by their children. This is the explanation put forward by Chinese theorists as early as the eighteenth century: 'Wife's brothers are *chiu* to one's own children. The father adopts the language of his children, and he also calls his wife's brothers *chiu*.'[2] But what about *yi*? Here the extension is made from the lower generation to the higher and it has to be admitted that, through a kind of 'reverse teknonymy', it is the children who adopt the speech of their father.[3]

In his general study of 1937 Fêng adds three more examples to the five discussed in his 1936 work. The term *shên*, in the vocative, applies to the father's younger brother's wife, and to the husband's younger brother's wife. The extension to the junior generation dates from the Sung period. Lastly, there is the extension of the terms *kung* and *p'o* from grandparents to the husband's parents. In all these cases, Fêng appeals to teknonymy, which he considers sufficiently universal in China, and sufficiently ancient (attested to since 489 B.C.), to be accepted as the explanation.[4]

Fêng is perhaps right, but there must be some reservations as to the considerable range he gives the notion of teknonymy, which he uses as a sort of panacea. The appearance of teknonymy and its intervention in any particular case themselves also pose problems. Let us dwell on this point a moment.

II

The term teknonymy was invented by Tylor to describe the custom whereby

---

[1] Fêng, 1936, p. 64.   [2] Quoted by Fêng, ibid. p. 62.
[3] ibid. p. 65.   [4] ibid. 1937, pp. 200–3.

a person is called the father, mother, grandfather or grandmother, etc., of one of his descendants instead of by his own name. Lowie accepts this meaning in his treatment of the institution,[1] and he interprets it as resulting from a terminological deficiency, viz., either the language has no specific term for the relative in question, or else the term cannot be used, provisionally or definitively, for reasons of etiquette. Fêng is not the first ethnologist to give the term a wider meaning, and this in itself does not raise any objection. All the same, however, it must be noticed that to call a woman 'So-and-so's mother', for example, is not the same thing as calling her 'mother', i.e., calling her *by the name of her child*, or *by the name given her by her child*. The two forms should doubtless be distinguished; and whereas Fêng's discussion deals exclusively with the second form, the observation he invokes in witness to the antiquity of teknonymy in China[2] comes under the first. Let us leave this first form to one side, since it plays no rôle in explaining the practices in question, and ask ourselves how the second can be interpreted. As this form of teknonymy is in current usage in our own society, it is our own customs which can most usefully be examined.

Suppose a household is composed of the children, the father, the mother and the mother's sister. For some years, this sister has only been referred to by the children's mother (her sister) and the children's father (her brother-in-law), as 'auntie', the 'baby' name given her by her nephews and nieces. How can this be interpreted? There are three possible explanations.

If the children enjoy the greatest prestige of any members of the group, the parents acknowledge the fact by adopting their terminology. By contrast, the parents can adopt the terminology of the children without compromising the aunt's prestige and thereby their own generation's prestige (thus a father, speaking to his children of their mother, will say 'your mother', or 'mother', to avoid using the direct term of address that he himself uses, i.e., his wife's first name, which is prohibited to the children). Finally, there is a third interpretation. With regard to the woman named, each partner commands a different system of references, such that she is known as 'sister', 'sister-in-law', and 'aunt'. When two members of the group are engaged in conversation and wish to refer to her they must either use their own system or adopt that of the interlocutor, neither of which is satisfactory. The children's transformation of the term of reference to the term of address, i.e., 'aunt' changed to 'auntie', provides a solution to this difficulty. In short, 'auntie' has the appearance of a personal name with regard to the person designated, and an impersonal term from the point of view of the person using it (i.e., it does not imply a particular kinship relationship). Therefore, we have two explanatory principles, the one based on affective reasons (prestige), the other on logical reasons (the necessity of finding a term common to all the systems of reference). The first principle admits of two contrasting interpretations.

[1] Lowie, 1961, pp. 107–9.
[2] Ch'en Ch'i speaks of his wife as 'Ch'ang's mother', Fêng, 1937, p. 202.

It can be seen that the problem of teknonymy is not a simple one, and that the particular principle, or the modality of such a principle, to be used must be determined for any given case.[1]

The difficulty is even more serious when two opposite forms of teknonymy are simultaneously invoked, as by Fêng. A man calls his brother-in-law *chiu*, using his children's parlance, but calls his mother's sister *yi*, using his parent's parlance. Under what conditions can these two opposite procedures coexist? It is true that their respective date of appearance are separated by some fifteen centuries. But then the concomitant changes in the Chinese family would need to be determined. The general appeal to teknonymy does not provide a solution to the problems posed by the extension of the terms. Teknonymy, and each of its highly varying forms, must have a reason, or rather, as the case may be, its reasons, and there is no justification for resorting to it as an arbitrary principle.

In the case of *yi*, one is sorely tempted to disagree with Fêng. We have said that the extension of the term to the mother's sister is ancient, apparently dating from the sixth century B.C., and this alone should be enough to isolate it from other cases studied.[2] To account for this, Fêng as we have seen, has had to advance the hypothesis of a veritable 'reverse teknonymy'. Granet suggests an explanation in terms of the son's marriage with the father's widow, and he quotes examples discussed by Fêng, and emphasizes that they are brought up by the chroniclers only to suffer indignant condemnation.[3] But if a thing has to be condemned, it follows that it must have been practised. The son's marriage with the father's widow was practised in the geographical areas, at least, since Fêng and Granet refer to criticisms levelled by ancient scribes against the Hsiung-nu, a pastoral population on the northern steppes, precisely because they married the father's widow. If we add, what Granet clearly saw, that marriage with the stepmother fits easily in the same system as permits marriage with the son's widow, or bride,[4] and that the latter can be correlated in turn with preferential marriage with the wife's brother's daughter, recognition must be given to a remarkably suggestive group of facts, all tending towards the same conclusion. In thus accepting the explanation by teknonymy, Granet *overdetermines* this conclusion.

---

[1] According to Fei Hsiao-Tung (1938, p. 135) the women of Kiangsu start by using their husbands' terminology for their parents-in-law (except for the father-in-law, who is designated by a special and immutable term, *činpa*), and only after they have had children do they start using the general terminology used by children. That the problem of appellations in China is more complex than is usually covered by the term teknonymy (even given Fêng's wide meaning of it) is also suggested by one of Hsu's studies. The spoken nomenclature seems to be consistently different from the written nomenclature, and its primary use is to express concrete situations: 'When addressing a son of mother's brother, one uses a brother term. When referring to the same person, one uses a term which differentiates the latter from a true brother' (Hsu, 1942, p. 250). There are then 'different categories of terms [which] may be correlated with specific social requirements' (ibid. p. 256).

[2] Fêng, 1937, p. 199.   [3] Granet, 1930; 1939, pp. 65–6.

[4] ibid. pp. 66–73

III

This is the conclusion that Granet had no hesitation in setting forth in the unnecessarily complicated form of the hypothesis of an eight-class system, interpolated between the four-class system of archaic times and the modern freedom. We have already emphasized and criticized the speculative character of this reconstruction. However, reduced to its simplest expression, viz., that in China there was a period when, or there were regions in which, there was marriage with the mother's brother's daughter, to the exclusion of marriage with the father's sister's daughter, the hypothesis, it must be admitted, retains a certain value, although for reasons which are not exactly those invoked by Granet. Of Granet's reasons we shall keep only two, viz., the dichotomy of affines into *hun* and *yin*, which other writers unfortunately have not discussed, and the existence of the Kachin system to the south of China. Had Granet known of the Gilyak system, so similar to the Kachin system and located to the north of China in a position corresponding to that occupied by the Kachin in the south, had he been in a position to add the Lushai-Kuki and Naga systems,[1] and had he analysed the Tibetan system, he would have been justified in ascribing to his hypothesis (at least in the simplified form we have retained) a much greater value. Indeed, it might be said that, peripheral to the whole of China, and thus suggesting an archaic survival, are the same marriage rules and the same kinship system. But, for this reason also, Granet would perhaps have begun to doubt his chronology. We shall return below to this aspect of the question.

By a curious paradox, Granet's harshest critic makes a remarkable contribution to his thesis. In a recent article Hsu[2] indisputably established the modern existence of marriage with the mother's brother's daughter in China; firstly, on the basis of observations published by Kulp[3] and Fei,[4] and, more importantly, on his own field work in northern China, western Yunnan and Kunming. In all these regions the preferred (but not obligatory) marriage is with the mother's brother's daughter, and the type absolutely condemned is that with the father's sister's daughter. The first is usually called 'follow (paternal) aunt marriage', and the second, 'return home marriage'.[5] We shall skip the somewhat naïve discussion of the functional value of the distinction, and keep solely to the facts. In the village of Kaihsienkung studied by Fei, the two types of marriage are distinguished as

[1] Making a comparison with the social organization of the Yao on the Indo-Chinese frontier, who sanction marriage between third cousins, Fortune notes: 'This rule is in strong contrast to the unilateral patrilineal exogamy for all China, coupled with prohibition of patrilateral cross-cousin marriage which the Chinese observe, without disapproval of marriage with first cousins on the maternal side' (Fortune, 1939, p. 348). This Yao rule should be compared with the similar system of the Naga, the secondary character of which is clearly affirmed (cf. ch. XVII, § II). The subdivision of the clan into lineages (*fong*), so typical of the development of Naga society, is also seen among the Yao.
[2] Hsu, 1945, pp. 83–103.   [3] Kulp, 1924.   [4] Fei, 1939.
[5] Hsu, 1945, p. 84.

'up the hill' marriage and 'reverting marriage.[1] In the town in the western Yunnan described by Hsu, an informant gave marriage with the mother's brother's daughter as representing 'as high as 70 per cent of all marriages',[2] an exaggerated percentage according to Hsu, although he recognizes that 'such marriages are certainly very frequent'.[3] In Fukien also, marriage with the mother's brother's daughter is in current usage, while marriage with the father's sister's daughter is considered as repugnant or even illegal.[4] Every informant from north China questioned by Hsu condemned marriage with the patrilateral cousin as equivalent to 'the return of bone and flesh',[5] a formula which will be commented upon below.[6] Hsu tries to explain the preference for the matrilateral cousin. He argues for the archaic existence of marriage between bilateral cross-cousins, and the development of the unilateral type under the influence of certain unfavourable factors in the previous formula, e.g., the growing predominance of the father-son relationship, the development of ancestor worship, etc. Although Hsu stresses that his hypothesis is based on a different set of facts and line of argument than Granet's, he is no less obliged to recognize that his is the same hypothesis.[7] The hypothesis is less important than the facts. But these facts must be fitted into the framework of such general structural laws of kinship systems as we have so far been able to isolate.

The two systems concerned (marriage with the bilateral cross-cousin, and marriage with the mother's brother's daughter) are correlated with the two elementary formulas of restricted exchange and of generalized exchange. It will be remembered that both can develop normally from an original division of the group into exogamous moieties. However, we also know that restricted exchange can successfully continue in a more complex structure only if the latter is characterized by a disharmonic regime. If the original structure, or subsequent structures, are subjected to a harmonic regime, the system can only become more complex by a transition to generalized exchange. These considerations, applied to China, mean firstly that a system of bilateral marriage can evolve towards a system of unilateral marriage, but only if the initial structure is harmonic, i.e., patrilineal and patrilocal or matrilineal and matrilocal. Let us note immediately that these conditions make the hypothesis whereby marriage with mother's brother's daughter emerged from a system of alternate generations, as a more complex form out of a simpler form, very doubtful if not unacceptable. In fact, a system of alternate generations is, by definition, the expression of a disharmonic regime. Of course, bilateral marriage does not imply a system of alternate generations, although, apart from patrilateral marriage, the inverse relationship is true.

Marriage with the matrilateral cross-cousin, postulated by Granet and verified by Hsu, can thus be isolated from a moiety system only if these moieties were originally harmonic either in the paternal or in the maternal

[1] Fei, 1939, pp. 50–1.	[2] Hsu, 1945, p. 91.	[3] loc. cit.	[4] Lin, 1945–7, p. 94.
[5] Hsu, 1945, p. 98.	[6] cf. chs. XXIII and XXIV.	[7] Hsu, 1945, p. 101 and n. 64.

line. Granet has collected inconclusive evidence, though probable to a degree, of a matrilineal element in the archaic Chinese family, an element which is held to have disappeared at a rather early date and made way for a purely patrilineal system. If matrilateral marriage succeeded bilateral marriage historically, it must be admitted that the archaic family was matrilineal, not only as to name or local group but absolutely (harmonic regime); and further, that it remained so until the appearance of generalized exchange, which is otherwise inexplicable. The truth of this is such that, when Granet's system of eight classes is formulated, we see that it rests on the development of the matrilineal principle (four matrilocal groups instead of two), the patrilineal elements (moieties) remaining unchanged (cf. Figs. 57 and 58). Since Granet explains the appearance of the eight-class system as a result of the progressive predominance of the agnatic principle, there is a contradiction which is not the least obstacle to his theory. Must we accept then that a harmonic regime, matrilineal and matrilocal, was suddenly converted into another harmonic regime, patrilineal and patrilocal? There is nothing permitting this hypothesis, and in any case the result would be a system of generalized exchange, but with four classes, and not eight. However, as it is envisaged, Granet's reconstruction leads nowhere.

Only one path remains open if these contradictory data are to be interpreted. This is the path to which Granet seemed to have been drawn, in the introduction to *Danses et légendes*, but only to repudiate it immediately. It consists in admitting that the Chinese facts offer traces and survivals of two systems, which coexisted, at least during a certain period, as the expressions either of distinct cultures and regions, or of social differentiation which, pushed to such a point, would suggest that nobles and peasants were descended from heterogeneous population strata.[1] Indeed, as Granet always perceived, the two systems are contrasted in the practices of two classes: it is the villages which exchange women, while oblique marriage has always been a feudal privilege only. Is it absolutely necessary to transform this social coexistence into an historical sequence?

IV

One essential fact, as we see it, must in any case be underlined. The oblique marriage of the feudal noble is a very archaic practice, one of our most ancient pieces of information on Chinese marriage, and certainly the most precise. Indeed, during the Chou period, the feudal noble married eight secondary wives as well as his principal wife: 'The *yin* were recruited in the following manner. The bride and the eight *yin* were divided into three groups,

---

[1] It is especially for this reason that another study of the Chinese system by Wu (1927, pp. 316–25) is not used here. This author starts from the notion, which is obviously erroneous, of a uniform system for the whole of China. He then endeavours to interpret the folk systems as deviations from the norm of the written systems, a point of view justly criticized by Fei (1936–7, pp. 125–48).

with three women in each group. The first group consisted of the bride, one of her younger sisters or younger half-sisters, *ti*, and one of her older brother's daughters, *chih*. These three women constituted the principal group. Two other feudal states of the same sibname as the bride each supplied a principle *yin*, a *ti*, and a *chih*. Thus there were three groups and nine women in all. The contribution to the *yin* by other states had to be entirely voluntary, and could not be solicited, for it was not proper to ask children of others to become the dishonourable *yin*.'[1] The custom of marriage with the wife's elder brother's daughter disappeared in the third century B.C., and the T'ang Code, promulgated during the period A.D. 627–83, made statutory the prohibition of marriages between members of different generations.[2] The ancient commentators seem to have given various explanations of the right to the wife's niece, and Granet and Fêng have adopted divergent interpretations. 'Three daughters', Granet recalls, 'form a "treasure", for "three" in China is the round number . . . It is better therefore . . . to add one of their nieces to the two sisters allowed to make up the threesome.'[3] Otherwise there would be a risk of depriving an affine of all the means of alliance available to the present generation. This would be an 'indiscreet use of compensatory practices'.[4] According to the commentators quoted by Fêng, the aim of marriage with the wife's niece was to ensure numerous descendants for the feudal noble: 'A niece, rather than a second younger sister was included in the *yin*, in order to create a difference in the blood, so that if the two sisters failed to bear issue, a niece of different blood might bear a son.'[5] This interpretation is based on the *Pai hu t'ung*, a work attributed to Pan Ku, who lived between A.D. 32–92.[6] At so late a period it is curious to note such a determinedly matrilineal interpretation, for it is only through the mother that the brother's daughter can differ from her aunts. Be that as it may, the causes put forward by Fêng and Granet are obviously rationalizations. Fêng can well note that not one case of marriage with the wife's brother's daughter has been reported since the beginning of the Western Han period (206 B.C.–A.D. 8), and stress that some specialists suspect that the practice of the *yin* was an invention of scholars of the Han period.[7] The custom has too many parallels in other regions of the world, and coincides too readily with other characteristics of archaic Chinese society, to be treated as anything but a fundamental structural phenomenon of the system studied.

For different reasons again, this is what neither Granet nor Fêng does. Granet's anxiety to arrange all the facts within an evolutionary series, and to derive complex forms (or what he considers as such) from simple forms (or what he considers as such), leads him to neglect completely the objectively archaic nature of oblique marriage. In Granet's system, the latter is only

---

[1] Fêng, 1937, pp. 187–8; cf. also Granet, 1920, *passim*; 1939, pp. 70–1, 130–3; Werner and Tedder, 1910, p. 24.
[2] Fêng, 1937, p. 196 and n. 86.   [3] Granet, 1939, p. 132.   [4] ibid. p. 130.
[5] Fêng, 1937, p. 188.   [6] ibid. p. 273.   [7] ibid. p. 190 and n. 71.

one stage and an almost final one in an already long evolution, the beginnings and expansion of which are, for him, lost in the dark recesses of time. At the same time, the feudal period appears as a late, almost recent, phenomenon, preceded by a long era of clan organization, while our earliest possible contact with Chinese society, the Shang culture, finds us in the very midst of feudalism, or what one might well call hypertrophied feudalism.[1] All that we know of Chinese society shows us an evolution, *grosso modo*, from a feudal stage with lineages preponderating towards a clan-like organization from which the patrilineal family progressively emerges, not the contrary. The development and increasingly rigorous conception of the rule of exogamy confirm this view, as Fêng has clearly shown.[2]

In this case, however, feudal institutions, or what we can perceive of them, ought to represent our most valuable sources of information, the starting-point of any attempt to interpret the archaic kinship system, the pivot around which the structure of this system must be organized. Marriage with the wife's brother's daughter would then be one of our few keys to this system. Fêng, however, is bent on closing all outlets in this direction. Far from seeing marriage with the wife's niece as a fact of prime significance, he constantly tends to minimize its importance, reducing it to an anomaly, or an insignificant consequence of other institutions, for example the sororate: 'When the sororate is practised extensively, it may be accompanied by marriage with the wife's brother's daughter, because if the wife has no marriageable sister her brother's daughter is a good substitute. There are indications of such a practice in feudal China among the nobility.'[3] But it is a 'highly arbitrary' practice, amounts to 'legalized incest', and has therefore never 'become very prevalent even among the nobility . . . [for] the practice actually ran counter to the generation-principle ideology of this period'.[4] What period? we might ask ourselves, for Fêng has traced the development of the principle of the equivalence of generations, which, as he himself says, reached its culminating point under the T'ang, i.e., a millennium after the period he indicates as marking the disappearance of the form of marriage in question.

Fêng asserts that this form of marriage was never frequent, but he gives no proof of this assertion. He recognizes that the petty nobility must have practised it, that the government ministers adopted it in certain verified cases, and that there has been discussion on whether the literati were or were not entitled to it. Consequently it is not so rare and extraordinary a custom,[5]

---

[1] Creel, 1935–6, pp. 46 et seq.; 1937b, *passim;* Yetts, 1939, p. 75.
[2] Fêng, 1937, pp. 174–5.   [3] ibid. p. 187.   [4] ibid. p. 189; cf. also p. 191.
[5] Marriage with the matrilateral cross-cousin has been noted by Hsu in a village on the south coast of Manchuria, a village in which he notes two significant cases of incest, one between the father and son's wife, the other with the father's brother's son's wife (Hsu, 1940b, pp. 126–8). Such incest is condemned, on the one hand, in the name of supernatural sanctions which befall those guilty of oblique unions (father-in-law and daughter-in-law, daughter and father, etc.), and for reasons of order in the terminology: 'What can she call her father now'? (ibid. p. 127.) All this suggests less repugnance for oblique unions than Fêng maintains.

as it was obviously in the interest of commentators of the T'ang epoch and later to make out.

However, the fact that some archaic customs could have had a very wide diffusion, and that sometimes they might have lasted many centuries, receives strange confirmation in a work written by a seventeenth-century author, Ch'en Ting, and translated into English by Shryock.[1] This young Chinese had the experience of marrying into a noble family of a people whom he calls the Miao, from south China. These people were divided into four clans and 'were bound by marriage ties, generation after generation'.[2] When an elder daughter was married, she was accompanied by eight bridesmaids, or concubines. 'This', says the author, 'preserved the ancient custom of the nobles marrying nine girls at one time.'[3] He dwells on the archaism and conservatism of the Miao: 'Their customs were primitive, resembling the customs of the Three Kingdoms.'[4] In point of fact, the eight Miao concubines were not divided into three lots, but into two. They lived in the side buildings behind the third hall, 'four on each side'.[5] They were not necessarily younger than the principal wife, and nothing indicates that some belonged to a different generation: 'Of these eight concubines, half belonged to the clan of my wife, and half were selected from well-to-do families. According to their ages, my wife came exactly in the middle. The eldest was four years older than my wife, and the youngest four years younger, there being a difference of one year between their successive ages.'[6] This is all quite different from the *yin* marriage, and the author puts on his own gloss when he declares that all these traits are 'according to the Chou ritual'.[7] But let us not forget that this is the second half of the seventeenth century, and even if we admit that customs at least two millennia old must have changed considerably, the persistence of essential traits after so long a period does not suggest for certain that they were originally uncommon and almost abnormal. Ch'en Ting, and the popular tradition to which he refers, are sociologically more meaningful than Fêng in this statement, at the conclusion of the work: 'The practice of the three dynasties, long discussed in China [was] unexpectedly preserved on the frontiers. An old proverb says, "when ceremony has been lost, seek it among the uncultivated". Now we cannot find it among the uncultivated, but among the Miao. It is really deplorable!'[8]

One detail in Ch'en Ting's description deserves special attention. It is the assertion that the four Miao clans are 'bound by marriage ties, generation after generation', the first wife's elder daughter having to marry the first wife's elder son of one of the other families. The author does not give any information on the type of reciprocity in force, but let us not forget that this is Yunnan, the region where Hsu now finds a considerable proportion of marriages with the mother's brother's daughter, and on the border of Kachin country. There is consequently a strong temptation to imagine these four

---

[1] Shryock, 1934, pp. 524–47.   [2] ibid. p. 531.   [3] loc. cit.   [4] ibid. p. 532.
[5] ibid. p. 533.   [6] ibid. p. 544.   [7] ibid. p. 531.   [8] ibid. p. 547.

clans united in a cycle of generalized exchange. If, as Ch'en Ting asserts so insistently, this was the survival of an archaic practice, we would also have a possible solution to the problem of exogamy being cancelled, among the Hsia and the Shang, after the fifth generation, viz., clan *A* cannot take its wives from within the clan, but must receive them from clan *B*, which receives them from clan *C*, which receives them from clan *D*. Consequently, five generations are necessary and sufficient for a complete cycle of exchange; clan *A*, which has given a woman, regains this woman in the fifth generation as the granddaughter's granddaughter, of the initial great-great-grandfather.

At the same time, we can see a possible interpretation of a quite remarkable feature of the kinship system noted by Fêng: 'During the first two centuries A.D., with cross-cousin marriage already long in abeyance, father's sister's sons were designated as *wai* (outside), e.g., *wai hsiung ti*, and mother's brother's sons as *nei* (inside), e.g. *nei hsiung ti*.'[1] This asymmetry appears subsequently to the similar practice in the *Êrh ya*, which classifies the two types of cross-cousin under the term *shêng*, but is testified to by the *Yi Li*, the nomenclature of which nevertheless conforms to that of the *Êrh ya*. It has been seen that this nomenclature (and notably the extension of the term *shêng*) suggests marriage between bilateral cross-cousins. In this context it is impossible to understand the transitory asymmetry noted by Fêng. The father's sister's son and the mother's brother's son are external close relatives on the same grounds. Both are *piao* (equivalent of *wai*), neither can be *chung* (internal close relative, equivalent of *nei*). But if the texts appear contradictory only because they reflect two different systems, and if the second of these systems is of the type with marriage with the matrilateral cross-cousin, then the asymmetry is elucidated. If we assume a clan *A*, the mother's brother's son belongs to clan *B*, *the closest* in the one-way cycle of generalized exchange, while the father's sister's son belongs to clan *D*, or *n*, in any case to *the most distant* in the same cycle. As the asymmetry of cross-cousins, and the measurement of a cycle of exogamy by a fixed number of generations, are connected in several systems which in general are peripheral to China,[2] there is, we feel, a very strong possibility that such a system also existed in China in an archaic form. In the light of these considerations, we can now return to the question of marriage with the wife's elder brother's daughter.

We have said why this type of marriage must be the cornerstone of any attempt at reconstructing a primitive system. We have retained Granet's intuition that such a type can be correlated with marriage with the mother's brother's daughter. Finally, we have seen that this latter type of marriage exists nowadays in China, and that there are many indications suggesting that it had a very early date of appearance. What kinship system permitting marriage with the wife's brother's daughter (the theory of 'legalized incest' is only one interpretation, in terms of a later system) also gives the suggestion

---

[1] Fêng, 1937, p. 117; cf. also Granet, 1939, pp. 31–2.   [2] cf. ch. XXIII.

of another form of marriage, that with the mother's brother's daughter? It is a system which is well known elsewhere and can still be studied in detail since it still exists in certain regions of the world, notably in California. Typologically speaking, it is a Miwok system, named after the group in which it has been best described.[1] As the present work is not, and is not intended to be, a historical reconstruction or a geographical description, but a typological analysis, we shall perhaps be allowed to try to interpret the vestigial form by reference to the complete type.

[1] Kroeber himself has not hesitated to compare the Chinese system with the Californian systems, in stating that the primitive Chinese system seems to be of the Cocopa type. (Kroeber, 1933, pp. 155-7).

CHAPTER XXII

Oblique Marriage

I

The kinship system of the Miwok Indians, who inhabit the Sierra Nevada in California, has been studied in a number of publications by Gifford. His description of it in his *Miwok Moieties*[1] is today a classic. The system employs thirty-four terms, twenty-one of which merge individuals of different generations. Thus Gifford could legitimately write: 'One of the striking features of the Central Sierra Miwok terms of relationship is the disregard of generations.'[2] This fundamental feature must be correlated with the social organization, which is characterized by exogamous patrilineal moieties, called respectively 'water moiety' and 'land moiety'. It should also be correlated with the rules of marriage, which include the mother's brother's daughter and the wife's brother's daughter among a man's authorized spouses. According to Gifford, the peculiarities of the system, exogamy apart, are explained 'by the right of marriage to certain of the wife's relatives and descent in the male line'.[3] This is held to be especially the case with the psychological and terminological assimilation of brothers. While the mother and her sisters are distinguished by the terms *üta* meaning mother, *tomu* or *ami*, mother's older sister, and *anisü* meaning mother's younger sister, the father and his brother are classified under the single term *üpü*, which finds expression 'in the practice of a man marrying his brother's widow and thus becoming the father of his brother's children'.[4] The assimilation of the mother's younger sister and father's brother's wife under *anisü*, if the latter is younger than the mother, and the mother's older sister and the father's brother's wife under *tomu* (or *ami*, among the Big Creek), if the latter is older than the mother, is easily explained in terms of remarriage with the deceased wife's sister.

A more difficult problem is posed by the extension of the term *anisü*, which means mother's younger sister, mother's brother's daughter and father's brother's wife, if the latter is younger than the mother. *Anisü* and *tomu* have for reciprocals *añsi* and *tune*, which mean son and daughter. Moreover, the children of the cousin-*anisü* are called brothers and sisters, as is normally the case with children of other types of *anisü*. Gifford has repeatedly maintained

---

[1] Gifford, 1916, pp. 139–94.   [2] ibid. p. 170.   [3] ibid. p. 183.   [4] loc. cit.

the thesis that these extensions are explained by the marriage with the wife's brother's daughter. My mother's brother's daughter is my father's potential spouse, as are also my mother's sister, and my father's brother's wife. Gifford remarks: 'The reflection, in the term *anisü*, of this form of marriage: namely, of a man to his wife's brother's daughter is indicative of its antiquity.'[1]

Other extensions prompt the same conclusion. They are *wokli*, for wife's brother and sister, and for wife's brother's son and daughter; and the reciprocal of *wokli*, *kawu*, for the sister's husband, and the father's sister's husband. In fact, the one custom is reflected in the extension of twelve terms: *anisü, añsi, kaka, kawu, kole, lupuba, tatci, tete, tune, tcale, üpsa* and *wokli*. The whole cross-cousin terminology, which comprises six terms (i.e., two for the mother's brother's son and daughter, and four for the father's sister's son and daughter, these terms being specialized in terms of the speaker's sex), 'seems to be based entirely on this form of marriage'.[2]

The fact that the preferred type of marriage is between *añsi* and *anisü* implies that a man can marry his mother's brother's daughter, in certain cases at least, and several examples of this type of marriage have been collected by Gifford.[3] But in no circumstances can a man marry his cousin *lupuba*, i.e., his father's sister's daughter. According to Gifford, whatever the popularity of the first type of marriage, it is not expressed by any terminological extension. At the very most there is a prohibition on conversation between a man and his mother's brother's wife, which suggests her assimilation to the step-mother, who is always taboo in California. But, if the twelve terminological assimilations explicable by marriage with the wife's brother's daughter are contrasted with the complete absence of peculiarities in the nomenclature relating to marriage with matrilateral cross-cousin, the conclusion must be reached that 'the former is the more primitive of the two'.[4] What then is 'the key to the mystery of the one-sided Miwok cross-cousin marriage'?[5] It is that on occasion a man, in favour of his son, forgoes his wife's brother's daughter, who is also this son's matrilateral cousin. Marriage with the cross-cousin is thus held to be only a recent and secondary form, derived from another form of preferential marriage, based on membership of the same patrilineage. For this reason it would not yet have had time to be reflected in the terminology.[6] Gifford concludes: 'If Miwok cross-cousin marriage had arisen in any other way than the hypothetical way already outlined it is hard to imagine why it should be restricted to only one pair of cross-cousins. The very fact that it is so restricted strengthens the theory of origin primarily through the passing on of a privilege in the male line'.[7] Kroeber has accepted this interpretation: 'The Miwok men marry their mother's brother's daughters, but Mr. Gifford concludes very convincingly that the original form of marriage is that of a man to his wife's brother's daughter, because twelve Miwok terms are in accord with this type of

---

[1] Gifford, 1916, p. 186.   [2] ibid. p. 187.   [3] ibid. p. 189.   [4] ibid. p. 191.
[5] ibid. p. 193.   [6] loc. cit.   [7] loc. cit.

marriage and none with cross-cousin marriage.'[1] Kroeber, moreover, endeavours to explain marriage with the wife's brother's daughter as the result of moiety exogamy in a patrilineal system: marriage with the wife's daughter, practised in the neighbouring tribes (Costañoan and Yurok), becomes impossible, because the wife's daughter belongs to the same moiety as her stepfather. Failing the wife's sister, polygyny is possible only with the wife's brother's daughter, who becomes the closest substitutable relative.[2]

There is no need to say that this is Rivers through and through. Gifford admits as much when, having rejected Lowie's incomplete but methodologically sound interpretation of moiety exogamy,[3] he adds: 'Marriage custom and terminology among the Miwok would seem, therefore, to support Dr. Rivers's contention.'[4] The methodological bases of Rivers's interpretation will be criticized elsewhere.[5] In the present case, one further question arises, viz., if moiety exogamy, simultaneous and successive polygyny, and patrilineal descent all tend towards the marriage with the wife's brother's daughter, is it acceptable that they should have nothing to say about the original wife? By definition, marriage with the wife's brother's daughter is a secondary marriage, in that it presupposes a previous marriage. What explanation is to be given for the silence of the system as regards the original marriage, when it is so voluble as to the secondary marriage?

In the second place, Gifford regards preferential marriage with the mother's brother's daughter (matrilateral cross-cousin) as a mystery, the key to which must be sought. He himself, however, cautions against 'the futility of using English terms of relationship with natives when discussing native customs'.[6] Marriage with the unilateral cousin is strange only for groups which regard both types of cousin as identical. By contrast, we have seen that, far from being a mystery, marriage with the matrilateral cousin provides an explanatory principle, and that, wherever we encounter it, we can be assured that the kinship system under consideration functions according to the formula of generalized exchange. When this type of marriage is found in connexion with another type, there is the further task of discovering a structure in terms of which both types can be considered as equivalent.

With regard to descent, a system of patrilineal moieties, as Kroeber clearly saw, constitutes the necessary and sufficient condition for the assimilation of these two potential spouses. But such a system would also include the patrilateral cousin, and her brother's daughter. Yet these last two are eliminated by a formula of generalized exchange which, as well as or instead of moieties, as will be recalled, involves a system of harmonic groups (patrilineal and patrilocal, or the contrary), between which arises a one-way circulation of spouses. The only other thing to be interpreted is the neglect of the factor of generation. For this to be brought about, it is necessary and sufficient for these groups to form lineages instead of classes, and for the

---

[1] Kroeber, 1917, p. 357.   [2] ibid. 1925, p. 459.   [3] cf. ch. IX.
[4] Gifford, 1916, p. 188.   [5] cf. ch. XXVII.   [6] Gifford, 1916, p. 189.

notion of lineage to be strongly enough implanted as to take priority over the notion of generation. It can then be said that lineage *A* provides women to lineage *B*, which provides women to lineage *C*, etc., returning to lineage *A*. The one important point is that the possible spouse shall belong to the required lineage. The generation is secondary and is not taken into consideration unless because of age or for reasons of convenience. In such a system, the matrilateral cousin is a possible spouse, to the exclusion of the patrilateral cousin, and the wife's brother's daughter is also a possible spouse. Why only these? It is because the possible spouse in the generation above is the mother, who is normally prohibited, or her younger sisters, *anisü*, who are identified with the possible spouse by the terminology. But, as one of Gifford's female informants significantly says, among the women of the prescribed lineage there are some who are nevertheless 'too much like his mother'.[1] Theoretically, despite the age difference, one should be able to resort to the

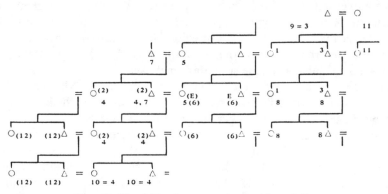

Fig. 67. The Miwok system (reduced model).

E : Masculine Ego
(E): Feminine Ego

The numbers without brackets indicate the assimilations made by E. The bracketed numbers indicate the assimilations made by (E).

grandmother (father's mother) and the wife's brother's son's daughter, as included in the class of potential spouses. The Miwok have decided not to do so, but the natives of Pentecost[2] have carried the logic of a similar system to this extent.

Let us therefore construct the reduced model of a patrilineal system with lineages, a system conforming to the formula of generalized exchange, and requiring only that a given lineage receive its wives from the lineage to its immediate right (Fig. 67). The lineage to male Ego's left is the lineage of his 'sons-in-law', and to female Ego's left, the lineage of her 'children',

[1] Gifford, 1916, p. 190.   [2] Swanton, 1916, pp. 455–65.

while the lineage to the right is the lineage of the 'fathers-in-law', and for both man or woman, the lineage of the 'mother'. In such a system, marriage with the mother's brother's daughter represents the simplest formula, but this does not imply that it is the most commonly used. From the lineage viewpoint the wife's brother's daughter represents an equally possible spouse, but this does not mean that she is married exclusively.

Be that as it may, these conditions account for all the features of the Miwok system, without appealing to particular causes which necessarily vary with each group and which reduce a harmonious whole to a pile of anomalies.

II

Let us summarize. From marriage with the matrilateral cross-cousin, to the exclusion of marriage with the patrilateral cousin, we can immediately infer a system of generalized exchange, one which thus involves more than two exchange groups. Consequently, among the Miwok, there is something more than moieties.[1] From the marriage with the wife's brother's daughter, the conclusion can be reached that the exchange groups are, like the moieties, based on father-right, and thus that here there is a harmonic regime, as is always the case with a simple system of generalized exchange. Finally, from the coexistence of the two types of marriage, it can be concluded that the exchange groups are lineages, i.e., structures oriented in terms of descent rather than in terms of generations. All these characteristics of the system can be deduced from the facts collected by Gifford in 1916. His discovery, published ten years later, of patrilineal and patrilocal lineages playing exactly the same rôle as could be attributed to them on a purely theoretical basis, must accordingly be hailed as a crucial experiment. Indeed, Gifford has found, among the Miwok, indisputable traces of the joint family or *nena*: 'The lineage name is always a place name . . . The lineage was a landowning group . . . Each *nena* is exogamous . . . Both lineages and moieties are patrilineal.'[2] And further: 'The lineage was anciently among the Miwok a political group, each lineage dwelling at its ancestral home, with the men of the lineage normally bringing their wives to the hamlet to live and the women of the hamlet normally marrying out of the hamlet.'[3] In a later article, Gifford eliminated all possible doubt as to the existence of the lineages.[4] At the same time, and perhaps without fully realizing it, he gave the *coup de grâce* to all the earlier attempts at interpretation.

Let us then examine the equations which, according to him, reflect marriage with the wife's brother's daughter and relate them to the schema in Fig. 67.

---

[1] That moiety exogamy does not play a determining rôle, in contrast to what Kroeber believed, clearly emerges from Gifford's statement that 'even among the Northern Sierra Miwok at Elk Grove, among whom the moiety system does not seem to exist, *añsi-anisü* marriages were the custom' (Gifford, 1916, p. 389).

[2] ibid. 1926, p. 389.   [3] ibid. p. 390.   [4] ibid. 1944, pp. 376–81.

1   Mother's brother's daughter   =   mother, stepmother, mother's sister
2   Father's sister's daughter or   =   son or daughter, stepson or step-
    son (feminine Ego)   daughter, sister's son or daughter
3   Mother's brother's son   =   mother's brother
4   Father's sister's daughter or   =   sister's daughter or son
    son (masculine Ego)
5   Father's sister   =   older sister
6   Brother's child (feminine   =   brother or sister
    Ego)
7   Father's sister's husband   =   sister's husband
8   Wife's brother's child   =   wife's brother or sister
9   Mother's brother   =   grandfather
10 Sister's child (masculine Ego)   =   grandchild
11 Mother's brother's wife   =   grandmother
12 Husband's sister's child   =   grandchild.

In his 1922 work,[1] Gifford, who still keeps wholly to his historic interpretations, treats equations 1 to 4 as the direct results, and equations 5 to 12 as the indirect results, of marriage with the wife's brother's daughter.[2] If one refers to the model of Fig. 67, which, however, is completely constructed, for reasons of simplicity, on the basis of mother's brother's daughter marriage (which we consider equivalent, as far as the system is concerned), it can be seen that: equations 1 and 3 identify men and women of my mother's lineage, as old as or older than Ego; equation 8, men and women of my mother's lineage, as old as or younger than Ego; equation 11, Ego's mother's brother's wife and grandmother (mother's mother) in so far as they are female members of the same lineage; equation 6, men and women of Ego's lineage, as old as or younger than Ego (feminine Ego); equation 7, men of 'sons-in-law' lineage, as old as or older than Ego; equation 4, men and women of 'sons-in-law' lineage as old as or younger than Ego (masculine Ego); equation 2, men and women of the lineage in which Ego finds her husband, and to which Ego (feminine) gives her children; equation 12 groups men and women of the one lineage (daughter's husband and children, feminine Ego); equation 5 groups the women of Ego's lineage (father's sisters and sisters, masculine Ego). Finally, equation 9 accords with 3, and equation 10 accords with 4. In every case, consequently, Gifford's equations are completely explained in terms of a cycle of patrilineages united according to the formula of generalized exchange.[3] At the very most the existence of a

---

[1] Gifford, 1922.   [2] ibid. pp. 248–50.

[3] A characteristic feature of the Miwok system is the extreme paucity of terms for grandparents. There are only three terms, viz., grandfather, grandmother and grandchild. (Kroeber, 1917, p. 356.) The reduced model would require more since the father's father belongs to my lineage; the mother's father and the father's mother, to my mother's lineage; and the mother's mother, to the wife's mother's lineage. The irregularities manifested in the grandparent's and the grandchildren's generations seem attributable to the intervention

differentiation can be noted within the lineage (as moreover, in the kinship nomenclature, within the principal generations) between older and younger members, normally in Ego's generation. We have discussed this problem earlier.[1] At this point we need only recall that this common differentiation is bound up, not so much with a certain type of marriage, as with the co-existence of two types of marriage which place two men, belonging to consecutive generations, in competition for the same woman (in the present case, the wife's brother's daughter, the father's potential spouse, is also the mother's brother's daughter, the son's potential spouse). The general solution, of which the Miwok merely afford a particular application, is then to distinguish the wife into an older sister (who is subject to the special claim of the generation immediately above) and a younger sister (who is subject to the claim of her own generation). Once again, we see that not one, but two, types of marriage are functionally connected with the system. In other words, Miwok social structure, characterized by patrilocal patrilineages, the two types of preferred marriage, and the terminological system of equations, form an indissoluble whole, and it is pointless to ascribe a special rôle to any particular aspect.

Let us adduce a further proof. From two female informants, one the daughter of the other, Gifford collected the list of the respective kinship relationships of ninety-one inhabitants of Big Creek, and of some other persons. In all, 122 persons were taken into account, and on this basis Gifford again established complex equations involving twenty-three terms. Anyone who has worked on kinship problems in the field knows how deceptive this procedure usually is, firstly, because native thought is interested more in the objective order of the system than in the subjective order of genealogies,[2] and secondly, because a system described by informants or deduced from questions is rarely reflected in concrete situations, and this leads to the appearance of lacunas and contradictions. To a certain extent there is always conflict between system and reality. Nevertheless, we have related the equations inferred by Gifford[3] to the reduced model of Fig. 67. Although it

---

[1] cf. ch. XIII.   [2] On this point, cf. Hocart, 1937, pp. 345–51.
[3] Gifford, 1916, pp. 174–81.

---

of moieties. In all systems characterized by lineages plus moieties, there are terms which, to borrow a striking expression from Deacon's informants on Ambrym, 'are not straight'. We shall return later to this phenomenon, which is certainly striking among the Miwok. Kroeber notes that a quarter, at least, of the kinship terms apply to persons belonging to either moiety, and from this he draws the conclusion that moieties are of recent introduction (Kroeber, 1925, p. 457). Gifford notes: 'In California, the evidence seems to indicate that there is no fundamental connexion between moieties on the one hand and bifurcation on the other. To be sure, all groups which have moieties bifurcate the uncle class, but many fail to bifurcate the grandparent class. Thus, in some tribes with moieties, paternal and maternal grandparents are called by a single term, although they are of opposite moieties.' (Gifford, 1922, p. 282.) Compare this with Kroeber: 'The distribution both of types of kinship systems and of special traits of kinship designations fails to agree with the distribution of these moieties.' (Kroeber, 1917, pp. 382–3.)

already constitutes a system in relation with a system, and although all marriages have been reduced to the simplest type (mother's brother's daughter), which Gifford asserts is without terminological correspondence, we find the following correlations (Fig. 68) (on the premise that there is a correlation when a term is applied to individuals of the same status, with respect to lineage and generation, or occupying the same position as a member, male or female, of the same lineage):

Kinship Term	Number of Relationships equated by Gifford	Number of correlations
ama	5	3
ami	5	3
anisü	5	5
añsi	4	4
apasti	2	2
atce	2	?
ene	2	2
haiyi	3	3
hewasu	2	2
kaka	5	5
kawu	4	3
kolina	3	3
kumatsa	1	–
manisa	1	–
oiyame	2	2
olo	5	4
papa	7	3
tatci	1	–
tete	3	3
tune	2	2
üpsa	2	2
üpü	2	2

Consequently, in thirteen cases there is a complete correlation between the equations and the system, and in four other cases the correlation is of the order 3/5, 3/4 and 4/5. Four cases remain (*atce, papa, kumatsa* and *manisa*) in which the correlation is doubtful, and, in the last two the reason for this is that only one meaning is given for each term. In these circumstances, cannot the terminological system be said to express, and equally well, marriage with the matrilateral cousin as much as marriage with the other possible spouse? Admittedly, the system of correlations which we end up with admits of uncertainties and contradictions. The contrary would be surprising, considering that the data were collected at a time when the social structure could no longer be regarded as intact. But if reference is made to the schema it will be seen that the doubtful cases are so grouped that it is possible to encircle the two symmetrical sectors in which they appear. These sectors correspond to the lineages and generations furthest from Ego, i.e., exactly the two zones in which a certain degree of confusion could legitimately

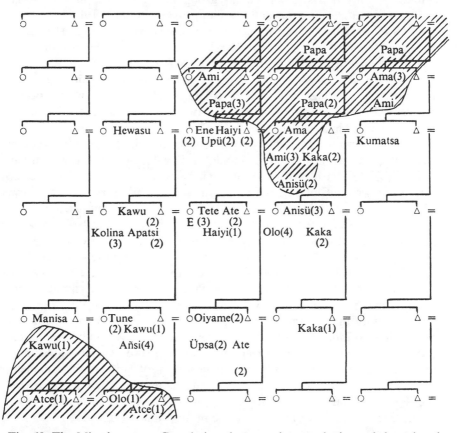

Fig. 68. The Miwok system. Correlations between the genealogies and the reduced model.

be expected. By contrast, in the immediate vicinity of Ego the correlations are rigorous. Clearly, therefore, the system must be understood and interpreted in terms of the total structure (and a structure like the one which we have first deduced and then experimentally verified).

III

It is not our intention to undertake a comparison between the archaic Chinese culture and Miwok society, nor even to use the kinship system of the Miwok in order to infer the system likely to have existed in the former. All the same, however, it must be noted that the Miwok type is not isolated or exceptional. It is in the middle of a wider group, the so-called Penutian group, which over and above the Miwok includes their neighbours, the Wintun, Maidu, Costañoan and Yokut. Lastly, the kinship system seems to have a functional connexion with the whole Penutian group culture, since, in California, 'culture centres and kinship centres are approximately identical.'[1]

Of all the systems the Miwok not only has preserved the greatest number of archaic features, but appears the least specialized,[2] although not the most typical.[3] Generally speaking, the kinship systems of the Penutian group seem to be characterized by the extreme poverty of the terminology[4] and asymmetrical marriage with the matrilateral cross-cousin, which occurs nowhere else in California.[5] These are two fairly remarkable similarities with what can be reconstructed of the Chinese system. However, it would be idle to attempt to press the comparison, or to seek to develop it in other directions, such as the existence, among the Yurok,[6] northern neighbours of the Miwok, of husbands/sons-in-law along with patrilocal marriage, so reminiscent of the Chinese situation.[7] Our sole intention has been to show, without preoccupation with historical or geographical comparisons, that there is a connexion between marriage with the mother's brother's daughter and marriage with the wife's brother's daughter; that, far from one being explainable in terms of the other, the two modalities appear as elements of a total structure, which can be restored; and that, whenever these two forms of marriage are found, or at the very least wherever their simultaneous presence can be inferred, the conclusion can thus be reached that there is a total structure of the same type, i.e., a collection of patrilineages, whether or not divided into moieties, and interconnected by a system of generalized exchange. We have directed our attention to the Miwok system, rather than to any other, only because its modernity permits verification of the argument. This system, the simplest formula of which was provided by the Gilyak and the Kachin, is clarified, in China, by certain of Granet's information, which seems literally to be borrowed from the more primitive groups:

'All the members, however distantly related, of families with the same surname, were called "younger or older" (= brothers); all members of families with different surnames were called "Fathers-in-law" or "Sons-in-law". They went further, and considered all the rules of what might be called "international public law" as the simple rules governing relations between affines (*hun, yin*).'[8]

Let us determine the implications of such a system with regard to marriages. It means a conjugal relationship, not between individuals, but between lineages, i.e., a given patrilineage treats the sisters of another patrilineage

[1] Gifford, 1922, p. 283. [2] ibid. pp. 228–9. [3] ibid. p. 207. [4] ibid. Kroeber, 1925.
[5] Gifford, 1922, p. 256.   [6] Kroeber and Waterman, 1934, pp. 1–15.
[7] Granet, 1939, pp. 142–3.   [8] ibid. p. 149; cf. also 1932, pp. 208–9.

as its actual or potential 'wives'. With regard to the Yuma, neighbours of the Miwok, Halpern also notes that the original social unit was the patrilocal patrilineage, in which wives figured under the title of 'foreigners': $u\cdot n^{y} \cdot i$.[1] As against a sequence of men, viz., father's father's father, father's father, father, son, son's son, etc., there is thus a sequence of women, viz., father's father's father's sister, father's father's sister, father's sister, son's sister, etc., from another lineage. The *connubium* is between the lineages considered as entities. In such a system there is an immediate confusion of generations: on the one side, 'sons-in-law', on the other, 'fathers-in-law'; on one side 'daughters-in-law', on the other, 'wives'. What must be explained, consequently, is not why generations are merged by the terminology, but why, to a certain extent, which varies according to the system, they are distinguished. The system, considered as such, confines itself to placing all the women of the fathers-in-law lineage in the same perspective. That a man of the sons-in-law lineage lays claim to *any* woman of the fathers-in-law lineage (class of grandmothers, stepmothers, cousins, or wife's nieces) or some *particular* woman, is the indication of a more or less rational system; that he lays claim to *only one woman*, or to *several*, is the indication of a more or less *reasonable* system; at this point, recourse must be had not only to the general kinship structure, but also to the whole social organization of the group considered. The more the individual claims to be completely representative of his lineage, i.e., in a feudal regime, the more ready will he be, on his own behalf, to put into effect the total claim which is actually for the benefit of the lineage. Granet, incomparable when it comes to the sociology of the feudal spirit, understood this admirably when interpreting 'oblique' marriages as a manifestation of the spirit of immoderation.[2] But even in a more primitive and reasonable (and doubtless also more rational) society, i.e., the Gilyak, in which a formally analogous total kinship structure apparently does not provide for marriage with the wife's brother's daughter (but only with the mother's brother's daughter), the wife's brother's daughter nevertheless receives the same term as the fiancée.[3]

Glimpses of the rivalries of patrilineages, wholly imbued with the feudal spirit, and furiously engaged in what Granet has so magnificently evoked in his *Danses et légendes*, i.e., struggles for prestige in which the cornering of women must have played no mean role, are to be seen in the most archaic phase of Chinese history, from the time of the Shang. We have elsewhere tried to evoke the social structure of the Shang from certain characteristics of their art,[4] and it is precisely this type of society which we were able to infer. The fact that, among the Shang, brother seems to have inherited from brother, clearly corresponds to a regime in which the solidarity of the lineage has not yet made room for the agnatic family, which was introduced by the Chou.

We are thus brought to the hypothesis of the coexistence, in ancient

---

[1] Halpern, 1942, p. 440.
[3] ch. XVIII.
[2] Granet, 1939, pp. 70–4, 130–3.
[4] Lévi-Strauss, 1945*b*.

China, of two kinship systems: the first, practised by the peasants, and based on a real or functional division into exogamous moieties, the exchange of sisters, and marriage between bilateral cross-cousins; the other, of feudal inspiration, and based on cycles of alliance between patrilineages (distributed or not into exogamous moieties), and marriage with the matrilateral cross-cousin and niece. That is, a system of restricted exchange and a system of generalized exchange. We have given the theoretical and practical reasons why these two systems must be of a simpler type than those postulated by Granet, and why it is impossible that the latter should have evolved, in the manner proposed by Granet, from the former. Consequently one must either admit their original heterogeneity, and acknowledge their coexistence in different regions or environments, or else contemplate the reverse sequence (which is the only one logically possible), with the restricted system being later than the generalized system, the latter then being the more archaic form. Before sketching a general picture of the features of Far Eastern kinship systems, we have yet to compare the Chinese facts more closely with those of neighbouring regions.

CHAPTER XXIII

Peripheral Systems

I

A comparative linguistic study of Tibetan and Chinese kinship systems had led Benedict to conclusions closely akin to ours, notably to the hypothesis that marriage with the matrilateral cross-cousin constitutes an essential archaic feature of this area. His analysis, which is guided by different considerations from those so far invoked by us, is so conclusive in its result that it seems absolutely necessary to reproduce its principal steps.

Like the Chinese nomenclature, the Tibetan employs basic and secondary terms. There are twenty-four basic terms, twelve masculine, nine feminine and three neuter, these latter used exclusively for relatives younger than Ego. This is also a characteristic of other Tibeto-Burman languages,[1] and is perhaps related to the absence of kinship terms for younger relatives which we have already noted in the Chinese systems.[2]

It is unnecessary to describe the system in detail, but one initial point should be mentioned. One finds *khu* for the father's brother, and *ne* for the mother's sister. These terms are derived from the Tibeto-Burman roots *$k'u$ and *ni – *nei, meaning 'mother's brother' and 'father's sister' respectively, which we have encountered in several systems in Assam and Burma, either with these meanings, or with the equivalent meaning of 'father-in-law' and 'mother-in-law'. Benedict explains the shifting of the root *$k'u$, from the mother's brother (who is also wife's father) to the father's brother, in terms of the peculiarly Tibetan existence of fraternal polyandry. Under this regime the father's brother is also mother's husband, and as a consequence he tends to occupy the predominant place, resulting from the combination of two statuses, which falls to the mother's brother under a regime of cross-cousin marriage.[3] This explanation is possible. It is not entirely satisfactory, but we would have to be better informed on Tibetan rules of marriage than we are if we were to start debating the point. However, some remarks are possible. In the past, fraternal polyandry was undoubtedly a very widespread institution in Central Asia, disappearing, in most groups, only in recent times. Briffault took delight in gathering together all the information on

[1] Benedict, 1941, p. 314.   [2] cf. p. 347, n. 3.   [3] Benedict, 1941, pp. 317–18.

this.[1] The Tibetan terminological transference ought to have parallels elsewhere, at least in vestigial form. By contrast, the Gilyak practise fraternal polyandry[2] without giving the father's brother a special place in the terminology. Actually, one other hypothesis would account better for this characteristic of the Tibetan terminology, viz., the transition from a matrilineal organization to the present patrilineal organization. In the first case, it is the maternal uncle, and in the second, the paternal uncle, who occupies the foremost position alongside the father in the family household, and the transference of the one term from the one to the other would thus be perfectly clear. In our opinion, this terminological evolution constitutes the strongest possible argument that might be produced in favour of the former existence of matrilineal descent in Tibet.

The new term introduced to designate the mother's brother, *shañ*, is used in combination with *tsha*, e.g., *shañ-tsha*, 'sister's son', and *tsha-shañ*, 'nephew and uncle on the mother's side'. This latter term appears in a historical work with the meaning of 'son-in-law and brother-in-law'. Here we find a familiar equation between sister's son and daughter's husband, suggestive of marriage with the matrilateral cross-cousin; and another equation which, as we have seen, is also a constant of the system, between mother's brother and wife's brother,[3] in no way requires to be interpreted in terms of teknonymy, as Benedict, following Fêng, seeks to do. This point has already been discussed.[4] Another aspect, typical of cross-cousin marriage, is the skeletal nature of the nomenclature of alliance.

Among the secondary terms, *skud* (*skud-po*, brother-in-law, father-in-law) is of particular interest. Benedict derives it from *khu*, mother's brother, whence *skud*, 'children of mother's brother in relation to him'. That is, a nephew who marries his mother's brother's daughter sees the latter's son (*skud*) become his wife's brother.[5] Not only is preferential marriage with the mother's brother's daughter found in Tibetan, but also the corresponding social structure made up of patrilineal exogamous lineages, as clearly emerges from Benedict's examination of the terms: *spun*, cousin; *-phu*, older brother; *tshan*, cousin; *-tsha*, nephew or niece, especially sister's child (man speaking), and grandchild. Benedict very convincingly establishes the equivalence of the Tibetan distinction between *phu-spun* and *tsha-tshan* and the opposition, already known to us, between the Kuki terms *pu*, 1, and *tu*, 2 (Fig. 69), i.e., the pair of opposites typical of systems of generalized exchange, and traced by us from the Kachin (*dama* and *mayu*) through the Chinese (*hun* and *yin*) to the Gilyak (*imgi* and *axmalk*).

It is necessary, however, to regard with considerable reserve Benedict's treatment of the Tibetan and Kuki systems as systems of the Omaha type. The Omaha type clearly poses quite different problems, as we shall show in another work. It will also be recalled that any effort to show that 'the ultimate

---

[1] Briffault, 1927, vol. I, p. 669 et seq.   [2] Sternberg, n.d., p. 107.
[3] Benedict, 1941, p. 322.   [4] cf. above p. 348 et seq.   [5] Benedict, 1941, pp. 323–4.

explanation of both the Tibetan and Kuki terminologies is to be sought in the practice of . . . teknonymy'[1] is useless and redundant, as we have established in the preceding chapters. The essential facts which hold good are: marriage with the matrilateral cross-cousin, the exogamous patrilineage (*rus-pa*) as the fundamental social unit, and the respect shown in the avuncular relationship by the honorific use (as among the Lakher and the Lushai) of the term for the maternal uncle.

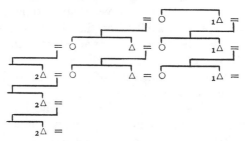

Fig. 69. Tibetan and Kuki systems.

Benedict found proof of these inferences in the text of an eighteenth-century Italian traveller, Desideri, who draws a primary distinction between the 'Rupá-cik' (*rus-pa cig*, literally 'one bone') and the 'Scia-cik' (*ça-cig*, literally 'one flesh'):

> 'The Thibettans recognize two classes of kinship. The first are called relations of the Rupa-cik, or of the same bone; the second, relations of the Scia-cik, or of the same blood. They recognize, as relations of Rupa-cik, or of the same bone, those who descend from a common ancestor, however remote, even when they have been divided into different branches during many generations. Relations of the Scia-cik, or the same blood, are those created by legitimate marriages. The first, though it may be exceedingly distant, is looked upon as an absolute and inviolable bar to matrimony . . . The second is also a bar to marriage in the first degree of relationship . . . but marriage (sic) with a first cousin on the mother's side is allowed, and frequently occurs.' [2]

This rule is confirmed, for the Bhotia, by the 1911 Census of India:

> 'It is not considered right that a man should marry his father's sister's daughter, but he may marry a cousin on his mother's side, mother's brother's daughter, or mother's sister's daughter. The reason given is that the bone descends from the father's side and the flesh from the mother's. Should cousins on the paternal side marry, it is said that the bone is pierced resulting in course of time in various infirmities.'[3]

To this, Benedict adds Gorer's evidence on the Lepcha, who believe that

---

[1] ibid. pp. 326–7.   [2] De Filippi, 1932, p. 192.   [3] O'Malley, n.d., V, p. 326.

the father's semen produces the bones and the brain, and the mother's vaginal secretions, the blood and the flesh. Benedict himself cites the Burmese *a ruì*, 'bone, lineage', and the Nyi Lolo *hngə-pu*, 'bone' *ve t'i hngə*, 'one family', literally 'family one bone', with the corresponding division of the Lolo of Western China into 'Black Bone' and 'White Bone'. If we consider that the 'theory of the bone and the flesh' is found from India to Siberia,[1] that it also exists in vestigial form, among the Mongols and the Turks of Russia,[2] that it is common in China,[3] and finally, that it appears in India from the time of the *Mahābhārata*,[4] we shall acknowledge that we are indebted to the old Italian traveller for the elucidation of an absolutely fundamental notion, the key to any attempt at reconstructing kinship systems in a geographical area of considerable dimensions, but in which widely dispersed survivals suggest an ancient homogeneity that, in these chapters, gradually re-forms before our eyes.

This is clearly the direction also taken by Benedict in comparing the Tibetan system with the archaic Chinese system which he reconstructs from the *Shih ching* (*c.* 800–600 B.C.). From his analysis, we will single out only the four terms with which we have already been long occupied: *ku* and *chih*, *chiu* and *shêng*, which he restores to the archaic forms, with the following connotations:

ko (*ku*)	father's sister, mother-in-law
t'iwət (*chih*)	brother's child (woman speaking)
g'i̯ôg (*chiu*)	mother's brother, father-in-law
seng (*shêng*)	sister's child (man speaking).

Not only do the terms *ko* and *g'i̯ôg* correspond functionally to the Tibeto-Burman roots **ku* and **ni–*nei*, but Benedict is able to establish the direct affinity of the archaic Chinese *g'i̯ôg* and the Tibeto-Burman **k'u*.[5] The archaic Chinese system and the Tibetan system are thus not only structurally similar but are linguistically connected.

Benedict's reconstruction gives only one term for cross-cousins, viz., *sĕng* (*shêng*), 'mother's brother's son, father's sister's son' (man speaking), which the *Êrh ya* also defines as 'sister's son'. It will be remembered that Fêng considers this to be a later interpretation, and the result of an interpolation.[6] Benedict takes his stand on Mencius (who gives *sĕng*, son-in-law) in showing that, on the contrary, *sĕng* is the basic term for 'sister's son' (man speaking) and 'son-in-law' in reciprocal relationship with *g'i̯ôg*, 'mother's brother, father-in-law'.

A similar pair of reciprocal terms is found in *ko* 'father's sister', and

[1] Shirokogoroff, 1935, p. 65.

[2] Hudson, 1938, pp. 18, 78, 84, 86; Vladimirtsov, 1948, p. 56 et seq.

[3] 'In the exogamic clans of China the very same terms are used as in Tibet to indicate the distinction between kinsmen "of the same flesh" – that is to say, belonging to the family of the wife – and "of the same bone", or of the same kinship class as the husband' (Briffault, 1927, vol. I, p. 672); cf. also Hsu, 1945, pp. 83–103.

[4] cf. ch. XXIV.　　[5] Benedict, 1941, p. 333.　　[6] Fêng, 1937, p. 171; Benedict, 1941, p. 336

t'iwət-d'iet, 'brother's child' (woman speaking). Benedict derives *shêng* from a verb *sĕng*, 'to bring into life, bear, produce', while the primary meaning of *t'iwət* is 'to go out', from which comes 'to produce, beget'.[1] Comparing these terms with the Gilyak *pandf*, comprising the *imgi* and *axmalk* in relationship to one another, which is a participial form of the middle voice of the verb *pan*, 'to be born', corresponding to the active *van* 'to beget, to produce',[2] there is indeed a temptation to go far beyond the sphere to which Benedict's conclusion is limited: 'We thus are presented, in general, with an exceptionally well-defined picture of an ancient cultural stratum, underlying both the Chinese and Tibeto-Burman cultures, in which cross-cousin marriage was a conspicuous feature.'[3] This should be understood, naturally, as marriage with the matrilateral cross-cousin, i.e., the system of generalized exchange.

Lolo terminology contains the same hybrid characteristics. Certainly, the most frequent type of marriage seems to be between cross-cousins, *o zie a sa*, which must be understood as bilateral cousins. This latter feature is confirmed by the terminology in various ways:

o pu	=	wife's father's father, mother's father
a ma	=	wife's father's mother, mother's mother, father's father's sister
sa mo	=	son's wife, sister's daughter, wife's brother's daughter.

There is, however, a distinction between two types of father-in-law:

o gni	=	mother's brother
i pi	=	father's sister's husband

and there are two types of mother-in-law:

a bər	=	father's sister
gni gni	=	mother's brother's wife.

This clearly shows that, if both types of cross-cousin can equally be chosen as spouse, they are not, as might be expected from the preceding equations, bilaterally identified.

In fact, the Lolo system has some features in common with the Kachin system, such as an exorbitant bride-price; the prolonged stay of the young wife with her family; the right of female lineages to succeed, and – as among the Naga – the pacificatory intervention of female lineages between allied and enemy clans; the succession of the youngest son to the real estate; and the levirate. At the other extreme of the area under consideration, the Lolo also show signs of Manchu organization, e.g., the hierarchization of relatives around the hearth, a typical feature also of the Kachin household;[4] the

---

[1] ibid. p. 337.   [2] Personal communication from R. Jakobson, cf. p. 298, n. 3.
[3] Benedict, 1941.   [4] Carrapiett, 1929, p. 12.

prohibition between older brother and younger brother's wife; and, last but not least, the division of collateral lines into older and younger, with the equations:

vi o = older brother, father's older brother's son
i i = younger brother, father's younger brother's son.[1]

When dealing with the Manchu, we shall establish the correlation between these many phenomena. At this point it will suffice to have given this further indication of the continuity of systems peripheral to the Chinese system.

II

Superficially, the Tungus kinship system contains no mystery. Sternberg and Shirokogoroff both report bilateral cross-cousin marriage, and the exchange of sisters between clans. Sternberg returns to these simple characteristics on several occasions[2] and Shirokogoroff confirms them. He says that up to the present the custom of exchanging women is one of the preferred methods for obtaining a wife. Among several other Tungus groups, it is practically the only way to get married.[3] Furthermore, marriage is said to be possible with the elder sister's daughter, and sexual relations are sanctioned with the father's younger brother's wife, which implies, as Sternberg says, 'marriage by exchange and sexual relations between consecutive generations',[4] clearly indicated by the equation: father's brother (*atki*) = elder brother. Consequently, all this suggests that we are faced with a simple system of restricted exchange. The facts must be examined much more closely for the discovery to be made that this apparent simplicity is a dangerous illusion.

From our viewpoint two Tungus groups are of particular importance. These are, on the one hand, the northern Tungus, who most likely occupied the whole of eastern China north of the Yangtse till the third millennium B.C., when they began to be driven back towards the north by the Chinese from western China,[5] and on the other, the Manchu, a group of Tungus origin, and intimately associated with Chinese life and institutions. Both have been studied by Shirokogoroff, but unfortunately in publications which are full of obscurities.

First let us consider the Northern Tungus, who are divided into exogamous and patrilineal clans: 'It is very often of common occurrence that two clans are bound by a systematic exchange of women, so that the mother's clan provides the women.'[6] Thus among the Birarčen the clans are paired: Maakagir exchanges its women with Malakul, Dunänkän with Mōkogir.

---

[1] Lin, 1945–7, pp. 89–93. The last structural feature – the distinction between the older and the younger branches of the same lineage – is also found among the Annamese with the distinction between *anh* and *em* (cf. Spencer, 1945).
[2] Sternberg, n.d., pp. 62–3; 1912, p. 327.   [3] Shirokogoroff, 1924, p. 69.
[4] Sternberg, n.d., pp. 55–6, 144.   [5] Shirokogoroff, 1923.   [6] ibid. 1929, p. 212.

The same situation is found among the Tungus of Transbaikalia, where the exchange pairings are Turujagir and Godigir, and Čilčagir and Kindigir.

Passing to the Kumarčen group, the situation is much less clear. Two old clans, Man'agir and Uilagir, may originally have stood in a relationship of restricted exchange, but later each of them is thought to have had to split, under the pressure of a growing population, giving rise to the two clans Učatkan and Govair which, although new clans, continued to be subject to the rule of exogamy: whence the following rules of marriage (Fig. 70):

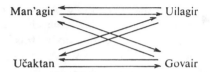

Fig. 70. Tungus marriage rules.

Man'agir	men marry	Govair and Uilagir women
Uilagir	men marry	Učatkan and Man'agir women
Učatkan	men marry	Govair and Uilagir women
Govair	men marry	Učatkan and Man'agir women.[1]

Man'agir and Učatkan on the one hand, Uilagir and Govair on the other, remain reciprocally prohibited, because of the former kinship which united them before the split. The question in these circumstances is the reason for the split. We shall find proof that when splitting occurs (as among the Naga), it is to allow intermarriage. For the moment we shall merely make a comparison with the Mao Naga, who are divided into four clans: Doe, Kopumai, Yena, Bekom, grouped into exogamous pairs. Doe and Kopumai on the one hand, Yena and Bekom on the other, cannot intermarry (Fig. 71).

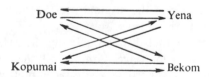

Fig. 71. Mao Naga marriage rules.

'The people themselves refer this to a common relationship.'[2]

Moreover, it is strange that the system described by Shirokogoroff should appear so clearly as a system of generalized exchange, or more exactly, that he – most probably following the theoretical explanations of his informants – should have described a system of restricted exchange in terms of generalized exchange. There could even be a system of generalized exchange of the Murngin type, if the continuous double cycle corresponded to a subdivision

[1] ibid. pp. 212–13.   [2] Hodson, 1923, p. 73.

of four clans into eight subsections, each cycle uniting four of these eight subsections. We hasten to emphasize that there is nothing in the available information to allow any such hypothesis, which if verified, would provide extraordinarily favourable evidence in support of Granet's theory. But the facts lead us in another direction. Shirokogoroff offers, namely, another version of the social history of the Kumarčen. The latter, he says in another passage from the same work, are divided into three old and three young clans. The first comprise the Man'agir, the Uilagir, and the Gagdadir, which he has not previously mentioned. The second group include the Učatkan, the Govair, and the Gurair which are also newcomers to us. As the Man'agir clan produced the Učatkan, and the Uilagir the Govair, the Gagdadir must have produced the Gurair. Shirokogoroff explains this in terms of the following tradition: 'There were two brothers Man'agir and Učatkan, of whom Učatkan was the junior. Therefore marriage is prohibited between the *man'agir* and the *učatkan*, and also between the *uilagir* and the *govair* . . . The clans *učatkan* and *govair* do not intermarry with the clans which have produced them, as their offshoots.'[1] The same situation repeats itself in the other groups.

This information is remarkable in several respects. Firstly, the singular resemblances to the social mythology of the Kachin will be noted,[2] viz., clans descended from brothers, the distinction between older and younger clans influencing the rules of marriage, and finally the asymmetrical number of the original social units, so suggestive of generalized exchange. Further, the Tungus tradition is by no means clear. If Man'agir and Učatkin are descended from two brothers, the second cannot be regarded as an offshoot of the first. The situation could be seen more easily as three clans descended from three older brothers, the three clans descended from the younger brothers being identified with the major clans, as Kachin mythology suggests, or simply as three clans descended from three brothers and later divided. In both cases, the asymmetry of the original social structure could only allow a system of generalized exchange.

The clearest indications that this was actually the case are to be found in the present regulation of marriage. Among all the Tungus groups, says Shirokogoroff, the marriage of cross-cousins has a preferential value. Among the Barguzin and the Nerchinsk, the *gusin* (mother's brother) can claim as wife his *juvda*, who is defined as a daughter of Ego's clanswomen, herself a member of the mother's and grandmother's clan. By contrast, marriage with the mother's brother is prohibited by the Tungus of Manchuria, just as is the marriage of a man with his mother's sister. But marriages with members of older or younger generations, if they are not directly related through the mother and the sister, are sanctioned, and even regarded as desirable. Marriage with the father's sister's children is permitted, as among the Manchu. However, the Tungus consider this type of marriage as being unprolific and

[1] Shirokogoroff, 1929, p. 131.   [2] ch. XV.

generally void of male descendants.[1] 'Father's sister's children' must obviously mean only the female patrilateral cousin, otherwise the two assertions that cross-cousin marriage has a preferential value and that matrilateral marriages are desirable 'if there is no direct relationship through the mother and the sister' (which entails that the choice falls upon the mother's brother's daughter and the mother's brother's son's daughter) would be meaningless. The majority of Tungus groups, by prohibiting a woman's marriage with the mother's brother, while sanctioning it with the mother's brother's daughter, attest to the survival of a system of generalized exchange even in the present situation where restricted exchange certainly predominates.

It is possible that the evolution of one type into the other was imposed by nomadism, since it is difficult for nomadic clans to conform to a system in which rules of residence count as much as rules of descent, and the harmonious functioning of which depends to such an extent on the spatial arrangement of the groups. Shirokogoroff believes that during their migrations the clans were obliged to travel in pairs, so as to respect the laws of exogamy, the veritable 'backbone of the Tungus social organization'.[2] It would obviously be much more difficult for them to travel in threes, or in greater numbers. Everything therefore suggests a regression from generalized exchange to restricted exchange.

III

An examination of the Manchu system leads us to the same conclusion. But here we have to cope with peculiar difficulties, which Shirokogoroff's minute study of this system does not always allow us to overcome. The Manchu system can indeed be regarded as the 'Chinese puzzle' in the theory of kinship systems. We are first faced with an often inextricable mixture of formulas of restricted and generalized exchange; secondly, perhaps, with a transition from matrilineal descent to patrilineal descent; and finally, with the reshaping of all the factors of the primitive system under the influence of the Chinese system, the broad classificatory principles of which have been superimposed on the ancient forms. The result is a virtually unlimited number of kinship terms, formed for the most part by the combination and recombination of simpler terms, so that in most cases it is impossible to discern the terms, or the roots, which make up the elementary nomenclature without the linguist's help – which would be most welcome here.

As the starting-point for our venture into this labyrinth, we shall choose one aspect, which itself is obscure, of the Chinese system. The *Shu Ching* classifies kinship terms according to the *chiu t'zŭ*, 'the nine grades of kindred'. What is meant by these nine grades has been the subject of debate among

[1] Shirokogoroff, 1929, p. 213.
[2] ibid. p. 210; cf., in ch. XXVII, the analogous hypothesis formulated by McConnel to account for a similar development among the aborigines of Cape York peninsula.

classical commentators. The old school wishes to reserve the terms included in the nine grades for clan relatives, i.e., nine generations, four above, and four below Ego's. By contrast, the new school sees the nine grades as embodying four groups of paternal relatives (the father, his ascendants, descendants and male collaterals; the father's sisters and their descendants; Ego's sisters and their descendants: Ego's daughters and their descendants), three groups of maternal relatives (mother's father and mother; mother's brothers; mother's sisters), and two groups of wife's relatives (wife's father; wife's mother).[1]

It is notable that, according to the viewpoint adopted, the classification of relatives in the Manchu system tallies almost exactly with both interpretations. Shirokogoroff explains that the clan, or *mokun*, is divided into classes (*dalan*), and if one wants to know the exact position of a person in the *mokun*, one immediately asks: 'Which is your class?'[2] These classes can number as many as seven, i.e., three generations above, and three generations below Ego's generation, and they group clan relatives as non-clan relatives, in accordance with the subdivision of the class into *ahuta dalen* (people of my clan), and *mini dalen* (people of my clan and of other clans).

This division of the family group into seven horizontal grades corresponding to generations has its counterpart, at least theoretically, in a division into seven vertical columns, representing the descendants of Ego's parent's brothers and sisters, of Ego's brothers and sisters, and of Ego. It is not exactly a question of lineages, for we shall have occasion to show that the terms expressing this division travel, as it were, from lineage to lineage, and can only define what we would rather call a 'linear series'. Thus we have two groups of terms, one group indicating generation, the other linear series.[3]

This system, which at first sight seems obscure, is clarified when compared with the social organization of the Western Turco-Mongols, who seem to have been better described. The Kazak, namely, possess a double organization, into vertical lineages and (horizontal) generation classes, which is very similar to the Manchu system. The legendary founder of the Great Order likewise had two sons, Taraq and Abaq, each the founder of an *uru* bearing his name, and grouping all his patrilineal descendants. At the same time, says Hudson, these two *uru* form a first genealogical stratum, *A*.[4] The process is repeated in the following generation, each of Abaq's four sons in turn founding an *uru* composing a lineage, the four together forming a second genealogical stratum, *B*. In the succeeding generation we find thirty-two *uru* forming a genealogical stratum, *C*, and so on.

The important point is that the *uru* of the higher strata do not disappear in producing the *uru* of the lower strata, but continue to exist as autonomous

[1] Fêng, 1937, pp. 204–5.   [2] Shirokogoroff, 1924, p. 44.

[3] For this whole discussion, and the diagrammatic representation of the Manchu system, the reader is referred to the first part of this work (ch. XIII), in which we draw a parallel between the Manchu and the Dieri systems.

[4] Hudson, 1938, p. 20.

units. Genealogically, an *uru* of *C* stratum, for example, is formed from the descendants of an *uru* of *B* stratum, which itself results from the subdivision of an *uru* of *A* stratum. Consequently, it might be supposed that the *A uru* no longer exist in the following stratum, except in the form of the *B uru* which are derived from them, and so on. This is not so: the 'parent *uru*' survive indefinitely alongside the 'offspring *uru*'.

Each *uru* is thus defined both as an autonomous lineage, and as the emanation of a certain generation class. That this is almost exactly equivalent to the Manchu *dalan* emerges clearly from Hudson's observation, which parallels the one just quoted from Shirokogoroff: 'When meeting anyone the first question was always 'What is your *uru*?' and in reply one gave the name of the last and smallest subdivision which one thought would be familiar to the questioner.'[1] Some studies list no fewer than 760 linear groups, intersected by seventeen generation classes.

The generation indicators in the Manchu system are:

tajeje	father's father's father
jeje	father's father
amata	father
ahuta, ejute	my brothers, my sisters
duj	son
omolo	grandson
tomolo	son's son's son.

The linear series indicators are:

eskundi	descendants of the father's brothers
nahundi	descendants of the mother's brothers
tehemdi	descendants of the mother's sisters
dalhidi	my brothers' descendants
inadi	my sisters' descendants
enendi	my descendants.

These six terms are interesting in several respects, firstly because there are only six of them, when seven would normally be expected: the corresponding term for the father's sister's descendants is missing. Later we shall see that it really does exist (*tarsidi*), although it has almost disappeared, hence its non-appearance in the terminology. This difference in the treatment accorded the father's sister's children and her grandchildren is in itself revealing. Secondly, the classification of relatives into seven linear series is very like the *chiu t'zŭ* according to the second interpretation given of it. Among the Manchu, we find the four groups corresponding to the paternal relatives in the *chiu t'zŭ*, and two of the three maternal groups. In addition, the Manchu system sets up a special series for Ego's brothers (who are

[1] ibid. p. 22.

regarded as descendants of the father by the Chinese). This subdivision is necessitated by the fact that the direct lineage starts from Ego in the Manchu system, instead of including the father and his ascendants as in the *chiu t'zǔ*. On the other hand, the Manchu classification does not allow for the wife's relatives, this being explained by the practice of cross-cousin marriage. It should be noted, however, that the Manchu nomenclature for affines introduces specific terms, at least as regards the husband's family (but not the wife's family, in which the usual kinship terms predominate): *ejgen*, husband; *purhu*, husband's sister; *eše*, husband's brother; *aša*, *uhun*, husband's brother's wife.[1]

Over and above these two groups of linear and generation indicators, we find a third group, corresponding, it seems, to the Chinese determinants:

haha	male (*hahadi*, my sons)
sargan	female (*sargan*, my wife, *sargandi*, my daughters)
ahu, amba	elder
to, fiango	younger
koro	distant.

A fourth group of simple or composite terms play the part of elementary terms. Some are direct borrowings from the Chinese nomenclature of reference or address:

mafa	grandfather
mama	grandmother
ama	father
ena, eme	mother
ečke	father's brother
ku	father's sister:
ku-nejne,	father's mother
kugu,	father's sister
kui,	father's sister's husband
ku-mafa,	father's father's sister's husband
nakču	mother's brother:
nakučihe,	mother's brother's wife
tehe	father's mother's sister
teheme,	mother's sister
wu	wife
wuheme,	father's brother's wife
wuhehe,	younger brother's wife
wurun,	son's wife, son's son's wife
gehe	elder sister
non	younger sister
ongosi	son, heir

[1] Shirokogoroff, 1924, tables IV and X, pp. 38, 43.

hodolion	daughter's husband
efu	elder sister's husband
meja	younger sister's husband.

The more distant degrees are expressed descriptively by the combination of two or more terms from these four categories. In this respect, the Manchu system is not exactly the same as the Chinese system, in which, except for certain cases, the elementary term provides a stable core to which the determinants are either prefixed or suffixed.

The four types of terms are combined freely, and the last group of terms can just as well be employed as determinants as can those of the other groups. In this way, there are, for example: *dalhi gehe*, father's brother's daughter (older than Ego), or father's father's brother's son's daughter; *dalhi omolo sargandi*, brother's son's daughter; *fiango nejne*, mother's mother's younger sister; *koro omolo hodolion*, son's daughter's husband; *nahundi omolo duj*, mother's brother's son's son's son; *nahundi eskundi ejun*, mother's mother's brother's son's daughter; *tehemdi ina wurun*, mother's mother's sister's son's son's son's wife, etc.[1]

Many of these terms are of Chinese origin, e.g., *jeje, nejne, ku, efu, meja*. Shirokogoroff notes that most of the purely Manchu terms are found in the maternal clan. The simple terms are seen to provide the rough outline of a structure of generalized exchange (Fig. 72).

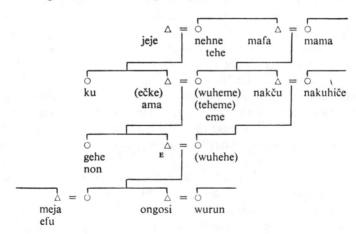

Fig. 72. Aspect of the Manchu system.

Particularly remarkable are the combinations of indicators of linear series. In principle, as we have said, these terms designate members of the one lineage. Their prototype is the term *dalhidi*, formed of the suffix *di* (abbreviation of *duj*, son) and the root *dala, dalan*, meaning the 'link', the

---

[1] ibid. tables I to X.

'knee'[1] and also indicating a certain subdivision of the clan. Shirokogoroff has very clearly reconstructed the development of Manchu society. Originally, there were a certain number of localized, exogamous units, the *hala*. Hand in hand with territorial expansion these *hala* subdivided into new exogamous units, the *gargan*, known by the names of various colours. In turn, the *gargan* gave rise to the *mokun*, which have no proper name and are the present exogamous units: 'The general prohibition is *to marry within the mokun*. If in some given place there are no girls to be married and a clan is very numerous, the Manchus . . . practise the division of the clan into two new exogamic units (*mokun*). Then the marriage between the members of these units becomes possible.'[2] We have seen that the *mokun*, and the allied *mokun*, are in turn divided into classes (*dalan*), each corresponding to a generation. However, the etymology of the term *dalhidi* shows that the class is more than just a class, being also the stage at which a lineage breaks away from the main trunk.

This being granted, we may expect to gather valuable information on the pairing of linear terms since the lineages are always seen to be distinguished and identified, separated and reunited, in terms of the marriage rules. It is significant that the term *dalhidi*, son, grandson, etc., of Ego's class (as Shirokogoroff has clearly seen) is also used for sons-in-law and daughters-in-law.[3] The following combinations are also found: *nahundi eskundi*; *nahundi eskundi dalhidi*; *nahundi dalhidi*; *tehemdi ina*; *dalhi eskundi*.

Let us consider, for example, the *nahundi*. Generally these are the mother's brother's descendants, but we also find them in the patrilineage of the father's mother: *nahundi ečke*, father's mother's brother's son, *nahundi eskundi*, father's mother's brother's son's son, *nahundi eskundi dalhidi*, father's mother's brother's son's son's son, etc. This assumes that the father himself has married a *nahundi*, in which case alone do the two series coincide. Indeed, the mother must be the father's mother's brother's daughter for the mother's lineage and the father's mother's lineage to overlap. A similar argument can be made in the other cases: *tehemdi* (mother's sisters' lineage), *inadi* (sister's lineage), etc.

We have called attention to the absence of a linear series indicator for the father's sister's descendants. There exists, however, a term *tarsi*, which, says Shirokogoroff, is very rarely used,[4] and refers to the relationship of an individual to the descendants of the women of the older class of the father's clan, and to the descendants of the men of the mother's class and clan. But it is doubtful whether this symmetry is primitive, given the existence of a very rare form of marriage, designated by the verb *tarsi-lambi*, an expression which Shirokogoroff says can be translated as 'I am marrying my *tarsi*, i.e., my father's sister's daughter.'[5] There is a strong prejudice against this type of marriage, but foremost among preferred spouses we find *nahundi ejun*

---

[1] Shirokogoroff, 1924, pp. 46–7   [2] ibid. p. 65.   [3] ibid. p. 47, n. 2.
[4] ibid. p. 70, n. 1.   [5] ibid. p. 70.

(matrilateral cross-cousins).[1] It is possible, as Shirokogoroff would have it, that the Manchu passed from matrilineal descent to patrilineal descent,[2] but it is useless to appeal to this hypothesis in order to explain the asymmetry, so strikingly attested to, between the two cross-cousins. What we find is simply the formula of generalized exchange, latent in a system which today has all the appearances of restricted exchange.

But these appearances should not deceive. Shirokogoroff can indeed write: 'The exchange of women is the most favourite form of marriage . . . A clan gives a woman to another clan and this one gives also in exchange a woman to the first clan . . . A man of the clan A marries a woman of the clan B and the clan A gives as wife the sister of this man to the woman's brother of the clan B.'[3] It must be added that the Manchu do not care for marriages between clans which are already allied, because such marriages do not help to increase alliances. Consequently there is a very clear tendency to maintain the wide cycles of generalized exchange.[4] Moreover, the Gold kinship terms which Lattimore collected[5] coincide with the Manchu terms collected by Shirokogoroff. This indicates that the Manchu system must be much more closely akin to the Gold system (the Gold are Tungus), i.e., to generalized exchange, than emerges from the Russian sociologist's commentary.

The Koryak also seek to expand to the full the alliances between families united by marriage by prohibiting the brothers of a given family from marrying the sisters of another family. The end desired is the multiplication of ties. When these facts are considered, there seems to be little reason to share Jochelson's scepticism as regards former Koryak practices. At the present time the Koryak have a matrimonial prohibition extending to second cousins. Jochelson is surprised by this divergence from Kamchadale practices, which include marriage between cousins (Krasheninnikov), marriage with a mother and her daughter (Steller), and sororal polygyny (Steller), customs which are proscribed by the Koryak. Krasheninnikov clearly says that the Reindeer Koryak marry their cousins, aunts and stepmothers, but Jochelson doubts that as marked a change as that attested to by the modern prohibitions could have occurred in the space of 150 years. He recognizes, however, that the myths allude to these now prohibited forms of marriage.

The myths certainly refer to a practice in which women, perhaps sisters, exchange husbands. This feature should also put us on the alert, because of its southern Asiatic equivalent, viz., that among the Lakher two sisters married at the same time can exchange husbands.[6] The same custom is found

---

[1] ibid. pp. 67–8.　　　　[2] ibid. pp. 48–9, 70, n. 1.　　　　[3] ibid. p. 71.

[4] Shirokogoroff mentions a prohibition which he obscurely calls 'facultative' relating to the marriage with a clan already linked to that of the suitor 'by some relationship of clans or religious connexion or some degree of relationship within the mother's clan' (ibid. p. 65). It can be wondered if there is not here a prohibition of the Gilyak type, or *tuyma axmalk*. If this is so, the generalized exchange characteristic of the Manchu system would be strengthened by it.

[5] Lattimore, 1933.　　　　　　　　　　　　　　　[6] Parry, 1932, p. 311.

in neighbouring groups. The myths also assume the practice of marriage between cousins.[1] An old Koryak man justifies his marriage with a certain village, because 'the union between my family and my children's mother's family must not be interrupted.'[2] All this suggests a former system of generalized exchange.

That the Manchu system is still in a state of fluctuation between two marriage formulas is also suggested by the splitting of the generations in Ego's class and his parents' class into older and younger. It will be remembered how we interpreted this phenomenon.[3] But in the case of the Manchu, we have better than a hypothesis. The Manchu house comprises several rooms. On the southern and northern sides of each of these rooms are two heated platforms on which the members of the family sleep in prescribed places. Members of the same class must be placed in alternate order, according to the formula (0, Ego's class; −1, −2, younger classes; +1, +2, older classes, etc.):

> First room: platform on the northern side: +1; −1; +1; 0; −1;
> First room: platform on the southern side: 0; −1; −1; 0;
> Second room: platform on the southern side: 0; −1; +1 and 2.

Shirokogoroff has shown that this special arrangement is related to sexual prohibitions and privileges. The wives of the younger members of Ego's class are prohibited, while he can joke with the real or potential wives of the older members of the class, and even have premarital sexual relations with them. Speaking more generally: 'All women of the senior class and all women of my own class, who are the wives of the men older than I, I do not call by their personal proper names and I have sexual rights with them but . . . all wives of the men who are younger than me . . . are strictly prohibited to me.'[4] In other words, as among the Naga, two marriage formulas are available, and one part of the women in my generation follows the same path as my wife, while the other follows a different path. Also as among the Naga, this alternative entails a distinction between father and father's brother, mother and mother's sister, relatives who, indeed, can found different lineages. Of course, the mother's brother is also the protector of his nephews and nieces, who love him dearly and sing him the song:

> *Nakču nakču* love (me)
> seven small bread fried
> (If) seven small bread I eat
> *nahan* (will be) full befouled.[5]

One can see all the analogies between this system and, for example, that of the Ao Naga. In both cases there is a proliferation into pairs of exogamous

---

[1] Jochelson, 1908, pp. 150, 156, 160, 225, 294, 297, 736, 737, 738, 750.   [2] ibid. p. 750.
[3] cf. chs. XIII and XVII.   [4] Shirokogoroff, 1924, pp. 100–1.
[5] Because of the resultant indigestion (ibid. p. 145).

units;[1] in both cases, an apparent restricted exchange conceals latent tendencies towards generalized exchange; in both cases, while both cross-cousins are nominally equivalent, one is avoided and the other preferred; the kinship systems exhibit the same complexity, owing to the fact that since the marriages of two brothers or of two sisters do not necessarily conform to the same type brothers or sisters should be distinguished, at the parents' level and at Ego's level, because of the different lineages to which they, or their descendants, can belong. In both systems, finally, the most stable terminological series is constructed on the model of matrilateral marriage (Fig. 73).

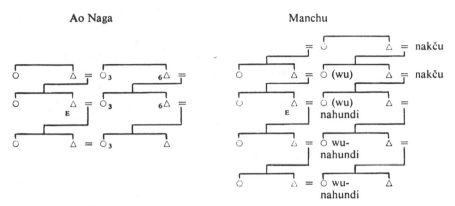

Fig. 73. Comparison between the Manchu and Ao Naga systems.

This aspect of the social organization of the Naga is remarkably akin to that found among the Olcha of the Amur River, who are divided into two moieties, each subdivided into six clans. Zolatarev writes on this subject: 'These data revealed the connexion of the *ngarka* custom not only with dual organization but also with a system of closed marriages requiring three clans, which makes the problem very complicated. It seems to me that formerly the Gilyak also had a dual organization, which was forced out by the intro-duction of the three clan system.'[2] The *ngarka* custom, or rivalry in eating, derives from the Gilyak *ngarka pud,.* 'the entertainment of the sons-in-law'. We believe we have gathered enough proof that the system of generalized exchange is the primary form without discussing Zolotarev's opinion to the contrary. But this remarkable recurrence of a juxtaposition of dual and tripartite organizations, already encountered among the Naga, must be remembered. The distinction made by the Chukchee between the paternal lineage, 'those who come from the penis' and the maternal lineage, 'those who

[1] Some clans are still linked by the memory of a common origin, and are called *kapči*, 'double twin'. The men alone use the term. Among the Tungus, in which the process of the formation of new clans is far from finished, nearly all the clans have their *kapči* (Shirokogoroff, 1924, pp. 66–7).

[2] Zolotarev, 1937, p. 129.

come from the womb',[1] seems to be a transposition of the classification, with which we are now familiar, between the 'side of the bone' and the 'side of the flesh'. The assimilation of the fourth degree in the ascending or descending order of generations, and the common designation 'bond' or 'joining'[2] in the collateral line, moreover, call to mind the fundamental structure of the Chinese system. Marriage between cousins is frequent, as among the Aleutians in the past, who, Veniaminov indicates, preferred the uncle's daughter as wife.[3] However far gone its decomposition, the Aleutian kinship system preserves a distinction between 'cross' and 'parallel'. The existence of only one term for cross-cousins, *asagax*, suggests that the terms of alliance were used by preference.[4] Inheritance of the mother's brother's wife, and possible relations with her during her husband's lifetime, indicate matrilineal descent. Krasheninnikov[5] confirms the custom of matrilateral marriage among the Kamchadale, and it has also been confirmed for the Ainu.[6] However, the fact that marriage between two brothers and two sisters is prohibited among the Ainu,[7] as among the Koryak, suggests that generalized exchange, if it ever did exist, has been reduced to a vestige in all these groups. The kinship systems preserve no trace of it, and belong among highly impoverished types, the study of which cannot be undertaken here. In fact, we know that (restricted) exchange of women is at present practised by the Chukchee.[8]

Despite these necessary reservations, an outline of the overall structure of the Asiatic picture emerges. In the extreme North and South, the Gilyak and Kachin systems mirror each other as two simple forms of generalized exchange. The parallelism is repeated between the Naga and the Tungus-Manchu systems, which, for their part, reveal the same mixture of restricted and generalized exchange. Actually, the Manchu system seems to be an Ao Naga system as revised and corrected by Confucian China. In the middle, finally, we have the Chinese system, the ancient features of which are suggestive of restricted exchange, barely masking indisputable vestiges of generalized exchange (Fig. 74). If this distribution is interpreted in diffusionist terms, it clearly suggests that, from eastern Siberia to Burma, generalized exchange was the most archaic form, and that restricted exchange, appearing subsequently, has not yet reached the peripheral areas.

IV

However, a diffusionist conception of the distribution of kinship systems in Asia is condemned to failure from the very start. Prehistoric Chinese culture may have been first represented in North China. Culturally, however, the Chinese are southerners.[9] If Shang civilization really did develop in north-

---

[1] Bogoras, 1904–9, p. 537.
[2] ibid. p. 539.
[3] Veniaminov, vol. III, p. 76.
[4] Jochelson, 1933, pp. 69–71.
[5] Krasheninnikov, 1819, vol. II, p. 124.
[6] Batchelor, 1901, p. 228.
[7] ibid. p. 229.   [8] Bogoras, 1904–9, p. 578.
[9] Maspero, 1927, pp. 19–21.

eastern China, it is in the proximity of its ancient area of expansion that we today find the system which seems best to have preserved certain characteristics attested to by the first chroniclers. Following these chroniclers, we have indicated that the Shang rule of exogamy ceased after the fifth generation. It is still the same today among the Manchu: when necessary, the exogamous clan is subdivided into two *mokun*, which become the new exogamous units. 'To create such a division it is quite enough to fix two groups of clan members, who have two different ancestors in the fifth senior class, and form of them two exogamic groups (*mokun*), with separate spirits, rites and shamans. However, the division of the clan must be authorized by the clan meeting after very long discussion.'[1] A similar system is found among the Yakut, who

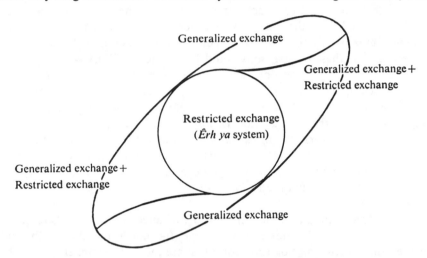

Fig. 74. Distribution of elementary forms of exchange in the Far East.

are organized into clans (*aga-usa*), which are subdivided into *nasleg* and *ulu* and with the rule of clan exogamy suspended after the ninth generation.[2] The same formula is found among the Kazak, who are divided into *uru*, patrilineal groups, and *aul*, patrilocal groups, with the limit of the exogamy of the *uru* being fixed at the seventh generation.[3] Finally, the Buriat had a similar rule, with a limit of nine generations in the male line, giving us to believe that matrilateral marriages were possible.[4]

The modern Manchu rule seems to illustrate customs the survival of which in archaic China is attested to by the chroniclers. Thus, one is led to imagine the Chinese kinship system, at the beginning of the historical period, as at a stage very similar to that still predominating among the Naga and the Manchu, viz., generalized exchange having already largely given way to restricted exchange, but still subsisting in preferential forms of marriage. Restricted

[1] Shirokogoroff, 1924, pp. 65–6.   [2] Czaplicka, 1914, pp. 55–6; Hudson, 1938, p. 98.
[3] ibid. p. 43.   [4] ibid. pp. 99–100.

exchange would have begun to cause the division of the clans and lineages into exchange organizations, the recentness of the process and its emergent character being attested to by the five-generations rule.

Let us not forget that among the Gilyak, who are still subject to generalized exchange, we have met a similar rule relating to two generations, the existence of which is explained by the desire to introduce a certain free play or flexibility into marriage exchanges. The Manchu have been seen to evince the same desire.

It would be interesting to discover whether the hypothesis of a Chinese kinship system of Manchu-Naga type round about the Shang period might be confirmed in other fields. Like the Naga, archaic China allowed new 'houses' to be formed by the detachment, in each generation, of a son who went and founded another lineage with a new name.[1] It is also possible that archaic China was familiar with the 'men's house' which is so typical of the Naga area.[2] If these comparisons could be extended, China would have to admit of the following development: a proto-archaic system, similar to the Kuki, Kachin, Tibetan and Gilyak systems, i.e., based on generalized exchange; next, a development of the type exemplified by the southern Naga, the Olcha, the Tungus and the northern Manchu, with more or less strong traces of generalized exchange, attested to by certain marriage preferences, or the survival of tripartite organizations, a state roughly corresponding to the days following the Shang period; then, finally, the system of the *Êrh Ya* and the *I Li* in which restricted exchange seems to have finally triumphed.

Are we forced to grant that generalized exchange arose somewhere in the centre of eastern Asia and spread towards the north and the south, and further that there was not time for its subsequent development from the central zone to reach the peripheral regions? In our opinion, three reasons militate against such an interpretation. We shall pass rapidly over the first, which rests on theoretical considerations, viz., that a functional system, e.g., a kinship system, can never be interpreted in an integral fashion by diffusionist hypotheses. The system is bound up with the total structure of the society employing it, and consequently its nature depends more on the intrinsic characteristics of such a society than on cultural contacts and migrations. To speak of diffusion in connexion with facts of this type is tantamount to saying that the whole society had diffused, which would only amount to shifting the problem.

More particularly, in the case now before us, the diffusionist interpretation can only be an artificial one. It does not account for two essential facts. Generalized exchange in a simple form (marriage with the mother's brother's daughter) exists even today in many regions of China, as a live institution, too important to be spoken of as a vestige. Conversely, even in the simplest

---

[1] Maspero, 1927, p. 123; Granet, 1926, pp. 14, 174.
[2] Maspero, 1927, pp. 130–2; Granet, 1926, pp. 52, 291, 333.

forms of generalized exchange (e.g., Kachin, Kuki, Gilyak systems) we have encountered certain features which have recurred too regularly to be explained as anomalies or vestiges. We have perceived in these features (the rôle of the bride's maternal uncle, and sometimes the rôle of the bridegroom's paternal aunt), which have been regarded by all the writers concerned, from Sternberg to Mills, as survivals of matrilineal descent, the sign of the existence within generalized exchange of embryonic but persistent notions connected with a reality of another order.

Consequently, an historico-geographical interpretation would be much too simplistic. Of all the systems considered, the Chinese is undoubtedly the most highly developed, but it is so just as Chinese society is itself the most highly developed society in the eastern part of Asia. And yet the Chinese system has preserved, in a very pure form, the formula of generalized exchange which strictly speaking it has thus never transcended. Likewise, it cannot be said that the Kuki, the Kachin, or the Gilyak systems have not yet been reached by the wave of restricted exchange, for they contain the germ of restricted exchange, and this germ must develop spontaneously, independent of all outside influence. The three types of kinship system that we have encountered – the Kachin-Gilyak type with generalized exchange; the Manchu-Naga type with a mixture of generalized and restricted exchange; and the Chinese type of the *Érh Ya* with restricted exchange – seem, therefore, to be three modalities of a single structure, rather than three stages of a single cultural migration. In the form which we regard as the simplest we find all the characteristics which will only subsequently be developed.

A question of considerable theoretical interest is then posed. So far we have regarded restricted exchange and generalized exchange as specific types, representative of heterogeneous forms of marriage and kinship systems. The analysis of the Murngin system, and the formidable complexity encountered by a culture in its specific attempt to make the formulas of restricted and generalized exchange coincide, could only confirm us in this conception.

We now come to a different finding. It became clear to us that restricted exchange could succeed generalized exchange, or at the very least coexist with it, as the result of an autonomous development. Moreover, we have spoken of the 'simple formula' of generalized exchange, and in fact, from this point of view, the Kuki, Kachin and Gilyak systems are simple systems. Yet these *simple* systems never succeed in presenting us with an absolutely *pure* formula. There is always a foreign element mixed in with it. What is this extrinsic element? We know that, when it develops, it acts as a factor in the production of restricted exchange, or at any rate prompts the development of a system which has all the appearances of restricted exchange. Is this extrinsic factor therefore restricted exchange itself, already and inevitably present when generalized exchange originates? Must it then be admitted that if restricted exchange originates and develops in a practically pure form (so much so that its conversion to generalized exchange poses problems as complex as those which the study of the Murngin system has led us to tackle), the converse is nevertheless not true, and that generalized exchange is always less real in that it is indissolubly tied to the other form? Does the allogenous element which we have discerned possess, on the contrary, specific characteristics which assume the appearance of restricted exchange by reason of a simple phenomenon of convergence? In this latter case, what is its nature, where does it come from, and to what does it correspond? Such are the problems which still remain for us to resolve.

3. India

CHAPTER XXIV

Bone and Flesh

I

In passing from the kinship systems of the Far East to those of India, we do not, strictly speaking, move into a new field. From Tibet and Assam to Siberia, and throughout China, we have met, as the 'Leitmotiv' of the indigenous theory of marriage, the belief that the bones come from the father's side and the flesh from the mother's side. From protohistoric times India has had the same belief, and provides in fact the oldest expression of it, since, as already mentioned, the idea is found in the *Mahābhārata*.[1] This recurrence of a fundamental theme is of considerable interest. It will be recalled that in Tibet the distinction between 'relatives of the bone' and 'relatives of the flesh' is objectively linked with the formula of generalized exchange. It has probably been the same in China and Siberia. What must be emphasized here is that the distinction is incompatible with a system of restricted exchange. The distinction is based, in fact, not on individuals – father and mother, who would each contribute their part in forming the child's body – but on groups, or lineages, the co-operation of which, in and through the marriage alliance, is required to form the paired unit which the Tibetans call *tsha-shañ* and the Gilyak call *pandf*, 'those who are born', and which, among the Chinese also, owes its existence to the alliance of *hun* and *yin*. In a system of restricted exchange, each group is both 'bone' and 'flesh,' since, to employ the language of the Schools, it gives fathers and mothers at the same time and in the same respect. In a system of generalized exchange each group also gives fathers and mothers, but no longer in the same respect. For example, in relation to a group *A*, a group *B* is the giver of mothers and nothing more, while *A* is, for itself and for *B*, only the giver of husbands (although for a third group *D*, it is also the giver of wives). Therefore two given groups, *A* and *B*, *B* and *C*, *C* and *n*, and *n* and *A*, always form, in relation to one another (i.e., with respect to the *pandf* descended from both), a pair of oppositions in which one group is 'bone' exclusively, and the other 'flesh' exclusively. If this analysis is accepted, it must be concluded that the distinction 'of bone and of flesh', whenever it is met with

[1] XII, 306.

393

in this or in an equivalent form, entails a strong probability of the existence, formerly or at the present time, of a system of generalized exchange.

Examples of such a system, in fact, are not lacking in India. To reduce the cost of marriage, says Hodson, a number of castes practise marriage by exchange. There are two forms of this. One is known as *adala badala*, *santa*, or *golowat*, in which son and daughter marry daughter and son. The other, which is more popular, is called *tigadda* or *tiptha*, and consists of a triangular system: an *A* man marries a *B* woman, a *B* man a *C* woman, and a *C* man and *A* woman. In the Punjab the same system involves four groups.[1] This is also the same system that Grigson reports for the Gond. The Maria Gond are divided into clans, related to each other as *dadabhai*, 'brother-clan', or as *akomama*, 'wife-clan'.[2] But, contrary to what Russell and Hira Lal believe, this division does not necessarily coincide with a division into moieties. There are triangular arrangements, which are incompatible with dual organization.[3]

Thus the Usendi clan receives its wives from the Guma clan, which receives its wives from the Jugho clan, which is itself united by a similar relationship with the Usendi clan. The Jate, Tokalor and Hukur clans maintain *connubium* with the Marvi clan, which is 'wife-clan' of the Usendi clan, which itself has

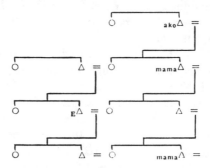

Fig. 75. Aspect of the Gond system.

marriage relationships with Jate, Tokalor and Hukur. The term *akomama* is revealing, for if the use of *ako* as a reciprocal term between mother's father and daughter's son is ignored, it can be established that the term *akomama* is formed by the juxtaposition of two kinship terms, viz., *ako*, which designates the mother's father, and *mama*, which connotes simultaneously the mother's brother, the wife's father, and the wife's brother's son,[4] i.e., the *akomama* are the exact equivalent of the Kachin *mayu ni* or the Gilyak *axmalk* (Fig. 75).

---

[1] Hodson, 1934, p. 36; cf. also Hutton, 1946, p. 139: 'Marriage by exchange, either direct or (the more popular form) three-cornered, is practised in the same areas' [the United Provinces].   [2] Grigson, 1938, p. 237.

[3] Even Russell's description, which reports organizations with five 'moieties', permits the inference that there is no question of dual organizations (Russell and Hira Lal, 1906, pp. 39–143).   [4] Grigson, 1938, p. 245.

But, even in an *akomama* clan, one cannot marry the wife's older sister, the wife's mother (among the Gond, the wife passes to her husband's clan), or any woman who is, with respect to the wife's older sister or the wife's mother, in the sister, aunt, or niece relationship. Thus, the preferred marriage is with the cross-cousin, and this type of marriage is regarded as the best 'because the family which has given a daughter to another family in marriage in one generation should have this obligation repaid by getting her back as a wife for a son of the next generation, and because such family arrangement obviates the necessity of paying the much heavier bride-price required for getting a bride from a new and unrelated family'.[1] These marriages are called *gudapal* or marriages of 'tribe-milk'.[2] It is curious that in these conditions the most frequent marriage is not with the mother's brother's daughter but with the father's sister's daughter, even though the system has been extended to the former type of marriage, 'which merely means the borrowing of a wife from the same family for two successive generations'.[3] Thus a formula which superficially conforms to generalized exchange functions in a way contrary to that demanded by the theory. It is apparent contradictions of this order which make India, as will be seen below, a privileged case for studying the solution to the difficulties pointed out at the end of the preceding chapter and which are of the same, but less pronounced, type.

The system found on the western frontiers seems to be simpler in that if a man gives a sister, aunt, niece or cousin in exchange, he avoids paying the price of his own marriage. Accordingly, we have a system of restricted exchange. However, as a long chain of exchanges in which '*A* gives to *B*, who gives to *C*, who gives to *D*, who gives to *A*'[4] often intervenes, we are, in fact, faced with a system of generalized exchange.

But as has been reported for the Gond, and as is also evident from the analysis of their kinship system,[5] which is partially oriented to restricted exchange and partially to generalized exchange, we find in fact, as among the Naga and the Tungus, a thorough mixing of the two formulas. As in these systems also, India offers the investigator a sort of hierarchy of groupings, some endogamous and others exogamous. It will be recalled that among the Angami Naga for example the exogamous function gradually shifted from the *kelhu* to the *thino*, and from the *thino* to the *putsa*.[6] The Manchu have a similar system with their *hala*, *gargan* and *mokun*. The *kelhu*, like the *hala*, were formerly exogamous organizations, and the *thino* is

[1] ibid. p. 247.   [2] loc. cit.
[3] loc. cit. Only marriage with the father's sister's daughter is categorically attested to by Rao (1910, p. 794).   [4] O'Brien, 1911, p. 433.
[5] Grigson, 1938, pp. 308-9. The importance of the Gond is that they seem to have preserved vestiges of an archaic culture. They have in common with the Naga not only certain kinship features but also the men's house (Hodson, 1922, pp. 57-8). They share this last feature with the Oraon, the Maler (ibid.), the Kondh and the Kurumba (ibid.; cf. Thurston, 1909, under these last two names). According to Hutton (1946, p. 22), the Maria Gond exhibit Mongolian affinities. See also (ibid. pp. 24-7) the parallel between the cultures of Assam and Orissa.   [6] ch. XVII.

barely so any longer. It seems that the Manchu *gargan* is no longer exogamous, and that the *mokun* itself is exogamous only for the short period of five generations.[1] These structures are strikingly similar to the Hindu system of endogamous castes (but which were formerly exogamous), *gotra* which recently became exogamous – but strictly so – and *sapiṇḍa* groups which, like the *mokun* – although in a different way (but in part only) bilateral – are reproduced every five generations. Can the similarity be pushed further and a reinterpretation of the notion of caste be suggested? The original forms of grouping from which castes are derived are called *varna* in Sanskrit, which means 'colour'. This fact was at one time used to prove that the organization was promulgated by the Aryan invaders on the basis of racial discrimination. Hocart has maintained a more likely hypothesis, which gives the 'colours', symbols of the four *varna*, a religious significance and a ritual function.[2] Nevertheless, in the light of the preceding considerations the fact cannot be ignored that the Manchu *gargan*, subdivisions of the *hala*, originally exogamous but now endogamous, *are designated by the names of colours.*[3]

This detail is all the more disturbing because the division of the Lolo into two hierarchized groups, 'White Bones' and 'Black Bones', already referred to in Chapter XXIII, recurs in exactly the same form and with the same names among the Kazak at the other extreme of Asia.[4] The Kazak aristocracy was designated by the name 'White Bones' (*aq syjek*) and the commoners were called 'Black Bones' (*kara syjek*). It is possible that the 'White Bones' constituted one or several lineages, real or theoretical. Marriages were not unknown between the two groups, although as a rule they were condemned. And so the question is posed whether, and to what extent, these divisions can be regarded as castes. It is very likely that besides the pure 'White Bones' there were hybrid 'White Bones', resulting from hypergamous marriages. With regard to the Lolo, we are clearly faced with castes in that 'White Bones' and 'Black Bones' can marry only among themselves, and 'when a woman of the Black Bones is found to have relations with a man of the White Bones, both of them are put to death'.[5] Among the Lolo, in fact, the 'Black Bones' are the nobility and the 'White Bones' an inferior class. Furthermore – and a refinement which immediately calls India to mind – if they can eat the same food, they should not however use the same plate.[6] These observations should be compared with the status differentiations, so common in Assam, which are marked by peculiarities of dress, e.g., the 'people with the black cape' and the 'people with the blue cape'. One cannot but be struck by the similarity of such systems with the distinction in the Ṛigveda between the 'light groups' and the 'dark groups': *arya varna* and *dasa varna*.

---

[1] ch. XXIII.   [2] Hocart, 1938, p. 46 et seq.   [3] ch. XXIII, p. 384
[4] Hudson, 1938, p. 55 et seq.   [5] Lin, 1945–7, p. 87.
[6] ibid. pp. 88–9. On 'the union of the five colours', the symbol of marriage, cf. Granet, 1926, pp. 154–5, 496–8, 503.

II

The similarity between the Hindu and the Manchu 'colour groups' would be more striking still if, as Senart suggests,[1] the term *varna* meant originally not 'caste' but 'estate' or 'class'. This would mean that in the time of the Brāhmanas there was a large number of tribes or clans corresponding both to the later distinction into castes (*jati*), and to a smaller division into classes (*varna*). It is difficult to determine whether these classes were the basis of a hierarchy of statuses, coextensive with the whole social group, or whether they corresponded to different groups but of unequal status. Only in the latter case is there a vague possibility of comparison with the Manchu organization. Since it derives from 'an identical scheme', the social structure of the ancient peoples of Iran, who were divided into four Pishtra, the Athrava corresponding to the Brahmin, the Rathaestha to the Kshatriya, the Vastriya to the Vaisya, and the Huiti, which appeared later, to the Sudra, most favour the first interpretation. One has the impression of being faced with a structural type rather than with the subdivision of a particular social group.[2] Nevertheless, our analysis of Kachin and Naga societies has shown how in a harmonic regime with generalized exchange the transition from a concrete distribution, explicable in terms of geography and history, to a generalized formal model, or vice versa, is easily accomplished. It will be recalled that it is hypergamy which effects this transformation.[3]

The sources supporting the former existence of caste exogamy clearly link exogamy and hypergamy. *The Laws of Manu*, to which reference must be made on this subject, explicitly say: 'A Sudra woman alone (can be) the wife of a Sudra, she and one of his caste (the wives) of a Vaisya, those two and one of his own caste (the wives) of a Kshatriya, those three and one of his own caste (the wives) of a Brāhmana.'[4] This information must be compared with two sets of facts: on the one hand, the marriage systems of the 'Old Kuki' in which the beautiful symmetry of the Kachin system (already affected, however, by the privilege of the noble families to lay claim to double alliances) disappears to the benefit of certain groups accumulating multiple alliances,[5] and on the other hand, the tendency of groups of northern Asia – the Manchu, Koryak and Gilyak – towards the multiplication of alliances.[6] Marriage by purchase provides an escape from the rules of generalized exchange among the Gond and among the groups on the western frontiers of India, as it also does among the Gilyak and to a certain extent in the cultures of Assam and Burma. In this way the accumulation of alliances is made possible for the groups which are economically and socially the most powerful. Granet has very convincingly retraced a similar development in

[1] Senart, 1896, ch. 2; Hutton, 1946, p. 59.
[2] Benveniste, 1932; 1938. See also Sunjana, 1888; Held, 1935, p. 40.
[3] ch. XVI.
[4] *The Laws of Manu*, IV, 12–13 (Bühler, 1886); cf. Risley, 1891, vol. I, p. xli; Hutton 1946, pp. 46–7.   [5] ch. XVII.   [6] ch. XXIII.

feudal China.[1] This gives us an opportunity to call attention to another similarity, associated with the previous considerations, between the marriage systems of ancient India and of the Far East.

It will be recalled that in feudal China the tendency to increase alliances is expressed especially in the privilege of the Chou noble to have three lots of wives: '*It is a rule* that a noble must marry *only* once, thus allying himself with *only one sing*. *It is a fact* that the wives of the same feudal lord very often had different and sometimes very diverse "names".'[2] And even when, as the rule requires, the three lots of wives can be claimed from the same *sing*, they must none the less belong to different houses.[3] In these noble marriages, which in fact allow – and also to a certain extent legally allow – the accumulation of alliances, the contribution of the subordinate nobles must be entirely voluntary and not solicited.[4] A striking parallel is met with in ancient India. Manu sanctions only four forms of marriage. One, called *arsha*, is a marriage by exchange against cattle (the buffalo prestations in the marriage exchanges of Assam and Burma are reminiscent of this). The three other forms are marriage by gift. There is an important distinction, however, between Brahma and Daiva marriages on the one hand, and the Prājāpatya marriage on the other, viz., the first two are based on the voluntary gift, while in the third the suitor asks for the hand of the young girl.[5] For this reason Prājāpatya marriage is regarded as inferior: 'According to Hindu ideas, marriage is a gift, and it loses a part of its value if the gift is not voluntary, but solicited.'[6] This statement, which is confirmed by Lanman's analyses,[7] holds our attention for two reasons. Firstly, it casts doubts on the early character of the interpretation by the Chinese commentators, which appears to be a rationalization, of the necessity of the voluntary gift for *yin* marriages. In the second place – and if it is admitted that *arsha* marriage, as is highly likely, was more or less of the Kachin-Lakher type, i.e., not a marriage by exchange as opposed to marriage by gift, but a marriage by gift *accompanied* by an exchange – it is very surprising that all the forms of marriage sanctioned by Manu are of the 'marriage by gift' type. In fact, this type is unknown to sociologists, and Lowie, for example, makes no mention of it in his analysis of 'means of acquiring a mate'.[8] In the literal sense of the term, marriage by gift would be a marriage without reciprocity and it cannot be seen how human society could function under the conditions that it presupposes.

It is only in a system of generalized exchange that marriage can assume, for the uninstructed observer, the superficial appearance of a gift. In a system of restricted exchange, the immediately perceivable aspect is that of the exchange of a daughter against a daughter, or brother's sister against son's wife. In a system of generalized exchange, by contrast, the transfer is

[1] Granet, 1939, ch. III.   [2] ibid. p. 131.   [3] Fêng, 1937, pp. 187–8.
[4] ch. XXI.   [5] *The Laws of Manu* III, 21–41 (Bühler, 1886).
[6] Banerjee, 1896, p. 78.   [7] Lanman, 1913.   [8] Lowie, 1961, pp. 17–26.

never directly reciprocal. It seems that the 'parents-in-law' group give a woman – and give her without receiving anything in exchange – at least on the part of the 'sons-in-law' group. The operation thus has all the appearances of a gift, and of a non-solicited gift, since the latter is founded on a pre-established order. In this connexion, Kachin practice can be compared with Hindu theory, viz., the *mayu ni* who are sounded out react ill-humouredly, make a show of refusing, and make extravagant demands. But when they have a girl to marry, they are the ones who take the initiative, and appeal to possible husbands, by hanging out women's clothes.[1] Among the Gilyak, orthodox marriage (based on generalized exchange) is a marriage *by right*, to which is opposed negotiated marriage based on purchase.[2]

A former system of generalized exchange, presumably already in a state of disintegration since its true nature is no longer understood, offers then the most satisfactory ground for explaining the origin of a theory of marriage by gift such as that met with in the *Laws of Manu*. We have indicated elsewhere the close similarity between several Australian systems and certain Asiatic systems.[3] This similarity can be seen here also: 'A man expects to marry as a matter of course the daughter of his mother's younger brother, his *KALA* . . . A full *KALA* likes to give his daughter to his sister's son, and he may insist on his wife betrothing her daughter to this man. That is to say, a man has a right to expect such a betrothal but he cannot claim the girl.'[4] The same writer adds that when a woman betroths her daughter under these conditions 'no return is expected. It is a gift . . . If (a woman) should have a daughter of reasonable age . . . she *must* give.'[5] Finally, McConnel calls marriage based on the direct exchange of sisters an 'exchange by arrangement',[6] as opposed to orthodox marriage (with the mother's brother's daughter), which she calls 'gift-exchange'.[7] Thus, here we have a universal characteristic of generalized exchange.

These considerations are of vital importance in understanding the development of generalized exchange, from the east to the west of the Euro-Asiatic world, and the relationships which unite preferential marriage with the mother's brother's daughter and so-called marriage 'by purchase'. It is striking that the four other forms of marriage known in India, and which appeared later than the previous four (or were of different origin) are, firstly, marriage by purchase (*asura*), the other three being marriages resulting from established fact, viz., mutual affection (*gandharva*), capture (*rakshasa*), and rape while asleep or unconscious (*paisacha*).[8] Our ideas on this will be discussed in another work. Here we shall mention only the curious similarity between Hindu and Chinese theory, which confirms once again that the two domains are, with regard to marriage systems, closely related, and that a common archaic structure must have existed to account for these similarities.

---

[1] ch. XVI.   [2] ch. XVIII.   [3] ch. XIII.   [4] McConnel, 1940, p. 448.
[5] Underlined in the text (ibid. pp. 449–50).   [6] ibid. p. 451.   [7] loc. cit.
[8] Banerjee, 1896, p. 82.

III

A parallelism of the same type appears with the problem of the exogamy of the *sapiṇḍa*. Caste exogamy, the most ancient form of Hindu exogamy and which has now disappeared, is contrasted with that of the *sapiṇḍa*, the most recent form.

The *sapiṇḍa* group is a bilateral grouping comprising relatives in both the paternal and the maternal lines. It includes an equal number of generations in both lines among which marriage is prohibited. According to the *Laws of Manu*, the rule of exogamy is extended to the sixth degree: 'The *sapiṇḍa* relationship ceases with the seventh person.'[1] There is, however, an asymmetry between the two lineages: 'The *sapiṇḍa* relationship ceases after the fifth ancestor in the maternal line, and after the seventh in the paternal line.'[2] It seems that *sapiṇḍa* exogamy did not begin to develop systematically until after the eighth century A.D.[3] It is calculated that towards the seventeenth century there were no fewer than 2,121 girls prohibited by *sapiṇḍa* exogamy. This figure is arrived at by assuming that it is the suitor's first marriage, that each household has only one son and one daughter, and by ignoring children of a previous marriage or those adopted.[4] At the end of the eighteenth century, Kāśīnātha, the author of the *Dharma-Sindhu*, introduced the notion of oblique or 'unequal marriage', which he condemns. Examples of this would be marriages with the wife's sister's daughter, or with the father's brother's wife's sister, neither of whom is *sapiṇḍa*: 'But from the point of generation the former is like his daughter, while the latter is in the place of uncle's wife.'[5] Nevertheless, there are texts which permit oblique marriages, certain forms of which are actually practised in the south-east of India (e.g., with the sister's daughter). Thus, more than ten centuries later, we see in outline a development similar to that which must have led to the prohibition of oblique marriage in the China of the T'ang.[6]

Nevertheless, it is not to this particular point that we wish to draw attention, but to the characteristics of the *sapiṇḍa* group proper. These characteristics are four in number: the *sapiṇḍa* group is a ritual group; it recognizes bilateral kinship; its structure has two critical aspects, corresponding respectively to the fourth and to the seventh generations; finally, it is certainly related, even if obscurely, to the system of kinship and marriage. On these four grounds it is impossible not to be struck by the similarity of the problems posed by the *sapiṇḍa* group in India, and by the mourning system and the *chao mu* order in China.

The word *piṇḍa* signifies a 'small ball of rice offered to the dead', for the *piṇḍa* sacrifice is offered in the first place to the father, to the grandfather, and to the great-grandfather. The three ascendants prior to the great-grandfather have right only to the *lepa* of the *piṇḍa*, i.e., to the grains of rice that fall from the hand when it is washed. The limit of exogamy at the

---

[1] *The Laws of Manu*, V, 60 (Bühler, 1886). [2] Banerjee, 1896, p. 58.
[3] Karandikar, 1929, pp. 194–5.   [4] ibid. p. 208.   [5] ibid. p. 212.   [6] ch. XXI.

seventh generation would thus be the transposition, on the plane of marriage, of the rules of sacrifice: the first generation offers the rice, the next three receive it, and the last three are given the *lepa*, making seven generations in all.[1] Thus, as in the Chinese feudal temple, we have two circles of ancestors, viz., those who have the right to a full homage, *piṇḍa*, or individual tablets, and those who can only lay claim to a lesser worship, *lepa*, or altar and platform constructed outside the temple proper.[2] If the founder of the lineage, who is always present, is left aside, there are in fact four generations in the feudal temple, and two outside, which with the sacrificer give a total of seven generations.

Like the Chinese terminology, in which must be seen a reflection of the mourning grades, the *sapiṇḍa* group thus appears, firstly as a ritual group, and only secondarily as a factor of kinship and marriage: 'One of the most striking aspects of *sapiṇḍa* relationship is the participation in the mortuary rites.'[3] A second similarity is immediately seen between the *sapiṇḍa* group and the Chinese mourning categories, viz., that they are both bilateral organizations.

Held has rightly noted that *sapiṇḍa* exogamy is based on kinship, rather than on a definite type of social organization: 'It extends so far, that no conceivable clan organization can function by its side.'[4] Actually, it is not so much the extension of *sapiṇḍa* exogamy which makes it impossible in a clan system, but its bilateral character, or more exactly, the particular form of bilaterality on which it is based, setting the agnates and their wives side by side, the mother at the father's side, the grandmother with the grandfather, and the great-grandmother with the great-grandfather. In every conceivable system of clan exogamy, spouses are members of different clans and consequently cannot be represented side by side. A problem of the same order is posed by the *chao mu* order for anyone who, following Granet, tries to interpret it in terms of clan organization: in the ancestral temple also, the wives' tablets appear beside those of their husbands, and – after a certain time, it is true – the sacrificer's wife must participate in the offerings jointly with her husband. Thus we are faced with a dilemma: either the object of the *chao mu* order (and of the specific characteristics of the *sapiṇḍa* group) is to express a dialectic of clan alliances, in which case the presence of women is inconceivable, or they express a bilateral conception of kinship, which is incompatible with clan organization. It could be assumed, it is true, that both systems date from a period in which the wife passed to the husband's clan. Granet expressly proposed this hypothesis in order to resolve the Chinese difficulties, and there would be no lack of material for the same interpretation to be extended to India.

But the *sapiṇḍa* group, like the *chao mu* order, is intimately bound up with the system of mourning, and the nature of this system, in India as in China,

---

[1] ibid. p. 180; Hutton, 1946, p. 53, n.2.   [2] ch. XX.
[3] Held, 1935, p. 70.   [4] ibid. p. 69.

is to require the participation, not only of agnates and their wives, but of paternal relatives and maternal relatives, 'internal' relatives and 'external' relatives in China, *jati* and *bandhu* in India.[1] Let us consider afresh the Chinese table of mourning grades. Even with the great importance attributed by Chinese culture to the distinction between clan relatives and non-clan relatives, and the theoretical exclusion of the latter, these nevertheless have the right to the last grade of mourning, *ssŭ ma*, with a possible increase from three to five months.[2] Furthermore, clanswomen are included in the mourning nomenclature, and are therefore not lost to their clan because of marriage. In India as in China maternal relatives are given a subordinate rank by their reduced right to mourning on the one hand, and on the other by the unequal number of generations required to perpetuate exogamy in both lines. But there is the same partial recognition of both lineages.

We may also note that in both systems the fifth and the seventh are the crucial generations. According to his rank, the Chou noble performs the rites to four or to seven generations of ancestors. The seventh generation is the absolute limit of the cult, and in India it is the absolute limit of the prohibition of marriage as well as of the cult. It will be recalled that in China mourning is extended to the fifth generation, and that in the Shang period the limit of exogamy was also fixed at the fifth generation. The full *piṇḍa* sacrifice also includes four generations (with the difference, in the computation, that India includes the sacrificer's generation, while China counts from the first ancestor), and the exogamy of maternal relatives ceases at the fifth generation. In the funeral rites the ancestor of the fifth generation (father's great-grandfather) is identified with the mythical ancestors and loses his right to an individual worship.[3] It is exactly the same in the Chinese ancestral temple, in which the tablets of the ancestors prior to the father's great-grandfather are deposited in a stone chest under the collective name of *tzu*. The same conceptual system with a quinary basis appears to underlie these family correlations: Chinese thought recognizes five colours, five sounds, five flavours, five perfumes, five notes, five directions and five planets;[4] India distinguishes five peoples in the world and five cardinal points, man has five 'breaths', the world is made of five mortal and five immortal elements.[5]

There is more than this. Following a study by Caland, Held relates what the prescribed orientation in the ritual is. East is to the front of the sacrificer, south on his right, and west behind him. But north is not regarded as being on his left, for it is one of the regions of the Gods, who cannot be 'to the left', because the right side is the auspicious side, while the left is the inauspicious side. East is the divine region *par excellence*, and hence the custom of marking the sacrificial enclosure by lines traced on three sides only, the front which faces the east being left open.[6]

[1] On this last point see Held, 1935, pp. 70–1; Hocart, 1924, pp. 103–4.
[2] Fêng, 1937, pp. 180–1.   [3] Held, 1935, pp. 96, 134.   [4] Bodde, 1939, p. 202.
[5] Held, 1935, pp. 120–1.   [6] ibid. p. 139.

All these characteristics coincide remarkably with the *chao mu* order, except for the inversion of north and south respectively. In the feudal temple the founding ancestor is indeed placed to the east, but his son is to the north, i.e., on his left (*chao*), and his grandson to the north, i.e., on his right (*mu*). It will be recalled that *chao* is the more honoured place, *mu* coming only second. But the coincidence of the Hindu and the Chinese orientation becomes complete if it is noted that the Chinese system is oriented with regard to the founder, and the Hindu system with regard to the officiant. Right and left are thus reversed because the perspective is not the same. In reality, the two structures are identical.

IV

Let us add to these facts the many indications from ancient India supporting the hypothesis of marriage with the matrilateral cross-cousin. The Ṛigveda says: 'They have offered you fat mixed with ghee, this is your share, as the maternal-uncle's daughter or the paternal-aunt's daughter is one's share in marriage.'[1] Arjuna's marriage has a large place in the Purāṇas. Arjuna marries Subhadrā, Kṛishṇa's sister, and Subhadrā is Vāsudeva's daughter, Vāsudeva being Kunti's brother, and Kunti Arjuna's mother.[2] It is true that in other versions Arjuna's maternal uncle is called Kaṁsa, and is presented sometimes as Arjuna's mother's brother and sometimes as her parallel cousin. Nevertheless, Karandikar considers that this is a late inter-pretation attempting to make the sacred texts coincide with contemporary prohibitions.[3] Other marriages between cross-cousins are mentioned in the *Harivaṁśa Purāṇa*.

Karandikar and Hocart tried to draw additional support from the genealogy of the Sākya[4] as found in the *Mahāvaṁsa*. This text would have Gautama descended from two successive generations of marriages between cross-cousins while he himself is held to have married Devadatta, his cross-cousin. But this is a late southern interpretation contradicted by northern traditions which represent Gautama and Devadatta as being parallel cousins.[5] The text of the *Mahāvaṁsa* is no less clear that cross-cousin marriage existed in Ceylon in the early centuries of the Christian era.[6]

Be that as it may, the *Śatapatha Brāhmaṇa* favourably mentions marriage in the third generation,[7] and its prohibition appears in the *Laws of Manu* as an innovation: for approaching three women who are similar to the sister, viz., the father's sister's daughter, the mother's sister's daughter, and the

[1] Karandikar, 1929, p. 14; Hutton, 1946, p. 54.

[2] Karandikar, 1929, p. 21; Held, 1935, pp. 161, 177, 187.

[3] Karandikar, 1929, pp. 14–15, 21; E. Benveniste has drawn my attention to a text from the *Mimamsa* (Renou, 1947, pp. 213–14) which provides a good example of this type of interpretation.

[4] Karandikar, 1929; Hocart, 1923.   [5] Emeneau, 1939.   [6] Held, 1935, pp. 78–9.

[7] Karandikar, 1929, pp. 180–2.

mother's brother's daughter, a lunar penitence had to be performed.[1] This then is proof that these marriages were still practised. And they probably continued up to a much later period. For example, Nārada, a writer of the sixth century A.D., prohibits marriage with seventeen persons, but cross-cousins are not included. The same omission is noted in the *Smṛitis* and in the thirteenth century, Devana, the writer of the *Smṛiti-Chandrika*, again gives the question a special chapter entitled: 'The defence of marriage with one's maternal uncle's daughter.' This defence relies on the fact that in Brāhma marriage the wife acquires the husband's father's *gotra*; consequently, the father's sister and the mother are not members of their brothers' *gotra*, and are not their *sapiṇḍa*; cross-cousin marriage is therefore not a *sapiṇḍa* marriage, and its prohibition is based only on custom. Nārada, like Mādhava who maintained the same thesis in the fourteenth century, is a writer from the Deccan. But if Mādhava bases the legitimacy of cross-cousin marriage in the south on local custom, he also invokes the specific characteristics of Brāhma marriage to extend his thesis to the northern regions. Mādhava, like Devana, expressly prohibits marriage between parallel cousins.[2]

When we consider these facts, and the many similarities that have been emphasized between family structure and the organization of mourning, in China and in ancient India, it is not surprising to see Held, following Hodson's lead and preceding Granet by only a few years, formulating a hypothesis for ancient India which coincides in the smallest details with that propounded by the writer of the *Catégories matrimoniales*. It is difficult to believe that Granet knew of Held's book without citing it, and if the parallelism between the two writers is fortuitous it is only the more striking. Held preceded Granet by four years in being the first to formulate (and departing from Hodson on these points) two ideas of basic theoretical value: firstly, that a system of generalized exchange (which he calls a 'circulative system') can be founded on dual organization, and, secondly, that generalized exchange is compatible with both matrilineal and patrilineal descent. In fact, Held very clearly understood that the nature of descent is a secondary characteristic of kinship systems, which can preserve a formal stable structure despite the conversion from one type of descent to the other. If necessary, the proof can be found in Eggan's study of the Choctaw system,[3] in which he establishes that a matrilineal system of the Crow type is transformed into a system of the Omaha type when it becomes patrilineal. In other words, the structural unit must be regarded as a Crow-Omaha system, in which the mode of descent introduces only secondary distinctions.

To explain the characteristics of the Hindu system, and the preference for the matrilateral cousin, Held like Granet, thus developed the hypothesis of a double mode of descent, patrilineal and matrilineal; and the system which

---

[1] *The Laws of Manu*, XI, 172 (Bühler, 1886, p. 466); Karandikar, 1929.
[2] ibid. pp. 195–203; Hutton, 1946, pp. 54–5.
[3] Eggan, 1937, pp. 34–52.

he reconstructs is identical – presumably because he attempts to account for the same phenomena – to Granet's eight-class system (Fig. 76).

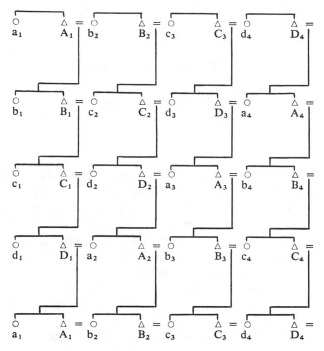

Fig. 76. Hindu system (after Held, 1935).

But it also raises the same difficulties.[1]

[1] Held's system is superficially more complex than Granet's in that it requires sixteen classes instead of eight. In fact, however, it is reducible to the same formula, for it is obvious that couples 1 and 3, and 2 and 4 represent respectively two patrilineal moieties. The hypothesis of a former system with marriage classes of the Australian type seems also to have misled Hutton (1946, pp. 55–6).

This chapter and those which follow were already set in type when I learned of two works by Kapadia (1947) and Elwin (1947), and an article by Brough (1946–7, pp. 32–45). Certain points in our argument could be improved by being stated more precisely and by being developed in the light of these important works.

CHAPTER XXV

Clans and Castes

I

Held's attempted reconstruction depends on three arguments: the majority of Hindu systems make a distinction between the two types of cross-cousin, which is shown by a marked preference for the matrilateral cross-cousin; some groups advocate marriage with the mother's brother's daughter, while prohibiting marriage in the maternal clan; finally, the social structure of India suggests a bilateral organization based on the recognition of both matrilineal and patrilineal descent. As the next chapter is devoted to matrilateral marriage in India, we shall begin by examining the two remaining points which pose problems of not only local but theoretical interest.

The Toda material[1] has brilliantly confirmed that 'there exists in India a patrilineal system of relationship, intersected by a latent matrilineal one'.[2] Toda society comprises two great endogamous divisions, each subdivided into exogamous and patrilineal *mod*. There is a second subdivision into *poljo:ḷ*, which are exogamous and matrilineal groups: 'This network of relations in the female line cuts across *mod* divisions, and divides the *to:rδas* at present into five exogamous sets of *poljo:ḷ*, the *töüvil* into six . . . No man may marry or have intercourse with any woman who is related to him through a wholly male line or through a wholly female line.'[3] Cross-cousin marriage results from this complex organization. Consequently Rivers was mistaken in thinking that he had shown that among the Toda the *poljo:ḷ* included all the members of the clan (*mod*), relatives being divided up into members of the same *mod* and members of the same *poljo:ḷ*. It was Rivers who was in error, not the natives.[4]

The function of the matrilineal clans is to regulate marriage and mourning obligations. The patrilineal clans regulate the choice of names and the rules of inheritance and marriage.[5] Generally Emeneau is of the opinion that south India is characterized by the exogamous patrilineal clan, with prohibitions in the matrilineal line which vary according to the community:

---

[1] cf. ch. VIII.   [2] Held, 1935, p. 53.   [3] Emeneau, 1937, p. 104.
[4] Nevertheless see Rivers, 1907, p. 622, in which another interpretation is already fore-shadowed.   [5] Emeneau, 1941, p. 169.

'[This] point . . . is of more fundamental importance for the understanding of South Indian ethnology than that about cross-cousin marriage.'[1] We have to go as far as Malabar, all the same, in order to find markedly matrilineal institutions, which does not indicate that Rivers's hypothesis on the Malabar origin of the Toda is justified, when he writes: 'It is clear that the general South Indian situation sketched above provides a sufficient basis for the Toda developments.'[2] This general picture gives predominance to patrilineal clans with a locally systematized development of matrilineal clans.

Aiyappan has proposed a similar interpretation of cross-cousin marriage among the matrilineal Nayar, but the relationship between the two modes of descent must be reversed: 'Cross-cousin marriage among them is the result of an unconscious change to patrilineal conditions.'[3] The same situation is evident among the Coorg, where cross-cousin marriage seems to result from the intersection of exogamous patrilineal clans (*oka*) with a limited matrilineal system.[4] It would be easy to give other examples of it.

There is no question, therefore, of denying the co-existence of both modes of descent in certain regions of India. This is incontestable. But how can Held say that in such a system 'marriage within the (matrilineal) clan of the mother is prohibited and allowed at the same time within the (patrilineal) clan of the mother', under the pretext that 'with this system of relationship each individual belongs to two clans, viz., to his father's patrilineal and to his mother's matrilineal clan.[5] This is to forget that, if the mother's patrilineal clan is sanctioned, the father's sister's matrilineal clan is also sanctioned, i.e., the father's sister's daughter is a possible spouse for the same reason as is the mother's brother's daughter. It is perfectly clear that the Toda practise bilateral cross-cousin marriage,[6] and so do the Coorg.[7] For an eight-class system to appear, which sanctions marriage with the matrilateral cross-cousin while prohibiting it with the patrilateral cross-cousin, it must in fact (unless it comes out of nothing) follow upon a four-class system which is already based on generalized exchange, i.e., a system which sanctions and prohibits precisely the same types of marriage. The sub-division into eight classes changes nothing and adds nothing. As we have shown in discussing Granet's work, it is a gratuitous and redundant hypothesis.

Granet, however, was obliged to resort to this hypothesis because he had postulated the earlier existence in China of a four-class system (based on restricted exchange). Held followed the same course, but for another reason. According to Russell, certain tribes of central India, such as the Bhil, the Maratha and the Kunbi, prohibit marriage in the mother's clan while recommending it with the mother's brother's daughter.[8] Consequently, Held looked for a system answering to the following conditions: a dichotomy of cross-cousins into matrilateral and patrilateral, and the differentiation of

<hr>

[1] ibid. p. 174, n. 26. [2] ibid. p. 175. [3] Aiyappan, 1934, p. 282.
[4] Emeneau, 1938, pp. 126–7. [5] Held, 1935, pp. 53–4. [6] Rivers, 1907; Emeneau, 1937.
[7] ibid. 1939, p. 127. [8] Held, 1935, pp. 52–3.

the matrilateral cousin with respect to other women of the maternal clan. He found it in the splitting of a simple system of generalized exchange (such as Hodson described) into a bilateral system, but still based on generalized exchange.

Even if he were right, it would then have been necessary for generalized exchange to exist as the condition of the derivative system. Held is locked in the same circularity as Granet, viz., that in order to explain certain anomalies (or peculiarities, regarded as such) of a simple system, both of them presuppose the earlier existence of a more complex system, of which the simple system is taken to be a sort of residue or vestige, without realizing that the former could only have come into being as a development of the latter, which must therefore have existed before it. Held can be given credit for his penetrating criticism of the notion of descent, without accepting his final conclusions. Because the mode of descent never constitutes an essential feature of a kinship system, it does not follow that 'bilineal characteristics are normal for a primitive organization'.[1] If Held means then that no human society absolutely ignores one of the lines, this is nothing new.[2] If, however, he means that all human groups trace descent through both lines in determining marriage rules, nothing is more incorrect, and numerous examples could be given of groups in which descent is (with regard to marriage) either entirely patrilineal or entirely matrilineal, and even of groups in which, where a precise rule of descent is lacking, a strictly unilateral theory of conception is invoked.[3]

From the discovery of bilateral organizations, it would be wrong to conclude that the lines from which descent is traced are confused or merged. Except for very rare exceptions, all known organizations are unilateral, but certain of them (and by no means the majority) are unilateral twice instead of once, which confirms rather than contradicts the fundamental nature of the idea of unilaterality. In the particular case of India there are both patrilineal and matrilineal systems. It is natural therefore that some groups should be simultaneously both, while the majority remain either the one or the other. Because patrilineal and matrilineal organizations exist side by side in Assam, as Hodson notes, it is not to be concluded, without forcing the notion, that 'matri- and patrilineal systems are interwoven with one another',[4] in the same sense as they are, for example, among the Toda, for in Assam it is not the same groups which exhibit the two types of organization.

It is possible that ancient India was matrilineal. Some entire regions are still so. Furthermore, there are certain peculiarities which are common to both ancient India and ancient China, notably the transmission of the name and the clan in the uterine line,[5] and it is curious that in Tibet (where the probabilities of a former matrilineal organization are very strong) the lineages

---

[1] Held, 1935, p. 56.
[2] ch. VIII.
[3] Lévi-Strauss, 1943b, pp. 398–409.
[4] Held, 1935, pp. 51–2.
[5] ibid. p. 73; Hutton, 1946, p. 129.

should have been designated in the Han period by the *ming* of the father and the *hsing* of the mother, i.e., the opposite of what took place in China.[1]

The fact that in India and in China, for certain archaic dynasties at least, the feminine line of descent is better known to us than the masculine, has no great value in itself, but the coincidence of two anomalies is more significant than if they were isolated cases.[2] Be that as it may, there is certainly no trace of matrilineal survivals among the Aryans.[3] If, with Hutton, it were supposed that a patrilineal Aryan society was grafted on to a pre-Aryan matrilineal base, the presence of both types could be easily explained. But probably things are not as simple as this. We have pointed out the structural affinities between Hindu society and the groups from both extremities of the Far East described in the previous chapters, which are generally patrilineal, but whose system of kinship and marriage (generalized exchange) is in fact compatible with a matrilineal organization. It is possible, and even probable, that sociologists who defend the theory that all human societies have passed from a matrilineal stage to a patrilineal stage have been victims of an optical illusion, and that, in fact, any human group might, in the course of centuries, develop alternately matrilineal or patrilineal characteristics, without the most fundamental elements of its structure being profoundly affected by it. To assert, as did Held, the universality or the priority of bilateral organization, is to perpetuate the illusion of traditional sociology in giving a decisive value to the mode of descent. If the mode of descent does not determine the essential characteristics of the systems (which are structural phenomena), it must not be allowed to play the leading part behind barely transfigured features.

Let us return to Russell's observation on the marriage system in central India. Can we take as the starting-point for the reconstruction of an archaic system facts coming from the central provinces, which are certainly not those in which primitive institutions can be best preserved? Thurston does not mention the Bhil, and he is content to note the existence of the Kunbi in South India.[4] But, for the Maratha rules of marriage, he refers to the Bant who are matrilineal.[5] Faced with Russell's observations, the first problem is to know what exactly he meant.[6] With regard to the Gond of Bastar, on whom we now have some modern studies, he expressed himself as follows. Marriage is prohibited between persons related in the male line, but the exogamous rules do not create any other obstacle, and a man could marry any relative in the maternal line. Nevertheless, there are special rules which prohibit marriage with certain types of relative.[7] To interpret this ambiguous text, reference must be made to Grigson, who shows that even in the *akomama* clan a man cannot marry his wife's older sister, his wife's mother, or a woman who is sister, aunt, or niece to his wife. Because the *akomama* clan is the

---

[1] Granet, 1939, p. 105, n. 1. [2] Held, 1935, pp. 73–4; Paranavitana, 1933, p. 240.
[3] Lumley, 1937, pp. 411–22. [4] Thurston, 1909, vol. IV, p. 118.
[5] ibid. vol. V, p. 14; vol. I, p. 123. [6] Russell and Hira Lal, vol. I, p. 87. [7] loc. cit.

mother's clan,[1] this amounts to saying that it is prohibited, except in the case of the matrilateral cross-cousin who nevertheless belongs to it. This is exactly the same situation reported by Russell for the Bhil, the Maratha and the Kunbi.

Generally speaking, it is certainly not necessary to resort to a complex system of marriage classes to justify either the prohibition on marriage with a certain relative, or – in a system of generalized exchange – the restriction of the preferential union to one, two, or several members of the 'wife-givers'' lineage. This point has already been considered in a previous chapter.[2] More particularly, with regard to the Gond, it is quite inconceivable, if such a system had existed, that it would have escaped an observer of Grigson's quality. Systems with marriage classes are not clouded in any mystery; natives who have them regard them as profane, and willingly and freely discuss them. Furthermore, they are often capable of developing a theoretical conception of them.[3] When a system of classes exists, it must be perceived. If several observers fail to mention it, the only reasonable conclusion is that the group considered does not possess it.

Actually, Held does not assert the present-day existence of an eight-class system. He merely infers its former existence from the marriage rules reported by Russell. But here a methodological question arises. It is legitimate to formulate the hypothesis of a former system of classes when facts which are found in the field of kinship nomenclature or in other fields (ritual, mourning, etc.) cannot be explained by the current situation without referring them to a vanished context of which they are held to be the vestiges. But in the case being considered the context invoked by Held (an eight-class system) adds absolutely nothing to the situation as given by the contemporary observer. It is a question of explaining a precise and living fact, viz., the preferential union with the mother's brother's daughter to the exclusion of the other members of the maternal clan. This double rule, positive and negative, could be the expression of an eight-class system. The only conclusion that may be drawn from this relationship is either that the groups considered have an eight-class system and have it at the present time, or else – if observation fails to disclose this system – that such a rule can function without a corresponding system of classes.

In this work we have constantly insisted that marriage classes constitute only one of the possible methods for establishing a system of reciprocity; and that this method consists in interpreting the reciprocity specifically in terms of 'classes,' whereas it is always possible to express it in terms of 'relations'. Both methods are always and everywhere available to the human mind, but for some odd reason some sociologists are fascinated by what we should like to call Australian Aristotelianism. They are convinced that, in the field of family and kinship, the logic of classes represents a more simple and primitive method of thought than the logic of relations. Here they show

[1] ch. XXIV.   [2] ch. XXII.   [3] ch. IX

themselves to be remarkably ignorant of developments in contemporary psychology, and to show little respect for the information collected in the field. Actually, *a class system can never be postulated*. If it exists, it must be directly visible. If it has existed, it can be inferred only from vestiges which are strictly inexplicable in terms of the present-day situation. Some of these vestiges are periodic phenomena. In this sense – but in this sense only – Held and Granet's venture seems legitimate, if not successful. Another useful indication is the extent of the kinship nomenclature, which must be a function of the complexity of the system. If we know that the Murngin have classes, it is not only because the natives say so, but because the extension of the nomenclature to seventy-one terms exactly confirms the degree of complexity of the system, as could have been deduced from the forty-one-term nomenclature of the Aranda systems or from the twenty-one-term nomenclature of the Kariera systems. The proto-archaic Chinese system must have had a very restricted nomenclature,[1] and the information that we have on the Hindu nomenclature, which is unfortunately fragmentary, suggests a similar condition.[2] An additional argument is provided by the terminological distinction between the mother's brother and the father's sister's husband.[3] Reduced nomenclatures are perfectly suited to simple systems of generalized exchange,[4] but they remove all probability from hypotheses favourable to the existence of complex systems.

II

One of the reasons prompting the formulation of these hypotheses is the multiplicity of exogamous groupings in India both at the present time and in the past. We have already examined two of these groupings, the caste and the *sapiṇḍa* group. To these we must add the *gotra*.

In principle, the *gotra* is a patrilineal grouping and it is always exogamous. On both these grounds it seems to duplicate the caste, which even in Manu's time functioned as an exogamous unit, and which even today seems to have remained exogamous in north India. It is largely because he was perplexed by this duality that Held believed he had found a neat solution in treating the *gotra* as a former matrilineal clan, which became patrilineal in the course of time, but which in its original form could have co-existed with the patrilineal caste to form a bilateral organization.[5] Held found confirmation that the caste had always constituted a patrilineal clan in the double meaning of the term *jati*, which designates both the caste (as an appellation presumably older than *varna*), and, in the *Mahābhārata*, the paternal relatives, as opposed to *bandhu*, for the maternal relatives.[6]

How then are the late appearance of the *gotra* and its exogamy to be explained? Manu deals with the two exogamous groups of caste and *sapiṇḍa*,

[1] ch. XXIII. [2] Rivers, 1907; Hocart, 1928, pp. 179–204. [3] Held, 1935, p. 77.
[4] ch. XVI. [5] Held, 1935, pp. 73–4, 82, 85. [6] ibid. p. 71, n. 1.

but makes no mention of *sagotra* marriage except with respect to the three great castes.[1] It is only Gautama who lays down that the guilt of one who has sexual relations with the wife of a friend, a sister, a woman belonging to the same *gotra*, or with the wife of a pupil, a daughter-in-law, or with a cow, is as great as that of one who violates the bed of his *guru*.[2] Manu gives the same list except with regard to the *gotra*.[3]

And even in the Sūtras the violation of the exogamy of the *gotra* is still given as a secondary sin. It was not until the third century that the rule of the prohibition of the *gotra* acquired a rigid character and that its violation became an inexpiable sin.[4] In the sixth century, Nārada lays down the rule that marriage with a *sagotra* girl is a sin for which castration is the only adequate punishment. Gradually, the prohibition of the paternal *gotra* is extended to the maternal *gotra*, and to the mother's brother's daughter, though the latter point is still open to discussion. The rule of exogamy seems definitely established only from the thirteenth century.[5]

The question is further complicated by the refinements which took place in the exogamous rules, principally in central and northern India and in Bengal. The Dumāl of Bihar and Orissa have three types of divisions: the *gōt* or clan; the *barga*, the eponymous section; and the *mitti* or local ancestral group. Marriage is prohibited only when the three divisions coincide, but in practice it is only the *barga* which counts, for it is the only division which exists in sufficient numbers.[6] Similarly, there are three types of section in Bengal: totemic, eponymous and territorial.[7] *Tambuli* is an exogamous system depending on both the *gotra* and the family name; the prohibition of marriage is absolute only when the two coincide.[8] The same rule applies among the Babhan when territorial sections and sections bearing the patronym of a saint coincide. The territorial section is absolutely prohibited, but the patronymic section is unimportant.[9]

What relationship is there between these different categories and the *gotra*? Risley regards the territorial section, a local group (*mūl*), as older than the *gotra*, which he assimilates to the patronymic sections; the latter do not always exist, whereas the division into *mūl* is general.[10] Karandikar's interpretation is quite different in that he assimilates *gotra*, *mūl*, and the groupings known according to region as *gōt*, *khul*, *intiperulu*, *tārvād*, etc.,[11] and for whom Hindu exogamy is consequently reduced, on the one hand to the *sapiṇḍa*, and on the other to the *gotra*.

However, two different types of grouping must be understood by *gotra*, a conclusion which is clear enough when the works of Karandikar and Risley are compared. Risley sees the *gotra* as groups named after saints, and, as an argument in favour of the historical priority of the territorial sections over

---

[1] *The Laws of Manu*, III, 5 (Bühler, 1886).   [2] Gautama, XXIII, 12 (Bühler, 1897).
[3] Karandikar, 1929, pp. 110–11.   [4] ibid. p. 126.   [5] ibid. pp. 128–30.
[6] Russell and Hira Lal, 1906, vol. II, pp. 530–1; Hutton, 1946, pp. 50–1.
[7] Risley, 1891, vol. I, p. liii.   [8] ibid. vol. II, p. 292.   [9] ibid. vol. I, p. 29.
[10] ibid. pp. 30, 285.   [11] Karandikar, 1929, Preface.

the *gotra*, he points out that the former are very numerous, while the 'Brahmin' *gotra* are less so and form a system which can be borrowed en bloc.[1] However, other writers call attention to the large number of *gotra* (up to 335 per clan) and their continual multiplication.[2] The difficulty is cleared up when, following Karandikar, two sorts of *gotra* are distinguished: on the one hand, local or eponymous, patronymic or matronymic groups of which there are great numbers, and on the other hand the *gotra* in the narrow sense as defined by the rule of exogamy: 'No persons belonging to the same *gotra* and reciting the same *pravara* can be mated together.'[3] *Gotra* defined by common *pravara* are few, there being about ten according to Karandikar and twenty-four to forty-two according to Banerjee, and they constitute, not eponymous sections, but ritual schools.[4] It is obviously these ritual schools that Risley regards as borrowed from the Brahman en bloc, and to which he attributes a recent origin. We will leave them to one side.

This distinction leads Karandikar to a general conception based essentially on the late character of *gotra* exogamy, according to which there is a transition from a period in which *sagotra* marriage is not mentioned, to its incidental prohibition, then (with Baudhāyana and Guatama) to the stipulation of penances to which the guilty parties, but not the child of such a union, are liable, or even to the prescription of a simple interruption of the offending relationships, free from any other penance, except in the case where a child has been born. In this period *sagotra* marriage is still a venial sin compared with the marriage of the younger before the older.[5] It is only Gautama who formally denounces *sagotra* marriage: 'The principle of sept exogamy was there. Some had adopted it in full. Some may have been wavering; while a few might have been averse to it. Such is the state of things seen from the Sutra works collectively.'[6]

Thus the Indo-Aryans, it is maintained, progressively elaborated the notion of *gotra*, religious school and exogamous grouping, by conforming to the exogamous formula on the model offered by the division of the conquered populations into *mūl, kul, tārvād*, etc. The 'great *gotra*', to use a simplified formula, are of Brahmanic origin and recent appearance. This is why the other castes do not have 'great *gotra*' proper, and why they must either fabricate them in imitation of the Brahmans or affiliate themselves to those of the latter. However, concurrent with the 'great *gotra*' and prior to them, many different types of grouping already existed in which archaic and exogamous formations can still be recognized. These 'little *gotra*' must not be confused with the 'great *gotra*'. It is only on this condition, and in relation to the 'great *gotra*' exclusively, that one can accept Karandikar's conclusions, according to which the *gotra* – which has nothing to do with inheritance, property rights, or the organization of authority – could not be an ancient

---

[1] Risley, 1891, vol. I, p. 30; Hutton, 1949, pp. 49–53.   [2] Adam, 1936, pp. 533–47.
[3] Karandikar, 1929, p. 22.   [4] ibid. ch. IV; Banerjee, 1896, p. 55.
[5] Karandikar, 1929, pp. 115–18.   [6] ibid. p. 119.

clan: 'Gotra institution was not based upon ancestry, and at least in its early stages the Brahmin law-givers were fully conscious of the artificialness of the organization and all their social legislations, excepting the marriage legislation were based upon the unit of the family and not of the gotra.'[1]

The 'little *gotra*', by contrast, *mūl, mitti, kul* or *gōt*, sometimes territorial groups and sometimes lineages, clans or subdivisions of the clan, sometimes patrilineal and sometimes matrilineal, have, at least in central and northern India, exogamous rules of great complexity. Some groups simply prohibit marriage in the paternal *gotra*, many add the maternal *gotra*, and others go even further. Risley and Russell describe cases which could be arranged into a continuous series, comprising from two or three to eight or nine prohibited *gotra*. Thus the Bai of Bhagalpur have two types of prohibition in that marriage is prohibited with a woman of the same *mūl*, of the *mūl* of one's mother, or of the *mūl* of one's father's mother, and with a woman whose mother or father's mother belongs to a *mūl* prohibited by the preceding rules,[2] i.e., if *a, b* and *d* are prohibited to *A*, *p* is also, since *p*'s mother's mother is *d* (Fig. 77).

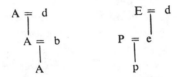

Fig. 77. Marriage prohibitions among the Bai.

The Jat of the Punjab, in addition to Ego's section, prohibit three others: those of his mother, his mother's mother and his father's sister's husband.[3] The Bargwar Goala exclude seven local groups (*dih*) both on the paternal and on the maternal side.[4] The Goala of Bihar (North India) prohibit marriage in the following sections: Ego's; his mother's; his mother's mother's; his mother's mother's mother's; his father's mother's; his father's mother's mother's; his father's mother's mother's mother's. Among the Satmulia or Kishnaut Goala of Bhagalpur, the prohibited *mūl* are: Ego's; his mother's; his mother's mother's; his mother's mother's mother's; his father's mother's; his father's father's mother's; and his mother's father's father's father's mother's. To these the Naomulia add Ego's father's mother's mother's and his father's mother's mother's mother's. Furthermore, there is the rule: *chachera, mamera, phurphera, masera, ye char nata bachake shadi hota hai,* 'The line of paternal uncle, maternal uncle, paternal aunt, maternal aunt,— these four relationships are to be avoided in marriage.'[5]

[1] Karandikar, 1929, pp. 88–9.
[2] Risley, 1891, vol. I, p. 51.
[3] Russell and Hira Lal, 1891, vol. III, p. 233.
[4] Risley, 1891, vol. I, p. lviii.
[5] ibid. pp. 285–6.

These prohibitions are particularly interesting because the Jat are divided into two types of moiety, one territorial ('high-country' and 'low-country') the other based on a mythical ancestry ('ship-gotra' and 'kashib-gotra').[1] The four prohibited lineages do not coincide with an eight-class system, or with a four-class system of restricted exchange (in which the father's sister's husband is in the mother's class), or with a four-class system of generalized exchange (which prescribes marriage in the mother's class). This is a good example of how impossible it is to interpret *gotra* prohibitions as the sign of a former marriage class system.

How are such complicated rules to be understood? Firstly, let us note that they are all of the same type, the only difference being that a varying number of sections, *mūl* or *gotra*, are involved. We can take it as established that these sections were originally the real exogamous units, and the only

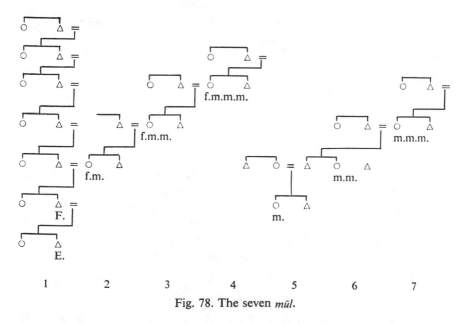

Fig. 78. The seven *mūl*.

ones, but that because exogamy, as it were, developed more rapidly than social differentiation, more and more sections had to be brought in to adapt the old institutions to the new rules. The patrilineal (or matrilineal) section was the original dress of exogamy, but exogamy grew more quickly than its clothes, and the sections had to be put end to end so as to cover the same body.

What then is the cause of this rapid development of exogamy? We have only to consider the prohibited *mūl* to see that we are dealing with a difficult, and often clumsy, attempt to interpret *sapiṇḍa* exogamy in terms of earlier

[1] Rose, 1914, vol. II, p. 375; Bray, 1925, pp. 30–3.

institutions. This is clearly evident from Risley's statement that the rule
defining the prohibited degrees is usually calculated to the fourth generation.[1]
It can be assumed that this adaptation was not always easy: 'Each caste has
made suitable modifications in the rules in making them applicable to itself.'[2]
Furthermore, Banerjee draws attention to the persistent struggle against
the tendency of families or lineages to make their own private law.[3] As late
even as the fifteenth century in the north of India the conflict between the
gotra and the *sapiṇḍa* systems can still be seen. Raghunandana defends a
theory according to which marriage is possible if the girl is three *gotra*
removed although within the fifth and the seventh *sapiṇḍa* degrees (Fig. 79).[4]

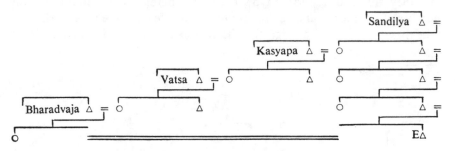

Fig. 79. Prohibited degrees in north India.

Furthermore, it will be noted from Risley's and Russell's tables that generally
the father's father's father's wife's section and the mother's father's father's
wife's section are not included in the prohibitions, thus leaving open this
form of compromise. Another indication of the same conflict is the curious
rationalization by which certain tribes still practising matrilateral marriage
justify it by disparaging the maternal lineage as too insignificant to merit
a special prohibition. Thus the Santal, who incline towards matrilateral
alliances, have the proverb: 'No man heeds a cow-track, or regards his
mother's sept.'[5]

III

Can any conception be formed of the relationships which unite the three
archaic exogamous institutions of caste, *gotra*, and *sapiṇḍa* group, and of
their respective places in the great structural system which we are trying to
define for Indo-Asiatic society? If we suppose, as so many analogies suggest,
that ancient India was a clan society, united into one or several systems of
generalized exchange, the task is perhaps not impossible. The study of
Kachin society has shown how there can co-exist, on the one hand, in the
countryside and among the common people, clans perpetuating an ancient

---

[1] Risley, 1891, vol. I, p. 286.   [2] Karandikar, 1929, p. 221.
[3] Banerjee, 1896, ch. VI.   [4] Karandikar, 1929, pp. 204–5.
[5] Risley, 1891, vol. I, pp. xlix–l.

model, and, on the other hand, in a feudal aristocracy, bigger and better-articulated groupings permitting the play of hierarchies and rivalries. Are these groupings former clans which subsequently become differentiated and specialized? This is possible, and even probable. If India had undergone an analogous development, it could be said that castes and clans (the castes themselves presumably ancient clans) were at one time exogamous groupings governed by generalized exchange, but that, because of an incipient exclusiveness, the castes maintained the essentially aristocratic formula of generalized exchange, and that this exclusiveness condemned the stagnating clans to develop independently towards restricted exchange. The outlines at least of one such development are known. Risley says that in the north of Mambhum, the Rampai and Domkatai sections are held in such poor esteem that the members of other sections refuse to give them their daughters in marriage, although they have no objection to receiving wives from them. Consequently, in this region the Babhan of the above-mentioned sections are forced to exchange women among themselves, although their daughters can find husbands in all sections outside their own.[1]

Thus intercaste marriages tend to the formation of new castes and to the development of the initial model, the latter being less 'racial' than 'cultural'.[2] For, as we have tried to show with regard to Kachin society, the five great fundamental groups of which can be regarded as castes and which are still exogamous, generalized exchange can in fact facilitate the integration of groups of different ethnic origins, as well as lead to the development of differences within an ethnically homogeneous society. That caste may be something over and above an historical residue, and that in one way it forms a functional unit, is clearly brought out by certain of Risley's observations. For example, even at the present time some incompletely 'Brahmanized' Dravidian tribes practise intertribal marriage. But the children of these unions are members of neither the paternal nor the maternal group. They form a new endogamous unit, the name of which often denotes the precise type of crossing of which it is the expression. The Munda have no fewer than nine groups of this type. The Mahili have five of them, and regard themselves as the descendants of a Munda and a Santal.[3] These subdivisions tend to form autonomous groups and to disguise their origin behind an occupational or territorial name.

Because they are hypergamous, castes tend then to be formed by a process of diversification. Clans, by contrast, are increased by fission. In this respect there is little doubt that the *gotra* is to the clan what the *thino* is to the *khelu*, or the *putsa* to the *thino*, among the Naga, or the *mokun* to the *gargan* among the Manchu. The *mūl* of the Goala of Bihar are sometimes subdivided into local sections. In this case, exogamy is transferred from the *mūl* to the subsection (*purukh*), the most convenient and the most restricted group having

---

[1] ibid. vol. I, p. 31.   [2] Nesfield, 1885.
[3] Risley, 1891. vol. I, p. xxxvii.

the largest place.[1] Senart also deals with the subdivision of the *gotra* as a function of exogamous requirements.[2] Adam describes the tribes of Nepal, again divided into clans (*thar*), some of which at least have lost their exogamous nature in favour of the *gotra* which compose them. It is often not possible to distinguish the *gotra*, which are in fact lineages, from the clans; new *gotra* continually appear.[3] Was there formerly a minimum distance required for the formation of new *gotra*, as we have found for the sub-clans of the Tungus, the Buriat and the Kazak? This might well be claimed on the basis of evidence from the Sūtras that 'the *gotra* begins with the grandson',[4] which is more understandable on such a hypothesis than is Held's hypothesis of a matrilineal origin of the *gotra*. On this subject we can refer to Risley's statement that (among the Goala) not only is marriage prohibited between two families for several generations, but the members of each family cannot marry into the *thar* or exogamous section of the other.[5] However, this does not, of course, preclude the *gotra* from having been patrilineal in some cases and matrilineal in others, depending on the type of clan from which they had sprung in particular regions. But a general hypothesis concerning this seems neither useful nor probable.

The archaic clans thus presumably underwent two forms of development. Some must have been perpetuated as castes by becoming specialists, while others must have gradually – but incompletely – disappeared in favour of more restricted units such as eponymous sections or territorial groups. Because of their aristocratic nature the former would have developed towards hypergamy and then towards endogamy, while the latter would have been more lastingly exogamous. But endogamy pure and simple would be inconceivable in that it would exclude all reciprocity. Thus the *sapiṇḍa* group can be regarded as the functional equivalent, in endogamous castes, of the subdivision of exogamous clans into unilineal groupings. It is true that the *sapiṇḍa* group is bilateral, but it preserves the germ of its patrilineal origin in the inequality established between the two lines. Moreover, it has not been sufficiently enphasized that an endogamous group can apply only bilateral impediments, otherwise it would be reduced to two or more exogamous sections.

But if endogamy precipitated the formation of bilateral groups in India, it must not be forgotten on that account that bilaterality is latent in any system of generalized exchange. The Gilyak *pandf*, the Chinese couple *hun-yin*, or the Tibetan *tsha-shan*, are the 'affines' who are at the same time 'those who are born together', maternal and paternal relatives treated as a unit. Both 'bone' and 'flesh' are necessary to make a human being. We have shown the progressive formation of feminine lineages in certain aspects of Kachin law and Tungus mythology. In Kachin law at least feminine lineages

---

[1] Risley, 1891, vol. I, p. 285. [2] Senart, 1896, p. 35.
[3] Adam, 1936, p. 537. In the same sense, Hutton, 1946, p. 45.
[4] Held, 1935, p. 73. [5] Risley, 1891, vol. I, p. lviii.

have a more than virtual existence. In one way it can be said that the Kachin wife, like the Hindu wife, receives a 'stridhana', the daughters in both cases having a preferential right to inherit it.[1] Furthermore, in both cases this preferential right gives claim essentially to the goods received as tokens of parental, and more especially of fraternal, love: 'What (was given) before the (nuptial) fire, what (was given) on the bridal procession, what was given in token of love, and what was received from her brother, mother, or father, that is called the six-fold property of a woman.'[2] Even in China, which is so strictly patrilineal, feminine lineages have a preferential right over certain types of goods.[3] India provides the example of an exceptional development of bilateralism, but differs only in degree, not in kind, from the systems which we have thought capable of comparison with it.

By asserting that this bilaterality is latent or manifest in all systems of generalized exchange, we are by no means recanting our previous criticism of the hypothesis of a universal bilateralism.[4] We have distinguished two forms of bilateralism: on the one hand, both lineages are recognized as having a more or less similar rôle, although their respective importance may differ in degree. In this sense, we are willing to admit the existence of a universal bilateralism. But, on the other hand, Held reaches the same conclusion by reference to an entirely different system, viz., that of the specialization of both lineages, pushed to the point where the social status of each individual results from the combination of two or four factors distributed 'in mosaic', as the geneticists say, and according to the formula of the veritable sociological 'Mendelism' which gives rise to the system of alternate generations. Although it is certainly possible to pass from the former type to the latter, through a continuous series of intermediaries, it must not be forgotten that this second type is an extreme form of specialization. It does not necessarily follow from the generality of the virtual form that the developed form is universal. An ingenious mind could presumably interpret every system of kinship and marriage in terms of marriage classes, just as a formal logician can give a syllogistic appearance to every form of mental activity. It does not follow that either is in fact the result of such mechanisms.

What picture then can we form of the development of the social structure of India? A system of clans sometimes patrilineal and sometimes matrilineal, but in either case governed by generalized exchange, facilitated either the hierarchical integration of a group of conquerors or the gradual differentiation of statuses within a homogeneous society. In this connexion it is not unimportant to note that Aryan society seems to have been organized as a harmonic regime, i.e., with patrilineal and patrilocal groups, in other words satisfying the theoretical conditions of a system of generalized exchange.[5] By taking a purely historical point of view, Hutton, like Senart, concluded that the origin

---

[1] ch. XVI.   [2] *The Laws of Manu*, IX, 194 (Bühler, 1886); Banerjee, 1896, pp. 31, 268.
[3] Granet, 1939, pp. 158–9.   [4] ch. VIII.
[5] cf. Sen Gupta, 1924, pp. 40–3, 53–6; 1938.

of the caste system was probably pre-Aryan. The Indo-European invaders, it is maintained, were content to crystallize a system of pre-existing prohibitions into a type of social hierarchy. From this came the scheme of Manu with the four *varna* organized within a hypergamous structure.[1] If, as Mitra suggests,[2] the four *varna* must be differentiated into two groups, the *dwija* or 'twice born' and the *sudra*, with a subdivision of the former group into three sections, we could recognize even more easily the model of the tripartite organizations which still exist among the Naga.

Which of the two hypotheses referred to in the previous paragraph is preferable is the historian's concern. We have seen that as far as the theory of generalized exchange is concerned they are equivalent. This is the same as saying that the notion of caste has a functional value independent of its historical origin. The gradual differentiation of statuses would have led to a dual development. Firstly, for the aristocratic clans (either by ethnic origin or by social rivalry), a development initially towards hypergamy and then towards endogamy, with the concomitant constitution of the exogamous group *within* the caste (on account of endogamy), and consequently obligatorily *bilateral* (without which the caste would retrogress to the clan), the *sapinda*. Secondly, for the client or subjugated clans, a partial development from generalized exchange towards restricted exchange (on account of hypergamy, which gradually excludes them from the extended cycles),[3] with the successive subdivision of the same clans firstly into 'little *gotra*' and then into more restricted units of the *purukh* type. The two developments are thus divergent. The former is marked by a synthetic character[4] which is expressed in the fact that the new castes are engendered by intercaste marriages. The other is marked by an analytic character which results from the gradual disappearance of the clans in favour of secondary groupings, which themselves give way to groupings of an even more subordinate type.

But, concurrently with the progressive organization of Hindu society, these two lines of development tend to converge, or more exactly they have to be functionally adapted to each other. The aristocratic castes are endowed with artificial divisions, more religious than social in nature, the 'great *gotra*' being governed by a rule of exogamy modelled on the *gōt*, *mūl* or *kul*, while the commoners or latecomers try to adapt their stationary exogamous system to the complicated requirements of the *sapinda* rule by progressively adding new sections to those originally prohibited. A further development leads to the imitation by the commoners of the 'Brahmanic *gotra*', either in that they set up for themselves ritual schools like those of their priests or

---

[1] Hutton, 1933, pp. 437–8.   [2] Preface to Bose, 1934*a*, p. iii.

[3] Marriage between bilateral cross-cousins was certainly practised in the fourth or fifth century B.C. (Pusalker, 1934.) Manu prohibits the marriage of cross-cousins as much as that between children of two sisters. It was thus not unknown.

[4] According to Risley (1891, vol. I, p. xxxi) the impulse which leads to the formation of castes has in no way lost its force, and it can be studied at work in many districts in India, even at the present time.

that they affiliate themselves to those already in existence.[1] This leads then to the complicated system of North India and of Bengal, viz., a singular accumulation of castes, *gotra*, eponymous or patronymic sections, and local groups. The situation has all the appearances of a complex former system of marriage classes. We hope to have shown that these appearances are illusory, and that only the hypothesis of an archaic simple system of generalized exchange, confirmed by many present-day facts and by otherwise incomprehensible vestiges, clarifies what up till now has been a very confused picture.

[1] In the region of Chota Nagpur, Risley reports numerous examples of the deliberate and conscious process by commoner tribes to 'Brahmanize' themselves. The *gotra* system is borrowed and imitated. These tendencies already existed in Manu's time (Risley, 1891, vol. I, pp. xv–xviii; Karandikar, 1929, p. 222).

CHAPTER XXVI

Asymmetric Structures

I

However, if we hope to find vestiges of ancient conditions preserved, it is best that we turn to South India. With regard to the study of elementary structures, to which this work is limited, India – and especially South India – is exceptionally interesting for two reasons. The first is the frequency of cross-cousin marriage. The second is because the three known modalities of cross-cousin marriage, viz., marriage with the bilateral cross-cousin, with the mother's brother's daughter, and with the father's sister's daughter, are to be found there.

In Part I of this work we established that an elementary kinship structure governed by a law of restricted exchange is directly expressed in preferential marriage between bilateral cross-cousins. In Part II it has been shown that an elementary kinship structure governed by a law of generalized exchange is also directly expressed in preferential marriage between sister's son and brother's daughter (marriage with the mother's brother's daughter). But, at the same time, it was evident, from the examination of the marriage customs and the kinship terminology, that if this latter system is found in sufficiently *simple* forms to be isolated, it is never found in a strictly *pure* form, and that a heterogeneous element is always mixed with it which cannot be reduced to the law of generalized exchange, and which exhibits, at least superficially, the characteristics of restricted exchange.

From this study of a large region of the world in which both systems are found side by side we hope that this difficulty, and at the same time other problems closely associated with it, can be cleared up. In point of fact we have not yet encountered, at least theoretically, the third modality of cross-cousin marriage, viz., marriage with the patrilateral cross-cousin, which is common in India. If it is acknowledged, as we believe we have proved, that restricted exchange and generalized exchange constitute two simple systems (i.e., inexplicable in terms of other systems), the close association of the three modalities of cross-cousin marriage can be theoretically interpreted in two different ways: either patrilateral cross-cousin marriage is the product of a sort of fission of restricted exchange, resulting from its contact with generalized exchange; or it constitutes a third specific type of reciprocity which cannot be reduced to either restricted exchange or generalized exchange, and which must be defined by its own characteristics, on a par with and independently of the other two. In the first case, it will be maintained that restricted exchange (which, let us not forget, is the bilateral form of reciprocity) splits, as it were, when it comes close to the unilateral form constituted by generalized exchange: the matrilateral modality is isolated, attracted and assimilated. The patrilateral modality subsists alone in an independent form, because it is irreducible. If the second hypothesis is the right one, we shall have to recognize that our analysis is incomplete, and apply ourselves to the definition of the third type.

Some introductory remarks are necessary. In one sense, the fission of restricted exchange always occurs. In an exogamous dual organization, for example, all the male members of one moiety and all the female members of the other are theoretically bilateral cousins, but not in the same way. For any two given individuals matrilateral and patrilateral ties can most probably always be discovered, but it does not follow that they are related in the same degree in both lines. In fact, a considerable proportion of such individuals will undoubtedly be bilateral cross-cousins, but in the first or second degree in one line, and in the third, fourth or fifth in the other. Sometimes the distance in one line will be sufficiently great for it to be practically ignored. This is why the rule of restricted exchange should be formulated circumstantially: it prescribes marriage with the cross-cousin who is either mother's brother's daughter and *at the same time* father's sister's daughter or who is *indifferently* one or the other. The terms must be understood in a classificatory sense. Thus, without any alteration of its nature, every system of restricted exchange admits of a certain coefficient of fission which can be regarded as normal, and which for each group could be calculated in terms of the marriage custom and demographic statistics. So long as this fission is neutral, so to speak – i.e., so long as both types of unilateral cross-cousin are regarded as mutually equivalent substitutes for bilateral cross-cousins – the phenomenon may be regarded as negligible as far as theoretical analysis is concerned.

When we speak of fission of restricted exchange, we are thinking of another type of phenomenon. The fission is, as it were, elective. In other words, instead of the group passively accepting the substitutes or the equivalents which are the by-products of the mechanical functioning of the system, it voluntarily and systematically seeks out one type of cousin to the exclusion of the other. It will be recalled that this elective fission is latent in certain Australian systems which, while conforming to the model of restricted exchange, assert a marked preference for the true matrilateral cousin (Kariera). These systems of restricted exchange are thus affected by a determinable coefficient of generalized exchange. But, contrary to what a superficial analysis might suggest, this type of fission never results in an equal preference for both types. Quite to the contrary, the preference for one entails the exclusion of the other. If the matrilateral cousins are sought after, the patrilateral cousins are not made available to others, since it is the same individuals who, according to the perspective in which they are considered, are the matrilateral cousins of *D* and the patrilateral cousins of *B*. In other words, a bilateral cousin is not the result of the addition of two unilateral cousins, but is one and the same individual.

If such members of a system of restricted exchange establish a preference for a certain type of cousin, they do not therefore make the other type available. They gradually oblige all the other members of the group to conform to their choice. The tendency of a system of restricted exchange towards asymmetry can thus never produce a fission, but only a conversion. For the group as a whole this conversion is manifested in the generalization of preferential marriage with one or the other unilateral cousin. This slightly abstruse analysis leads to an important conclusion, viz., that the fission of restricted exchange cannot be conceived as resulting from the influence of mechanical factors, such that it reduces a group addicted to bilateral marriage into two groups practising respectively the two forms of unilateral marriage. The fission is never real; it can be only ideological. If it exists, it cannot be in the group, but in the minds of members of the group, and for a given group it must operate in only one direction. The hypothesis of fission implies then: (1) that some groups with restricted exchange have changed over to patrilateral marriage, and others to matrilateral marriage; (2) that this change took place in terms of a logical opposition, consciously or unconsciously conceived in the native mind, between the two types of unilateral cousin. Thus, our first hypothesis amounts to an explanation, in time and in space, of the theoretical relationships on which the second is based.

II

This position with regard to the problem is confirmed by the facts. If the two unilateral modalities of cross-cousin marriage automatically resulted from a fission of the bilateral form, it ought to be expected that both of them would be encountered with the same approximate frequency. But this is by no means the case. On the contrary, all the experts on India emphasize that matrilateral marriage is clearly more frequent than patrilateral marriage. What is the nature of this difference?

Let us take, for example, the tabulation of the rules of cross-cousin marriage in India as compiled by Frazer.[1] Of a total of sixteen groups, fourteen clearly incline towards marriage with the matrilateral cousin. These are the Gowari, Agharia, Andh, Bahna, Kaikari, Kharia, Kohli, Chandknahe, Kurmi, Mahar, Maratha, Chero, Iraqi and Kunjra. One group, the Gond, has a predilection for the father's sister's daughter, while another, the Golla, practises both forms but lays the stress on marriage with the patrilateral cousin.

[1] Frazer, 1919, vol. II, p. 126.

In the Appendix to his famous article, 'The Marriage of Cousins in India',[1] Rivers reports that marriage with the mother's brother's daughter is general in Telugu country, where it is known by the name of *menarikam*, and in Malabar, Cochin and Travancore, where the Brahmans themselves have adopted it. Several Brahman groups from the Telugu- and Canara-speaking regions have done so, too. In the Madras Presidency, the same form of marriage exists among the Konga Vellala, the Kunnavan, the Kondh and the Kallan, who also practise bilateral marriage. In Bengal, matrilateral marriage is preferred by the Kaur and the Karan, to whom must be added the Chero, the Iraqi and the Kunjra of the North-Western Provinces. These last two groups formally prohibit marriage with the father's sister's daughter. This latter type, says Rivers, is 'less common'.[2] It exists only rarely in a preferential form which distinguishes it clearly from bilateral marriage, which is reported in thirteen groups from Madras, the Central Provinces and the North-West, Bombay and Bengal.

Hodson has drawn up a table of groups which allow bilateral marriage, and those which sanction only marriage with the mother's brother's daughter. The first category comprises fifty names, the second sixty-three. But only Bombay and the Central Provinces are examined. To appreciate fully the predominance of matrilateral marriage it must be borne in mind that in South India, 'the classic home of cousin-marriage',[3] large groups such as the Kuruba and the Komati prescribe this form of marriage.[4] Even in North India, matrilateral marriage occurs among the Chero, Baiga, Gidhiya, Karan, Kaur, Birhor and Bhotia, with, moreover, details which bring these last systems close to those of Tibet, Assam and Burma.

Karandikar[5] gives forty-two groups from South India and the Central Provinces which have cross-cousin marriage. All, with the exception of ten (seven bilateral, three patrilateral), declare a matrilateral preference. Thus there is no doubt that marriage with the mother's brother's daughter is by far the most frequent.

This preponderance is sufficient demonstration that cross-cousin marriage in India, contrary to what Rivers was tempted at least to accept,[6] cannot be a by-product of dual organization. Koppers has recently revived this aspect of the question, and has very convincingly shown, following Niggemeyer,[7] the pseudomorphic nature of the Hindu divisions into moieties.[8] Niggemeyer had suggested that, wherever a division of the group into 'Great' and 'Small', 'Superior' and 'Inferior', etc., is found in India, there is a distinction based on the more or less complete assimilation of two groups to Hinduism. These pseudo-moieties are, in fact, habitually endogamous. It is true that there are at least three groups with exogamous moieties: the Korava, the Bilimagga of Mysore and the Janappan of Madras. The organization of the

---

[1] Rivers, 1907, p. 625 et seq.   [2] ibid. p. 627.   [3] Hodson, 1925, p. 170.
[4] ibid. pp. 168–71.   [5] Karandikar, 1929.   [4] Rivers, 1907, pp. 622–3.
[7] Niggemeyer, 1933, p. 407–61, 579–619.   [8] Koppers, 1944, pp. 72–92, 97–119.

Janappan and Bilimagga is not entirely clear,[1] but that of the Korava is worth describing. The Korava are divided into three sections, the first two of which are reputedly composed of pure Korava, and the third of natives married outside the caste, and their descendants. These three sections are again divided into two exogamous moieties called respectively *Pothu* and *Penti*, i.e., 'male' and 'female'. The first of the three sections is *Pothu*, the second and the third are *Penti*. Thurston adds, 'the Pothu section is said to have arisen from men going in search of brides for themselves, and the Penti from men going in search of husbands for their daughters.'[2] This asymmetry precludes all possible interpretation of the system as a dual organization. The *Pothu* and the *Penti*, 'sons-in-law' and 'fathers-in-law', reproduce the division characteristic of systems of generalized exchange.

We have interpreted the pseudo-dualism of the Gond of Bastar in the same way.[3] Under these conditions, it is significant that the Bhuiya of Orissa, who practise village exogamy, are divided into *kutumb*, or villages where the members are prohibited spouses, and *bandhu*, villages in which marriage can be contracted.[4] Because the social organization of the Bhuiya is harmonic, viz., patrilineal and patrilocal, and *bandhu* designates maternal relatives,[5] there is a double reason to conclude upon a system of generalized exchange.

The apparent dualism of the Munda is no less illusory. Each Munda village is divided into two groups of *khut*, called *paharkhut* and *munhakhut* respectively. The first provides the religious chief, the second the secular chief: the first is regarded as 'older', the other as 'younger'; the first is regarded as superior, and the other as inferior. Both *khut* of a village belong to the same clan or *kili*, have the same totem, and cannot intermarry. Marriage can take place only between *khut* belonging to different villages and clans, and according to the following rules, viz., if a marriage takes place between two corresponding *khut* of two different villages, other marriages of the same type are sanctioned within the limits of the same generation, but a prohibition ensues for the following generations which lasts as long as the first couples live and even as long as both *khut* preserve the social relationships derived from the intermarriage. Conversely, if a marriage has taken place between *paharkhut* of one village and *mundakhut* of another, this type of marriage is prohibited in the following generation, while that between two *paharkhut*, and that between two *mundakhut*, are allowed.[6] These peculiar rules can be expressed by the formula on p. 427, in which *M* designates the marriage; 1, 2, 3, the successive generations; and *p* and *m* both types of *khut*, respectively.

One might be tempted to interpret the system as an Aranda system. This would be theoretically possible (by marriage with the mother's mother's brother's son's daughter, or with the mother's mother's brother's daughter's daughter or with the father's father's sister's son's daughter or with the

---

[1] Thurston, 1909, vol. I, p. 240; vol. II, p. 448.   [2] Thurston, 1909, vol. III, pp. 449–50.
[3] ch. XXIV.   [4] Koppers, 1944; Roy, 1935.   [5] ch. XXV.
[6] Koppers, 1944, pp. 81–3; *Encyclopaedia Mundarica*, vol. VIII, pp. 2333–80.

$$M_3 \ (p = m) \qquad = f\left[M_2 \ \begin{matrix} (p = p) \\ (m = m) \end{matrix}\right]$$

$$f\left[M_2 \ \begin{matrix} (p = p) \\ (m = m) \end{matrix}\right] = f\left[M_1 \ (p = m)\right]$$

father's father's sister's daughter's daughter), if we did not know that, during the period of marriage between two *mundakhut*, the *paharkhut* of one village can contract marriage with either *khut* of the other village and vice versa, which excludes a matrilineal dichotomy being superimposed on the double patrilineal dichotomy into *khut* and into *kili*. In these circumstances the simplest interpretation is that of a system originally based on marriage with the father's sister's daughter, as can be seen from Figs. 80 and 81. Here also we are faced with a pseudo-dualism, which in this case

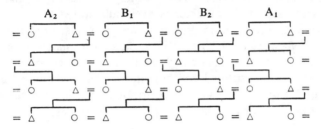

Fig. 80. Munda system.

A and B designate the *khut*; 1 and 2 designate the villages or their clan.

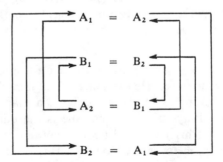

Fig. 81. Munda marriage transcribed in terms of the Aranda system.

masks a system of patrilateral marriage. The cases examined thus suggest that marriage with the mother's brother's daughter, and marriage with the father's sister's daughter, are two specific forms, and that the apparent dualism of certain Hindu societies is explained either by religious considerations, as Niggemeyer and Koppers believe, or as the result of the accidental convergence, in specific and limited cases, of these two types of marriage, whether actually existing or latent.

III

Facts of another type, which are at the basis of Rivers's hypothesis in favour of an ancient dualism in India must also be considered. Rivers ultimately abandoned this interpretation, at least in part, in order to support Richards's economic interpretation,[1] which is certainly no more satisfactory. But it is the facts themselves which deserve attention.

What we are dealing with here is the particularly close relationship that is met with in India between the nephew and the mother's brother, especially on the occasion of the nephew's marriage.[2] On the subject of the Tamil-speaking Kallan and of certain Telugu, Frazer says: 'Failing a cousin of this sort, he must marry his aunt or his niece or any near relative.'[3] In some cases, marriage with the sister's daughter is even substituted for or preferred to marriage with the cross-cousin. In numerous groups, such as the Vallamba, the Konga Vellala, etc., which practise cross-cousin marriage, if the young husband, because of his age, is unable to give his wife children, his brother, father or uncle is substituted for him in this task. Among the Korava, Koracha, or Yerukala of South India, the mother's brother usually claims his sister's daughter for his son:

> 'The value of a wife is fixed at twenty pagodas. The maternal uncle's right to the first two daughters is valued at eight out of twenty pagodas, and is carried out thus: if he urges his preferential claim, and marries his own sons to his nieces, he pays for each only twelve pagodas; and, similarly, if he, from not having sons, or any other cause, forgo his claim, he receives eight pagodas of the twenty paid to the girl's parents by anybody else who may marry them.'[4]

Nevertheless, among these same Korava, the uncle is not obliged to give his nieces to his sons in marriage. He can marry them himself: 'In this tribe, as in a number of other tribes in southern India, a man has the option of marrying his niece, always provided that she is the daughter of his *elder* sister; the daughter of his *younger* sister he may not take to wife, unless indeed he should happen to be a widower.'[5] This preference for his niece, which is on occasion greater even than that for the cross-cousin, is specially marked among the Telugu- or Canarese-speaking castes of Mysore, with the result that nieces married to their uncle change their status, in relation to this uncle's son, from that of cross-cousins to that of mother's sisters and

---

[1] Rivers, 1915; Richards, 1914, pp. 194–8.　　　　　　　　　　[2] cf. ch. IX.
[3] Frazer, 1919, vol. II, p. 105.　　　　　　　　　　　　　　　　[4] ibid. p. 109.
[5] loc. cit. The differentiation between the older and younger sister in consanguineous marriages (cf. ch. I) is to be compared with this.

thus become prohibited spouses. The Sanyasi, a Telugu-speaking caste of itinerant mendicants, sanction marriage with the cross-cousin only when marriage with the niece is impossible.[1] The Holeya and the Madiga of Mysore, two particularly primitive groups, formally prohibit marriage with parallel cousins, who are classified as brothers and sisters. The same assimilation is met with among the Golla, an illiterate caste from Mysore, which treats marriage between parallel cousins as a form of incest, and also among the Devanga, a caste of weavers from Mysore, among the castes of the Kannada linguistic group, such as the Kappiliyan and the Annupan, and finally, among the Oriya-speaking groups, who are not Dravidians. The first two groups at least advocate the following marriages in order of preference: firstly, the elder sister's daughter; only then the patrilateral cross-cousin, and in her absence, the matrilateral cross-cousin; finally, and in the absence of the first three types, the younger sister's daughter. Thus cross-cousin marriage seems to be intercalated between two forms of avuncular marriage. There is no doubt that in India, as also in South America, the two forms are closely associated.

It is not only facts of this order which attracted Rivers's attention. For example, when he writes: 'A careful examination of the evidence would seem to show that the relation between uncle and nephew at marriage is especially a feature of Dravidian society',[2] he has in mind other phenomena concerning the particularly close assistance that the nephew receives from the uncle on the occasion of his marriage, that is to say precisely 'in those ceremonies in which we should expect them to be prominent, if the uncle-nephew relation be a survival of the marriage regulation'.[3]

Among certain tribes such as the Koi, Yerkala and Paraiyan, these relationships still co-exist with cross-cousin marriage. Among others, such as the Tiyyan and Idaiyan, in which cousin marriage does not exist – or no longer exists – the uncle nevertheless has a right to compensation at the time of his nephew's marriage. These and similar customs have often been interpreted as survivals of mother-right, and Rivers does not entirely exclude this interpretation, which Lowie was to criticize so decisively some years later.[4] Nevertheless, Rivers regarded it as insufficient, on account of the similar part played in numerous cases by the father's sister or her husband. For example, how are we to understand the part played by the (bridegroom's) father's sister's husband in Iraqi marriage, unless an earlier regulation is invoked by which the mother's brother is at the same time the father's sister's husband, as is the case in a system of marriage between bilateral cross-cousins?[5] Thus, on the basis of the regions of the world which have been considered, it must be admitted that the special relationship between uncle and nephew can have different origins. We are faced with one of 'these cases of complex causation' that Rivers believes 'to be the rule in

[1] ibid. p. 114.   [2] Rivers, 1907, p. 618.   [3] ibid. p. 613.   [4] Lowie, 1919.
[5] Rivers, 1907, p. 615.

sociology'.[1] When this relationship is found associated with an extant or vestigial state of matrilineal descent it can be seen as an aspect of the rôle devolving upon the uncle as his nephew's natural protector. But in India, where matrilineal descent has a much more limited area of distribution than cross-cousin marriage, and where matrilineal descent began to disappear at a much earlier date than cross-cousin marriage, it is possible that the maternal uncle's rôle is a survival of cross-cousin marriage rather than of matrilineal descent. Thus this special rôle must be explained, it is argued, as the expression of the survival of the maternal uncle's rôle as potential father-in-law.[2]

Rivers's thesis would have some force if a rigorous correlation were established between patrilateral and matrilateral marriage on the one hand, and the intervention in the marriage of the father's sister's husband and the mother's brother respectively on the other. If this correlation existed, it would be difficult to avoid the conclusion that it is the potential father-in-law who appears each time. But such is not the case. Specifically, with regard to the Iraqi, the example which Rivers takes as his basis, Rivers himself indicates unequivocally that they marry the mother's brother's daughter, which makes the part played by the father's sister's husband (who is different from the mother's brother, according to the hypothesis) inexplicable, unless appeal is made – as Rivers was obliged to do, but without any proof – to an earlier state of bilateral marriage[3] which today has disappeared. And how will we argue in the case of the Kachin? It will be recalled that they have a simple system of generalized exchange. In the marriage ceremony *the bride's* mother's brother and *the bridegroom's* father's sister, both of whom the system absolutely excludes as spouses, have simultaneous parts to play. Furthermore, the bridegroom's mother's brother (who is also the bride's father) does not play any rôle in the marriage; actually he cannot even be present. The symmetrical nature of the structure uniting the bridegroom and the bride, the bridegroom's father's sister and the bride's mother's brother, in the absence of all possibility of the merging of functions, is obviously the key to the situation (Fig. 82).

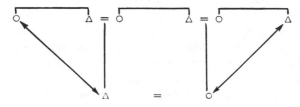

Fig. 82. Father's sister and mother's brother.

---

[1] Rivers, 1910, p. 57.   [2] ibid. 1907, pp. 616–17.   [3] ibid. p. 615.

Let us add that either the father's sister or the father's sister's husband, depending on the particular case, has a rôle to play. At a pinch Rivers's interpretation would account for the second case, but is useless in the first. By contrast, it can be understood that in societies in which masculine authority is firmly established the father's sister, who is always the essential person, is represented by her husband who acts in her place.

IV

We shall quickly mention several other objections which warrant attention. Rivers interprets phenomena which Radcliffe-Brown has since shown (and basing himself, at least in part, on the same facts, for in addition to India Rivers refers to Fiji) must be correlated with a regime of patrilineal descent,[1] as vestiges of matrilineal descent (or as facts identical to those that would be expected from this mode of descent). He also seems to take it for granted that a relationship of reciprocal assistance is the characteristic attitude between the son-in-law and the father-in-law. This is by no means so, and for a double reason. Among the Naga, although they practise cross-cousin marriage, the maternal uncle, the potential father-in-law, is strictly avoided. And, conversely, in many African, Melanesian and American groups, whether they have cousin marriage or not, there is opposition, and not parallelism, between the respective attitude of the nephew and the uncle on one hand, and of the father-in-law and the son-in-law on the other. In one case solidarity and affection are found, and in the other reserve and restraint. If the facts referred to by Rivers were the vestiges of a former system of bilateral cross-cousin marriage, there would be an odd contradiction between the rôle played by the bride's maternal uncle (her potential father-in-law) at the time of marriage, and the attitude of the Hindu wife in respect to her father-in-law, i.e., the latter is expressed by the root, *vij*, the general sense of which is 'trembling at', and is applied also to the reaction of men at the roaring of a lion, of birds at the sight of a falcon, or to the feelings of the monk who has forgotten the Buddha.[2]

But there is an infinitely more serious difficulty. The special relationship of tenderness or of fear which exists in innumerable cultures between the nephew and the maternal uncle, has fascinated sociologists to such a point that too often they plunge headlong at it like the bull at the matador's cape, without concerning themselves with the exact nature of the reality that it covers, and it may be suspected that Rivers himself was a victim of such rashness. We shall not deal with the whole question of the maternal uncle here; the solution has been outlined in another work.[3] Let us merely recall that Lowie has established that the avuncular relationship is present in both patrilineal and matrilineal regimes; that Radcliffe-Brown has differentiated two different forms of it; and that we ourselves have suggested that these

[1] Radcliffe-Brown, 1924. [2] Coomaraswamy, 1942. [3] Lévi-Strauss, 1945*a*, pp. 33–53.

two forms, in their turn, must be differentiated into four modalities. It is necessary, moreover, to distinguish a special case, India and South America being characteristic examples, in which cross-cousin marriage is associated with the mother's brother having a matrimonial privilege over the sister's daughter. In this case, the maternal uncle is then an actual or potential brother-in-law, whether he himself marries Ego's sister, or whether Ego's wife's maternal uncle is, at the same time, Ego's wife's sister's husband.

We have already cited examples of Hindu groups which practise this form of marriage, and who even prefer it in some cases to cross-cousin marriage. It is illustrated in numerous customs. Thus among the Korava: 'A man can marry his sister's daughter, and, when he gives his sister in marriage, he expects her to produce a bride for him. His sister's husband accordingly pays Rs. 7-8-0 out of the Rs. 60 of which the bride-price consists, at the wedding itself, and Rs. 2-8-0 more each year until the woman bears a daughter.'[1] The kinship terminology emphasizes the nature of the actual or potential brother-in-law, who among the Korava (who also practise the exchange of daughters) is both maternal uncles:

'At the conclusion (of a feast) the future bridegroom's people inquire if the girl has a maternal uncle, to whom the purchase money should be paid . . . But, as a matter of fact, the whole of it is never paid. A few instalments are sometimes handed over, but generally the money is the cause of endless quarrels. When, however, the families are on good terms, and the husband enjoys the hospitality of his wife's maternal uncle or vice versa it is a common thing for one to say to the other after drinking: See, brother-in-law, I have paid you two madas today, so deduct this from the vōli (purchase price)'.[2]

The term for brother-in-law, used here by the husband to address his wife's maternal uncle, expresses a kinship relationship which can but need not exist, but which is implied in the system as a permanent virtuality. It is highly likely that the rule mentioned above, according to which a man can marry only his older sister's daughter but not his younger sister's daughter, is intended to avoid the possible conflict between father and son, the younger sister's daughter remaining available for her matrilateral cross-cousin, which conforms to the regulation of marriage in force among the Korava.

There are thus two types of relationship between the uncle and the nephew. There is, on the one hand, the assistance given by the uncle to his nephew when he marries, and, on the other hand, the maternal uncle's matrimonial privilege over his sister's daughter, which also creates for him a special type of relationship with his matrilateral nephew. If it is at least theoretically possible to associate the former type of relationship with matrilineal descent, it is obviously impossible in the case of the latter, for the maternal uncle would bear the same name or belong to the same exogamous group (in any

[1] Thurston, 1909, vol. III, pp. 486–7.   [2] ibid. p. 478.

case to the same moiety) as his sister's daughter, and consequently could not marry her. For this reason the matrilineal Nayar expressly prohibit it. The marriage privilege of the mother's brother over the sister's daughter is conceivable only in a regime of patrilineal descent, or in a regime which does not yet admit of systematic descent. The Brazilian natives themselves justified it to the sixteenth-century missionaries by a unilineal theory of conception, reserving for the father the only active rôle.[1] By contrast, these two types of relationship which are often co-existent and which, when descent is definitive, seem to be marked by contradictory characteristics, are harmoniously based when they are interpreted in the light of the structure of exchange, which is at the basis of both avuncular and cross-cousin marriage.

There exists, in fact, a still more simple structure of reciprocity than that found between two cross-cousins, viz., that which results from the claim that a man who has given his sister can make on the sister's daughter (Fig. 83).

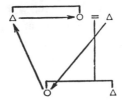

Fig. 83. Avuncular privilege.

The sister's daughter is the first substitute possible when the new brother-in-law has no sister to exchange. This relationship is often very clear in native thought. Thus in western Papua, where patrilineal descent occurs, men arrange marriages usually on the basis of an exchange of daughters. If one of the partners has neither a daughter nor an unmarried sister to give in exchange when the contract is concluded, he will very probably have to agree to give the first daughter born to him.[2]

Even where the exchange of sisters has been practised by the older generation, nothing prevents it being continued and prolonged between the two men who have exchanged their sisters by an exchange of their daughters. But two types of men always have virtual authority over the same woman, viz., her father and her brother. Therefore we immediately have four possible schemes of reciprocity: the exchange of sisters by or for the brothers, either in the older generation or in the younger generation; the exchange of daughters by fathers; and finally, the exchange of a sister against a daughter, or of a daughter against a sister. Furthermore, the four schemes can co-exist, a man not being restricted to only one daughter or to only one sister, but being able to have several of them with nothing to prevent them from being exchanged according to different modalities.

[1] Lévi-Strauss, 1943*b*, pp. 398–409. [2] Lyons, 1924, p. 58.

If, as in Fig. 83, the mother's brother claims his sister's daughter, he is immediately put into a debit position with respect to his nephew, since by this fact the nephew is deprived of a woman to exchange for a wife.

As already noted, the double right of the uncle over the niece and of Ego over his cousin, which is found in the elementary structures of reciprocity, can be in conflict in the case of bilateral cross-cousin marriage. For in this case a man and his son claim the same woman. The same thing occurs in the case of the uncle's privilege over the matrilateral niece, and of Ego's over his patrilateral cross-cousin. We have already given examples of this among the Korava, Koracha, or Yerukala of South India. But the uncle can also discharge his debt in two ways: either by giving his nephew one of his wives or by giving him the right to inherit his wife after his death, as often happens in Africa,[1] or by giving him his daughter to marry, i.e., the matrilateral cross-cousin. Thus, exchange can take place between the nephew and the uncle, i.e., in an oblique way, between two successive generations, and in this case the uncle, in relation to his nephew, gives up his status as mother's brother and acquires the different status of actual or potential brother-in-law. This status of potential brother-in-law is the common basis of both avuncular marriage and the assistance given by the uncle to the nephew at the time of marriage. Both are thus corollaries of the more fundamental structure of exchange.

v

The assertions in the preceding paragraph must be understood in a symbolic sense; they have no more than metaphorical value. In point of fact, nothing is further from our mind than to wish to explain unilateral cross-cousin marriage as a consequence of the avuncular privilege or vice versa, as Kirchhoff has tried to do for South America.[2] If both types of marriage exist simultaneously, it can be only by reason of the total structure of the system, which accounts for both, and from the theoretical point of view it is entirely unimportant if in some given group there are reasons to suppose that the father has transferred his right to his son, that the uncle has discharged his debt by giving a daughter, or that the father himself has taken his son's potential wife. All these reasons are mutually contradictory, and in our opinion they constitute a mythological view of social history. To suppose that they have operated in some specific cases is no reason at all to suppose that this action has occurred everywhere in only the one form or in the same order. The ultimate explanation cannot be sought in this direction.

[1] And also in Siberia and on the north-west coast of North America. It is striking that in these two regions – and for the reason which has just been indicated – the uncle and the brother-in-law represent the same type of risks and consequences. For the same reason and in the same way they represent the perilous element of Aleutian life (Jochelson, n.d.; cf. particularly stories nos. 6, 12, 13, 17, 24, 39, 49, 54, 58, 65). In Tlingit stories the maternal uncle continually fears his nephew as the rival in love for his younger wife and seeks to kill him (Swanton, 1909). And the same situation is found in South America on the Xingú (Lévi-Strauss, 1948c).   [2] Kirchhoff, 1932, pp. 41–70.

Here again we find a problem which we have already posed with regard to the Chinese and the Miwok systems, concerning the relationship between matrilateral cousin marriage and marriage with the wife's brother's daughter. In every case where 'parallel marriage' and 'oblique marriage' co-exist, there is neither contradiction nor opposition – nor a relationship of causality – between the two forms of exchange. The fact that a man receives another man's sister as his wife does not imply that he no longer has the right to receive his daughter, but quite the contrary. This is because the fact of receiving, if it involves an obligation to give, also implies a renewed right, which is always being revived, to receive again. As Granet, who takes a better view here than in his attempt to derive oblique marriage from parallel marriage, and furthermore quoting an orator of an ancient address, puts it: '*In welcoming* new relationships *with ritual presents* old relationships must not be *left idle*.'[1] We shall add to this Leenhardt's clear statement evoking the mythological origin of Kanaka alliances:

> 'In the beginning there was the *vibe*, the alliance of Nerhè and Rheko, the former of the Ver totem, the latter of the Iule totem. They exchanged their sisters, and had it been a bargain they would have called it quits. But this exchange is not a bargain, it is an arrangement for the future, a social contract: the child that each has by the woman received goes back to take the place that this woman has left among her mother's people; from generation to generation new gaps are filled alternately in the same way.'[2]

In many groups marriage involves a series of interminable obligations on the part of the son-in-law. Conversely, the fact that one has ceded to another a value as great as his sister or his daughter, involves him in unending renewed payments, such as will ensure the maintenance of an alliance for which much has already been sacrificed. Nothing would be more dangerous than to break the bond, for then there would no longer be any source of support. Marriage alliance always involves a choice between those with whom one is allied and on whom henceforth one relies for friendship and help, and those with whom an alliance is declined or ignored and with whom ties are severed. In one way, then, one is the slave of one's alliance, since it is established at the price of transferring irreplaceable, or almost irreplaceable, goods, viz., sisters and daughters. From the moment that one is bound by it everything must be done to maintain and develop it. In the same way as for many primitives a gift requires new gifts, and a benefit received establishes a right to an uninterrupted series of new benefits, so also the gaining of a sister puts one in a privileged position to obtain the daughter also. The gift or the exchange of daughters creates a relationship of affinity; it can also be said that the bond of affinity, already established by marriage with the sister, is a ground for later claiming the daughter.

[1] Granet, 1939, p. 116.   [2] Leenhardt, 1930, p. 71.

Wherever a simple method of direct or indirect exchange is practised, based on the elementary structures of reciprocity created by the cession of sisters and daughters, the brothers-in-law relationship, or, as we would prefer to say, the relationship of affinity, has an importance characterized by an acute ambiguity. The brothers-in-law depend on one another in a truly vital way, and this mutual dependence can create alternatively, and sometimes also simultaneously, collaboration, confidence and friendship, or else distrust, fear and hate. Most often, arbitration between these opposed sentiments is ensured by a strictly fixed social behaviour and a whole system of obligations and reciprocal prohibitions, of which the parents-in-law taboo (including under this term all those designated in English as 'in-laws') is only one element.

But the avuncular privilege, a veritable 'uncle-affinity,' is itself only an element in a more complex situation. When we examined the simple systems of generalized exchange (i.e., those based on marriage with the mother's brother's daughter), we drew attention to the abnormal rôle played by the bride's maternal uncle, which is an apparent contradiction to the orientation of the system.[1] This rôle is not accompanied by a corresponding rôle for the bridegroom's maternal uncle, for in these systems the latter is the bride's father, and it is as such that he appears in the marriage ceremony (when he is not, as among the Kachin, strictly excluded from it). In systems of generalized exchange the two maternal uncles are two clearly distinct persons belonging to different lineages, and the relationship which unites a man with his maternal uncle (and which obliges the latter *to give him* his daughter in marriage) is totally different from that relationship which unites a girl with her maternal uncle (and which allows the latter, to use a simplified formula, *to obstruct* his niece's marriage). Under these conditions, and when these ideas are transposed to India, we must carefully consider a certain number of facts:

(1) From observations reported by Rivers it follows that both maternal uncles, or the bridegroom's or the bride's uncle alone, depending on the case, have parts to play in the marriage ceremony. Rivers has completely ignored these differences.

(2) Among the different modalities of cross-cousin marriage, it is that of matrilateral marriage (corresponding thus to generalized exchange) which is by far the most frequent.

(3) When the description given by Rivers of sixty-seven groups in which the maternal uncle has a part to play in the marriage is analysed, it is discovered that in thirty-two groups at least the uncle concerned is the *bride's mother's brother*.[2] A great number of cases are uncertain, but, given this already considerable proportion, it can be inferred that the part played by the bride's maternal uncle is by far the more frequent. India

---

[1] chs. XVIII and XXIII.　　　　　　[2] Rivers, 1907, Appendix.

thus verifies the surprising correlation, already established elsewhere, between generalized exchange and the rôle of 'creditor' played by the bride's matrilineage.

A much more precise and systematic expression of this 'creditor' rôle of the maternal relatives, which so struck Hocart, is found in the two forms of marriage of the uncle with the sister's daughter and of the brother's son with the sister's daughter (marriage with the father's sister's daughter). It is towards these developed forms of a very general phenomenon that we must turn in order to try to arrive at an interpretation of the apparent anomalies of generalized exchange. The avuncular privilege has just been analysed. We shall now examine marriage with the patrilateral cross-cousin.

CHAPTER XXVII

Cycles of Reciprocity

I

Cross-cousin marriage conceals two problems. The first is posed by the differentiation of cross-cousins and parallel cousins in spite of their equal degree of proximity. We believe that we have provided the solution to this in Part I. However, it seems as if we have only helped to make another problem more difficult, for cross-cousins are not always and everywhere regarded as equivalent, even though, as regards our solution of the first problem, they satisfy the same requirements. It is true that there are many groups in which marriage takes place indiscriminately with the mother's brother's daughter or the father's sister's daughter. In this case, furthermore, the cross-cousin, being a bilateral cousin, normally answers to both relationships. But other societies prescribe marriage with the father's sister's daughter and prohibit it with the mother's brother's daughter, whereas in other places still, it is the contrary which occurs. If the distribution of these two forms of unilateral marriage is considered, it will be noted that the second type is much more common. This is, in our view, a significant fact. And even in groups with systems based on restricted exchange, it can be said that the mother's brother's lineage has a privileged position.

It is here that the second problem appears. Our whole theory of marriage is based on the fact that cross-cousins have a common quality which distinguishes them from parallel cousins. Yet not only is there a differentiation between cousins but this discrimination penetrates within the theoretically homogeneous category of cross-cousins. Have we thus established the distinction of cousins into cross and parallel only to see it come to nothing? If it were to appear that both types of cross-cousin differed from each other as much as they differ as a whole from parallel cousins, the distinction we have proposed between the two groups would lose nearly all its significance.

Sociologists have long been aware of this difficulty. They find it hard to excuse cross-cousin marriage for having raised the problem of the difference between children of collaterals of the same sex and children of collaterals of different sexes, and then adding the further problem of the difference between the mother's brother's daughter and the father's sister's daughter. Consequently, having decided that the distinction between cross-cousins and parallel cousins was meaningless, they have generally refrained from giving even a completely negative answer to the preference for one or the other of the two cross-cousins;[1] or, if they have done so, their explanation is based on considerations which are often absurd.

McConnel has suggested a geographical and economic explanation to account for the difference between the Kendall-Holroyd Wikmunkan in northern Australia, who allow either unilateral cousin, but never the bilateral cousin, and who prefer the mother's brother's daughter, and their eastern neighbours, the Kandyu, who tolerate only the father's sister's daughter. Her argument goes that the tie with the maternal clan is closer in tribes living in the fertile coastal region where the clans are more or less sedentary, while the bush life of the Kandyu and their habits as semi-nomadic hunters involves a loosening of inter-clan ties and a strengthening of the solidarity of the paternal clan, 'a woman being glad to identify herself with her hereditary ground and clan by giving her daughter to her brother's son'.[2]

Elkin has made short work of this fantasy by showing that the situation as found in Cape York cannot be generalized, in that neighbouring regions, geographically similar to those which McConnel associates with patrilateral marriage, recognize only matrilateral marriage.[3] But Elkin himself has taken no less dangerous a path in explaining the preference (which is increasing according to him) for matrilateral marriage by the desire of the aborigines to find a mother-in-law as far away as possible 'both in geographical position and relationship',[4] because of the parents-in-law prohibition.

It seems that if we wish to avoid these anecdotic explanations there are only two courses open. Sometimes a change from matrilineal to patrilineal descent has been invoked, but this proves absolutely nothing. It does not take into account the fact, which we have already stressed, that cross-cousin marriage does not require any unilateral theory of descent for its existence. On the other hand, Frazer has suggested an answer resting on the economic rivalry between brother and sister, each trying with varying degree of success according to the society involved, to obtain a wife for his or her son.[5] Thus, 'a father is more anxious to get his niece for nothing for his son than to give his daughter for nothing to his nephew'.[6] Nevertheless this is what happens in the great majority of cases, for even Frazer admits that marriage with the mother's brother's daughter is the more frequent type. Over and above the danger which lies, as we have shown, in thinking of marriage by exchange in economic terms, we would thus be faced with an exceptional feminist victory, rare to say the least in primitive societies, and passing singularly unnoticed.

[1] Lowie, 1961, ch. II.

[2] McConnel, 1940, p. 438. It will be recalled that Shirokogoroff formulated an analogous hypothesis with regard to the Tungus (ch. XXIII).

[3] Elkin, 1940*b*, pp. 382–3.   [4] ibid. p. 432; Elkin, 1931*b*, pp. 302–9.

[5] Frazer, 1919, vol. II, pp. 121–5.   [6] ibid. p. 121.

If one of the marriages were regularly and constantly preferred to the other, we could still inquire into the secondary differences between cross-cousins which, without affecting their fundamental opposition to parallel cousins, would nevertheless explain a subsequent distinction between the two types. But, once again, this is not the case. Sometimes cross-cousins are regarded as being interchangeable, and sometimes as being different. When they are regarded as being different it is not for the same reason, since groups which favour the matrilateral cousin are more numerous than those which recommend the patrilateral cousin. Sociologists can hardly be blamed for believing that this was all purely arbitrary and that the explanation – if there were one – would relate solely to historical and contingent phenomena. Logically the problem seems to admit of no solution. To the extent that one can conceive the possibility of explaining marriage with the bilateral cross-cousin, to the exclusion of the parallel cousin, or of understanding the exclusion of the bilateral cousin in favour of either unilateral cousin, or, finally, of resolving the problem of the continual exclusion of one unilateral cousin in favour of the other, so it seems impossible to find one principle which simultaneously accounts for the exclusion of parallel cousins, for the preference for bilateral cross-cousins, for the prohibition of one or the other unilateral cross-cousin, and in particular, for the fact that when one of them is prohibited, it is more often (but without any regularity) one than the other.

The logic, however, must be there if kinship systems are really systems, and if, as our whole work has attempted to show, formal structures, consciously or unconsciously apprehended by the human mind, constitute the indestructible basis of marriage institutions, of the incest prohibition whereby the existence of these institutions is made possible, and of culture itself, the advent of which is constituted by the incest prohibition.

In chapters XII and XV we have shown the fundamentally different structures to which marriage with the bilateral cross-cousin and with the mother's brother's daughter (i.e., with the matrilateral cross-cousin) correspond. In the former case, the marriage system is regulated by a law of restricted exchange: if an *A* man marries a *B* woman, a *B* man marries an *A* woman. In the latter case, the system is based on a law of generalized exchange: if an *A* man marries a *B* woman, a *B* man marries a *C* woman. In formulating these two laws, and in illustrating their consequences, we have already provided two answers to the group of questions just listed. Indeed, with the law of generalized exchange, we have given a theoretical basis to matrilateral cross-cousin marriage, i.e., that type of unilateral cousin marriage which has the wider distribution. Consequently, the difference between the two types of marriage, viz., bilateral or ambivalent marriage (i.e., indiscriminately recognizing either cousin as a possible spouse) and marriage with the mother's brother's daughter – the father's sister's daughter being excluded – becomes perfectly clear. Bilateral marriage is based on direct or restricted exchange; marriage with the mother's brother's daughter is based on indirect or generalized exchange.

At the same time, we have answered the question why matrilateral marriage is very rarely found in a system with marriage classes, whereas, by contrast, marriage classes appear in the majority of cases in which bilateral marriage occurs. In chapter XIII we have shown that direct exchange is possible only in what we have called disharmonic regimes, i.e., in which residence and descent separately follow the father's and the mother's lines, while indirect exchange arises, as the only possible mode of integration of groups, in harmonic regimes, i.e., in which descent and residence are at once paternal and patrilocal, or maternal and matrilocal respectively.

We have also seen that disharmonic regimes alone are capable of providing a regular process of reproduction by segmentation from moieties to subsections. Harmonic regimes are unstable regimes which can acquire an autonomous structure only when they reach the stage of systems of generalized exchange with n sections. Prior to this stage, the continuity is concealed within dual organization. Later it is corrupted and distorted (as in the Murngin system) by the inevitable contamination of the principle of alternation. There is thus a basic difference between direct and indirect exchange in that the former is extremely productive as regards the number of systems which can be based upon it, but functionally is relatively sterile. This is what we have expressed above by emphasizing that a four-section system in itself represents no development on a moiety system as regards the integration of the group. This same characteristic can be expressed in another way. The development of restricted exchange goes hand in hand with the admission of an even greater number of local groups participating in the exchange, e.g., two in a Kariera system and four in an Aranda system. Organic development (i.e., development in the degree of integration) goes hand in hand with a mechanical development (i.e., the numerical increase in the number of participants). Conversely, generalized exchange, while relatively unproductive in the matter of system (since it can engender only one single pure system), is very fruitful as a regulating principle: the group remaining unchanged in extent and composition, generalized exchange allows the realization of a more supple and effective solidarity within this mechanically stable group.

Consequently, we understand why, as soon as a unilateral preference arises, the degree of kinship, i.e., the notion of relationship, preponderates, while wherever bilateralism is to the fore, it is the system, i.e., inclusion or exclusion within or outside the class, which plays the leading rôle. In our opinion, this is where to look for the answer to the problem of the functional relationship between marriage classes and kinship systems in Australia. Believing that he had established a latent conflict between the two, Radcliffe-Brown concluded that the kinship system alone was important, and he denied marriage classes any functional value with regard to the regulation of marriage. By contrast we have shown that there is a remarkable parallelism between classes and degrees of kinship, and the reason for it can now be seen, viz., that even if a marriage system is based on direct exchange it cannot entirely disregard the latent potentialities of indirect exchange, and vice versa. For example, the Kariera system is undeniably a system of direct exchange since it is based on the exchange of sisters and daughters. However, a certain coefficient of generalized exchange is introduced into the system in so far as the real matrilateral cross-cousin is regarded as the preferred spouse. The Kariera system is symmetrical, but with, as it were, a slight tendency to become warped as long as this warping does not endanger the specific equilibrium of the system. A certain freedom always exists in this respect, no marriage system being able to function in an absolutely rigorous way, since this would presuppose a statistical equality of the sexes, an invariability of the life expectancy of individuals, and an equal stability of marriages, all of which can only exist as limiting factors. This freedom is taken advantage of in order to achieve, through marriages, the best possible integration of the local group, without endangering the integration, which is sought as a more essential end, of the two types of complementary local groups.

Thus, disharmonic systems have naturally developed towards organizations with marriage classes, because, in such systems, direct exchange is the simplest and most effective process for ensuring the integration of the group. Of course, this development is not necessary. In South America we know of numerous examples of systems without marriage classes which feature marriage with the bilateral cross-cousin. However, if the elements of the organization into marriage classes are given, in the form of dual organization, then it can be predicted that all development towards integration will be through the subdivision of the two original classes into sections and subsections, as has taken place in Australia. It cannot be said *a priori* that this development must occur absolutely, and many groups practising direct exchange never pass beyond the stage of dual organization. On the contrary, if the initial regime is harmonic, the odds will be against it, i.e., against the formation of an organization with marriage classes. The repetition of the initial process of dichotomy, ending with dual organization, will be fruitless indefinitely. No further integration will occur, and the process, if set in motion, will mark time indefinitely, alternately transforming local groups into unilineal lineages and unilineal lineages into local groups, without changing the number of social units involved or the type of connexion between them. This is why the majority of the groups practising indirect exchange, in the form of marriage with the mother's brother's daughter, cling to the consideration of the degree of kinship, and so rarely resort to a distribution into marriage classes.

II

These considerations can be expressed in another way. The whole structure of cross-cousin marriage is based on what we might call a fundamental quartet, viz., in the older generation, a brother and a sister, and in the following generation, a son and a daughter, i.e., all told, two men and two women; one man creditor and one man debtor, one woman received and one given. If we were to envisage this quartet as constructed in a system of marriage between parallel cousins, an essential difference would appear. The quartet would then include an uneven number of men and women, i.e., three men and one woman in the case of marriage between cousins descended from brothers, and three women and one man in the case of marriage between cousins descended from sisters. In other words, as we have established in chapter IX, the structure of reciprocity could not be set up. But, from the fact that any system of cross-cousin marriage permits the formation of a structure of reciprocity, it does not follow that these systems are strictly equivalent and interchangeable. No doubt they are in the case of the direct exchange of daughters or sisters, which leads to the fact that all cross-cousins are bilateral, but they cease to be such in the case of marriage with one or the other unilateral cousin.

Let us construct the two quartets corresponding to marriage with the mother's brother's daughter and marriage with the father's sister's daughter (Fig. 84). In a purely formal way, the former is a 'better structure' than the

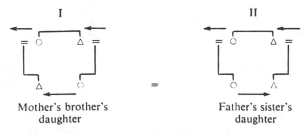

Fig. 84. Mother's brother's daughter and father's sister's daughter.

latter, in the sense that it is the most complete development conceivable of the principle of crossing, on which the very notion of cross-cousins is based. In cross-cousin marriage it seems as if there were a special virtue – the nature of which, moreover, we have determined – attached to what we have called asymmetrical pairs, i.e., those formed by a brother and a sister, as opposed to symmetrical pairs formed respectively by two brothers or two sisters. The native mind is clearly aware of this, since it commonly gives a special name to the unique grouping of brother and sister, called 'the beautiful-ones' by the Wintu,[1] this immediately calling to mind the *neparii* or 'sacred unity' of New Caledonia,[2] the *tuagane* of Manua,[3] or the *veiwekani* of Fiji.[4]

If we generalize this notion of the asymmetrical pair, we can say that the quartet constructed on marriage with the mother's brother's daughter is

[1] Lee, 1940, p. 605.   [2] Leenhardt, 1930, p. 65.   [3] Mead, 1930, pp. 41–2.
[4] Hocart, 1929, pp. 33–4.

formed of four of these pairs: a brother and a sister; a husband and a wife; a father and a daughter; and a mother and a son. In other words, however the structure is analysed, men and women appear in regular alternation, as must do those from whom cross-cousins (and more generally, potential spouses in a dual organization) are descended. The quartet of marriage with the matrilateral cousin is the systematic application, to all degrees of kinship, of the formal alternation of sex on which the existence of cross-cousins depends.

The structure of the second quartet, though it certainly has the same overall value, is less satisfactory. Interpreting it in the same way as the previous structure, we find only two asymmetrical pairs, viz., brother and sister, and husband and wife, and two symmetrical pairs, viz., father and son, mother and daughter. Accordingly, this structure conforms, as it were, to only half the archetype, while the other half retains the fundamental relationship of symmetry of the pairs on which the existence of parallel cousins depends.

Admittedly, this analysis is based on external characteristics and is hence devoid of explanatory value. But this is not the case with the difference in the functioning of the two systems, which is itself a result of these apparently insignificant peculiarities of the structures. Each quartet implies the existence of three marriages, i.e., two in the ascending generation and one in the descending generation. If our theory of cross-cousin marriage is correct, this last marriage is a function of those which occurred in the previous generation. Precisely because of the difference in structure to which we called attention in the previous paragraph, the three marriages of quartet No. I are all oriented in the same direction, while those of quartet No. II reveal a change to the opposite direction when we turn from the older to the younger generation. What does this mean? It means that quartet No. I is what we might call an *open structure*, inserted naturally and necessarily within structures of the same type (as is evident from the principle of generalized exchange): the various cessions and acquisitions of wives, by which the quartet is constituted, presuppose a whole chain of cessions and acquisitions on which, to the final analysis, a wider but self-sufficient system of the same type can be built. By contrast, quartet No. II is a *closed structure*, within which a cycle of exchange opens and closes in the following manner: a woman is ceded in the ascending generation, a woman is acquired in the descending generation, and the system returns to a point of inertia. Let us express this essential difference in another way. Let Ego be a man in the descending generation. In schema No. I, his marriage is merely a link in a chain, the previous link being his sister's marriage, and the succeeding link his wife's brother's marriage. All marriages in the group are connected in this way. In schema No. II Ego's marriage is merely the counterpart to the cession of the father's sister by the father in the ascending generation. With Ego's marriage, which is like a restitution, the transaction is, as it were, terminated.

Ego's sister's marriage is an integral part of another transaction which has no connexion with the previous one. On this occasion, the transaction figures under the heading of Ego's father's marriage. Again, Ego's brother's marriage is connected with a third transaction, the ceding of the sister by the wife's father, a transaction completely independent of the two other transactions. Of course, these expressions have only metaphorical value, but they allow us to see at once the fundamental difference between marriage with the mother's brother's daughter and marriage with the father's sister's daughter. We have defined the former as an application of a principle of generalized exchange, as opposed to marriage with the bilateral cousin which derives from a principle of restricted exchange. Marriage with the father's sister's daughter is equally opposed to bilateral marriage. But an essential characteristic distinguishes it at the same time from marriage with the mother's brother's daughter. Marriage with the father's sister's daughter, like marriage with the mother's brother's daughter, derives from a principle of exchange, but a principle, in its case, of *discontinuous* exchange.

What is meant by this? Instead of constituting an overall system, as bilateral marriage and marriage with the matrilateral cousin each do in their respective spheres, marriage with the father's sister's daughter is incapable of attaining a form other than that of a multitude of small closed systems, juxtaposed one to the other, without ever being able to realize an overall structure. There is a law of restricted exchange which we have formulated as follows: if A marries B, B marries A. There is a law of generalized exchange, as follows: if A marries B, B marries C. However, as against these two continuous forms of reciprocity, we now find a discontinuous form for which there is no law. This system results rather from the methodical application in every case of a rule or formula, the mathematical expression of which we have given in the previous chapter in connexion with the Munda system.

The use of this formula gives a satisfactory result in the sense that, with it, a loan always involves a repayment, and a marriage, which means a loss for a family group, has its counterpart in a marriage which constitutes a gain for the same group: a sister ceded and lost by the father brings in return a spouse for the son. But nowhere is the group as a whole engaged; a total structure of reciprocity never emerges from the juxtaposition of these local structures. Bilateral marriage, like unilateral marriage with the mother's brother's daughter, ensures the best possible solidarity of family groups allied by marriage. Moreover, this solidarity extends to the whole social group, in achieving a structure: dual organization, marriage classes, or system of relationships. By contrast, if marriage with the father's sister's daughter fulfils the first function, it never satisfies the second. The integration of the group does not proceed from the participation of every individual and biological family in a collective harmony. It results both mechanically and precariously from the sum of particular ties by which a family is linked with one family or another. Instead of the real unity of a single thread under-lying the whole social fabric, there is an artificial unity of bits and pieces, proceeding from the fact that two interconnected elements are each coupled with a third element.

Theoretically speaking, this difference is reflected in the fact that there is no formula for marriage with the patrilateral cousin; the system is no more than the statement and repetition of the obvious rule by which it operates. More exactly, it is not a system, but a procedure. The rule of marriage with the father's sister's daughter is doubtless no more incompatible with an organization into marriage classes, answering to the principle of restricted exchange, than is the rule of marriage with the mother's brother's daughter. Indeed, the law of restricted exchange represents the integration of these two rules into one rule, the rule of bilateral marriage, by sister or daughter exchange. But, in this case, there is no equivalence between the system of classes and the rules of marriage, since the latter always add, as we have seen, a principle of differentiation which could not be deduced from the system of classes in itself. We have resolved this difficulty in the case of marriage with the matrilateral cousin by formulating the principle of generalized exchange, which enabled us to define a class system answering strictly to this particular form of marriage.

Nothing like this is possible for marriage with the father's sister's daughter. The notion of discontinuity expresses its peculiar nature but does not constitute its law. There, and only there, might Radcliffe-Brown's assertion, that the kinship relationship alone determines the marriage, be applied. Nevertheless the assertion would still remain inexact. Here as elsewhere what determines marriage is not the kinship relationship in itself, but the fact that this kinship relationship, by changing into alliance, allows the formation of a structure of reciprocity. Of the three forms of cross-cousin marriage, marriage with the father's sister's daughter merely provides the most crudely empirical method of arriving at this result.

It is easy to understand the reason for this. In another chapter we have observed that the relation, at least potential, of a structure of reciprocity precedes the emergence of cross-cousins. It is enough that a man who has ceded his sister to another man should lay claim to the daughter to be born of this marriage even before the child's birth. A woman has been ceded, another woman (and the first to take her place in the alliance constellation) is, or will be, restored. This is theoretically the simplest possible expression of reciprocity, and can be juxtaposed with direct sister exchange, precede it, or be substituted for it, as the case may be. It is clear that this avuncular privilege does not take one further aspect of the problem into account, viz., the marriage of the maternal uncle's son, whether he is already born, or is yet to be born. This aspect can be integrated in various ways: by the denial of the right, pure and simple, as in those Australian and South American societies in which the elders systematically corner the young women of the group; or by the father's surrender of his right to his niece in favour of his son, as in certain groups in South India; or, finally, through the assumption that, because of the uneven rate of population increase (often modified by voluntary intervention) father and son can both be satisfied by marrying two sisters, one being niece to the father and the other cousin to the son. We have shown how the Korava rule whereby one can marry only the elder sister's daughter is explained by an attempt to give two successive generations an equal share of wives belonging to the one generation.[1]

Thus it can be seen that a structure of reciprocity can always be defined from two different perspectives: a parallel perspective, i.e., in which all marriages occur between members of the same generation, and an oblique perspective, whereby a marriage between members of the same generation is counter-balanced by a marriage between members of two consecutive generations (sometimes not consecutive, as in several Australian and Melanesian tribes). It is also possible for the group to admit of both perspectives simultaneously, as do certain tribes in South India and South America which have both avuncular and cross-cousin marriage. Finally, it can be seen how the 'parallel' perspective allows a state of equilibrium to be realized at all times, every man of a given generation always having, at least theoretically, a corresponding member of the opposite sex in his own generation, while the 'oblique' perspective involves a perpetual disequilibrium, each generation having to speculate on the following generation because it has itself been encroached upon by the previous generation.

It is clear that marriage with the father's sister's daughter accommodates better to an initial position of the problem of reciprocity in 'oblique' perspective than does its matrilateral counterpart. Envisaged from this point of view, we can interpret it plausibly as the marriage resulting from the fact that a man who has ceded his sister claims in exchange his sister's daughter, as yet unborn, for himself or his son. This definition of the marriage with the father's sister's daughter already emerges from Fig. 84. Furthermore, it is possible to prove it experimentally. Among the South Indian tribes which practise this form of marriage, it results, the observers tell us, from a claim by the mother's brother over his sister's daughter on behalf of his son. The same tribes which practise marriage with the father's sister's daughter provide the best examples of marriage with the sister's daughter. In other words, both forms of marriage are found together, and in certain Telugu-speaking groups, marriage with the cousin is actually a substitute for marriage with the niece. A study of the facts thus tallies with the theoretical analysis in presenting the former as a function of the latter. Among the Tottiyan and many others, the fact that the father takes the place of his son who is still too young to fulfil his conjugal duties is added confirmation of this view.

From the psychological and logical points of view, the two unilateral

---

[1] Not in terms of the levirate, as Chattopadhyay believed with regard to a similar feature from North India (Chattopadhyay, 1922).

perspectives express different attitudes. The 'parallel' perspective has more satisfactory results as regards the regularity of the structure and the affective atmosphere it helps to create. However, it requires the deferment of the exchange, so that the settlement is not to the benefit of the same people as bore the burden of the sacrifice, in short, so that the exchange mechanism shall function in relation to the whole group and not just to the individuals immediately interested. By contrast, the 'oblique' perspective results from what is at once a greedy and individualistic attitude. The giver seeks compensation immediately, or as quickly as possible, in a form which shall maintain in the highest degree the concrete and substantial tie between what has been given and what should be returned. What he values is not so much the immediate credit as the right of pursuit. This is clear in the case of avuncular marriage. But these primitive characteristics continue to exist, even when the right is ceded by the father to his son: for example, the fact that wherever there is marriage with the father's sister's daughter, in India, this privilege is reflected in such an anxious and literal claim that irregular marriages, in which the husband is sometimes still but a child, are common, clearly expresses the tie, which exists in this form of marriage, between the claim and the object claimed.

Our use here of the term 'primitive' is not meant to assert the chronological priority of marriage with the father's sister's daughter over other forms of cross-cousin marriage, but expresses, rather, an intrinsic characteristic. Marriage with the father's sister's daughter, like marriage with the sister's daughter, represents from the logical as much as from the psychological point of view the simplest and most crudely concrete application of the principle of reciprocity. By no means does it follow that it must be the oldest. Consequently we do not explain why this form of marriage is less frequent in terms of an alleged survival characteristic which would be difficult to verify. Rather, as the previous analysis establishes, it constitutes an abortive form. The claiming of the sister's daughter by the maternal uncle or by his son is premature on two scores: firstly, because it is a speculation on an as yet unrealized future, and secondly, and more particularly, because it precipitately closes the cycle of reciprocity and consequently prevents the latter from ever being extended to the whole group. Even when it is closed (and possessing, for this reason, its functional value) it will never exceed the stunted form of so many precocious plants. It will be but a small cycle, not of a large number of alliances found in the aggregate (restricted exchange) or in a chain (generalized exchange), but of two only.

If, then, in the final analysis, marriage with the father's sister's daughter is less frequent than that with the mother's brother's daughter, it is because the latter not only permits but favours a better integration of the group, whereas the former never succeeds in creating anything but a precarious edifice made of juxtaposed materials, subject to no general plan, and its discrete texture is exposed to the same fragility as each of the little local structures of which ultimately it is composed. If another image be preferred, it can be said that marriage with the father's sister's daughter contrasts with other forms of cross-cousin marriage as an economy based on exchange for cash contrasts with economies practising operations òn deferred terms. For this reason, it is incapable of turning to account the security provided by marriage classes, the guarantee given to each individual that there shall be a permanent exchange value for what he has ceded, in the class of possible spouses, just as the banknote is the assurance of the permanent presence of gold in the public treasury's coffers. Marriage with the patrilateral cousin is indeed a form of marriage by exchange, but such an elementary form that the exchange can only just be described as an exchange in kind, since the substantial identity of the thing claimed and the thing ceded is pursued, through the sister, in her own daughter. It represents the Cheap-Jack in the scale of marriage transactions.

III

From all this, the difficulty dogging us from the beginning of the study of generalized exchange is clarified, and at the same time new aspects come to light. We have encountered a single logical conception of the opposition between marriage with the mother's brother's daughter and marriage with the father's sister's daughter throughout the whole area of generalized exchange, extending from Assam to Indonesia and from Burma to eastern Siberia. The Batak of Sumatra forbid marriage with the father's sister's daughter, saying 'How is it possible that water can flow up to its source?'[1] On the other hand, the Lubu of the western part of Sumatra justify marriage with the mother's brother's daughter by invoking the proverb, 'the leech rolls towards the open wound'.[2] It will be recalled that Tibet and China condemn marriage with the patrilateral cross-cousin as being a 'return of bone and flesh' which runs the risk of 'piercing the bones' if it occurs. The Gold of Siberia distinguish, in the same way, between marriage which 'carries away the blood', and marriage which 'brings it back'. The Chinese contrast marriages which 'follow (paternal) aunt' and marriages which 'return home', one being called 'marriage which shows the side', the other 'marriage in return'.[3] A similar image appears in a Naga myth: when the tiger parts company for ever with man, his brother who has beaten him in a race by a piece of treachery, he leaves him the following precepts as final and supreme advice: 'When you pluck shoots from stumps in the "jhums" to stop them growing always pull away from the stump. Always use a hoe for weeding.

---

[1] Frazer, 1919, vol. II, p. 166.

[2] ibid. pp. 166–7. It is all the more legitimate to compare the two formulas since the Lubu show signs of recent Batak influence. The mother's brother's daughter, the preferred spouse, is called in both languages *boru tulang* (Loeb and Toffelmier, 1939, p. 216).

[3] cf. ch. XXI and XXIII.

Never marry women of your own clan.'[1] The contrast underlying all these formulas is obviously that of a progressive as opposed to a regressive move, or of a natural as opposed to an abnormal move.

However, our foregoing analyses have shown that there is more to this proverbial folklore than threadbare images serving to cover a prohibition and a prescription. In all these cases (and as usual) primitive thought shows itself to be more trustworthy than are some sociologists. Rivers, for example, goes so far to as say: 'It is very difficult to see how such a regulation could have had any direct psychological foundation – to conceive any motive which should make the marriage of the children of brother and sister desirable, while the marriage of the children of two brothers and of two sisters is so strictly forbidden.'[2] The same writer concludes that, as regards cross-cousin marriage, 'it would seem impossible to find any adequate direct psychological explanation in motives of any kind, whether religious, ethical, or magical',[3] and that it must be regarded as 'meaningless',[4] except as a survival or vestige. Rivers, though, would never have gone so far in this direction as writers who, like him, evoke 'the arbitrary manner in which primitive people divided first cousins into marriageable (non-incestuous) and non-marriageable (incestuous) groups',[5] but who ridicule him for having, like Frazer, made cross-cousin marriage the 'divining rod for greater mysteries in social organization'.[6] One is staggered by such obtuseness and levity when a moment's serious consideration of the formulas just recalled would have been sufficient to reveal not only the cause of cross-cousin marriage, but also the specific nature of its various modalities.

For all these formulas express the same truth in various forms: a human group need only proclaim the law of marriage with the mother's brother's daughter for a vast cycle of reciprocity between all generations and lineages to be organized, as harmonious and ineluctable as any physical or biological law, whereas marriage with the father's sister's daughter forces the interruption and reversal of collaborations from generation to generation and from lineage to lineage. In one case, the overall cycle of reciprocity is co-extensive with the group itself both in time and in space, subsisting and developing with it. In the other case, the multiple cycles which are continually created fracture and distort the unity of the group. They fracture this unity because there are as many cycles as there are lineages, and they distort it because the direction of the cycles must be reversed with each generation.

Biological laws have been invoked above, and there would be real piquancy in showing scorners of primitive logic that, by differentiating marriage relationships into 'types' with characteristic properties, primitive logic is proceeding no differently than does the biologist who classifies relationships between the sexes among the ciliates into from six to twenty-eight different formulas,[7] or the geneticist, who differentiates between five and seven types

---

[1] Mills, 1937, p. 266.   [2] Rivers, 1907, p. 623.   [3] ibid. p. 624.   [4] loc. cit.
[5] Loeb and Toffelmier, 1939, p. 184.   [6] loc. cit.   [7] Jennings, 1942, p. 113.

of consanguineous marriage, according to the average rate of appearance of recessive characteristics in each type.[1] Differentiations in no way inferior to primitive subtleties are then seen to appear between degrees of proximity which are customarily identified in popular thought: the results of union with the father's sister are not the same as those of union with the mother's sister; in genetics, the father's brother and the mother's brother receive different statuses, as also do cross- and parallel cousins. The empiricism of some contemporary sociologists merely repeats, on a different plane, the mistake of an outmoded idealism, and it must be answered in the same way:

'It is, therefore, from the history of nature and human society that the laws of dialectics are abstracted. For they are nothing but the most general laws of these two aspects of historical development, as well as of thought itself . . . [Hegel's] mistake lies in the fact that these laws are foisted on nature and history as laws of thought, and not deduced from them . . . The universe, willy-nilly, is made out to be arranged in accordance with a system of thought which itself is only the product of a definite stage of evolution of human thought. If we turn the thing around, then everything becomes simple, and the dialectical laws that look so extremely mysterious in idealist philosophy at once become simple and clear as noonday.'[2]

The laws of thought – primitive or civilized – are the same as those which are expressed in physical reality and in social reality, which is itself only one of its aspects.

Matrilateral marriage represents the most lucid and fruitful of the simple forms of reciprocity, whereas patrilateral marriage, in its twofold aspect as an avuncular privilege and as marriage with the father's sister's daughter, furnishes its poorest and most elementary application. But there is another side to the coin. Socially and logically, marriage with the mother's brother's daughter provides the most satisfactory formula. From an individual and psychological viewpoint, however, we have repeatedly shown that it is a risky venture. It is a long-term speculation which continually verges on bankruptcy, if the unanimity of the collaborations and the collective observance of the rules should ever come into default. The system of patrilateral marriage is a safer operation precisely because its aims are less ambitious. We might well say that it is the safest of marriage arrangements compatible with the incest prohibition. In relation to the formula of restricted exchange, which occupies a middle position, we must therefore oppose 'short cycle systems' and 'long cycle systems'. Patrilateral marriage (with firstly the avuncular privilege, and then marriage with the father's sister's daughter) permits the realization of the shorter cycle, but also, as regards its functional value, the more limited one; whereas matrilateral marriage offers a formula of inexhaustible potentialities for the formation of more and more extensive

[1] Hogben, 1933, pp. 63–5.   [2] Engels, 1940, pp. 26–7.

cycles. At the same time, it can be seen that the length of the cycle is in inverse ratio to its security (Figs. 84 and 85).

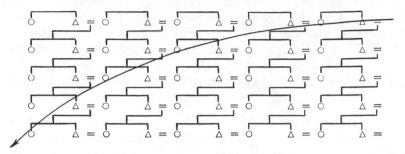

Fig. 85a. Cycle of reciprocity. Marriage with the mother's brother's daughter (long cycle).

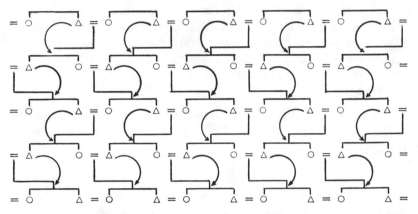

Fig. 85b. Cycle of reciprocity. Marriage with the father's sister's daughter (short cycle).

The rôle and nature of the allogeneous factor which is constantly found in association with simple forms of generalized exchange can then be understood. Groups which have not hesitated to plunge into that great sociological venture, the system of generalized exchange, which is so richly promising and productive of results but also so full of hazards, have remained obsessed by the patrilateral formula, which offers none of these advantages but does not entail the same dangers. We do not mean that the patrilateral formula is more primitive than the other, or that human societies have passed from the latter to the former. But we believe, on the basis of the facts brought together in the preceding chapters, that the two formulas constitute an indissoluble pair of opposites, the two poles of the simple formula of reciprocity, and that the one cannot be thought of without the other, at least unconsciously. The application of these formulas, however, is an entirely different matter. Some societies which are very poor in the field of social organization have been able to satisfy themselves with patrilateral marriage and its limited possibilities, without ever contemplating the adventure of matrilateral marriage. But, even among those which have undertaken it most resolutely, none has been able to rid itself completely of the disquiet engendered by the risks in the system, and they have held fast, sometimes vaguely, sometimes categorically, to that pledge of security which is provided, depending on the group, by a certain coefficient, or even by a symbol, of patrilaterality.

India has shown itself to be the least audacious in this respect, since patrilateral marriage, and in both its forms, here borders on the other type of marriage. Furthermore, this explicit patrilaterality is surrounded by a diffuse fringe, marked by the rôle of the maternal uncle – especially the bride's maternal uncle – in the marriage ceremony. The Gilyak adhere strictly to matrilateral marriage; nevertheless, the right of the bride's maternal uncle to receive a part of the bride-price, in the form of a sister or a daughter,[1] places this Siberian tribe at the limit of patrilaterality. The groups of Assam and Burma which practise marriage with the mother's brother's daughter also provide, it will be recalled, its most complete and systematic formula; but even among these the patrilateral obsession still makes itself felt, although more reservedly, in the otherwise inexplicable sharing of the bride's uncle in the profits of the marriage prestations.[2] Thus, the apparent anomaly which, throughout the study of generalized exchange, has presented this form of exchange as mixed with an obscure element which appeared at first sight to pertain to restricted exchange,[3] amounts, in fact, to a typical characteristic of the structure of systems of generalized exchange. We have already defined this characteristic by saying that there are simple systems of generalized exchange but that these systems are never pure. Doubtless, it is possible to form an ideal conception of a pure system. But human societies have never achieved this degree of abstraction; they have always thought of generalized exchange in contrast with – and therefore, at the same time, in association with – the patrilateral formula, the latent intervention and underlying presence of which provides an element of security, from which none of these societies has even been bold enough completely to free itself.

If this interpretation is correct, two conclusions emerge. Firstly, the appearances of restricted exchange which puzzled us in our study of the systems of India, Burma, Assam, Tibet, China, Mongolia and Siberia, do not in fact pertain to this form of exchange. The bilaterality is a secondary result, a product of the convergence of two forms of unilaterality which are always present and given. The criticism of the pseudo-dual organizations of India had already allowed us to foresee this result. In the second place, and as a consequence, the problem of the relative priority of the formulas of generalized and restricted exchange in India and in China is an illusory problem,

---

[1] cf. ch. XVIII.   [2] cf. chs. XVI and XVII.

[3] We thus anticipated Lane (1961) in perceiving the 'restricted' aspects of generalized exchange; but we did not draw the same absurd inferences as this writer.

for if the matrilateral formula alone exerts a positive action, the patrilateral formula always exists, in a negative form, alongside it, as the second term of a correlative pair. It can be said that the two formulas are eternally coexistent. All the historical hypotheses imaginable will never succeed in providing anything more than the incomplete and approximate transfiguration of a dialectical process.[1]

Ghosts are never invoked with impunity. By clinging to the phantom of patrilateral marriage, systems of generalized exchange gain an assurance, but they are consequently exposed to a new risk, since patrilateral marriage is not only the counterpart of matrilateral marriage but also its negation. Within systems of reciprocity, marriage with the father's sister's daughter – short cycle – is to marriage with the mother's brother's daughter – long cycle – what incest is to the entirety of systems of reciprocity. To speak in mathematical terms, incest is the 'limit' of reciprocity, i.e., the point at which it cancels itself out. And what incest is to reciprocity in general, such is the lowest form of reciprocity (patrilateral marriage) in relation to the highest form (matrilateral marriage). For groups which have reached the subtlest but also the most fragile form of reciprocity, by means of marriage between sister's son and brother's daughter, marriage between sister's daughter and brother's son represents the omnipresent danger but irresistible attraction of a 'social incest', more dangerous to the group, even, than biological incest, which latter will never compromise the security of the system because it cannot be conceived of as a solution. It may be understood, then, how it is that in all the above-mentioned formulas both types of marriage are associated as well as opposed; that the reasons for proclaiming the excellence of the one are the same as those for abhorring the other; and, finally, that these formulas are literally the same as those employed in archaic texts, such as the *Ko-ji-ki*, and the *Nihongi*, to brand incest: 'Making rice-fields on the mountain, making hidden conduits run on account of the mountain's height: today indeed (my) body easily touches the younger sister.'[2] For a system of generalized exchange, to marry the father's sister's daughter or to sleep with the sister is, on the same grounds, to reverse a cycle of reciprocity, which is tantamount to destroying it, 'making water flow up to its source'; in a word, it is incest.

After this, the force with which certain peoples who practise matrilateral marriage have condemned patrilateral marriage cannot cause any surprise. The one is not only the opposite and the negation of the other, but it also brings nostalgia and regret for it. Frazer and Thurston[3] have quoted, as an antiquarian curiosity, a text from the *Kanyaka Purana*, the sacred book of the Komati, which, by its apocalyptic tone, offers the best proof of the

---

[1] These observations answer in advance Leach's criticism that I indulge too much in historical reconstructions.

[2] Chamberlain, 1932, p. 358; Ashton, 1896, vol. I, pp. 323–4.

[3] Frazer, 1919, vol. II, pp. 110–12; Thurston, 1909, vol. III, pp. 317–18.

ambivalence already suggested by theoretical analysis. It concerns the solemn sacrifice of one hundred and two *gotra*, who prefer to throw themselves into the flames rather than allow the indescribably beautiful Vasavambika to make a marriage calculated to save the kingdom but contrary to the sacred rule of the *menarikam* (marriage between sister's son and brother's daughter). The one hundred and two *gotra*, with Vasavambika at their head marched proudly towards one hundred and three fire-pits, but not before making their children promise to give their 'daughters in marriage to sons of their father's sisters even though the young men should be black-skinned, plain, blind of one eye, senseless, of vicious habits, and though their horoscopes should not agree, and the omens be inauspicious'.[1] They warned them that, if they failed in their duty, they would lose their possessions and that misfortune would fall upon their families. Furthermore, the caste received full powers to excommunicate delinquents and to prohibit them from entering the town. As for Vasavambika she promised those who violated the sacred custom dumpy daughters 'with gaping mouths, disproportionate legs, broad ears, crooked hands, red hair, sunken eyes, dilated eye-balls, insane looks, broad noses, wide nostrils, hairy bodies, black skin, and protruding teeth'.[2] These curses, hurled against those who prefer sister's daughters to brother's daughters, are by no means inconsequential. They express, with incomparable force, decisive differences in structure, which are such that the choice made between them by a society affects its destiny for ever.

[1] Frazer, 1919, vol. II, p. 111.   [2] ibid. pp. 111–12.

Conclusion

The future life will be but a repetition of the present, but all will then remain in the prime of life, sickness and death will be unknown, and there will be no more marrying or giving in marriage.

Andaman myth, after E. H. Man, *On the Aboriginal Inhabitants of the Andaman Islands* (London, n.d., pp. 94–5.)

CHAPTER XXVIII

The Transition to Complex Structures

I

In the course of this work we have steadfastly avoided historical reconstructions. We have attempted to follow the precept, formulated but so
poorly observed by Rivers, that 'the nature of systems of relationship depends
on forms of social structure rather than on differences of race',[1] or to speak
the language of the linguist, we have attempted to define areas of affinity,
not routes of migration. It is all the more significant that our attempt has
led us, without prior design or foreknowledge of this result, to confine our
attention to one region of the world, vast no doubt but continuous, and with
easily definable boundaries. This region extends from eastern Siberia in the
north to Assam in the south, and from India in the west to New Caledonia
in the east.

As the reader must have realized, we have so little confined ourselves to
this area that we have continually borrowed examples from other regions.
Accordingly it is not our intention to challenge the existence of elementary
kinship structures in other parts of the world, especially Africa and America.
In both these continents, cross-cousin marriage and other forms of preferential
union are abundantly represented. Nevertheless, as far as we know at
present, generalized exchange in its simple form appears only within the
limits of the area considered, where several examples of it are provided.
Furthermore, between these various modern and geographically localized
occurrences, we have been able to establish a continuous series of intermediate types, which provide a basis for the hypothesis of a much vaster,
and altogether exceptional, archaic extension of this form of exchange.

As regards restricted exchange, the situation is perhaps not so striking.
In Africa, the exchange of wives is a characteristic feature of Pygmy society,
where elements, at least, of dual organization are also encountered, as in
Polynesia. Brilliantly clear examples of dual organization are found in North
America, and for some years we have known that it occupies no less a place
in South America. However, some reservations must be made. It has long
been noted that moiety systems are practically absent from Africa. Elsewhere

---

[1] Rivers, 1914, vol. II, p. 10.

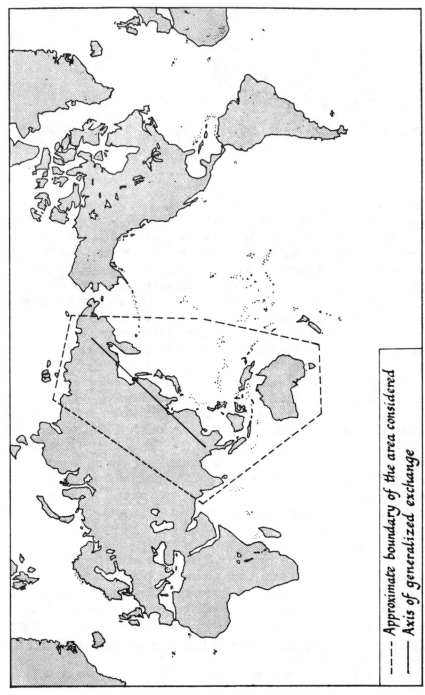

Fig. 86. Approximate boundary of the area considered and axis of generalized exchange.

---- Approximate boundary of the area considered
—— Axis of generalized exchange

their real nature and, in particular, their homogeneity, have been closely discussed by specialists on Polynesia and America.[1] There is nothing comparable in either Africa or America to the precision and clarity found in the study of Australian societies. More especially, it is not essential to consider these continents, unless on exceptional grounds and to illustrate some detail of a custom or institution. The area to which we have been spontaneously confined in the course of our analysis has an extraordinary density of kinship systems answering to the definition of elementary structures. It allows all types to be considered and gives several examples of each type. These examples are the richest and most lucid, and approximate most closely to the demands of a theoretical demonstration. Thus we have a privileged area, the general aspect of which we cannot avoid examining.

First let us consider it in terms of generalized exchange. We have been led in Part II to define an axis of generalized exchange running from south-west to north-east, i.e., from western Burma to eastern Siberia, the two end positions being taken up by the two simple forms encountered in our inquiry, viz., the Kachin and Gilyak systems. Near these two end positions we find hybrid systems which are remarkably similar in their structural detail, viz., the various Naga systems in the south, the Tungus and Manchu systems in the north. The middle of the axis between the latter is entirely given over to the Chinese system, which, as we have attempted to show, still reveals, even after a very complex evolution, an archaic structure of generalized exchange, sometimes in an astonishingly vivid form, and accounting for at least some of its present aspects. Several intermediate systems placed on the axis or in its immediate vicinity, in the exact place required by theoretical analysis, confirm the accuracy of this scheme.

What happens on either side of the axis? To the west, as distant as central Asia, we have found characteristic features of the structure of the northern systems, such as the periodic extinction of the rule of exogamy, which we have also related to the rhythm of the reproduction of clans and sub-clans in Naga society. An observation by Constantine Porphyrogenitus, which we owe to the friendly interest of Roman Jakobson, may permit us to push the frontier further back. The Petcheneg were divided into eight stems, each commanded by a chief who was succeeded by a cousin or a cousin's son 'so as to avoid the functions of chief being perpetuated in only one family of a clan, and to ensure collaterals of their right of inheritance and the transmission of honours'.[2] This strange rule would be easily explained if the rhythm of the extinction of exogamy, which we have traced as far as the Kazak,[3] had previously existed among the Petcheneg without compromising the political authority of the original clan. While the latter would lose its exogamous character in favour of its derivative sub-clans, authority would rest with the main unit, and be wielded in succession by each of the sub-clans, which are cousins to each other. The lack of information about the former

[1] cf. ch. VI.   [2] ch. 37.   [3] cf. ch. XXIII.

organization of the family and the rules of marriage in central and western Asia allows only hypotheses to be made on this point, as on others. Finally, again in the region to the west of the axis, India has provided us with examples of systems in which, as it were, generalized exchange miscarries into patrilaterality.

To the east of the axis stretches a zone of migrations, invasions and conquests leaving little hope of finding the old systems in position. However, there is no possible question about a vast part of Indonesia. To the matrilateral Batak and Lubu – the former with a peculiar suppression of the patrilateral prohibition after three generations, reminiscent of the periodic phenomena evoked in the previous paragraph – must be added the following regions: Nias, Ceram, Tanimbar, Kei, Flores, Sumba, and the Moluccas, where there is clear evidence of marriage with the mother's brother's daughter.[1] But suddenly we reach the border marking the commencement of restricted exchange. Forms of bilateral marriage are to be observed in Endeh and Manggarai, on Flores, Kisar, Aru, Leti, Moa and Lakor.[2] The past existence of marriage classes of the Aranda type with sister exchange has been postulated for Java before the Hindu conquest. These classes are thought still to survive, at least in vestigial form, in Sumatra, in eastern Indonesia, and might thus once have had a continuous distribution as far as New Guinea. Their presence in ancient times is allegedly testified to still by a bilateral social organization, though without the clan, in the whole area considered, especially in certain districts of Flores and Alor. In Borneo and Celebes there are still enclaves which are predominately matrilineal or predominantly patrilineal.[3] Such attempts at reconstruction should be accepted with great caution.

In any case the Fijian system provides valuable information. It has long been regarded as a characteristic example of bilateral cross-cousin marriage. Recent studies limit this interpretation and make it more precise. In the western part of Viti Levu, the relations between *mbito* patrilineal groups are sufficiently suggestive of generalized exchange. However, generally speaking, cross-cousin marriage is reported to be less common than formerly appeared and to take place mainly with the patrilateral cousin.[4] As a growing patrilaterality accompanies the decline of generalized exchange in India, it could be that the same occurrence in Fiji marks the eastern frontier of the area predominantly given over to this form of exchange.

There is a great temptation to draw an axis of restricted exchange from the base of the axis of generalized exchange and perpendicular to it, running north-west to south-east, from South India to New Caledonia and passing through Australia. For this attractive framework to be viable, however, it must be shown that Hindu systems are bilateral, and we have seen that

[1] Loeb, 1933, pp. 16–50.   [2] loc. cit.
[3] loc. cit.; Bertling, 1936, pp. 119–34; Kennedy, 1937, p. 290; 1939, p. 167.
[4] Capell and Lester, 1941, p. 319; 1945, p. 171.

their apparent bilaterality is pseudomorphic. The moiety organizations of India superficially resemble those of Australia, but actually their nature is different. Moreover, Australia is alone in providing pure forms of restricted exchange, as compared with Assamese groups with dual organization in which it is found only in hybrid forms. Consequently, the region embracing South India, Assam, a part of Sumatra and Australia cannot be treated as an axis of restricted exchange in the sense that we spoke of an axis of generalized exchange. It is merely the area in which restricted exchange is most frequent.

Can even this be taken as true? The extreme poles of this area, South India and Australia, share striking similarities, but the resemblance occurs precisely where restricted exchange disappears. The Hindu moiety systems differ from the moiety systems of the Australian aborigines. On the other hand, both regions have the patrilateral system in common, in the form of the Munda system in India, and – if our interpretation of it is correct – the Mara-Anula system in Australia. Besides, there are many indications favouring the existence of marriage between non-consecutive generations in ancient India – either with a 'grandmother', or with a 'granddaughter' – and this has known parallels in Australia and Melanesia. But these forms pertain to structures as far removed from restricted exchange as is possible, to systems which, in comparison with the previous systems, have so far been classed as 'aberrant', but the examination of which has gradually forced upon us the notion of generalized exchange. Consequently, this comparison, far from leading, as it were, to 'the Australianization' of India, would oblige us rather to 'de-Australianize' Australia itself, i.e., to give even more attention than we have done so far to this residue made up of apparently heterogeneous systems. There has been an attempt to minimize their importance because they refused to be reduced to the Kariera and Aranda types. On the contrary, it is these latter types which should take their place in a more complex and, this time, heuristic classification.[1]

The extent to which the methodologically indispensable distinction between restricted and generalized exchange strains the data of the experiment can be seen. There is a privileged territory for restricted exchange, embodying Australia and its Asian and Melanesian prolongations. There is also a privileged territory for generalized exchange, the Burma-Siberia axis. But, just as matrilateral marriage, the simple form of generalized exchange, has continually appeared to us as suffering from a sort of patrilateral corruption, we now see that restricted exchange, if it can exist in simple forms, is never pure either. Even in Australia it is embedded in a context of matrilateral or patrilateral systems.

Accordingly, we should resist to the very end any historico-geographical interpretation which would make restricted or generalized exchange the discovery of some particular culture, or of some stage in human development.

[1] Radcliffe-Brown did this in his 1951 article.

Wherever there is restricted exchange there is generalized exchange, and generalized exchange itself is never free of allogeneous forms. The difference derives from the fact that the contamination of generalized exchange seems to be one of its intrinsic properties; it shows itself in every system, in customs and institutions which are contradictory to the system. When faced with the same phenomena, observers as varied as Hutton, Sternberg and Junod, to mention only a few, have been prompted by the anomalies not only to ask themselves the same question, whether patrilineal societies did not once pass through a matrilineal stage, but to give exactly the same answer. We hope we have contributed to the dissipation of this illusion.[1] The contamination of restricted exchange, on the other hand, takes an extrinsic form. Each system is simple and coherent, but is continually besieged by other systems based upon principles which are foreign to it.

Can the reason be given for this difference? Undoubtedly, yes, if we keep to the ideas advanced in chapter VIII, and consider that the three elementary structures of exchange, viz., bilateral, matrilateral and patrilateral, are always present to the human mind, at least in an unconscious form, and that it cannot evoke one of them without thinking of this structure in opposition to – but also in correlation with – the two others. Matrilateral and patrilateral marriage represent the two poles of generalized exchange, but they are opposed to each other as the shortest and the longest cycles of exchange, and both are opposed to bilateral marriage as the general to the particular – since mathematics confirms that, in all combinations with several partners, the game for two should be treated as a particular case of the game for three.[2] At the same time, bilateral marriage has the characteristic of alternation in common with patrilateral marriage, whereas it resembles matrilateral marriage in that both allow a general solution, and not a collection of partial solutions, as is the case with patrilateral marriage. The three forms of exchange thus constitute four pairs of oppositions (Fig. 87).

II

Nevertheless, a problem does remain, relating at least in part to cultural history. The study of a limited area of the world, comprising India, the Far East and Australia, is both necessary and sufficient to define the fundamental laws of kinship and marriage. It is necessary, since no other region combines all possible cases, or gives such clear examples of some of these cases. It is sufficient, for if the rest of the world reproduces a few simple cases and, in particular, exhibits more complex situations, these simple cases are generally less favourable than those which we have selected for our argument, and the complex situations can all be reduced to the three elementary forms, inde-

[1] Junod, 1962, vol. I, p. 267; and, for Sternberg and Hutton, chs. XVII and XVIII of this work.

[2] Von Neumann and Morgenstern, 1944, p. 47. It can be seen that as far back as 1949 I gave notice of this reduction of restricted to generalized exchange, the significance of which has been somewhat exaggerated by Maybury-Lewis and by Leach (1961b).

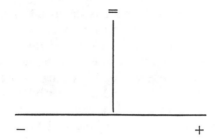

Fig. 87. System of oppositions between the elementary forms of marriage.

= Bilateral marriage; no cycle; formula: A $\leftrightarrow$ B

− Patrilateral marriage; short cycle; formula: $\begin{cases} A \rightarrow B \\ A \leftarrow B \end{cases}$

+ Matrilateral marriage; long cycle; formula: A $\rightarrow$ B $\rightarrow$ C

pendently transformed or intercombined, which we have set out to define.

Does this logical priority correspond to an historical privilege? It is for the cultural historian to inquire into this. Confined as we are to a structural analysis, we need give only a brief justification of the proposition just advanced, and according to which complex kinship structures – i.e., not involving the positive determination of the type of preferred spouse – can be explained as the result of the development or combination of elementary structures. A special and more developed study is to be devoted to these complex structures at a later date. We shall consider in turn the east and west of the privileged area, i.e., Oceania and America on the one hand, Africa and Europe on the other.

Strictly speaking, the six-class systems of the Ambrym-Pentecost type[1] relate to the study of elementary structures. Although they involve a positive determination of the class of the preferred spouse we have reserved them for another work because of their great complexity, which makes them a limiting case. Even a superficial examination shows them to be the result of the combination of a dualistic and a triadic rule of reciprocity, the intention being to make these coincide. This has been accomplished at the cost of extreme difficulties in application, and of new contradictions which are henceforth inherent in these systems. As the combination of the principles of restricted and generalized exchange seems to us to be at the basis of the so-called Crow-Omaha systems of America (which do not always involve a determination of the prescribed spouse), we prefer that the eastern area of complex structures should start to the south of Melanesia.

A further reason prompts us to this decision. Melanesia, as a whole, seems to be infinitely less characterized by bilateral organization than has generally been asserted. New Guinea and its neighbouring regions present, to an

---

[1] Deacon, 1927, pp. 325–42, and the later articles by Radcliffe-Brown (1927), and B. Z. Seligman (1927).

extraordinary degree, what Williams has described as 'sex affiliation', i.e., a differentiation of status between brother and sister, the brother following the paternal line and the sister the maternal line.[1] It is impossible to interpret this phenomenon in terms of restricted exchange, but it becomes very clear when envisaged in terms of generalized exchange, since in matrilateral as in patrilateral marriage the brother and the sister have different matrimonial destinies. The study of sexual affiliation, without cross-cousin marriage, thus allows the definition, throughout the whole Melanesian world, of a sort of 'fault' of generalized exchange, the significance of which seems even greater when it is noted that it borders that wide zone of breakdown of kinship structures which is the Polynesian world. The whole eastern area, the 'Oceanic-American' area as it might be called, thus forms a sort of theatre in which restricted and generalized exchange meet each other, sometimes in conflict, sometimes in harmony. If this hypothesis is correct, the question of bilateral marriage in South America should be carefully re-examined.

III

In contrast to the eastern area, which is characterized by the juxtaposition of the two elementary forms of exchange, the western area, i.e., the Euro-African *bloc*, seems to give free rein to irregularly developed forms, which however all relate exclusively to generalized exchange. This is strictly true for Europe, where we believe not even traces of bilaterality can be revealed. There is no doubt that Africa provides sporadic manifestations of restricted exchange, e.g. the Pygmies, the Hehe, certain Bantu-speaking peoples, the Nuer, the Lobi, etc.[2] But, apart from the fact that these manifestations are often embryonic, and would all require careful examination, Africa is known to be the elected territory for a type of marriage which we have not yet encountered in its most pronounced form: marriage by purchase.

The study of the Kachin and the Gilyak has taught us that marriage by purchase is not incompatible with systems of generalized exchange. It has also shown us that the formula of purchase provides a solution to certain difficulties inherent in generalized exchange and allows them to be overcome. It remains to be proved that marriage by purchase, in its very essence, relates to this elementary structure, and, in a way, constitutes a supple and developed form of it.

We are all familiar with the discussion on the nature of bride-price or *lobola* in Africa, particularly among the Bantu. The *lobola* is neither a dowry – since it does not accompany the bride, but goes to the bride's family – nor a payment; indeed, the woman is never subject to appropriation; she cannot be sold, nor can she be put to death. She remains under the jealous protection of her family, and if she deserts her husband for a just motive, he cannot

---

[1] Williams, 1932, pp. 51–81; cf. ch. VIII of our work.   [2] cf. ch. VIII.

reclaim the *lobola*.[1] What then is *lobola*? In South Africa it consists above all of cattle, and for the Bantu, 'cattle are the most important medium for all ritual relations between human groups'.[2] They assume this rôle of mediary, firstly 'between groups of living men in compensation for and purification from homicide', secondly 'between the living group and the group of the dead in sacrifice',[3] and finally between the groups involved in the marriage. By the terms of the prohibition of incest, a woman cannot have children in her own group. Accordingly, either she must be transferred to a neighbouring group or a man from another group must come to her.[4] Whether descent is matrilineal or patrilineal (and among the Bantu there are both possibilities), both groups, owing to the prohibition of incest, are placed in a state of reciprocal interdependency. The transfer of *lobola* does not represent a unilateral purchase. As the counterpart to the daughter, it affirms the bilaterality of the link.

But, at the same time, it is more than this. The completion of the marriage rites does not put an end to reciprocal obligations between the groups. The reality of the alliance is attested to during the whole marriage by a series of services offered and rendered, and of gifts demanded and received. But once *lobola* is received it immediately commences a new cycle. The main reason that it cannot be seen as a payment is that it is never consumed, except on occasion and in part for sacrificial ends. Scarcely is it received than it is re-invested for a wife for the brother or cousin of the young bride. As a thread runs through a piece of fabric, *lobola* creates an unlimited series of connexions between members of the same group, and between different groups. The Seligmans have described this aspect of bride-price as a total prestation in another region of Africa: 'A boy who has no sister will be poor.'[5] Again: 'Every Shilluk youth is interested in the marriage of his sister and of his father's sister's daughter, for he receives cattle resulting from their bride-wealth and without cattle he cannot himself marry . . . Thus a man has every reason to desire his sister's marriage to be stable.'[6] But the multiplication of ties between the groups has a counterpart in the consolidation of ties within the group. Among the Azande, 'as boys hope to marry they must be obedient and work for their fathers, who will give them spears paid for their sisters'.[7] Consequently, the bond between fathers and sons is tied up with the bond between the allied families. The groom works for his parents-in-law, and he receives the counter-prestation of his gifts from his wife in the manifold forms of cooking, gardening, procreation of children and sexual gratification. The exchange of services takes place in both directions, and the double circulation of women and cattle according to an alternating rhythm ensures the union of groups and of generations through the years.

A particularly significant light is cast on the real nature of the marriage tie in these African systems by the special respect shown, in many groups,

[1] Hoernlé, 1925*b*, p. 490.   [2] ibid. p. 481.   [3] ibid. p. 483.   [4] loc. cit.
[5] Seligman and Seligman, 1932, p. 62.   [6] ibid. p. 62.   [7] ibid. p. 514.

in the relationship between the husband and the wife's brother's wife, whom the Thonga solemnly call the 'great mukoñwana'.[1] Among the Shilluk, this sister-in-law is included in the category of *ora* (relatives by marriage who should be respected), and the Seligmans say: 'It is clear that she stands in a relationship quite different from that of a wife's sister or a brother's wife. But no reasons were discovered for treating her as a mother-in-law.[2] Among many primitive peoples, parents-in-law are indeed known to be subject to special taboos as regards the daughter-in-law, and even more often, the son-in-law. But Junod adds an additional detail to his description, viz., that the Thonga show as much respect for the 'great mukoñwana' as for a mother-in-law, and more. Therefore the first interpretation given by Junod, that the sister-in-law is a presumptive mother-in-law (because of a marriage privilege over the wife's brother's daughter), is not satisfactory. It is even less satisfactory when it is considered that the husband enjoys the privilege of familiarity with his wife's brother, who, by the same principle, should be considered as a presumptive father-in-law and consequently be treated with respect.

The explanation sought by the Seligmans is to be found in another of Junod's remarks. The *lobola* paid for the girl is immediately used to acquire a wife for this girl's brother. The wife's brother's wife has thus been obtained with the same cattle as this wife. She has been bought with her husband's cattle. In our opinion, one need look no further for the reasons for the special attitude of the husband towards his 'great mukoñwana'. Any contact or intimacy between them would have been socially dangerous. The cycle of *lobola* would be prematurely and irrevocably closed, the development of the theoretically infinite series of prestations and counter-prestations would come to nothing, the whole system of connexions would have proved a failure. Thus the difficult relationship between the husband and his sister-in-law has a twofold consequence: on the one hand, sexual relationships between them are prohibited, and are likened to incest; on the other hand, an apparent paradox allows the husband the possibility of claiming her as wife in the case of a separation in which the fault is found to rest with the wife. This latter possibility exists, at least, among the BaRonga.[3] But, says Junod, recourse to this desperate solution is only had when there is no other possibility, and everywhere it is regarded as a great misfortune. More often than not, the wife's family is forced to substitute another daughter of the group for the 'great mukoñwana', and this substitution is called 'to put a log across the road'.[4] It is uncommon for her to be accepted by the husband, for 'one does not jump over the log'.[5]

It can be seen that the wife's brother's wife embodies two persons, and it is not surprising to see her assume this character of sacred object, in the nature of which she participates by her very ambiguity. This double character clearly appears if an attempt is made to isolate the letter of the system, its

[1] Junod, 1962, vol. I, pp. 241–2.					[2] Seligman and Seligman, 1932, p. 60.
[3] Junod, 1962, vol. I.					[4] ibid. p. 243.					[5] loc. cit.

abstract character, as it were, its arithmetic, from the more concrete realities which underlie it. From a theoretical viewpoint, the wife is obtained by cattle, which are used to buy the sister-in-law, who is the symbol or surety of the cattle. She can therefore be claimed, if the recipient party shows itself incapable, through default of the woman, of carrying out its part of the contract. This is the formal aspect of the system of *lobola*, its mechanical and non-human expression. In this connexion, it is not unprofitable to note that *lobola* has increasingly tended to take the form of a commercial transaction.[1] However, the basic reality is something else entirely: I have obtained my wife by transferring cattle, and the woman has been delivered to me only because her family, in turn, count on the cattle as the means of receiving a further wife for a member of that group. This wife, the 'great mukoñwana', is thus in some ways the final reason for the whole operation. Everything takes place as if, instead of being at the end of the process, she were at its origin, or as if I had exchanged the 'great mukoñwana' for my wife. And actually I have exchanged her, since she is my cattle, consequently of my flesh, and symbolically at least of my clan. Furthermore, although abstract legality allows me to claim her as an item of property, morality prevents me from approaching her, for the same reason that I cannot approach a kinswoman, and adulterous relationships with her are regarded as incestuous.

This incestuous character of participation in the cattle is most clearly established by Hoernlé's following remarks, which were made without reference to the problem just discussed: 'Among the Pondo, the Zulu and the Herero, tribesmen may drink milk only with members of their own sib. Among the Zulu and the Pondo, to drink milk with a member, or members of another sib is tantamount to pledging blood-brotherhood with that sib, and would prevent a man from marrying a woman of that sib.'[2] The same writer adds that, in several south-eastern Bantu tribes, a woman after marriage cannot partake of the milk of her husband's cattle for a period; she would harm both herself and her husband's people by doing so. Only after her husband's ancestors have signified their satisfaction with the new member of the kraal is it safe for her to share in the milk. In the meantime, she drinks the milk from a cow brought from her own home, which is an indispensable part of the things that she brings to her marriage.[3] Junod reports that the woman made over against the cattle, and the woman bought with these same cattle, are called 'twins'. [4]

These observations are vital because they unequivocally illustrate the arbitrament between kinship and alliance which constitutes the prohibition of incest. At the beginning of the article from which we have just quoted, Hoernlé shows that there is a substantial identity in the native mind between the clan and its cattle. To drink milk is to share in the very nature of the

[1] Hoernlé, 1925*b*, p. 490.   [2] ibid. p. 481.   [3] ibid. p. 482.
[4] Junod, 1962, vol. I.

group. For the woman this would mean being placed straight away in the abnormal situation of the 'great mukoñwana', and playing on the ambiguity of the positions of wife – *who is exchanged for the cattle*, but is exchanged even in the process of resisting (one recalls the ritual squabbles over refusal of the *lobola*) – and of sister *who is the cattle*, since the cattle themselves are the group. Thus, we see that *lobola* acquires a further meaning, more concrete and hence probably deeper, no longer merely symbolical but real. Let us follow the progress of the *lobola* cycle through the groups. There inevitably comes a time when the cattle will return, as it were, to the kraal, and when, after purchase upon purchase and exchange upon exchange, the cattle which I transferred in order to obtain a wife will return to my group with the departure of a daughter. Theoretically, at least, the possibility is not even excluded of the return process being carried out directly and without intermediary. Put another way, the 'great mukoñwana', who is my potential wife, might be not merely the symbolical embodiment of my own flesh and blood, or, in other words, of my cattle; she might possibly – and this time, actually – be my cousin or sister.

If our analysis is correct, *lobola* is nothing more than an indirect and developed form of marriage by exchange. More exactly, it constitutes one of the many operational techniques whereby the exchange which we have regarded as inherent in the institution of marriage can be expressed in a large society composed of multiple groups. There is scarcely need to show that the process whereby the woman provided as a counterpart is replaced by a symbolical equivalent is better adapted to the conditions of a society with a high population density than is direct exchange. Indeed, it is possible to conceive of two formulas of real exchange. One formula is that by which the exchange takes place directly between two individuals, or two restricted groups of individuals, and then there is the risk of marriage never joining more than two groups at once, and of linking them into pairs of families, each pair forming a discrete totality within the general group (restricted exchange). The other formula is that by which the exchange takes place among several sections of the community, presupposing the intentional or accidental realization of an overall structure, which is not always given. In the absence of a structure of this type (exogamous moieties or marriage classes), the practice of *lobola* establishes a flexible system, because the exchanges, instead of being present and immediate, are potential and deferred.

Marriage by purchase is thus compatible with all forms of exchange. But the solitary prohibition on the 'great mukoñwana' is enough to prevent the formation of a short cycle, and to guarantee that the cattle, spears or hoes shall complete a wide circuit during which several families will have given sisters and daughters without receiving wives. What do they receive in their stead? The guarantee, in the form of special goods, that they themselves shall find wives. Cattle, spears and hoes are thus veritable *mayu ni*, or 'wife-givers', to use the Kachin expression. The only difference is that these 'wife-givers', instead of being defined as a concrete section of the social group over whose daughters one has prior claim, are represented by symbolical equivalents, by *tokens*, or even more exactly, by *debts*, recoverable from any family whatsoever, *on condition that this family can be brought into relation with Ego's family in the long cycle.* If cousin marriage remains sanctioned, purchase will simply reconstitute a simple formula of generalized exchange, viz., marriage with the mother's brother's daughter, with the wife's brother's daughter or – in matrilineal descent – with the mother's brother's wife.[1] If cousin marriage is forbidden, purchase does not contradict generalized exchange: it extends and broadens its formula, by enforcing, through the gradual augmentation of prohibited degrees, the formation of longer and longer, and theoretically at least unlimited, cycles. The substitution of wife-purchase for the right to the cousin thus allows generalized exchange to break away from its elementary structure, and favours the creation of a growing number of increasingly supple and extended cycles. At the same time, the rule of circulation for privileged goods imposes a rhythm upon henceforth improvised cycles, determines their course, and attests at any moment to the credit or debit state of the balance-sheets.

IV

We have just seen that the structure of exchange is not solidary with the prescription of a preferred spouse. And even if the increase of prohibited degrees eliminates first, second and third cousins from among the possible spouses, the elementary forms of exchange which we have attempted to define will still continue to function. A sufficiently dense society, in which the families were all seeking to extend their alliances, would spontaneously form a long cycle. If the statistics of a large number of marriages reveal, in certain cases at least, distant kinship relationships between the spouses, these relationships will, of necessity, be predominantly matrilateral. By contrast, a society in a state of crisis, in which the policy as regards alliances was dominated by an immediate concern for obtaining or maintaining guarantees, would reveal on analysis a high coefficient of patrilaterality even if this could not be directly established, or only in certain cases and for distant degrees of kinship. These observations are essential for anyone wishing to extend to the European world the general principles of interpretation postulated in this work. Hocart noted that medieval Europe offered some sort of the alternate generations system in the custom of giving the grandfather's name to the grandson. From this he was at least tempted to infer the existence of a former

---

[1] On the frequency of these forms of marriage in South Africa, cf. Eiselen, 1928, pp. 413–28; Junod, 1962, vol. I, *passim.*

Indo-European marriage between bilateral cross-cousins.[1] Nothing justifies such a hypothesis. But we know that the system of alternate generations is not connected with it, and that this system can as well result from patrilateral marriage. To understand the phenomenon pointed out by Hocart, it is sufficient to picture medieval society as having a permanent or temporary tendency to shorten the marriage cycles, probably because of the general instability. This shortening must inevitably have raised the coefficient of patrilateral marriages, even if this patrilaterality was established at such a remote degree of kinship that the participant families need have had no knowledge of it, and this was certainly not the case for noble or royal marriages, which were constantly concerned with maintaining the balance. Unbeknown even to the conscious activity of the group, a high rate of patrilaterality must gradually impose upon collective thought its specific rhythm of a periodic reversal of all the cycles.[2] The alternation of first names is easily explained as a sort of game, or aesthetic formulation, based upon the unconscious realization of an as yet crude and faintly outlined structural phenomenon.

Consequently, there is no need for us to reconstruct some archaic state in which Indo-European society practised cross-cousin marriage, or even recognized a division into exogamous moieties, to be able to give a rapid outline interpretation of the structure of European kinship systems. We need only note that Europe, in its present state, or in the still recent past, provides, or provided, a body of structural features all relating to what we have called generalized exchange, the functional relationships of which are still observable in the study of simple forms of this type of exchange. What are these features?

First and foremost is the Germanic classification of kinsmen and affines into *speermagen* and *schweitmagen* on the one hand, and *spillmagen* and *kunkelmagen* on the other: paternal relatives and maternal relatives, 'relatives by the spear and the sword' and 'relatives by the distaff and the spindle'. With this we again encounter the Indo-Oriental distinction between 'relatives of the bone' and 'relatives of the flesh', between 'wife-givers' and 'wife-takers'. We have said why in our opinion this classification is compatible only with a system of generalized exchange. Only in such a system are maternal relatives maternal and nothing else with respect to paternal relatives, with the latter in an equally univocal position with respect to maternal relatives. By contrast, in a system of restricted exchange the two groups simultaneously possess both attributes with respect to each other.[3] The recurrence of this typical classification from Germany to Wales would in itself justify the inclusion of Europe in the area of generalized exchange.

---

[1] Hocart says that the primitive form would well have been a system of alternate generations in which grandfather = grandson, and that this system seems to be obscurely connected with cross-cousin marriage (1928, p. 203).

[2] cf. chs. XXVI and XXVII.   [3] cf. ch. XXIII.

The study of simple forms of generalized exchange in Burma and Assam has permitted us to establish a correlation between these forms and the appearance of a division of the society into extensive unilateral groups which most probably derive from clans, but have special characteristics such as status differentiation together with ethnic, linguistic or functional peculiarities, or peculiarities of custom. These groups are exogamous, and their hierarchial distribution forces them to practise hypergamy. Kachin mythology represents them as descended from brothers, either singly or in pairs.[1] We have interpreted Hindu castes, and perhaps also Iranian 'social classes', as products of a structure of the same type. However, it is consistent with the facts to postulate the existence of this structure in a much wider area. Herodotus (IV, 5–6) describes it among the Scythians, with characteristics (founding brothers, twin sections, etc.) reminiscent of Kachin mythology, even down to the details. Dumézil, who cites Hindu parallels in this connexion, has been able to trace its expansion to the Caucasus.[2] If we add that the same passage in Herodotus reports inheritance by the younger brother among the Scythians, and that as far away as Ireland there is a similar practice, the custom of *geilfine* or the 'white-headed boy', meaning the fifth son, the favoured heir – as among the Kachin – of the family property,[3] then a remarkable homogeneity, which only the notion of generalized exchange has allowed us to comprehend, must be recognized as extending from the Siberian-Burman axis to western Europe.

But there is more. The exceptionally close relationship between the maternal uncle and his sister's son, which Tacitus described among the Germans, and which found considerable vitality in the *chanson de geste* a thousand years later, poses the same problem of a pseudo-matrilineal cast to a regime of father-right, to the solution of which we have gradually been led by the study of Burmese, Siberian and Hindu societies.[4] The broad structural features indicated locally by the distinction between 'bone' and 'flesh', 'sword' and 'distaff', completely exclude the hypothesis of a former dual organization which understandably attracted Hocart and Dumézil. It is once more a question of the ambivalent relationship uniting maternal relatives, who are only maternal relatives, and paternal relatives who receive wives without providing any, at least to the same partners. After our study of the Kachin system we have seen the emergence, as a corollary to generalized exchange, of the assertion of feminine rights which is so typical also of Germanic and Celtic institutions. Finally, even the Kachin *sumri* or 'precious goods' and the Gilyak *šagund* or 'vital nerves', in both cases protectors of the hearth

---

[1] cf. ch. XVI.   [2] Dumézil, 1930, pp. 125–6; 1945, pp. 146 et seq.

[3] This is Bergetto's status in John Ford's play *'Tis Pity She's a Whore* (published with introduction and notes by Havelock Ellis, London, 1888, p. 114), and it is not unimportant to note that it adds a dramatic element to the incestuous situation between his bride Annabella and her brother.

[4] cf. ch. XXVII. In this we diverge therefore from the dualistic interpretation advanced by Dumézil (1924, p. 277).

received by the husband from his wife's family, have their equivalent in ancient Europe. Among the Germans, the bride brings certain goods to her husband in return for the bride-price, which comprises an ox, a saddled horse, a shield, spear and sword. Tacitus relates that this interchange of gifts was recognized as establishing the most solemn bond, and as having a sacred value making them indeed 'the deities of marriage'.[1]

But in order to reduce European rules of marriage to a structure of generalized exchange it is not enough to establish the resemblances to simple forms. The differences must also be accounted for, i.e., the gradual evolution of European systems from a probable archaic stage, in which alliances were made in terms of directional cycles with $2+n$ partners (the simple formula of generalized exchange), to the modern state of indetermination which achieves a result of the same order by means of a small number of negative prescriptions. Without treating the problem fully, we shall briefly indicate the direction in which the answer should be sought.

One conclusion immediately emerges from the study of simple forms of generalized exchange: that, kept in the simple state, they are not viable.[2] Generalized exchange leads to hypergamy, i.e., the participants in the great cycle of exchange, gradually gaining differences in status from the very fact of the formula of exchange, can only receive spouses from partners occupying a superior or an inferior position in the hierarchy. It will be recalled that the appearance of this critical phase is still attested to for ancient India. Let us take the most common case in which the rule prescribes marriage with a woman of an immediately inferior status. How do women of the highest class get married? In a system of generalized exchange, the continuity of the link is ensured by a single cycle of exchange which connects all constituent elements of the group as partners. No interruption can occur at any point in the cycle without the total structure, which is the basis of social order and individual security, being in danger of collapse. The Kachin system reveals generalized exchange at the precise moment when this dramatic problem makes its appearance.

There must be a solution to this problem. We have already encountered one, in which groups united by a cycle of generalized exchange are subdivided, often two by two, into more restricted formations, pairs of which commence to exchange. The evolution of the Assamese and Chinese systems and the Tungus and Manchu systems, give varied illustrations of this process. Local systems of restricted exchange begin to function within a total system of generalized exchange, and gradually replace it. The group gives up a *simple* form of generalized exchange for an equally *simple* form of restricted exchange. But it can also preserve the principle of generalized exchange by renouncing a *simple* form for a *complex* form. This is the European development.

Firstly, let us consider the case in which the contradiction inherent in the

---

[1] *Germania*, ch. 18.   [2] cf. ch. XVI.

hypergamous rule in some way rigidifies the cycle of generalized exchange. The cycle is interrupted, the indefinite chain of prestations and counter-prestations seizes up. The partners mark time, and, placed in a position where it is impossible for them to fulfil their prestations, keep their daughters by marrying them to their sons, until a miracle sets the whole machine going again. Needless to say, such a process is contagious. It must gradually reach every member of the body social, and change hypergamy to endogamy. Only India has systematically and durably adopted this solution. However, the whole area provides rough and provisional skeletal forms of this solution. Such is the eclectic attitude of Iran, which associates a quite supple class endogamy with sporadic marriage between near relatives,[1] or the Egyptian practice of consanguineal marriages. However, if our interpretation of the latter is correct,[2] it is echoed in Iran and even in Greece, in the custom of the daughter-heir, who, in the absence of a male heir, marries a close relative. In fact, the Egyptian or Polynesian marriage with the older sister, to the exclusion of the younger sister, seems merely an extreme form of female inheritance. In western Europe, patristic literature and, later, Elizabethan drama, reveal the extent and duration of the vacillations of the public conscience on the question of consanguineal marriages.

However, another solution is equally possible, and it is this which has ultimately left its mark on the European system. Since generalized exchange engenders hypergamy, and hypergamy leads either to regressive solutions (restricted exchange or endogamy), or to the complete paralysis of the body social, an arbitrary element will be introduced into the system, a sort of sociological *clinamen*, which, whenever the subtle mechanism of exchange is obstructed, will, like a *Deus ex machina*, give the necessary push for a new impetus. India clearly conceived the idea of this *clinamen*, although it finally took a different path and left the task of developing and systematizing the formula of it to others. This is the *swayamvara* marriage, to which a whole section of the Mahābhārata is devoted.[3] It consists, for a person occupying a high social rank, in the privilege of giving his daughter in marriage to a man of any status, who has performed some extraordinary feat, or better still, has been chosen by the girl herself. How else would she proceed, since, as a king's daughter in any hypergamous system she would be denied any spouse if the social rule were strictly observed? Undoubtedly, *swayamvara* marriage as described in epic poetry and folklore, from Assam to central and western Europe, is largely a myth. Yet the transfiguration into mythological form conceals a real problem, and probably positive institutions as well. Even in the Middle Ages, Welsh law distinguished between two forms of marriage, *rod o cenedl*, 'gift by kindred' and *lladrut*, 'stolen, secret or furtive', the former being the surrender of the woman by her family, the latter, the gift of the woman by herself.[4] Can we not recognize here, in their probable

[1] Benveniste, 1932, pp. 117, 125; Mazaheri, 1938, pp. 113, 131.   [2] cf. ch. I.
[3] Roy, 1883-6, vol. I.   [4] Ellis, 1926, vol. I, p. 393.

juxtaposition over a long period, the logical and perhaps historical starting-point and point of arrival of the evolution of generalized exchange?

It is interesting to note that Dumézil, while engaged in the study of problems very different from those taken up here, was also induced to propose a connexion between *swayamvara* marriage (or very similar customs) and the hypergamous structure of Indo-European society. He compares the Scandinavian legend of the marriage of Skadhi, who was left free to choose a husband from any one of several hidden candidates, and who selected an old man by mistake, with the story from the Mahābhārata (III, 123–5) of Princess Sukanyā, married in obedience to her duty to the elderly ascetic Cyavana, and who, given the privilege of another choice from among three indistinguishable candidates, all young and handsome, discovered among them him who had been her original husband. Dumézil is especially interested by the fact that, in both versions, the proceedings connected with the choice are machinated by divine personages, whom he identifies with the patrons of the third social function, 'here candidates are piteously got rid of, there the candidate is comically chosen'; and at this juncture he poses the question whether 'perhaps there was an ancient tie between this third function, and a type of marriage in which the woman chose her husband freely'.[1] Undoubtedly there would be a risk in citing another section of the Mahābhārata (Swayam-varaparva), where Princess Krishna, whom her father and brother put up as the prize to a competition, is carried off from the gathering of warrior princes by a Brahman of high birth disguised in ordinary clothing; for the violent exclamation of the defeated competitors that 'the *swayamvara* is for the Kshatriyas', accompanied by an appeal to the most venerable tradition,[2] seems to have a clearly different meaning here, full of the spirit of endogamy. And yet *swayamvara*, the marriage of chance, merit, or choice, can really only have meaning if it gives a girl from a superior class to a man from an inferior class, guaranteeing at least symbolically that the distance between the statuses has not irremediably compromised the solidarity of the group, and that the cycle of marriage prestations will not be interrupted. This is why the lower classes have a major interest in the *swayamvara*, because for them it represents a pledge of confidence. Thus they become the jealous guardians of the rules of the game and right up to contemporary folklore, the drama – or the comedy – of *swayamvara* marriage will lie alternatively, according to the viewpoint of the narrator, either in the opportunity offered to natural gifts, or in the adroitness of the great in getting round the law.

Undoubtedly, *swayamvara* marriage has a basis in general or in previous institutions. Its appearance would have been inconceivable but for the latent conflict between the ostensibly matrilateral orientation of systems of generalized exchange, and the patrilateral nostalgia which secretly undermines them, or, in other words, but for the unconscious belief in the security of

[1] Dumézil, 1945, p. 179.
[2] Roy, 1883–6, vol. I, Adi Parva, CLXII; Dutt, 1917, CXCI–7.

short-cycle systems which is always found in societies engaged in the hazards of long-cycle systems. Indeed, since our study of the Kachin system we have seen that this internal contradiction is expressed in a resurgence of feminine lines, and an assertion of female rights, sanctioned by custom. It remains no less the case that, with *swayamvara* marriage, the three basic characteristics of modern European marriage were introduced in, to borrow the Welsh expression, a 'furtive, secret', and almost fraudulent manner. These characteristics are: freedom to choose the spouse within the limit of the prohibited degrees; equality of the sexes in the matter of marriage vows; and finally, emancipation from relatives and the individualization of the contract.

CHAPTER XXIX

The Principles of Kinship

I

Thus, it is always a system of exchange that we find at the origin of rules of marriage, even of those of which the apparent singularity would seem to allow only a special and arbitrary interpretation. In the course of this work, we have seen the notion of exchange become complicated and diversified; it has constantly appeared to us in different forms. Sometimes exchange appears as direct (the case of marriage with the bilateral cousin), sometimes as indirect (and in this case it can comply with two formulas, one continuous, the other discontinuous, corresponding to two different rules of marriage with the unilateral cousin). Sometimes it functions within a total system (this is the theoretically common characteristic of bilateral marriage and of matrilateral marriage), and at others it instigates the formation of an unlimited number of special systems and short cycles, unconnected among themselves (and in this form it represents a permanent threat to moiety systems, and as an inevitable weakness attacks patrilateral systems). Sometimes exchange appears as a cash or short-term transaction (with the exchange of sisters and daughters, and avuncular marriage), and at other times more as a long-term transaction (as in the case where the prohibited degrees include first, and occasionally second, cousins). Sometimes the exchange is explicit and at other times it is implicit (as seen in the example of so-called marriage by purchase). Sometimes the exchange is closed (when marriage must satisfy a special rule of alliance between marriage classes or a special rule for the observance of preferential degrees), while sometimes it is open (when the rule of exogamy is merely a collection of negative stipulations, which, beyond the prohibited degrees, leaves a free choice). Sometimes it is secured by a sort of mortgage on reserved categories (classes or degrees); sometimes (as in the case of the simple prohibition of incest, as found in our society) it rests on a wider fiduciary guarantee, viz., the theoretical freedom to claim any woman of the group, in return for the renunciation of certain designated women in the family circle, a freedom ensured by the extension of a prohibition, similar to that affecting each man in particular, to all men in general. But no matter what form it takes, whether direct or indirect, general or special, immediate or deferred, explicit or implicit, closed or open, concrete or symbolic, it is exchange, always exchange, that emerges as the fundamental and common basis of all modalities of the institution of marriage. If these modalities can be subsumed under the general term of exogamy (for, as we have seen in Part I, endogamy is not opposed to exogamy, but presupposes it), this is conditional upon the apperception, behind the superficially negative expression of the rule of exogamy, of the final principle which, through the prohibition of marriage within prohibited degrees, tends to ensure the total and continuous circulation of the group's most important assets, its wives and its daughters.

The functional value of exogamy, defined in its widest sense, has been specified and brought out in the preceding chapters. This value is in the first place negative. Exogamy provides the only means of maintaining the group as a group, of avoiding the indefinite fission and segmentation which the practice of consanguineous marriages would bring about. If these consanguineous marriages were resorted to persistently, or even over-frequently, they would not take long to 'fragment' the social group into a multitude of families, forming so many closed systems or sealed monads which no pre-established harmony could prevent from proliferating or from coming into conflict. The rule of exogamy, applied in its simplest forms, is not entirely sufficient to the task of warding off this mortal danger to the group. Such is the case with dual organization. With it there is no doubt that the risk of seeing a biological family become established as a closed system is definitely eliminated; the biological group can no longer stand apart, and the bond of alliance with another family ensures the dominance of the social over the biological, and of the cultural over the natural. But there immediately appears another risk, that of seeing two families, or rather two lineages, isolate themselves from the social continuum to form a bi-polar system, an indefinitely self-sufficient pair, closely united by a succession of intermarriages. The rule of exogamy, which determines the modalities for forming such pairs, gives them a definite social and cultural character, but this social character is no sooner given than it is disintegrated. This is the danger which is avoided by the more complex forms of exogamy, such as the principle of generalized exchange, or the subdivision of moieties into sections and subsections in which more and more numerous local groups constitute indefinitely more complex systems. It is thus the same with women as with the currency the name of which they often bear, and which, according to the admirable native saying, 'depicts the action of the needle for sewing roofs, which, weaving in and out, leads backwards and forwards the same liana, holding the straw together'.[1] Even when there are no such procedures, dual organization is not itself ineffective. We have seen how the intervention of preferred degrees of kinship within the moiety, e.g., the predilection for the real cross-cousin, and even for a certain type of real cross-cousin, as among

[1] Leenhardt, 1930, pp. 48, 54.

the Kariera, provides the means of palliating the risks of an over-automatic functioning of the classes. As opposed to endogamy and its tendency to set a limit to the group, and then to discriminate within the group, exogamy represents a continuous pull towards a greater cohesion, a more efficacious solidarity, and a more supple articulation.

This is because the value of exchange is not simply that of the goods exchanged. Exchange – and consequently the rule of exogamy which expresses it – has in itself a social value. It provides the means of binding men together, and of superimposing upon the natural links of kinship the henceforth artificial links – artificial in the sense that they are removed from chance encounters or the promiscuity of family life – of alliance governed by rule. In this connexion, marriage serves as model for that artificial and temporary 'conjugality' between young people of the same sex in some schools and on which Balzac makes the profound remark that it is never superimposed upon blood ties but replaces them: 'It is strange, but never in my time did I know brothers who were "Activists". If man lives only by his feelings, he thinks perhaps that he will make his life the poorer if he merges an affection of his own choosing in a natural tie.'[1]

On this level, certain theories of exogamy which were criticized at the beginning of this work find a new value and significance. If, as we have suggested, exogamy and the prohibition of incest have a permanent functional value, co-extensive with all social groups, surely all the widely differing interpretations which have been given for them must contain an atom of truth? Thus the theories of McLennan, Spencer and Lubbock have, at least, a symbolical meaning. It will be recalled that McLennan believed that exogamy had its origin in tribes practising female infanticide, and which were consequently obliged to seek wives for their sons from outside. Similarly, Spencer suggested that exogamy began among warrior tribes who carried off women from neighbouring groups. Lubbock proposed a primitive opposition between two forms of marriage, viz., an endogamous marriage in which the women were regarded as the communal property of the men of the group, and an exogamous marriage, which reckoned captured women as the private property of their captor, thus giving rise to modern individual marriage. The concrete detail may be disputed, but the fundamental idea is sound, viz., that exogamy has a value less negative than positive, that it asserts the social existence of other people, and that it prohibits endogamous marriage only in order to introduce, and to prescribe, marriage with a group other than the biological family, certainly not because a biological danger is attached to consanguineous marriage, but because exogamous marriage results in a social benefit.

Consequently, exogamy should be recognized as an important element – doubtless by far the most important element – in that solemn collection of

---

[1] 'The conjugal regard that united us as boys, and which we used to express by calling ourselves "Activists" . . .' Balzac, vol. X, 1937, pp. 366, 382.

manifestations which, continually or periodically, ensures the integration of partial units within the total group, and demands the collaboration of outside groups. Such are the banquets, feasts and ceremonies of various kinds which form the web of social life. But exogamy is not merely one manifestation among many others. The feasts and ceremonies are periodic, and for the most part have limited functions. The law of exogamy, by contrast, is omnipresent, acting permanently and continually; moreover, it applies to valuables – viz., women – valuables *par excellence* from both the biological and the social points of view, without which life is impossible, or, at best, is reduced to the worst forms of abjection. It is no exaggeration, then, to say that exogamy is the archetype of all other manifestations based upon reciprocity, and that it provides the fundamental and immutable rule ensuring the existence of the group as a group. For example, among the Maori, Best tells us:

> 'Female children of rank, as also male children of that status, were given in marriage to persons of important, powerful tribes, possibly of a quite unrelated people, as a means of procuring assistance from such tribes in time of war. In this connexion we can see the application of the following saying of older times: "*He taura taonga e motu, he taura tangata e kore e motu*" ("A gift connexion may be severed, but not so a human link"). Two peoples may meet in friendship and exchange gifts and yet quarrel and fight in later times, but intermarriage connects them in a permanent manner.'[1]

And, further on, he quotes another proverb: '*He hono tangata e kore e motu, kapa he taura waka, e motu*', 'A human joining is inseverable, but not so a canoe-painter, which can be severed.'[2] The philosophy contained in these remarks is the more significant because the Maori were by no means insensible to the advantages of marriage within the group. If both families quarrelled and insulted each other, they said, this would not be serious, but merely a family affair, and war would be avoided.[3]

II

The prohibition of incest is less a rule prohibiting marriage with the mother, sister or daughter, than a rule obliging the mother, sister or daughter to be given to others. It is the supreme rule of the gift, and it is clearly this aspect, too often unrecognized, which allows its nature to be understood. All the errors in interpreting the prohibition of incest arise from a tendency to see marriage as a discontinuous process which derives its own limits and possibilities from within itself in each individual case.

Thus it is that the reasons why marriage with the mother, daughter or sister can be prevented are sought in a quality intrinsic to these women.

---

[1] Best, 1929, p. 34.   [2] ibid. p. 36.   [3] ibid. 1924, vol. I, p. 447.

One is therefore drawn infallibly towards biological considerations, since it is only from a biological, certainly not a social, point of view that motherhood, sisterhood or daughterhood are properties of the individuals considered. However, from a social viewpoint, these terms cannot be regarded as defining isolated individuals, but relationships between these individuals and everyone else. Motherhood is not only a mother's relationship to her children, but her relationship to other members of the group, not as a mother, but as a sister, wife, cousin or simply a stranger as far as kinship is concerned. It is the same for all family relationships, which are defined not only by the individuals they involve, but also by all those they exclude. This is true to the extent that observers have often been struck by the impossibility for natives of conceiving a neutral relationship, or more exactly, no relationship. We have the feeling – which, moreover, is illusory – that the absence of definite kinship gives rise to such a state in our consciousness. But the supposition that this might be the case in primitive thought does not stand up to examination. Every family relationship defines a certain group of rights and duties, while the lack of family relationship does not define anything; it defines enmity:

'If you wish to live among the Nuer you must do so on their terms, which means that you must treat them as a kind of kinsman and they will then treat you as a kind of kinsman. Rights, privileges and obligations are determined by kinship. Either a man is a kinsman, actually or by fiction, or he is a person to whom you have no reciprocal obligations and whom you treat as a potential enemy.'[1]

The Australian aboriginal group is defined in exactly the same terms:

'When a stranger comes to a camp that he has never visited before, he does not enter the camp, but remains at some distance. A few of the older men, after a while, approach him, and the first thing they proceed to do is to find out who the stranger is. The commonest question that is put to him is "Who is your *maeli* (father's father)?" The discussion proceeds on genealogical lines until all parties are satisfied of the exact relation of the stranger to each of the natives present in the camp. When this point is reached, the stranger can be admitted to the camp, and the different men and women are pointed out to him and their relation to him defined . . . If I am a blackfellow and meet another blackfellow that other must be either my relative or my enemy. If he is my enemy I shall take the first opportunity of killing him, for fear he will kill me. This, before the white man came, was the aboriginal view of one's duty towards one's neighbour . . .'[2]

Through their striking parallelism, these two examples merely confirm a universal situation:

[1] Evans-Pritchard, 1940, p. 183.   [2] Radcliffe-Brown, 1913, p. 151.

'Throughout a considerable period, and in a large number of societies, men met in a curious frame of mind, with exaggerated fear and an equally exaggerated generosity which appear stupid in no one's eyes but our own. In all the societies which immediately preceded our own and which still surround us, and even in many usages of popular morality, there is no middle path. There is either complete trust or complete mistrust. One lays down one's arms, renounces magic, and gives everything away, from casual hospitality to one's daughter or one's property.'[1]

There is no barbarism or, properly speaking, even archaism in this attitude. It merely represents the systematization, pushed to the limit, of characteristics inherent in social relationships.

No relationship can be arbitrarily isolated from all other relationships. It is likewise impossible to remain on this or that side of the world of relationships. The social environment should not be conceived of as an empty framework within which beings and things can be linked, or simply juxtaposed. It is inseparable from the things which people it. Together they constitute a field of gravitation in which the weights and distances form a co-ordinated whole, and in which a change in any element produces a change in the total equilibrium of the system. We have given a partial illustration at least of this principle in our analysis of cross-cousin marriage. However, it can be seen how its field of application must be extended to all the rules of kinship, and above all, to that universal and fundamental rule, the prohibition of incest. Every kinship system (and no human society is without one) has a total character, and it is because of this that the mother, sister, and daughter are perpetually coupled, as it were, with elements of the system which, in relation to them, are neither son, nor brother, nor father, because the latter are themselves coupled with other women, or other classes of women, or feminine elements defined by a relationship of a different order. Because marriage is exchange, because marriage is the archetype of exchange, the analysis of exchange can help in the understanding of the solidarity which unites the gift and the counter-gift, and one marriage with other marriages.

It is true that Seligman disputes that the woman is the sole or predominant instrument of the alliance. She cites the institution of blood brotherhood, as expressed by the *henamo* relationship among the natives of New Guinea.[2] The establishment of blood-brotherhood does indeed create a bond of alliance between individuals, but by making them brothers it entails a prohibition on marriage with the sister. It is far from our mind to claim that the exchange or gift of women is the only way to establish an alliance in primitive societies. We have shown elsewhere how, among certain native groups of Brazil, the community could be expressed by the terms for 'brother-in-law' and 'brother'. The brother-in-law is ally, collaborator and friend; it is the term given to adult males belonging to the band with which an

---

[1] Mauss, 1925, p. 138. [2] B. Z. Seligman, 1935, pp. 75–93.

alliance has been contracted. In the same band, the potential brother-in-law, i.e., the cross-cousin, is the one with whom, as an adolescent, one indulges in homosexual activities which will always leave their mark in the mutually affectionate behaviour of the adults.[1] However, as well as the brother-in-law relationship, the Nambikwara also rely on the notion of brotherhood: 'Savage, you are no longer my brother!' is the cry uttered during a quarrel with a non-kinsman. Furthermore, objects found in a series, such as hut posts, the pipes of a Pan-pipe, etc., are said to be 'brothers', or are called 'others', in their respective relationships, a terminological detail which is worth comparing with Montaigne's observation that the Brazilian Indians whom he met at Rouen called men the 'halves' of one another, just as we say 'our fellow men'.[2] However, the whole difference between the two types of bond can also be seen, a sufficiently clear definition being that one of them expresses a mechanical solidarity (brother), while the other involves an organic solidarity (brother-in-law, or god-father). Brothers are closely related to one another, but they are so in terms of their similarity, as are the posts or the reeds of the Pan-pipe. By contrast, brothers-in-law are solidary because they complement each other and have a functional efficacy for one another, whether they play the rôle of the opposite sex in the erotic games of childhood, or whether their masculine alliance as adults is confirmed by each providing the other with what he does not have – a wife – through their simultaneous renunciation of what they both do have – a sister. The first form of solidarity adds nothing and unites nothing; it is based upon a cultural limit, satisfied by the reproduction of a type of connexion the model for which is provided by nature. The other brings about an integration of the group on a new plane.

Linton's observation on blood-brotherhood in the Marquesas helps to place the two institutions (blood-brotherhood and intermarriage) in their reciprocal perspectives. Blood-brothers are called *enoa*: 'When one was *enoa* with a man, one had equal rights to his property and stood in the same relation to his relatives as he did.'[3] However, it emerges very clearly from the context that the *enoa* system is merely an individual solution acting as a substitute, while the real and effective solution of the relations between the groups, i.e., the collective and organic solution of intermarriages, with the consequent fusion of the tribes, is made impossible by the international situation. Although vendettas may be in progress, the institution of *enoa*, a purely individual affair, is able to ensure a minimum of liaison and collaboration, even when marriage, which is a group affair, cannot be contracted.

Native theory confirms our conception even more directly. Mead's Arapesh informants had difficulty at first in answering her questions on possible infringements of the marriage prohibitions. However, when they eventually did express a comment the source of the misunderstanding was clearly

[1] Lévi-Strauss, 1948a.   [2] Montaigne, 1962, vol. I, ch. XXXI ('Des Cannibales').
[3] Linton, 1945, p. 149

revealed: they do not conceive of the prohibition as such, i.e., in its negative aspect; the prohibition is merely the reverse or counterpart of a positive obligation, which alone is present and active in the consciousness. Does a man ever sleep with his sister? The question is absurd. Certainly not, they reply: 'No, we don't sleep with our sisters. We give our sisters to other men, and other men give us their sisters.'[1] The ethnographer pressed the point, asking what they would think or say if, through some impossibility, this eventuality managed to occur. Informants had difficulty placing themselves in this situation, for it was scarcely conceivable: 'What, you would like to marry your sister! What is the matter with you anyway? Don't you want a brother-in-law? Don't you realize that if you marry another man's sister and another man marries your sister, you will have at least two brothers-in-law, while if you marry your own sister you will have none? With whom will you hunt, with whom will you garden, whom will you go to visit?'[2]

Doubtless, this is all a little suspect, because it was provoked, but the native aphorisms collected by Mead, and quoted as the motto to the first part of this work, were not provoked, and their meaning is the same. Other evidence corroborates the same thesis. For the Chukchee, a 'bad family' is defined as an isolated family, 'brotherless and cousinless'.[3] Moreover, the necessity to provoke the comment (the content of which, in any case, is spontaneous), and the difficulty in obtaining it, reveal the misunderstanding inherent in the problem of marriage prohibitions. The latter are prohibitions only secondarily and derivatively. Rather than a prohibition on a certain category of persons, they are a prescription directed towards another category. In this regard, how much more penetrating is native theory than are so many modern commentaries! There is nothing in the sister, mother, or daughter which disqualifies them as such. Incest is socially absurd before it is morally culpable. The incredulous exclamation from the informant: 'So you do not want to have a brother-in-law?' provides the veritable golden rule for the state of society.

III

There is thus no possible solution to the problem of incest within the biological family, even supposing this family to be already in a cultural context which imposes its specific demands upon it. The cultural context does not consist of a collection of abstract conditions. It results from a very simple fact which expresses it entirely, namely, that the biological family is no longer alone, and that it must ally itself with other families in order to endure. Malinowski supported a different idea, namely, that the prohibition of incest results from an internal contradiction, within the biological family, between mutually incompatible feelings, such as the emotions attached to sexual relationships and parental love, or 'the sentiments which form naturally

[1] Mead, 1935, p. 84. [2] loc. cit. [3] Bogoras, 1904–9, p. 542.

between brothers and sisters'.[1] These sentiments nevertheless only become incompatible because of the cultural rôle which the biological family is called upon to play. The man should teach his children, and this social vocation, practised naturally within the family group, is irremediably compromised if emotions of another type develop and upset the discipline indispensable to the maintenance of a stable order between the generations: 'Incest would mean the upsetting of age distinctions, the mixing up of generations, the disorganization of sentiments and a violent exchange of rôles at a time when the family is the most important educational medium. No society could exist under such conditions.'[2]

It is unfortunate for this thesis that there is practically no primitive society which does not flagrantly contradict it on every point. The primitive family fulfils its educative function sooner than ours, and from puberty onwards – and often even before – it transfers the charge of adolescents to the group, with the handing over of their preparation to bachelor houses or initiation groups. Initiation rituals confirm this emancipation of the young man or girl from the family cell and their definitive incorporation within the social group. To achieve this end, these rituals rely on precisely the processes which Malinowski cites as a possibility solely in order to expose their mortal dangers, viz., affective disorganization and the violent exchange of rôles, sometimes going as far as the practice, on the initiate's very person, of most unfamilial usages by near relatives. Finally, different types of classificatory system are very little concerned to maintain a clear distinction between ages and generations. However, it is just as difficult for a Hopi child to learn to call an old man 'my son', or any other assimilation of the same order, as it would be for one of ours.[3] The supposedly disastrous situation that Malinowski depicts in order to justify the prohibition of incest, is on the whole, no more than a very banal picture of any society, envisaged from another point of view than its own.

This naïve egocentrism is so far from being new or original that Durkheim made a decisive criticism of it years before Malinowski gave it a temporary revival in popularity. Incestuous relationships only appear contradictory to family sentiments because we have conceived of the latter as irreducibly excluding the former. But if a long and ancient tradition allowed men to marry their near relatives, our conception of marriage would be quite different. Sexual life would not have become what it is. It would have a less personal character, and would leave less room for the free play of the imagination, dreams and the spontaneities of desire. Sexual feeling would be tempered and deadened, but by this very fact it would compare closely with domestic feelings, with which it would have no difficulty in being reconciled. To conclude this paraphrase with a quotation: 'Certainly, the question does not pose itself once it is assumed that incest is prohibited; for the conjugal order, being henceforth outside the domestic order, must necessarily develop in a

---

[1] Malinowski, 1934, p. lxvi.   [2] ibid. 1927, p. 251.   [3] Simmons, 1942, p. 68.

divergent direction. This prohibition clearly cannot be explained in terms of ideas which obviously derive from it.'[1]

Must we not go even further? On the very occasion of marriage, numerous societies practise the confusion of generations, the mingling of ages, the reversal of rôles, and the identification of what we regard as incompatible relationships. As these customs seem to such societies to be in perfect harmony with a prohibition of incest, sometimes conceived of very rigorously, it can be concluded, on the one hand, that none of these practices is exclusive of family life, and, on the other hand, that the prohibition must be defined by different characteristics, common to it throughout its multiple modalities. Among the Chukchee, for example:

> 'the age of women thus exchanged is hardly considered at all. For instance, on the Oloi River, a man named QI'mIqai married his young son five years old to a girl of twenty. In exchange he gave his niece, who was twelve years of age, and she was married to a young man more than twenty years old. The wife of the boy acted as his nurse, fed him with her own hands and put him to sleep.'[2]

The writer also cites the case of a woman who, married to a two-year old baby and having a child by 'a marriage companion', i.e., an official and temporary lover, shared her attentions between the two babies: 'When she was nursing her own child, she also nursed her infant husband . . . In this case the husband also readily took the breast of his wife. When I asked for the reason of the wife's conduct, the Chukchee replied, "Who knows? Perhaps it is a kind of incantation to insure the love of her young husband in the future".'[3] At all events, it is certain that these apparently inconceivable unions are compatible with a highly romantic folklore, full of devouring passions, Prince Charmings and Sleeping Beauties, shy heroines and triumphant loves.[4] We know of similar facts in South America.[5]

However unusual these examples may appear, they are not unique, and Egyptian-style incest probably represents only the limit. They have their parallel among the Arapesh in New Guinea, among whom infant betrothals are frequent, the two children growing up as brother and sister. But this time the age difference is on the side of the husband:

> 'An Arapesh boy grows his wife. As a father's claim to his child is not that he has begotten it but rather that he has fed it, so also a man's claim to his wife's attention and devotion is not that he has paid a bride-price for her, or that she is legally his property, but that he has actually contributed the food which has become flesh and bone of her body.'[6]

Here again, this type of apparently abnormal relationship provides the psychological model for regular marriage: 'The whole organization of

[1] Durkheim, 1898, p. 63. [2] Bogoras, 1904-9, p. 578. [3] loc. cit.
[4] ibid. pp. 578-83. [5] Means, 1931, p. 360. [6] Mead, 1935, p. 80.

society is based upon the analogy between children and wives as representing a group who are younger, less responsible, than the men, and therefore to be guided. Wives by definition stand in this child-relationship . . . to all of the older men of the clan into which they marry.'[1]

Likewise, among the Tapirapé of central Brazil, depopulation has brought about a system of marriage with young girls. The 'husband' lives with his parents-in-law and the 'wife's' mother is responsible for woman's work.[2] The Mohave husband carries the little girl that he has married on his shoulders, busies himself with household duties, and generally speaking acts both as husband and *in loco parentis*. The Mohave comment upon the situation cynically, and ask, sometimes even when the person concerned is present, whether he has married his own daughter: ' "Whom are you carrying around on your back? Is that your daughter?" they ask him. When such marriages break up, the husband often has a manic attack.'[3]

I myself have been present, among the Tupí-Cawahib of the upper Madeira, in central Brazil, at the betrothal of a man about thirty years old with a scarcely two-year-old baby, still in its mother's arms. Nothing was more touching than the excitement with which the future husband followed the childish frolics of his little fiancée. He did not tire of admiring her, and of sharing his feelings with the onlookers. For some years his thoughts would be filled with the prospect of setting up house. He would feel strengthened by the certainty, growing alongside him in strength and beauty, of one day escaping the curse of bachelorhood. Henceforth, his budding tenderness is expressed in innocent gifts. According to our standards, this love is torn between three irreducible categories, viz., paternal, fraternal, and marital, but in an appropriate context it reveals no element of disquiet or defect, endangering the future welfare of the couple, let alone the whole social order.

We must decide against Malinowski and those of his followers who vainly attempt to support an outmoded position,[4] in favour of those, like Fortune and Williams, who, following Tylor, found the origin of the incest prohibition in its positive implications.[5] As one observer rightly puts it: 'An incestuous couple as well as a stingy family automatically detaches itself from the give-and-take pattern of tribal existence; it is a foreign body – or at least an inactive one – in the body social.'[6]

No marriage can thus be isolated from all the other marriages, past or future, which have occurred or which will occur within the group. Each marriage is the end of a movement which, as soon as this point has been reached, should be reversed and develop in a new direction. If the movement ceases, the whole system of reciprocity will be disturbed. Since marriage is the condition upon which reciprocity is realized, it follows that marriage

---

[1] Mead, 1935, pp. 80–1. [2] Wagley, 1940, p. 12. [3] Devereux, 1939, p. 519.
[4] Seligman, 1931–2, pp. 250–76.
[5] Fortune, 1932, pp. 620–2; Williams, 1936, p. 169; Tylor, 1889.
[6] Devereux, 1939, p. 529.

constantly ventures the existence of reciprocity. What would happen if a wife were received without a daughter or a sister being given? This risk must be taken, however, if society is to survive. To safeguard the social perpetuity of alliance, one must compromise oneself with the chances of descent (i.e., in short, with man's biological substructure). However, the social recognition of marriage (i.e., the transformation of the sexual encounter, with its basis in promiscuity, into a contract, ceremony or sacrament) is always an anxious venture, and we can understand how it is that society should have attempted to provide against the risks involved by the continual and almost maniacal imposition of its mark. The Hehe, says Brown, practise cross-cousin marriage, but not without hesitation, for if cross-cousin marriage allows the clan-line to be maintained, it risks it in the case of a bad marriage, and informants report: 'Thus some forbid their children to marry a cousin.'[1] The ambivalent attitude of the Hehe towards a special form of marriage is the pre-eminent social attitude towards marriage in any of its forms. By recognizing and sanctioning the union of the sexes and reproduction, society influences the natural order, but at the same time it gives the natural order its chance, and one might say of any culture of the world what an observer has noted of one of them: 'Perhaps the most fundamental religious conception relates to the difference between the sexes. Each sex is perfectly all right in its own way, but contact is fraught with danger for both.'[2]

Marriage is thus a dramatic encounter between nature and culture, between alliance and kinship. 'Who has given the bride?' chants the Hindu hymn of marriage: 'To whom then is she given? It is love that has given her; it is to love that she has been given. Love has given; love has received. Love has filled the ocean. With love I accept her. Love! let her be yours.'[3] Thus, marriage is an arbitration between two loves, parental and conjugal. Nevertheless, they are both forms of love, and the instant the marriage takes place, considered in isolation, the two meet and merge; 'love has filled the ocean'. Their meeting is doubtless merely a prelude to their substitution for one another, the performance of a sort of *chassé-croisé*. But to intercross they must at least momentarily be joined, and it is this which in all social thought makes marriage a sacred mystery. At this moment, all marriage verges on incest. More than that, it is incest, at least social incest, if it is true that incest, in the broadest sense of the word, consists in obtaining by oneself, and for oneself, instead of by another, and for another.

However, since one must yield to nature in order that the species may perpetuate itself, and concomitantly for social alliance to endure, the very

---

[1] Brown, 1934, p. 28. [2] Hogbin, 1935, p. 330.

[3] Banerjee, 1896, p. 91. As to marriage considered as bordering upon incest, compare the following, written in a completely different spirit: 'Profound sentiment [between husband and wife] would have seemed odd and even "ridiculous", in any event unbecoming; it would have been as unacceptable as an earnest "aside" in the general current of light conversation. Each has a duty to all, and for a couple to entertain each other is isolation; in company there exists no right of the *tête-à-tête*.' (Taine, 1876, p. 133.)

least one must do is to deny it while yielding to it, and to accompany the gesture made towards it with one restricting it. This compromise between nature and culture comes about in two ways, since there are two cases, one in which nature must be introduced, since society can do everything, the other in which nature must be excluded, since it rules from the first – before descent and its assertion of the unilineal principle, and before alliance, with its establishment of prohibited degrees.

IV

The multiple rules prohibiting or prescribing certain types of spouse, and the prohibition of incest, which embodies them all, become clear as soon as one grants that society must exist. But society might not have been. Have we therefore resolved one problem, as we thought, only to see its whole importance shifted to another problem, the solution to which appears even more hypothetical than that to which we have devoted all our attention? In actual fact, let us note, we are not faced with two problems but with only one. If our proposed interpretation is correct, the rules of kinship and marriage are not made necessary by the social state. They are the social state itself, reshaping biological relationships and natural sentiments, forcing them into structures implying them as well as others, and compelling them to rise above their original characteristics. The natural state recognizes only indivision and appropriation, and their chance admixture. However, as Proudhon has already observed in connexion with another problem, these notions can only be transcended on a new and different level: 'Property is non-reciprocity, and non-reciprocity is theft... But common ownership is also non-reciprocity, since it is the negation of opposing terms; it is still theft. Between property and common ownership I could construct a whole world.'[1] What is this world, unless it is that to which social life ceaselessly bends itself in a never wholly successful attempt to construct and reconstruct an approximate image of it, that world of reciprocity which the laws of kinship and marriage, in their own sphere of interest, laboriously derive from relationships which are otherwise condemned to remain either sterile or immoderate?

However, the progress of contemporary social anthropology would be of small account if we had to be content with an act of faith – fruitful no doubt, and in its time, legitimate – in the dialectic process ineluctably giving rise to the world of reciprocity, as the synthesis of two contradictory characteristics inherent in the natural order. Experimental study of the facts can join with the philosophers' presentiments, not only in attesting that this is what happened, but in describing, or beginning to describe, how things happened.

In this regard, Freud's work is an example and a lesson. The moment the claim was made that certain extant features of the human mind could be

[1] Proudhon, 1897, vol. VI, p. 131.

explained by an historically certain and logically necessary event, it was permissible, and even prescribed, to attempt a scrupulous restoration of the sequence. The failure of *Totem and Taboo*, far from being inherent in the author's proposed design, results rather from his hesitation to avail himself of the ultimate consequences implied in his premises. He ought to have seen that phenomena involving the most fundamental structure of the human mind could not have appeared once and for all. They are repeated in their entirety within each consciousness, and the relevant explanation falls within an order which transcends both historical successions and contemporary correlations. Ontogenesis does not reproduce phylogenesis, or the contrary. Both hypotheses lead to the same contradictions. One can speak of explanations only when the past of the species constantly recurs in the indefinitely multiplied drama of each individual thought, because it is itself only the retrospective projection of a transition which has occurred, because it occurs continually.

As far as Freud's work is concerned, this timidity leads to a strange and double paradox. Freud successfully accounts, not for the beginning of civilization but for its present state; and setting out to explain the origin of a prohibition, he succeeds in explaining, certainly not why incest is consciously condemned, but how it happens to be unconsciously desired. It has been stated and restated that what makes *Totem and Taboo* unacceptable, as an interpretation of the prohibition of incest and its origins, is the gratuitousness of the hypothesis of the male horde and of primitive murder, a vicious circle deriving the social state from events which presuppose it. However, like all myths, the one presented in *Totem and Taboo* with such great dramatic force admits of two interpretations. The desire for the mother or the sister, the murder of the father and the sons' repentance, undoubtedly do not correspond to any fact or group of facts occupying a given place in history. But perhaps they symbolically express an ancient and lasting dream.[1] The magic of this dream, its power to mould men's thoughts unbeknown to them, arises precisely from the fact that the acts it evokes have never been committed, because culture has opposed them at all times and in all places. Symbolic gratifications in which the incest urge finds its expression, according to Freud, do not therefore commemorate an actual event. They are something else, and more, the permanent expression of a desire for disorder, or rather counter-order. Festivals turn social life topsy-turvy, not because it was once like this but because it has never been, and can never be, any different. Past characteristics have explanatory value only in so far as they coincide with present and future characteristics.

Freud has sometimes suggested that certain basic phenomena find their explanation in the permanent structure of the human mind, rather than in its history. For example, anxiety would result from a contradiction between what the situation demands and the means at the individual's disposal to

[1] Kroeber, 1939, pp. 446–51.

deal with it, for example, by the helplessness of the new-born child before the afflux of external stimuli. Anxiety would thus appear before the differentiation of the super-ego: 'It is highly probable that the immediate precipitating causes of primal regression are quantitative factors such as an excessive degree of excitation and the breaking through of the protective shield against stimuli.'[1] Indeed, the severity of the super-ego is in no way related to the degree of severity experienced. Inhibition thus gives proof of an internal and not an external origin.[2] To us these views alone seem capable of giving an answer to a question posed very disturbingly by the psycho-analytic study of children, namely that among young children 'the feeling of sin' appears more precise, and better formed, than the individual history of each case would suggest. This would be explained if, as Freud supposed, it were possible for inhibitions in the broadest sense (disgust, shame, moral and aesthetic demands) to be 'organically determined and . . . occasionally . . . produced without the help of education'.[3] There would be two forms of sublimation, one derived from education and purely cultural, the other 'a lower form', proceeding by an autonomous reaction and appearing at the beginning of the latency period. It might even be that in these exceptionally favourable cases it would continue throughout life.[4]

These bold assumptions concerning the thesis of *Totem and Taboo*, and the accompanying hesitations, are revealing. They show a social science like psychoanalysis – for it is one – still wavering between the tradition of an historical sociology, looking, as Rivers did, to the distant past for the reason for the present-day situation – and a more modern and scientifically more solid attitude, which expects a knowledge of its future and past from an analysis of the present. Moreover, the latter is clearly the practitioner's point of view. But it cannot be overemphasized that the path followed in delving into the structure of the conflicts to which a sick man is prone, in order to recreate its history and so arrive at the initial situation around which all subsequent developments took place, is contrary to that of the theory as presented in *Totem and Taboo*. In the one case, the progression is from experience to myths, and from myths to structure. In the other, a myth is invented to explain the facts, in other words, one behaves like the sick man instead of diagnosing him.

V

Despite these presentiments, only one social science has reached the point at which synchronic and diachronic explanation have merged, because synchronic explanation allows the reconstitution of the origin of systems and their synthesis, while diachronic explanation reveals their internal logic and perceives the evolution which directs them towards an end. This social

---

[1] Freud, 1959, p. 94.
[2] ibid. 1930, p. 116.
[3] ibid. 1938, pp. 583–4.
[4] ibid. p. 625.

science is linguistics, regarded as a phonological study.[1] When we consider its methods, and even more its object, we may ask ourselves whether the sociology of the family, as conceived of in this work, involves as different a reality as might be believed, and consequently whether it has not the same possibilities at its disposal.

The diversity of the historical and geographical modalities of the rules of kinship and marriage have appeared to us to exhaust all possible methods for ensuring the integration of biological families within the social group. We have thus established that superficially complicated and arbitrary rules may be reduced to a small number. There are only three possible elementary kinship structures; these three structures are constructed by means of two forms of exchange; and these two forms of exchange themselves depend upon a single differential characteristic, namely the harmonic or disharmonic character of the regime considered. Ultimately, the whole imposing apparatus of prescriptions and prohibitions could be reconstructed *a priori* from one question, and one alone: in the society concerned, what is the relationship between the rule of residence and the rule of descent? Every disharmonic regime leads to restricted exchange, just as every harmonic regime announces generalized exchange.

The progress of our analysis is thus close to that of the phonological linguist. What is more, if the incest prohibition and exogamy have an essentially positive function, if the reason for their existence is to establish a tie between men which the latter cannot do without if they are to raise themselves from a biological to a social organization, it must be recognized that linguists and sociologists do not merely apply the same methods but are studying the same thing. Indeed, from this point of view, 'exogamy and language . . . have fundamentally the same function – communication and integration with others'.[2] It is to be regretted that after this profound remark its author makes off in another direction, and assimilates the incest prohibition to other taboos, such as the prohibition on sexual relations with an uncircumcised boy among the Wachagga, or the inversion of the hypergamous rule in India.[3] The incest prohibition is not a prohibition like the others. It is *the* prohibition in the most general form, the one perhaps to which all others – beginning with those cited above – are related as particular cases. The incest prohibition is universal like language, and if it is true that we are better informed on the nature of the latter than on the origin of the former, it is only by pursuing the comparison to its conclusion that we can hope to get to the meaning of the institution.

Modern civilization has acquired such a mastery of the linguistic instrument and of means of communication, and makes such a diversified use of them, that we have, as it were, immunized ourselves against language, or at least so we believe. We see language as no more than an inert medium, in itself ineffective, the passive bearer of ideas on which the fact of expression

[1] Trubetzkoy, 1933; 1939.   [2] Thomas, 1937, p. 182.   [3] ibid. p. 197.

confers no additional characteristic. For most men, language represents without falsifying. But modern psychology has refuted this simplistic conception: 'Language does not enter into a world of accomplished objective perceptions merely to give purely external and arbitrary signs or "names" to individual given objects which are clearly delimited from one another; but it is itself a mediator in the formation of objects. It is in one sense the supreme denominator.'[1] This more accurate view of linguistic fact is not a discovery or a new invention. It merely places the narrow perspectives of the civilized white adult in a vaster, and consequently more valid, human experience, in which 'the naming mania' of the child, and the study of the profound upheaval produced in backward subjects by the sudden discovery of the function of language, corroborate observations made in the field; from which it emerges that the conception of the spoken word as communication, as power, and as action represents a universal feature of human thought.[2]

Certain facts taken from psychopathology already tend to suggest that the relations between the sexes can be conceived as one of the modalities of a great 'communication function' which also includes language. For certain sufferers from obsessions, noisy conversation seems to have the same significance as an unbridled sexual activity. They themselves speak only in a low voice and in a murmur, as if the human voice were unconsciously interpreted as a sort of substitute for sexual power.[3] But, even if one is prepared to accept and use these facts only with reservation (and here we call upon psychopathology only because, like infantile psychology and social anthropology, it allows a more comprehensive way of experiencing the social universe), it must be acknowledged that they receive striking confirmation from certain observations on primitive customs and attitudes. One need only recall that in New Caledonia 'the evil word' is adultery, for 'word' should probably be interpreted as meaning 'act'.[4] More significant evidence is also available. For several very primitive peoples in the Malay Archipelago, the supreme sin, unleashing storm and tempest, comprises a series of superficially incongruous acts which informants list higgledy-piggledy as follows: marriage with near kin; father and daughter or mother and son sleeping too close to one another; incorrect speech between kin; ill-considered conversation; for children, noisy play, and, for adults, demonstrative happiness shown at social reunions; imitating the calls of certain insects or birds; laughing at one's own face in the mirror; and finally, teasing animals, and in particular, dressing a monkey as a man, and making fun of him.[5] What possible connexion could there be between such a bizarre collection of acts?

Let us make a short digression. In a neighbouring region, Radcliffe-Brown came across only one of these prohibitions. The Andaman Islanders believe

---

[1] Cassirer, 1933, p. 23.
[2] ibid. p. 25; 1944, p. 31 et seq.; Leenhardt, 1946; Firth, 1939, p. 317.
[3] Reik, 1931, p. 263.   [4] Leenhardt, 1946, p. 87.
[5] Skeat and Blagden, 1906, vol. II, p. 223; Schebesta, 1929, *passim*; Evans, 1923, pp. 199–200; 1937, p. 175.

that the tempest is provoked by killing a cicada, or by making a noise when it sings. As the prohibition seems to exist in isolation, and since he avoids all comparative study, in the name of the principle that every custom is explainable by an immediately apparent function, the English anthropologist treated this example on a purely empirical basis: the prohibition, he argues, proceeds from the myth of the ancestor who killed a cicada; it cried out, and night appeared. Consequently, according to Radcliffe-Brown, this myth expresses the difference in value between night and day in native thought. Night creates fear, this fear is reflected in a prohibition, and, as night cannot be acted upon, it is the cicada which becomes the object of the taboo.[1]

If this method were to be applied to the complete system of prohibitions as listed above, each prohibition would require a different explanation. But why then does native thought group them under the one heading? Either native thought must be accused of being incoherent, or we must search for the common characteristic which, in a certain respect, makes these apparently heterogeneous acts express an identical situation.

A native remark puts us on the track. The Pygmies of the Malay Peninsula consider it a sin to laugh at one's own face in a mirror, but they add that it is not a sin to ridicule a real human being since he can defend himself. This interpretation obviously also applies to the dressed-up monkey which is treated as a human being when it is teased, and looks like a human being (just as does the face in the mirror), although it is not really one. This interpretation can also be extended to the imitation of the calls of certain insects or birds, 'singing' creatures, no doubt, like the Andamanese cicada. By imitating them, one is treating an emission of sound which 'sounds' like a word as a human manifestation when it is not. Thus, we find two categories of acts definable as an immoderate use of language: the first, from a quantitative point of view, to play noisily, to laugh too loudly, or to make an excessive show of one's feelings; the second, from a qualitative point of view, to answer sounds which are not words, or to converse with something (mirror or monkey) which is human only in appearance.[2] These prohibitions are all thus reduced to a single common denominator: they all constitute a *misuse of language*, and on this ground they are grouped together with the incest prohibition, or with acts evocative of incest. What does this mean,

[1] Radcliffe-Brown, 1933, pp. 155–6, 333.

[2] The same definition can be made to include all actions classified by the Dayak as *djeadjea* or forbidden, viz., ' "giving a man or animal a name that is not his or its . . . or to say something about him that is contrary to his nature; for example, that a louse dances, or a rat sings, or a fly goes to war . . .; or to say of a man that he had a cat or some other animal for a mother or wife". To bury any living animal and say "I am burying a man." ' (Hardeland, 1859, s.v.; cf. Caillois, 1959.) However, we believe that these acts relate to the positive interpretation which we propose, rather than Caillois's interpretation based on disorder, or 'counter-order' (ibid. ch. III). 'Mystic homosexuality' appears to us a false category since homosexuality is not the prototype of 'the misuse of communications', but is one of its particular cases, for the same reason (but in a different sense) as are incest and all the other acts just enumerated.

except that women themselves are treated as signs, which are *misused* when not put to the use reserved to signs, which is to be communicated?

In this way, language and exogamy represent two solutions to one and the same fundamental situation. Language has achieved a high degree of perfection, while exogamy has remained approximate and precarious. This disparity, however, is not without its counterpart. The very nature of the linguistic symbol prevented it from remaining for long in the stage which was ended by Babel, when words were still the essential property of each particular group: values as much as signs, jealously preserved, reflectively uttered, and exchanged for other words the meaning of which, once revealed, would bind the stranger, as one put oneself in his power by initiating him, something of oneself and acquires some power over the other. The respective attitudes of two individuals in communication acquire a meaning of which they would otherwise be devoid. Henceforth, acts and thoughts become mutually solidary. The freedom to be mistaken has been lost. But, to the extent that words have become common property, and their signifying function has supplanted their character as values, language, along with scientific civilization,[1] has helped to impoverish perception and to strip it of its affective, aesthetic and magical implications, as well as to schematize thought.

Passing from speech to alliance, i.e., to the other field of communication, the situation is reversed. The emergence of symbolic thought must have required that women, like words, should be things that were exchanged. In this new case, indeed, this was the only means of overcoming the contradiction by which the same woman was seen under two incompatible aspects: on the one hand, as the object of personal desire, thus exciting sexual and proprietorial instincts; and, on the other, as the subject of the desire of others, and seen as such, i.e., as the means of binding others through alliance with them. But woman could never become just a sign and nothing more, since even in a man's world she is still a person, and since in so far as she is defined as a sign she must be recognized as a generator of signs. In the matrimonial dialogue of men, woman is never purely what is spoken about; for if women in general represent a certain category of signs, destined to a certain kind of communication, each woman preserves a particular value arising from her talent, before and after marriage, for taking her part in a duet. In contrast to words, which have wholly become signs, woman has remained at once a sign and a value. This explains why the relations between the sexes have preserved that affective richness, ardour and mystery which doubtless originally permeated the entire universe of human communications.

But that atmosphere of feverish excitement and sensitivity which engendered symbolic thought, and social life, which is its collective form, can still with its far-off vision kindle our dreams. To this very day, mankind has always

---

[1] 'Our scientific civilization . . . tends to impoverish our perception' (Köhler, 1937 p. 277).

dreamed of seizing and fixing that fleeting moment when it was permissible to believe that the law of exchange could be evaded, that one could gain without losing, enjoy without sharing. At either end of the earth and at both extremes of time, the Sumerian myth of the golden age and the Andaman myth of the future life correspond, the former placing the end of primitive happiness at a time when the confusion of languages made words into common property, the latter describing the bliss of the hereafter as a heaven where women will no longer be exchanged, i.e., removing to an equally unattainable past or future the joys, eternally denied to social man, of a world in which one might *keep to oneself*.

Appendix

Rhodes University
Grahamstown
South Africa

Dear M. Lévi-Strauss,

Thank you for your letter. I can write an article, if you wish, offering a justification for some of the views with which you are not in agreement. I cannot, however, estimate how many words would be needed. I would include an analysis of the Dieri system which does not seem to me to be complicated. Here are a few of the points that I would try to make clear.

(1) As I pointed out forty years ago the kinship divisions of Australian tribes may exist as named divisions or may exist without names. The analysis of Australian systems requires the examination of the divisions whether they are named or not.

The four classes of the Dieri system which I pointed out in 1914 can be seen if you will examine the kinship terms. If Ego is of class A, then this class includes all the men he calls yenku, niyi, ngatata and kanini; class B includes those he calls kami, nadada and kadi; class C includes his kaka, taru and tidnara, and class D his ngapari, ngatamura and paiera. When you examine the Dieri system in the light of these four kinship divisions it is neither aberrant nor complicated.

You contrast the Aranda system with the Mara. But the Aranda have a system of four semi-moieties each consisting of a certain number of local clans. In Aranda they are not named and in Mara they are. Further, you fail to take account of alternative marriages which are a regular feature of marriage systems of the Aranda type. In Aranda as in Mara-Anyula the *standard* marriage is with a daughter of a mother's female cross-cousin, and the first *alternative* marriage is with the daughter of a *distant* mother's brother and a *distant* father's sister.

(2) The most widespread system of divisions in Australia is into two endogamous moieties or alternating generation divisions. There are very few tribes in which this dual division does not exist, the Yaralde and Ungarinyin being the best authenticated instances. These divisions are very rarely named, the only two known examples being in Western Australia where they are named totemically, e.g., Birangumat and Djuamat. They exist in tribes that have no named classes, such as what I call the Kukata type, Elkin's southern Luritja.

It is this division into endogamous moieties that lies at the very foundation of all the 'class' systems. When you speak, on page 190, of 'un problème théorique assez inquiétant: quelle est la relation entre les systèmes à deux moietiés et les systèmes a quatre classes' the problem is not correctly formulated. When to the system of endogamous moieties (alternating generation divisions) you add exogamous moieties, either patrilineal or matrilineal, there results a system of four divisions. The problem, therefore, is why these four divisions are sometimes named and sometimes not.

(3) You write (p. 205) of 'deux méthodes de détermination du conjoint – la méthode des classes et la méthode des relations'. But the 'classes' or divisions are only groupings of relations, whether named or not. There are therefore not two methods of arranging marriage but only one. In the actual arrangement of marriages the local clans or hordes play a predominant part. This is so not only in such tribes as the Yaralde and Kukata which have no class systems but also in the tribes that do have class systems.

(4) To my mind a very important question is whether or not a system permits a man to marry the daughter of a woman of his own local clan. The only tribes about which I am *certain* that such marriages are permitted are those of the Kariera cluster. All other tribes about which we have fully adequate knowledge avoid such close marriages, but they do so in different ways. The Karadjeri, Yir-Yoront and Murngin prohibit marriage with the daughter of any 'father's sister', and since marriage is preferred with the daughter of the

499

mother's brother it follows that these tribes cannot practise the exchange of sisters. There are a number of tribes that forbid marriage with the daughter of a 'near' 'father's sister' and also with the daughter of a 'near' mother's brother, but permit marriage with the daughter of distant relatives of these kinds and therefore can practise the exchange of sisters. Examples are the Kukata (no moieties or classes except endogamous generation divisions), the Ompela (patrilineal moieties), Kumbaingeri (four 'classes') and the Murinbata. This kind of marriage is also, of course, forbidden in tribes that have a system of marriage between second cousins (Aranda type of marriage). It is important to note that in the Aranda tribe there is an objection to marriage of a man with the son's daughter of a 'father's father's sister' of his own clan (local group), though the standard marriage is with son's daughter of 'father's father's sister' (aranga).

I do not regard the statement by Miss McConnel about the Kandju as being acceptable. There is no authentic example of patrilateral cousin marriage anywhere in Australia, meaning by that a system in which a man marries the daughter of a father's sister but may not marry the daughter of a mother's brother, own or classificatory.

This will give you some slight idea of what I might write about. I am concerned only with what the Australian systems really are and how they work, and not with their origin or development. If I wished to propose a historical hypothesis it would be one relating to the different ways in which different Australian tribes have provided systems which avoid marriages of a man with the daughter of a woman (father's sister) or his own patrilineal local clan. Methods of doing this which have not been used in Australia can be found in Melanesia (New Ireland, Ambrym, etc.).

I should like very much to see your paper for the New York meeting. Would it be possible to send me a duplicate copy? I should greatly appreciate that as I cannot be at the meeting.

With kind regards,

Yours sincerely,
A. R. RADCLIFFE-BROWN

P.S. The clue to the Wik-munkan system seems to lie in the custom by which a man has an assigned wife's mother's mother who will be a 'sister' of the father's mother, thus avoiding marriage with daughter of own or near 'father's sister' (*pinya*).

Typology of Australian Marriage Systems
  I. Systems with marriage of first cousin (actual or nominal).
      1. With bilateral cousin marriage and exchange of sisters.
          (a) systems in which a man may marry the daughter of his *own* father's sister or *own* mother's brother. Kariera type.
          (b) Systems in which a man marries the daughter of a *classificatory* mother's brother or father's sister but may not marry the daughter of a *near* father's sister.
              Varieties – Kumbaingeri, of N. S. Wales, Ompela of Queensland, Murinbata of Arnhem Land, Kukata of S. Australia.
      2. With matrilateral marriage without exchange of sisters.
          Karadjeri (four classes), Yir-Yoront (patrilineal moieties).
          Murngin (eight classes).
  II. Systems of marriage with *second* cousins with exchange of sisters. The widespread form is that in which the *standard* form of marriage is between children of two female cross-cousins.

There are systems which do not fall under this classification such as the Yaralde. If there were a system with patrilateral marriage it would constitute a type I.3.

Bibliography

BIBLIOGRAPHY

Abel, T. M. 'Unsynthetic Modes of Thinking among Adults: A Discussion of Piaget's Concepts.' *American Journal of Psychology*, vol. XLIV, pp. 123–32. 1932.

Adam, L. 'The Social Organization and Customary Law of the Nepalese Tribes.' *American Anthropologist*, vol. XXXVIII, pp. 533–47. 1936.

Aiyappan, A. 'Cross-Cousin and Uncle-Niece Marriages in South India.' *Congrès International des Sciences Anthropologiques et Ethnographiques*, pp. 281–2. London, 1934.

Allee, W. C. 'Social Dominance and Subordination among Vertebrates.' *Levels of Integration in Biological and Social Systems. Biological Symposia*, vol. VIII. 1942.

Amelineau, E. 'Essai sur l'évolution historique et philosophique des idées morales dans l'Égypte ancienne.' *Bibliothèque de l'École pratique des Hautes Études. Sciences religieuses*, vol. VI. Paris, 1895.

Armstrong, W. E. 'Report on the Suau-Tawala'. *Papua: Anthropology Report*, no. 1. 1920–1.

Ashton, W. G. *Nihongi.* 2 vols. London, 1896.

Balzac, H. de. *Louis Lambert.* (*Œuvres Complètes*, vol. X.) Paris, 1937.

Banerjee, G. N. *The Hindu Law of Marriage and Stridhana.* Calcutta, 1896.

Barbeau, C. M. 'Iroquoian Clans and Phratries.' *American Anthropologist*, vol. XIX, pp. 392–405. 1917.

Barnes, H. 'Marriage of Cousins in Nyasaland.' *Man*, vol. XXII, no. 85, pp. 147–9. 1922.

Barnett, H. G. 'The Coast Salish of Canada.' *American Anthropologist*, vol. XL, pp. 118–41. 1938*a*.

——'The Nature of the Potlatch.' *American Anthropologist*, vol. XL, pp. 349–58. 1938*b*.

Barton, R. F. 'Reflection in Two Kinship Terms of the Transition to Endogamy.' *American Anthropologist*, vol. XLIII, pp. 540–9. 1941.

——'The Religion of the Ifugaos.' *Memoirs of the American Anthropological Association*, no. 65, pp. 1–219. 1946.

Basov, M. 'Structural Analysis in Psychology from the Standpoint of Behaviour.' *Journal of Genetic Psychology*, vol. XXXVI, pp. 267–90. 1929.

Batchelor, J. *The Ainu and Their Folklore.* London, 1901.

Bateson, G. 'Social Structure of the Iatmül People of the Sepik River.' *Oceania,* vol. II, pp. 245–91. 1931.

——*Naven.* Cambridge, 1936.

Baur, E., Fischer, E. and Lenz, P. *Menschliche Erblichkeitslehre und Rassenhygiene.* Munich, 1927.

Benedict, P. K. 'Tibetan and Chinese Kinship Terms.' *Harvard Journal of Asiatic Studies,* vol. VI, pp. 313–37. 1941.

Benveniste, E. 'Les Classes sociales dans la tradition avestique.' *Journal asiatique,* vol. CCXXI, pp. 117–34. 1932.

——'Traditions indo-iraniennes sur les classes sociales.' *Journal asiatique,* vol. CCXXX, pp. 529–49. 1938.

Berndt, R. M. ' "Murngin" (Wulamba) Social Organization.' *American Anthropologist,* vol. LVII, pp. 84–106. 1955.

Bertling, C. T. 'Huwverbod op grond van verwantschapsposities in Middel Java.' *Indisch Tijdschrift van het Recht,* vol. CXLIII, pp. 119–34. 1936.

Best, E. *The Maori.* 2 vols. Wellington, 1924.

——'The Whare Kohanga (the "Nest House") and Its Lore.' *Dominion Museum Bulletin,* no. 13, pp. 1–72. 1929.

Birket-Smith, K. *The Eskimos.* London, 1936.

Bishop, H. L. 'A Selection of ŠiRonga Proverbs.' *The South African Journal of Science,* vol. XIX. 1922.

Blondel, C. *La Conscience morbide.* Paris, 1914.

Blumenbach, J. F. 'Beyträge zur Naturgeschichte.' *Anthropological Treatises of J. F. Blumenbach.* London, 1965.

Boas, F. 'The Social Organization and the Secret Societies of the Kwakiutl Indians.' *Report of the United States National Museum (1895),* pp. 311–738. 1897.

——'The Eskimo of Baffin Land and Hudson Bay.' *Bulletin of the American Museum of Natural History,* vol. XV, pt. I, pp. 1–570. 1901.

——'Introduction.' *Handbook of American Indian Languages. Bulletin of the Bureau of American Ethnology,* vol. XL (pt. I, 1908), pp. 1–83. 1911.

Bodde, D. 'Types of Chinese Categorical Thinking.' *Journal of the American Oriental Society,* vol. LIX, pp. 200–19. 1939.

Bogoras, W. 'The Chukchee.' *Memoirs of the American Museum of Natural History,* no. 11, pp. 1–733. 1904–9.

Bose, J. K. 'Dual Organization in Assam.' *Journal of the Department of Letters, University of Calcutta,* vol. XXV. 1934*a.*

——'Social Organization of the Aimol Kukis.' *Journal of the Department of Letters, University of Calcutta,* vol. XXV, pp. 1–9. 1934*b.*

——'The Nokrom System of the Garos of Assam.' *Man,* vol. XXXVI, no. 54, pp. 44–6. 1936.

——'Marriage Classes among the Chirus of Assam.' *Man,* vol. XXXVII, no. 189, pp. 160–2. 1937.

Brainard, P. 'The Mentality of a Child Compared with that of Apes.' *Journal of Genetic Psychology*, vol. XXXVII, pp. 268–93. 1930.

Bray, D. 'The Jat of Baluchistan.' *Indian Antiquary*, vol. LIV, pp. 30–3. 1925.

Briffault, R. *The Mothers*. New York, 1927.

Brough, J. 'The Early History of the Gotras.' *Journal of the Royal Asiatic Society*, pp. 32–45, 76–90. 1946–7.

Brown, G. G. 'Hehe Cross-Cousin Marriage.' *Essays Presented to C. G. Seligman*, ed. E. E. Evans-Pritchard *et al*. London, 1934.

Buck, P. H. 'Samoan Material Culture.' *Bulletin of the Bernice P. Bishop Museum*, no. 75, pp. 1–724. 1930.

Bühler, G. *Institutes of the Sacred Law. Sacred Books of the East*, ed. F. M. Müller, vol. II. Oxford, 1886–97*a*.

——*The Laws of Manu. Sacred Books of the East*, ed. F. M. Müller, vol. XXV. Oxford, 1886–97*b*.

Bühler, K. 'L'Onomatopée et la fonction représentative du langage.' *Psychologie du Langage*, pp. 101–19. 1933.

Caillois, R. *Man and the Sacred*. Glencoe, Ill., 1959.

Capell, A. and Lester, R. H. 'Local Divisions and Movements in Fiji.' *Oceania*, vol. XI, pp. 313–41. 1941.

—— ——'Kinship in Fiji.' *Oceania*, vol. XV, pp. 171–200. 1945.

Carpenter, C. R. 'A Field Study of the Behaviour and Social Relations of Howling Monkeys (*Alouatta palliata*).' *Comparative Psychology Monographs*, vol. X, no. 2. 1934.

——'A Field Study in Siam of the Behaviour and Social Relations of the Gibbon (*Hylobates lar*).' *Comparative Psychology Monographs*, vol. XVI, no. 5. 1940.

——'Sexual Behaviour of Free Range Rhesus Monkeys (*Macaca mulatta*)'. *Comparative Psychology Monographs*, vol. XVIII. 1942.

Carrapiett, W. J. S. *The Kachin Tribes of Burma*. Rangoon, 1929.

Cassirer, E. 'Le Langage et la construction du monde des objets.' *Psychologie du Langage*, pp. 18–44. 1933.

——*An Essay on Man*. New Haven, 1944.

Chamberlain, B. H. *Ko-ji-ki, Records of Ancient Matters*. Transactions of the Asiatic Society of Japan, supplementary vol. X, pp. 1–369. 1932.

Chattopadhyay, K. P. 'Levirate and Kinship in India.' *Man*, vol. XXII, no. 25, pp. 36–41. 1922.

Chen, T. S. and Shryock, J. K. 'Chinese Relationship Terms.' *American Anthropologist*, vol. XXXIV, pp. 623–69. 1932.

Clark, E. 'The Sociological Significance of Ancestor-Worship in Ashanti.' *Africa*, vol. III, pp. 431–70. 1930.

Codrington, R. H. *The Melanesians*. Oxford, 1891.

Colbacchini, A. A. and Albisetti, C. *Os Bororós orientais*. São Paulo, 1942.

Cole, F. C. 'Family, Clan and Phratry in Central Sumatra.' *Essays in*

Anthropology Presented to A. L. Kroeber, ed. R. H. Lowie. Berkeley, 1936.

Coomaraswamy, A. K. '*Saṁvega*: "Aesthetic Shock".' *Harvard Journal of Asiatic Studies,* vol. VII, pp. 174–9. 1943.

Cooper, J. M. 'Incest Prohibitions in Primitive Culture.' *Primitive Man,* vol. V, pp. 1–20, 1932.

Cosquin, E. *Études folkloriques.* Paris, 1922.

Couvreur, P. S. *Li Ki.* 2 vols. Paris, 1916.

Creel, H. G. 'On the Origins of the Manufacture and Decoration of Bronze in the Shang Period.' *Monumenta Serica,* vol. I, pp. 46 et seq. 1935–6.

——'Studies in Early Chinese Culture.' *American Council of Learned Societies, Studies in Chinese and Related Civilizations,* first series, no. 3. Baltimore, 1937*a*.

——*The Birth of China.* New York, 1937*b*.

Czaplicka, M. A. *Aboriginal Siberia.* Oxford, 1914.

Dahlberg, G. 'Inbreeding in Man'. *Genetics,* vol. XIV, 421–54. 1929.

——'Inzucht bei Polyhybridität bei Menschen.' *Hereditas,* vol. XIV, pp. 83–96. 1930–1.

——'On Rare Defects in Human Populations with Particular Regard to In-breeding and Isolate Effects.' *Proceedings of the Royal Society of Edinburgh,* vol. LVIII, pp. 213–32. 1937–8.

Davenport, W. 'Nonunilinear Descent and Descent Groups.' *American Anthropologist,* vol. LXI, pp. 557–72. 1959.

Davidson, D. S. 'The Basis of Social Organization in Australia.' *American Anthropologist,* vol. XXVIII, pp. 529–48. 1926.

——'The Family Hunting Territory in Australia.' *American Anthropologist,* vol. XXX, pp. 614–31. 1928*a.*.

——*The Chronological Aspects of Certain Australian Social Institutions.* Philadelphia, 1928*b*.

——'The Geographical Distribution Theory and Australian Social Culture.' *American Anthropologist,* vol. XXXIX, pp. 171–4. 1937.

Davis, H. and Warner, W. L. 'Structural Analysis of Kinship.' *American Anthropologist,* vol. XXXVII, pp. 291–313. 1935.

Davy, D. *La Foi jurée.* Paris, 1922.

Deacon, A. B. 'The Regulation of Marriage in Ambrym.' *Journal of the Royal Anthropological Institute,* vol. LVII, pp. 325–42. 1927.

——*Malekula: A Vanishing People in the New Hebrides.* London, 1934.

Delay, J. *Les Dissolutions de la mémoire.* Paris, 1942.

Dennis, W. 'Infant Reaction to Restraint: An Evaluation of Watson's Theory.' *Transactions of the New York Academy of Science,* vol. II, pp. 202–18. 1940*a*.

——'Does Culture Appreciably Affect Patterns of Infant Behaviour?' *Journal of Social Psychology,* vol. XII, pp. 305–17. 1940*b*.

——'The Socialization of the Hopi Child.' *Language, Culture and Personality:*

Essays in Memory of Edward Sapir, ed. L. Spier *et al.* Menasha, 1941.

'Der sexuelle Anteil an der Theologie der Mormonen.' *Imago*, vol. III. 1914.

Deshaies, L. 'La Notion de relation chez l'enfant.' *Journal de Psychologie*, vol. XXXIV, pp. 112–33. 1937.

Devereux, G. 'The Social and Cultural Implications of Incest among the Mohave Indians.' *Psychoanalytic Quarterly*, vol. VIII, pp. 510–33. 1939.

Diderot, D. *Le Neveu de Rameau. Œuvres*. Paris, 1935.

Doke, C. M. 'Social Control among the Lambas.' *Bantu Studies*, vol. II, no. 1. 1923.

Drower, E. S. *The Mandaeans of Iraq and Iran*. Oxford, 1937.

Dubois, H. M. 'Monographie des Betsileo.' *Travaux et mémoires de l'Institut d'Ethnologie*, vol. XXXIV, pp. 1–510. 1939.

Dumézil, G. 'Le Festin d'immortalité.' *Annales du Musée Guimet, Bibliothèque d'Études*, vol. XXXIV. 1924.

——'La Préhistoire iranienne des castes.' *Journal asiatique*, vol. CCXVI, pp. 109–30. 1930.

——*Naissance d'archanges*. Paris, 1945.

Durkheim, D. 'La Prohibition de l'inceste et ses origines.' *Année sociologique*, vol. I, pp. 1–70. 1898.

Dutt, R. C. *The Mahābhārata and Rāmāyana*. London, 1917.

East, E. M. *Heredity and Human Affairs*, New York, 1938.

Eggan, F. 'Historical Change in the Choctaw Kinship System.' *American Anthropologist*, vol. XXIX, pp. 34–52. 1937.

Eiselen, W. 'Preferential Marriage: Correlation of the Various Modes among the Bantu Tribes of the Union of South Africa.' *Africa*, vol. I, pp. 413–28. 1928.

Elkin, A. P. 'The Kopara. The Settlement of Grievances.' *Oceania*, vol. II, pp. 191–8. 1931*a*.

——'Social Organization in the Kimberley Division, North-Western Australia.' *Oceania*, vol. II, pp. 296–333. 1931*b*.

——'The Social Organization of South Australian Tribes.' *Oceania*, vol. II, pp. 44–73. 1931*c*.

——'The Dieri Kinship System.' *Journal of the Royal Anthropological Institute*, vol. LXI, pp. 493–8. 1931*d*.

——'Marriage and Descent in East Arnhem Land.' *Oceania*, vol. III, pp. 412–15. 1933.

——'Anthropology and the Future of the Australian Aborigines.' *Oceania*, vol. V, pp. 1–18. 1934.

——*Studies in Australian Totemism*. Oceania Monograph, no. 2. Sydney, 1937*a*.

——Review of W. Lloyd Warner, *A Black Civilization*. *Oceania*, vol. VIII, pp. 119–20. 1937*b*.

Elkin, A. P. 'Sections and Kinship in Some Desert Tribes of Australia.' *Man*, vol. XL, pp. 21–4. 1940*a*.

——*Kinship in South Australia*. Sydney, 1940*b*.

——'Native Languages and the Field Worker in Australia.' *American Anthropologist*, vol. XLIII, pp. 89–94. 1941.

——'Murngin Kinship System Re-examined and Remarks on Some Generalizations.' *American Anthropologist*, vol. LV, pp. 412–19. 1953.

Ellis, H. *Sexual Selection in Man*. Philadelphia, 1906.

Ellis, T. P. *Welsh Tribal Law and Custom in the Middle Ages*. 2 vols. Oxford, 1926.

Elwin, V. 'A note on the Theory of Symbolism of Dreams among the Baiga.' *British Journal of Medical Psychology*, vol. XVI, pp. 237–54. 1939.

——*The Muria and their Ghotul*. Oxford, 1947.

Emeneau, M. B. 'Toda Marriage Regulations and Taboos.' *American Anthropologist*, vol. XXXIX, pp. 103–12. 1937.

——'Kinship and Marriage among the Coorgs.' *Journal of the Royal Asiatic Society of Bengal* (Letters), vol. IV, pp. 123–47. 1938.

——'Was There Cross-Cousin Marriage among the Śākyas?' *Journal of the American Oriental Society*, vol. LIX, pp. 220–26. 1939.

——'Language and Social Forms: A Study of Toda Kinship Terms and Dual Descent.' *Language, Culture and Personality: Essays in Memory of Edward Sapir*, ed. L. Spier *et al*. Menasha, 1941.

Engels, F. *Dialectic of Nature*. New York, 1940.

Evambi, R. K. 'The Marriage Customs of the Ovimbundu.' *Africa*, vol. XI, pp. 342–8. 1938.

Evans, I. H. N. *Studies in Religion, Folk-lore, and Customs in British North Borneo and the Malay Peninsula*. Cambridge, 1923.

——*The Negritos of Malaya*. Cambridge, 1937.

Evans-Pritchard, E. E. 'Exogamous Rules among the Nuer.' *Man*, vol. XXXV, no. 7, p. 11. 1935.

——*The Nuer*. Oxford, 1940.

Fei, H. T. 'The Problem of the Chinese Relationship System.' *Monumenta Serica*, vol. II, pp. 125–48. 1936–7.

——Review of H. Y. Fêng, *The Chinese Kinship System. Man*, vol. XXXVIII, no. 153, p. 135. 1938.

——*Peasant Life in China*. London, 1939.

Fêng, H. Y. 'Teknonymy as a Formative Factor in the Chinese Kinship System.' *American Anthropologist*, vol. XXXVIII, pp. 59–66. 1936.

——'The Chinese Kinship System.' *Harvard Journal of Asiatic Studies*, vol. II, pp. 141–275. 1937.

Fenichel, O. *The Psychoanalytical Theory of Neurosis*. New York, 1945.

Ferris, G. S. *Sanichar, the Wolf-Boy of India*. New York, 1902.

Filippi, F. de. *An Account of Tibet, The Travels of Ippolito Desideri of Pistoia, S.J., 1712–1727*. London, 1932.

Firth, R. *Primitive Economics of the New Zealand Maori*. New York, 1929.
——'Marriage and the Classificatory System of Relationship.' *Journal of the Royal Anthropological Institute*, vol. LX, pp. 235–68. 1930.
——*We, the Tikopia*. London, 1936.
——*Primitive Polynesian Economy*. London, 1939.
Flinders-Petrie, W. M. *Social Life in Ancient Egypt*. London, 1923.
Foley, J. P. Jr. 'The "Baboon-boy" of South Africa.' *American Journal of Psychology*, vol. LIII, pp. 128–33. 1940.
Ford, J. *'Tis Pity She's a Whore*. London, 1888.
Forde, C. D. 'Kinship in Umor – Double Unilateral Organization in a Semi-Bantu Society.' *American Anthropologist*, vol. XLI, pp. 523–53. 1939*a*.
——'Government in Umor: A Study of Social Change and Problems in a Nigerian Village Community.' *Africa*, vol. XII, pp. 129–61. 1939*b*.
——*Marriage and the Family among the Yakö in S. E. Nigeria*. London School of Economics Monographs in Social Anthropology, no. 5. 1941.
Fortune, R. F. *Sorcerers of Dobu*. London, 1932.
——'Incest'. *The Encyclopedia of the Social Sciences*. New York, 1935.
——'Introduction to Yao Culture.' 'Yao Society: A Study of a Group of Primitives in China.' *Lingan Science Journal*, vol. XVIII, pp. 343–55. 1939.
Frazer, J. G. *Folklore in the Old Testament*. 3 vols. London, 1919.
Freud, S. *Civilization and its Discontents*. London, 1930.
——'Infantile Sexuality', in *Three Contributions to the Theory of Sex*. New York, 1938.
——*Totem and Taboo*. London, 1950.
——*Inhibitions, Symptoms and Anxiety*. London, 1949.

Gayton, A. H. 'Yokuts and Western Mono Social Organization.' *American Anthropologist*, vol. XLVII, pp. 409–26. 1945.
Gesell, A. *Wolf-Child and Human Child*. New York, 1940.
Gifford, E. W. 'Miwok Moieties.' *University of California Publications in American Archaeology and Ethnology*, vol. XII, pp. 130–94. 1916.
——'California Kinship Terminologies.' *University of California Publications in American Archaeology and Ethnology*, vol. XVIII. 1922.
——'Miwok Lineages and the Political Unit in Aboriginal California.' *American Anthropologist*, vol. XXVIII, pp. 389–401. 1926.
——'Miwok Lineages.' *American Anthropologist*, vol. XLVI, pp. 376–81. 1944.
Gilhodes, C. 'Marriage et condition de la femme chez les Katchin, Birmanie.' *Anthropos*, vol. VIII, pp. 363–75. 1913.
——*The Kachins: Religion and Customs*. Calcutta, 1922.
Godden, G. M. 'Naga and Other Frontier Tribes of North-East India. *Journal of the Royal Anthropological Institute*, vol. XXVI, pp. 161–201. 1896.
——'Naga and Other Frontier Tribes of North-East India. Contd.' *Journal of the Royal Anthropological Institute*, vol. XXVII, pp. 22–51. 1897.

Goldenweiser, A. A. 'Remarks on the Social Organization of the Crow Indians.' *American Anthropologist*, vol. XV, pp. 281–94. 1913.

Goodenough, W. 'A Problem in Malayo-Polynesian Social Organization.' *American Anthropologist*, vol. LVII, pp. 71–83. 1955.

Granet, M. *La Polygnie sororale et le Sororat dans la Chine féodale.* Paris, 1920.

——*Danses et légendes de la Chine ancienne.* 2 vols. Paris, 1926.

——*Chinese Civilization.* London, 1930.

——*Festivals and Songs of Ancient China.* London, 1932.

——'Catégories matrimoniales et relations de proximité dans la Chine ancienne.' *Annales sociologiques*, série B, fasc. 1–3. Paris, 1939.

Griaule, M. 'Jeux Dogons.' *Travaux et Mémoires de l'Institut d'Ethnologie*, vol. XXXII, pp. 1–290. 1938.

Grigson, W. *The Maria Gonds of Bastar.* Oxford, 1938.

Guillaume, P. 'Le Développment des éléments formels dans le langage de l'enfant.' *Journal de Psychologie*, vol. XXIV, pp. 203–29. 1927.

——'Recherches sur l'usage de l'instrument chez les singes.' *Journal de psychologie*, vol. XXVIII, pp. 481–555. 1931.

——'Recherches sur l'usage de l'instrument chez les singes.' *Journal de psychologie*, vol. XXXI, pp. 497–554. 1934.

——'Recherches sur l'usage de l'instrument chez les singes.' *Journal de psychologie*, vol. XXXIV, pp. 425–48. 1938.

——and Meyerson, J. 'Quelques recherches sur l'intelligence des singes.' *Journal de psychologie*, vol. XXVII, pp. 92–7. 1930.

Gurdon, P. R. T. *Some Assamese Proverbs.* Shillong, 1896.

——*The Khasis.* London, 1914.

Gusinde, M. *Die Feuerland-Indianer.* Vienna, 1931.

Haeckel, J. 'Clan Reziprozität und Clan-Antagonismus in Rhodesia und deren Bedeutung für das Problem des Zweiklassensystems.' *Anthropos*, vol. XXX, supplement, pp. 654ff. 1938.

Haldane, J. B. S. *Heredity and Politics.* London, 1938.

Halpern, A. M. 'Yuma Kinship Terms.' *American Anthropologist*, vol. XLIV, pp. 425–41. 1942.

Hanson, O. *A Grammar of the Kachin Language.* Rangoon, 1896.

——*The Kachins: Their Customs and Traditions.* Rangoon, 1913.

Hart, C. W. M. 'The Tiwi of Melville and Bathurst Islands.' *Oceania*, vol. I, pp. 167–80. 1930*a*.

——'Personal Names among the Tiwi.' *Oceania*, vol. I, pp. 280–90. 1930*b*.

Head, W. R. *Handbook of the Haka Chin Customs.* Rangoon, 1917.

Held, G. J. *The Mahābhārata: An Ethnological Study.* Amsterdam, 1935.

Henry, J. Review of C. Nimuendajú, *The Apinayé. American Anthropologist*, vol. XLII, pp. 337–8. 1940.

Herskovits, M. J. 'The Social Organization of the Bush-Negroes of Surinam.' *Proceedings of the XXIII International Congress of Americanists*, pp. 713–27. 1928.

——'The Ashanti *ntoro:* A Re-examination.' *Journal of the Royal Anthropological Institute*, vol. LXVII, pp. 287–96. 1937.

Hertz, H. F. *A Practical Handbook of the Kachin or Chingpaw Language etc. with an Appendix on Kachin Customs, Laws and Religion.* Rangoon, 1915.

Hocart, A. M. 'Buddha and Devadatta.' *Indian Antiquary*, vol. LII, pp. 267–72. 1923.

——'Maternal Relations in India Ritual.' *Man*, vol. XXIV, no. 76, pp. 103–4. 1924.

——'The Indo-European Kinship System.' *Ceylon Journal of Science* (Section G), vol. I, part 4, pp. 179–204. 1928.

——'Lau Islands, Fiji.' *Bulletin of the Bernice P. Bishop Museum*, vol. LXII, pp. 1–240. Honolulu, 1929.

——*The Progress of Man.* London, 1933.

——'Covenants.' *Man*, vol. XXXV, no. 164, pp. 149–51. 1935.

——'Kinship Systems.' *Anthropos*, vol. XXXII, pp. 345–51. 1937.

——'Les Castes.' *Annales du Musée Guimet.* Bibliothèque de vulgarisation, vol. LIV, pp. 1–274. 1938.

Hodson, T. C. *The Primitive Culture of India.* Royal Asiatic Society, James G. Forlong Fund, vol. I. London, 1922.

——*The Naga Tribes of Manipur.* London, 1923.

——'Notes on the Marriage of Cousins in India.' *Man in India*, vol. V, pp. 163–75. 1925.

——*Aspects of the Census of India, 1931.* Congrès International des Sciences Anthropologiques et Ethnographiques. London, 1934.

Hoernlé, A. W. 'The Social Organization of the Nama Hottentots of South-west Africa.' *American Anthropologist*, vol. XXVII, pp. 1–24. 1925a.

——'The Importance of Sib in the Marriage Ceremonies of the South-western Bantu.' *South African Journal of Science*, vol. XXV, pp. 481–92. 1925b.

Hogben, L. T. *Genetic Principles in Medicine and Social Science.* London, 1931.

——*Nature and Nurture.* New York, 1933.

Hogbin, H. I. 'The Sexual Life of the Natives of Ontong Java (Solomon Islands).' *Journal of the Polynesian Society*, vol. XL, pp. 23–34. 1931a.

——'Tribal Ceremonies at Ontong Java (Solomon Islands)'. *Journal of the Royal Anthropological Institute*, vol. LXI, pp. 27–55. 1931b.

——'Polynesian Ceremonial Gift Exchange.' *Oceania*, vol. III, pp. 13–39. 1932.

——'Native Culture in Wogeo: Report of Field Work in New Guinea.' *Oceania*, vol. V, pp. 308–37. 1935.

——'The Hill People of North-Eastern Guadalcanal.' *Oceania*, vol. VIII, pp. 62–89. 1937.

Hose, C. and McDougall, W. *The Pagan Tribes of Borneo.* 2 vols. London, 1912.

Howitt, A. W. 'Australian Group-Relationships.' *Journal of the Anthropological Institute,* vol. XXXVII, pp. 279–89. 1907.

Hsu, F. L. K. Review of M. Granet, 'Catégories Matrimoniales et relations de proximité dans la Chine ancienne.' *Man,* vol. XL, no. 183, pp. 157–8. 1940*a*.

——'The Problem of Incest Tabu in a North China Village.' *American Anthropologist,* vol. XLII, pp. 122–35. 1940*b*.

——'Concerning the Question of Matrimonial Categories and Kinship Relationship in Ancient China.' *T'ien Hsia Monthly,* vol. XI, pp. 242–69, 353–62. 1940–1.

——'The Differential Function of Relationship Terms.' *American Anthropologist,* vol. XLIV, pp. 748–56. 1942.

——'Observations on Cross-Cousin Marriage in China.' *American Anthropologist,* vol. XLVII, pp. 83–103. 1945.

Hudson, A. E. 'Kazak Social Structure.' *Yale University Publications in Anthropology,* no. 20, pp. 1–109. 1938.

Hume, D. 'Of the Dignity of Human Nature.' *Essays, Moral, Political and Literary,* in *David Hume: Philosophical Works,* ed. T. H. Green and T. H. Grose, Vol. III. London, 1886.

Hutton, J. H. *The Sema Nagas,* London, 1921*a*.

——*The Angami Nagas.* London, 1921*b*.

——*Caste in India.* Cambridge, 1946.

Isaacs, S. *Intellectual Growth in Young Children.* London, 1930.

——*Social Development in Young Children.* London, 1933.

Itard, J. E. *The Wild Boy of Aveyron.* New York, 1962.

Jakobson, R. 'Observations sur le classement phonologique des consonnes.' *Proceedings of the Third International Congress of Phonetic Sciences,* pp. 34–41. 1938.

——*Kindersprache, Aphasie und allgemeine Lautgesetze.* Uppsala, 1941.

Jennings, H. S. *Genetics.* New York, 1935.

——'The Transition from the Individual to the Social Level.' *Levels of Integration in Biological and Social Systems. Biological Symposia,* vol. VIII. 1942.

Jochelson, W. *Contes aléoutes,* ed. R. Jakobson. nos. 34–5. MS. in New York Public Library. n.d.*a*.

——*Aleutian Ethnographical and Linguistic Material.* MS. in New York Public Library. n.d.*b*.

——'The Koryak.' *Memoirs of the American Museum of Natural History,* no. 10, pp. 1–811. 1908.

——'The Yukaghir and the Yukaghirized Tungus.' *Memoirs of the American Museum of Natural History,* no. 13, 1–454. 1910–26.

——*History, Ethnology and Anthropology of the Aleut.* Publications of the Carnegie Institution of Washingon, no. 432. 1933.

Johnson, C. S. *Patterns of Negro Segregation.* New York, 1943.

Josselin de Jong, J. P. B. de. *Lévi-Strauss's Theory on Kinship and Marriage.* Mededelingen van het Rijksmuseum voor Volkenkunde, no. 10. Leiden, 1952.

Junod, H. A. *The Life of a South African Tribe.* 2 vols. New York, 1962.

Kaberry, P. M. 'The Abelam Tribe, Sepik District, New Guinea. A Preliminary Report.' *Oceania*, vol. XI, pp. 233–57; 345–67. 1941.

——'Law and Political Organization in the Abelam Tribe, New Guinea.' *Oceania*, vol. XII, pp. 209–25, 331–63. 1942.

Kapadia, K. M. *Hindu Kinship.* Bombay, 1947.

Karandikar, S. V. *Hindu Exogamy.* Bombay, 1929.

Kellogg, W. N. 'More about the "Wolf-Children" of India.' *American Journal of Psychology*, vol. XLIII, pp. 508–9. 1931.

——'A further Note on the "Wolf-Children" of India.' *American Journal of Psychology*, vol. XLVI, pp. 149–50. 1934.

Kennedy, R. 'A Survey of Indonesian Civilization.' *Studies in the Science of Society presented to A. G. Keller*, ed. G. P. Murdock. New Haven, 1937.

——'The "Kulturkreislehre" Moves into Indonesia.' *American Anthropologist*, vol. XLI, pp. 163–9. 1939.

Kirchhoff, P. 'Verwandtschaftsbezeichnungen und Verwandtenheirat.' *Zeitschrift für Ethnologie*, vol. LXIV, pp. 41–70. 1932.

Klein, M. *The Psychoanalysis of Children.* London, 1932.

Kluckhohn, C. 'Theoretical Bases for an Empirical Method of Studying the Acquisition of Culture by Individuals.' *Man*, vol. XXXIX, no. 89, pp. 98–103. 1939.

——'The Personal Document in Anthropological Science.' *The Use of Personal Documents in History, Anthropology and Sociology.* Social Science Research Council Bulletin, no. 53. 1945.

Köhler, W. *The Mentality of Apes.* New York, 1928.

——'La Perception humaine.' *Journal de psychologie*, vol. XXVII, pp. 5–30. 1930.

——'Psychological Remarks on Some Questions of Anthropology.' *American Journal of Psychology*, vol. I, pp. 271–88. 1937.

Kohts, N. 'Recherches sur l'intelligence du chimpanzé par la méthode du "choix d'après modèle".' *Journal de psychologie*, vol. XXV, pp. 255–75. 1928.

——'Les Habitudes motrices adaptatives du singe inférieur.' *Journal de psychologie*, vol. XXVII, pp. 412–47. 1930.

——'La Conduite du petit du chimpanzé et de l'enfant de l'homme.' *Journal de psychologie*, vol. XXXIV, pp. 494–531. 1937.

Koppers, W. 'India and the Dual Organization.' *Acta Tropica*, vol. I, pp. 72–92, 97–119. 1944.

Kowalewsky, M. *Tableau des origines et de l'evolution de la famille et de la propriété.* Stockholm, 1890a.

——'Marriage among the Early Slavs.' *Folklore,* vol. I, pp. 463–80. 1890b.

——'La Famille matriarcale au Caucase.' *L'Anthropologie,* vol. IV, pp. 259–78. 1893.

Krasheninnikoff, S. P. *Description of the Land Kamchatka.* 2 vols. St. Petersburg, 1819.

Kreezer, G. and Dallenbach, K. M. 'Learning the Relation of Opposition.' *American Journal of Psychology,* vol. XLI, pp. 432–41. 1929.

Kroeber, A. L. 'California Kinship Systems.' *University of California Publications in American Archaeology and Ethnology,* vol. XII, pp. 339–96. 1917.

——*Handbook of the Indians of California.* Bulletin of the Bureau of American Ethnology, no. 78, pp. 1–941. 1925.

——'Process in the Chinese Kinship System.' *American Anthropologist,* vol. XXXV, pp. 151–7. 1933.

——'Basic and Secondary Patterns of Social Structure.' *Journal of the Royal Anthropological Institute,* vol. LXVIII, pp. 299–310. 1938.

——'Totem and Taboo in Retrospect.' *American Journal of Sociology,* vol. XLV, pp. 446–51. 1939.

——'Stepdaughter Marriage.' *American Anthropologist,* vol. XLII, pp. 562–70. 1940.

——'The Societies of Man.' *Levels of Integration in Biological and Social Systems. Biological Symposia,* vol. VIII. 1942.

——and Waterman, T. T. 'Yurok Marriages.' *Publications in American Archaeology and Ethnology,* vol. XXV, pp. 1–14. University of California, 1934.

Kruse, A. 'Mundurucu Moieties.' *Primitive Man,* vol. VII, pp. 40–7. 1934.

Kulp, D. H. *Country Life in South China.* New York, 1925.

Kyriakos, M. 'Fiançailles et mariage à Mossoul.' *Anthropos,* vol. VI, pp. 774–84. 1911.

Labouret, H. 'Les Tribus du Rameau Lobi.' *Travaux et mémoires de l'Institut d'Ethnologie,* vol. XV. 1931.

Lane, B. S. 'Structural Contrasts between Symmetric and Asymmetric Marriage Systems: A Fallacy.' *Southwestern Journal of Anthropology,* vol. XVII, pp. 49–55. 1961.

Lanman, C. R. 'Hindu Law and Custom as to Gifts.' *Anniversary Papers by Colleagues and Pupils of George Lyman Kittredge.* Boston, 1913.

Lattimore, O. 'The Gold Tribe: "Fishskin Tatars" of the Lower Sungari.' *Memoirs of the American Anthropological Association,* no. 40, pp. 1–77. 1933.

Lawrence, W. E. 'Alternating Generations in Australia.' *Studies in the Science of Society Presented to A. G. Keller,* ed. G. P. Murdock. New Haven, 1937.

Leach, E. *Political Systems of Highland Burma*. London, 1954.

——*Rethinking Anthropology*. London School of Economics Monographs on Social Anthropology, no. 22. London, 1961*a*.

——'Asymmetric Marriage Rules, Status Difference, and Direct Reciprocity: Comments on an Alleged Fallacy.' *Southwestern Journal of Anthropology*, vol. XVII, pp. 343–50. 1961*b*.

Lee, D. D. 'The Place of Kinship Terms in Wintu·' Speech.' *American Anthropologist*, vol. XLII, pp. 604–16. 1940.

Leenhardt, M. 'Notes d'ethnologie néo-calédonniene.' *Travaux et mémoires de l'Institut d'Ethnologie*, vol. VIII. 1930.

——'Ethnologie de la parole.' *Cahiers Internationaux de Sociologie*, vol. I. 1946.

Leighton, D. and Kluckhohn, C. *Children of the People*. Cambridge, 1948.

Lévi-Strauss, C. 'Contributions à l'étude de l'organization sociale des Indiens Bororo.' *Journal de la Société des Américanistes de Paris*, vol. XXVIII, pp. 269–304. 1936.

——'Guerre et commerce chez les Indiens de l'Amérique du Sud.' *Renaissance*, vol. I, pp. 122–39. 1943*a*.

——'The Social Use of Kinship Terms among Brazilian Indians.' *American Anthropologist*, vol. XLV, pp. 398–409. 1943*b*.

——'The Social and Psychological Aspects of Chieftainship in a Primitive Tribe: The Nambikwara of Western Mato Grosso.' *Transactions of the New York Academy of Sciences*, series 2, vol. VII, pp. 16–32. 1944.

——'L'Analyse structurale en linguistique et en anthropologie.' *Word*, vol. I, pp. 33–53. 1945*a*.

——'Le Dédoublement de la Représentation dans les Arts de l'Asie et de l'Amérique.' *Renaissance*, vol. III, pp. 33–53. 1945*b*.

——*La Vie familiale et sociale des Indiens Nambikwara*. Paris, 1945*a*.

——'The Tupí-Cawahíb.' *Handbook of South American Indians*, ed. J. Steward, vol. III. Bureau of American Ethnology. Washington, D.C., 1948*b*.

——'The Tribes of the Xingu.' *Handbook of South American Indians*, ed. J. Steward, vol. III. Bureau of American Ethnology. Washington, D.C., 1948*c*.

——*The Savage Mind*. London, 1966.

Lévy-Bruhl, L. *Le Surnaturel et la nature dans la mentalité primitive*. Paris, 1931.

——*La Mythologie primitive*. Paris, 1935.

Lin, Y. H. 'The Kinship System of the Lolo.' *Harvard Journal of Asiatic Studies*, vol. IX, pp. 81–100. 1946.

Linton, R. 'Marquesan Culture.' *The Individual and His Society*, ed. A. Kardiner. New York, 1945.

Loeb, E. M. 'Patrilineal and Matrilineal Organization in Sumatra: The

Batak and the Minangkabau.' *American Anthropologist*, vol. XXXV, pp. 16–50. 1933.

Loeb, E. M. and Toffelmier, G. 'Kin Marriage and Exogamy.' *Journal of General Psychology*, vol. XX, pp. 181–228. 1939.

Lowie, R. H. 'Exogamy and the Classificatory, System of Relationships.' *American Anthropologist*, vol. XVII, pp. 223–39. 1915.

——'The Matrilineal Complex.' *University of California Publications in American Archaeology and Ethnology*, vol. XVI, pp. 29–45. 1919.

——Review of W. J. Perry, *The Children of the Sun. American Anthropologist*, vol. XXVI, pp. 86–90. 1924.

——'Some Moot Problems in Social Organization.' *American Anthropologist*, vol. XXXVI, pp. 321–30. 1934.

——*Traité de sociologie primitive*. French translation, E. Métraux. Paris, 1935.

——'American Culture History.' *American Anthropologist*, vol. XLII, pp. 409–28. 1940.

——*Primitive Society*. New York, 1961.

Lubbock. J. *The Origin of Civilization and the Primitive Condition of Man*. London, 1870.

——*Marriage, Totemism and Religion*. London, 1911.

Lumley, F. E. 'Indo-Aryan Society.' *Studies in the Science of Society Presented to A. G. Keller*, ed. G. P. Murdock. New Haven, 1937.

Luria, A. R. 'The second Psychological Expedition to Central Asia.' *Journal of Genetic Psychology*, vol. XLIV. 1934.

Luttig, H. G. *The Religious System and Social Organization of the Herero*. Utrecht, 1934.

Lyons, A. P. 'Paternity Beliefs and Customs in Western Papua.' *Man*, vol. XXIV, no. 44, pp. 58–9. 1924.

McConnel, U. 'Social Organization of the Tribes of Cape York Peninsula, North Queensland.' *Oceania*, vol. X, pp. 54–72, 434–55. 1940.

McGraw, M. B. *The Neuromuscular Maturation of the Human Infant*. New York, 1944.

McLennan, J. F. *Primitive Marriage*. Edinburgh, 1865.

Maine, H. J. S. *Dissertations on Early Law and Custom*. New York, 1886.

Malinowski, B. *Sex and Repression in Savage Society*. London, 1927.

——*The Sexual Life of Savages*. London, 1929.

——'Introduction' to H. I. Hogbin, *Law and Order in Polynesia*. London, 1934.

Man, E. H. *On the Aboriginal Inhabitants of the Andaman Islands*. London, n.d. [1885.]

Maslow, A. H. 'Comparative Behaviour in Primates, VI: Food Preferences of Primates.' *Journal of Comparative Psychology*, vol. XVI, pp. 187–97. 1933.

Maspero, G. *Contes populaires de l'Égypte ancienne*. Paris, 1889.

Maspero, H. *La Chine antique*. Paris, 1927.

Mauss, M. 'Essai sur le don: Forme et raison de l'échange dans les sociétés archaïques.' *Année sociologique*, n.s., vol. I, pp. 30–186. 1925.

Maybury-Lewis, D. H. P. 'Parallel Descent and the Apinayé Anomaly.' *Southwestern Journal of Anthropology*, vol. XVI, pp. 191–216. 1960.

Mazaheri, A. A. *La Famille iranienne aux temps anté-islamiques.* Paris, 1938.

Mead, M. 'The Social Organization of Manua.' *Bulletin of the Bernice P. Bishop Museum*, no. 76, pp. 1–218. 1930.

——*Sex and Temperament in Three Primitive Societies.* New York, 1935.

——'A Twi Relationship System.' *Journal of the Royal Anthropological Institute*, vol. LXVII, pp. 297–304. 1937.

Means, P. A. *Ancient Civilizations of the Andes.* New York, 1931.

Métraux, A. 'The Ethnology of Easter Island.' *Bulletin of the Bernice P. Bishop Museum*, no. 160. pp. 1–432. 1940.

——L'Île de Pâques. Paris, 1941.

——'La Vie sociale de L'Île de Pâques.' *Anales del Instituto de Etnografía Americana*, Universidad Nacional de Cuyo. 1942.

Miller, G. S. 'The Primate Basis of Human Sexual Behaviour.' *Quarterly Review of Biology*, vol. VI, pp. 379–410. 1931.

Mills, J. P. *The Lhota Nagas.* London, 1922.

——*The Ao Nagas.* London, 1926.

——*The Rengma Nagas.* London, 1937.

Molina, C. de. 'An Account of the Fables and Rites of the Yncas.' *Narratives of the Rites and Laws of the Incas*, ed. C. R. Markham. London, 1873.

Montaigne, M. de. *Essais.* 2 vols. Paris, 1962.

Mookerji, R. K. 'The Nokrom System of the Garos of Assam.' *Man*, vol. XXXIX, no. 167, p. 168. 1939.

Morgan, L. H. *Systems of Consanguinity and Affinity of the Human Family.* Smithsonian Contributions to Knowledge, vol. XVII, no. 218. Washington, 1871.

Muller, H. F. 'A Chronological Note on the Physiological Explanation of the Prohibition of Incest.' *Journal of Religious Psychology*, vol. VI, pp. 294–5. 1931.

Murdock, G. P. 'Rank and Potlatch among the Haida.' *Yale University Publications in Anthropology*, no. 13, pp. 3–20. 1936.

——'Double Descent.' *American Anthropologist*, vol. LX, pp. 555–61. 1942.

Murdock, G. P. 'Correlations of Matrilineal and Patrilineal Institutions,' in *Studies in the Science of Society Presented to A. G. Keller*, ed. G. P Murdock. New Haven, 1937.

——'Cognatic Forms of Social Organization.' *Social Structure in South-East Asia.* Viking Fund Publications in Anthropology, no. 29. 1960.

Murray, M. A. 'Marriage in Ancient Egypt.' *Congrès international des sciences anthropologiques, Comptes rendus.* London, 1934.

Needham, R. 'A Structural Analysis of Purum Society.' *American Anthropologist*, vol. LX, pp. 75–101. 1958.

——'Patrilateral Prescriptive Alliance and The Ungarinyin.' *Southwestern Journal of Anthropology*, vol. XVI, pp. 274–91. 1960*a*.

——'A Structural Analysis of Aimol Society.' *Bijdragen tot de Taal-, Land- en Volkenkunde*, vol. 116, pp. 81–108. 1960*b*.

——'Notes on the Analysis of Asymmetric Alliance.' *Bijdragen tot de Taal-, Land- en Volkenkunde*, vol. 117, pp. 93–117. 1961.

Nelson, E. W. 'The Eskimo about Bering Strait.' *Annual Report, Bureau of American Ethnology*, vol. XVIII, pp. 3–418. 1896–7.

Nesfield, J. C. *Brief View of the Caste System of the Northwestern Provinces and Oudh*. Allahabad, 1885.

Niggemeyer, H. 'Totemismus in Vorderindien.' *Anthropos*, vol. XXVIII, pp. 407–61, 579–619. 1933.

Nimuendajú, C. *The Apinayé*, ed. R. H. Lowie and J. M. Cooper. *The Catholic University of America Anthropological Series*, vol. VIII. 1939.

Nissen, H. W. 'A Field Study of the Chimpanzee.' *Comparative Psychology Monographs*, vol. VIII, no. 1. 1931.

——and Crawford, M. P. 'A Preliminary Study of Food-Sharing Behaviour in Young Chimpanzees.' *Journal of Comparative Psychology*, vol. XXII, pp. 383–419. 1936.

O'Brien, A. J. 'Some Matrimonial Problems of the Western Border of India.' *Folklore*, vol. XXII, pp. 426–48. 1911.

Olson, R. L. 'Clan and Moiety in Native America.' *University of California Publications in American Archaeology and Ethnology*, vol. XXX, pp. 351–422. 1933.

O'Malley, L. S. S. *Census of India, 1911*, vol. V. Delhi, n.d.

Paranavitana, S. 'Matrilineal Descent in the Sinhalese Royal Family.' *Ceylon Journal of Science* (Section G), vol. II, pp. 235–40. 1933.

Parry, N. E. *The Lakhers*. London, 1932.

Perry, W. J. *The Children of the Sun*. London, 1923.

Piaget, J. 'Psycho-pédagogie et mentalité enfantine.' *Journal de psychologie*, vol. XXV, pp. 38–40. 1928*a*.

——*Judgment and Reasoning in the Child*. London, 1928*b*.

——*The Child's Conception of the World*. London, 1929.

——*Plays, Dreams and Imitation*. London, 1951.

Pink, O. 'The Landowners in the Northern Division of the Aranda Tribe, Central Australia.' *Oceania*, vol. VI, pp. 275–322. 1936.

Playfair, A. *The Garos*. London, 1909.

Porteus, S. D. *The Psychology of a Primitive People*. London, 1931.

Proudhon, P. J. *Solution du probléme social. Œuvres*, vol. VI. Paris, 1897.

Pusalker, A. D. 'Critical Study of the Work of Bhāsa, with Special Reference to the Sociological Conditions of His Age.' *Journal of the University of Bombay*, vol. II. 1934.

Radcliffe-Brown, A. R. 'Three Tribes of Western Australia.' *Journal of the Royal Anthropological Institute*, vol. XLIII, pp. 143–70. 1913.

——'The Relationship System of the Dieri Tribe.' *Man*, vol. XIV, no. 33, pp. 53–6. 1914.

——'The Mother's Brother in South Africa.' *The South African Journal of Science*, vol. XXI, pp. 542–55. 1924.

——'The Regulation of Marriage in Ambrym.' *Journal of the Royal Anthropological Institute*, vol. LVII, pp. 343–8. 1927.

——*The Social Organization of Australian Tribes*. Oceania Monograph, no. 1. Sydney, 1931.

——*The Andaman Islanders*. Cambridge, 1933.

——'Patrilineal and Matrilineal Succession.' *Iowa Law Review*, vol. XX, pp. 286–303. 1935*a*.

——'On the Concept of Function in Social Science.' *American Anthropologist*, vol. XXXVII, pp. 394–402. 1935*b*.

——'On Social Structure.' *Journal of the Royal Anthropological Institute*, vol. LXX, pp. 1–12. 1940.

——'Murngin Social Organization.' *American Anthropologist*, vol. LIII, pp. 37–55. 1951.

Radin, P. 'The Autobiography of a Winnebago Indian.' *University of California Publications in American Archaeology and Ethnology*, vol. XVI, pp. 381–473. 1920.

Rao, C. H. 'The Gonds of the Eastern Ghauts.' *Anthropos*, vol. V, pp. 791–7. 1910.

Raum, O. F. 'Female Initiation among the Chaga.' *American Anthropologist*, vol. XLI, pp. 554–65. 1939.

Reichard, G. A. *Navaho Religion: A Study in Symbolism*. MS. in New York Public Library. n.d. [*Navaho Religion: a study of symbolism*. 2 vols. (Bollingen Series, XVIII.) New York, 1950.]

Reik, T. *Ritual*. London, 1931.

Renou, L. *Anthologie sanskrite*. Paris, 1947.

Richards, A. I. *Hunger and Work in a Savage Tribe*. London, 1932.

——'Reciprocal Clan Relationships among the Bemba of N. E. Rhodesia.' *Man*, vol. XXXVII, no. 222, pp. 188–93. 1937.

——*Land, Labour and Diet in Northern Rhodesia*. Oxford, 1939.

Richards, F. J. 'Cross-Cousin Marriage in South India.' *Man*, vol. XIV, no. 97, pp. 194–8. 1914.

Rink, H. J. *The Eskimo Tribes*. London, 1887.

Risley, H. H. *The Tribes and Castes of Bengal*. 4 vols. Calcutta, 1891.

Rivers, W. H. R. 'The Marriage of Cousins in India.' *Journal of the Royal Asiatic Society*, pp. 611–40. 1907.

——'The Father's Sister in Oceania.' *Folklore*, vol. XXI. 1910.

Rivers W. H. R. *The History of Melanesian Society.* 2 vols. Cambridge, 1914.
——'Marriage'. *Encyclopaedia of Religion and Ethics*, vol. 8, pp. 423–32. Edinburgh, 1915.
Rose, H. A. *Glossary of the Tribes and Castes of the Punjab and North-West Frontier Province.* 3 vols. Punjab, 1914.
Roy, P. C. *The Mahābhārata.* 11 vols. Calcutta, 1883–6.
Roy, S. C. *The Hill Bhūiyās of Orissa.* Ranchi, 1935.
Russell, R. V. and Hira Lal, R. B. *Tribes and Castes of the Central Provinces of India.* 4 vols. London, 1906.

Salisbury, R. F. 'Asymmetrical Marriage Systems.' *American Anthropologist*, vol. LXVIII, pp. 639–55. 1956.
Sartre, J. P. *Critique de la raison dialectique.* Paris, 1960.
Schapera, I. *The Khoisan Peoples of South Africa.* London, 1930.
Schebesta, P. *Among the Forest Dwarfs of Malaya.* London, 1929.
——*Among Congo Pygmies.* London, 1933.
——*Revisiting My Pygmy Hosts.* London, 1936.
Searl, M. N. 'Some Contrasted Aspects of Psychoanalysis and Education.' *British Journal of Educational Psychology*, vol. II, pp. 276–95. 1932.
Séchehaye, M. A. *Symbolic Realization.* New York, 1950.
Seligman, B. Z. 'Cross-Cousin Marriage.' *Man*, vol. XXV, no. 70, pp. 114–21. 1925.
——'Bilateral Descent and the Formation of Marriage Classes.' *Journal of the Royal Anthropological Institute*, vol. LVII, pp. 349–76. 1927.
——'Asymmetry in Descent with Special Reference to Pentecost.' *Journal of the Royal Anthropological Institute*, vol. LVIII, pp. 533–58. 1928.
——'The Incest Barrier: Its Rôle in Social Organization.' *British Journal of Psychology*, vol. XXII, pp. 250–76. 1931–2.
——'The Incest Taboo as a Social Regulation.' *The Sociological Review*, vol. XXVII, pp. 75–93. 1935.
——Review of H. Y. Fêng, *The Chinese Kinship System. American Anthropologist*, vol. XLI, pp. 496–8. 1939.
Seligman, C. G. *The Melanesians of British New Guinea.* Cambridge, 1910.
——and Seligman, B. Z. *Pagan Tribes of the Nilotic Sudan.* London, 1932.
Senart, E. C. M. *Les Castes dans l'Inde.* Paris, 1896.
Sen Gupta, N. C. 'Early History of Sonship in India.' *Man*, vol. XXIV, nos. 32 and 42, pp. 40–3, 53–6. 1924.
——Putrikā-putra, or the Appointed Daughter's Son in Ancient Law.' *Journal of the Royal Asiatic Society of Bengal* (Letters), vol. IV. 1938.
Shakespear, J. *The Lushei Kuki Clans.* London, 1912.
Sharp, L. 'Ritual Life and Economics of the Yir-Yoront of Cape York Peninsula.' *Oceania*, vol. V, pp. 19–42. 1934.
——'Semi-Moieties in North-Western Queensland.' *Oceania*, vol. VI, pp. 158–74. 1935.

Shirokogoroff, S. M. 'Anthropology of Northern China.' *Journal of the Royal Asiatic Society* (North China Branch), extra vol. III. 1923.

——'Social Organization of the Manchus: A Study of the Manchu Clan Organization.' *Journal of the Royal Asiatic Society* (North China Branch), extra vol. III, pp. 1–194. 1924.

——*Social Organization of the Northern Tungus.* Shanghai, 1929.

——*The Psychomental Complex of the Tungus.* London, 1935.

Shryock, J. K. 'Ch'en Ting's Account of the Marriage Customs of the Chiefs of Yunnan and Keichou.' *American Anthropologist*, vol. XXXVI, pp. 524–47. 1934.

Simmons, L. W. (ed.). *Sun Chief.* New Haven, 1942.

Singh, J. A. L., and Zingg, R. M. *Wolf-Children and Feral Men.* New York, 1942.

Skeat, W. W. and Blagden, C. O. *Pagan Races of the Malay Peninsula.* 2 vols. London, 1906.

Spencer B. and Gillen, F. J. *Native Tribes of Central Australia.* London, 1899.

Spencer, H. *Principles of Sociology.* 3 vols. London, 1882–96.

Spencer, R. F. 'The Annamese Kinship System.' *Southwestern Journal of Anthropology*, vol. I, pp. 284–310. 1945.

Spier, L. *Yuman Tribes of the Gila River*, Chicago, 1933.

Squires, P. C. ' "Wolf-Children" of India.' *American Journal of Psychology*, vol. XXXVIII, pp. 313–15. 1927.

Stack, E. and Lyall, C. J. *The Mikirs.* London, 1908.

Stanner, W. E. H. 'A Note upon a Similar System among the Nangiomeri.' *Oceania*, vol. III, pp. 416–17. 1933a.

——'The Daly River Tribes: A Report of Field Work in North Australia.' *Oceania*, vol. III, pp. 377–405. 1933b.

——'Murinbata Kinship and Totemism.' *Oceania*, vol. VII, pp. 186–216. 1936.

Steller, Georg Wilhelm. *Beschreibung von dem Lande Kamtschatka.* Frankfurt and Leipzig, 1774.

Sternberg, L. *The Social Organization of the Gilyak.* MS. in Library of the American Museum of Natural History. New York, n.d.

——*Specimens of Gilyak Folklore* (in Russian). St. Petersburg, 1904.

——'The Turano-Ganowanian System and the Nations of North-East Asia.' *Memoirs of the International Congress of Americanists.* London, 1912.

Stevenson, H. N. C. 'Feasting and Meat Division among the Zahau Chins of Burma.' *Journal of the Royal Anthropological Institute*, vol. LXVII, pp. 15–32. 1937.

Sumner, W. G. 'The Yakuts. Abridged from the Russian of Sieroshevski.' *Journal of the Royal Anthropological Institute*, vol. XXXI, pp. 65–110. 1901.

Sunjana, D. D. P. *Next of Kin Marriages in Old Iran.* London, 1888.

Swanton, J. R. 'The Social Organization of American Tribes.' *American Anthropologist*, vol. VII, pp. 663–73. 1905a.

Swanton, J. R. 'Contributions to the Ethnology of the Haida.' *Memoirs of the American Museum of Natural History*, vol. VIII, pp. 1–300. 1905*b*.
——'A Reconstruction of the Theory of Social Organization.' *Boas Anniversary Volume*. New York, 1906.
——Tlingit Myths and Texts. *Bulletin of the Bureau of American Ethnology*, no. 39, pp. 1–451. 1909.
——'The Terms of Relationship of Pentecost Island.' *American Anthropologist*, vol. XVIII, pp. 455–65. 1916.

Taine, H. A. *Les Origines de la France contemporaine*. London, 1876.
Teit, J. 'The Thompson Indians of British Columbia.' *Memoir of the American Museum of Natural History*, vol. II, pp. 163–392. 1900.
Thomas, W. I. *Primitive Behaviour*. New York, 1937.
Thomson, B. H. *The Fijians: A Study of the Decay of Custom*. London, 1809.
Thomson, D. F. 'The Joking Relationship and Organized Obscenity in North Queensland.' *American Anthropologist*, vol. XXXVII, pp. 460–90. 1935.
Thurnwald, R. 'Bánaro Society: Social Organization and Kinship System of a Tribe in the Interior of New Guinea.' *Memoirs of the American Anthropological Association*, vol. III, no. 4, pp. 251–391. 1916.
——'Pigs and Currency in Buin.' *Oceania*, vol. V, pp. 119–41. 1934.
Thurston, E. *Castes and Tribes of Southern India*. 7 vols. Madras, 1909.
Todd, J. A. 'Redress of Wrongs in Southwest New Britain.' *Oceania*, vol. VI, pp. 401–40. 1936.
Trevitt, J. W. 'Notes on the Social Organization of North-East Gazelle Peninsula, New Britain.' *Oceania*, vol. X, pp. 350–9. 1939.
Trubetzkoy, E. N. 'La Phonologie actuelle.' *Psychologie du langage*, pp. 227–46. 1933.
——*Grundzüge der Phonologie*. Prague, 1939.
Tylor, E. B. 'On a Method of Investigating the Development of Institutions: Applied to Laws of Marriage and Descent.' *Journal of the Anthropological Institute*, vol. XVIII, pp. 245–72. 1889.
——*Primitive Culture*. London, 1871.

Valentine, C. W. 'The Innate Basis of Fear.' *Journal of Genetic Psychology*, vol. XXXVII, pp. 394–420. 1930.
van Waters, M. 'The Adolescent Girl among Primitive People.' *Journal of Religious Psychology*, vol. VII, pp. 75–120. 1913–14.
van Wouden, F. A. E. *Sociale Structuurtypen in de Groote Oost*. Leiden, 1935. [English edition, translated from the Dutch by Rodney Needham, preface by G. W. Locher: *Types of Social Structure in Eastern Indonesia*. (Koninklijk Instituut voor Taal-, Land- en Volkenkunde Translation Series, vol. 11.) The Hague, 1968.]
Vega, G. de la. *Histoire des Incas*. 2 vols. Paris, 1787.

Veniaminov, I. E. *Notes on the Islands of Unalaska District*, vol. III.

Vladimirtsov, B. *Le Régime social des Mongols*. Paris, 1948.

Volkor, T. 'Rites et usages nuptiaux en Ukraine.' *L'Anthropologie*, vol. II, pp. 160–84, 537–87. 1891.

von Feuerbach, P. J. A. *Caspar Hauser*. 2 vols. Boston, 1833.

von Fürer-Haimendorf, C. 'The *Morung* System of the Konyak Nagas.' *Journal of the Royal Anthropological Institute*, vol. LXVIII, pp. 349–78. 1938.

von Martius, C. F. P. *Beiträge zur Ethnographie und Sprachenkunde Amerikas zumal Brasiliens*. 2 vols. Leipzig, 1867.

von Neumann, J., and Morgenstern, O. *Theory of Games and Economic Behaviour*. Princeton, 1944.

Vygotski, L. S. 'The Problem of the Cultural Development of the Child.' *Journal of Genetic Psychology*, vol. XXXVI, pp. 415–34. 1929.

Wagley, C. 'The Effects of Depopulation upon Social Organization as Illustrated by the Tapirapé Indians.' *Transactions of the New York Academy of Sciences*, series 2, vol. III, pp. 12–16. 1940.

Wallon, H. 'Le Réel et le mental: à propos d'un livre récent.' *Journal de psychologie*, vol. XXXII, pp. 455–89. 1934.

Warner, W. L. 'Morphology and Functions of the Australian Murngin Type of Kinship: Part One.' *American Anthropologist*, vol. XXXII, pp. 207–56. 1930.

——'Morphology and Functions of the Australian Murngin Type of Kinship: Part Two.' *American Anthropologist*, vol. XXXIII, pp. 172–98. 1931.

——'Kinship Morphology of Forty-one North Australian Tribes.' *American Anthropologist*, vol. XXXV, pp. 63–86. 1933.

Webb, T. T. 'Tribal Organization in Eastern Arnhem Land.' *Oceania*, vol. III, pp. 406–17. 1933.

Wedgwood, C. H. 'Cousin Marriage.' *Encyclopedia Britannica*. London, 1936*a*.

——'Exchange Marriage'. *Encylopedia Britannica*. London, 1936*b*.

Wehrli, H. J. 'Beitrag zur Ethnologie der Chingpaw (Kachin) von Ober-Burma.' *Internationales Archiv für Ethnographie*, vol. XVI, supplement. Leiden, 1904.

Werner, E. T. C. and Tedder, H. R. 'Descriptive Sociology – Chinese.' *Descriptive Sociology*, ed. H. Spencer, vol. IX. London, 1910.

Westermarck, E. A. *The History of Human Marriage*. 2 vols. London, 1891.

——'Recent Theories of Exogamy.' *Sociological Review*, vol. XXVI, pp. 22–40. 1934*a*.

——*Three Essays on Sex and Marriage*. London, 1934*b*.

Williams, F. E. *Orokaiva Society*. Oxford, 1930.

——'Sex Affiliation and Its Implications.' *Journal of the Royal Anthropological Institute*, vol. LXII, pp. 51–81. 1932.

——*Papuans of the Trans-Fly*. Oxford, 1936.

Wu, C. C. 'The Chinese Family: Organization, Names, and Kinship Terms.' *American Anthropologist*, vol. XXIX, pp. 316–25. 1927.

Yerkes, R. M. 'A Program of Anthropoid Research.' *American Journal of Psychology*, vol. XXXIX, pp. 181–99. 1927.
——'Social Behaviour in Infrahuman Primates.' *Handbook of Social Psychology*, ed. C. A. Murchison. Worcester, 1935.
——and Elder, S. H. 'Œstrus Receptivity and Mating in Chimpanzee.' *Comparative Psychology Monographs*, vol. XIII, no. 5. 1936.
Yetts, W. P. *The Cull Chinese Bronzes*. London, 1939.

Zingg, R. M. 'More about the "Baboon-boy" of South Africa." *American Journal of Psychology*, vol. LIII, pp. 455–62. 1940.
Zolotarev, A. M. 'The Bear Festival of the Olcha.' *American Anthropologist*, vol. XXIX, pp. 113–30. 1937.
Zuckerman, S. *The Social Life of Monkeys and Apes*. London, 1932.

General Index

The index to the French text, in both the first and second editions, includes the names of authors, peoples, and physical features only. The present general index, newly compiled for this edition by the Editor, has been made more comprehensive by the addition of numerous topical indications. Certain entries, relating to matters of special importance in the argument, provide analytical references as well. The index should thus serve as an elementary theoretical concordance.